VIRGINIA'S LOST WILLS
An Index

Wesley E. Pippenger

HERITAGE BOOKS
2018

HERITAGE BOOKS

AN IMPRINT OF HERITAGE BOOKS, INC.

Books, CDs, and more—Worldwide

For our listing of thousands of titles see our website
at
www.HeritageBooks.com

Published 2018 by
HERITAGE BOOKS, INC.
Publishing Division
5810 Ruatan Street
Berwyn Heights, Md. 20740

International Standard Book Number
Paperbound: 978-0-7884-5812-5

TABLE OF CONTENTS

INTRODUCTION

For this study, a "lost record" is considered in two ways: first, as an item from a location where court records have been destroyed, and second for records that are found in unexpected places—oftentimes far from their point of origin. One might consider this work about wills and their whereabouts. Also abstracts or transcripts of wills have been noted when found published in periodicals.

Numerous sources have been consulted, and these are listed under Abbreviations. Many wills may be found digitized and accessed online at the Library of Virginia. Wills that are identified from chancery suits are typically not included if they that originate from the same county as the court copy of a will. Of the wills that have been copied from chancery causes, a single suit reference is normally given; however, the will may be found in multiple suits. Many previous to 1800 are included. In using the burned record county database at the Library, not all items show the specific source for the copy, so the reference given here is merely "BRCD." As such, these items may be downloaded from the website.

Users may note that the format used herein is the same this compiler used to create the 10-volume series of *Index to Virginia Estates, 1800-1865*, commissioned by the Virginia Genealogical Society. Duplicate entries have been removed from the subject work, which focuses on data previous to 1800.

Locating records of this type seems a never-ending task, as different projects come and go and generate different forms of finding aids. Any additions or changes are welcome.

Wesley E. Pippenger
Tappahannock, Virginia

ABBREVIATIONS

BRCD	Library of Virginia, Online Burned Record Counties Database
C	*The Chesopiean*, Norfolk, Va.
CA	Library of Virginia, Burned Jurisdiction Records Database, Court of Appeals
CF	Chancery Cause, Final File
CFH	*Central Virginia Heritage*, Charlottesville, Va.
CHS	*Chesterfield Historical Society Journal*
CL	James Branch Cabell Library, Virginia Commonwealth University, Richmond, Va.
CM	Prince William County Court Minutes, at Brentsville, 1843-1848; court date
Cocke	William Ronald Cocke III, *Hanover County Chancery Wills and Notes* (Columbia, Va., 1940)
Crozier	William Armstrong Crozier, *Virginia County Records, Vol. III: Williamsburg Wills, Being Transcriptions From the Original Files at the Chancery Court of Williamsburg* (New York: The Genealogical Association, 1906). Soon after Crozier's compilation, a fire in Williamsburg destroyed the surviving Chancery Court records.
CW	Colonial Williamsburg Foundation, John D. Rockefeller, Jr. Library, Special Collections Section, Williamsburg, Va.: (1) Helen M. Anderson Papers, 1818-1918; (2) Baylor Papers; (3) Richard Corbin Papers, 1746-1825; (4) Deneufville Papers, 1785-1836; (5) Elizabeth G. Elliott Collection; (6) Fontaine -Maury Papers; (7) Garrett Family Papers; (8) Rev. Scervant Jones Papers, 1834-1854; (9) Ludwell Papers, 1676-1879; (10) Neale Family Papers, 1835-1873; (11) Francis Nicholson Papers, [and Addition One], 1695/6-1765; (12) Dixon Family Papers, 1789-1941; (13) Philibert Papers; (14) Robinson Family Papers; (15) Dickinson Family Papers, 1778-1845
D&W	Deeds and Wills. 17th century estate records of Surry County were generally omitted from *Torrence*, as found in D&W Books 1 through 6.
DAR	Daughters of the American Revolution Library, Washington, D.C., Manuscripts Collection
DB	Deed Book
DCA	District of Columbia, Office of Public Record, Archives, Washington, D.C.; Box Number of Original Will
DC-R	Library of Virginia, Burned Jurisdiction Records Database, District Court, Richmond
DC-W	Library of Virginia, Burned Jurisdiction Records Database, District Court, Williamsburg
FC	*Filson Club History Quarterly*, Louisville, Ky.
FDC	Fredericksburg District Court Records, 1793-1798, at the courthouse in Fredericksburg; case number cited; L indicates law action, V indicates appeal, and H indicates chancery action
Filson	Filson Historical Society, Louisville, Ky.
Finley	Carmen Finley Papers (collections of the Caldwell, Finley, Minear and McFarling families), Sonoma State University, Rohnert Park, Calif.

Fleet	Beverley Fleet, *Virginia Colonial Abstracts (The Original 34 Volumes Reprinted in 3)* (Baltimore, Md.: Genealogical Publishing Co., 1988); as part of Volume 3 of the above, Beverley Fleet compiled a list of Virginia-related items, 1607-1850, found at the Huntington Library in San Marino, California. These are chiefly at pages 545-559, and are cited as "Fleet, Huntington Data."
G1	Eugenia G. Glazebrook and Preston G. Glazebook, *Virginia Migrations, Hanover County: Volume I (1823-1850), Wills, Deeds, Depositions, Invoices, Letters, and Other Documents of Historical and Genealogical Interest*
G2	Eugenia G. Glazebrook and Preston G. Glazebook, *Virginia Migrations, Hanover County: Volume II (1743-1871), Wills, Deeds, Depositions, Letters, Marriages, Obituaries, Estates for Sale, Absentee Land Owners, and Other Documents of Historical and Genealogical Interest*
GC	Library of Virginia, Burned Jurisdiction Records Database, General Court
GSTV	*Genealogical Society of Tidewater Virginia Bulletin*
HC	Library of Virginia, Burned Jurisdiction Records Database, High Court of Chancery
HCD	Richmond City, Hustings Court Deeds, Books 1, 2 and 3, were not included in *Torrence*, when he indexed wills and administrations up to 1800
HCHS	*Henrico County Historical Society Newsletter*
HHS	*Hanover County Historical Society Bulletin*
HSF	Yearbook of the Historical Society of Fairfax County, Virginia
K	Kentucky Historical Society
KQB	*Bulletin of the King & Queen County Historical Society in Virginia*
KWHSB	*Bulletin of the King William County Historical Society of Virginia*
LC	Land Causes
LCH	*Louisa County Historical Magazine*
LP	Loose papers at the county or city cited; may be followed by another abbreviation
LP:date	Library of Virginia, Legislative Petition with date
LVA	Library of Virginia, Richmond, Va. Includes entries from LVA card catalog drawer, "Microfilm, Wills from Lost Will Books, 1801-XXXX" before 1866, and other sources.
M	Maryland State Archives, Hall of Records, Annapolis, Maryland. Probate Records, Colonial Index for the Prerogative Court of Maryland; cite Liber and folio, or other entry
ME	Maine Historical Society
Mason	College of William and Mary, Earl Gregg Swem Library, Manuscripts Division, George Mason Papers
Mason	Polly Cary Mason, *Records of Colonial Gloucester County, Virginia*; Volume
MVG	Virginia Genealogical Society, *Magazine of Virginia Genealogy*; title changed with Volume 22 from the *Virginia Genealogical Society Quarterly*

N	Peter Wilson Coldham, comp., *North American Wills Registered in London, 1611-1857* (Baltimore: Genealogical Publishing Co., 2007); entries followed by the will identifier from the Public Record Office (PRO) in London.
NHS	*Northumberland County Historical Society Bulletin*
NNHM	*Northern Neck of Virginia Historical Magazine*
NVG	Marty Hiatt, Editor, *Northern Virginia Genealogy*
OB	Order Book
PGM	*Pennsylvania Genealogical Magazine*, Philadelphia, Pa.
PWR	Prince William Reliquary, published by the Prince William Public Library System, Ruth E. Lloyd Information Center (RELIC) for Genealogy and Local History, Bull Run Library, Manassas, Va.; Volume:Number, page
RB	Record Book
Rappahannock*	is used to indicate the county that was established in 1656 but became extinct in 1692 when it was divided into Essex and Richmond counties
Records	Henrico County Miscellaneous Records, multiple volumes
Shepherd	Samuel Shepherd, *The Statutes at Large of Virginia, from October Session 1792 to December Session 1706, inclusive, in Three Volumes (New Series) Being a Continuation of Hening* (Richmond, Samuel Shepherd, 1836).
SV	*Southside Virginian*
Swem	Earl Gregg Swem Library, College of William and Mary, Williamsburg, Va.: (1) George W. Southall Papers, 1807-1904; (2) Charles Campbell Papers, 1743-1896; (3) Jerdone Papers, 1753-1890, 1771-1845; (4) Prentis Family Papers
Prentis	Prentis Family Papers, Manuscripts Department, Earl Gregg Swem Library, College of William and Mary, Williamsburg, Va.
Sweeny	William Montgomery Sweeny, *Wills of Rappahannock County, Virginia, 1656-1692* (Lynchburg: J.P. Bell Co., 1947)
t	Typescript copy
T:	Correction or addition to Clayton Torrence's *Virginia Wills and Administrations*
THS	*Tazewell County Historical Society Newsletter*
TQ	*Tyler's Quarterly*
TVF	Virginia Lee Hutcheson Davis, Editor, *Tidewater Virginia Families*
ur	Unrecorded record in the loose papers of the location cited
UT	Barker Texas History Center, University of Texas, Austin, Tex.
UVA	University of Virginia, Alderman Library, Manuscripts Division, Charlottesville, Va.
Valentine	Valentine Museum, Richmond, Va.
VAN	*Virginia Appalachian Notes*, Roanoke, Va.

V:	Virginia Historical Society, Richmond, Va. Because many call numbers are long or note multiple folders, a plus sign (+) is sometimes inserted in the reference code
VCR	*Virginia County Records* (New York, NY: 1909)
VCRP	Library of Virginia, Virginia Colonial Records Project, Survey Report No. Many entries are for mariners or others who are about to embark on a voyage to Virginia, or have recently returned from Virginia.
VG	John Frederick Dorman, Editor, *The Virginia Genealogist*
VGS Bulletin	*Virginia Genealogical Society Bulletin*
VGSQ	*Virginia Genealogical Society Quarterly*, by the Virginia Genealogical Society; renamed with Volume 22 to the *Magazine of Virginia Genealogy*
VMHB	Virginia Historical Society, *Virginia Magazine of History and Biography*
VTG	*Virginia Tidewater Genealogy*, published quarterly by the Tidewater Genealogical Society, Hampton, Va.
W&D	Wills & Deeds
W&D1794	Caroline County Wills and Deeds, 1794-1859
W&P1742	Caroline County Wills and Plats, 1742-1830
Washington	Bushrod Washington, *Reports of Cases Argued and Determined in the Court of Appeals of Virginia, Volume 1* (Richmond: Thomas Nicolson, 1798).
WB	Will Book
WB 1724	Charles City County Will Book 1724/5 February 3 to 1731 June 2; photocopy at the Virginia Historical Society; original volume at the Library of Virginia
Weisiger	(1) Benjamin B. Weisiger, III, *Burned County Data, 1809-1848, as Found in the Virginia Contested Election Files* (Athens, Ga.: Iberian Publishing Co., 1986)
Wills	Library of Virginia, Westmoreland County Loose Original Wills, 1755-1800; see microfilm Reel #28a; card reference.
Winfree	Waverly K. Winfree, *The Laws of Virginia, Being a Supplement to Hening's The Statutes at Large, 1700-1750* (Richmond: The Virginia State Library, 1971)
WVHM	*West Virginia Historical Magazine*, Charleston, W.Va.
WMQ	*William & Mary College Historical Quarterly*, First Series
WMQ2	*William & Mary College Historical Quarterly*, Second Series
X	Drawer X, Fairfax County Circuit Court Archives, Fairfax, Va.; primarily original records but may be photocopies

VIRGINIA'S LOST WILLS: An Index

NAME	LOCATION	TYPE	YEAR	REFERENCE(S)
A				
Abbes, Edward		Will	1637	VCRP, Survey #03978
Abbott, Roger, in Culpeper Co.	Frederick	Will	1809	CF1835-159
Abbott, Thomas	James City	Will	1692	V:Mss1 L51 f676-682
Able, James	Prince William	Will	(nd)	CF1880-022
Abney, Dannet	Halifax	Will	1756	DB5, p. 94
Abney, Dannitt	Hanover	Will	1757	V:Mss1 Sp716 a 8
Abney, Reuben	Halifax	Will	1809	V:Mss1 Sp716 a 3984+
Abraham, Mordecai	King William	Account	(nd)	Note[1]
Acker, Nicholas, in DC	Fairfax	Will	1878	CF1881-033
Acree, Joshua	Hanover	Will	1777	LVA Acc. #27286a
Acree, Jossua [sic], of St. Paul's Parish	Hanover	Will	1777	Fleet, Huntington Data
Acree, Thomas	Hanover	Will	1858	Fleet, Huntington Data
Acree, Thomas	Hanover	Will	1858	LVA Acc. #41008, r4609
Acres, Richard	Spotsylvania	Will Ref.	1823	VGS Bulletin VII, p. 95
Acrill, Hannah, in Charles City Co.	Henrico	Will	1778	CF1792-019; BRCD
Acrill, Hannah, of Westover Parish	Charles City	Will	1778	MVG 39:4, p. 257
Acrill, William	Charles City	Exor. Bond	1783	VG 14, p. 184
Adams, Ann, of Westham, Eng.		Will	1744	V:Mss1 Ad198 a 1-2
Adams, Francis P., c/o George	Fairfax	Guard.	1817	X
Adams, Gabriel	Fairfax	Will	1844	LVA Acc. #343683, 2:38
Adams, Gabriel	Fairfax	Will	1844	X
Adams, Gabriel	Fairfax	Inventory	1844	X
Adams, Gabriel	Fairfax	Account	1853	X
Adams, Hannah, in Fairfax Co.	Arlington	Will	1823	CF1829-002
Adams, Henry, of Southampton Co.	Williamsburg	Will Ref.	1800	Crozier, p. 5
Adams, James		Will	1755	VCRP, Survey #04648
Adams, John	Halifax	Will	1833	LVA Acc. #38038-12
Adams, John	Fairfax	Account	1852	X
Adams, John, in Bedford Co.	Franklin	Will	1856	CF1873-010
Adams, John L., in Pittsylvania Co.	Campbell	Will	1849	CF1853-025
Adams, Lydia, in Hampshire Co.	Frederick	Will	1831	CF1859-101
Adams, Peter	Surry	Inventory	1687	T:D&W3, p. 86b
Adams, Richard	Richmond City	Will	1800	V:Mss1 Ad194 a 1
Adams, Richard		Will	1800	GC
Adams, Richard (GC)	Richmond City	Will	1800	LVA Acc. #28458
Adams, Richard, in Richmond	Petersburg	Will	1800	CF1848-019
Adams, Robert, of Fairfax Co.	Williamsburg	Will Ref.	1789	Crozier, p. 5
Adams, Samuel	Fairfax	Will	1791	LVA Acc. #343683, 2:38
Adams, Samuel	Fairfax	Sale	1843	X
Adams, Samuel	Fairfax	Inventory	1843	X
Adams, Samuel, in Bedford Co.	Campbell	Will	1847	CF1871-035
Adams, Samuel, in Fairfax Co.	Arlington	Will	1805	CF1829-002
Adams, Sarah, c/o George	Fairfax	Guard.	1817	X
Adams, Thomas	Augusta	Will	1784	V:Mss2 Ad195 a 1
Adams, Thomas		Will Ref.	1788c	V:Mss1 M3855 a 5499+

---

[1] LVA, U.S. Circuit Court Records, Box 82, *Anderson's Exors. v. Lawrence' Exors.* (1811).

NAME	LOCATION	TYPE	YEAR	REFERENCE(S)
Adams, William	Fairfax	Appraisal	1812	NVG 6, p. 625
Addams, James	Charles City	Inventory	1692	VGSQ 17:2, p. 43
Addington, Frances W., in Norfolk	Portsmouth	Will	1879	CF1908-029
Addonson, John	Lancaster	Will	1665	LVA Acc. #26678
Addums, James	Charles City	Inventory	1692	D&W1692, p. 150
Addy, Nicholas, of London		Will	1642	VCRP, Survey #06891
Adkins, Daniel	Henrico	Inventory	1771	Records, Vol. 7, p. 2143
Adkins, John W., in Goochland Co.	Powhatan	Will	1863	CF1871-020
Adkins, Rebecca	Prince George	Will	1801	SV 9:1, p. 17
Agnew, Park, in Alexandria	Campbell	Will	1910	CF1911-030
Akin, James	Henrico	Will	1774	Note[1]
Akin, Seldon, in MS	Henrico	Will	1896	CF1897-059
Albridgton, Richard	York	Will	1683	TQ 09:3, p. 209
Alcock, Richard, in Amherst Co.	Lynchburg	Will	1820	CF1823-039
Alderson, Catherine	Richmond	Will	1844c	V:Mss1 D3743 b
Aldridge, James	Prince George	Will	1860	SV 10:1, p. 15
Alexander, George, in Fairfax Co.	Arlington	Will	1784	CF1818-030
Alexander, Gerard	Stafford	Will	1761	LVA Acc. #22965
Alexander, Gerrard, in Fairfax Co.	Arlington	Will	1791	CF1818-030
Alexander, Gustavus Brown	King George	Will	1856	V:Mss1 M1795 c 94-133
Alexander, Henry	Monroe	Will	1783	V:Mss1 C1716 a627+
Alexander, John	Stafford	Will	1677	LVA Acc. #22965-3
Alexander, John	Stafford	Will	1677	TQ 21:2, p. 122
Alexander, John	Stafford	Will Ref.	1763	Washington, p. 36
Alexander, John	Stafford	Will	1768	Note[2]
Alexander, John	Stafford	Will	1768	LVA Acc. #22965
Alexander, John	Stafford	Will	1775	Note[3]
Alexander, John, Capt., Gent.	Stafford	Will	1677	Note[4]
Alexander, John, in Campbell Co.	Bedford	Will	1838	CF1873-107
Alexander, John, of St. Paul's Parish	Stafford	Will	1768	Fleet, Huntington Data
Alexander, John, of Stafford Co.	Fairfax	Will	1677	X
Alexander, John, Sr.	Stafford	Will	1763	LVA Acc. #41008, r4614
Alexander, Philip	Fairfax	Will	1790	V:Mss1 Se485 a 77-80
Alexander, Philip Thornton	King George	Will	1783	FDC L575-132
Alexander, Rawleigh	Northumberland	Will	1804	CF1812-001
Alexander, Robert	Stafford	Will Ref.	1703	Washington, p. 35
Alexander, Robert	Stafford	Will	1704	Note[5]
Alexander, Robert	Stafford	Will	1704	LVA Acc. #22965-3
Alexander, Robert	Stafford	Will	1735	LVA Acc. #22965
Alexander, Robert	Stafford	Will Ref.	1735	Washington, p. 35
Alexander, Robert	Stafford	Will Ref.	1735	Hening, Vol. 6, p. 399
Alexander, Robert	Stafford	Will	1736	Note[6]

---

[1] Henrico County Miscellaneous Records, Vol. 4, p. 1287.

[2] Prince William County Land Causes, 1789-1793, p. 90.

[3] Fairfax County Land Causes, 1812-1832, p. 118.

[4] Prince William County Land Causes, 1789-1793, p. 221.

[5] LVA Acc. #22965-3, Alexandria Town Trustees Minute Book.

[6] LVA Acc. #22965-3, Alexandria Town Trustees Minute Book.

NAME	LOCATION	TYPE	YEAR	REFERENCE(S)
Alexander, Robert	Caroline	Will	1819	Note[1]
Alexander, Robert, in Alexandria Co.	Prince William	Will	1859	CF1883-016
Alexander, Robert, in Fairfax Co.	Arlington	Will	1793	CF1812-019
Alexander, Robert, of Stafford Co.	Prince William	Will	1736	Note[2]
Alexander, William B., in MO	Arlington	Will	1846	CF1896-010
Alexander, William B., in MO	Alexandria	Will	1848	CF1896-010
Alford, Aaron E.	Fairfax	Inventory	1876	X
Alford, John	New Kent	Will	1726	TVF 3:2, p. 116
Alford, John	New Kent	Will	1726	MVG 25:3, p. 77
Alford, John	New Kent	Will	1726	VMHB 23, p. 420
Alford, John, of Rockingham Co.	Augusta	Will	1810	CF1817-044
Allan, James, Sr.	Fredericksburg	Will	1799	DCWA, p. 124
Allan, Jarret L.	Culpeper	Will	1877	CF1885-021
Allan, John	Richmond City	Will	1863	Fleet, Huntington Data
Allason, William	Fauquier	Will	1793	CF1814-003
Allason, William	Fauquier	Will	1800	LVA Acc. #24062
Allen, Anne	Brunswick	Will	1783	SV 3, p. 113
Allen, Arthur, Gent.	Surry	Will Ref.	1668	Winfree, p. 364
Allen, Christian, Sr., in Henrico Co.	Powhatan	Will	1829	CF1870-010
Allen, Edward	Nansemond	Will	1816	Note[3]
Allen, Elizabeth	Culpeper	Will	1818	CF1833-003
Allen, Elizabeth Lowry	James City	Will	1815	Swem(1):f121-123
Allen, Isham	Henrico	Inventory	1774	Note[4]
Allen, James	Hanover	Will	1765	V:Mss6:1 AL547:7
Allen, James	Hanover	Will	1772	VG 46, p. 254
Allen, James, of Hanover Co.	Cumberland	Will	1772	CF1798-006
Allen, James W.	Fairfax	Account	1851	X
Allen, Jesse	Buckingham	Will	1782	BRCD
Allen, Jesse, in Buckingham Co.	Lynchburg	Will	1782	CF1826-076
Allen, John C., in Cumberland Co.	Prince Edward	Will	1835	CF1893-044
Allen, Joseph	New Kent	Estate Ref.	1736	Hening, Vol. 4, p. 539
Allen, Joseph, in Richmond	Albemarle	Will	1862	CF1906-070
Allen, Leroy P., in MO	Mecklenburg	Will	1851	CF1870-014 CC
Allen, Martha W., in Norfolk Co.	Portsmouth	Will	1855	CF1867-011
Allen, Nancy	Fairfax	Inventory	1860	X
Allen, Nancy	Fairfax	Sale	1860	X
Allen, Nancy, in Cumberland Co.	Prince Edward	Will	1862	CF1893-045
Allen, Richmond, of New Kent Co.	Williamsburg	Will Ref.	1808	Crozier, p. 5
Allen, Samuel	Cumberland	Will	1774	WB2, p. 148
Allen, Samuel, in Amherst Co.	Lynchburg	Will	1799	CF1822-048
Allen, Thomas	James City	Will	1832	Note[5]
Allen, Thomas	Fairfax	Appraisal	1859	X
Allen, Thomas	Fairfax	Sale	1859	X
Allen, Tobias, in Middlesex Co.	Essex	Will	1801	CF1811-015

---

[1] Wesley E. Pippenger, *John Alexander: A Northern Neck Proprietor, His Family, Friends, and Kin* (Baltimiore, Md.: Gateway Press, Inc., 1990), p. 234; copy from Fredericksburg District Court Chancery, *Henry P. Alexander v. John P. Miller*.

[2] Prince William County Land Causes, 1789-1793, p. 224.

[3] LVA, Land Office Revolutionary War Military Certificate Papers, Reel 1, frame 964.

[4] Henrico County Miscellaneous Records, Vol. 7, p. 2223.

[5] LVA, Land Office Revolutionary War Military Certificate Papers, Thomas Allen, Folder 18.

NAME	LOCATION	TYPE	YEAR	REFERENCE(S)
Allen, William	Elizabeth City	Will	1731	TVF 8:2, p. 116
Allen, William	Elizabeth City	Will	1731	TQ 19, p. 110
Allen, William	Albemarle	Will	1754	V:Mss6:1 AL547:2
Allen, William Hunt	Buckingham	Will	1806	LP:27 DEC 1825
Allen, William, in Elizabeth City Co.	Amelia	Will	1731	CF1764-004
Allen, William, of New Kent Co.	Williamsburg	Will Ref.	1808	Crozier, p. 5
Allen, William, of Stafford Co.	Fauquier	Will	1741	Note[1]
Allen, William, pilot	Amelia	Will	1731	Note[2]
Allexon, Jasper, mariner [Ellixon]		Will	1706	VCRP, Survey #03891
Allgood, John		Estate Ref.	1808	Shepherd, Vol. 3, p. 419
Allgood, John	Dinwiddie	Will	1823	VG 16, p. 269
Allin, Silvester		Will	1636	VCRP, Survey #03973
Allison, Ann, in Richmond	Henrico	Will	1861	CF1889-104
Allison, Harrison	Fairfax	Will	1832	NVG 8, p. 1092
Allison, John	Fairfax	Account	1845	X
Allison, Mary	Arlington	Will	1786	CRA:4
Allison, Mary Craig, of Alexandria	D.C.	Will	1830	DCA: Box 10
Allison, William	Fauquier	Will	1793	LVA Acc. #24062
Allman, Thornton, Sr. [Almon]	King William	Will	1878	CF1909-003
Allmutt, James, in MD	Frederick	Will	1786	CF1818-163
Allocate, Thomas	Warwick	Will	1726	BRCD
Almon, John	Northumberland	Will	1795	CF1821-001
Alsop, Gilbert	Stafford	Will	1708	WB1699, p. 409
Alstot, John	Rockingham	Will Ref.	1783	LVA:1159583
Ambler, Charles E., in WV	Fauquier	Will	1876	CF1903-060
Ambler, Edward, Col., in Rappa. Co.	Culpeper	Will	1846	CF1873-016
Ambler, Jaquelin	Richmond City	Will	1798	T:HCD2
Ambler, Richard, of York Town	James City	Will	1765	V:Mss1 Am167b
Ames, John	Nansemond	Will	1865	CF1883-007
Ames, Okes, of Bristol Co. MA	Arlington	Will	1887	WB10:097; File #728A
Amiss, Gabriel, in Frederick Co.	Fauquier	Will	1770	CF1791-012
Anderson, Abraham	Frederick	Will	1805	LVA Acc. #37817
Anderson, Alexander	Hanover	Will Abstract	1821	Cocke:1
Anderson, Alexander	Hanover	Will	1822	CF1835-005
Anderson, Andrew	Essex	Will	1764	T: firstname not Hudson
Anderson, Beverley	King & Queen	Will	1822c	V:Mss1 M1752a92-108
Anderson, Beverley	King & Queen	Will	1868	V:Mss3 K5893 a 69-86
Anderson, Beverley	King & Queen	Will	1868	LVA Acc. #24187
Anderson, Charles	Prince George	Will	1718	DB1713, p. 289
Anderson, Christian		Will	1848	UVA Acc. #12553
Anderson, Dabney, of Caroline Co.	Louisa	Appraisal	1735	CF1804-011
Anderson, Edward	King & Queen	Will (N)	1830	CF1855-003
Anderson, Elizabeth	Louisa	Will	1794	V:Mss6:1 An247:4
Anderson, Francis T., in Rockbridge Co.	Bedford	Will	1887	CF1897-016
Anderson, Genet	Hanover	Will	1834	CF1846-001
Anderson, Genet	Hanover	Will	1842	Cocke:2
Anderson, Genet	Hanover	Will	1861	CF1885-012

---

[1] Fauquier County Land Causes, 1759-1807, p. 358.
[2] Amelia County Land Causes, 1744-1769, p. 180.

NAME	LOCATION	TYPE	YEAR	REFERENCE(S)
Anderson, Genet, Sr.	Hanover	Will	1833	CF1885-012
Anderson, George M.	Richmond City	Will	1834	V: Mss1 W9801 a640
Anderson, Hanisford, Sr., King & Queen	Essex	Will	1892	CF1912-013
Anderson, Henry, of Hanover Co.	Augusta	Will	1783	BRCD
Anderson, J., in Chesterfield Co.	Prince Edward	Will	1850	CF1864-003
Anderson, James		Estate Ref.	1798	Note[1]
Anderson, James B., in Cumberland Co.	Prince Edward	Will	1856	CF1864-001
Anderson, John	Hanover	Will Abstract	1800	Cocke:2
Anderson, John	Hanover	Will	1800	CF1835-007
Anderson, John	Mathews	Will	1808	Note[2]
Anderson, John	Caroline	Will	1813	TQ 19:3, p. 159[3]
Anderson, John	Gloucester	Estate Ref.	1832	Note[4]
Anderson, John	Fairfax	Will	1872	X
Anderson, John H.	Caroline	Will	1855	W&D1794, p. 73
Anderson, John H.	Caroline	Will	1861	W&D1794, p. 83
Anderson, John, of Mathews Co.	Williamsburg	Will Ref.	1808	Crozier, p. 5
Anderson, John, of Taylor's Creek	Hanover	Will	1800	TQ 20:4, p. 239
Anderson, John T.	Hanover	Will	1863	CF1899-040
Anderson, John T., of *Verdon*	Hanover	Will	1864	Cocke:4
Anderson, Jordan, Sr., Chesterfield Co.	Prince Edward	Will	1815	CF1864-003
Anderson, Joseph A., of St. Paul's Par.	Hanover	Will	1823	Cocke:39
Anderson, Mathew	Louisa	Will	1833	V:Mss6:1 An247:4
Anderson, Ninian	Arlington	Will	1791	CRA:55
Anderson, Ninian	Arlington	Sale	1792	CRA:73
Anderson, Pauncey	Louisa	Will	1781	V:Mss6:1 An247:4
Anderson, Peter S., in Cumberland Co.	Prince Edward	Will	1852	CF1864-001
Anderson, Philip B.	King & Queen	Will	1862	CF1862-001
Anderson, Robert		Will	1793	Note[5]
Anderson, Robert	Hanover	Will	1853	Cocke:6
Anderson, Robert	Hanover	Will	1853	CF1879-021
Anderson, Robert	James City	Will	1871	CF1873-005
Anderson, Robert, of Hanover Co.	Goochland	Inventory	1793	Fiduciaries 1793 A
Anderson, Susanah, of St. Paul's Par.	Hanover	Will	1724	LVA Acc. #25854
Anderson, Thomas	Hanover	Will	1794	LVA Acc. #21047
Anderson, William	Hanover	Estate Ref.	1794	Shepherd, Vol. 1, p. 332
Anderson, William	Hanover	Estate Ref.	1794	LP:25 NOV 1794
Anderson, William	Hanover	Estate Ref.	1795	Shepherd, Vol. 1, p. 417
Anderson, William, in Eng.	Albemarle	Will	1795	CF1833-002
Anderson, William, of King William Co.	Louisa	Inventory	1719	CF1804-006
Anderton, George	Surry	Inventory	1765	T: from Anderson
Andis, Henry	Rockingham	Estate Ref.	1830	LP:02 DEC 1840
Andrews, Elizabeth	Chesterfield	Will (U)	1843	LVA:1140179
Andrews, John, in Loudoun Co.	Fairfax	Will	1766	X
Andrews, John, merchant		Will	1616	VCRP, Survey #03111

---

[1] LVA, Revolutionary War Rejected Claims, James Anderson, Folder 24.

[2] LVA, U.S. Circuit Court Records, Box 157, *Kemp v. Hudgins* (1855).

[3] From suit *Anderson v. Anderson*.

[4] LVA, Revolutionary War Rejected Claims, John Anderson, Folder 25.

[5] W.P. Anderson, *Anderson Family Records* (1936), p. 36.

NAME	LOCATION	TYPE	YEAR	REFERENCE(S)
Andrews, John, of Williamsburg	James City	Will	1833	Swem(1):f124
Andrews, Lewis, in Orange Co.	Louisa	Will	1858	CF1896-017
Andrews, Mary Blair	Williamsburg	Will	1820	Note[1]
Andrews, Mary Blair	Williamsburg	Will	1820	LVA Acc. #28458
Andrews, Mary Blair	Williamsburg	Will	1820	VG 29, pp. 205, 252
Andrews, Mary Blair	Williamsburg	Will	1820	V:Mss6:1 H3833:1
Andrews, Robert	Williamsburg	Will Ref.	1803	Crozier, p. 5
Andrews, Robert	Williamsburg	Will	1804	Note[2]
Andrews, Robert	Williamsburg	Will	1804	MVG 24:1, p. 82
Andrews, Samuel, in Spotsylvania Co.	Henrico	Will	1870	CF1910-044
Andrews, Samuel, in Spotsylvania Co.	Louisa	Will	1870	CF1896-022
Andrews, Thomas, Sr.	Surry	Will	1693	T: correct from Andros
Andrews, William		Will	1721	VCRP, Survey #04665
Andrews, William	Dinwiddie	Will	1770	LVA Acc. #25828
Andrick, Joseph, in Shenandoah Co.	Rockingham	Will	1892	CF1893-084
Anglin, Adrian, in Buckingham Co.	Henry	Will	1777	CF1801-002
Annandale, Thomas	Westmoreland	Will	1792	Note[3]
Anthony, Betsy W.	Hanover	Will	1840	BRCD
Anthony, Charles		Will	1615	VCRP, Survey #03109
Anthony, David, of Middlesex Co.		Will	1676	VCRP, Survey #03558
Anthony, Elizabeth	Campbell	Will	1801	LVA Acc. #37102
Applewaite, Henry	Isle of Wight	Will	1770	LVA Acc. #24194
Archbell, John, mariner		Will	1692	VCRP, Survey #03759
Archer, Ann	Fairfax	Dower	1830	X
Archer, Edward	Norfolk City	Will	1771	V:Mss1 W3395 a 704+
Archer, Edward, of Norfolk Borough	Williamsburg	Will Ref.	1771	Crozier, p. 5
Archer, John, in Richmond	Dinwiddie	Will	1856	CF1866-010
Archer, Mary C., in Cumberland Co.	Amelia	Will	1849	CF1858-003
Archer, Mary Chastain Cocke	Cumberland	Will	1841	V:Mss1 A4247 a 206+
Archer, Mary Chastain Cocke	Cumberland	Will	1841	UT
Archer, Obadiah	Hanover	Will	1859	CF1876-030
Arell, David	Alexandria	Will Ref.	1796	Shepherd, Vol. 2, p. 65
Arell, David [Pheby Moore]	Fairfax	Dower	1803	X
Argent, George		Will	1654	VCRP, Survey #04114
Arlington, Michael		Will	1719	VCRP, Survey #04343
Armistead, Anderson, in MD	Campbell	Will	1874	CF1882-025
Armistead, Booth	Elizabeth City	Will	1742	TQ 06:4, p. 251
Armistead, Elizabeth, of Mathews Co.	Williamsburg	Will Ref.	1815	Crozier, p. 5
Armistead, John	Gloucester	Will Ref.	1734	Hening, Vol. 6, p. 405
Armistead, John	Fauquier	Will	1788	Note[4]
Armistead, John	Prince William	Will	1788	Note[5]
Armistead, John	Caroline	Will Ref.	1789	LP:10 NOV 1789
Armistead, John		Estate Ref.	1794	Shepherd, Vol. 1, p. 331
Armistead, John, in Caroline Co.	Fauquier	Will	1788	CF1815-048

---

[1] LVA, Treasurer's Office Material, 7th Stack (E5). Box "James River and Kanawha Co. Guaranteed Bonds. Wills and Certificates..." Accession #28458.

[2] LVA, Land Office Revolutionary War Military Certificate Papers, Robert Andrews, Folder 3.

[3] Westmoreland County Wills, 1755-1800, Reel 28a, #41.

[4] Fauquier County Land Causes No. 2, 1816-1833, p. 49.

[5] Prince William County Land Causes, 1793-1811, p. 478.

NAME	LOCATION	TYPE	YEAR	REFERENCE(S)
Armistead, John, in PA	Fauquier	Will	1788	CF1816-008
Armistead, John S., in Charlotte Co.	Campbell	Will	1845	CF1860-008
Armistead, Robert	York	Will	1737	TQ 06:4, p. 249
Armistead, Robert	Caroline	Will	1767	BRCD
Armistead, Robert		Will	1767	LVA Acc. #22656
Armistead, Robert, in Elizabeth City Co.	Williamsburg	Will Ref.	1742	Crozier, p. 5
Armistead, Susan, in Charlotte Co.	Campbell	Will	1854	CF1861-002
Armistead, Theodorick, in Norfolk Co.	Princess Anne	Will	1812	CF1816-022
Armistead, William	Gloucester	Will Ref.	1755	Hening, Vol. 8, p. 487
Armistead, William	Prince William	Will	1755	LC 1805-1816, p. 413
Armistead, William	Gloucester	Will	1785	TQ 24, p. 45
Armistead, William, in Amherst Co.	Lynchburg	Will	1810	CF1826-002
Armistead, William, of Blisland Parish	New Kent	Will	1793	BRCD
Armistead, William, of Kingston Parish	Gloucester	Will	1756	Note[1]
Armitradeing, Christian	Northampton	Will (N)	1650	D&W1645, p. 219
Armstrong, Archibald, in Augusta Co.	Bath	Will	1801	CF1824-002
Armstrong, Ellis	Essex	Will	1840	V:Mss1 W2296 a 297+
Armstrong, Zachariah P.	Hanover	Will	1889	CF1893-002
Arnall, Henry	Hanover	Will	1835	Cocke:7
Arnell, Henry	Hanover	Will	1835	CF1860-001
Arnett, David, of King William Co.	Louisa	Will	1738	BRCD
Arnold, James	Orange	Will	1816	V:Mss1 B9468 a 12-16
Arrington, John	Appomattox	Will	1846	BRCD
Arrington, John, in Appomattox Co.	Campbell	Will	1846	CF1856-002
Arthur, Barnabas, in Bedford Co.	Lynchburg	Will	1815	CF1821-060
Arthur, Charles R.	Richmond City	Will	1797	T:HCD2, p. 308
Arundel, Jemima	Fairfax	Account Ref.	1849	X
Asbury, Henry	Westmoreland	Will	1707	V:Mss1 C2468 a2357+
Asbury, Henry	Richmond	Will	1813	NNHM 23:1, p. 2471
Asbury, Joseph, in Hampshire Co.	Frederick	Will	1819	CF1827-153
Ashby, J. William, in Stafford Co.	Prince William	Will	1891	CF1899-025
Ashby, John, Capt.	Prince William	Will	1789	VG 09, p. 147
Ashby, John, in Fauquier Co.	Frederick	Will	1789	CF1827-010
Ashby, Robert B., in Warren Co.	Frederick	Will	1838	CF1878-006
Ashby, Robert, in Fauquier Co.	Frederick	Will	1792	CF1817-042
Ashby, Thomas	Frederick	Will	1752	UVA MSS 7257
Ashley, Edmund	Princess Anne	Inventory	1720	T: correct from Edward
Ashmore, Mary, of Dettengen Parish	Prince William	Will	1748	TQ 20:1, p. 52
Ashmore, William	Prince William	Will	1834	CF1867-004
Ashton, James	Stafford	Will	1687	VMHB 10, p. 292
Ashton, James, in Stafford Co.	London	Will	1687	N:PROB11/1701
Ashton, James, Maj.	Stafford	Estate Ref.	1690	OB: 09 SEP 1690
Ashton, James, of Stafford Co.	London	Will	1687	VCRP, Survey #03739
Ashton, John, of Stafford Co.	Rappahannock*	Will Abstract	1682	VMHB 10, p. 293
Ashton, John W., in Fairfax Co.	King George	Will	(nd)	CF1844-006
Ashton, John W., in Fairfax Co.	King George	Will	(nd)	CF1844-006
Ashton, Peter	Stafford	Will Ref.	1669	VMHB 10, p. 293
Ashwell, John, in Bedford Co.	Franklin	Will	1846	CF1859-052

---

[1] Prince William County Land Causes, 1805-1816, p. 413.

NAME	LOCATION	TYPE	YEAR	REFERENCE(S)
Askins, John		Estate Ref.	1786	Hening, Vol. 12, p. 363
Aston, Walter	Charles City	Will	1667c	V:Mss5:9 B9965:1
Aston, Walter, of *Cawsey's Gare*	Charles City	Will Abstract	1666	VMHB 50, p. 259
Atchison, Margaret	Fairfax	Sale	1860	X
Atchison, Margaret	Fairfax	Account	1860	X
Atkins, Anthony	Surry	Will	1781	T: not Inventory
Atkins, John	James City	Will	1624	VMHB 11, p. 153
Atkins, Lewis	Gloucester	Estate Ref.	1832	Note[1]
Atkins, Martha	Henrico	Will	1778	Note[2]
Atkins, Micah	Arlington	Will	1799	CRA:285
Atkinson, Charles	Caroline	Will	1842	Weisiger 1:072
Atkinson, Francis, mariner		Will	1695	VCRP, Survey #04717
Atkinson, George	Prince William	Will Ref.	1844	CM:04 MAR 1844
Atkinson, George	Prince William	Will Ref.	1844	CM:01 APR 1844
Atkinson, Lemuel	Surry	Will	1797	T: correct from Samuel
Atkinson, Roger	Dinwiddie	Will	1800	PRO T 79/7 r235
Atkinson, Roger	Dinwiddie	Will	1800	Note[3]
Atkinson, Thomas	Sussex	Will	1774	LVA Acc. #31070
Atkinson, Thomas W.	New Kent	Will	1880	CF1882-015
Atkinson, William, the younger		Will	1613	VCRP, Survey #03108
Atores, Amaro	Surry	Will	1677	T:D&W2, p. 141b
Attwood, Edward	Princess Anne	Will	1709	LVA Acc. #44103
Attwood, William	Princess Anne	Will	1720	LVA Acc. #44103
Atwood, James	Culpeper	Will	1781	V:Mss2 Sp457 b
Aungier, John, clerk		Will	1692	VCRP, Survey #03760
Austin, John, Jr.	Hanover	Will	1815	LVA Acc. #24645a
Austin, Reubin	Chesterfield	Will	1797	V:Mss2 Au775 a 1
Austin, Thomas	Hanover	Will	1802	LVA Acc. #21929
Austin, Thomas	Hanover	Will	1802	V:Mss2 Au777 a 1
Austin, Thomas, in York Co.	James City	Will	1866	CF1881-002
Averett, Rudd, in Charlotte Co.	Lunenburg	Will	1849	CF1855-032
Avery, Billy Haly	Prince George	Will	1802	Note[4]
Avery, George	Surry	Will	1692	T:D&W4, p. 269b
Avery, Thomas	Surry	Inventory	1676	T:D&W2, p. 115b
Avory, Mary	Prince George	Will	1767	LVA Acc. #19939
Awbrey, Chandler	Westmoreland	Wil	1756	V:Mss1 Sco857 a 13-27
Awbrey, Henry	Essex	Will	1694	D&W1692, p. 311
Awbrey, Thomas	Loudoun	Will	1787	WBC, p. 258
Awbrey, Thomas, in Loudoun Co.	Frederick	Will	1787	CF1827-136
Awmiller, George, in Shenandoah Co.	Frederick	Will	1803	CF1823-203
Aylett, Elizabeth	King William	Will	1835	V:Mss1 Sco857 a 13-27
Aylett, Judith Page Waller	King William	Will	1859	V:Mss1 Ay445 b902
Aylett, Judith Page Waller	King William	Will	1860	V:Mss1 Ay445 a 57
Aylett, Philip	King William	Will	1848	V:Mss1 Ay445 b902
Aylett, William	King William	Will	1733	LVA Acc. #24194-26

---

[1] LVA, Revolutionary War Rejected Claims, Lewis Atkins, Folder 24.
[2] Henrico County Miscellaneous Records, Vol. 7, p. 2383.
[3] LVA, U.S. Circuit Court Records, Box 63, *Hanson v. Atkinson* (1804).
[4] LVA, Land Office Revolutionary War Military Certificate Papers, William H. Avery, Folder 26.

NAME	LOCATION	TYPE	YEAR	REFERENCE(S)
Aylett, William	King William	Will	1780	MVG 26:3, p. 169
Aylett, William	King William	Will	1808	MVG 26:3, p. 169
Aylett, William, in King William Co.	Bedford	Will	1782	CF1835-051
Aylett, William, of St. John Parish	King William	Will	1780	Note[1]
Aylett, William Roane	King William	Will	1900	V:Mss2 G6388 b
Aylward, William, merchant		Will	1707	VCRP, Survey #03897
Ayre, Thomas	Fairfax	Will	1873	CF1881-050

---

[1] LVA, Land Office Revolutionary War Military Certificate Papers, William Aylett, Folder 29.

NAME	LOCATION	TYPE	YEAR	REFERENCE(S)

B

NAME	LOCATION	TYPE	YEAR	REFERENCE(S)
Babbicum, Katherine	Henrico	Will	1721	Records, Vol. 2, p. 521
Baber, Edward		Will	1655c	V:Mss1 B1166a
Baber, Eliz. Cross Jepp Strachey		Will	1672c	V:Mss1 B1166a
Backhurst, Bolling	Charles City	Will	1786	LP, box 51, folder 271
Bacon, Ebenezer, of Alexandria	Arlington	Will	1867	CF1877-001
Bacon, Elizabeth, in Mecklenburg Co.	Lunenburg	Will	1849	CF1856-004
Bacon, Lyddal	Lunenburg	Will	1775	CF1829-038
Bacon, Richard, seaman		Will	1687	VCRP, Survey #03740
Baer, Sallie Ann, in MD	Roanoke	Will	1874	CF1892-037
Bagby, Richard	King & Queen	Will	1855	CF1877-001
Bagby, Richard, in King & Queen Co.	Petersburg	Will	1855	CF1858-031
Bage, Thomas	Surry	Inventory	1700	T: correct from will
Bage, Thomas	Surry	Will	1796	T: correct from 1795
Bagley, Granderson, of Nottoway Co.	Amelia	Will	1806	BRCD
Bagley, Hugh	Surry	Inventory	1693	T:D&W4, p. 309a
Bagly, Thomas	Surry	Inventory	1713	T: correct from Baly
Bagnall, Roger	Isle of Wight	Will	1647	VMHB 6, p. 41
Bailey, Anselm	Surry	Will (U)	1806	VTG 13:2, p. 54
Bailey, Anselm	Surry	Will Abstract	1806	VG 13, p. 51
Bailey, Benjamin	Surry	Will	1780	T: correct from 1779
Bailey, Carr	Fauquier	Will	1771	CF1809-056
Bailey, Daniel, of Westmoreland Co.	Williamsburg	Will Ref.	1786	Crozier, p. 6
Bailey, James, of Westmoreland Co.	Williamsburg	Will Ref.	1784	Crozier, p. 6
Bailey, Joseph, Sr.	Henrico	Will	(nd)	Fleet, Huntington Data
Bailey, Robert	Surry	Inventory	1719	T: correct from Balee
Bailey, Thomas	Surry	Inventory	1777	T: correct from 1771
Bailey, Thomas T.	Albemarle	Will	1832	LVA Acc. #43838
Bailey, William	Halifax	Will	1862	V:Mss1 B1565 a 72-79
Bain, David A., in Portsmouth	Isle of Wight	Will	1866	CF1874-021
Baird, John, in Prince George Co.	Petersburg	Will	1825	CF1845-019
Baird, John, of Prince George Co.	Petersburg	Will	1825	CF1837-027
Baird, John William, of Pr. George Co.	Petersburg	Will	1834	CF1843-031
Baird, John William, Prince George Co.	Petersburg	Will	1834	CF1851-026
Baker, Amy	Essex	Will Abstract	1745	Fleet 2:327
Baker, Benjamin, of Nansemond Co.	Southampton	Will	1785	CF1806-002
Baker, Bolling, in FL	Henrico	Will	1882	CF1884-007
Baker, Brooks	Charlotte	Will	1821	V:Mss1 Sp516 a 1745+
Baker, Brooks	Charlotte	Will	1826	V: K110W448R651946
Baker, David	Nansemond	Will Ref.	1786	LP:03 NOV 1786
Baker, Elizabeth, of Nansemond Co.	Williamsburg	Will Ref.	1801	Crozier, p. 6
Baker, G.W., in Frederick Co.	Warren	Will	1865	CF1918-018
Baker, Heironimus, in Shenandoah Co.	Frederick	Will Ref.	1795	CF1820-112
Baker, James, Sr., in Henry Co.	Lynchburg	Will	1820	CF1822-050
Baker, Jerman, in Cumberland Co.	Henrico	Will	1828	CF1884-007
Baker, John	Louisa	Estate Ref.	1790	Hening, Vol. 13, p. 224
Baker, John	Rockingham	Will	1827	LVA:1159583 t
Baker, Martin	Hanover	Will	1821	VG 45, p. 56
Baker, Martin	Hanover	Will	1836	CF1891-026
Baker, Martin, of Hanover Co.	Louisa	Will	1821	CF1833-006
Baker, Martin, of Hanover Co.	Louisa	Will	1821	VG 45, p. 56

NAME	LOCATION	TYPE	YEAR	REFERENCE(S)
Baker, Martin, of Orange Co.	Hanover	Will	1836	Cocke:9
Baker, Michael, Sr., of Rockingham Co.	Augusta	Will	1803	CF1821-044
Baker, Samuel	Rockingham	Will	1858	LVA:1159583 t
Baker, Samuel	Rockingham	Will	1858	MVG 49:1, p. 73
Baker, Samuel Martin	Hanover	Will	1890	V:Mss1 B1787 a83-92
Baker, Thomas		Will	1698	VCRP, Survey #04783
Baker, Thomas, apothecary		Will	1654	VCRP, Survey #04111
Baker, William	King William	Inventory	1703	RB1, p. 117
Baker, William H.	Nansemond	Estate Ref.	1793	LP:21 DEC 1809
Baker, William H., of Nansemond Co.	Southampton	Account	1801	CF1803-001
Baldwin, Lemuel H., in NY	Prince William	Will	1894	CF1897-006
Balfour, James	Charles City	Will	1742	TQ 19:4, p. 218
Balfoure, William, chirurgeon		Will	1686	VCRP, Survey #03737
Ball, Burgess	Loudoun	Will	1800	V:Mss1 B2105 a 32-41
Ball, Elijah	New Kent	Will	1892	CF1909-001
Ball, Elizabeth Ann, in Chesterfield Co.	Henrico	Will	1820	CF1837-002
Ball, George	King & Queen	Will Ref.	(nd)	VG 27, p. 27
Ball, James	Lancaster	Will Ref.	1754	Hening, Vol. 10, p. 469
Ball, James, in Lancaster Co.	Richmond	Will	1826	CF1851-004
Ball, John	Stafford	Will Ref.	1722	WBK, p. 35
Ball, John	Lancaster	Will	1772	LVA Acc. #23554
Ball, John, in Amherst Co.	Lynchburg	Will	1817	CF1823-044
Ball, John, in Fairfax Co.	Arlington	Will	1766	CF1845
Ball, John, of Overwharton Parish	Stafford	Will	1722	VGS Bulletin VI, p. 53
Ball, Margaret	Lancaster	Will	1783	LVA Acc. #23554
Ball, Miriam, of Alexandria, wid/o John	D.C.	Will	1843	DCA: Box 16
Ball, Richard	Lancaster	Will	1726	LVA Acc. #23554
Ball, William	Lancaster	Will	1680	LVA Acc. #23554
Ballard, Elizabeth	Charles City	Inventory	1726	D&W1724, p. 152
Ballard, Elizabeth	Charles City	Will	1726	D&W1724, p. 131
Ballard, Francis	Charles City	Inventory	1727	D&W1724, p. 168
Ballard, Francis	Charles City	Account	1728	D&W1724, p. 198
Ballard, Thomas	Stafford	Will Partial	1730	LVA Acc. #20487, p. 35
Ballard, William, in Bedford Co.	Lynchburg	Will	1817	CF1825-002
Ballendine, John	Fairfax	Will	1782	ME
Ballenger, Francis	Fairfax	Account	1840	X
Ballenger, Francis	Fairfax	Inventory	1844	X
Ballenger, Francis	Fairfax	Sale	1844	X
Ballew, Abraham, mariner		Will	1709	VCRP, Survey #04357
Balley, George	Lancaster	Will	1677	WB1674, p. 28
Ballou, Charles Anderson	Halifax	Will	1865	V:Mss2 B2145 b
Ballow, Elizabeth	Cumberland	Will	1826c	V:Mss1 N1786 a 6725+
Ballow, Elizabeth	Cumberland	Inventory	1826c	V:Mss1 N1786 a 6725+
Balthis, Erasmus, in Shenandoah Co.	Washington	Will	1870	CF1888-015
Baly, Daniel	Surry	Inventory	1680	T: correct from 1679
Baly, Joseph	Lancaster	Will	1675	LP
Bamer, Francis	Surry	Will	1729	T: correct from Barner
Bandfield, John	Accomack	Will	1764	BRCD
Banister, John	Dinwiddie	Will	1788	LVA Acc. #28392
Banister, John	Dinwiddie	Will	1788	V:Mss2 M4516 b

NAME	LOCATION	TYPE	YEAR	REFERENCE(S)
Banister, John	Dinwiddie	Will	1788	Note[1]
Banister, John, of Dinwiddie Co.	Williamsburg	Will Ref.	1788	Crozier, p. 6
Bankhead, James	Westmoreland	Will	1785	Wills #25
Bankhead, William	Westmoreland	Will	1788	Wills #32
Banks, Adam	Madison	Will	1816	Fleet, Huntington Data
Banks, Andrew	King & Queen	Will	1829	Swem(1):f150
Banks, Bartholomew, in MI	Henrico	Will	1883	CF1893-008
Banks, Clement, in Jefferson Co.	Frederick	Will	1825	CF1830-346
Banks, Gerard	Stafford	Will	1787	FDC L564-20
Banks, Horatio N., in MI	Henrico	Will	1882	CF1893-008
Banks, James, of Bristol Parish	Prince George	Will	1733	DB1733, p. 567
Banks, John	Surry	Will (U)	1780	LVA:1048937
Banks, John	Surry	Will (U)	1780	VG 13, p. 52
Banks, John	Surry	Will (U)	1780	VTG 13:2, p. 54
Banks, John, in Richmond	Henrico	Will	1809	CF1893-008 CC
Banks, Josiah	Mathews	Estate Ref.	1835	Note[2]
Banks, Judith	Caroline	Will Ref.	1778	Hening, Vol. 9, p. 575
Banks, Linn	Madison	Will	1812	LVA Acc. #21156
Banks, Lucy, wid/o Benjamin	Surry	Will Abstract	1845	VG 13, p. 52
Banks, Lucy, wid/o Benjamin	Surry	Will (U)	1845	VTG 13:3, p. 127
Banks, Ralph	King & Queen	Estate Ref.	1735	Hening, Vol. 5, p. 214
Banks, Ralph		Estate Ref.	1759	Hening, Vol. 7, p. 293
Banks, Townley	King & Queen	Will	1817	BRCD
Banks, William	King & Queen	WII Ref.	1709	Hening, Vol. 7, p. 293
Banks, William	King & Queen	Will Ref.	1709	Hening, Vol. 5, p. 214
Banks, William	King & Queen	Will	1709	TQ Vol. 16, p. 21
Banks, William L.	James City	Will	1814	Swem(1):f154
Banton, Rebecca	Lancaster	Will	1754	LP
Barber, John	Arlington	Inventory	1798	CRA:260
Barber, John	Arlington	Account	1799	CRA:290
Barber, Richard	Frederick	Will	1777	T: correct from James
Barbour, James	Culpeper	Will	1775	FDC L562-26
Barcroft, Thomas		Will	1728	VCRP, Survey #07112
Bard, David	Surry	Will	1688	T:D&W4, p. 43a
Barden, James	Fairfax	Account	1854	X
Barden, John	Fairfax	Account	1845	X
Barham, Anthony		Will	1641	VCRP, Survey #03989
Barham, Anthony	Warwick	Will Ref.	1644	VG 21, p. 33
Barham, Charles, of Martin's Hundred	James City	Will Ref.	1682	Winfree, p. 367
Barham, Frances	New Kent	Will	1851	CF1871-006
Barham, William	Surry	Account	1774	T: not inventory
Barker, John	Fauquier	Will	1793	T: correct from Baker
Barker, Richard B.	Hanover	Will	1868	CF1871-001
Barker, Richard C.	Hanover	Will	1862	Cocke:5
Barker, William	Lancaster	Will	1710	LP
Barksdale, Claiborne, Sr., Charlotte Co.	Lynchburg	Will	1825	CF1850-004
Barlow, Samuel, mariner		Will	1716	VCRP, Survey #04145

[1] LVA, Land Office Surveys, Bk. 30, p. 131.
[2] LVA, Land Office Revolutionary War Military Certificate Papers, Josiah Banks, Folder 28.

NAME	LOCATION	TYPE	YEAR	REFERENCE(S)
Barlow, William K.	Hanover	Will	1844	Cocke:10
Barlow, William K.	Hanover	Will	1844	CF1855-002
Barnes, Cassandra	Fairfax	Account	1845	X
Barnes, George	Charles City	Will	1784	Note[1]
Barnes, George	Charles City	Will	1784	LP, box 21, folder 271
Barnes, Henry	Charlotte	Will	1795	WB1, p. 403
Barnes, Jacob, in NC	Southampton	Will	1811	CF1817-021
Barnes, John	Surry	Will	1691	T:D&W4, p. 202a
Barnes, John	Henrico	Will	1720	Records, Vol. 2, p. 493
Barnes, John	Nansemond	Will	1834	BRCD
Barnes, John	Fairfax	Inventory	1845	X
Barnes, Martin, in Madison Co.	Culpeper	Will	1824	CF1834-001
Barnes, Martin, in Madison Co.	Culpeper	Will	1824	CF1832-005
Barnett, Charles L., in Montgomery Co.	Roanoke	Will	1849	CF1857-003
Barnett, James, in NC	Mecklenburg	Will	1850	CF1880-018 CC
Barnett, Robert	Amherst	Will	1787	WB3, p. 35
Barnett, Septimia, in Charlottesville	Albemarle	Will	1892	CF1893-065
Barnum, Annie, in MD	Culpeper	Will	1896	CF1900-018
Barr, Jane	Prince George	Will	1823	VGSQ 14, p. 122
Barr, Jane	Prince George	Will	1823	Note[2]
Barr, John	Northumberland	Will Abstract	1777	Hening, Vol, 9, p. 320
Barr, John, in Hampshire Co.	Frederick	Will	1818	CF1821-121
Barret, Caroline M., in AL	Henrico	Will	1872	CF1883-022
Barret, Mary		Will	1746	LVA Acc. #23409-IX
Barret, William	James City	Will	1786	MVG 31:4, p. 348
Barrett, William E.	James City	Admin.	1820	Swem(1):f145
Barrett, William, of James City Co.	York	Will	1786	CF1799-002
Barrick, James B.	Hanover	Will Abstract	1854	Cocke:10
Barrick, James B.	Hanover	Will	1854	CF1890-014
Barrick, Martha	Hanover	Will Abstract	1886	Cocke:10
Barrick, Martha	Hanover	Will	1888	CF1890-014
Barron, Richard		Will Ref.	1787	Note[3]
Barrow, Absalom H., of MO	Lunenburg	Will	1847	CF1866-057
Barrow, William L., in Doddridge Co.	Dinwiddie	Will	1858	CF1869-006
Barrow, William, Sr., in Henry Co.	Franklin	Will	1848	CF1856-012
Barry, Eliza, of Georgetown DC	Arlington	Will	1880	WB10:005; File #701A
Barry, William	Charles City	Inventory	1731	D&W1724, p. 335
Barton, Edward	Prince William	Will Ref.	1712	DBL, p. 84
Baskervill, George, in NC	Mecklenburg	Will	(nd)	CF1871-008 CC
Baskervill, George, in NC	Mecklenburg	Will	1863	CF1882-016 CC
Baskerville, John	Appomattox	Estate Ref.	1835	Note[4]
Bass, Edward	Chesterfield	Will	1834	LVA Acc. #21463
Bass, Edward, in Chesterfield Co.	Powhatan	Will	1834	CF1835-001
Bass, William, in Amelia Co.	Lynchburg	Will	1793	CF1824-024
Bass, William, in Chesterfield Co.	Powhatan	Will	1839	CF1872-024

---

[1] LVA, Charles City County Loose Papers, Box 21, Folder 271.

[2] LVA, U.S. Circuit Court Records, Box 150, *Gibson v. Barr* (1845).

[3] LVA, Land Office Revolutionary War Military Certificate Papers, Richard Barron, Folder 38.

[4] LVA, Land Office Revolutionary War Military Certificate Papers, John Baskerville, Folder 13.

NAME	LOCATION	TYPE	YEAR	REFERENCE(S)
Bassett, Betty Carter Browne	Hanover	Will	1816	V:Mss1 B2944 a 460
Bassett, George Washington	Hanover	Will	1878	V:Mss1 B2944 a 1630
Bassett, William	New Kent	Will	1671	V:Mss2 B2948 b 1-3
Basye, Edmund	Culpeper	Will	1799	Note[1]
Basye, Edmund	Fredericksburg	Will	1799	Note[2]
Bates, John, Jr.	Essex	Will	1733	Fleet 2:300
Batt, Thomas	Elizabeth City	Will	1738	D&W1737, p. 50
Batt, Thomas, Sr.	Elizabeth City	Will	1718	Note[3]
Battaile, John, of St. Mary's Parish	Essex	Will	1708	VMHB 41, p. 177
Battaile, Lawrence	Caroline	Will	1773	BRCD
Batte, Henry	Prince George	Will Abstract	1727	VGS Bulletin IV, p. 72
Batte, Robert, in Prince George Co.	Petersburg	Will	1807	CF1833-030
Batte, William	Prince George	Will	1755	WB1750, p. 545
Batte, William	Prince George	Will	1755	NGSQ 60, p. 209
Batte, William	Prince George	Will Abstract	1755	VGS Bulletin IV, p. 71
Batte, William	Prince George	Will	1762	NGSQ 60, p. 209
Batte, William, Jr.	Prince George	Will Ref.	1762	VGS Bulletin IV, p. 71
Battersby, Elizabeth	Buckingham	Will	1768	LVA Acc. #21046
Battle, Robert	Prince George	Will	1807	BRCD
Battle, William, in Greensville Co.	Brunswick	Will	1789	CF1809-003
Baugh, Sarah	Brunswick	Will	1792	V:Mss1 Sh8185aSect.1
Baugh, William	Chesterfield	Bond	1751	LVA:104594
Baugh, William	Chesterfield	Bond	1754	LVA:104594
Baugh, William	Chesterfield	Account	1758	LVA:104594
Baugh, William	Chesterfield	Account	1771	LVA:104594
Baughan, John, Maj.	Essex	Will	1776	CF1809-006
Baughan, Thomas	Buckingham	Will	1828c	V:Mss1 B3262 a16-90
Baxter, Edward, of Westover Parish	Charles City	Will	1726	D&W1724, p. 111
Baxter, John	Prince George	Will Abstract	1801	Note[4]
Baxter, John	Prince George	Will	1801	SV 3:1, p. 7
Baxter, John, of Prince George Co.	Sussex	Will	1801	LVA[5]
Baxter, John S., in IA	Rockingham	Will	1853	CF1885-165
Baxter, Joseph, in PA	Rockingham	Will	1841	CF1885-165
Baxter, Thomas	Petersburg	Will	1878	LVA Acc. #22969b
Bayley, John	Prince William	Will	1861	CF1878-012
Bayley, Sally	Caroline	Will	1825	W&D1794, p. 19
Bayley, Thomas	Henrico	Will	1723	Records, Vol. 2, p. 575
Baylis, John, in Prince William Co.	Frederick	Will	1764	CF1777-001
Bayliss, George	Fairfax	Will	1885	CF1890-011
Baylor, George	Caroline	Will	1785	W&P1742, p. 34
Baylor, George, in Augusta Co.	Bath	Will	1848	CF1866-001
Baylor, Gregory, of Drysdale Parish	King & Queen	Will	1782	Fleet 2:345

---

[1] He died in Kentucky in 1804; from copy in Fredericksburg Circuit Court; may have been in now lost Culpeper County Will Book after 1813; also see Otto Basye, *The Basye Family in the United States* (1950), p. 194.

[2] He died in Kentucky in 1804; from copy in Fredericksburg Circuit Court; may have been in now lost Culpeper County Will Book after 1813; also see Otto Basye, *The Basye Family in the United States* (1950), p. 194.

[3] Elizabety City County Deeds, Inventories & Orders, 1715-1721, p. 158.

[4] LVA, Prince George County Land Book, 1802, p. 24.

[5] LVA, Sussex County Loose Papers, 1754-1870, box 228, filed with the answer of the defendant in the chancery cause of *Williams' Administrator v. Baxter's Executor* (1818).

NAME	LOCATION	TYPE	YEAR	REFERENCE(S)
Baylor, Gregory, of Drysdale Parish	King & Queen	Will	1785	TQ 19:3, p. 161
Baylor, John	Caroline	Will	1772	W&P1742, p. 18
Baylor, John	Caroline	Will	1808	Note[1]
Baylor, John	Caroline	Will	1808	LVA Acc. #41008, r4608
Baylor, John	Caroline	Will	1808	Note[2]
Baylor, John	King & Queen	Estate Ref.	1835	Note[3]
Baylor, John, of *New Market*	Caroline	Will	1773	VMHB 24, p. 367
Baylor, John, of *New Market*	Caroline	Will	1808	Fleet, Huntington Data
Baylor, John Roy, Dr., of *Locust Hill*	Caroline	Will	1894	V:Mss1 B5645 a6-11
Baylor, Louisa Henrietta	Caroline	Will	1899	V:Mss1 B3445 b 131+
Baylor, Maria	Caroline	Will	1850	W&D1794, p. 59
Bayly, Anselme	Surry	Will	1688	T:D&W4, p. 73a
Bayly, Henry	Henrico	Will	1667	Records, Vol. 1, p. 35
Bayly, Pierce, of Loudoun Co.	Frederick	Will	1800	CF1822-157
Bayly, Richard	Northampton	Will	1661	T: correct from Baly
Baynham, Joseph	Louisa	Will	1786	Note[4]
Baynton, John		Will	1690	VCRP, Survey #03747
Beach, Lewis	Fairfax	Will	1853	X
Beach, Lewis	Fairfax	Plat	1868	X
Beach, Lewis [Mildred]	Fairfax	Dower	1868	X
Beach, Peter	Stafford	Will	1702	WB1699, p. 143
Beach, Peter	Stafford	Will	1706	WB1699, p. 359
Beadles, Elizabeth, in Rockingham Co.	Greene	Will	1858	CF1881-005
Beagnal, Josiah, in Nansemond Co.	Isle of Wight	Will	1782	CF1816-011
Beal, John	Hanover	Will Abstract	1836	Cocke:11
Beal, John	Hanover	Will	1837	BRCD
Beale, John	Richmond City	Will	1792	T:HCD1, p. 614
Bear, Jacob	Rockingham	Will	1787	V:Mss1 B3804 a7-10
Bear, Jacob	Rockingham	Will	1787	V:Mss1 B3804 a1-2
Beard, David	Rockingham	Will	1850	CF1862-006
Beard, James D.	Rockingham	Will	1857	CF1862-006
Beard, James, of Rockingham Co.	Augusta	Will	1790	CF1838-048
Beard, Jonathan, in Baltimore Co. MD		Will	1806	LVA Acc. #24194
Beard, Richard, of Norfolk Borough	Williamsburg	Will Ref.	1817	Crozier, p. 5
Beard, William		Will	1646	VCRP, Survey #03992
Beare, Charles, mariner		Will	1729	VCRP, Survey #04657
Beasley, Martha E., in Pr. George Co.	Brunswick	Will	1897	CF1907-005
Beasley, Richard R., in Pr. George Co.	Brunswick	Will	1862	CF1907-005
Beaton, Thomas B., in Norfolk Co.	Portsmouth	Will	1854	CF1870-013
Beazley, Adam	Caroline	Will	1810	W&P1742, p. 91
Beazley, Bridget	Buckingham	Will Abstract	1792	VGS Bulletin V, p. 66
Beazley, Bridget	Buckingham	Will	1793	LVA Acc. #25971b
Beazley, James	Orange	Will	1798	FDC V567-121
Beazley, John	Buckingham	Will	1782	VGS Bulletin V, p. 66
Beazley, John	Buckingham	Will	1782	LVA Acc. #24608a

---

[1] LVA, U.S. Circuit Court Records, Bk. 20, Richmond, p. 187
[2] Fredericksburg City Record of Cases Decided, Nov. 1, 1820, p. 132
[3] LVA, Land Office Revolutionary War Military Certificate Papers, John Baylor, Folder 4.
[4] Louisa County Wills Not Fully Proved, 1757-1902, p. 5.

NAME	LOCATION	TYPE	YEAR	REFERENCE(S)
Beazley, John	Buckingham	Will	1782	LVA Acc. #30722
Beazley, John	Buckingham	Will	1782	V:Mss2 B3868 a 1
Beazley, Thomas L., in Richmond	Hanover	Will	1848	CF1855-003
Becker, Jacob, in NY	Henrico	Will	1862	CF1885-021
Becket, Sarah	Henrico	Will	1813	VGSQ 18:3, p. 79
Beckett, Ann C., in OH	Albemarle	Will	1871	CF1886-024
Beckham, John, in Culpeper Co.	Fauquier	Will	1831	CF1866-076
Beckley, Susannah, in Amherst Co.	Lynchburg	Will	1819	CF1826-044
Beckley, William	Prince George	Will	1819	LVA Acc. #27394
Beckwith, Jennings	Fairfax	Will	1867	CF1890-017
Beckwith, Jonathan, in Richmond Co.	Essex	Will	1824	CF1831-024
Beckwith, William E.	Fairfax	Will	1866	CF1867-046
Beddingfield, Nathaniel	Elizabeth City	Will	1798	D&W34, p. 406
Bedford, Benjamin, in Cumberland Co.	Powhatan	Will	1772	CF1796-002
Bedinger, Katherine H.	Alexandria	Will	1866	CF1902-033
Beedle, Harriett T.	Prince William	Will	1871	CF1875-031
Beeler, Christopher, in Hampshire Co.	Frederick	Will	1779	CF1821-119
Beeling, William	Rockingham	Will	1845	CF1857-008
Beesley, Samuel, merchant		Will	1727	VCRP, Survey #04645
Beeson, Edward, in Berkeley Co.	Frederick	Will	1817	CF1823-283
Beheathland, John		Will	1639	VCRP, Survey #03985
Belcher, Francis	Amelia	Will	1782	T: correct from Edward
Belcher, Francis, of Amelia Co.	Franklin	Will	1822	WB2, p. 512
Bell, David	Goochland	Will	1744	LVA Acc. #28962
Bell, George	Hanover	Will	1779	MVG 31:4, p. 347
Bell, George, of Hanover Co.	Richmond City	Will	1779	BRCD
Bell, George W., in Prince Edward Co.	Lunenburg	Will	1856	CF1865-005
Bell, James	Augusta	Will	1752	MVG 29:3, p. 188
Bell, John	Fauquier	Will	1743	Note[1]
Bell, John	Richmond City	Will	1791	T:HCD1, p. 572
Bell, John	Caroline	Will	1804	LVA Acc. #20407
Bell, Nathan	Hanover	Will	1835	CF1835-001
Bell, Nathan	Hanover	Will Abstract	1840	Cocke:11
Bell, Robert H., in Lynchburg	Bedford	Will	1894	CF1910-028
Bell, Stephen	Surry	Will	1792	T: correct from 1789
Bell, Thomas	Orange	Will	1798	FDC L564-110
Bell, Thomas	Northumberland	Will	1835	CF1857-007
Bell, William	Northumberland	Will	1773	CF1804-004
Bell, William	Orange	Will	1780	LVA Acc. #20407
Bell, William	Mathews	Estate Ref.	1806	Note[2]
Bell, William, of Norfolk	London	Will	1795	N:PROB11/1257
Belsches, Judy	Louisa	Inventory	1768	LVA Acc. #21607
Belsches, Patrick	Louisa	Will	1764	LVA Acc. #21607
Benear, Henry H., in Fauquier Co.	Rappahannock	Will	1852	CF1859-005
Benington, Richard, carpenter		Will	1612	VCRP, Survey #03107
Benn, Christian, of Nansemond Co.	Williamsburg	Will Ref.	1799	Crozier, p. 5
Bennett, Charles	Fairfax	Will	1839	X

[1] Fauquier County Land Causes 1, 1809-1815, p. 382.
[2] LVA, Revolutionary War Rejected Claims, William Bell, Folder 22.

NAME	LOCATION	TYPE	YEAR	REFERENCE(S)
Bennett, Charles, of Alexandria	Arlington	Will	1835	CF1852-001
Bennett, Everard	Halifax	Will	1827	V:Mss1 B4395 a 38-40
Bennett, John	Isle of Wight	Will	1770	VMHB 6, p. 38
Bennett, Joseph	Fairfax	Plat	1770	X
Bennett, Malinda, of Albemarle Co.	Rockingham	Marriage A.	1821	LVA:1159583
Bennett, Rice, in Cumberland Co.	Lynchburg	Will	1773	CF1820-004
Bennett, Richard		Will Partial	1750	Note[1]
Bennett, Richard, Gov.	Nansemond	Will	1675	VMHB 38, p. 77
Bennett, Richard, Gov.	Nansemond	Will	1675	LVA Acc. #25574
Bennett, Richard, Gov., in Eng.	Nansemond	Will	1675	VMHB 37, p. 77
Bennett, Richard, in Pittsylvania Co.	Bedford	Will	1811	CF1843-014
Bennett, Richard, in Pittsylvania Co.	Lynchburg	Will	1811	CF1827-061
Bennett, Richard, of Nansemond River	London	Will	1676	N:PROB11/351
Bennett, Richard, of Nansemond River		Will	1676	VCRP, Survey #03560
Bennett, Richard, Sr., Pittsylvania Co.	Lynchburg	Will	1811	CF1833-014
Bennett, William, in PA	Henrico	Will	1895	CF1900-057
Benskin, Henry		Will	1692	VCRP, Survey #03757
Benson, Rachel	Princess Anne	Will	1717	D&W3, p. 193
Bensten, James, in Norfolk Co.	Portsmouth	Will	1868	CF1903-031
Benthall, Robert, in MD	Portsmouth	Will	1870	CF1882-004
Bentley, Thomas, of Illinois Co.	Henrico	Will	1785	MVG 29:3, p. 188
Benwell, William Sarney, mariner		Will	1775	VCRP, Survey #04798
Berkeley, Betty Landon	Hanover	Will	1866	CF1897-006
Berkeley, Carter	Hanover	Will	1839	CF1857-002
Berkeley, Carter	Hanover	Will	1842	Cocke:15
Berkeley, Carter	Hanover	Will	1842	CF1857-002
Berkeley, Edmund	Hanover	Will	1868	CF1900-002
Berkeley, Edmund	Hanover	Will	1868	V:Mss1 B4555 b 8-24
Berkeley, Lewis	Hanover	Will	1836	CF1858-001
Berkeley, Lewis	Hanover	Will	1836	Cocke:16
Berkeley, William	Fairfax	Will	1762	NVG 6, p. 629
Berkeley, William, Sir		Will Ref.	1676	Note[2]
Berkley, Barbary	Fairfax	Will	1785	X
Berkley, Barbary, in Loudoun Co.	Fairfax	Will	1785	CF1848-012
Berkley, Benjamin	Fairfax	Will	1817	NVG 5, p. 458
Berkley, Benjamin	Fairfax	Will	1817	X
Berkley, Julia	Fairfax	Will	1850	X
Berkley, Julia, in Frederick Co.	Fairfax	Will	1855	CF1857-030
Bernard, Elizabeth Thacker	Hanover	Will	1863	V:Mss2 B4566 a 1
Bernard, Elizabeth Thacker	Hanover	Will	1863	LVA Acc. #21835
Bernard, Robert	Gloucester	Will	1742	V:Mss1 B4568 a 1
Bernard, Robert	Gloucester	Will	1742	LVA Acc. #25966
Bernard, Robert, of Kingston Parish	Gloucester	Will	1742	VG 12, p. 149
Bernard, Thomas	Warwick	Inventory	1651	Records 1648, p. 21
Bernard, William	Gloucester	Estate Ref.	1704	Hening, Vol. 4, p. 457
Bernard, William	King George	Will	1783	FDC H569-31
Berney, John		Will	1697	VCRP, Survey #06053

---

[1] From Duke University, Kilby Papers, Item 167.

[2] Minutes of the Council and General Court of Virginia, p. 535.

NAME	LOCATION	TYPE	YEAR	REFERENCE(S)
Berry, Edward	Rappahannock*	Will Ref.	1684	Sweeny, p. 8
Berry, William	King George	Will	1721	OB1721, p. 2
Berry, William	Richmond	Will	1721	FDC L564-128
Berry, William, of Richmond Co.	King George	Will	1721	VG 01, p. 5
Berryman, Elizabeth G.	Prince William	Will	1836	CF1867-004
Berryman, Gilson	Stafford	Will	1750	V:Mss2 B4598 c
Berryman, John	Stafford	Will	1722	V:Mss2 B4598 c
Berryman, John	Lancaster	Will	1787	V:Mss2 B4598 c
Berryman, John, of Lancaster Co.	Williamsburg	Will Ref.	1787	Crozier, p. 5
Berryman, Willoughby Newton	Northumberland	Will	1807	CF1825-004
Best, Thomas	Nansemond	Will	1683	LVA Acc. #32064
Best, Thomas	Nansemond	Will	1683	V:Mss2 B4645 a 1
Best, Thomas	Nansemond	Will	1683	DAR MSS 297 b1 f17
Best, Thomas	Nansemond	Will	1683	LVA Acc. #30715
Best, Thomas	Nansemond	Will	1683	BRCD
Best, Thomas	Nansemond	Will	1683	VG 24, p. 3
Best, William	Warwick	Inventory	1651	Records 1648, p. 24
Bettes, Elisha, in Botetourt Co.	Roanoke	Will	1825	CF1870-003
Betts, Elisha	Lunenburg	Will	1784	CF1834-061
Betts, Elisha	Lunenburg	Will	1784	CF1816-012
Betts, Royston, Jr.	Northumberland	Will	1841	Note[1]
Betts, Royston, Jr.	Northumberland	Will	1841	CF1842-003
Betts, Sarah, in Roanoke Co.	Lynchburg	Will	1857	CF1857-039
Betzold, David, of Alexandria	Fairfax	Will	1858	CF1859-032
Bevan, Samuel, of Baltimore MD	Arlington	Will	1892	WB10:194; File #753A
Beveridge, Noble	Loudoun	Will	1845	V:Mss2 B46798 a 1
Beveridge, Noble, in Loudoun Co.	Fauquier	Will	1842	CF1855-057
Beverley, Byrd	Norfolk City	Will		V:Mss1 B4678 a 4604+
Beverley, Euphrasie Maria Louisa	Richmond City	Will	1858	V:Mss1 B4678 a 4604+
Beverley, Harry	Spotsylvania	Will	1730	FDC V559-25
Beverley, Marie Carter	D.C.	Will	1817	V:Mss1 B4678 a 4604+
Beverley, Robert	Middlesex	Will	1687	V:Mss2 B4675 a 2
Beverley, Robert	Middlesex	Will	1687	V:Mss2 B4675 a 1
Beverley, Robert	Middlesex	Will	1687	V:Mss2 B4675 a 3
Beverley, Robert	Spotsylvania	Will	1733	FDC L387-69
Beverley, Robert	Spotsylvania	Will Ref.	1733	Hening, Vol. 8, p. 280
Beverley, Robert	Essex	Will	1800	FDC L564-4
Beverley, Robert, Gent.	King & Queen	Will Ref.	1722	Winfree, p. 228
Beverley, Robert, the elder	Middlesex	Estate Ref.	1766	Hening, Vol. 8, p. 227
Beverley, William	Williamsburg	Will	1756	FDC L567-158
Beverley, William B., in Essex Co.	Arlington	Will	1866	CF1870-050
Beverley, William Bradshaw	Loudoun	Will	1866	V:Mss1B4678 b929-17,193
Beverly, William B., in Essex Co.	Fauquier	Will	1866	CF1898-050
Beverly, William, of *Blandfield*	Essex	Will	1755	VMHB 22, p. 297
Bevis, William, mariner		Will	1717	VCRP, Survey #04336
Bew, Rigault		Will	1698	VCRP, Survey #04782
Bias, Mary C.	Bath	Will	1874	CF1882-010
Bicknall, William	Amherst	Will	1780c	GSTV 6, p. 23

---

[1] Northumberland County District Court Orders, Deeds, [Wills], 1789-1825 [1849], p. 495.

NAME	LOCATION	TYPE	YEAR	REFERENCE(S)
Bicksler, Benjamin F., in WI	Fairfax	Will	1885	CF1909-034
Biggs, Richard, of West & Shirley 100s		Will	1626	VCRP, Survey #03114
Bilbro, William, of Botetourt Co.	Augusta	Will	1807	CF1832-006
Bilisoli, Antione, in Norfolk Co.	Portsmouth	Will	1845	CF1889-021
Billingsley, George		Will	1681	M: L4 f118
Billups, Austin, in Dinwiddie Co.	Petersburg	Will	1823	CF1837-017
Billups, George	Gloucester	Will Partial	1673	Mason, Vol. 2
Billups, George	Gloucester	Will Partial	1673	V:Mss2 B4975 a 1
Billups, George	Gloucester	Will Partial	1705	Mason, Vol. 2
Billups, John	Gloucester	Will Abstract	1785	Note[1]
Billups, John, Drisdale Parish, Caroline	Berkeley	Will	1781	WB1:212
Billups, Richard, of Gloucester Co.	Williamsburg	Will Ref.	1752	Crozier, p. 6
Billups, Richard, of Kingston Parish	Gloucester	Will Abstract	1752	Mason, Vol. 2
Binford, James M., in Norfolk Co.	Portsmouth	Will	1855	CF1868-012
Binford, William	Prince George	Inventory	1761	DB1759, p. 161
Binford, William A., in Hanover Co.	Powhatan	Will	1852	CF1881-013
Bingham, George, in Orange Co.	Greene	Will	1829	CF1858-004
Bingham, Roscow Cole		Estate Ref.	1788	Hening, Vol. 12, p. 693
Bingham, Stephen		Will	1759	LP:08 NOV 1787
Bingham, Stephen, of St. John Par.	King William	Will	1759	TQ 10, p. 48
Binns, Charles	New Kent	Will	1853	CF1888-008
Binns, Daniel	New Kent	Sale	1814	LVA Acc. #20543
Binns, Daniel	New Kent	Account	1814	LVA Acc. #20543
Binns, Elizabeth	Surry	Will	1784	WB12, p. 19
Binns, John Alexander, in Loudoun Co.	Frederick	Will	1813	CF1851-096
Binns, Thomas, of New Kent Co.	Williamsburg	Will Ref.	1800	Crozier, p. 5
Birchet, Robert, of Bristol Parish	Prince George	Will	1760	DB1759, p. 179
Birchett, Peter, Sr., Prince George Co.	Petersburg	Will	1856	CF1876-078
Birchett, Susan, in Prince George Co.	Petersburg	Will	1831	CF1844-026
Birchfield, John, in Montgomery Co.	Roanoke	Will	1855	CF1877-021
Bird, Armistead	Henrico	Will	1771c	V:Mss4 V8 g
Bird, Armistead	King & Queen	Will	1772	VG 18, p. 24
Bird, Phillomon, of Farnham Parish	Richmond	Will	1752	Fleet 2:329
Bird, Robert	King & Queen	Will	1696	VG 17, p. 166
Bird, Robert	Henrico	Will	1696c	V:Mss4 V8 g
Bird, Robert		Will	1796	LVA Acc. #25817
Bird, Robert	Henrico	Will	1796c	V:Mss4 V8 g
Bird, Robert A.		Will	1768	LVA Acc. #25817
Bird, Robert Armistead	Henrico	Will	1768	V:Mss4 V8 g
Bird, Robert Armistead	King & Queen	Will	1768	VG 17, p. 268
Bird, Robert, of St. Stephen's Parish	King & Queen	Will	1796	VG 18, p. 27
Bird, Thomas	Surry	Will	1688	T:D&W4, p. 99a
Bird, William	Henrico	Will	1716c	V:Mss4 V8 g
Bird, William, Jr.	King & Queen	Will Ref.	1835	Note[2]
Bird, William, of St. Stephen's Parish	King & Queen	Will	1716	VG 17, p. 266
Birt, Elizabeth, of New Kent Co.	Charles City	Will	1833	Swem(1):f80
Biscoe, Robert	Lancaster	Will	1747	D&W1743, p. 180

---

[1] Mason, *Records of Colonial Gloucester County, Virginia*, Vol. 2.

[2] LVA, Land Office Revolutionary War Military Certificate Papers, Thomas Lipscomb, Folder 5.

NAME	LOCATION	TYPE	YEAR	REFERENCE(S)
Bishop, David	Surry	Will (U)	1830	VTG 13:3, p. 125
Bishop, David	Surry	Will Abstract	1830	VG 13, p. 52
Bishop, George, in Jefferson Co.	Frederick	Will	1819	CF1829-030
Bishop, James	Prince George	Will	1825	SV 9:1, p. 7
Bishop, James	Prince George	Will	1825	VGSQ 14, p. 123
Bishop, James	Prince George	Will	1825	LP:11 DEC 1830
Bishop, John	Prince George	Will	1813	BRCD
Bishop, John, in PA	Frederick	Will	1814	CF1831-199
Bishop, John, in Prince George Co.	Petersburg	Will	1813	CF1847-037
Bishop, Mary	Surry	Will (U)	1760	LVA:1048937
Bishop, Mary	Surry	Will (U)	1760	VTG 13:2, p. 52
Bishop, Mary	Surry	Will Abstract	1760	VG 13, p. 52
Bissill, William		Will	1713	VCRP, Survey #04360
Bittinger, Edmund G., Rev., U.S.N.	Fairfax	Will	1888	LVA Acc. #343683, 2:38
Black, David	Dinwiddie	Will Ref.	1781	LP:22 DEC 1807
Black, David, s/o Dr. David, of Blandford	Petersburg	Estate Ref.	1808	Shepherd, Vol. 3, p. 417
Black, Jane, in Fluvanna Co.	Albemarle	Will	1860	CF1886-032
Black, Jeremiah S., of York Co. PA	Arlington	Will	1883	WB10:046; File #715A
Black, John	Charles City	Inventory	1693	D&W1692, p. 163
Black, John	Albemarle	Will	1854	Fleet, Huntington Data
Black, Rebekah	Augusta	Will	1802	Note[1]
Blackburn, Christopher	Caroline	Estate Ref.	1834	Note[2]
Blackburn, Richard	Prince William	Will	1757	Note[3]
Blackburn, Richard, Col.	Prince William	Will	1757	TQ 31:1, p. 38
Blackburn, Roland	Henrico	Inventory	1767	Records, Vol. 6, p. 1981
Blackburn, William	Charles City	Inventory	1729	D&W1724, p. 237
Blackburn, William	Charles City	Account	1729	D&W1724, p. 260
Blackmore, Mary E.	Fauquier	Will	1882	CF1903-056
Blacknall, George	Norfolk City	Will	1857	V:Mss1 P3496c505-510
Blacknall, Mary Catherine, of GA	Nansemond	Will	1884	CF1899-009
Blacknell, Charles, of Gloucester Co.	York	Will	1762	LP 1792 Box 8
Blacknell, Charles, of Kingston Parish	Gloucester	Will	1762	MVG 31:4, p.345
Blackwell, Joel	Lunenburg	Will	1856	CF1857-018
Blackwell, Joel	Lunenburg	Will	1856	V:Mss1 AL546 a 18-26
Blackwell, John, the elder	New Kent	Will Ref.	1717	Hening, Vol. 8, p. 641
Blackwell, Samuel	Northumberland	Will	1786	CF1804-014
Blain, William	Rockingham	Will	1830	CF1845-010
Blaine, George, in Nelson Co.	Lynchburg	Will	1811	CF1834-032
Blair, Ann	Richmond City	Will	1794	T:HCD2, p. 150
Blair, James, in Richmond	Hanover	Will	1835	CF1841-013
Blair, James, of Prince George Co.	Mecklenburg	Will	1771	CF1791-003
Blair, John	Williamsburg	Will	1800	LVA Acc. #28458
Blair, John	Williamsburg	Will	1800	V:Mss6:1 H3833:1
Blair, John	Williamsburg	Will	1800	Note[4]
Blair, John Durbarrow	Richmond City	Will	1823	V:Mss2 B5753 b

---

[1] Augusta County Wills, Bk. 1-A, pp. 43-44, proved 7 APR 1802 in Staunton District Court.
[2] LVA, Land Office Revolutionary War Military Certificate Papers, Christopher Blackburn, Folder 40.
[3] Prince William County Land Causes, 1805-1816, p. 360.
[4] LVA, Treasurer's Office Material, "James River and Kanawha County Guaranteed Bonds, Wills and Certificates," Acc. #28458.

NAME	LOCATION	TYPE	YEAR	REFERENCE(S)
Blair, John, Hon.	Williamsburg	Will	1800	VG 29, p. 206
Blair, John S., in Lynchburg	Campbell	Will	1868	CF1871-040
Blair, Mary Winston	Richmond City	Will	1826	V:Mss2 B5753 b
Blakemore, Edward	Lancaster	Will	1777	LP
Bland, John, Jr., of Stratton Major Par.	King & Queen	Will	1846	CF1892-001
Bland, John, merchant		Will	1680	VCRP, Survey #06086
Bland, Richard, of Westover Parish	Prince George	Will Abstract	1720	VMHB 37, p. 160
Bland, Spencer	King & Queen	Will	(nd)	V:Mss1 M1752a92-108
Bland, Spencer	King & Queen	Will	1838	Note[1]
Bland, Spencer	King & Queen	Will Partial	1838c	Fleet 2:355
Bland, Theodorick	Prince George	Account	1784c	V:Mss1 B6108 a32-37
Bland, Theodorick	Prince George	Will	1789	VMHB 37, p. 161
Bland, Theodorick, Col.	Prince George	Will	1789	VMHB 3, p. 315
Bland, Theodowick, Prince George Co.	Petersburg	Will	1859	CF1874-055
Bland, Thomas	King & Queen	Will	1807	V:Mss3 K5893 a 69-86
Bland, Thomas	King & Queen	Will	1807	Note[2]
Blankenship, Joel	Chesterfield	Will	1789	WB4, p. 598
Blankinship, Branch	Chesterfield	Will (U)	(nd)	LVA:1140179
Blanks, James	Charles City	Will	1793	Note[3]
Blanks, Nicholson	Charles City	Account	1728	D&W1724, p. 200
Blanton, Alexander M., Cumberland Co.	Prince Edward	Will	1869	CF1894-004
Blanton, J., in Cumberland Co.	Prince Edward	Will	1852	CF1860-018
Blatt, John	Fairfax	Estate Ref.	1783	Hening, Vol. 13, p. 108
Blayton, Esther Virginia	New Kent	Will	1894	CF1899-005
Blessing, Henry, in Wythe Co.	Bland	Will	1873	CF1895-007
Blessing, Jacob, in Washington Co.	Smyth	Will	1830	CF1841-005
Blevin, Richard, mariner		Will	1695	VCRP, Survey #06049
Blick, Elijah H.H., in Brunswick Co.	Dinwiddie	Will	1877	CF1909-005
Blick, Thomas	Brunswick	Will	1773	CF1788-003
Blight, Robert	Prince George	Will	1710	SV 11:2, p. 70
Blincoe, Martha S., in Loudoun Co.	Arlington	Will	1849	CF1878-044
Blincoe, Sybil	Fairfax	Will	1869	CF1904-040
Blincoe, Thomas, in Loudoun Co.	Frederick	Will	1806	CF1817-064
Blount, Wilson, in Fincastle	Augusta	Will	1817	CF1830-105
Blow, Richard	Surry	Admin.	1687	T:D&W3, p. 97a
Blow, Richard		Will	1833c	Swem
Blow, Samuel	Surry	Will	1799	T: correct from 1796
Blue, Uriah, in Hampshire Co.	Frederick	Will	(nd)	CF1819-070
Blundell, John	Northumberland	Will	1792	Note[4]
Blundon, Seth	Northumberland	Will	1798	CF1815-015
Blunt, Francis	Hanover	Will	1851	Cocke:19
Blunt, Francis	Hanover	Will	1851	CF1878-034
Blunt, Richard	Sussex	Will	(nd)	TVF 13:2, p. 58
Blunt, Richard	Sussex	Will	1774	VTG 13:2, p. 58
Blunt, Richard, Sr.	Surry	Will	1747	VTG 18:1, p. 47

[1] Beverly Fleet, *Virginia Colonial Abstracts*, King and Queen County County, Vol. 14, 5th Collection, p. 90.
[2] LVA, Land Office Revolutionary War Military Certificate Papers, Christopher Bland, Folder 26.
[3] LVA, Charles City County Loose Papers, Box 51, Folder 271.
[4] Northumberland County District Court Orders, Deeds, [Wills], 1789-1825, p. 289.

NAME	LOCATION	TYPE	YEAR	REFERENCE(S)
Blunt, William, in Isle of Wight Co.	Portsmouth	Will	1820	CF1892-003
Boa, Caven, of Alexandria	Arlington	Inventory	1799	CRA:291
Board, John, in Bedford Co.	Lynchburg	Will	1787	CF1839-008
Boardyman, Richard	Charles City	Inventory	1724	D&W1724, p. 13
Boatwright, Leonard	Cumberland	Will	1856	V:Mss1 B6304a105-107
Bobby, Thomas	Charles City	Will Ref.	1721	TQ 19, p. 221
Bocock, James B., in Lynchburg	Bedford	Will	1899	CF1906-091
Bocock, Willis P., in AL	Bedford	Will	1885	CF1906-091
Boggess, Robert	Fairfax	Inventory	1817	X
Boggess, Robert	Fairfax	Will	1817	X
Bohannon, Ambrose	Gloucester	Will	1753	LVA Acc. #21104
Bohannon, Ambrose	Williamsburg	Will Abstract	1776	Fleet 2:345
Bohannon, Ambrose, of Essex Co.	Williamsburg	Will	1753	Crozier, p. 5
Bohannon, Ambrose, of Kingston Par.	Gloucester	Will Ref.	1753	VG 19, p. 116
Bohannon, Ambrose, So. Farnam Par.	Williamsburg	Will Abstract	1800	Crozier, p. 8
Bohannon, Isaac	King & Queen	Will	1843	LP
Bohannon, John	Gloucester	Will	1843	CF1888-004
Bohannon, Thomas N.	Prince William	Acct. Ref.	1843	CM:03 JUL 1843
Bolling, Archibald, in Campbell Co.	Lynchburg	Will	1826	CF1834-012
Bolling, Blair, of Richmond	Powhatan	Will	1839	CF1850-016
Bolling, John	Prince George	Will	1744	LVA Acc. #22483
Bolling, John	Bedford	Will	1757	V:Mss1 B6368 b 1-3
Bolling, John	Chesterfield	Will Abstract	1757	VMHB 22, p. 215
Bolling, John, Jr.		Will	1755	LVA Acc. #22483c
Bolling, Robert	Prince George	Will Ref.	1748	Hening, Vol. 8, p. 291
Bolling, Robert	Dinwiddie	Will	1749	LVA Acc. #20076
Bolling, Robert	Dinwiddie	Will	1777	LVA Acc. #20076, p. 5
Bolling, Robert	Dinwiddie	Will	1791	LVA Acc. #41772
Bolling, Robert, of Bristol Parish	Prince George	Will	1747	LVA Acc. #20076
Bolling, William	Goochland	Will	1845	CF1846-011
Bolton, Alexander	Charles City	Inventory	1725	D&W1724, p. 62
Bolton, Charles, in NC	Lynchburg	Will	1803	CF1826-088
Bond, William	Essex	Will	1776	CF1800-002
Bondry, William		Will	1700	LVA Acc. #22077
Bondurant, Joseph	Buckingham	Will	1835	LP:06 FEB 1843
Bondurant, Thomas Moseley	Buckingham	Will	1860	LVA Acc. #24513
Bonison, Abia	Lancaster	Will	1685	LP
Bonison, Abya	Lancaster	Will	1663	LP
Bonner, Jesse	Dinwiddie	Will	1803	LVA Acc. #27293-13
Bonnet, Edward	Henrico	Inventory	1742	Records, Vol. 4, p. 1171
Bonney, Nathan	Princess Anne	Will	1802	SV 15:2, p. 89
Booker, Ann	Essex	Will	1774	Fleet 2:304
Booker, Ann	King & Queen	Will	1778	V:Mss3 K5893 a 69-86
Booker, Edward	Amelia	Will	(nd)	UVA MSS 4756
Booker, Elizabeth	Amelia	Will	1826	V:Mss2 B6445 a 1
Booker, Isaac	King & Queen	Will	1841	CF1858-006
Booker, Martha, w/o Richard	York	Will	1742	TQ 18:3, p. 171
Booker, Parrish	Goochland	Will	1822	CF1835-008
Booker, Richard	Prince Edward	Estate	(nd)	UVA MSS 4756
Booker, Richard Lawson, of LA	Cumberland	Will	1839	CF1861-001
Booker, William Marshall	Amelia	Will	1802	V:Mss2 B64471 a 1

NAME	LOCATION	TYPE	YEAR	REFERENCE(S)
Boon, Annie E., in Augusta Co.	Staunton	Will	1896	CF1899-011
Boon, William, of King George Co.	Augusta	Will	1795	CF1855-034
Booth, Edwin G., Sr., in Richmond	James City	Will	1886	CF1908-014
Booth, Frances R.	Nottoway	Will	1885c	V:Mss1 W7547a15,041
Booth, Isaac, in Lawrence Co. AR	Floyd	Will Abstract	1838	VGS Bulletin VIII, p. 65
Booth, John		Will	1694	VCRP, Survey #04711
Booth, Rodham H.	Northumberland	Will	1842	Note[1]
Booth, Thomas, of Hanover Co.	Williamsburg	Will Ref.	1756	Crozier, p. 6
Booth, William P.	Northumberland	Will	1869	CF1874-004
Boothe, George, in Amelia Co.	Bedford	Will	1767	CF1812-010
Borden, Benjamin	Frederick	Will	1742	UVA Acc. #5635
Borden, Benjamin, of Orange Co.	Augusta	Will	1753	CF1834-041
Borum, Edmond, of Kingston Parish	Mathews	Will	1798	TVF 10:2, p. 91
Borum, Edmond, of Kingston Parish	Mathews	Will	1803	BRCD
Boseman, Harman	Charles City	Inventory	1725	D&W1724, p. 29
Boseman, Harman, of Westover Par.	Charles City	Will	1725	D&W1724, p. 28
Boseman, John	Charles City	Inventory	1727	D&W1724, p. 165
Boseman, Mary	Charles City	Will (N)	1726	D&W1724, p. 111
Boseman, Mary	Charles City	Inventory	1726	D&W1724, p. 114
Bosher, Charles James	King William	Will	1857c	V:Mss4 K5898 b
Bosher, William	Hanover	Will	1869	CF1878-028
Bosher, William	Hanover	Will	1870	CF1874-040
Bosman, Mary	Charles City	Will	1726	D&W1724, p. 111
Boss, Peter, in Loudoun Co.	Frederick	Will	1818	CF1822-185
Boswell, Benjamin, mariner		Will	1744	VCRP, Survey #04625
Boswell, Ellen J.	Lunenburg	Will	1880	CF1888-013
Boswell, John, of Louisa Co.	Hanover	Will	1788	G1:1
Boswell, Machen, of Mathews Co.	Williamsburg	Will Ref.	1794	Crozier, p. 6
Boswell, Thomas, of Ware Parish	Gloucester	Will	1797	BRCD
Boswell, William	Louisa	Will Abstract	1750	VGS Bulletin VIII, p. 16
Boteler, Ann F., in Jefferson Co.	Frederick	Will	1827	CF1830-182
Botterill, George, in MD	Henrico	Will	1872	CF1889-125
Botts, Anthony	Prince William	Will	1884	CF1899-005
Botts, Edward B.	Dinwiddie	Will	1845	CF1846-001
Botts, Seth	Stafford	Will	1776	WBN, p. 323
Botts, Seth, of Overwharton Parish	Stafford	Will	1776	TQ 33:4, p. 249
Boucher, Daniel	Isle of Wight	Will	1668	W&D1661, p. 53
Boughan, Thomas, in Buckingham Co.	Essex	Will	1828	CF1837-020
Boughton, Benjamin	Stafford	Will	1842	V:Mss1 T2118 d11382+
Boughton, Benjamin	Stafford	Will	1842	V:Mss1 T2118 d11390
Boughton, John	Essex	Will	1811	V:Mss1 T2118 d9783+
Bouldin, Frances W.V. Flournoy	Charlotte	Will	1900	V:Mss1 B6638 a2812+
Bouldin, Thomas Tyler	Charlotte	Will	1869	V:Mss1 B6638 a2264
Boult, John	Princess Anne	Will	1799	SV 12:3, p. 118
Boulware, Agathy	Caroline	Will	1829	LVA Acc. #23786
Boulware, Cornelia to John L. Slaughter	King & Queen	Marriage	1864	LP
Boulware, Elliott	Caroline	Will	1829	LVA Acc. #23786
Boulware, Muscoe	Caroline	Will	1843	Weisiger 1:074

---

[1] Northumberland County District Court Orders, Deeds, [Wills], 1789-1825 [1849], p. 494.

NAME	LOCATION	TYPE	YEAR	REFERENCE(S)
Bourdon, Henry	Dinwiddie	Will	1863	CF1872-006
Bourn, John	Louisa	Will	1813	V:Mss1 B2346 a 1157
Boush, Goodrich, of Norfolk Borough	Williamsburg	Will (N)	1782	Crozier, p. 8
Boush, John, of Norfolk Borough	Williamsburg	Will Abstract	1792	Crozier, p. 9
Boushell, William, Sr., of Norfolk Co.	Williamsburg	Will Abstract	1795	Crozier, p. 10
Bowden, Lemuel J., in Norfolk	James City	Will	1864	CF1872-002
Bowdoin, John T.		Will	1821	UVA Acc. #640
Bowe, John	Hanover	Will	1809	CF1834-003
Bowe, John	Hanover	Will	1809	Cocke:21
Bowe, Nathaniel	Hanover	Will	1830	CF1842-009
Bowe, Nathaniel	Hanover	Will	1830	Cocke:20
Bowe, Nathaniel, in Hanover Co.	Henrico	Will	1830	CF1831-004
Bowe, William	Hanover	Will	1816	Cocke:22
Bowe, William	Hanover	Will	1816	CF1834-003
Bowen, James, of Fauquier Co.	Arlington	Will	1815	CF1867-018
Bowen, Peter B., in Culpeper Co.	Fauquier	Will	1860	CF1891-030
Bowers, Christian, in Rockingham Co.	Roanoke	Will	1875	CF1889-008
Bowie, James, of *Braehead*	Caroline	Estate Ref.	1801	LP:24 DEC 1801
Bowie, John, in Culpeper Co.	Rappahannock	Will	1810	CF1842-009
Bowie, John, in Culpeper Co.	Rappahannock	Will	1810	CF1841-003
Bowker, James, of New Kent Co.	London	Will	1704	N:PROB11/479
Bowler, John [Boulware]	Caroline	Guard. Appt.	1799	BRCD
Bowler, William [Boulware]	Caroline	Guard. Appt.	1799	BRCD
Bowles, Anderson	Hanover	Will	1840	CF1885-007
Bowles, Anderson	Hanover	Will	1840	CF1874-031
Bowles, Benjamin	Hanover	Will	1780	V:Mss2 B68175 a 1
Bowles, Elisabeth	Hanover	Will	1804	CF1842-003
Bowles, Elizabeth	Hanover	Wll (N)	1804	Cocke:23
Bowles, Irvine S., in Bedford Co.	Roanoke	Will	1862	CF1872-034
Bowles, Jesse R.	Hanover	Will	1887	CF1910-007
Bowles, Jesse T.	Hanover	Will	1880	CF1885-007
Bowles, John	Albemarle	Will	(nd)	LVA Acc. #35914
Bowles, Joseph H.	Hanover	Will	1896	CF1903-025
Bowles, Susan D., in Hanover Co.	Henrico	Will	1851	CF1889-022
Bowles, Thomas	Hanover	Will	1820	CF1842-003
Bowles, Thomas	Hanover	Will	1820	Cocke:23
Bowles, Thomas	Hanover	Will	1820	V:Mss1 B6817 a 11-13
Bowles, Thomas	Hanover	Will	1840	Note[1]
Bowles, William, in Montgomery Co.	Lynchburg	Will	1798	CF1815-015
Bowlware, John, Jr.	Essex	Will Abstract	1743	Fleet 2:302
Bowman, David	Rockingham	Will	1846	CF1854-001
Bowman, Edward	Henrico	Will	1722	Records, Vol. 2, p. 555
Bowman, Isaac, in Shenandoah Co.	Frederick	Will	1826	CF1837-080
Bowman, John, Sr., of Rockingham Co.	Augusta	Will	1816	CF1820-018
Bowry, Henry	Charles City	Admin.	1834	Swem(1):f80
Bowry, John, Sr.	Charles City	Will	1825	Swem(1):f80
Bowyer, Thomas, of Botetourt Co.	Augusta	Will	1785	CF1819-044
Boyce, Richard, in Hampshire Co.	Frederick	Will	1791	CF1827-210

---

[1] Inez M. Bowles, *Thomas Bowles, Hanover County, Virginia*, p. 7

NAME	LOCATION	TYPE	YEAR	REFERENCE(S)
Boyd, Alexander C., in Botetourt Co.	Bedford	Will	1821	CF1850-012
Boyd, Alexander, Sr.	Dinwiddie	Will Ref.	1824	LP:02 DEC 1824
Boyd, Andrew, in Botetourt Co.	Bedford	Will	1820	CF1850-012
Boyd, David, in Northumberland Co.	Frederick	Will	1781	CF1814-049
Boyd, David, of Northumberland Co.	Williamsburg	Will Abstract	1781	Crozier, p. 9
Boyd, Elizabeth Hill	Berkeley	Will	1840	V:Mss1 B9967 b259+
Boyd, Hamilton, in Lynchburg	Bath	Will	1881	CF1891-006
Boyd, James, in Granville Co. NC	Mecklenburg	Will	1814	CF1825-005
Boyd, James, of Botetourt Co.	Augusta	Will	1816	CF1836-008
Boyd, Robert	King & Queen	Will	1821	Fleet 2:353
Boyd, Robert	King & Queen	Will	1821	Note[1]
Boyd, Robert B.	King & Queen	Will	1838	Note[2]
Boyd, Robert B.	King & Queen	Will	1869	Fleet 2:354
Boyd, Spencer	Williamsburg	Will Abstract	1778	Fleet 2:345
Boyd, Spencer, of King & Queen Co.	Williamsburg	Will Abstract	1779	Crozier, p. 7
Boyd, Spencer, of King & Queen Co.	Williamsburg	Will Abstract	1779	Crozier, p. 7
Boyess, George		Will	1686	T: not Rappahannock[3]
Boykin, Francis, Sr., of Isle of Wight Co.	Williamsburg	Will Abstract	1805	Crozier, p. 9
Boze, William T., in Richmond	Henrico	Will	1898	CF1898-037
Brack, Richard, of James City Co.	Williamsburg	Will Abstract	1789	Crozier, p. 6
Bracken, Sarah M.	Gloucester	Will	1824	Note[4]
Bracken, Sarah M.	Gloucester	Will	1824	LVA Acc. #26317a
Brackett, Ludwell	Amelia	Will	1814	V:Mss1 N1786 a 5268+
Brackett, Ludwell, of Amelia Co.	Cumberland	Will	1804	CF1832-016
Bradban, John	Charles City	Inventory	1729	D&W1724, p. 271
Bradbourn, John	Charles City	Will	1729	D&W1724, p. 265
Bradby, James Allen	Surry	Will	1802c	V:Mss1 W3273 b
Bradenham, John, of New Kent Co.	Williamsburg	Will Abstract	1795	Crozier, p. 10
Bradenham, John, of New Kent Co.	Williamsburg	Will Abstract	1795	Crozier, p. 10
Bradford, Anna	Charles City	Account	1725	D&W1724, p. 42
Bradford, Emily	Culpeper	Will	1874	CF1878-062
Bradford, John, mariner		Will	1716	VCRP, Survey #04144
Bradford, Joseph, in Madison Co.	Fauquier	Will	1812	CF1815-046
Bradford, Richard	Charles City	Account	1724	D&W1724, p. 41
Bradford, Richard	Charles City	Will Ref.	1725c	D&W1724, p. 41
Bradford, Richard, Capt.	Charles City	Will Ref.	1724	D&W1724, pp. 41, 215
Bradford, Richard, in Granville Co. NC	Caroline	Will (U)	1757	VGS Bulletin IV, p. 50
Bradley, Ann M.	Fairfax	Guard. Bond	1840	X
Bradley, Benjamin	Charles City	Will	1768	D&W1766, p. 63
Bradley, James, of Charles City Co.	Williamsburg	Will Abstract	1803	Crozier, p. 10
Bradley, John	Lancaster	Will	1715	LP
Bradley, Randall, late of Hanover Co.	D.C.	Will	1871	DCA:Box 44
Bradley, William	Fairfax	Inventory	1775	X
Bradshaw, Ann Maria, in MD	Roanoke	Will	1854	CF1868-016
Bradshaw, Charles	Cumberland	Will	1761	WB1, p. 217

---

[1] Beverly Fleet, *Virginia Colonial Abstracts*, King and Queen County County, Vol. 14, 5th Collection, p. 87.

[2] Beverly Fleet, *Virginia Colonial Abstracts*, King and Queen County County, Vol. 14, 5th Collection, p. 87.

[3] Refer to Sweeny, p. 9, where the compiler lists wills given in *Torrence* that have not been found of record in Rappahannock County.

[4] LVA, Land Office Revolutionary War Military Certificate Papers, Robert Thurston, Folder 15.

NAME	LOCATION	TYPE	YEAR	REFERENCE(S)
Bradshaw, Jordan	Goochland	Will	1795	CF1803-001
Bradshaw, Richard, in MD	Roanoke	Will	1842	CF1868-016
Bragg, Eliza W., in Petersburg	Amelia	Will	1893	CF1900-007
Bragg, Isabella, in Wake Co. NC	Petersburg	Will	1877	CF1885-037
Bragg, Thomas, in Culpeper Co.	Rappahannock	Will	1822	CF1841-001
Braithwaite, William H.	James City	Will	1893	CF1898-001
Brame, Mary	Caroline	Will	1819	W&P1742, p. 108
Brame, Nicholas	Essex	Will (N)	1721	DB16, p. 277
Branch, Benjamin, collector	Chesterfield	Estate Ref.	1806	Shepherd, Vol. 3, p. 275
Branch, Benjamin, Jr., in Dinwiddie Co.	Lunenburg	Will	1824	CF1837-013
Branch, Christopher, Jr.	Henrico	Inventory	1665	Records, Vol. 1, p. 31
Branch, Elizabeth	Isle of Wight	Will	1816	Crozier, p. 8
Branch, Henry, of Southampton Co.	Williamsburg	Will Abstract	1808	Crozier, p. 11
Branch, Polly, of Southampton Co.	Williamsburg	Will Abstract	1814	Crozier, p. 8
Branch, William, in Albemarle Co.	Washington	Will	1892	CF1907-024
Brander, Louisiana Harris Adkins	Richmond City	Will	1875c	V:Mss1 H3202 c 165+
Bransford, James	Powhatan	Will	1781	CF1793-001
Branson, Invidesse R., in Amherst Co.	Lynchburg	Will	1886	CF1889-036
Brantley, Edward	Isle of Wight	Will	1717	Note[1]
Brawner, Basil, in Alexandria	Fairfax	Will	1893	CF1910-025
Brawner, William	Prince William	Will	1869	CF1869-011
Braxton, Carter	King William	Estate Ref.	1809	LP:10 DEC 1812
Braxton, Corbin, Dr., in King William Co.	Henrico	Will	1872	CF1898-030
Braxton, George	King & Queen	Will Ref.	1749	KQB:8
Braxton, George, of King & Queen Co.	Augusta	Will	1749	CF1819-013
Braxton, George, the elder	King & Queen	Will Ref.	1726	Hening, Vol. 8, p. 474
Braxton, Mary E.	King William	Will	1888	BRCD
Braxton, Mary W., in King William Co.	Fairfax	Will	1844	CF1851-008
Braxton, William Armistead	King William	Will	1865	BRCD
Braxton, Wm. Armistead, in King Wm.	Henrico	Will	1865	CF1890-040
Bray, Angelica	James City	Will Ref.	1717	Hening, Vol. 4, p. 371
Bray, Charles	Essex	Will	1772	CF1803-003
Bray, David, Jr.	James City	Will Ref.	1731	Hening, Vol. 4, p. 371
Bray, David, of Wilmington Parish	James City	Will Ref.	1717	Hening, Vol. 6, p. 412
Bray, David, Sr.	James City	Will Ref.	1717	Hening, Vol. 4, p. 371
Bray, David, the elder		Will Ref.	1717	Winfree, p. 381
Bray, James	Williamsburg	Will	1725	CW M-1561
Bray, James	Williamsburg	Will Ref.	1725	VGS Bulletin VIII, p. 41
Bray, James	James City	Will Ref.	1753	Hening, Vol. 6, p. 413
Bray, James, the elder		Will Ref.	1725	Winfree, p. 381
Bray, Thomas		Estate Ref.	1751	Hening, Vol. 6, p. 413
Bray, Thomas, the elder		Will Ref.	1700	Winfree, p. 381
Bray, William		Will Ref.	1753	Hening, Vol. 6, p. 413
Breazeal, Drury	Henrico	Inventory	1771	Records, Vol. 7, p. 2129
Breazeal, Henry	Henrico	Inventory	1764	Records, Vol. 6, p. 1915
Brechin, Sarah, of St. Paul's Parish	Hanover	Dower	1731	VGS Bulletin VII, p. 52
Bredin, John	Rockingham	Estate Ref.	1802	Shepherd, Vol. 2, p. 373

---

[1] Isle of Wight County Deeds, Wills, Great Book, 1717-1726, p. 90 (second pagination); Torrence lists only inventory.

NAME	LOCATION	TYPE	YEAR	REFERENCE(S)
Breedlove, William	King William	Will	1803	Note[1]
Brengle, Maria, in MD	Henry	Will	1893	CF1905-008
Brent, Christopher N., in DC	Fauquier	Will	1831	CF1832-052
Brent, Daniel Carroll	Stafford	Will	1815	Note[2]
Brent, George	Stafford	Will	1778	LVA Acc. #41008, r4614
Brent, George	Stafford	Will	1778	LVA Acc. #23373
Brent, George, in Loudoun Co.	Frederick	Will	1785	CF1820-021
Brent, George Lee	Stafford	Will	1818	Land Office[3]
Brent, George, of Overwharton Parish	Stafford	Will	1778	Fleet, Huntington Data
Brent, George, of Overwharton Parish	Stafford	Will	1778	LVA Acc. #22783
Brent, George, of Woodstock	Stafford	Will	1700	VMHB 18, pp. 96, 321
Brent, Giles	Stafford	Will	1672	RB1671, pp. 63, 461
Brent, Henry	Fairfax	Will	(nd)	X
Brent, Hugh	Lancaster	Will	1671	LP
Brent, Mary	Westmoreland	Will Ref.	1658	VMHB 16, p. 211
Brent, Mary	Westmoreland	Will	1663	VMHB 16, p. 98
Brent, Mary H.P.	Nelson	Will	1833	MVG 41:4, p. 302
Brent, Robert, of Woodstock	Stafford	Will	1721	VMHB 18, p. 444
Brent, Thomas C., in Wash. Co. MD	Culpeper	Will	1832	CF1872-009
Brent, William	Stafford	Will Ref.	1742	Hening, Vol. 5, p. 292
Brent, William	Stafford	Will Ref.	1818	Note[4]
Brewer, John	Dinwiddie	Will	1798	VGSQ 10:1, p. 3
Brewer, John	Fairfax	Inventory	1817	X
Brewer, John	Fairfax	Will	1817	X
Brewer, John, grocer		Will	1636	VCRP, Survey #03974
Brewer, John, of Nansemond Co.	Williamsburg	Will Abstract	1814	Crozier, p. 6
Brewer, Sackfield	Charles City	Will	1699	D&W1724, p. 144
Brewer, Samuel, in Norfolk Co.	Portsmouth	Will	1855	CF1861-002
Brewton, William	Surry	Will	1739	T: not Stafford
Bridewell, Lewis	Prince William	Will	1846	V:Mss1 L5486 a
Bridger, John, of Smithfield	Williamsburg	Will Abstract	1795	Crozier, p. 8
Bridger, Martha, w/o John, Isle of Wight	Williamsburg	Will Abstract	1789	Crozier, p. 7
Bridgewater, Joseph	Henrico	Will	1762	Records, Vol. 6, p. 1881
Bridgewater, William	Henrico	Will	1718	Records, Vol. 2, p. 363
Bridgewater, [blank]	Henrico	Will Partial	1763	Records, Vol. 6, p. 1897
Bridgforth, M. Jane	Lunenburg	Will	1888	CF1899-002
Bridgforth, Thomas, St. Ann's Parish	Essex	Will	1764	Fleet 2:331
Briesey, William	Henrico	Inventory	1676	Records, Vol. 1, p. 55
Briggs, Henry, Sr., in Southampton Co.	Princess Anne	Will	1807	CF1830-003
Briggs, Margery	Surry	Inventory	1688	T:D&W4, p. 57a
Briggs, Richard	Brunswick	Will	1840	CF1842-022
Bright, Charles, in Bedford Co.	Lynchburg	Will	1819	CF1832-035
Bright, Peter	Bath	Will	1873	CF1907-004
Brightwell, Randall	King William	Will Ref.	1702	RB1, p. 292
Brightwell, Reynold	King William	Will	1702	RB2, p. 13

---

[1] King William County Record Book 1, p. 150.

[2] LVA, Land Office Revolutionary War Military Certificate Papers, William Brent, Folder 15; also Land Office Caveat Papers, 1858-1896

[3] LVA, Land Office Revolutionary War Military Certificate Papers, William Brent, Folder 14.

[4] LVA, Land Office Revolutionary War Military Certificate Papers, William Brent, Folder 14.

NAME	LOCATION	TYPE	YEAR	REFERENCE(S)
Brillhart, Daniel, in Montgomery Co.	Roanoke	Will	1844	CF1868-011
Brim, John	Middlesex	Inventory	1711	WBA, p. 251
Brinckley, John	Nansemond	Will Ref.	1724	Hening, Vol. 4, p. 529
Brinker, Henry	Frederick	Will	1772	MVG 28:3, p. 190
Brinkerhoff, L.D., in Fredericksburg	Culpeper	Will	1877	CF1883-055
Brinkley, Michael	Nansemond	Will	1762	VG 21, p. 39
Brinn, John	Fairfax	Will	1822	X
Brisco, William	James City	Will Abstract	(nd)	Duvall
Briscoe, James	Westmoreland	Will	1797	Wills #44
Briscoe, William	Middlesex	Will	1700c	V:Mss1 Am167b
Britt, William	Goochland	Will	1787	LVA Acc. #28582
Britton, George, in Fairfax Co.	Fauquier	Will	1818	CF1848-040
Broache, Isaac	King & Queen	Will	(nd)	VMHB 46, p. 265
Broache, Isaac	King & Queen	Will	(nd)	V:Mss1 C5217 b 813+
Broaddus, Rebecca	Caroline	Will	1833	W&D1794, p. 29
Broaddus, Thomas	Caroline	Will	1787	W&P1742, p. 38
Broadhurst, John, the younger		Will	1701	VCRP, Survey #04118
Broadribb, William	James City	Will	1703	WMQ 14:1, p. 35
Broadribb, William	James City	Will	1703	V:Mss1 Am167b
Broadwater, Charles	Prince William	Will	1734	WBC, p. 33
Broadwater, Charles	Fairfax	Account	1816	X
Broadwater, Charles	Fairfax	Sale	1816	X
Broadwater, Charles	Fairfax	Inventory	1816	X
Brock, Archibald, in Rockingham Co.	Greene	Will	1868	CF1877-004
Brock, Elizabeth	Fredericksburg	Will	1797	DCWA, p. 77
Brock, John C.	Hanover	Will	1864	CF1877-020
Brock, John P.	Hanover	Will	1823	Fleet, Huntington Data
Brock, William	Princess Anne	Will	1801	SV 15:2, p. 87
Brockenbrough, Austin, of Essex Co.	Richmond	Will	1858	CF1871-001
Brockwell, Edward B.	Prince George	Will	1885	BRCD
Brockwell, Edward B., in Pr. Geo. Co.	Petersburg	Will	1885	CF1891-035
Broders, Jon H.	Fairfax	Will	1860	X
Brodnax, William H.	Dinwiddie	Will	1834	V:Mss2 B7856 a 1
Brodwater, Caleb	Accomack	Will	1833	LVA Acc. #28954
Bronaugh, William	Fairfax	Sale	1775	X
Bronaugh, William	Fairfax	Inventory	1775	X
Broocke, Lewis, in King & Queen Co.	Essex	Will	1832	CF1833-007
Brooke, Francis Taliaferro	Spotsylvania	Will	1851	V:Mss2 B7908 d
Brooke, George, of *Mantapike*	King & Queen	Will	1782	VMHB 11, p. 95
Brooke, George, of St. Stephen's Parish	King & Queen	Will	1782	VGS Bulletin VII, p. 88
Brooke, George, of St. Stephen's Parish	King & Queen	Will	1782	Note[1]
Brooke, Humphrey	Culpeper	Will	1763	VMHB 12, p. 102
Brooke, Humphrey	Fauquier	Will Abstract	1802	VMHB 15, p. 202
Brooke, James, in PA	Frederick	Will	1822	CF1849-032
Brooke, John	Essex	Will	1788	VMHB 12, p. 100
Brooke, Matthew W., Prince William Co.	Fauquier	Will	1816	CF1866-008
Brooke, Paulin, of York River	London	Will	1748	N:PROB11/759
Brooke, Paulin, of York River	London	Will	1748	VCRP, Survey #04635

---

[1] LVA, U.S. Circuit Court Records, Bk. 17 (Richmond), p. 17.

NAME	LOCATION	TYPE	YEAR	REFERENCE(S)
Brooke, Richard	Essex	Will	1708	DB13, p. 106
Brooke, Richard	King & Queen	Will	1817	Note[1]
Brooke, Richard	King & Queen	Will	1817	Note[2]
Brooke, Richard	King & Queen	Will	1817	Fleet 2:353
Brooke, Robert H.	Fauquier	Will	1872	CF1880-011
Brooke, Robert H.	Fauquier	Will	1872	CF1888-032
Brooke, Robert, of St. Anne's Parish	Essex	Will	1790	VMHB 12, p. 223
Brooke, Sarah Taliaferro	Essex	Will	1764	VMHB 12, p. 322
Brooke, William	Essex	Will	1767	VMHB 12, p. 323
Brooke, William	Essex	Will	1779	VMHB 12, p. 103
Brooke, William	King & Queen	Will	1804	Note[3]
Brooke, William, of King & Queen Co.	Williamsburg	Will Abstract	1804	Crozier, p. 9
Brooke, William, of St. Anne's Parish	Essex	Will	1735	VMHB 12, p. 216
Brooke, Zacharias	Henrico	Will	1738	Records, Vol. 4, p. 1063
Brookes, Thomas	Henrico	Will	1696	RB5, p. 610
Brooking, William, Sr., of Petsworth Par.	Gloucester	Will	1703	BRCD
Brooks, James	Southampton	Will (U)	1759	BRCD
Brooks, James G., in Richmond	Bedford	Will	1881	CF1896-026
Brooks, John	Mathews	Will	1848	LVA Acc. #25818
Brooks, William to Evelilna Garrett	King & Queen	Marriage	1838	LP
Brothers, John, Sr.	Nansemond	Estate Ref.	1692	Hening, Vol. 5, p. 73
Brown, A.H.	Culpeper	Will	1879	CF1889-002
Brown, Basil	King William	Will	1813	BRCD
Brown, Benajah	Buckingham	Will	1814	Note[4]
Brown, Benajah, of Buckingham Co.	Cumberland	Will	1814	Judgments 1857 AUG
Brown, Benjamin, of Hanover Co.	Augusta	Will	1781	CF1816-035
Brown, Benjamin, Jr., St. Martin's Par.	Hanover	Will	1781	VG 10, p. 22
Brown, Bennett	Essex	Will	1789	CF1810-005
Brown, Beverly	Brunswick	Will	1791	CF1809-003
Brown, Beverly	Brunswick	Will	1791	CF1819-013
Brown, Beverly	Brunswick	Will	1791	CF1809-006
Brown, Bolar B., in TX	Bath	Will	1873	CF1889-001
Brown, Daniel	Lynchburg	Will	1817	V:Ms1 Ea765 a225-229
Brown, Daniel, Sr., in Cumberland Co.	Culpeper	Will	1833	CF1845-019
Brown, Elijah T.	Bath	Will	1861	CF1878-004
Brown, Elizabeth	Lancaster	Will	1715	LP
Brown, Elizabeth E., in Albemarle Co.	Louisa	Will	1858	CF1891-028
Brown, Eugene Vannoy, of Caroline Co.	D.C.	Will	1892	DCA: Box 129
Brown, Francis, of South Farnham Par.	Rappahannock*	Will	1691	V:Mss2 B8131 a 1
Brown, Francis, of South Farnham Par.	Rappahannock*	Will	1691	Sweeny, p. 147
Brown, Frederick R., in Henry Co.	Franklin	Will	1895	CF1897-030
Brown, George, in Brunswick Co.	Lunenburg	Will	1840	CF1851-003
Brown, George Newman	Prince William	Will	1814	CF1836-003
Brown, Gideon H., in Rappahannock Co.	Culpeper	Will	1884	CF1901-007

---

[1] Beverly Fleet, *Virginia Colonial Abstracts*, King and Queen County County, Vol. 14, 5th Collection, p. 85.

[2] LVA, U.S. Circuit Court Records, Bk. 17 (Richmond), p. 118.

[3] LVA, U.S. Circuit Court Records, Bk. 17 (Richmond), p. 117.

[4] LVA, Cumberland Co. Loose Papers, box 30 (Circuit Court, August Term 1857), *Ford et al. v. Boston*.

NAME	LOCATION	TYPE	YEAR	REFERENCE(S)
Brown, Henry J.	Buckingham	Will	1854	Note[1]
Brown, Henry J., of Powhatan Co.	Cumberland	Will	1854	CF1859-022
Brown, Isabella McCall	Henrico	Will	1837	Note[2]
Brown, Israel	Lunenburg	Will	1760	CF1796-010
Brown, James	Warwick	Will	1707	LVA Acc. #20027
Brown, James, in Hanover Co.	Louisa	Will	1806	CF1823-002
Brown, James, in Scotland	Lynchburg	Will	1817	CF1828-070
Brown, James, of St. Paul's Parish	Hanover	Will	1806	LVA Acc. #24677a-10
Brown, Jesse		Will	1770	WB2, p. 357
Brown, John	Princess Anne	Will	1802	SV 15:2, p. 89
Brown, John B., of Alexandria	D.C.	Will	1867	DCA: Box 39
Brown, John D.G.	Hanover	Will	1867	CF1895-015
Brown, John, Dr.	York	Will	1726	DB4, p. 150
Brown, John G., in Fayette Co. KY	Culpeper	Will	1835	CF1851-003
Brown, John, of Williamsburg	York	Will Ref.	1723	D&B4 1729, p. 150
Brown, Joseph	Stafford	Will	1806	Note[3]
Brown, Joseph B., in Norfolk Co.	Portsmouth	Will	1886	CF1902-004
Brown, Margaret, in Scotland	Lynchburg	Will	1817	CF1828-070
Brown, Michael	Wythe	Will	1849	MVG 29:3, p. 190
Brown, Milo [Harriet]	Fairfax	Renounce	1893	X
Brown, Milton	Hanover	Will	1852	CF1854-001
Brown, Milton M.	Hanover	Will	1852	Cocke:94
Brown, Milton M.	Hanover	Will	1852	CF1873-004
Brown, Molly	Fauquier	Will	1796	CF1796-001
Brown, Mordecai, in Petersburg	Culpeper	Will	1840	CF1851-003
Brown, Noah	Dinwiddie	Will	1798	VG 16, p. 168
Brown, Peter E.	Dinwiddie	Will	1843	CF1863-001
Brown, Richard	Lancaster	Will	1717	LP
Brown, Richard	Fairfax	Will	1745	LVA Acc. #343683, 2:38
Brown, Richard	Pittsylvania	Will Part	1784	LVA Acc. #42957
Brown, Richard Dixson	Warwick	Estate Ref.	1787	LP:19 NOV 1787
Brown, Robert	Warwick	Will	1696	V:Mss3 C3807 a 66
Brown, Robert	Warwick	Will Ref.	1780	LP:19 NOV 1787
Brown, Samuel	Grayson	Will		DB1:216
Brown, Sarah, in Culpeper Co.	Rappahannock	Will	1830	CF1860-005
Brown, Tarlton, Sr., in Henry Co.	Franklin	Will	1828	CF1849-026
Brown, William	James City	Will	1816	Swem(1):f181
Brown, William, Dr.	Arlington	Inventory	1792	CRA:85
Brown, William, Dr., of Alexandria	Arlington	Will	1792	CRA:59
Brown, William Hunt	Frederick	Will (U)	1865	LVA:1117621
Brown, William, in Brunswick Co.	Lunenburg	Will	1813	CF1832-003
Brown, William, in Lynchburg	Amherst	Will	1812	CF1852-001
Brown, William, in Pr. George Co.	Brunswick	Will	1776	CF1809-003
Brown, William, in Smith Co. TN	Buckingham	Estate Ref.	1835	VG 28, p. 121
Brown, William, of James City Co.	Williamsburg	Will Abstract	1776	Crozier, p. 11

---

[1] LVA, Cumberland Co. Loose Papers, box 31 (Chancery Causes, August Term 1859), *Peyton A. Brown v. Brown's Exors.*
[2] James River and Kanawha County Deeds, Bk. 2, p. 95.
[3] Fredericksburg Superior Court of Chancery, Land Causes and Appeals, 1817-1819, pp. 247, 325

NAME	LOCATION	TYPE	YEAR	REFERENCE(S)
Brown, William, of Kingston Parish	Mathews	Will	1792	Note[1]
Brown, William, of Lynchburg	London	Will	1815	N:PROB11/1565
Brown, William, of Prince George Co.	Brunswick	Will	1766	CF1809-003
Brown, William, of Prince George Co.	Petersburg	Will	1776	CF1841-033
Brown, William, of Surry Co.	Williamsburg	Will Abstract	1786	Crozier, p. 11
Browne, Andrew, mariner		Will	1702	VCRP, Survey #04121
Browne, Basil	King & Queen	Will	1813	LP
Browne, Basil, in King William Co.	Essex	Will	1813	CF1836-013
Browne, Benjamin, of Surry Co.	Williamsburg	Will Abstract	1819	Crozier, p. 11
Browne, Bennett, of *Hill Park*	Essex	Will	1788	Fleet 2:347
Browne, Daniel, Sr.	Essex	Will	1708	DB13, p. 148
Browne, Edward	Lancaster	Will	1663	LP
Browne, Edward	Surry	Inventory	1680	T: correct from 1679
Browne, John, of James City Co.	Williamsburg	Will Abstract	1794	Crozier, p. 11
Browne, Judith Carter, of *Elsing Green*	King William	Will	1801	V:Mss2 B2946 b 9-13
Browne, Martha	Henrico	Will Ref.	1721	Records, Vol. 2, p. 517
Browne, William	Surry	Will	1705	V:Mss2 B8187 a 1
Browne, William	Surry	Will	1786	LVA Acc. #24194
Browne, William	Surry	Will	1799	LVA Acc. #24194
Browne, William Burnet, of *Elsing Green*	King William	Will Ref.	1804	Shepherd, Vol. 3, p. 57
Browne, William, of James City Co.	Williamsburg	Will Abstract	1808	Crozier, p. 11
Browning, James	Henrico	Will	1772	Records, Vol. 7, p. 2181
Browning, William L., in Culpeper Co.	Rappahannock	Will	1877	CF1897-017
Brownlee, Nancy		Will	1800c	UVA Acc. #6688
Brubaker, Brubaker	Rockingham	Will	1804	CF1860-045
Bruce, Alexander, in Nottoway Co.	Lunenburg	Will	1795	CF1822-008
Bruce, Charles	King George	Will	1754	V:Mss1 B8306 b1-27
Bruce, Charles	King George	Will	1754	V:Mss1 B8306 a36-42
Bruce, Charles	Charlotte	Will	1889	V:Mss1 B8306 b28-439
Bruce, Charles	Orange	Inventory		V:Mss1 B8306 a36-42
Bruce, George	Richmond	Will	1715	V:Mss1 B8306 b1-27
Bruce, George	Richmond	Will	1715	V:Mss1 B8306 a36-42
Bruce, Henry	Richmond	Will	1727	V:Mss1 B8306 b1-27
Bruce, Henry	Richmond	Will	1727	V:Mss1 B8306 a36-42
Bruce, James C., in NC	Dinwiddie	Will	1865	CF1869-005
Bruce, William	Richmond	Will	(nd)	V:Mss1 B8306 a36-42
Bruce, William Moore, of Norfolk Co.	Williamsburg	Will Abstract	1794	Crozier, p. 8
Brumbelow, Frances	Brunswick	Will	1818	SV 3:3, p. 112
Brumley, William	New Kent	Will	1845	CF1868-003
Brumskill, John, of Fairfield	Caroline	Will	1762	FDC L387-63
Brumskill, William	Caroline	Will	1771	Note[2]
Brumskill, William	Caroline	Will	1771	FDC L387-63
Brushwood, Ann C.	King & Queen	Will	1852	CF1871-002
Bryan, John	Richmond City	Will	1786	T:HCD1, p. 65
Bryan, Thomas	Rockingham	Will	1793	CF1856-002
Bryan, William, of Botetourt Co.	Augusta	Will	1806	CF1821-003
Bryant, George, in DC	Alexandria	Will	1863	CF1893-001

---

[1] LVA, Land Office Revolutionary War Military Certificate Papers, William Brown, Folder 32.
[2] Caroline County Appeals and Land Causes, 1777-1807, p. 483.

NAME	LOCATION	TYPE	YEAR	REFERENCE(S)
Bryant, George, in DC	Arlington	Will	1863	CF1893-001
Bryant, Lucy W.	James City	Will	1870	CF1872-010
Bryant, Parmenas, in Nelson Co.	Lynchburg	Will	1823	CF1826-030
Bryers, Edward	Henrico	Will	1744	Records, Vol. 4, p. 1279
Buchan, Robert, clerk	Stafford	Will	1804	FDC L571-62
Buchan, Robert, clerk	Stafford	Will	1804	FDC L571-64
Buchan, Robert, Overwharton Parish	Stafford	Will	1804	Note[1]
Buchanan, D., in Richmond	Henrico	Will	1898	CF1901-036
Buchanan, George	Smyth	Will	1842	CF1857-009
Buchanan, James	Henrico	Will	1787	LVA Acc. #28458
Buchanan, James, in Wythe Co.	Smyth	Will	1816	CF1843-013
Buchanan, James, in Wythe Co.	Smyth	Will	1816	CF1866-024
Buchanan, James, in Wythe Co.	Smyth	Will	1816	CF1852-005
Buchanan, John, in Augusta Co.	Bedford	Will	1769	CF1850-012
Buchanan, John, in Wythe Co.	Smyth	Will	1816	CF1846-005
Buckels, Robert, in Berkeley Co.	Frederick	Will	1790	CF1819-101
Buckner, Baldwin, of Gloucester Co.	Williamsburg	Will Abstract	1778	Crozier, p. 6
Buckner, Elizabeth, of *Mill Hill Farm*	Caroline	Will	1787	LVA Acc. #22782
Buckner, Elizabeth Taliaferro	Caroline	Will	1786	V:Mss2 B8572 a 1
Buckner, George, Capt., of *Braynefield*	Caroline	Will Ref.	1828	VMHB 64, p. 363
Buckner, George, Capt., of *Braynefield*	Caroline	Will	1828	Note[2]
Buckner, John	Stafford	Will	1748	V:Mss2 B8574 a 1
Buckner, John	York	Will	1748	TQ 21:3, p. 175
Buckner, William	Caroline	Will	1788	TQ 21:3, p. 177
Bucktrout, Horatio N., in Norfolk	James City	Will	1848	CF1890-008
Bulkeley, Arthur, merchant		Will	1645	VCRP, Survey #03991
Bullett, Thomas, in Fauquier Co.	Bath	Will	1778	CF1836-009
Bullett, Thomas, of Fauquier Co.	Augusta	Will	1778	CF1825-080
Bullifant, Philip	York	Will	1803	CF1828-002
Bullifant, Philip	York	Will	1803	MVG 31:4, p. 358
Bullifant, Philip, in Williamsburg	York	Will	1803	BRCD, DC-W
Bullington, Josiah	Henrico	Will	1785	Records 1774, p. 110
Bullock, David, in Henrico Co.	Louisa	Will	1833	CF1843-012
Bullock, Edward	Hanover	Will	1753	TVF 12:2, p. 116
Bullock, Edward	Hanover	Will	1756	V:Mss2 B8764 a 1
Bullock, Edward, in Greene Co. GA	Hanover	Will	1756	LVA Acc. #26907
Bullock, Edward, of St. Martin's Parish	Hanover	Will	1756	LVA Acc. #25628
Bullock, James	Bedford	Estate Ref.	1784	Hening, Vol. 13, p. 104
Bullock, Reuben E., in Fluvanna Co.	Louisa	Will	1870	CF1874-014
Bullock, Thomas	Isle of Wight	Will	1787	SV 11:3, p. 114
Bullock, William		Will	1650	VCRP, Survey #03999
Bulluck, Thomas	Isle of Wight	Will (U)	1788	LVA:1161459
Bumber, George, late King George Co.	D.C.	Will	1878	DCA:Box 68
Bunch, Burwell G.	Louisa	Will	1871	CF1906-002
Bunting, William, of Norfolk Co.	Williamsburg	Will Abstract	1801	Crozier, p. 7
Burchell, John	Clarke	Will	1859c	V:Mss1 T2197 a 54-61
Burchell, Norval W., in DC	Fairfax	Will	1899	CF1910-048

---

[1] LVA, U.S. Circuit Court Records, Virginia District, Box 142, *Buchan v. Buchan & Seddon* (1838).
[2] Fredericksburg District Court Chancery, File 304.

NAME	LOCATION	TYPE	YEAR	REFERENCE(S)
Burfoot, Thomas, Sr., Chesterfield Co.	Amelia	Will	1820	CF1838-007
Burge, Drury		Estate Ref.	1801	Shepherd, Vol. 2, p. 345
Burge, Drury, in Charlotte Co.	Lynchburg	Will	1796	CF1818-004
Burge, John	Charles City	Inventory	1693	VGSQ 17:3, p. 105
Burgess, Edward	King William	Will	1705	RB2, p. 46
Burgess, Edward, in Stafford Co.	Fauquier	Inventory	1723	CF1789-018
Burgess, Edward, in Stafford Co.	Fauquier	Will	1759	CF1783-004
Burgess, Edward, in Stafford Co.	Fauquier	Will	1759	CF1789-018
Burgess, Hannah, in Greene Co. NY	Fairfax	Will	1835	CF1881-003
Burgess, R.U., in Southampton Co.	Portsmouth	Will	1888	CF1901-021
Burgh, Thomas	Prince George	Will	1752	SV 8:2, p. 64
Burgh, Thomas, of Prince George Co.	Amelia	Will	1752	CF
Burkart, Joseph W., Elizabeth City Co.	D.C.	Will	1890	DCA:Box 118
Burke, Henry	Caroline	Will	1777	TQ 33:2, p. 114
Burke, John	Essex	Will	1788	CF1807-002
Burke, John, of *Burke's Tavern*	Caroline	Will	1790	TQ 33:2, p. 115
Burke, Silas	Fairfax	Guard. Acct.	1844	X
Burke, Thomas H.	Caroline	Will	1829	TQ 33:2, p. 114
Burke, Thomas Henry	Caroline	Will	1829	LVA Acc. #22870
Burks, George	Buckingham	Will	1838	MVG 49:3, p. 178
Burn, James	Fairfax	Admin. Bond	1750	X
Burnell, Francis	New Kent	Will	1669	V:Mss2 B2946 b 9-13
Burnett, Margaret	Hanover	Will	1834	Cocke:30
Burnett, Margaret	Hanover	Will	1834	CF1837-004
Burnett, Richard P.	New Kent	Will	1878	CF1889-009
Burnett, Robert	Lunenburg	Will	1847	CF1871-067
Burnette, Richard	Hanover	Will	1833	CF1837-004
Burnley, Hardinia	Hanover	Will	1835	CF1838-003
Burnley, John	Hanover	Will	1779	CF1871-022
Burnley, John	Hanover	Will	1780	LVA Acc. #36195, r99
Burnley, John, in Great Britain	Hanover	Will	1778	CF1871-022
Burnley, John, in London, Eng.	Hanover	Will Abstract	1785	Cocke:24
Burnley, John, of Hanover Co.	London	Will	1780	N:PROB11/1061
Burnley, Samuel G., in Fluvanna Co.	Albemarle	Will	1875	CF1887-012
Burras, Jacob, in Caroline Co.	Louisa	Will	1742	CF1768-001
Burras, Thomas	Orange	Will	1789	V:Mss1 G8855 b 124+
Burrass, Jacob [of Goose Pond]	Caroline	Will	1742	LVA Acc. #32230
Burrell, William, planter		Will	1648	VCRP, Survey #03996
Burroughs, Jacob, in Caroline Co.	Louisa	Will	1742	CF1768-001
Burroughs, James, in Franklin Co.	Bedford	Will	1861	CF1894-053
Burrow, John	Dinwiddie	Will	1778	LVA Acc. #27477
Burrow, John	Dinwiddie	Will	1797	BRCD
Burrow, John, in Orange Co. NC	Dinwiddie	Will, 1778	1797	VG 14, p. 152
Burrow, Philip, Sr.	Dinwiddie	Will	1778	LVA Acc. #27464
Burrow, Philip, Sr., in Orange Co. NC	Dinwiddie	Will, 1778	1797	VG 14, p. 150
Burrus, Henry	Caroline	Will	1840	Weisiger 1:075
Burrus, John	Caroline	Will	1778	FDC L565-19
Burrus, Sally, in Amherst Co.	Lynchburg	Will	1813	CF1831-002
Burruss, Jacob [Burroughes]	Caroline	Will	1742	VGSQ 13:2, p. 47

NAME	LOCATION	TYPE	YEAR	REFERENCE(S)
Burruss, Samuel	Caroline	Will	1828	Note[1]
Burruss, Thomas	Caroline	Will	1824	W&P1742, p. 17
Burt, Philip, of York Co.	Williamsburg	Will Abstract	1798	Crozier, p. 7
Burton, Benjamin	Fairfax	Will	1808	X
Burton, Benjamin	Fairfax	Inventory	1816	X
Burton, May	Orange	Will	1828	UVA MSS 702
Burton, May, in Orange Co.	Greene	Will	1827	CF1868-002
Burton, May, in Orange Co.	Greene	Will	1827	CF1884-002
Burton, May, in Orange Co.	Greene	Will	1828	CF1893-007
Burton, Philip, in Amherst Co.	Lynchburg	Will	1804	CF1822-013
Burton, Robert	Richmond City	Will	1807	BRCD, DC-R
Burton, Robert	Richmond City	Will	1837	BRCD
Burton, Robert, in Bedford Co.	Lynchburg	Will	1819	CF1827-001
Burton, William	Northampton	Will	1770	LVA Acc. #24194
Burton, William	Stafford	Will	1778	MVG 26:4, p. 264
Burwell, B.L., in NY	Powhatan	Will	1874	CF1909-080
Burwell, Carter	James City	Will	1756	LVA Acc. #24801
Burwell, George Harrison		Account	1784	V:Mss1 B8306 b1349+
Burwell, James	York	Will Ref.	1718	Hening, Vol. 8, p. 481
Burwell, James B., in Richmond Co.	Essex	Will	1811	CF1845-022
Burwell, James B., in Richmond Co.	Frederick	Will	1811	CF1824-190
Burwell, James B., in Richmond Co.	Frederick	Will	1811	CF1831-022
Burwell, James, of King's Creek	York	Will	1718	V:Mss6:1 B9582:4
Burwell, James, of Richmond Co.	Middlesex	Will	1811	CF1856-002
Burwell, James, of Richmond Co.	Frederick	Will	1818	CF1838-025
Burwell, Lewis	York	Estate Ref.	1736	Hening, Vol. 4, p. 534
Burwell, Lewis, in Henrico Co.	Roanoke	Will	1803	CF1846-009
Burwell, Lewis, of Richmond City	Augusta	Will	1803	CF1805-043
Burwell, Nathaniel	Gloucester	Will Ref.	1721	Note[2]
Burwell, Nathaniel	Gloucester	Will Ref.	1721	Hening, Vol. 8, p. 448
Burwell, Nathaniel	King William	Will	1802	Note[3]
Burwell, Robert, in Isle of Wight Co.	Frederick	Will	1777	CF1815-078
Burwell, Robert, in Isle of Wight Co.	Frederick	Will	1777	CF1815-060
Burwell, Robert, in Isle of Wight Co.	King & Queen	Will	1777	Note[4]
Burwell, Robert, in Isle of Wight Co.	King & Queen	Will	1777	WMQ 7, p. 311
Burwell, Robert, of Isle of Wight Co.	Williamsburg	Will Abstract	1777	Crozier, p. 10
Burwelll, Lewis, the Elder, of Botetourt	Augusta	Will	1804	CF1832-062
Bushby, William, in Washington DC	Arlington	Will	1810	CF1832-001
Bushong, John, in PA	Gloucester	Will	1886	CF1888-018
Bushrod, Thomas	Westmoreland	Will	1698	VG 18, p. 55
Butcher, John, of Alexandria	Arlington	Will	1811	CF1854-005
Butler, Catherine L.	Dinwiddie	Will	1858	CF1863-003
Butler, Epaphroditus	Isle of Wight	Will	1810	SV 11:3, p. 114
Butler, John		Will	1711	V:Mss1 B4678 a 4788
Butler, John	Prince George	Will	1778	BRCD

---

[1] Caroline County Land Causes, 1835-1913, Vol. 1, p. 29.
[2] *Proceedings of Clarke County Historical Association*, Vol. 4 (1944), p. 6.
[3] Franklin County, Ky. Deeds, Bk. F, p. 238
[4] LVA, U.S. Circuit Court Records, Box 24, *McDowell, Sterling v. Burwell* (1831).

NAME	LOCATION	TYPE	YEAR	REFERENCE(S)
Butler, John	Fairfax	Account	1836	X
Butler, John	King William	Will	1845	V:Mss1 Eu177 a 159
Butler, John, of Prince George Co.	Petersburg	Will	1778	CF1841-033
Butler, John, of Westmoreland Co.	Rappahannock*	Will Abstract	1677	VMHB 5, p. 286
Butler, John [of *Audalusia*]	Caroline	Will	1810	LVA Acc. #22892
Butler, Jonathan	Dinwiddie	Will	1844	CF1863-003
Butler, Lawrence	Frederick	Will	1811	TQ 13:4, p. 272
Butler, Reuben	King William	Estate Ref.	1806	LP:23 JAN 1836
Butler, Tobias		Will	1688	VMHB 3, p. 203
Butler, William	King William	Will	1861	CF1911-023
Butler, William	King William	Sale	1862	BRCD
Butler, William	King William	Account	1863	BRCD
Butler, William	King William	Account	1864	CF1911-023
Butt, Arthur, of Norfolk Co.	Williamsburg	Will (N)	1822	Crozier, p. 7
Butt, Josiah		Will Partial	1800	Fleet, Huntington Data
Butterworth, Benjamin, in Petersburg	Henrico	Will	1848	CF1889-001
Buttimore, Dennis, of Alexandria	D.C.	Will	1897	DCA:Box 167
Butts, Andrew J.	Staunton	Will	1898	CF1909-001
Byerly, John	Rockingham	Will	1831	CF1842-001
Byrd, Ariadne Price	Hanover	Will	1860	CF1876-017
Byrd, Mary, of *Westover*	London	Will	1819	N:PROB11/1620
Byrd, Mary Willing, of *Westover*	Charles City	Will	1814	Note[1]
Byrd, Mary Willing, of *Westover*	Charles City	Will	1814	V:Mss2 B9962 a 5
Byrd, Mary Willing, of *Westover*	Charles City	Will	1814	VMHB 6, p. 346
Byrd, Otway	Lunenburg	Will	1889	CF1895-008
Byrd, Thomas Taylor	Frederick	Will	1820	V:Ms11 B9968 c 1-2
Byrd, W. Carter, in Highland Co. OH	Lynchburg	Will	1818	CF1821-016
Byrd, William, I, of Westover Parish	Charles City	Will	1704	WMQ2 3, p. 246
Byrd, William, III	Charles City	Will	1777	V:Mss2 B9966 a 3
Byrd, William, III, in Charles City Co.	Lynchburg	Will	1774	CF1821-016
Byrd, William, III, of Westover Parish	Charles City	Will	1777	VMHB 38, p. 59
Byrd, William, of Westover Parish	Charles City	Will	1704	LVA Acc. #35434
Byrd, William, of Westover Parish	Charles City	Will	1704	VMHB 48, p. 331
Byrd, William, of Westover Parish	Charles City	Will	1743	V:Mss2 B9964 a 11
Byrd, William, of Westover Parish	Charles City	Will	1744	LVA Acc. #28412
Byrd, William, of *Westover*	Charles City	Will	1777	VMHB 9, p. 85
Byrne, James, in Petersburg	Culpeper	Will	1817	CF1839-014
Byrne, James, in Petersburg	Culpeper	Will	1817	CF1839-006
Byrne, James, in Petersburg	Fauquier	Will	1818	CF1866-076
Byrom, James	Essex	Will Abstract	1748	Fleet 2:302
Bywater, Abraham	Prince George	Will	1767	UVA MSS 8486
Bywater, Abraham, Martins Brandon	Prince George	Will	1768	LVA Acc. #26732
Bywaters, Robert	Culpeper	Will	1829	CF1836-002

---

[1] LVA, U.S. Circuit Court Records, Virginia District, Box 121, *Byrd [Charles] v. Byrd's Exors* (1826).

NAME	LOCATION	TYPE	YEAR	REFERENCE(S)

C

NAME	LOCATION	TYPE	YEAR	REFERENCE(S)
Cabaniss, Asa, in Nottoway Co.	Lunenburg	Will	1829	CF1839-004
Cabell, Ann, in Nelson Co.	Bedford	Will	1838	CF1844-041
Cabell, George, in Campbell Co.	Lynchburg	Will	1823	CF1827-028
Cabell, Joseph	Buckingham	Will	1798	VG 15, p. 298
Cabell, Joseph	Buckingham	Will	1798	LVA Acc. #28458
Cabell, Joseph C., in Nelson Co.	Albemarle	Will	1856	CF1874-005
Cabell, Landon, in Amherst Co.	Lynchburg	Will	1834	CF1871-003
Cabell, Powhatan B., of Pittsylvania Co.	Danville	Will	1860	WBA:180
Cabell, Samuel J., in Nelson Co.	Lynchburg	Will	1818	CF1828-039
Cabell, Samuel J., in Nelson Co.	Lynchburg	Will	1818	CF1823-029
Cabell, William, Dr.	Amherst	Will	1774	V:Mss1 C1118 a 1-2
Cady, Henry	Hanover	Will	1879	CF1884-026
Cady, Henry	Hanover	Will	1879	CF1897-013
Cady, Lucinda, in PA	Hanover	Will	1886	CF1900-027
Cady, Lucinda, of Hanover Co.	D.C.	Will	1890	DCA: Box 118
Cain, Peter	Prince George	Will	1830	SV 9:1, p. 22
Calaway, Hannah, in Scott Co.	Wise	Will	1892	CF1894-027
Caldwell, Andrew, in Berkeley Co.	Frederick	Will	1790	CF1819-075
Caldwell, John	Augusta	Will	1790	WB8, p. 179
Caldwell, John	Augusta	Will	1790	Finley
Caldwell, John	Augusta	Will	1795	Finley
Caldwell, John	Augusta	Will	1795	WB8, p. 291
Caldwell, John	Augusta	Will	1823	Finley
Caldwell, Joseph, in Loudoun Co.	Frederick	Will	1793	CF1834-059
Callaway, Hannah, in Scott Co.	Washington	Will	1886	CF1899-003
Callaway, James, in Amherst Co.	Lynchburg	Will	1795	CF1827-073
Callaway, James, in Amherst Co.	Lynchburg	Will	1795	CF1827-034
Callaway, James, in Bedford Co.	Lynchburg	Will	1809	CF1821-076
Callaway, James, in Bedford Co.	Lynchburg	Will	1809	CF1831-014
Callaway, James, in Bedford Co.	Lynchburg	Will	1809	CF1821-072
Callaway, William, Sr., in Bedford Co.	Lynchburg	Will	1821	CF1834-021
Callicot, James J., in Charlotte Co.	Lynchburg	Will	1823	CF1830-014
Callis, Betsey	Mathews	Guard. Acct.	1811	BRCD
Callis, James, in Lunenburg Co.	Franklin	Will	1798	CF1834-007
Callis, Lewis B.	Gloucester	Will	1841	CF1909-030
Callis, Robert, orphans of	Mathews	Guard. Acct.	1811	TVF 5:1, p. 39
Callis, William H.	Mathews	Guard. Acct.	1811	Note[1]
Calloway, Hannah	Wise	Will	1886	CF1890-025
Calthorpe, James	York	Will	1711	CF1841-007
Calvert, George, 3rd son of Lord Geo.		Will	1635	VCRP, Survey #03970
Calvert, George, in Fairfax Co.	Prince William	Will	1830	CF1834-008
Calvert, Maximilian, of Norfolk Borough	Williamsburg	Will Abstract	1782	Crozier, p. 13
Calvert, Ralls	Culpeper	Will	1814	CF1845-014
Calvert, Ralls, in Culpeper Co.	Rappahannock	Will	1814	CF1845-015
Calvert, Thomas, of Princess Anne Co.	Williamsburg	Will Abstract	1813	Crozier, p. 13
Camden, William, in Amherst Co.	Lynchburg	Will	1813	CF1816-005
Cameron, John	Lunenburg	Will	1815	V:Mss2 C1458 a 1

---

[1] Auditor of Public Accounts, Record Group 48, Box 756, Folder 1814-1815.

NAME	LOCATION	TYPE	YEAR	REFERENCE(S)
Camm, John	King & Queen	Will	1767	LVA Acc. #20953
Camm, John	King & Queen	Will	1767	LVA Acc. #24417
Camm, John	King & Queen	Will	1767	V:Mss3 K5893 a 69-86
Camm, John, of *North Bank*	King & Queen	Will	1766	Fleet 2:337
Camp, George	James City	Will	1761	LVA Acc. #24194
Camp, Rebecca, of James City Co.	Williamsburg	Will Abstract	1797	Crozier, p. 14
Campbell, Alexander S., in MD	Fauquier	Will	1890	CF1893-021
Campbell, America W.	Orange	Will	1862	UVA MSS 5346
Campbell, Angus, Capt.		Will	1809	UVA MSS 5067-a
Campbell, Archibald	Surry	Will Abstract	1805	VG 13, p. 52
Campbell, Archibald	Surry	Will (U)	1805	VTG 13:2, p. 55
Campbell, Arthur, in Knox Co. KY	Lee	Will	1812	LVA Acc. #38926
Campbell, Donald, of Norfolk Borough	Williamsburg	Will Abstract	1794	Crozier, p. 13
Campbell, Isaac, Rev.	Prince William	Will Ref.	1778	Note[1]
Campbell, J., in KY	Washington	Will	1880	CF1903-001
Campbell, James	Essex	Will	1774	Fleet 2:344
Campbell, James	Fairfax	Account	1829	X
Campbell, James, in Chesterfield Co.	Washington	Will	1814	CF1903-001
Campbell, James, in KY	Wise	Will	1880	CF1883-019
Campbell, James, of Essex Co.	Williamsburg	Will Abstract	1774	Crozier, p. 13
Campbell, Lawrence, in Amherst Co.	Lynchburg	Will	1814	CF1834-003
Campbell, Mary, in KY	Washington	Will	1884	CF1903-001
Campbell, Robert James Caulfield, Eng.	Albemarle	Will	1878	CF1888-021
Campbell, Sarah	King & Queen	Will	1796	Fleet, 2nd Collection
Campbell, Sarah, of King & Queen Co.	Williamsburg	Will Abstract	1798	Crozier, p. 14
Campbell, Walter, Sr., in MD	Richmond	Will	1872	CF1879-005
Campbell, William	Orange	Will	1823c	V:Mss1 B2346 a 24-251
Campbell, William, mariner		Will	1693	VCRP, Survey #03956
Campbell, William, sailor		Will Ref.	1693	VCRP, Survey #03955
Campbell, William, St. Stephen's Par.	King & Queen	Will	1805	Fleet 2:170
Cannop, John, mariner		Will	1706	VCRP, Survey #03893
Caphart, Rosana, of Richmond	Henrico	Will	1815	VGSQ 18:3, p. 80
Capps, Edward, Sr., of Lynhaven Parish	Princess Anne	Will	1801	SV 15:1, p. 36
Cardwell, Amelia G., in Charlotte Co.	Lunenburg	Will	1858	CF1868-013
Cardwell, Jane	Dinwiddie	Will	1796	VG 16, p. 165
Cardwell, John	King William	Will	1850	CF1925-002
Cardwell, John	King William	Account	1861	CF1925-002
Cardwell, William, in Charlotte Co.	Prince Edward	Will	1874	CF1912-020
Carey, Mylles	Warwick	Will	1667	LVA Acc. #24813-1
Carlin, James, in Alexandria	Rappahannock	Will	1882	CF1903-004
Carlton, Alice	Hanover	Will	1861	CF1880-016
Carlton, Ambrose	Richmond City	Will	1878	V:Mss1 C1972 a22-24
Carlton, Elizabeth	King & Queen	Will	1917	LP
Carlton, George K.	King & Queen	Will	1846	CF1860-002
Carlton, Isaac	King & Queen	Will	1824	Note[2]
Carlton, James Ryland	King & Queen	Will	1915	LP

---

[1] Prince William County Land Causes, 1793-1811, p. 149.

[2] Halifax County Chancery Suits, *Leonard Carlton, Exor. of William Carlton v. William Dews*; also see *The Southside Virginian*, Vol. V No. 1 (January 1987), pp. 31-37. Also see King & Queen Chancery CF1852-037.

NAME	LOCATION	TYPE	YEAR	REFERENCE(S)
Carlton, John	King & Queen	Will	1835c	V:Mss1 M1752a92-108
Carlton, John R., in Middlesex Co.	Essex	Will	1844	CF1879-027
Carlton, Lewis	King & Queen	Will	1819	CF1874-004
Carlton, Lewis	King & Queen	Will (N)	1861	LP
Carlton, Sebell	Essex	Will	1769	Fleet 2:339
Carlton, William	King & Queen	Will	1812	Note[1]
Carlyle, John	Fairfax	Will	1780	V:Mss1 C1995 a 37-39
Carmichael, Eliza, in NY	Fairfax	Will	1891	CF1909-009
Carmichael, Eliza, in NY	Fairfax	Will	1894	CF1910-026
Carn, Nicholas, of Rockingham Co.	Augusta	Will	1815	CF1825-127
Carnathan, John		Will	1702	VCRP, Survey #04119
Carney, James H., in Norfolk Co.	Portsmouth	Will	1854	CF1892-013
Carpenter, Charles	Culpeper	Will	1804c	V: F232 C9 S61
Carpenter, William W.	Hanover	Will	1866	CF1885-012
Carper, Frederick	Fairfax	Plat	1877	X
Carper, Frederick	Fairfax	Division	1877	X
Carr, Caldwell, in Loudoun Co.	Fauquier	Will	1855	CF1860-053
Carr, Dabney	Henrico	Will	1837	LVA Acc. #28458
Carr, Dabney	Henrico	Will	1837	Note[2]
Carr, Robert	Nansemond	Will	1773	LVA Acc. #34676
Carr, Robert	Nansemond	Will	1773	SV 12:3, p. 128
Carr, Thomas	King William	Will	1735	UVA MSS 7690-ah
Carr, Thomas, of *Topping Castle*	Caroline	Will	1738	UVA Acc. #4257
Carr, William	Prince William	Will	1791	Fleet, Huntington Data
Carr, William, in Prince William Co.	Fauquier	Will	1791	CF1873-037
Carr, William, of Prince William Co.	Arlington	Will	1791	Judgments 1818
Carraway, George S.	Hanover	Will	1888	CF1884-033
Carrel, Elizabeth	Surry	Will (U)	1847	VTG 13:3, p. 127
Carrell, Elizabeth	Surry	Will Abstract	1847	VG 13, p. 53
Carrington, C.S., in Rockbridge Co.	Washington	Will	1896	CF1898-007
Carrington, Joseph L., in Richmond	Henrico	Will	1887	CF1910-030
Carrington, Joseph L., in Richmond	Henrico	Will	1890	CF1912-045
Carrington, W.A., in TX	Mecklenburg	Will	1896	CF1906-038 CC
Carson, Charles S.	Washington	Will	1813	MVG 29:3, p. 190
Carter, Abram, late of Fluvanna Co.	D.C.	Will	1882	DCA:Box 78
Carter, Charles	King George	Estate Ref.	1766	Hening, Vol. 8, p. 214
Carter, Charles	Charles City	Will	1806	LVA Acc. #26820
Carter, Charles	Charles City	Will	1806	LVA Acc. #24194
Carter, Charles	Charles City	Will	1806	V:Mss2 C24534 a 1
Carter, Charles	Culpeper	Will	1819	LVA Acc. #25226
Carter, Charles, Dr.	Lancaster	Estate	1825c	LVA Acc. #24295
Carter, Charles, in Charles City Co.	Fairfax	Will	1806	CF1851-008
Carter, Charles L., of Fauquier Co.	D.C.	Will	1891	DCA: Box 123
Carter, Charles, of *Cleve*	King George	Will	1762	VMHB 31, p. 39
Carter, Charles, of *Cleve*	King George	Will Ref.	1762	Hening, Vol. 8, p. 436
Carter, Charles, of *Cleve*	King George	Estate Ref.	1766	Hening, Vol. 8, p. 218

---

[1] Halifax Co. Chancery Suits, *Leonard Carlton, Exor. of William Carlton v. William Dews*; also see *The Southside Virginian*, Vol. V No. 1 (January 1987), pp. 31-37. Also see King & Queen Chancery CF1852-037.
[2] LVA, Treasurer's Office Material, "James River and Kanawha County Guaranteed Bonds, Wills and Certificates," Acc. #28458.

NAME	LOCATION	TYPE	YEAR	REFERENCE(S)
Carter, Curtis, in Henrico Co.	Essex	Will	1850	CF1884-028
Carter, Eden	Loudoun	Will	1859	LVA Acc. #41008, r4610
Carter, Eden, in Williams Co. OH	Loudoun	Will	1857	Fleet, Huntington Data
Carter, Edward, in Fredericksburg	Frederick	Will	1792	CF1818-090
Carter, Edward, in Fredericksburg	Lynchburg	Will	1792	CF1822-018
Carter, Edward, of *Blenheim*	Albemarle	Will	1792	UVA MSS 807
Carter, Edward, of *Blenheim*	Albemarle	Will Abstract	1792	VMHB 44, p. 353
Carter, Edward, of Fredericksburg	Albemarle	Will	1792	CF1873-017
Carter, Emily H.	Fairfax	Guard. Bond	1817	X
Carter, George	Fairfax	Admin.	1742	V:Mss2 C2469 b
Carter, George		Will Ref.	1794	Shepherd, Vol. 1, p. 334
Carter, George	Hanover	Will	1862	CF1886-007
Carter, George P.	Hanover	Will	1878	CF1900-024
Carter, Gertrude	Fauquier	Will	1872	CF1894-076
Carter, James	Williamsburg	Will Abstract	1794	Crozier, p. 15
Carter, Jesse L., in Pittsylvania Co.	Henrico	Will	1880	CF1881-004
Carter, Jesse, Rev.	King & Queen	Account	1801	LVA Acc. #25251
Carter, John		Admin.	1747	V:Mss10: no. 187
Carter, John	Fairfax	Plat	1840	X
Carter, John	Fairfax	Division	1840	X
Carter, John, late of *The Trap*	Caroline	Will	1834	TVF 10:4, p. 226
Carter, Joseph	Prince George	Will	1760	DB1759, p. 150
Carter, Landon, in Richmond Co.	Fauquier	Will	1761	CF1805-058
Carter, Lawson H., in Franklin Co.	Bedford	Will	1849	CF1860-058
Carter, Peter, of Cameron Parish	Loudoun	Will	1794	NVG 3:4, p. 141
Carter, Robert	Lancaster	Will Ref.	1726	Hening, Vol. 8, p. 464
Carter, Robert	Lancaster	Will Ref.	1726	Hening, Vol. 8, p. 445
Carter, Robert	Fairfax	Plat	1822	X
Carter, Robert	Fairfax	Division	1822	X
Carter, Robert "King"	Lancaster	Will	1730	UVA MSS 13535
Carter, Robert "King"	Lancaster	Will	1730	V:Mss1 C2468 a9-26
Carter, Robert "King"	Lancaster	Will	1730	LVA Acc. #25840
Carter, Robert, of *Corotoman*	Lancaster	Will Ref.	1726	Winfree, p. 428
Carter, Robert Wormeley, Richmond Co.	Arlington	Will	1797	CF1814-008
Carter, Sally, of Stafford Co.	Arlington	Will	1809	CF1814-023
Carter, Samuel S., in Richmond	Henrico	Will	1832	CF1871-013
Carter, Sophia	Prince William	Will	1832	Note[1]
Carter, Thomas	Hanover	Estate Ref.	1801	LP:09 DEC 1834
Carter, Thomas O.B.	Fauquier	Will	1840	LVA Acc. #41008, r4608
Carter, Thomas O.B.	Fauquier	Will	1840	Fleet, Huntington Data
Carter, Thomas O.B., in Fauquier Co.	King George	Will	(nd)	CF1856-002
Carter, Thomas, Rev.	Warwick	Will	1837	BRCD
Cartwright, Jesse	Prince George	Will	1842	SV 9, p. 106
Cartwright, Marmaduke	Nansemond	Will	1885	BRCD
Cartwright, Rachael, Bladensburg MD	Arlington	Will	1869	WB9:185; File #672A
Carver, Fannie P.	Hanover	Will	1880	CF1882-005
Cary, Ann, of Gloucester Co.	Cumberland	Will	1788	CF1803-003
Cary, Archibald, in Chesterfield Co.	Lynchburg	Will	1787	CF1820-044

---

[1] LVA, U.S. Circuit Court Records, Virginia District, Box 205, *Carter & Wife v. Carter's Exors.* (1840).

NAME	LOCATION	TYPE	YEAR	REFERENCE(S)
Cary, Elizabeth, of Warwick Co.	Williamsburg	Will Abstract	1805	Crozier, p. 14
Cary, Henry, in Chesterfield Co.	Henrico	Will	1749	LVA Acc. #21434
Cary, Martha Ann, in Richmond	Lynchburg	Will	1878	CF1882-016
Cary, Mary	Surry	Will	1804	WMQ 20, p. 289
Cary, Miles	Warwick	Will	1667	LVA Acc. #21438-1
Cary, Miles, Gent.	Warwick	Will Ref.	1667	Winfree, p. 347
Cary, Miles, in Albemarle Co.	Henrico	Will	1849	CF1857-003
Cary, Miles, of *Ceeley*	Elizabeth City	Will Abstract	1752	Fleet 2:329
Cary, Richard, merchant		Will	1730	VCRP, Survey #04657
Cary, Sarah, in Frederick Co.	Rappahannock	Will	1861	CF1893-008
Cary, Sary to William Newsum	King & Queen	Marriage	1823	LP
Cary, Thomas, of Warwick Co.	Williamsburg	Will Abstract	1792	Crozier, p. 14
Cary, Thomas W., of Warwick Co.	Williamsburg	Will Abstract	1819	Crozier, p. 14
Cary, William, of *Mulberry Island*	Warwick	Will	1713	LVA Acc. #24813
Cary, Wilson, of *Ceeley*	Elizabeth City	Will Abstract	1752	Fleet 2:329
Cary, Wilson, of *Ceelys*	Elizabeth City	Will	1772	VMHB 10, p. 189
Cash, Howard	Amherst	Will	1772	VTG 7:4, p. 214
Cash, Howard	Amherst	Will	1772	GSTV 17, p. 214
Cash, James	King George	Will	1782	FDC L560-33
Cash, William	Westmoreland	Will	1708	FDC L560-33
Caskie, James, in Richmond	Fauquier	Will	1866	CF1885-002
Cason, Cornelius	Princess Anne	Will	1802	SV 15:2, p. 91
Cate, John	Prince George	Will	1839	SV 9:2, p. 57
Cathon, James	Warwick	Will	1696	TVF 1:1, p. 37
Cathon, James	Warwick	Will	1696	LVA Acc. #22067 p. 455
Catlett, Charles J., in Loudoun Co.	Arlington	Will	1844	CF1848-025
Catlett, John	Caroline	Will	1739c	V:Mss2 T1439 b
Catlett, John, in Frederick Co.	Warren	Will	1826	CF1840-003
Catlett, John, in Frederick Co.	Warren	Will	1826	CF1850-002
Catlett, John, of Gloucester Co.	Williamsburg	Will Abstract	1808	Crozier, p. 14
Catlett, Samuel Jones	King William	Will	1810	LP:18 DEC 1810
Catlett, Thomas	Caroline	Inventory	1739c	V:Mss2 T1439 b
Catlett, William	Essex	Will Ref.	1749	V:Mss2 M5348 a1
Catterton, Francis, in Orange Co.	Greene	Will	1834	CF1848-003
Catts, G. Henry	Prince William	Will	1887	CF1913-031
Cavanaugh, Philemon	Orange	Will	1744	FDC V390-17
Cavanaugh, Susannah, in Bedford Co.	Franklin	Will	1840	CF1849-045
Cavans, William, in Loudoun Co.	Frederick	Will	1804	CF1820-124
Cave, Belfield	Orange	Will	1811	V:Mss1 B2346 a 1151
Cave, Benjamin	Orange	Will	1762	V:Mss1 C3154 a 1-2
Cavendish, Alice Mann	Bath	Inventory	1858c	V:Mss2 M1326 b
Cavendish, William H.	Bath	Will	1818	V:Mss2 M1326 b
Cazenove, Anthony C., Alexandria Co.	Fairfax	Will	1852	CF1902-007
Cazenove, Anthony Charles	Fairfax	Will	1775	CF1902-007
Cecil, Witten	Tazewell	Will	1841	CF1876-051
Chadick, James	James City	Will	1811	Swem(1):f129
Chaffin, John Booker	Amelia	Inventory	1856	V:Mss2 C3468 b
Chaffin, Susan Adeline Willson	Amelia	Account	1865	V:Mss2 C3468 b
Chaffin, Susan Adeline Willson	Henrico	Will	1870	V:Mss2 C3468 b
Chalmers, Anna M., of Albemarle Co.	D.C.	Will	1782	DCA: Box 130
Chamberlain, John, planter	Essex	Will	1725	Fleet 2:244

NAME	LOCATION	TYPE	YEAR	REFERENCE(S)
Chambers, Sarah, in Prince William Co.	Smyth	Will	1813	CF1846-006
Chambers, Sarah, in Prince William Co.	Smyth	Will	1813	CF1846-010
Chambless, William, of Bristol Parish	Prince George	Will	1759	DB1787, p. 635
Chambliss, William, in Sussex Co.	Brunswick	Will	1802	CF1822-011
Champe, Jane, of Lamb's Creek	King George	Will	1767	VMHB 44, p. 276
Champe, John	King George	Will	1759	V:Mss10: no. 187
Champe, John, of Lamb's Creek	King George	Will	1763	VMHB 44, p. 274
Champe, William	Culpeper	Will	1784	VMHB 44, p. 280
Champion, Vienna	Prince George	Will	1852	SV 9:4, p. 159
Chandler, Bolling	Dinwiddie	Will	1884	CF1891-004
Chandler, Elizabeth, of Rockingham Co.	Augusta	Will	1847	CF1859-001
Chandler, Harman	New Kent	Will	1867	CF1878-002
Chandler, Robert	Caroline	Will	1803	V:Mss2 C3636 b
Chandler, Robert	Caroline	Inventory	1803c	V:Mss2 C3636 b
Chandler, Robert	Caroline	Will	1815	TQ 22:1, p. 53
Chandler, Rufus [of *Little Yale*]	Caroline	Will	1832	LVA Acc. #24120
Chandler, Timothy	Caroline	Will	1803	TQ 22:1, p. 50
Chandler, Timothy	Caroline	Will	1831	BRCD
Chandler, Timothy, of Caroline Co.	Rockbridge	Will	1825	CF1831-008
Chandler, Timothy, of Caroline Co.	Louisa	Will	1831	CF1836-010
Chandler, Timothy [of *Woodland*]	Caroline	Will	1803	V:Mss2 C3636 b
Chandler, William	Caroline	Inventory	(nd)	V:Mss2 C3636 b
Chandler, William	Caroline	Will	1821	TQ 22:1, p. 54
Chandler, William	Caroline	Will	1822	V:Mss2 C3636 b
Chapman, Aaron	James City	Will	1883	CF1888-005
Chapman, Constant	Fairfax	Will	1798	FDC V558-144
Chapman, George, in Prince William Co.	Fauquier	Will	1829	CF1838-045
Chapman, George, of *Thoroughfare*	Prince William	Will	1827	V:Mss1 C3676 a 5-8
Chapman, George, of *Thoroughfare*	Arlington	Will	1869	WB9:202; File #675A
Chapman, John	Spotsylvania	Will	1776	FDC L386-11
Chapman, Matilda Louisa Chapman	Charles Co. MD	Will	1866	V:Mss1 C3676 a 9-12
Chapman, Taylor, of Overwharton Par.	Stafford	Will	1749	D&W O, p. 80
Chapman, William, of Alexandria DC	London	Will	1801	N:PROB11/1352
Chappell, Jacob	Princess Anne	Will	1795	SV 15:2, p. 86
Chappell, John C.	Lunenburg	Will	1829	CF1836-032
Chappell, Robert W.	Petersburg	Will	1855	V:Mss1 B3445 b 131+
Chappell, William, in Sussex Co.	Dinwiddie	Will	1844	CF1855-003
Chareon, Anthony, of St. Anne's Parish	Albemarle	Will	1755	VMHB 37, p. 165
Charles, Kemp, of Warwick Co.	Williamsburg	Will Abstract	1782	Crozier, p. 12
Charles, Thomas	Warwick	Will	1795	BRCD
Charles, Thomas, in Warwick Co.	York	Will	1795	CF1808-001
Charles, Thomas, of Warwick Co.	York	Will	1795	MVG 31:4, p. 356
Charles, William	York	Will	1816	CF1823-001
Charlton, Stephen	Northampton	Will	1645	VMHB 77, p. 259
Charlton, Stephen	Northampton	Will	1645	V:Mss2 C3817 a 1
Charroon, Anthony	Buckingham	Will	1771	SV 3:3, p. 122
Charroon, Anthony	Buckingham	Will	1771	LVA Acc. #25971c
Chastain, Lewis, in KY	Bedford	Will	1814	CF1825-005
Cheatham, Thomas	Chesterfield	Will	1795	V:Mss1 T2478b146-147
Cheatham, Thomas	Lunenburg	Will	1876	CF1894-004
Cheek, Jacob	Bath	Will	1813	LVA Acc. #31648

NAME	LOCATION	TYPE	YEAR	REFERENCE(S)
Chelton, Nicholas [Shelton]		Will	1738	LVA Wills/Admin. DB
Chenoweth, John, in Berkeley Co.	Frederick	Will	1814	CF1851-087
Cherry, Priscilla, of Norfolk Co.	Williamsburg	Will Abstract	1816	Crozier, p. 12
Chesley, Philip, of York Co.	London	Will	1675	N:PROB11/347
Chesley, Phillip, of York Co.		Will	1675	VCRP, Survey #03554
Chetwine, Edward	Isle of Wight	Will Abstract	1649	VMHB 6, p. 246
Cheves, John	Prince George	Will Partial	1759	DB1759, p. 196
Chichester, George	Fairfax	Plat	1869	X
Chichester, George M., in Loudoun Co.	Arlington	Will	1835	CF1849-005
Chichester, John, of Lancaster Co.		Will	1753	VCRP, Survey #06596
Chichester, John, of Lancaster Co.		Will	1763	VCRP, Survey #04639
Chichester, Mary, of Loudoun Co.	D.C.	Will	1872	DCA: Box 46
Chichester, Richard		Will	1746	VCRP, Survey #04632
Chichester, Richard, in Fairfax Co.	Arlington	Will	1798	CF1849-005
Chichester, Richard McC., Fauquier Co.	Arlington	Will	1827	CF1879-008
Chichester, Richard McC., Fauquier Co.	Alexandria	Will	1827	CF1879-008
Chichester, Richard McC., Fauquier Co.	Arlington	Will	1829	CF1849-005
Chichester, Richard McCarty	Fauquier	Will	1830	CF1870-015
Chichester, Richard, of Fairfax Co.	London	Will	1803	N:PROB11/1394
Chichester, Richard, of Lancaster Co.	London	Will	1746	N:PROB11/745
Chichester, Sarah	Fairfax	Will	1826	CF1839-016
Chichester, Sarah Elizabeth	Loudoun	Will	1878c	V:Mss1 H2485 e 1-69
Chichester, Sarah, in Fairfax Co.	Arlington	Will	1825	CF1849-005
Chick, Pettus	Hanover	Will	1854	CF1859-012
Chick, Pettus W.	Hanover	Will	1854	CF1872-013
Chick, Pettus W.	Hanover	Will	1854	Cocke:34
Chieves, Joel	Prince George	Will	1842	SV 9:3, p. 106
Child, Salmon	Fairfax	Will	1866	CF1888-035
Childress, Lucy, in Amherst Co.	Lynchburg	Will	1795	CF1817-023
Childress, Spotswood	Hanover	Will	1858	Fleet, Huntington Data
Childress, Spotswood	Hanover	Will	1858	LVA Acc. #41008, r4609
Childs, James H.	Fauquier	Will	1878	V:Mss1 C4378 a 132+
Childs, William Lewis	Fauquier	Will	(nd)	V:Mss1 C4378 a 132+
Chiles, Henry	Spotsylvania	Will Ref.	1765	VMHB 19, p. 324
Chiles, Micajah	Caroline	Will Ref.	1734	VGS Bulletin VII, p. 9
Chiles, Pleasant	Caroline	Will	1825	LP:22 DEC 1831
Chilton, Charles P., in Culpeper Co.	Fauquier	Will	1869	CF1891-045
Chilton, Judith, in Campbell Co.	Lynchburg	Will	1830	CF1834-005
Chilton, R.S.	Culpeper	Will	1896	CF1906-021
Chilton, Richard, in Campbell Co.	Lynchburg	Will	1815	CF1826-081
Chilton, Richard, in Campbell Co.	Lynchburg	Will	1822	CF1852-025
Chilton, Richard, Jr., in Campbell Co.	Lynchburg	Will	1822	CF1834-005
Chilton, Susannah, in Loudoun Co.	Frederick	Will	1816	CF1828-182
Chinn, Caroline, of Prince William Co.	D.C.	Will	1898	DCA: Box 174
Chinn, Charles	Fauquier	Will	1787	K
Chinn, Rawleigh	Loudoun	Will	1816	V:Mss2 C4415 b
Chinn, Rawleigh, in Loudoun Co.	Frederick	Will	1816	CF1828-214
Chinn, Richard, in Loudoun Co.	Frederick	Will	1800	CF1818-122
Chinn, Robert, in Lancaster Co.	Richmond	Will	1821	CF1846-004
Chinn, Robert, in Lancaster Co.	Westmoreland	Will	1821	CF1845-013
Chisholme, Hugh	Hanover	Will	1837	CF1867-001

NAME	LOCATION	TYPE	YEAR	REFERENCE(S)
Chisholme, Hugh	Hanover	Will	1837	Cocke:36
Chiswell, John	Augusta	Will	1766	VGS Bulletin VII, p. 77
Chiswell, John	Hanover	Will	1766	VGS Bulletin VII, p. 77
Chiswell, John	Hanover	Will	1766	LVA Acc. #27257
Chiswell, John	Williamsburg	Estate Ref.	1766	Hening, Vol. 8, p. 270
Chowning, Eliza B.	Spotsylvania	Will	1862	V:Mss1 H2485 a 284+
Chowning, Eliza B.	Spotsylvania	Inventory	1863	V:Mss1 H2485 a 284+
Chrisman, C.	Rockingham	Will	1846	CF1852-012
Chrisman, Elias	York	Will	1812c	VTG 11:1, p. 21
Chrisman, Erasmus	Rockingham	Will	1846	CF1852-012
Christian, Ann	New Kent	Will	1855	Note[1]
Christian, Francis H., in Frederick Co.	Fauquier	Will	1788	CF1805-040
Christian, James, in Albemarle Co.	Lynchburg	Will	1759	CF1830-132
Christian, John, of New Kent Co.	Williamsburg	Will Abstract	1801	Crozier, p. 12
Christian, Matthias, of Norfolk Co.	Williamsburg	Will Abstract	1794	Crozier, p. 12
Christian, Michael, of Northampton Co.	Williamsburg	Will Abstract	1783	Crozier, p. 12
Christian, Moses	Tazewell	Will	1855	CF1866-013
Christian, Richard Allen	Middlesex	Will	1864	V:Mss1 J6496 a 1 151-1
Christian, Solomon		Will	1740	VCRP, Survey #04661
Christian, Thomas	Goochland	Estate	(nd)	UVA MSS 4756
Christian, William	Augusta	Will	1779	Fleet, Huntington Data
Christian, William	Augusta	Will	1779	LVA Acc. #41008, r4608
Christian, William	New Kent	Will	1802	LVA Acc. #24601d
Christie, Charles I., in PA	Hanover	Will	1838	CF1899-040
Christmas, Thomas, in Warren Co. NC	Hanover	Will	1769	LVA Acc. #26293
Christmas, Thomas, in Warren Co. NC	Henrico	Will Abstract	1769	VGS Bulletin III, p. 54
Christmas, Thomas, of St. Martin's Par.	Hanover	Will	1769	V:Mss2 C4646 a 1
Christmas, Thomas, of St. Martin's Par.	Hanover	Will	1769	VGS Bulletin III, p. 54
Chrystie, John, of York River		Will	1718	VCRP, Survey #04339
Chrystie, Thomas	Hanover	Will	1812	Note[2]
Chrystie, Thomas	Hanover	Will	1812	VG 15, p. 277
Chrystie, Thomas, Dr., of Hanover	Hanover	Will	1812	V:Mss1 C4695a368-376
Churchill, Charles [Churchwill]	Portsmouth	Will	1864	CF1901-030
Churchill, Sally, in Middlesex Co.	Williamsburg	Will (N)	1799	Crozier, p. 12
Churchill, Sarah	Middlesex	Will (N)	1799	Fleet 2:351
Churchill, Sarah, in Frederick Co.	Culpeper	Will	1814	CF1849-007
Churchill, Thomas E.	Middlesex	Will	1805	V:Mss2 P9305 b
Churchman, Henry J., in Augusta Co.	Staunton	Will	1881	CF1894-018
Circle, Peter, of Botetourt Co.	Augusta	Will	1818	CF1833-005
Citzers, Matthias	Frederick	Will (U)	1843	LVA:1117621
Claiborne, Augustine	Sussex	Will	1787	TQ 05:2, p. 127
Claiborne, Augustine	Sussex	Will	1787	V:Mss1 C5217 b 5-0
Claiborne, Herbert Augustine	Richmond City	Will	1840	V:Mss1 C5217 b 79-84
Claiborne, Leonard	Buckingham	Will	1840	SV 5:1, p. 5
Claiborne, Leonard	Buckingham	Will	1840	Election[3]
Claiborne, Mary	Sussex	Will	1799	TQ 05:2, p. 130

---

[1] New Kent County Wills, Bk. 1 (1864-1887), p. 225, at the courthouse only.

[2] LVA, Land Office Military Certificates, Box 35, Folder 28.

[3] LVA, Contested Election Papers, Buckingham County, 1840/41.

NAME	LOCATION	TYPE	YEAR	REFERENCE(S)
Claiborne, Mary Burnet Browne	New Kent	Will	1804	V:Mss1 C5217 b 34-35
Claiborne, Philip	King William	Will	1796c	V:Mss1 C5217 c 20-23
Claiborne, Philip Whitehead	King William	Will	1772	V:Mss1 C5217 c 20-23
Claiborne, Thomas	Stafford	Will	1735	WBM, p. 186
Claiborne, William	King William	Will	1705	RB2, p. 43
Claiborne, William		Will	1746	VCRP, Survey #04633
Claiborne, William Dandridge	King William	Will	1811	V:Mss1 C5217 c 20-23
Claiborne, William Dandridge	King William	Will Ref.	1811	VMHB 1, p. 323
Claiborne, William, of *Romancoke*	King William	Will Abstract	1705	VMHB 1, p. 318
Claiborne, William, of *Romancoke*	King William	Will	1746	V:Mss1 C5217 c 20-23
Clajon, Philanthropos, in Jamaica	Arlington	Will	1797	CF1811-016
Clanton, John	Sussex	Will	1778	Swem
Clark, Bolling	Dinwiddie	Will	1809	SV 7:2, p. 60
Clark, Bolling	Dinwiddie	Will	1809	BRCD
Clark, Bolling	Dinwiddie	Will	1809	Note[1]
Clark, Bolling, of Bath Parish	Dinwiddie	Will	1809	LVA Acc. #33248
Clark, Francis, in Louisa Co.	Goochland	Will	(nd)	CF1809-012
Clark, Isham	Bedford	Will	1822	LVA Acc. #21615f
Clark, James, in Campbell Co.	Lynchburg	Will	1802	CF1830-101
Clark, John	Halifax	Will	1827	V:Mss1 B1565 b 1-2
Clark, John, in Campbell Co.	Lynchburg	Will	1819	CF1829-023
Clark, Jonathan	King & Queen	Will	1834	LP
Clark, Jonathan, in King & Queen Co.	Essex	Will	1734	CF1787-004
Clark, Jonathan, of Drysdale Parish	King & Queen	Will Abstract	1734	Fleet 2:326
Clark, Jonathan, of Drysdale Parish	King & Queen	Will	1734	Fleet 2:201
Clark, Jonathan, of Drysdale Parish	King & Queen	Will	1734	LVA Acc. #21036
Clark, Robert, Sr.	Essex	Will	1790	CF1818-008
Clark, Sarah, wid., of Leeds, Fauquier	London	Will	1835	N:PROB11/1842
Clark, William D., in Orange Co.	Louisa	Will	1865	CF1898-077
Clark, William H., in Halifax Co.	Campbell	Will	1871	CF1905-009
Clark, William H., in Halifax Co.	Bedford	Will	1873	CF1888-025
Clark, William, in Alleghany Co.	Bath	Will	1868	CF1901-012
Clarke, Elizabeth C.	Hanover	Will	1865	CF1867-005
Clarke, Humphrey, cooper	Isle of Wight	Will Abstract	1655	VMHB 6, p. 253
Clarke, James, in Chesterfield Co.	Lynchburg	Will	1802	CF1834-012
Clarke, John, in Middlesex Co.	Essex	Will	1834	CF1851-022
Clarke, John, Jr., late of Gloucester Co.	London	Will	1757	N:PROB11/1833
Clarke, John, of Gloucester Co.		Will	1757	VCRP, Survey #04674
Clarke, Joseph, in Orange Co.	Louisa	Will	1839	CF1898-077
Clarke, Nathaniel, in SC	Henry	Will	1869	CF1914-001
Clarke, Richard	Amelia	Will	(nd)	UVA MSS 4756
Clarke, Robert	Essex	Will	1790	CF1808-010
Clarke, Robert	Richmond City	Will	1859	Fleet, Huntington Data
Clarke, Robert, Sr., of Essex Co.	Williamsburg	Will Abstract	1790	Crozier, p. 15
Clarke, Thomas, of York Co.	London	Will	1670	N:PROB11/332
Clarke, William	Hanover	Inventory	1802	G1:21
Clarke, William	Hanover	Settlement	1807	G1:23

---

[1] See *The Southside Virginian*, Vol. VII No. 2 (April 1989), pp. 60-1. LVA, filed in a suit to divide property, in Monroe Co., Miss. Emily J. Atkinson is petitioner.

NAME	LOCATION	TYPE	YEAR	REFERENCE(S)
Clarke, William	New Kent	Will	1847	BRCD
Clarke, William, in New Kent Co.	Henrico	Will	1847	CF1873-036
Clarkson, James L., in FL	Albemarle	Will	1894	CF1903-002
Clarkson, Mary, in Essex Co.	King & Queen	Will	1865	CF1880-012
Clary, Harwood	Brunswick	Will	1790	CF1811-003
Clary, Harwood	Brunswick	Will	1790	CF1801-001
Claud, Philip J.	Southampton	Will	1859	BRCD
Claud, Phillip J.	Southampton	Will	1844	MVG 31:4, p. 353
Clay, Henry	Henrico	Will	1748	V:Mss1 B7826a307-357
Clay, John	Hanover	Will	1782	WMQ2 14, p. 174
Clay, John	Hanover	Inventory	1790	G1:29
Clay, John	Hanover	Will, 1782	1802	G1:27
Clay, John, Rev.	Hanover	Will	1782	Note[1]
Clay, Odin G., in Campbell Co.	Henrico	Will	1888	CF1889-123
Clay, Stephen, s/o Robert		Will	1734	VCRP, Survey #04667
Clay, Thomas, in Dinwiddie Co.	Petersburg	Will	1812	CF1836-029
Clayborne, William	King William	Will Abstract	(nd)	VMHB 37, p. 279
Clayborne, William	King William	Will	1705	RB2, p. 42
Claybrooke, Thomas W., in TN	Louisa	Will	1868	CF1895-012
Clayton, Alice Bowyer Buggins		Will	1692	V:Mss5:9 B4554:1
Clayton, Elizabeth	King & Queen	Will	1847	LVA Acc. #22043
Clayton, James	King & Queen	Will	1820	MVG 22:4, p. 29
Clayton, James	King & Queen	Will	1820	LVA Acc. #20628
Clayton, Jasper, Sir		Will	1660	V:Mss5:9 B4554:1
Clayton, John	Gloucester	Will	1737	V:Mss5:9 B4554:1
Clayton, John	James City	Will	1737	V:Mss5:9 B4554:1
Clayton, John	James City	Will	1737	V:Mss1 J4105 a 12-16
Clayton, John, of Ware Parish	Gloucester	Will	1774	V:Mss1 J4105 a 12-16
Clayton, John, of Williamsburg	James City	Will	1737	LVA Acc. #29679
Clayton, Lucy M. Dixon Carpenter	Gloucester	Will	1827c	V:Mss1 C5217 b 2+
Clayton, Mary Thomson		Will	1692	V:Mss5:9 B4554:1
Clayton, Pike M.	King & Queen	Account	1854c	Fleet 2:393
Clayton, Pike M.	King & Queen	Account	1855	LVA Acc. #22043
Clayton, Samuel	King & Queen	Will	1818	Fleet, 3rd Collection
Clayton, Samuel	King & Queen	Will	1820	Fleet 2:267
Clayton, William, clerk, of New Kent Co.	Williamsburg	Will Abstract	1797	Crozier, p. 18
Cleare, Ambrose, of New Kent Co.	London	Will	1697	VCRP, Survey #04777
Cleare, Ambrose, of New Kent Co.	London	Will	1697	N:PROB11/441
Cleaver, Thomas		Will	1700	VCRP, Survey #04792
Cleek, James	Bath	Will	1879	CF1880-002
Cleek, Matthias	Bath	Will	1855	CF1874-008
Cleggs, Isaiah	King & Queen	Will	(nd)	LP
Clement, George W., in Pittsylvania Co.	Franklin	Will	1867	CF1881-057
Clement, George W., in Pittsylvania Co.	Henry	Will	1867	CF1881-008
Clement, Henry Haggard	Essex	Will Abstract	1794	Fleet 2:345
Clement, John	Hanover	Will	1749	HHS 31, p. 9
Clement, John, of St. Paul's Parish	Hanover	Will	1749	LVA Acc. #26888
Clements, Bede	Arlington	Will	1814	CF1816-008

---

[1] LVA, U.S. Circuit Court Records, Box 115, *Clay's Admin. v. Thomas Cocke* (1824).

NAME	LOCATION	TYPE	YEAR	REFERENCE(S)
Clements, Henry Haggard, of Essex Co.	Williamsburg	Will Abstract	1794	Crozier, p. 17
Clements, Isham	Amelia	Estate Ref.	1803	Shepherd, Vol. 2, p. 458
Clements, John	Essex	Will	1767	CF1823-015
Clements, John C., of Gloucester Co.	Lancaster	Will	1812	CF1848-008
Clements, John, of King William Co.	Louisa	Will	1767	Judgments 1823 MAY
Clements, Mace	Essex	Will	1806	TVF 2:3, p. 169
Clements, Pitman, of Essex Co.	Williamsburg	Will Abstract	1778	Crozier, p. 17
Clements, Pitman, of Essex Co.	Williamsburg	Will Abstract	1778	Fleet 2:345
Clements, William, in Richmond Co.	Essex	Will	1708	CF1845-023
Clemments, James	Prince George	Will	1837	SV 9:2, p. 55
Clemonds, Joseph W. [Clemmand]	Smyth	Will	1852	CF1860-030
Clendening, Samuel	Loudoun	Will	1859	UVA Acc. #2
Cleve, Thomas		Will	1697	VCRP, Survey #06054
Cleveland, Johnston, in Loudoun Co.	Fairfax	Will	1834	X
Cleveland, Johnston, in Loudoun Co.	Fairfax	Will	1834	CF1857-018
Clifton, Edward, of Westover Parish	Charles City	Will	1726	D&W1724, p. 76
Clopton, Frederick, in Clarke Co.	Frederick	Will	1854	CF1857-039
Clopton, John	James City	Will	1891	CF1907-018
Clopton, Jones C., Dr., of *Bloomsbury*	Essex	Sale	1851	V:Mss1 W2296 a 297+
Clopton, Robert, of Cumberland Co.	Williamsburg	Will Abstract	1793	Crozier, p. 16
Cloudas, John	Essex	Will	1791	CF1817-021
Clough, George	Hanover	Estate Ref.	1810	LP:20 DEC 1810
Clough, John T.	Hanover	Will	1867	CF1901-038
Clover, Williston	Fairfax	Will	1879	CF1885-006
Cluverius, Benjamin, of Abingdon Par.	Gloucester	Will	1748	BRCD
Cluverius, Benjamin, of Abingdon Par.	Gloucester	Will	1785	BRCD
Coapland, Mary C.	Dinwiddie	Will	1826	VGSQ 10:1, p. 3
Coates, Frances to James Durham	King & Queen	Marriage	1830	LP
Coates, James C., in Culpeper Co.	Rappahannock	Will	1864	CF1914-003
Coates, Thomas		Will	1749	LVA Wills/Admin. DB
Cobb, Benjamin, of Southampton Co.	Williamsburg	Will Abstract	1826	Crozier, p. 16
Cobb, John, of Southampton Co.	Williamsburg	Will Abstract	1792	Crozier, p. 16
Cobb, Michael, of Southampton Co.	Williamsburg	Will Abstract	1795	Crozier, p. 15
Cobbs, Joseph	Isle of Wight	Will	1653	VMHB 6, p. 251
Cobbs, Robert, in Campbell Co.	Lynchburg	Will	1829	CF1848-002
Cobbs, Thomas M., in Amelia Co.	Powhatan	Will	1840	CF1874-009
Cobbs, William	Bedford	Will	1844	UVA MSS 1792
Cochran, Catharine P., in Loudoun Co.	Fauquier	Will	1895	CF1903-055
Cochran, David, of New Castle	Hanover	Will	1792	TVF 10:1, p. 52
Cochran, William L., in Albemarle Co.	Fauquier	Will	1876	CF1908-010
Cock, Mary	Fairfax	Will	1891	X
Cocke, Abraham	Amelia	Will	1760	V:Mss2 C64502 a 1
Cocke, Allen, of Surry Co.	Williamsburg	Will Abstract	1802	Crozier, p. 15
Cocke, Ann Barraud, w/o John H.		Will	1816	UVA Acc. #640
Cocke, Benjamin		Will	1763	UVA Acc. #640
Cocke, Bowler	Henrico	Will	1771	V:Mss2 C64503 a 1
Cocke, Bowler	Henrico	Will	1771	V:Mss1 M3855 a 5499+
Cocke, Bowler, Jr.	Henrico	Will	1771	LVA Acc. #28350
Cocke, Cary Charles		Will	1885	UVA Acc. #640
Cocke, Catesby	Prince William	Will	1772	BRCD

NAME	LOCATION	TYPE	YEAR	REFERENCE(S)
Cocke, Catesby	Prince William	Will	1772	Note[1]
Cocke, Catesby, of Prince William Co.	London	Will	1773	VCRP, Survey #04693
Cocke, Catesby, of Prince William Co.	London	Will	1773	N:PROB11/985; BRCD
Cocke, Charles L., in Norfolk Co.	Portsmouth	Will	1854	CF1871-013
Cocke, Chastain	Powhatan	Will	1794c	V:Mss1 N1786 a 6593+
Cocke, Edward	Charles City	Division S.	1726	D&W1724, p. 145
Cocke, Edward	Charles City	Will	1726	D&W1724, p. 113
Cocke, Edward, of Surry Co.	D.C.	Will	1900	DCA:Box 191
Cocke, Edward, of Westover Parish	Charles City	Will	1726	D&W1724, p. 113
Cocke, Elizabeth, at Alexandria	Prince George	Will	1857	SV 10:1, p. 12
Cocke, Francis A., of Richmond	Hanover	Will	1857	CF1868-008
Cocke, Francis A., of Richmond	Hanover	Will	1857	Cocke:121
Cocke, Harrison H.	Dinwiddie	Will	1873	CF1879-016
Cocke, Hartwell, of Surry Co.	Williamsburg	Will Abstract	1772	Crozier, p. 18
Cocke, Hartwell, of Surry Co.	Williamsburg	Will	1772	UVA Acc. #640
Cocke, Henry, of Surry Co.	Williamsburg	Will Abstract	1777	Crozier, p. 15
Cocke, Herbert C., in Halifax Co.	Campbell	Will	1837	CF1838-005
Cocke, J.H.		Will	1817	UVA Acc. #640
Cocke, James, Jr.	Henrico	Will	1772	Note[2]
Cocke, James, Sr.	Henrico	Will	1775	Note[3]
Cocke, John Hartwell	Surry	Will	1791	UVA Acc. #640
Cocke, John Hartwell		Will	1861	UVA Acc. #640
Cocke, John Hartwell		Will	1865	UVA Acc. #640
Cocke, John, in Portsmouth	Isle of Wight	Will	1880	CF1884-004
Cocke, Joseph A.	Hanover	Will	1823	CF1860-013
Cocke, Joseph A.	Hanover	Will	1823	CF1842-008
Cocke, Lemuel, Jr.	Surry	Will	1795	T: correct from Samuel
Cocke, Littlebury	Charles City	Will	1773	Records 1766, p. 463
Cocke, Littlebury	Charles City	Inventory	1774	Note[4]
Cocke, Margaret	Henrico	Will	1719	Records, Vol. 2, p. 433
Cocke, Nicholas	Middlesex	Will	1678	V:Mss2 C6451 a 1
Cocke, Philip St. George	Powhatan	Will	(nd)	V:Mss2 C6452 a 1
Cocke, Philip St. George, Powhatan Co.		Will	1861	UVA Acc. #640
Cocke, Philip St. George, Powhatan Co.	Brunswick	Will	1862	CF1902-026
Cocke, Philip St. George	Powhatan	Will	1862	CF1896-006
Cocke, Pleasant	Prince George	Estate Ref.	1798	LP:06 DEC 1798
Cocke, Polly M.	Prince George	Will	1809	MVG 31:4, p. 352
Cocke, Polly M., in Pr. George Co.	York	Will	1809	CF1835-001
Cocke, Polly M., of Prince George Co.	Petersburg	Will	1809	CF1842-032
Cocke, Richard	Henrico	Will	1665	Rrecords, Vol. 1, p. 27
Cocke, Richard		Will Abstract		VMHB 44, p. 141
Cocke, Richard, Jr.		Will	1800	UVA Acc. #640
Cocke, Susanna	Surry	Will (N)	1784	WB12, p. 23
Cocke, Thomas	Prince George	Will	1840	BRCD
Cocke, Thomas, in Prince George Co.	Petersburg	Will	1840	CF1853-023

[1] Peter Wilson Coldham, *American Wills Proved in London* (1992), p. 256.

[2] Henrico County Proceedings of Commissioners ..., 1774-1782, p. 27.

[3] Henrico County Miscellaneous Records, Vol. 7, p. 2249.

[4] LVA, Charles City County Records, 1766-1774, p. 538.

NAME	LOCATION	TYPE	YEAR	REFERENCE(S)
Cocke, Thomas, in Prince George Co.	Petersburg	Will	1840	CF1844-040
Cocke, Thomas, of Prince George Co.	Southampton	Will	1750	DB1, p. 410
Cocke, Thomas P.	Prince George	Will	1832	BRCD
Cocke, Thomas P., Prince George Co.	Petersburg	Will	1832	CF1841-038
Cocke, William	Hanover	Will	1822	CF1842-008
Cocke, William	Hanover	Will	1822	CF1860-013
Cocke, William Fleming	Henrico	Inventory	1767	Records, Vol. 6, p. 1985
Cocke, William H.	Isle of Wight	Will	1823	UVA Acc. #38-463
Cocke, William, of *Lowground*	Henrico	Will Abstract	(nd)	VMHB 44, p. 145
Cocke, William, of St. Paul's Parish	Hanover	Will	1822	Cocke:38
Cockerham, Philip P., Mecklenburg Co.	Lunenburg	Will	1776	CF1780-001
Cockerill, Thompson	Madison	Will	1837	LVA Acc. #20061
Cockerille, Ann	Fairfax	Account	1846	X
Cockerille, Mary Ellen	Fairfax	Guard. Bond	1845	X
Cockerille, Sampson	Fairfax	Will	1791	CF1838-013
Cockley, Edward, cook		Will	1699	VCRP, Survey #06063
Cockran, Richard	King William	Will	1839	V:Mss1 Eu177 a 23-26
Cockran, Richard	King William	Will	1839	CF1875-001
Cockshudd, Jeffery, mariner		Will	1710	VCRP, Survey #04346
Codd, St. Leger, in Cecil Co. MD	Lancaster	Will	1708	WB9, p. 264
Coe, Edward, in Loudoun Co.	Frederick	Will	1815	CF1820-089
Coe, Spencer A., of Falls Church	D.C.	Will	1892	DCA: Box 130
Cofer, George, in Bedford Co.	Lynchburg	Will	1830	CF1830-148
Coffer, Francis	Fairfax	Will	1817	X
Coffman, Martin, in Shenandoah Co.	Frederick	Will	1805	CF1825-094
Cogbill, Harriet Randolph Boyd Dodson	Mecklenburg	Will	1884	V:Mss1 C6553 a 42
Coghill, Atwell	Caroline	Will	1824	W&P1742, p. 116
Cogswell, Susan M., of Plainfield NJ	Arlington	Will	1892	WB10:242; File #776A
Cohen, Myer M.	Richmond City	Inventory	1799	Note[1]
Coke, Richard	James City	Will	1844	Swem(1):f131
Colbert, Mary Ann, of Rappa. Co. VA	Arlington	Will	1887	WB10:132; File #732A
Colbert, William	Culpeper	Will	1864	CF1878-051
Colbert, William, in Culpeper Co.	Fauquier	Will	1864	CF1890-033
Coldstream, Henry	Stafford	Admin.	1692	OB: 13 SEP 1692
Cole, Jesse, in Williamsburg	James City	Will	1845	CF1876-002
Cole, John	Henrico	Will	(nd)	Records, Vol. 7, p. 2375
Cole, Leonard, mariner		Will	1700	VCRP, Survey #06069
Cole, William	Warwick	Will	1729	TVF 1:4, p. 175
Cole, William	Charles City	Will Ref.	1752	VG 14, p. 180
Cole, William	Prince George	Will	1804	BRCD
Cole, William		Estate Ref.	1806	Shepherd, Vol. 3, p. 229
Cole, William, in Prince George Co.	Petersburg	Will	1804	CF1845-048
Cole, William, of *Buckland*, Ch. City	Albemarle	Will	1750	LP
Cole, William, of *Buckland*	Charles City	Will	1750	MVG 31:4, p. 344
Cole, William, of Warwick Co.	Albemarle	Will	1729	LP
Cole, William, of Warwick Co.	Albemarle	Will	1729	MVG 31:4, p. 353
Coleman, Daniel	Cumberland	Estate	(nd)	UVA MSS 4756
Coleman, Edmund T., in Amherst Co.	Lynchburg	Will	1817	CF1840-005

---

[1] Richmond City Hustings Court Deeds, No. 2, 1792-1799, p. 539.

NAME	LOCATION	TYPE	YEAR	REFERENCE(S)
Coleman, Elizabeth	Stafford	Will P.	1683	OB:13 NOV 1683
Coleman, Francis	Caroline	Will	1771	TQ 20, p. 166
Coleman, Henry E., in Halifax Co.	Powhatan	Will	1837	CF1857-015
Coleman, Irma	Dinwiddie	Will	1865	CF1891-005
Coleman, James, Col.	Fairfax	Will	1817	CF1831-001
Coleman, James, in Loudoun Co.	Frederick	Will	1815	CF1821-188
Coleman, John	Bath	Will	1885	CF1890-008
Coleman, John David	Amherst	Will	1784	CF1805-005
Coleman, John, in Amherst Co.	Lynchburg	Will	1778	CF1831-034
Coleman, John, in Fairifax Co.	Frederick	Will	1815	CF1821-188
Coleman, John, of Petsworth Parish	Gloucester	Will Ref.	1732	Winfree, p. 373
Coleman, Lewis W.	Hanover	Will	1863	Cocke:40
Coleman, Lindsey, in Amherst Co.	Lynchburg	Will	1809	CF1837-016
Coleman, Lucy A.	Caroline	Will	1834	UVA MSS 38-470
Coleman, Lyttleton G.	Louisa	Will	1829	LVA Acc. #30405
Coleman, Samuel	Buckingham	Will	1803	MVG 22:4, p. 28
Coleman, Samuel	Buckingham	Will	1803	LVA Acc. #28849
Coleman, Samuel	Buckingham	Will	1803	VGSQ 14:3, p. 89
Coleman, Samuel	Buckingham	Will	1803	LVA Acc. #28194
Coleman, Samuel, of Norfolk Borough	Williamsburg	Will Abstract	1805	Crozier, p. 16
Coleman, Sarah	Fairfax	Sale	1806	X
Coleman, Stephen	Surry	Inventory	1693	T:D&W4, p. 291b
Coleman, Thomas	King & Queen	Will	1748	TVF 2:2, p. 70
Coleman, Thomas	King & Queen	Will	1748	LVA Acc. #25817
Coleman, Thomas	Henrico	Will	1748c	V:Mss4 V8 g
Coleman, Thomas and wife	Fairfax	Sale	1806	X
Coleman, Wyatt, in James City Co.	York	Will	1798	CF1835-001
Coleman, Wyatt, of Williamsburg	York	Will	1798	MVG 31:4, p. 348
Coles, Catharine, in Pittsylvania Co.	Campbell	Will	1848	CF1870-011
Coles, Mary Randolph Price	Louisa	Will	1847c	V:Mss1 D1124 b 3609+
Coles, Walter	Hanover	Will	1815	VMHB 58, p. 125
Collart, William, of Norfolk		Will	1776	VCRP, Survey #04800
Collcutt, William		Will (N)	1659	VCRP, Survey #03523
Colles, Thomas, shipwright		Will	1707	VCRP, Survey #03898
Collett, John, of Washington DC	London	Will	1822	N:PROB11/1659
Colley, Charles, Sr., of Hanover Co.	Goochland	Will	1811	CF1858-014
Collier, Alexander, mariner		Will	1739	VCRP, Survey #04653
Collier, Benjamin	Surry	Inventory	1768	T: correct from 1767
Collier, Hamlett, in KY	Mecklenburg	Will	1835	CF1842-004 CSC
Collier, John	Surry	Admin.	1679	T: correct from Coltier
Collier, Joseph	Surry	Will	1727	T: correct from John
Collier, Moody, of Southampton Co.	Williamsburg	Will Abstract	1815	Crozier, p. 15
Collingwood, Gerrard, mariner		Will	1732	VCRP, Survey #04660
Collins, Ann	Arlington	Partition	(nd)	CF1869-024
Collins, John	Surry	Will	1693	T:D&W4, p. 342b
Collins, John	Richmond City	Will	1794	T:HCD2, p. 135
Collins, Joyeux	King & Queen	Will	1843	CF1901-001
Collins, Thomas	Caroline	Will	1781	W&P1742, p. 30
Collins, Thomas, in Hampshire Co.	Frederick	Will	1824	CF1832-169
Collins, Thomas, in King & Queen Co.	Essex	Will	1826	CF1832-015
Collins, Thomas, Jr.	King & Queen	Will	1826	LP

NAME	LOCATION	TYPE	YEAR	REFERENCE(S)
Collins, Thomas, Jr., King & Queen Co.	Essex	Will	1826	CF1839-011
Collins, Thomas, s/o John	Spotsylvania	Will Abstract	1748	Fleet 2:302
Colson, Joseph	Brunswick	Will	1737	D&W1, p. 335
Colston, Edward, in Berkeley Co.	Fauquier	Will	1850	CF1857-008
Colston, Rawleigh, in Berkeley Co.	Frederick	Will	1823	CF1835-092
Colston, Rawleigh, of Berkeley Co.	London	Will	1827	N:PROB11/1722
Coltman, William, mariner		Will	1666	VCRP, Survey #03537
Colvill, Thomas	Fairfax	Will	1766	X
Combs, George	Henrico	Inventory	1724	Records, Vol. 2, p. 593
Combs, John, Jr.	Fauquier	Will	1781	CF1852-013
Combs, Leslie, in Fayette Co. KY		Will	1883	V:Mss2 C7335 a 1
Comer, Dennis	Fairfax	Will	1853	CF1866-037
Comer, Dennis	Fairfax	Account	1853	X
Comer, Dennis	Fairfax	Inventory	1853	X
Compton, John	Richmond City	Will (N)	1796	T:HCD2, p. 289
Compton, John	Richmond City	Will (N)	1796	FDC L567-38
Compton, John	Fairfax	Inventory	1817	X
Conly, Edmond C.	Fairfax	Will	1868	CF1894-004
Conner, Elias	Fairfax	Guard. Bond	1844	X
Conner, Jane Catharine	Fairfax	Guard. Bond	1844	X
Conner, Lewis	Dinwiddie	Will	1771	VGSQ 10:1, p. 6
Conner, Silas	Fairfax	Guard. Bond	1844	X
Connor, George	Caroline	Will	1844	W&D1794, p. 44
Connor, James			1729	LVA Wills/Admin. DB
Connor, Mary	Prince William	Will	1876	CF1894-020
Conrad, Isaac	Prince William	Inv. Ref.	1843	CM:03 JUL 1843
Conrad, Peter	Rockingham	Will	1800	LVA:1159583 t
Conrad, Peter	Rockingham	Bond	1801	LVA:1159583 t
Conrad, Peter, of Rockingham Co.	Augusta	Will	1800	CF1838-001
Conrad, Rebecca Holmes	Frederick	Will	1832	V:Mss1 C7637 a 302+
Conrad, Robert Y.	Winchester	Will	1875	LVA Acc. #40785, r180
Conrad, Robert Young	Frederick	Will	1833	V:Mss1 C7637 a 302+
Constable, Jonathan T.	Fairfax	Will	1876	X
Constantine, William	Essex	Will	1697	Note[1]
Contanceau, John	Northumberland	Will Original	1718	M: Box C folder 75
Convers, John		Will	1654	VCRP, Survey #03124
Converse, Amasa	Richmond City	Will	1872	V:Mss7:1 C7692:1
Conway, James	Northumberland	Will	1824	CF1834-010
Conway, James	Northumberland	Will	1824	Note[2]
Conway, Richard	Arlington	Will	1806	CF1815-001
Conway, Robert, of Alexandria	Arlington	Will	1806	CF1851-006
Conway, Seneca M., in WI	Northumberland	Will	1848	CF1853-008
Conway, Thomas [of Mt. Zion]	Caroline	Will	1827	W&D1794, p. 21
Coockin, William	Surry	Will	1677	T: correct from Coggin
Cook, Adam	Fairfax	Will	1868	X
Cook, John, shipwright, of Barbadoes	Williamsburg	Will Abstract	1765	Crozier, p. 18
Cook, Richard P.	New Kent	Will	1891	CF1893-002

---

[1] Refer to *Sweeny*, p. 9, where the compiler lists wills given in *Torrence* that have not been found of record in Rappahannock County.

[2] Northumberland County District Court Orders, Deeds, [Wills], 1789-1825 [1849], p. 461.

NAME	LOCATION	TYPE	YEAR	REFERENCE(S)
Cook, William, in Warren Co.	Rappahannock	Will	1843	CF1847-007
Cooke, Dawson	King & Queen	Will	1829	LVA Acc. #26529-16
Cooke, E.E.	Hanover	Will	1888	CF1893-004
Cooke, John	Hanover	Will	1862	CF1878-015
Cooke, John, merchant	Isle of Wight	Will	1703	CW M-1561
Cooke, Mordecai, Jr., of Gloucester Co.	Williamsburg	Will Abstract	1776	Crozier, p. 18
Cooke, Nathan, in PA	Frederick	Will	1801	CF1818-051
Cooke, Stephen, in Loudoun Co.	Arlington	Will	1815	CF1857-005
Cooke, Thomas	King & Queen	Will	1806	V:Mss1 M1752 a 65-91
Cooke, Thomas, Stratton Major Parish	King & Queen	Will	1804	Fleet 2:352
Cooke, Thomas, Stratton Major Parish	King & Queen	Will	1806	Swem(1):f204
Cooke, Thomas, Stratton Major Parish	King & Queen	Will	1806	Note[1]
Cooksey, Thomas S.	Fairfax	Account	1860	X
Coombs, John N., in Loudoun Co.	Fairfax	Will	1876	CF1881-026
Coon, Mathew, in Stafford Co.	Fauquier	Will	1731	CF1789-011
Cooper, Francis, of Lunenburg Co.	Mecklenburg	Will	1777	CF1825-032
Cooper, Frederick	Surry	Will	1806	Note[2]
Cooper, John, of James City Co.	Williamsburg	Will Abstract	1792	Crozier, p. 19
Cooper, Joseph	Fairfax	Guard. Bond	1840	X
Cooper, Joseph	Louisa	Will	1895	Note[3]
Cooper, Justinian	Isle of Wight	Will	1650	VMHB 6, p. 122
Cooper, Ruth, in Berkeley Co.	Frederick	Will	1851	CF1859-002
Cooper, Samson, of York Co., Eng.	Northumberland	Will	1659	LVA Acc. #22748
Cooper, Samuel		Will	1659	M: L1 f209
Cooper, Samuel, of *Cameron*	Fairfax	Will	1871	V:Mss1 C7887 a 83-96
Cooper, Sarah Maria Mason	Fairfax	Will	1890c	V:Mss1 C7887 a 97-150
Cooper, Thomas	Surry	Inventory	1688	T:D&W4, p. 51b
Copedge, John, of Queen Anne's Co.		Will	1709	CW M-1561
Copeland, Elisha	Nansemond	Estate Ref.	1791	LP:04 NOV 1793
Copenhaver, Frederick	Smyth	Will	1838	CF1837-003
Copin, George	Prince William	Will Ref.	1843	CM:04 DEC 1843
Copper, Elizabeth	Arlington	Will	1790	CRA:17
Copper, Elizabeth	Arlington	Account	1794	CRA:143
Coran, Patrick, of Petersburg	Prince George	Will	1816	SV 9:1, p. 19
Corbet, Richard	Princess Anne	Will	1720	T: correct from Corbell
Corbett, Frank E., of Alexandria	D.C.	Will	1900	DCA: Box 168
Corbin, A.R.	Culpeper	Will	1893	CF1895-016
Corbin, Alice	King & Queen	Will	1791	VG 35, p. 208
Corbin, Alice	King & Queen	Will	1791	TVF 12:3, p. 168
Corbin, Alice, in King & Queen Co.	Essex	Will	1792	CF1833-031
Corbin, Gawin	King & Queen	Will	1744	FDC L387-1
Corbin, Gawin	King & Queen	Division	1748	Fleet 2:417
Corbin, Gawin	Westmoreland	Will	1760	FDC L387-1
Corbin, Gawin	Westmoreland	Will Ref.	1761	Hening, Vol. 7, p. 458
Corbin, Gawin, of Cople Parish	Westmoreland	Will	1760	VMHB 30, p. 310
Corbin, Gawin, of Stratton Major Parish	King & Queen	Will	1744	Fleet 2:157

[1] Fleet, Beverly, *Virginia Colonial Abstracts*, King and Queen County County, Vol. 14, 5th Collection, p. 82.
[2] Surry County Wills, Etc., Bk. 2, p. 80.
[3] Louisa County Wills Not Fully Proved, 1757-1902, p. 15.

NAME	LOCATION	TYPE	YEAR	REFERENCE(S)
Corbin, Gawin, of Stratton Major Parish	King & Queen	Will	1744	WMQ 14:4, p. 285
Corbin, Henry	Buckingham	Will	1675	VMHB 29, p. 376
Corbin, Henry, on Rappahannock River	Buckingham	Will	1675	Fleet 2:156
Corbin, James M.	Culpeper	Will	1880	CF1886-028
Corbin, John, of *Gales*	Middlesex	Will Abstract	1800	VMHB 30, p. 404
Corbin, John Tayloe, of *Laneville*	King & Queen	Will	1794	Fleet 2:162
Corbin, Maria	King & Queen	Will	1797	Fleet 2:165
Corbin, Mary Waller	King & Queen	Will	1797	V:Mss2 C8114 b 11-13
Corbin, Priscilla, in Stafford Co.	Fauquier	Will	1855	CF1877-009
Corbin, Rebecca Parke, in K&Q Co.	Hanover	Will	1821	CF1861-028
Corbin, Rebecca Parke, in K&Q Co.	Hanover	Will	1824	Cocke:40
Corbin, Richard	King & Queen	Will	1709	Fleet, 1st Collection
Corbin, Richard, of *Laneville*	King & Queen	Will	1790	Fleet 2:160
Corbin, Richard, of *Laneville*	King & Queen	Will	1816	LVA Acc. #24194
Corder, Elias, in Richmond	Rappahannock	Will	1828	CF1878-013
Corderoy, William, merchant		Will	1667	VCRP, Survey #03540
Corker, William	Surry	Will (N)	1677	T: correct from Cocker
Corley, John P., of Nelson Co.	Augusta	Will	1818	CF1844-028
Corley, Minoah, in Fauquier Co.	Rappahannock	Will	1817	CF1842-008
Cornell, Samuel	Surry	Inventory	1680	T: correct from 1679
Cornick, Joel	Princess Anne	Will	1754	DB7, p. 590
Cornwall, Alexander, mariner		Will	1704	VCRP, Survey #04139
Cornwallis, Letitia		Will	1731	CW(14)
Cornwallis, Letitia		Will	1739	CW(14)
Cornwallis, Letitia		Will	1740	CW(14)
Cornwell, Constance, in Pr. Wm. Co.	Fairfax	Will	1825	CF1839-001
Cornwell, Jesse, in Pr. Wm. Co.	Fairfax	Will	1813	CF1839-001
Corprew, George R., in Pr. Anne Co.	Norfolk	Will	1825	CF1836-018
Corr, Thomas Roane	King & Queen	Will	1831	V:Mss1 C8177 a 32-38
Corran, Martha		Will	1805	BRCD, GC
Corran, Martha, in Fra.	Petersburg	Will	1805	CF1842-029
Correll, Teague		Will	1666	LVA Wills/Admin. DB
Correll, Teague		Inventory	1669	LVA Acc. #25364
Corrie, Hannah, in Richmond Co.	Essex	Will	1791	CF1846-013
Corrie, Hannah, of Richmond Co.	Williamsburg	Will Abstract	1792	Crozier, p. 17
Corrie, John	King & Queen	Estate Ref.	1789	TVF 11:2, p. 99
Cosby, John	Richmond City	Will	1859	Fleet, Huntington Data
Costigan, Margaret, in MD	Fairfax	Will	1890	CF1907-014
Costigan, William, in MD	Fairfax	Will	1888	CF1907-014
Cotten, Mary	Surry	Will	1729	T: correct from 1728
Cottrell, Peter	Henrico	Will	1816	LVA Acc. #26020
Cottrell, Samuel	Henrico	Will	1858	CF1887-029
Cottrell, William	King William	Will	1812	VGS Bulletin VII, p. 24
Cottrell, William [Cotterell]	King William	Will	1812	BRCD
Couch, Lucy A.	Lunenburg	Will	1876	CF1882-018
Couch, Margaret, in Richmond	Henrico	Will	1829	CF1885-007
Couch, Samuel	Goochland	Will	1799	MVG 29:3, p. 190
Couch, Samuel	Goochland	Will	1800	Note[1]

---

[1] Goochland County Deeds, Bk. 17, pp. 545-547.

NAME	LOCATION	TYPE	YEAR	REFERENCE(S)
Couch, Samuel	Goochland	Will	1800	DB17, p. 545
Couch, William T.	Lunenburg	Will	1868	CF1882-018
Couchman, Henry, in Hampshire Co.	Frederick	Will	1767	CF1830-268
Coulter, Peter, of Fairfax Co.	Prince William	Will	1829	LP
Council, Michael	Elizabeth City	Estate Ref.	1784	Hening, Vol. 13, p. 105
Countanceau, John	Northumberland	Will	1732	M: L21 f687-692
Coupland, James	Chesterfield	Estate Ref.	1772	Hening, Vol. 13, p. 101
Coutart, Peter, of Petersburg	London	Will	1809	N:PROB11/1501
Coutts, Patrick	Richmond City	Will Ref.	1776	Hening, Vol. 12, p. 385
Coutts, Patrick		Estate Ref.	1790	Hening, Vol. 13, p. 228
Coutts, William	Henrico	Will	1787	V:Mss2 C8376 a 1
Coutz, Jacob, in Loudoun Co.	Frederick	Will	1780	CF1828-245
Cowan, David, in Russell Co.	Washington	Will	1866	CF1879-012
Cowan, Elizabeth, in Bedford Co.	Lynchburg	Will	1811	CF1834-006
Cowan, Robert, in Bedford Co.	Lynchburg	Will	1803	CF1834-006
Cowardin, W.L., in Richmond	Henrico	Will	1888	CF1907-035
Cowherd, Tabitha, in Orange Co.	Louisa	Will	1855	CF1890-006
Cowles, Thomas	Charles City	Division	1774	Note[1]
Cowling, John	Fairfax	Will	1882	CF1897-006
Cowling, Samuel	Nansemond	Will	1857	CF1868-027
Cowne, Augustine	Culpeper	Will	1824	V:Mss2 C8393 a 1
Cox, Abner		Estate Ref.	1805	Shepherd, Vol. 3, p. 196
Cox, Andrew, of Nansemond Co.	London	Will	1764	N:PROB11/895
Cox, Andrew, of Nansemond Co.	London	Will	1764	VCRP, Survey #04680
Cox, Edward	Powhatan	Will	1791	CF1843-001
Cox, Frances A., in Westmoreland Co.	Northumberland	Will	1859	CF1866-011
Cox, Francis A., in Westmoreland Co.	Northumberland	Will	1859	CF1879-011
Cox, George	Henrico	Will	1722	Records, Vol. 1, p. 183
Cox, George	Goochland	Will	1728	VGS Bulletin VIII, p. 18
Cox, George	Powhatan	Will	1795	CF1822-029
Cox, George, in Goochland Co.	Henrico	Will	1728	LVA Acc. #26248
Cox, George, in Goochland Co.	Henrico	Will	1728	VGS Bulletin VIII, p. 18
Cox, George, of Henrico Co.	Goochland	Will	1728	DB1, p. 2
Cox, Gilbert, of Stafford Co.	D.C.	Will	1873	DCA: Box 50
Cox, Henry	Dinwiddie	Will	1862	CF1876-009
Cox, James L., in Westmoreland Co.	Arlington	Will	1845	CF1847-009
Cox, James S., in Pittsylvania Co.	Henry	Will	1828	CF1834-005
Cox, John	Rappahannock*	Will	(nd)	TQ 23:2, p. 114
Cox, John	Essex	Will	1765	DB9, p. 12
Cox, John P.	Dinwiddie	Will	1851	CF1870-020
Cox, Mary P.	Dinwiddie	Will	1833	CF1871-005
Cox, Matthew	Goochland	Will	1734	T: correct from Martha
Cox, Michael	Charles City	Inventory	1728	D&W1724, p. 204
Cox, Sem, of Richmond Co.	London	Will	1710	N:PROB11/523
Cox, Sem, of Richmond Co.		Will	1711	VCRP, Survey #04355
Cox, Thomas, in Currituck Co. NC	Norfolk	Will	1840	CF1842-008
Cox, Warner, in Albemarle Co.	Greene	Will	1857	CF1880-001
Cox, William	Northumberland	Will	1781	CF1835-006

---

[1] LVA, Charles City County Records, 1766-1774, p. 533.

NAME	LOCATION	TYPE	YEAR	REFERENCE(S)
Cox, William	Lee	Will	1800	Note[1]
Cox, William	Lee	Will	1800	Note[2]
Cox, William, in Dinwiddie Co.	Petersburg	Will	1826	CF1859-048
Crabtree, William, in Washington Co.	Smyth	Will	1816	CF1839-010
Cradle, Lucy	Mecklenburg	Will	1856	V:Mss1 B2924d533-538
Crafford, David	New Kent	Estate Ref.	1723	Winfree, p. 265
Crafford, David, of St. Peter's Parish	New Kent	Estate Ref.	1732	Winfree, p. 379
Crafford, David, of St. Peter's Parish	New Kent	Estate Ref.	1767	VGS Bulletin VII, p. 51
Crafford, Henry	Southampton	Will	1771	WB2, p. 436
Crafford, Robert	Surry	Will	1714	T: from Crawford
Craford, John, mariner		Will	1741	VCRP, Survey #04378
Craft, George, in Pittsylvania Co.	Franklin	Will	1868	CF1872-006
Crafton, Mary, in Franklin Co.	Roanoke	Will	1836	CF1848-008
Crafton, Stephen B.	Lunenburg	Will	1874	CF1899-013
Craghead, John, Sr., in Franklin Co.	Bedford	Will	1859	CF1886-024
Craig, Ebenezer, of Princess Anne Co.	Williamsburg	Will Abstract	1809	Crozier, p. 17
Craig, James	Lunenburg	Will	1795	CF1798-002
Craik, James	Fairfax	Will	1814	Gunston Hall
Craik, James	Fairfax	Inventory	1817	X
Craik, Maria D.	Fairfax	Inventory	1817	X
Craik, William	Arlington	Will	1807	CF1827-023
Craik, William, of Alexandria	D.C.	Will	1886	DCA: Box 96
Cralle, Baisel	Lunenburg	Will	1786	CF1794-004
Cralle, G.T., Sr., in Nottoway Co.	Prince Edward	Will	1879	CF1887-001
Crane, John		Account	1818c	V:Mss1 H7935 a 1
Cranford, Henry L., in DC	Fairfax	Will	1883	CF1900-008
Cranford, Henry L., in DC	Fairfax	Will	1897	CF1900-008
Craswell, James		Will	1720	LVA Acc. #21494
Craswell, James		Will	1720	OB5, p. 524
Crawford, David, in Amherst Co.	Lynchburg	Will	1802	CF1819-024
Crawford, John, in Amherst Co.	Lynchburg	Will	1818	CF1824-051
Crawford, Lucy, in Amherst Co.	Lynchburg	Will	1853	CF1858-041
Crawford, Norman	Dinwiddie	Will	1861	CF1882-023
Crawford, Rebecca	Rockingham	Will	1828	CF1859-008
Crawley, Samuel	Williamsburg	Will Ref.	1793	VGS Bulletin VIII, p. 37
Crawley, William	Amelia	Will	1738	BRCD
Creasy, John, Sr., in Bedford Co.	Lynchburg	Will	1820	CF1827-022
Creed, John, of Martin's Hundred	London	Will	1635	N:PROB11/167
Creed, John, of Martyns Hundred	London	Will	1635	VCRP, Survey #03971
Creed, William	Surry	Will	1687	T:D&W4, p. 35b
Creger, Lawrence, of Alexandria	D.C.	Will	1801	DCA:Box 1
Creigh, Thomas	Greenbrier	Will	1847c	V:Mss1 C5217 a 851+
Crenshaw, Chapman	Hanover	Will	1840	CF1876-007
Crenshaw, Chapman	Hanover	Will	1841	Cocke:41
Crenshaw, Charles	Hanover	Will	1790	BRCD
Crenshaw, Charles, in Hanover Co.	Lynchburg	Will	1790	CF1831-003
Crenshaw, Charles, of St. Martin's Par.	Hanover	Will	1825c	MVG 38:4, p. 298

---

[1] Lee County Loose Wills, 1794-1832, pp. 1-3 (original), formerly in missing Will Book 1, pp. 1-2.
[2] Lee County Loose Wills, 1784-1832, pp. 1-3; formerly in missing Will Book 1, pp. 1-2

NAME	LOCATION	TYPE	YEAR	REFERENCE(S)
Crenshaw, Daniel	Lunenburg	Will	1795	CF1851-004
Crenshaw, Edmund B.	Hanover	Estate Ref.	1845	Note[1]
Crenshaw, Nathaniel C., in Hanover Co.	Henrico	Will	1866	CF1907-003
Crenshaw, Susanna	Hanover	Will	1779	LVA Acc. #34346, r1126
Crenshaw, Susanna	Hanover	Will	1779	LVA Acc. #36102, r444a
Crenshaw, Susanna, in St. Martin's Par.	Hanover	Will	1779	LVA Acc. #27286b
Crenshaw, Susanna, of St. Martin's Par.	Hanover	Will	1779	Fleet, Huntington Data
Crew, Elllyson	Charles City	Will	1772	LVA Acc. #29567
Crew, Ellyson	Charles City	Will	1772	LP, box 51, folder 271
Crew, Joseph	Charles City	Account	1726	D&W1724, p. 145
Crew, Margaret	Warwick	Will	1688	Records 1687-1688
Crew, Margaret, of *Mulberry Island*	Warwick	Will	1687	LVA Acc. #24853
Crew, Sabra	Charles City	Inventory	1726	D&W1724, p. 87
Crew, Sabra	Charles City	Account	1730	D&W1724, p. 334
Crewes, William	Surry	Inventory	1691	T:D&W4, p. 227b
Crews, Joseph, in Amherst Co.	Lynchburg	Will	1802	CF1831-046
Crews, Susanna		Will	1779	LVA, misc. reel #4446
Creyke, Alice	Middlesex	Will	1684	Fleet 2:237
Creyke, Henry, Capt.	Middlesex	Will (N)	1684	Fleet 2:236
Crichlow, John, of Southampton Co.	Williamsburg	Will Abstract	1819	Crozier, p. 17
Crichton, William, of Southampton Co.	Williamsburg	Will Abstract	1801	Crozier, p. 16
Cridar, Martin		Will	1774	Note[2]
Critcher, Jadwin, of Cameron Parish	Fairfax	Will	1749	NVG 7, p. 926
Crittenden, William	Orange	Will	1841	V:Mss2 C8695 a 1
Crittenton, William	Henrico	Will Ref.	1793	Fleet 2:350
Crockett, Tilman, in Tazewell Co.	Roanoke	Will	1839	CF1860-005
Crockford, John	King & Queen	Will	1757	Fleet 2:330
Crockford, John, of King & Queen Co.	Middlesex	Will	1757	CF1791-002
Cromartie, Adam, mariner		Will	1741	VCRP, Survey #04376
Cropp, James, in Stafford Co.	Fauquier	Will	1832	CF1842-007
Croshaw, Richard	York	Will	1693	Fleet 2:235
Crosland, Joseph	Charles City	Inventory	1689	D&W1689, p. 78
Crosland, Joseph	Charles City	Inventory	1689	D&W1689, p. 87
Cross, Hardy	Nansemond	Will	1858	CF1866-007
Cross, Hardy, in Nansemond Co.	Portsmouth	Will	1858	CF1870-012
Cross, John	Charles City	Inventory	1731	D&W1724, p. 341
Cross, John	Lunenburg	Will	1791	CF1816-018
Cross, John	Hanover	Will	1823	Fleet, Huntington Data
Cross, John	Hanover	Will	1823	LVA Acc. #34269
Cross, John, in Westover Parish	Charles City	Will	1730	D&W1724, p. 333
Cross, John, of Lunenburg Co.	Mecklenburg	Will	1791	CF1817-008
Cross, John, of Westover Parish	Charles City	Will	1731	D&W1724, p. 333
Cross, Joseph	Hanover	Account	1791	LVA Acc. #34269
Cross, Joseph	Hanover	Will	1791	LVA Acc. #34269
Cross, Joseph, in Loudoun Co.	Frederick	Will	1779	CF1828-292
Cross, Joseph, in Loudoun Co.	Frederick	Will	1780	CF1818-157
Cross, Joseph, Sr.	Hanover	Will	1797	Fleet, Huntington Data

---

[1] LVA, Treasurer's Office Material, "James River and Kanawha County Guaranteed Bonds, Wills and Certificates," Acc. #28458.

[2] LVA, Northern Neck Plats and Certificates, John Cooper.

NAME	LOCATION	TYPE	YEAR	REFERENCE(S)
Cross, Joseph, Sr.	Hanover	Will	1797	LVA Acc. #27286d
Cross, Nathaniel	Hanover	Will	1859	CF1903-035
Cross, William, in NJ	Frederick	Will	1812	CF1818-157
Cross, William, of Nottoway Co.	Mecklenburg	Will	1802	CF1817-008
Croswell, James	Essex	Will	1720	LVA Acc. #21494
Crouch, Elizabeth, in WV	Bedford	Will	1875	CF1875-039
Croucher, Robert	York	Will (N)	1705	T: from Richmond Co.
Crow, John, mariner		Will	1710	VCRP, Survey #04347
Crowder, Ethel, in Petersburg	Dinwiddie	Will	1856	CF1882-007
Crump, Abner, of Powhatan Co.	D.C.	Will	1802	DCA:Box 18
Crump, Anderson	New Kent	Will	1852	CF1882-001
Crump, Anderson	New Kent	Will	1853	CF1881-015
Crump, Bartlee	New Kent	Will	1843	Swem(1):f217
Crump, Benedict, of New Kent Co.	Williamsburg	Will Abstract	1811	Crozier, p. 19
Crump, Charles Carter	New Kent	Will	1851	CF1867-006
Crump, Charles, of New Kent Co.	Williamsburg	Will Abstract	1809	Crozier, p. 19
Crump, Daniel F.	Fairfax	Will	1849	CF1881-039
Crump, Edmund	New Kent	Will	1849	CF1896-006
Crump, Henry Clay	New Kent	Will	1865	CF1887-010
Crump, John, of Hamilton Parish	Prince William	Will	1746	Note[1]
Crump, Mildred, in New Kent Co.	Henrico	Will	1838	CF1873-004
Crump, Robert	New Kent	Will	1806	MVG 22:4, p. 27
Crump, Robert	New Kent	Will	1806	LVA Acc. #24193a
Crump, Robert	New Kent	Will	1806	LVA Acc. #28122
Crump, Sarah Delia	Dinwiddie	Will	1880	CF1887-001
Crump, Sheldon	New Kent	Will	1835	Swem(1):f217
Crump, William	Franklin	Will	1835	Swem
Crump, William B.	New Kent	Will	1867	CF1882-024
Crutcher, Thomas, of Caroline Co.	Williamsburg	Will Abstract	1786	Crozier, p. 18
Crutcher, Thomas, of Drysdale Parish	Caroline	Will	1786	TQ 27:4, p. 280
Crutchfield, John	Spotsylvania	Will	1819	MVG 29:3, p. 190
Crutchfield, Thompson, in Botetourt Co.	Smyth	Will	1834	CF1847-014
Cryer, Elizabeth	Dinwiddie	Will	1811	VG 16, p. 257
Culbertson, James, in Scott Co.	Washington	Will	1884	CF1899-003
Cully, Abraham		Will	1694	VCRP, Survey #04712
Cully, Abraham, of Stafford Co.	London	Will	1694	N:PROB11/419
Culpeper, Alexander		Will	1691	CW(9)
Culpepper, Benjamin, in Norfolk Co.	Portsmouth	Will	1877	CF1900-022
Culton, James	Lee	Will	1800	Note[2]
Culton, James	Lee	Will	1800	Note[3]
Cumberland, George	Culpeper	Will	1863	CF1896-013
Cummings, George W.	Fairfax	Will	1886	CF1902-005
Cummings, Jane	Prince George	Will	1830	SV 9:1, p. 22
Cummings, John	Botetourt	Inventory	1778	V:Mss1 P9267 e 2298+
Cumpston, Edward H., of Alexandria	D.C.	Will	1885	DCA:Box 91
Cumpston, Mary Mitchell, of Salem	D.C.	Will	1891	DCA:Box 124

---

[1] Fauquier County Miscellaneous Records, 1759-1807, p. 360.
[2] Lee County Deeds, Bk. 1, 1793-1804, p. 160; original in Lee County Loose Wills, 1794-1832, pp. 117-118.
[3] Lee County Loose Wills, 1794-1832, pp. 117-118; Lee County Deeds, Bk. 1, 1793-1804.

NAME	LOCATION	TYPE	YEAR	REFERENCE(S)
Cunnard, Jonathan, in Loudoun Co.	Frederick	Will	1796	CF1828-236
Cunningham, Edward	Goochland	Will	1836	V:Mss1 C9175 a 4-15
Cunningham, Mary		Will	1767	BRCD, GC
Cunningham, Richard	Cumberland	Will	1812	V:Mss1 C9175 a 4-15
Cunningham, Richard	Cumberland	Inventory	1813	V:Mss1 C9175 a 4-15
Cunningham, Robert, in Hardy Co.	Frederick	Will	1802	CF1822-024
Cunningham, Robert, in Hardy Co.	Frederick	Will	1803	CF1819-121
Cunninghame, Mary	Gloucester	Will	1767	TVF 12:1, p. 41
Curd, Edward	Henrico	Will	1742	Records, Vol. 4, p. 1177
Curd, John, in Goochland Co.	Bedford	Will	1819	CF1870-170
Curle, Nicholas	Elizabeth City	Will	1714	LVA Acc. #30881
Curle, Nicholas Wilson, of Eliz. City Co.	London	Will	1772	N:PROB11/983
Curle, Nicholas Wm., of Eliz. City Co.		Will	1772	VCRP, Survey #04686
Curreell, Nicholas		Estate Ref.	1797	Shepherd, Vol. 2, p. 129
Currin, Rhoda, in Montgomery Co.	Roanoke	Will	1847	CF1853-013
Curry, James, in Monroe Co.	Bath	Will	1832	CF1844-001
Curtain, Daniel	Arlington	Will	1800	CRA:309
Curtis, Bartlett A.	Hanover	Will	1866	CF1872-026
Curtis, Bartlett A.	Hanover	Will	1866	CF1867-019
Curtis, Bartlett A.	Hanover	Will	1866	CF1878-037
Curtis, Chisley	Brunswick	Will	1796	CF1816-058
Curtis, Churchwell, in Mecklenburg Co.	Brunswick	Will	1812	CF1816-058
Curtis, Daniel P., in Warwick Co.	James City	Will	1857	CF1883-005
Curtis, Daniel P., in Warwick Co.	James City	Will	1857	CF1897-009
Curtis, Henry	Hanover	Will	1862	CF1867-019
Curtis, Henry, Dr.	Hanover	Will	1855	V:Mss1 C9434 a 306+
Curtis, Thomas Cary, in Warwick Co.	James City	Will	1851	CF1872-008
Custis, Daniel Parke	James City	Admin.	1758	LVA Acc. #22983(2)
Custis, Hancock	Accomack	Will	1727	V:Mss1 C9698 a 5
Custis, John	James City	Will	1750	LVA Acc. #26562
Custis, John	James City	Will	1750	Note[1]
Custis, John, Hon., of Williamsburg	London	Will	1753	N:PROB11/804
Custis, John, of Williamsburg	James City	Will	1750	LVA Acc. #22983-1
Custis, John, of Williamsburg		Will	1753	VCRP, Survey #04655
Custis, Thomas	Accomack	Will	1814	LVA Acc. #24194
Custis, William	Accomack	Will	1725	WMQ 23, p. 127
Cutchin, David, of Nansemond Co.	Isle of Wight	Will	1838	CF1853-007

---

[1] Custis Family Papers, from the P.C.C. Fos. 3.21, typescript.

NAME	LOCATION	TYPE	YEAR	REFERENCE(S)

D

NAME	LOCATION	TYPE	YEAR	REFERENCE(S)
Dabbs, Joseph	Lunenburg	Will	1748	CF1761-012
Dabney, Catherine W.	Louisa	Will	1841	LVA Acc. #41008, r4610
Dabney, Catherine W.	Louisa	Will	1841	Fleet, Huntington Data
Dabney, Charles	Louisa	Will	1833	Fleet, Huntington Data
Dabney, Charles	Louisa	Will	1833	LVA Acc. #41008, r4610
Dabney, Cornelius	Hanover	Will Abstract	1765	Note[1]
Dabney, Cornelius	Goochland	Will	1821	CF1839-001
Dabney, George	King William	Will	1729	V:Mss2 D1127 a 1
Dabney, George	King William	Will	1729	VG 21, p. 307
Dabney, George	King William	Will	1729	Finley
Dabney, George	King William	Will	1729	LVA Acc. #27738
Dabney, Mehetabel, in Henrico Co.	Hanover	Will	1855	CF1868-012
Dabney, Mehetabel, of Henrico Co.	Richmond City	Will	1835	Cocke:45
Dabney, Samuel, Montgomery Co. TN	Lynchburg	Will	1830	CF1830-061
Dabney, William	King William	Will	1767	WB1, p. 26
Dabney, William	King William	Will	1767	VG 06, p. 3
Dade, Cadwallader, of St. Paul's Parish	Stafford	Will	1761	LVA Acc. #22515-12
Dade, Cadwallader, of St. Paul's Parish	Stafford	Will	1761	WBO, p. 388
Dade, Sarah, rel/o Gilson Berryman	Stafford	Will Ref.	1761	VMHB 38, p. 188
Dailey, John, in TN	Washington	Will	1882	CF1888-085
Dailey, William	Brunswick	Will	1778	CF1791-009
Daingerfield, Margaret Boyd Vowell	Alexandria	Will	1887	V:Mss1 D3545 a 1,167
Daingerfield, William	Essex	Will	1767	Fleet 2:338
Daingerfield, William	Essex	Will	1769	WMQ 11, p. 69
Dalby, Thomas	King William	Will	1702	RB2, p. 8
Dale, Peter	Surry	Inventory	1676	T: correct from Dole
Dallas, Thomas	Prince William	Will	1756	V:Mss2 D1618 a 1
Dalton, James T., in Petersburg	Dinwiddie	Will	1894	CF1909-010
Dameron, Charles	Northumberland	Will (U)	1764	NHS 25, p. 48
Damron, Dunmore	Nelson	Will	1839	LVA Acc. #33303, r1075
Dance, Richardson J.	Dinwiddie	Will	1868	CF1890-003
Dance, William Spencer	Powhatan	Will	1858	V:Mss2 C1538 b
Dancy, Edward	Charles City	Inventory	1772	Records, p. 375
Dandridge, B.W.	New Kent	Will	1883	CF1886-003
Dandridge, Bartholomew, in Fra.	Arlington	Will	1799	CF1809-015
Dandridge, Bartholomew, of New Kent	Williamsburg	Will Abstract	1785	Crozier, p. 21
Dandridge, Nathaniel West	King William	Will Ref.	1743	Hening, Vol. 6, p. 321
Dandridge, Nathaniel West	Hanover	Will	1786	Note[2]
Dandridge, Nathaniel West	Hanover	Will	1786	VMHB 22, p. 96
Dandridge, Nathaniel West	Hanover	Inventory	1802	G1:39
Dandridge, Nathaniel West	Hanover	Will, 1791	1802	G1:37
Dandridge, Nathaniel West	Richmond City	Admin.	1813	TVF 10:3, p. 171
Dandridge, Unity	King William	Will Ref.	1753	Hening, Vol. 7, p. 296
Dandridge, Unity	King William	Estate Ref.	1766	Hening, Vol. 8, p. 224
Dandridge, William		Will Abstract	1743	Hening, Vol. 6, p. 322
Dandridge, Willinette	New Kent	Will	1882	CF1885-006

---

[1] William H. Dabney, *Sketch of the Dabneys of Virginia* (1888), p. 38.

[2] LVA, U.S. Circuit Court Records, Box 194, *Murdock v. Dandridge, Underwood* (1823).

NAME	LOCATION	TYPE	YEAR	REFERENCE(S)
Dandridge, Willinette	New Kent	Will	1882	CF1886-003
Daniel, Beverly, in NC	Mecklenburg	Will	1846	CF1851-009 CSC
Daniel, Frances, of Middlesex Co.	Williamsburg	Will Abstract	1808	Crozier, p. 21
Daniel, Giles	Isle of Wight	Will (U)	1804	SV 12:1, p. 37
Daniel, John	Prince George	Will	1801	SV 9:1, p. 16
Daniel, John Moncure	Stafford	Will	1813	Note[1]
Daniel, Joseph	Brunswick	Will	1794	CF1806-023
Daniel, Peter Vivian	Richmond City	Will	1860	V:Mss2 D2255 a 2
Daniel, Robert, in Berkeley Co.	Frederick	Will	1823	CF1825-081
Daniel, Thomas	Prince George	Will	1808	SV 9:1, p. 17
Daniel, William A., in Cumberland Co.	Culpeper	Will	1851	CF1852-001
Daniel, William S., in Jefferson Co.	Fairfax	Will	1849	CF1859-021
Dansie, Thomas, mariner		Will	1735	VCRP, Survey #04672
Darden, George W., in Nansemond Co.	Isle of Wight	Will	1880	CF1886-010
Darden, George W., in Nansemond Co.	Isle of Wight	Will	1880	CF1897-007
Darke, William, in Berkeley Co.	Frederick	Will	1801	CF1836-108
Darly, Aaron, in Loudoun Co.	Fairfax	Will	1879	CF1900-040
Darnall, Waugh	King George	Will	1726	WBA1, p. 55
Darnall, Waugh	King George	Will	1726	TQ 20, p. 169
Darnall, Waugh	Prince William	Will	1726	Note[2]
Darne, Amelia B.	Fairfax	Account	1851	X
Darne, Nicholas	Fairfax	Sale	1840	X
Darne, Nicholas	Fairfax	Account	1852	X
Darne, Richard H.	Fairfax	Plat	1855	X
Darneille, Elizabeth	Albemarle	Will	1830	MVG 31:4, p. 342
Darneille, Elizabeth	Albemarle	Will	1830	LVA Acc. #33216
Darneille, Elizabeth	Albemarle	Will (U)	1830	BRCD
Darracott, John	Hanover	Will Abstract	1835	Cocke:28
Darracott, John	Hanover	Will	1837	LVA Acc. #24677-31[3]
Darracott, John	Hanover	Will	1837	CF1871-022
Darracott, John, in Wilkes Co. GA	Hanover	Will	1793	VGSQ 21:3, p. 92
Darracott, William, in Hanover Co.	Louisa	Will	1792	CF1812-025
Darrell, Augustus	Fairfax	Will	1777	X
Darrell, George	Fairfax	Will	1771	X
Darrell, Sampson	Fairfax	Will	1777	X
Dauge, James	Princess Anne	Will	1719	D&W3, p. 275
Daughtrey, Rebecca F., in Norfolk	Portsmouth	Will	1889	CF1892-004
Davenport, Abraham, in Jefferson Co.	Frederick	Will	1820	CF1828-272
Davenport, Abram, in Jefferson Co.	Frederick	Will	1825	CF1827-173
Davenport, Frances, of *Elm Grove*	Augusta	Will	1810	V:Mss1 G 8855 e 5357
Davenport, James, of Cople Parish	Williamsburg	Will Abstract	1777	Crozier, p. 21
Davenport, William, in Spotsylvania Co.	Louisa	Will	1798	CF1844-025
Davers, Jertmyn		Will	1751	VCRP, Survey #04679
David, Addison, in Lynchburg	Bedford	Will	1817	CF1829-008
Davidson, Nathaniel		Will	1815	Swem
Davies, Robert, of Rockingham Co.	Augusta	Will	1804	CF1820-033

---

[1] LVA, U.S. Circuit Court Records, Virginia District, Box 142, *Buchan v. Buchan & Seddon* (1838).
[2] Prince William County Land Causes, 1789-1793, p. 359.
[3] LVA, Hanover County, Burnley Family Chancery Suit Papers, also see LVA, Misc. Reel #99.

NAME	LOCATION	TYPE	YEAR	REFERENCE(S)
Davies, Sollomon	Surry	Admin.	1680	T: correct from Davis
Davies, William		Will	1775	VCRP, Survey #04799
Davies, William, of King George Co.	London	Will	1775	N:PROB11/1011
Davis, Christopher		Admin.	1734	VG 4, p. 66
Davis, Christopher	Prince George	Admin. Bond	1734	VG 04, p. 66
Davis, Dawson, in Surry Co.	Isle of Wight	Will	1850	CF1879-002
Davis, Edward	Dinwiddie	Will	1758	LVA Acc. #27293-1
Davis, Edward	Dinwiddie	Will	1758	LVA Acc. #28657-8
Davis, Edward	Dinwiddie	Will	1758	VG 16, p. 163
Davis, Edward	Dinwiddie	Will	1806	LVA Acc. #21507
Davis, Elizabeth	King & Queen	Will	1839	Note[1]
Davis, Elizabeth	King & Queen	Will Abstract	1839	Fleet 2:355
Davis, Elizabeth M.	Middlesex	Will Abstract	1820	Fleet 2:353
Davis, Elizabeth M., of Middlesex Co.	Williamsburg	Will Abstract	1821	Crozier, p. 20
Davis, Elizabeth, of Nottoway Co.	Mecklenburg	Will	1813	CF1844-034
Davis, Elizabeth, of Nottoway Co.	Mecklenburg	Will	1813	CF1843-003 CSC
Davis, Elizabeth, of St. Paul's Parish	Hanover	Will	1748	Fleet, Huntington Data
Davis, Garland M., in Jefferson Co.	Frederick	Will	1848	CF1850-029
Davis, Henry	Hanover	Inventory	1787	BRCD
Davis, Henry, of Hanover Co.	Albemarle	Will	1773	LP
Davis, Henry, of St. Martin's Parish	Hanover	Will	1772	MVG 31:4, p. 346
Davis, Hugh	Prince William	Will Ref.	1843	CM:03 JUL 1843
Davis, Humphrey, Sr., in Mathews Co.	York	Will	1809	CF1811-001
Davis, J.H., in Cumberland Co.	Amelia	Will	1857	CF1888-011
Davis, Jacob	Northampton	Will	1768	T: correct from David
Davis, Jacob	Nottoway	Will	1794	BRCD
Davis, Jacob, of Nottoway Co.	Mecklenburg	Will	1794	CF1844-034
Davis, John	Brunswick	Will	1798	CF1833-019
Davis, John A.	New Kent	Will	1888	CF1896-001
Davis, John W.	Prince William	Will	1887	CF1895-003
Davis, Jordan A., in Lynchburg	Bedford	Will	1844	CF1859-038
Davis, Joseph, in Orange Co.	Greene	Will	1799	CF1856-004
Davis, Mary Ann, of New Kent Co.	Williamsburg	Will Abstract	1809	Crozier, p. 20
Davis, Mary G., in FL	Campbell	Will	1884	CF1884-018
Davis, Micajah, Jr., in Lynchburg	Bedford	Will	1858	CF1888-022
Davis, Moses	New Kent	Will	1688	LVA Acc. #41008, r4611
Davis, Moses	New Kent	Will	1688	Fleet, Huntington Data
Davis, Moses	New Kent	Will	1688	LVA Acc. #32048
Davis, Moses	New Kent	Will	1688	LVA Acc. #36102, r444a
Davis, Nancy, in Augusta Co.	Staunton	Will	1851	CF1899-003
Davis, Nancy, in Augusta Co.	Staunton	Will	1857	CF1889-007
Davis, Nehemiah	Fairfax	Will	1796	CF1838-011
Davis, Owen	York	Will	1706	Note[2]
Davis, Presley	Prince William	Will	1823	CF1858-001
Davis, Richard, of Overwharton Parish	Prince William	Will	1716	Note[3]
Davis, Richard, Sr.	Prince William	Will	1824	CF1890-017

---

[1] Beverly Fleet, *Virginia Colonial Abstracts*, King and Queen County County, Vol. 14, 5th Collection, p. 90.

[2] York County Land Causes, 1746-1769, p. 68.

[3] Prince William County Land Causes, 1793-1811, p. 313.

NAME	LOCATION	TYPE	YEAR	REFERENCE(S)
Davis, Shelton C., in Richmond	Henrico	Will	1879	CF1893-048
Davis, Staige, of Middlesex Co.	Williamsburg	Will Abstract	1812	Fleet 2:353
Davis, Staige, of Middlesex Co.	Williamsburg	Will Abstract	1813	Crozier, p. 20
Davis, Sterling, in TN	Lunenburg	Will	1856	CF1885-007
Davis, Thomas	Essex	Will	1718	V:Mss1 B4678 a 4604+
Davis, Thomas	Essex	Will	1799	CF1823-027
Davis, Virginia F.	Fairfax	Will	1853	X
Davis, Virginia F., in Frederick Co.	Fairfax	Will	1859	CF1901-002
Davis, William	Charles City	Inventory	1772	Records, p. 412
Davis, William	Isle of Wight	Will	1796	LVA Acc. #20038
Davis, William B., in King & Queen Co.	Essex	Will	1867	CF1887-003
Davis, William, in Campbell Co.	Lynchburg	Will	1829	CF1854-031
Davyes, Richard, planter		Will	1661	VCRP, Survey #03528
Dawkins, John, of Dettingen Parish	Prince William	Will	1746	Note[1]
Daws, John	Mecklenburg	Will	1819	Note[2]
Dawson, Benjamin		Will	1851	UVA MSS 3984-e
Dawson, Berryman [Benjamin]	Rockingham	Admin. Bond	1833	AB1
Dawson, Berryman [Benjamin]	Rockingham	Admin.	1833	MB14:076, 130
Day, James	Isle of Wight	Will Ref.	1701	VHMB 45, p. 195
Day, William	Henrico	Will	1771	Records, Vol. 7, p. 2141
Day, William O.	Hanover	Will	1878	CF1899-030
Deakins, Philip	Prince William	Inv. Ref.	1844	CM:04 MAR 1844
Deale, Elias, in Culpeper Co.	Rappahannock	Will	1819	CF1846-002
Dean, John, of Bath Co.	Augusta	Will	1811	CF1824-035
Dean, Joseph	Alexandria	Will	1818	NVG 4:1, p. 222
Deane, Sophia Caldwell	Richmond City	Will	1861	V:Mss1 W8945 b 1035+
Deans, James, merchant	Chesterfield	Will Abstract	1762	VMHB 23, p. 442
Deans, Josiah Herbert, in AL	Gloucester	Will	1881	CF1896-011
Dear, Edmund	Louisa	Will	1795	Note[3]
Dear, Phebe A.E., in Highland Co.	Rappahannock	Will	1898	CF1903-011
Deatley, James E., in Westmoreland Co.	King George	Will	(nd)	CF1848-003
Deatley, James E., in Westmoreland Co.	King George	Will	(nd)	CF1848-003
Deavers, Lewis	Fairfax	Guard. Bond	1845	X
Debell, William		Inventory	1740	LVA Acc. #24961-3
DeBell, Elizabeth	Fairfax	Inventory	1843	X
Debrell, Anthony	Buckingham	Will	1816	BRCD
DeButts, S. Welby, in Loudoun Co.	Fairfax	Will	1912	CF1915-047
Dedman, Samuel, in Mecklenburg Co.	Lunenburg	Will	1790	CF1810-020
Degge, Anthony	Surry	Will (U)	1784	VTG 13:2, p. 53
Degge, Anthony	Surry	Will (U)	1784	LVA:1048937
Degge, Anthony	Surry	Will (U)	1784	VG 13, p. 53
Deisher, Christian, of *Craig's Creek*	Botetourt	Will	1890	V:Mss2 D3685 b
Dejarnatt, Daniel, of *Fall Point*	Hanover	Will	1795	LVA Acc. #24838
Dejarnatte, William Y.	Hanover	Will	1817	Cocke:47
Dejarnett, Daniel	Hanover	Will	1795	Fleet, Huntington Data
Dejarnette, William	Hanover	Will	1817	CF1842-016

---

[1] Prince William County Land Causes, 1793-1811, p. 357.

[2] Incorrectly indexed as "John Day" in Mecklenburg County General Index to Wills.

[3] Louisa County Wills Not Fully Proved, 1757-1902, p. 18.

NAME	LOCATION	TYPE	YEAR	REFERENCE(S)
DeJarnette, Elliott	Spotsylvania	Will	1857	LVA Acc. #22870
DeLaCour, Claude	Albemarle	Will	1789	VMHB 37, p. 164
Delaney, John	Madison	Will	1803	CF1826-007
Delarue, Eugene	Hanover	Will	1896	CF1897-017
Delk, Roger	Surry	Admin.	1699	T:D&W5, p. 89a
Delke, Roger	Surry	Will	1693	T:D&W4, p. 309b
Demfield, John	Surry	Inventory	1688	T:D&W4, p. 43b
Deneale, George, in Alexandria Co.	Fairfax	Will	1818	CF1848-019
Deneale, John Earl	Fairfax	Guard. Acct.	1817	X
Deneale, Sibyl	Fairfax	Division	1783	X
Deneale, William	Fairfax	Will	1814	X
Deneale, William, sheriff	Fairfax	Account	1801	X
Deneufville, John A.	James City	Will	1874	CF1884-004
Deneufville, John A.	James City	Will	1874	CF1891-002
Deneufville, Peter Robert	James City	Will	1809	CW(4)
Denmead, Adam, in MD	Lynchburg	Will	1863	CF1870-031
Denney, William	Northumberland	Will	1793	CF1815-005
Dennis, Elizabeth, in Pr. Edward Co.	Bedford	Will	1861	CF1883-084
Dennis, Richard	Charles City	Will	1724	D&W1724, p. 14
Dennis, Richard	Charles City	Inventory	1725	D&W1724, p. 27
Dennis, Rob	Surry	Admin.	1687	T:D&W4, p. 24a
Dennis, William M., of James City Co.	Williamsburg	Will Abstract	1821	Crozier, p. 19
Dent, Thomas, in London, Eng.	Richmond City	Will	1817	MVG 26:2, p. 152
Denton, J. Barton	Hanover	Will	1897	CF1907-039
Denton, John	Frederick	Will	1767	WB3, p. 407
Depp, Peter	Powhatan	Will	1808	LVA Acc. #22554
Depriest, John, in Campbell Co.	Lynchburg	Will	1799	CF1834-035
Derick, Henry		Will	1677	VCRP, Survey #03713
Derickson, George, mariner		Will	1685	VCRP, Survey #03733
Dermont, Michael, of Stafford Co.	Prince William	Will	1733	LVA Allason Papers
Derring, James	Isle of Wight	Will	1785	WB9, p. 305
Deshazo, William		Account	1821c	V:Mss1 H7935 a 1
Desmond, Daniel	Norfolk City	Will	1814	LVA Acc. #24194
Devaughn, Samuel, in Washington DC	Arlington	Will	1867	CF1878-046
Dever, Nancy	Rockingham	Will	1863	CF1867-011
Deverall, Benjamin		Will	1720	VCRP, Survey #04641
Devereux, Eleanor E., in NY	Fairfax	Will	1893	CF1896-033
Devereux, Eleanor E., in NY	Fairfax	Will	1895	CF1896-033
Devereux, Jarrett	Goochland	Will	1819	CF1838-014
Dew, Thomas	King & Queen	Will	1843	V:Mss2 D5106 b
Dewell, Drury	Surry	Inventory	1794	WB1, p. 71
Dewell, Edward, of Warrasquoyke		Will	1640	VCRP, Survey #03988
Dewey, Stephen	Dinwiddie	Will	1770	SV 3:4, p. 154
Deyerle, Peter, in Montgomery Co.	Roanoke	Will	1813	CF1863-018
Diack, Alexander	Williamsburg	Will (N)	1789	Crozier, p. 22
Dibrell, Anthony	Buckingham	Will	1816	LVA Patteson Papers
Dibrell, Anthony	Buckingham	Estate	1816c	LVA Acc. #24295
Dickenson, Elisha	Fredericksburg	Will	1794	DCWBA, p. 42
Dickenson, Henry, in Russell Co.	Washington	Will	1867	CF1881-018
Dickenson, James H., in Russell Co.	Washington	Will	1894	CF1896-070
Dickenson, Robert P., in Russell Co.	Wise	Will	1890	CF1920-001

NAME	LOCATION	TYPE	YEAR	REFERENCE(S)
Dickerson, John	Bath	Will	(nd)	CF1837-009
Dickerson, John	Essex	Will	1778	CF1805-011
Dickerson, John, of York Co.	Williamsburg	Will Abstract	1801	Crozier, p. 20
Dickeson, John		Will	1801	CW(15)
Dickey, Edward, in Campbell Co.	Lynchburg	Will	1812	CF1819-036
Dickie, Barbara, form. King & Queen	Hanover	Will	1817	Cocke:52
Dickie, Barbara, in King William Co.	Hanover	Will	1845	CF1847-003
Dickinson, Ann "Nancy" Woolfolk	Caroline	Will	1840	MVG 34:2, p. 159[1]
Dickinson, Edmund		Will	1778	CW(15)
Dickinson, Edmund	York	Will	1778	CF1785-006
Dickinson, Francis		Will	1630	VCRP, Survey #03962
Dickinson, Henry, in Kanawha Co.	Bedford	Will	1871	CF1872-072
Dickinson, Jacob, of Nansemond Co.	Isle of Wight	Account	1799	CF1816-016
Dickinson, John, in Kanawha Co.	Bedford	Will	1868	CF1870-047
Dickinson, John J., in Kanawha Co.	Bedford	Will	1867	CF1872-072
Dickinson, John J., in Kanawha Co.	Bedford	Will	1868	CF1899-236
Dickinson, Martha	Bath	Will	(nd)	CF1837-009
Dickinson, Nathaniel	Hanover	Will	1840	Cocke:48
Dickinson, Nathaniel	Hanover	Will	1840	CF1872-014
Dickinson, Nathaniel	Hanover	Will	1840	CF1861-011
Dickinson, Nathaniel	Hanover	Will	1843	CF1846-003
Dickinson, Nathaniel	Hanover	Will	1843	CF1901-002
Dickinson, Thomas	Caroline	Will	1826	MVG 34:2, p. 159[2]
Dickinson, Thomas	Nottoway	Will	1858	V:Mss2 D5608 a 2
Dickinson, Thomas	Nottoway	Will	1858	V:Mss2 D5608 a 1
Dickinson, Thomas	Nottoway	Will	1860	CF1870-008
Dickinson, William, in Kanawha Co.	Bedford	Will	1861	CF1872-072
Dickinson, William, in Kanawha Co.	Bedford	Will	1865	CF1899-236
Dickinson, William M.	Caroline	Will	1851	W&D1794, p. 68
Dickson, Charles	Warwick	Inventory	1697	Records 1695, p. 456
Dickson, Robert, in Portsmouth	Isle of Wight	Will	1866	CF1874-018
Diddep, Thomas	Richmond City	Will	1863	MVG 37:1, p. 42
Digges, Cole	Hanover	Will	1817	MVG 29:3, p. 190
Digges, Cole	Hanover	Will	1817	Note[3]
Digges, Cole	Hanover	Will	1817	VGSQ 11:1, p. 7
Digges, Ludwell	Fauquier	Will	1836	CF1855-006
Digges, Ludwell	Fauquier	Will	1836	V:Mss1 B3658 a 5-20
Digges, Mary		Will	1825	Fleet, Huntington Data
Diggs, Edward	York	Will	1675	LVA Acc. #41686
Diggs, Edward		Will	1686	VCRP, Survey #03736
Diggs, John, in Nelson Co.	Albemarle	Will	1846	CF1885-006
Dill, Adolph, Sr., in Richmond	Henrico	Will	1867	CF1879-019
Dillard, John, in Campbell Co.	Lynchburg	Will	1863	CF1883-038
Dillard, Stephen H., in Hanover Co.	Henrico	Will	1829	CF1853-008
Dillard, Thomas, in Bedford Co.	Lynchburg	Will	1820	CF1827-060
Dinwiddie, Edward W., in Bedford Co.	Campbell	Will	1884	CF1909-031

---

[1] Caroline Co. Circuit Court Chancery, *Dickinson et al. v. Dickinson* (1845).

[2] Caroline Co. Circuit Court Chancery, *Dickinson et al. v. Dickinson* (1845).

[3] LVA, Land Office Caveats, Box 1858-1896.

NAME	LOCATION	TYPE	YEAR	REFERENCE(S)
Dinwiddie, John	King George	Will	1700	LVA Acc. #24865
Dinwiddie, John		Will	1725	VG 13, p. 51
Dinwiddie, John, Maj.	King George	Will	1700	VG 03, p. 51
Dinwiddie, John, merchant	King George	Will	1724	WB1A, p. 45
Dinwiddie, Robert		Will	1770	VCRP, Survey #04683
Dinwiddie, Robert		Will	1786	UVA MSS 3194-1
Dinwiddie, Robert, of Jackson River	Bath	Will	1796	TQ 14, p. 243
Dinwiddie, Robert, of Jackson River	Bath	Will	1796	TQ 14:4, p. 243
Dinwiddie, William		Will	1833	UVA MSS 3194-1
Dishman, John	Westmoreland	Will	1739	D&W9, p. 31a
Dishman, Samuel	Loudoun	Will	1847	V:Mss6:2 D6316:2
Dishman, Samuel, in Westmoreland Co.	Essex	Will	1727	CF1807-003
Diskin, John		Account	1735	M: L13 f248
Dismukes, James [of Port Royal]	Caroline	Will	1770	W&P1742, p. 14
Disney, John B.	Fairfax	Account	1848	X
Dison, Leonard	Henrico	Will	1733	Records, Vol. 3, p. 909
Dix, Walter	Essex	Will	1833	LP ur
Dixon, Anthony Tucker	Charles City	Will	1808	VGS Bulletin IV, p. 49[1]
Dixon, Anthony Tucker, Dr.	Charles City	Inventory	1808c	V:Mss1 C9434 a 269+
Dixon, George O., of Alexandria	D.C.	Will	1863	DCA:Box 31
Dixon, Henry	Chesterfield	Will	1804	SV 6:2, p. 68
Dixon, Henry	Chesterfield	Will	1804	LVA Wills/Admin. DB
Dixon, James		Estate Ref.	1794	Shepherd, Vol. 1, p. 335
Dixon, James	Arlington	Will	1800	CRA:314
Dixon, John	Gloucester	Will	1777	Note[2]
Dixon, John, in Canterbury, Eng.		Will	1758	FDC L392-76
Dixon, John, of Bristol, Eng.	Fredericksburg	Will	1758	LVA Acc. #32931
Dixon, John, of Ware Parish	Gloucester	Will	1789	Note[3]
Dixon, John, printer		Will	1804	CW(12)
Dixon, Josiah, mariner		Will	1699	VCRP, Survey #06062
Dixon, Michael	Mathews	Estate Ref.	1817	LP:10 DEC 1818
Dixon, Roger	Fredericksburg	Will	1772	LVA Acc. #32931
Dixon, Roger	Spotsylvania	Will	1772	V:Mss1 B2346 a 1096
Dixon, Samuel	Hanover	Estate Ref.	1809	LP:21 DEC 1809
Dixon, William, of Fairfax Co.	D.C.	Will	1886	DCA:Box 96
Dixson, Margery	Princess Anne	Will	1705	DB1, p. 432
Dobbins, Charles, in King & Queen Co.	Essex	Will	1790	CF1831-071
Dobie, Robert		Will	1777	Note[4]
Dobson, Edward, of Abingdon Parish	Gloucester	Will Abstract	1677	Mason, Vol. 2, p. 52
Dobson, John	Gloucester	Will	1833	LVA Acc. #30719
Dobyns, Daniel, of Richmond Co.	Williamsburg	Will Abstract	1784	Crozier, p. 22
Dobyns, Winifred, of Richmond Co.	Williamsburg	Will Abstract	1801	Crozier, p. 22
Dodd, William, of Botetourt Co.	Augusta	Will	1823	CF1832-088
Dodds, Joseph, of Alexandria	D.C.	Will	1852	DCA:Box 21
Dogan, Elizabeth	Prince William	Inv. Ref.	1843	CM:04 SEP 1843

---

[1] From Duke University, John R. Kilby Papers.

[2] LVA, U.S. Circuit Court Records, Box 195, *Murdock, Donald & Co. v. Dixon's Reps.* (1824).

[3] LVA, U.S. Circuit Court Records, Box 195, *Murdock, Donald & Co. v. Dixon's Reps.* (1824).

[4] Sussex County Order Book, 1777-1782, p. 48; Henrico County Miscellaneous Court Records, Vol. 7, 1770-1807, p. 2289.

NAME	LOCATION	TYPE	YEAR	REFERENCE(S)
Doles, Catharine	Surry	Will	1750	T: correct from Dales
Domelaw, Richard		Will	1624	VCRP, Survey #03113
Donald, Andrew, in Bedford Co.	Lynchburg	Will	1806	CF1821-051
Donald, Andrew, in Bedford Co.	Lynchburg	Will	1806	CF1843-001
Donaldson, William	Fairfax	Will	1816	X
Doniphan, Alexander	Stafford	Will	1768	TQ 26:4, p. 275
Donnan, Alexander	Petersburg	Will	1892c	V:Mss1 M3156 a 183+
Dorney, Mary J., in NY	Lynchburg	Will	1886	CF1899-035
Doss, James, Sr., in Pittsylvania Co.	Lynchburg	Will	1796	CF1818-017
Doswell, Benjamin T.	Caroline	Will	1828	W&P1742, p. 121
Doswell, Benjamin T.	Hanover	Will	1828	CF1834-006
Doswell, Benjamin T., of Caroline Co.	Hanover	Will	1828	Cocke:177
Doswell, James	Hanover	Will	1825	V:Mss1 D7424 b 1-5
Doswell, James Turner	Hanover	Will	1872	V:Mss1 D7424 b 17-19
Doswell, Lilly Ann	Hanover	Will	1861	CF1869-003
Doswell, Lilly Ann	Hanover	Will	1861	Cocke:53
Doswell, Thomas	Hanover	Will	1778	HHS 6, p. 4
Doswell, Thomas	Hanover	Will	1870c	V:Mss1 D7424 b 6-16
Doswell, Thomas Walker, of *Bullfield*	Hanover	Will	1889	V:Mss1 D7424 b 38-41
Douglas, William	Louisa	Account	(nd)	V:Mss2 D7476 b
Douglas, William	Louisa	Inventory	(nd)	V:Mss2 D7476 b
Douglas, William	Goochland	Will	1775	V:Mss1 D7475 a 40-44
Douglas, William	Louisa	Will	1798	V:Mss2 D7476 b
Douglas, William	Louisa	Exor. Bond	1798	V:Mss2 D7476 b
Douglass, Hugh, in Loudoun Co	Frederick	Will	1812	CF1821-011
Douglass, John	Orange	Will	1828	UVA MSS 702
Douglass, William, in Loudoun Co.	Frederick	Will	1783	CF1821-011
Douglass, William, of St. John Parish	King William	Will Ref.	1718	Winfree, p. 352
Dove, Henry, of Rockingham Co.	Augusta	Will	1801	CF1829-024
Dove, James	Richmond City	Account	1799	Note[1]
Dover, William, shipwright		Will	1706	VCRP, Survey #03894
Dow, Alexander	Fairfax	Inventory	1817	X
Dow, Alexander	Fairfax	Sale	1817	X
Dowdell, James G., in Loudoun Co.	Fauquier	Will	1888	CF1889-054
Dowden, William	Surry	Will	1782	T: correct from Dawson
Dowell, John	Louisa	Will	1760	V:Mss1 B2346 a 1158
Dowell, William, in Nottoway Co.	Lunenburg	Will	1818	CF1837-009
Dowles, William	Hanover	Will	1805	Cocke:154
Dowles, William	Hanover	Will	1861	CF1861-025
Downe, Nicholas		Will	1653	VCRP, Survey #04110
Downer, William	Caroline	Will	1808	TVF 4:2, p. 120
Downer, William	Caroline	Will	1808	BRCD
Downer, William, in Caroline Co.	Goochland	Will	1808	CF1817-001
Downman, John Bartholomew	Fauquier	Will	1859	V:Mss1 D7598 a 46-50
Downman, Raleigh	Elizabeth City	Will Ref.	1754	VMHB 78, p. 228
Downman, Raleigh, of Lancaster Co.		Will	1782	VCRP, Survey #04703
Downman, Rawleigh	Elizabeth City	Will	1754	Note[2]

---

[1] Richmond City Hustings Court Deeds, No. 2, 1792-1799, p. 588.
[2] Virginia Historical Society, Ball-Downman Papers, Vol. 78, p. 228.

NAME	LOCATION	TYPE	YEAR	REFERENCE(S)
Downman, Rawleigh Porteus	Prince William	Will	1801	VG 19, p. 083
Downman, Rawleigh William	Lancaster	Wil	1838	V:Mss1 D7598 a 42-45
Downs, James B.	Fauquier	Will	1894	CF1895-061
Downs, Robert	Henrico	Inventory	1758	Records, Vol. 6, p. 1775
Dozier, Joseph	Westmoreland	Will	1799	Note[1]
Dozier, Richard T., in Lancaster Co.	Northumberland	Will	1838	CF1854-009
Drake, James	Henrico	Will	1791	T: correct from Duke
Drake, Richard, in King George Co.	Westmoreland	Will	1780	Wills #18
Drake, Robert, in New Kent Co.	James City	Will	1865	CF1868-002
Drew, Juliet Jordan Shore	Richmond City	Will	1846	V:Mss1 C5217 b 813+
Drew, Richard	Surry	Admin.	1695	T:D&W5, p. 67a
Drew, Sarah, of Southampton Co.	Williamsburg	Will Abstract	1807	Crozier, p. 22
Drew, William	Surry	Will	1778	LVA Acc. #24194
Drew, William	Surry	Will	1778	LVA Acc. #27394
Drew, William	Berkeley	Will	1785	NUCMC Unidentified
Drew, William	Berkeley	Inventory	1796	NUCMC Unidentified
Drewry, Henry, in Chesterfield Co.	Hanover	Will	1886	CF1904-032
Drewry, Henry T., in Chesterfield Co.	Bath	Will	1868	CF1893-012
Drinkard, Mary	Charles City	Inventory	1771	Records, p. 331
Drinkard, William R., of Charles City Co.	Williamsburg	Will Abstract	1805	Crozier, p. 21
Drinkwater, John	Charles City	Will (N)	1693	VGSQ 17:2, p. 44
Drinkwater, John, of *Wynoke*	Charles City	Will (N)	1693	D&W1692, p. 153
Driskill, William B., in Charlotte Co.	Campbell	Will	1854	CF1873-040
Druitt, Jonathan		Will Ref.	1735	Hening, Vol. 7, p. 171
Drumont, James, mariner		Will	1667	VCRP, Survey #03538
Drumright, William, in GA	Mecklenburg	Will	1882	CF1889-008 CC
Drysdale, Hugh, Maj.	London	Will	1726	VCRP, Survey #04643
Drysdale, Hugh, Lt. Gov. of Va.	London	Will	1726	VG 34, p. 26
Duckworth, William	Frederick	Will	1761	Note[2]
Dudley, Elizabeth	Prince George	Will	1764	LVA Acc. #23423c
Dudley, George E., of Mathews Co.	Williamsburg	Will Abstract	1814	Crozier, p. 21
Dudley, John	Prince William	Will	1788	Fleet 2:201
Dudley, Richard	Essex	Will Ref.	1716	Fleet 2:326
Dudley, Richard, of South Farnham P.	Essex	Will	1717	Fleet 2:202
Dudley, William	Richmond	Will Abstract	1750	Fleet 2:303
Dudley, William	Caroline	Estate Ref.	1822	LP:04 DEC 1822
Duerson, R.C., in Spotsylvania Co.	Louisa	Will	1873	CF1889-002
Duff, Roger	Frederick	Will	1789	MVG 29:3, p. 190
Duff, Roger		Will	1789	Land Office
Duff, Samuel, in Russell Co.	Tazewell	Will	1829	CF1873-053
Duff, William	Prince William	Will	1745	Note[3]
Dugar, Reuben	King William	Will	1833	CF1868-001
Dugger, Ella, in LA	Mecklenburg	Will	1873	CF1893-017 CC
Dugger, Richmond, of Brunswick Co.	Mecklenburg	Will	1823	CF1855-015
Duke, Albert N., in Goochland Co.	Louisa	Will	1852	CF1874-002
Duke, Elizabeth	Charles City	Will	1729	D&W1724, p. 263

---

[1] Westmoreland County Original Wills, 1755-1800, Reel 28a, #45.
[2] Frederick County Land Book 1 (and Causes), 1758-1832, p. 1.
[3] Prince William County Land Causes, 1789-1793, p. 526.

NAME	LOCATION	TYPE	YEAR	REFERENCE(S)
Duke, Elizabeth	Charles City	Will	1729	D&W1724, p. 263
Duke, Elizabeth	Charles City	Inventory	1730	D&W1724, p. 290
Duke, James	Charles City	Account	1768	Records, p. 65
Dukes, John, in Culpeper Co.	Frederick	Will	1809	CF1836-114
Dulaney, Wm. Hedgeman, Shenandoah	Frederick	Will	1809	CF1821-023
Dulany, Bladen	D.C.	Will	1876	DCA:Box 60
Dulany, Bladen, in DC	Fauquier	Will	1857	CF1875-007
Dulany, Henry Grafton, in Loudoun Co.	Fairfax	Will	1889	CF1892-050
Dulany, Henry R.	Fairfax	Guard. Acct.	1848	X
Dulany, Henry Rozier	Arlington	Will	1839	CF1866-027
Dulany, John P., in Loudoun Co.	Fauquier	Will	1878	CF1908-046
Dulany, Rebecca A.	Fairfax	Guard. Acct.	1848	X
Dulin, Martha, of Gloucester Co.	Williamsburg	Will Abstract	1809	Crozier, p. 20
Dulin, Mary, in Loudoun Co.	Frederick	Will	1814	CF1830-138
Dulin, William, in Loudoun Co.	Frederick	Will	1812	CF1830-104
Dunbar, William, of Farnham Parish	Rappahannock*	Will	1687	Sweeny, p. 136
Duncan, W.A., in DC	Fairfax	Will	1888	CF1893-036
Duncanson, James, in Fredericksburg	Culpeper	Will	1791	CF1832-010
Duncle, John, of Rockingham Co.	Augusta	Will	1783	CF1815-012
Dundore, Mary	Rockingham	Will	1838	LVA Acc. #31256
Dunkan, John, mariner		Will	1714	VCRP, Survey #04363
Dunklee, William R., in OH	Washington	Will	1890	CF1906-136
Dunlap, Ann, in Rockbridge Co.	Bath	Will	1809	CF1842-003
Dunlap, James, in Rockbridge Co.	Bath	Will	1840	CF1842-003
Dunlap, John, in Rockbridge Co.	Bath	Will	1804	CF1842-003
Dunlop, Alexander	James City	Will	1880	CF1898-005
Dunlop, Alexander	James City	Will	1880	CF1916-014
Dunlop, John, in London, Eng.		Will	1830	V:Mss1 Sp687 c 8-13
Dunman, Joseph	Lunenburg	Will	1799	CF1816-015
Dunman, Joseph	Lunenburg	Will	1799	CF1805-007
Dunn, John	Warwick	Will	1790	V:Mss3 C3807 a 73
Dunn, Lanier, of Bath Co.	D.C.	Will	1911	DCA:Box 980
Dunn, Thomas B.	Hanover	Will	1859	Cocke:54
Dunn, Thomas B.	Hanover	Will	1859	CF1874-033
Dunn, Walter, of Middlesex Co.	London	Will	1820	N:PROB11/1629
Dunn, William	Southampton	Will (U)	1761	BRCD
Dunn, William	Caroline	Will	1839	Weisiger 1:071
Dunn, William M., in Jefferson Co.	Fairfax	Will	1854	CF1888-020
Dunn, William M., in DC	Fairfax	Will	1888	CF1888-020
Dunnington, Stephen A., in NY	Louisa	Will	1873	CF1887-032
Dunster, Robert	Isle of Wight	Will	1656	VMHB 6, p. 254
Dupray, Frances	Henrico	Admin.	1736	Records, Vol. 3, p. 1023
Dupuy, Asa	Prince Edward	Will	1847	V:Mss1 W3286 a 16-20
Dupuy, Asa	Prince Edward	Plat	1866	V:Mss1 W3286 a 16-20
Durfey, Goodrich	James City	Will	1869	CF1877-003
Durfey, Goodrich	James City	Will	1869	CF1882-008
Durham, James to Frances Coates	King & Queen	Marriage	1830	LP
Durrett, George	Caroline	Will	1812	W&D1794, p. 10
Durrett, George	Caroline	Will	1812	TQ 30:3, p. 208
Duryea, Nancy T., in NY	Henrico	Will	1889	CF1892-001
Dute, John	Surry	Inventory	1691	T:D&W4, p. 243a

NAME	LOCATION	TYPE	YEAR	REFERENCE(S)
Duval, Nathaniel H., in Chesterfield Co.	Henrico	Will	1871	CF1888-027
Duval, William	Buckingham	Will	1842	BRCD
Duval, William, in Buckingham Co.	Lynchburg	Will	1842	CF1860-025
Duval, William, of Gloucester Co.	Williamsburg	Will Abstract	1785	Crozier, p. 21
DuVal, Robert	Henrico	Will	1773	Dead Cases 1785 88-3
Duvall, Nathaniel H., in Chesterfield Co.	Louisa	Will	1871	CF1876-029
Dyel, William	Loudoun	Will	1766	M: L36 f350
Dyson, Francis	Nottoway	Will	1866	Judgments 1876

NAME	LOCATION	TYPE	YEAR	REFERENCE(S)

E

NAME	LOCATION	TYPE	YEAR	REFERENCE(S)
Eades, Joseph	Buckingham	Will	1827	BRCD
Eades, Joseph, in Buckingham Co.	Lynchburg	Will	1827	CF1845-019
Early, Joab	Putnam	Will	1860	V:Mss1 Ea765 b 9-10
Early, Joab	Putnam	Will	1865	V:Mss1 Ea765 b 9-10
Early, John	Orange	Will	1774	FDC L570-1
Early, Joshua, in Bedford Co.	Lynchburg	Will	1811	CF1833-039
Early, Thomas J., in Madison Co.	Albemarle	Will	1856	CF1895-084
Early, William, in Madison Co.	Greene	Will	1853	CF1888-005
Earnshaw, Isaac	King William	Will	1705	RB2, p. 48
Earsom, John	Hampshire	Will	1847	LVA Acc. #32231
Earsom, John, in Hampshire Co.	Frederick	Will	1790	CF1822-270
Earsom, Simon, in Hampshire Co.	Frederick	Will	1795	CF1822-270
Easby, Robert	Cumberland	Account	1759	WB1, p. 192
Easby, William, of Washington DC	Arlington	Will	1890	WB10:166; File #745A
East, David	Richmond City	Will	1787	T:HCD1, p. 156
East, Edward	Henrico	Inventory	1736	Records, Vol. 3, p. 979
East, Thomas	Louisa	Will	1782	Note[1]
Eastham, Philip, in Culpeper Co.	Rappahannock	Will	1823	CF1884-001
Eatherton, Mary A.	Hanover	Will	1861	CF1880-005
Eaton, Thomas	Elizabeth City	Will	1659	LP:18 DEC 1830
Eaton, Thomas	Elizabeth City	Will	1659	LVA Acc. #20496
Eaves, Mary Eliz. Harwood, in NY	Gloucester	Will	1896	CF1905-028
Eaves, Mary Eliz. Harwood, in NY	Gloucester	Will	1896	CF1903-035
Eckles, Solomon, of Cople Parish	Westmoreland	Will	1788	Wills #30
Eckles, Solomon, of Westmoreland Co.	Williamsburg	Will Abstract	1788	Crozier, p. 23
Eddins, Abraham, in Orange Co.	Greene	Will	1832	CF1852-003
Eddins, Abraham, in Orange Co.	Greene	Will	1832	CF1838-002
Eddins, William, in Orange Co.	Albemarle	Will	1875	CF1904-042
Edloe, Carter H.	Prince George	Will	1844	SV 9:3, p. 108
Edloe, Carter H., in Prince George Co.	Petersburg	Will	1844	CF1855-020
Edloe, Carter H., of Prince George Co.	Southampton	Will	1844	LP:11 DEC 1845
Edloe, John	Charles City	Account	1773	Note[2]
Edloe, Philip	Charles City	Will	1727	D&W1724, p. 153
Edloe, Philip	Charles City	Inventory	1727	D&W1724, p. 175
Edmonds, Courtney Ann, Alexandria Co.	Fauquier	Will	1839	CF1849-016
Edmonds, Elias	Northumberland	Settlement	1744	TVF 6:3, p. 184
Edmondson, Elizabeth, of *Hilford*	Charles City	Will	1790	BRCD
Edmondson, H.A., of Halifax Co.	D.C.	Will	1921	DCA: Box 687
Edmondson, William	Essex	Will Abstract	1774	Fleet 2:343
Edmonson, Thomas, of Essex Co.	Williamsburg	Will Abstract	1759	Crozier, p. 23
Edmund, Sam, the younger, Nelson Co.	Lynchburg	Will	1803	CF1850-022
Edmund, Samuel, in Nelson Co.	Lynchburg	Will	1821	CF1850-022
Edmunds, James A., in Pittsylvania Co.	Campbell	Will	1844	CF1875-018
Edmunds, James, in DC	Fairfax	Will	1880	CF1907-002
Edmunds, John, cutler		Will	1672	VCRP, Survey #03548
Edmunds, Susan W. Morton	Charlotte	Will	1864	V:Mss1 B6638 a2812+

---

[1] Louisa County Wills Not Fully Proved, 1757-1902, p. 21.

[2] LVA, Charles City County Records, 1766-1774, p. 445.

NAME	LOCATION	TYPE	YEAR	REFERENCE(S)
Edmunds, Thomas W.R., in KY	Amelia	Will	1834	CF1837-027
Edmundson, Upton, in Amelia Co.	Lunenburg	Will	1881	CF1812-012
Edsor, Joseph	Westmoreland	Will	1779	Wills #16
Edward, Warner	King William	Will	(nd)	BRCD
Edwards, Alpheus, of Charlottesville	D.C.	Will	1898	DCA:Box 175
Edwards, Andrew	Stafford	Will	1788	FDC L563-141
Edwards, Andrew	Stafford	Will	1788	VG 16, p. 307
Edwards, Brambley	Brunswick	Will	1817	LVA Wills/Admin. DB
Edwards, Brambley	Brunswick	Will	1817	SV 3:1, p. 38
Edwards, Catharine	Northumberland	Will	1831	Note[1]
Edwards, Elizabeth	Surry	Will	1771	T: correct from Mary
Edwards, Frances			1731c	LVA Wills/Admin. DB
Edwards, George	King William	Will	1867	LVA Acc. #28458
Edwards, Hartwell	Surry	Will Abstract	1801	VG 13, p. 53
Edwards, Hartwell	Surry	Will (U)	1801	VTG 13:2, p. 55
Edwards, Horace	James City	Will	1888	CF1896-015
Edwards, John		Will	1668	VCRP, Survey #03541
Edwards, John	Warwick	Settlement	1696	TVF 3:4, p. 228
Edwards, John	Warwick	Inventory	1697	Records 1695, p. 454
Edwards, John	Charles City	Inventory	1770	Records, p. 241
Edwards, John	Suffolk	Will (N)	1862	V:Mss2 Ed967 a 1
Edwards, Martha	Surry	Will	1795	WB1, p. 97
Edwards, Martha	Surry	P. of Atty.	1812	VG 13, p. 53
Edwards, Narcissa, in Southampton Co.	Brunswick	Will	1867	CF1871-033
Edwards, Thomas	Mathews	Will	1857	TVF 7:2, p. 97
Edwards, Thomas	Mathews	Will	1857	Superior Ct. Papers 1860s
Edwards, Warner	King William	Will	(nd)	CF1890-001
Edwards, William	Charles City	Inventory	1726	D&W1724, p. 79, 229
Edwards, William	Charles City	Inventory	1728	D&W1724, p. 229
Edwards, William	Bedford	Will	1757	DB1, p. 118
Edwards, William	Brunswick	Will	1781	CF1788-002
Edwards, William	Brunswick	Will	1781	CF1796-013
Edwards, William Newett	Surry	Account	1772	T: correct from Newet
Edwards, William, of Surry Co.	Williamsburg	Will Abstract	1797	Crozier, p. 24
Edzar, James, the younger		Estate Ref.	1789	Hening, Vol. 13, p. 96
Effinger, John F.	Rockingham	Will	1840	LP:04 FEB 1848
Effinger, John Ignatious	Shenandoah	Will	1837	V:Mss6:1 Ef443:1
Eggborn, Harriet H., in Culpeper Co.	Fairfax	Will	1854	CF1859-010
Eggleston, Edmund, in Cumberland Co.	Amelia	Will	1840	CF1886-011
Eggleston, Richard, of James City Co.	Williamsburg	Will Abstract	1794	Crozier, p. 23
Eggleston, Richard, Sr., Powhatan Co.	Amelia	Will	1781	CF1806-016
Eggling, Margaret A., in Goochland Co.	Henrico	Will	1869	CF1889-072
Eidson, Henry, in Campbell Co.	Lynchburg	Will	1819	CF1837-002
Eilbeck, Jonathan, of Norfolk	London	Will	1821	N:PROB11/1645
Elam, William P., in Petersburg	Prince Edward	Will	1874	CF1878-020
Elcan, Patrick Henry, Dr., *Elk Hall*	Buckingham	Will	1841	V:Mss1 El183 a 189+
Elder, Harrison J.	Lunenburg	Will	1876	CF1895-025
Elder, Thomas	Henrico	Will Ref.	1796	Shepherd, Vol. 2, p. 64

---

[1] Northumberland County District Court Orders, Deeds, [Wills], 1789-1825 [1849], p. 467.

NAME	LOCATION	TYPE	YEAR	REFERENCE(S)
Eldred, Harriet A.	James City	Will	1899	CF1903-006
Eldridge, Thomas	Surry	Will	1741	V:Mss2 El245 a 1
Eley, William, of Nansemond Co.	Williamsburg	Will Abstract	1791	Crozier, p. 23
Elgin, Eliza Rebecca	Fairfax	Guard. Bond	1843	X
Elgin, Gustavus	Fairfax	Account	1899	X
Eliason, William A., in Fairfax Co.	Arlington	Will	1829	CF1852-010
Elkin, Ralph	Stafford	Will P.	1690	OB: 09 SEP 1690
Elkins, David, in Culpeper Co.	Fauquier	Will	1828	CF1835-043
Elkins, David, Sr., in Culpeper Co.	Fauquier	Will	1828	CF1835-023
Eller, Henry, in Wythe Co.	Smyth	Will	1839	CF1845-009
Ellerson, J.H.	Hanover	Will	1891	CF1894-018
Ellett, Virginia	Richmond City	Will	1868	V:Mss3 El546 a Sect. 4
Ellicott, John M., in Chester Co. PA	Arlington	Will	1841	CF1852-006
Ellington, Emily, of Pr. Edward Co.	Amelia	Will	1827	CF1837-010
Elliott, Anthony		Will	1666	LVA Wills/Admin. DB
Elliott, Caleb	Essex	Will	1796	FDC V569-18
Elliott, Caleb, of Essex Co.	Williamsburg	Will Abstract	1797	Crozier, p. 22
Elliott, Cuton	York	Will	1816	MVG 31:4, p. 358
Elliott, Cuton	York	Will	1816	BRCD
Elliott, George, mariner		Will	1665	VCRP, Survey #03536
Elliott, Kemp P.		Will	1832	CW(5)
Elliott, Kemp P., in York Co.	James City	Will	1837	CF1897-009
Elliott, Morton	Caroline	Will	1827	CF1835-008
Elliott, Samuel	Fairfax	Admin. Bond	1816	NVG 6, p. 627
Ellis, Charles	Albemarle	Will	1760	V:Mss2 El59 c 17-18
Ellis, Charles	New Kent	Will	1899	CF1903-004
Ellis, George	Henrico	Will	1772	Records, Vol. 7, p. 2153
Ellis, Hardy, of Norfolk Co.	Williamsburg	Will (N)	1815	Crozier, p. 24
Ellis, Jacob	New Kent	Will	1888	CF1891-008
Ellis, Jesse	Henrico	Will	1783	WB1 1781, p. 69
Ellis, John		Will	1659	VCRP, Survey #03520
Ellis, John	Frederick	Will	1762	MVG 29:3, p. 191
Ellis, Joseph, of Norfolk Co.	Williamsburg	Will Abstract	1805	Crozier, p. 24
Ellis, Mary Fleming Lewis	Gloucester	Will	1818	VGS Bulletin V, p. 6[1]
Ellis, Mildred M., in Carroll Co.	Louisa	Will	1869	CF1887-014
Ellis, Samuel, of Norfolk Co.	Williamsburg	Will Abstract	1797	Crozier, p. 23
Ellis, Thomas, in Orange Co.	Louisa	Will	1816	CF1889-006
Ellis, William	Arlington	Will	1786	CRA:1
Ellis, William L.	Essex	Will	1859	Fleet, Huntington Data
Ellis, William L.	Essex	Will	1866	LVA Acc. #41008, r4608
Ellixon, Jasper, mariner [Allexon]		Will	1706	VCRP, Survey #03891
Ellzey, Lewis	Fairfax	Will	1785	X
Ellzey, Sarah, of Leesburg	Loudoun	Will	1853	V:Mss1 H2485 e 71-79
Ellzey, William	Fairfax	Plat	1879	X
Elmore, Elizabeth	Hanover	Will	1784	LVA Acc. #41008, r4609
Elmore, Elizabeth	Hanover	Will	1784	LVA Acc. #33139
Elmore, Elizabeth		Will		HHS 40, p. 6
Elmore, Thomas	Henrico	Inventory	1770	Records, Vol. 7, p. 2087

[1] From Duke University, William Patterson Smith Papers.

NAME	LOCATION	TYPE	YEAR	REFERENCE(S)
Elsey, Thomas	Stafford	Will	1680	LVA Steadman Coll.
Elsey, Thomas	Stafford	Will	1721	LVA Steadman Coll.
Elton, Robert	Surry	Inventory	1693	T:D&W4, p. 303a
Ely, Ann, in PA	Louisa	Will	1860	CF1899-031
Ely, George G., of Falls Church	D.C.	Will	1894	DCA:Box 145
Elzey, Thomas	Stafford	Will	1698	TQ 24, p. 275
Elzey, Thomas	Stafford	Will	1721	TQ 24, p. 276
Embry, William	Orange	Will	1759	V:Mss1 B2346 a 1152
Emerson, George W., in DC	Fairfax	Will	1869	CF1887-013
Emerson, John P., in Alexandria	King George	Will	1885	CF1905-006
Emmerson, Arthur, in Norfolk Co.	Portsmouth	Will	1842	CF1884-005
Emory, Robert, Rev., in MD	Fauquier	Will	1848	CF1892-038
Endee, Henry de, of LA	Cumberland	Will	1832	CF1857-012
England, William, in Cumberland Co.	Hanover	Will	1854	CF1886-024
England, William, in Cumberland Co.	Hanover	Will	1854	Cocke:31
English, James, of Alexandria	D.C.	Will	1879	DCA:Box 68
Engs, Philip W., in NY	Fauquier	Will	1875	CF1880-002
Enton, John, of *Covent Garden*		Will	1691	VCRP, Survey #03748
Epes, Archibald, in Prince George Co.	Petersburg	Will	1820	CF1834-022
Epes, Elizabeth	Henrico	Will	1678	RB2, p. 59
Epes, Francis	Nottoway	Will	1842	BRCD
Epes, Francis, in Nottoway Co.	Lunenburg	Will	1833	CF1842-009
Epes, Francis, Jr., in Nottoway Co.	Dinwiddie	Will	1858	CF1859-006
Epes, Francis, of Dinwiddie Co.	Brunswick	Will	1777	Superior Court 1822 APR
Epes, Francis, of Nottoway Parish	Amelia	Will Abstract	1789	VMHB 25, p. 405
Epes, Hamlin	Dinwiddie	Will	1774	Note[1]
Epes, John	Charles City	Account	1726	D&W1724, p. 135
Epes, John	Nottoway	Will Ref.	1816	VMHB 25, p. 405
Epes, John, Jr.	Charles City	Inventory	1725	D&W1724, p. 40
Epes, Peter	Prince George	Will	1807	BRCD
Epes, Peter, in Prince George Co.	Petersburg	Will	1807	CF1853-023
Epes, Peter, of Prince George Co.	York	Will	1807	CF1835-001
Epes, Sarah, Martins Brandon	Prince George	Will	1729	LVA Acc. #23423a
Epes, Tabitha	Charles City	Account	1726	D&W1724, p. 135
Epes, Thomas	Prince George	Will	1780	LVA Acc. #23684
Epes, William	Prince George	Will	1812	BRCD
Epes, William, in Prince George Co.	Petersburg	Will	1812	CF1853-023
Epes, William, of Dinwiddie Co.	Brunswick	Will	1762	Superior Court 1822 APR
Eppes, Archibald	Prince George	Will	1820	V:Mss1 F9156 a 5
Eppes, Archibald	Prince George	Will	1855	SV 10:1, p. 11
Eppes, Archibald, in Prince George Co.	Petersburg	Will	1820	CF1834-022
Eppes, Archibald, of *Appomattox Manor*		Will Ref.	1837	V:Mss1 Ep734 a 21
Eppes, Christian, of *City Point*	Prince George	Will	1799	LVA Acc. #27512b
Eppes, Christian, of *City Point*	Prince George	Will	1799	VMHB 21, p. 327
Eppes, Christian Robertson	Prince George	Will	1806	V:Mss1 F9156 a 5
Eppes, Christina	Prince George	Division	1806	LVA Acc. #27512
Eppes, Elizabeth Poythress, Broadway	Prince George	Will	1845	SV 9:3, p. 109
Eppes, Frances	Prince George	Will	1816	BRCD

---

[1] LVA, U.S. Circuit Court Records, Box 88, *Duncan v. Russell & Epes* (1815).

NAME	LOCATION	TYPE	YEAR	REFERENCE(S)
Eppes, Frances	Dinwiddie	Will	1834	SV 2:3, p. 109
Eppes, Frances, in Prince George Co.	Petersburg	Will	1816	CF1833-030
Eppes, Francis	Henrico	Will (N)	1678	OB1678, p. 65
Eppes, Francis	Dinwiddie	Will	1777	Note[1]
Eppes, Francis	Prince George	Will	1844	SV 9:3, p. 108
Eppes, Francis	Prince George	Will	1844	BRCD
Eppes, Francis, in Prince George Co.	Petersburg	Will	1844	CF1868-030
Eppes, Francis, the elder	Henrico	Will Ref.	1719	Hening, Vol. 8, p. 450
Eppes, John	Prince George	Will	1844	SV 9:3, p. 108
Eppes, Lewellin, Jr.	Henrico	Will	1743	Records, Vol. 4, p. 1227
Eppes, Lewellin, of Charles City Co.	Williamsburg	Will Abstract	1758	Crozier, p. 22
Eppes, Martha B.J.	Buckingham	Will	1861	BRCD
Eppes, Martha Burke Jones	Buckingham	Will	1861	LVA Acc. #29644
Eppes, Mary	Charles City	Inventory	1772	Records, p. 348
Eppes, Peter	Charles City	Inventory	1773	Records, p. 472
Eppes, Peter	Charles City	Will	1774	OB
Eppes, Peter, of Charles City Co.	Williamsburg	Will Abstract	1773	Crozier, p. 24
Eppes, Phebe	Prince George	Will	1850	SV 9:4, p. 158
Eppes, Richard	Prince George	Will	1794	V:Mss1 F9156 a 5
Eppes, Richard, in Prince George Co.	Petersburg	Will	1794	CF1834-022
Eppes, Richard, of *City Point*	Prince George	Will	1794	VMHB 21, p. 218
Eppes, Richard, of *City Point*	Prince George	Will Partial	1794	VMHB 22, p. 81
Eppes, Temple	Charles City	Admin.	1767	Records, p. 153
Eppes, Temple	Charles City	Account	1769	VG 14, p. 183
Eppes, William, in Dinwiddie Co.	Petersburg	Will	1794	CF1835-033
Esdale, James		Will	1772	M: Box E folder 20
Eskridge, George	Westmoreland	Will	1735	NNHM 12:1, p. 1077
Esley, Ann	Henrico	Will	1720	Records, Vol. 2, p. 483
Essell, Timothy	Surry	Inventory	1696	T: correct from Ezell
Estes, Abraham	Caroline	Will	1759	FDC L559-64
Estes, Abraham	Caroline	Will	1759	VMHB 61:472
Estes, John	Caroline	Will	1778	W&P1742, p. 26
Estes, Susannah H.S., in Caroline Co.	Lunenburg	Will	1854	CF1871-048
Estes, Susannah M.S.	Caroline	Will	1854	BRCD
Estes, Thomas, in Orange Co.	Louisa	Will	1861	CF1898-066
Etherington, Thomas	Norfolk	Will (N)	1687	DB5, p. 22a
Eubank, James [at Summit]	Caroline	Will	1830	W&P1742, p. 122
Eubank, John	Lunenburg	Will	1796	CF1809-012
Eubank, Richard	King William	Will	1871	CF1905-012
Eubank, Richard	King William	Account	1889	BRCD
Eubank, Warner, in Lancaster Co.	Northumberland	Will	1884	CF1900-003
Eubank, Warner, in Lancaster Co.	Northumberland	Will	1884	CF1900-003
Eustace, John	Northumberland	Will	1785	CF1793-002
Evans, Agnes	Prince George	Will	1833	SV 9:1, p. 23
Evans, Ann	Surry	Will	1711	T:D&W6, p. 93
Evans, Benjamin	Prince George	Will	1711	SV 10:3, p. 113
Evans, Charles R.	King & Queen	Will	1856	CF1868-008
Evans, Isaac, in Berkeley Co.	Frederick	Will	1793	CF1819-050

---

[1] LVA, Land Office Revolutionary War Military Certificate Papers, Frances Eppes, Folder 8.

NAME	LOCATION	TYPE	YEAR	REFERENCE(S)
Evans, John, blacksmith	Loudoun	Will	1767	MVG 29:3, p. 191
Evans, Mark	Lunenburg	Will	(nd)	CF1818-006
Evans, Peter, in Botetourt Co.	Roanoke	Will	1797	CF1839-003
Evans, Philip, in Washington DC	Arlington	Will	1816	CF1848-016
Evans, Sarah	Prince George	Will	1711	SV 10:3, p. 113
Evans, Susannah E., in PA	Fauquier	Will	1890	CF1894-063
Evans, William, of Southampton Co.	Williamsburg	Will Abstract	1804	Crozier, p. 24
Evens, Benjamin	Surry	Will	1729	T: correct from Evans
Evens, William	Surry	Will	1760	T: correct from Evans
Everett, Charles	Albemarle	Will	1848c	CFH 17:3, p. 64
Everitt, Joseph	Isle of Wight	Will (U)	1793	LVA:1161459
Ewell, Charles, in KY	Prince William	Will	1871	CF1875-048
Ewell, Charlotte, in Prince William Co.	Fauquier	Will	1823	CF1879-002
Ewell, Jesse, in Prince William Co.	Fauquier	Will	1805	CF1879-002
Ewell, Thomas	D.C.	Will	1796	DCA:Box 19
Ewell, Thomas Winder	Prince William	Will	1780	CF1839-003
Ewens, William, mariner		Will	1650	VCRP, Survey #04098
Ewing, Ebenezer, now of York Co.	Williamsburg	Will Abstract	1795	Crozier, p. 23
Ewing, George, in Wythe Co.	Smyth	Will	(nd)	CF1840-008
Ezard, Timothy	Surry	Admin.	1696	T:D&W5, p. 112a
Ezell, Buckner Davis	Brunswick	Will	1885c	V:Ms1 Ez333 a 60-70

NAME	LOCATION	TYPE	YEAR	REFERENCE(S)

F

NAME	LOCATION	TYPE	YEAR	REFERENCE(S)
Fairclaugh, Robert, shipmaster		Estate Ref.	1790	Hening, Vol. 13, p. 212
Fairfax, Berthia	Fairfax	Division	1879	X
Fairfax, Bryan, Baron	Fairfax	Will	1802	V:Mss2 H2463 d
Fairfax, Bryan, in Fairfax Co.	Arlington	Will	1802	CF1813-028
Fairfax, Denny, in Richmond Co.	Fauquier	Will	1802	CF1839-019
Fairfax, George W.	Fairfax	Plat	1872	X
Fairfax, George W.	Fairfax	Division	1872	X
Fairfax, George William	Fairfax	Will	1787	V:Mss2 F1619 b
Fairfax, George William, at *Belvoir*	Fairfax	Inventory	1774c	V:Mss2 F1619 b
Fairfax, George William, of Truro Parish	London	Will	1780	LVA Acc. #43792
Fairfax, George William, of Fairfax Co.		Will	1787	VCRP, Survey #04708
Fairfax, Henry	Prince William	Will	1847	CF1911-011
Fairfax, Henry	Prince William	Will	1847	CF1910-015
Fairfax, James W.	Fairfax	Division	1872	X
Fairfax, Jane, in Fairfax Co.	Arlington	Will	1805	CF1813-028
Fairfax, John T.	Fairfax	Division	1872	X
Fairfax, Priscilla	Fairfax	Will	1870	X
Fairfax, Reginald, in Richmond	Fairfax	Will	1863	CF1885-002
Fairfax, Sanford	Fairfax	Account	1860	X
Fairfax, Sanford	Fairfax	Division	1872	X
Fairfax, Sarah Cary	Fluvanna	Will Ref.	1811	V:Mss2 C2598 b
Fairfax, Thomas	Fairfax	Will	1846c	V:Mss2 H2463 d
Fairfax, Thomas, in Frederick Co.	Fauquier	Will	1782	CF1839-019
Fairfax, Thomas, Lord	Frederick	Will	(nd)	V:Mss2 H2463 d
Fairfax, Thomas, Lord	Frederick	Inventory	1782	VMHB 8, p. 11
Fairfax, Thomas, Lord	Frederick	Will	1782	V:Mss10: no. 117
Fairfax, Thomas, Lord	Frederick	Will	1782	LVA Acc. #25812
Fairfax, William	Fairfax	Will	1755	X
Fairfax, William	Fairfax	Will	1757	V:Mss2 H2463 d
Fairfax, William, on South Potomack	Fairfax	Will	1757	VMHB 4, p. 102
Fanning, David, of Annapolis, N.S.		Will	1825	LVA Acc. #25923
Fanning, Thomas, of Nansemond Co.	Isle of Wight	Will	1825	CF1829-020
Fargrason, Robert	Henrico	Will	1718	Records, Vol. 2, p. 399
Farinholt, Richard Lyons	York	Inventory	1857	V:Mss1 F2274 a 80-84
Farinholt, Richard Lyons	York	Will	1857	V:Mss1 F2274 a 80-84
Farinholt, Robert A.	New Kent	Will	1881	CF1892-008
Farinholt, Roberts, Sr.	King & Queen	Will	1833	LVA Acc. #26529-10
Farinholt, Willie J.	New Kent	Will	1887	CF1907-003
Faris, John	Henrico	Will	(nd)	DB1744, p. 30
Farish, Ellen D.	Culpeper	Will	1899	CF1907-024
Farish, George B., in Caroline Co.	Henrico	Will	1846	CF1871-003
Farish, James	Orange	Will	1828	V:Mss1 B2346 a 1153
Farish, James, in Orange Co.	Culpeper	Will	1828	CF1835-001
Farlee, William A., of Alexandria Co.	D.C.	Will	1887	DCA: Box 102
Farley, Drusella	Amelia	Will	1784	CF1800-029
Farley, Simon, of Island of Antigua	Williamsburg	Will Abstract	1756	Crozier, p. 25
Farley, Thomas	Montgomery	Will	1796	MVG 29:3, p. 191
Farne, Henry	Charles City	Will Ref.	1671	OB1672, p. 538
Farr, Richard	Henrico	Will	1718	Records, Vol. 2, p. 379
Farr, Richard R.	Fairfax	Account	1853	X

NAME	LOCATION	TYPE	YEAR	REFERENCE(S)
Farrar, John, in Chesterfield Co.	Powhatan	Will	1800	CF1835-004
Farrar, William	Goochland	Will	1812	CF1818-023
Farrar, William, of Henrico Parish	Henrico	Will Ref.	1676	Winfree, p. 326
Farriss, Jacob, in Cumberland Co.	Powhatan	Will	1837	CF1852-010
Farrow, William	Prince William	Will	1754	PWR 2:3, p. 68
Farrow, William	Prince William	Will	1754	LC 1793, pp. 12, 245
Fary, Joseph, merchant		Will	1695	VCRP, Survey #04716
Fassaker, Richard, of Stafford Co.	London	Will	1676	N:PROB11/351
Fassaker, Richard, of Stafford Co.		Will	1676	VCRP, Survey #03559
Faucett, Vincent W., of Middlesex Co.	Williamsburg	Will Abstract	1815	Crozier, p. 24
Faulcon, Nicholas, Sr.	Surry	Will	1793	T: correct from Jr.
Faulk, Christopher, in Berkeley Co.	Frederick	Will	1812	CF1831-150
Faulkner, Benjamin, Sr., planter	Halifax	Will	1783	TVF 5:2, p. 100
Faulkner, William	Fairfax	Division	1859	X
Faulkner, William	Fairfax	Plat	1859	X
Fauncett, Vincent W., of Middlesex Co.	Williamsburg	Will Abstract	1815	Fleet 2:353
Fauntleroy, John	Essex	Will	1765	Fleet 2:333
Fauntleroy, John	Richmond	Will	1794	TVF 12:4, p. 250
Fauntleroy, Moore G.	King & Queen	Will	1859	CF1876-004
Fauntleroy, Moore, in Richmond Co.	Essex	Will	1793	CF1808-007
Fauntleroy, Samuel G.	King & Queen	Will	1825	Note[1]
Fauntleroy, Samuel Gardner	King & Queen	Will	1899	V:Mss2 D5106 b
Fauntleroy, Thos. W., in Middlesex Co.	Campbell	Will	1876	CF1899-004
Fauntleroy, William, in Richmond Co.	Lynchburg	Will	1793	CF1822-018
Fauntleroy, William, in Richmond Co.	Culpeper	Will	1797	CF1888-022
Fauntleroy, William, of Lunenburg Par.	Richmond	Will	1757	VMHB 14, p. 220
Fauquier, Francis	York	Will	1768	WMQ 8, p. 171
Fauquier, Francis		Will	1771	VCRP, Survey #04691
Fauss, Mary, of New Kent Co.	Williamsburg	Will Abstract	1793	Crozier, p. 24
Faver, John	Essex	Will	1723	T: correct from Faner
Faw, Abraham, of Alexandria	Arlington	Will	1828	CF1860-025
Fawne, Thomas, chirurgeon		Will	1652	VCRP, Survey #04105
Feagan, William, in Pr. William Co.	Culpeper	Will	1809	CF1852-005
Fearn, John	Buckingham	Will	1782	VGSQ 19:3, p. 102
Featherstone, William	Charles City	Will	1718	D&W1724, p. 153
Feild, Abraham	Westmoreland	Will	1674	DB1665, p. 203
Feild, Theophilus	Mecklenburg	Will	1769	WB10, p. 324
Feilding, Ambrose		Will	1675	VCRP, Survey #03556
Feilding, Richard	Northumberland	Will	1667c	V:Mss1 C2468 a2357+
Fellgate, Tobias, of Westover	London	Will	1635	N:PROB11/167
Fellgate, Tobias, of Westover		Will (N)	1635	VCRP, Survey #03972
Fellix, Edward, mariner		Will	1729	VCRP, Survey #04371
Fellows, Lewis P., in NY	Fauquier	Will	1866	CF1880-002
Felpes, Humphrey	Surry	Will	1715	T: correct from 1714
Fendla, John	Lancaster	Will	1762	LP
Fenn, Daniel B.	Prince George	Will	1856	SV 10:1, p. 12
Fenn, Daniel B., of Prince George Co.	Petersburg	Will	1856	CF1876-078
Fenwick, Julia	D.C.	Will	1892	DCA:Box 138

---

[1] Beverly Fleet, *Virginia Colonial Abstracts*, King and Queen County County, Vol. 14, 5th Collection, p. 101.

NAME	LOCATION	TYPE	YEAR	REFERENCE(S)
Ferguson, Alexander	Franklin	Will	1818	UVA MSS 38-649
Ferguson, Alexander, in Franklin Co.	Lynchburg	Will	1818	CF1830-020
Ferguson, E.T., in Greensville Co.	Brunswick	Will	1884	CF1913-036
Ferguson, Joel	Lunenburg	Will	1788	CF1814-029
Ferguson, John	Essex	Will Abstract	1769	Fleet 2:339
Ferguson, Mary, late Sangster	Fairfax	Dower	1803	X
Ferish, George B.	Caroline	Will	1846	BRCD
Fern, Timothy	Isle of Wight	Will	1651	VMHB 6, p. 39
Fernando, William	Prince George	Estate Ref.	1847	LP:29 MAY 1852
Ferne, Thomas	Northumberland	Will Ref.	1693	OB5, pp. 85, 156
Ferrell, William, in Bedford Co.	Lynchburg	Will	1780	CF1827-074
Fewqua, Giles	Charles City	Inventory	1772	Records, p. 339
Ficklin, Anthony S., in Fauquier Co.	Culpeper	Will	1821	CF1878-001
Ficklin, Benjamin F., in Richmond	Albemarle	Will	1871	CF1902-002
Ficklin, Frances M., in Fauquier Co.	Culpeper	Will	1844	CF1878-001
Ficklin, Slaughter W., in Albemarle Co.	Charlottesville	Will	1886	CF1895-003
Ficklin, Strother, in Stafford Co.	Fauquier	Will	1827	CF1871-077
Field, Daniel, in Madison Co.	Culpeper	Will	1832	CF1852-007
Field, George B.	Gloucester	Will Abstract	1826	VGS Bulletin V, p. 8[1]
Field, Henry, Jr., in Culpeper Co.	Madison	Will	1787	CF1873-061
Field, Theophilus, of Prince George Co.	Henrico	Will	1769	Judgments 1784 MAR
Field, William S.	Culpeper	Will	1835	CF1877-009
Fielding, Ambrose	Northumberland	Inventory	1675	NNHM 37:1, p. 4256
Fielding, Edward	Northumberland	Will	1696	V:Mss F4604a2
Fielding, Henry, at London, Eng.	King & Queen	Will	1712	LVA Acc. #27285
Fielding, Henry, at London, Eng.	King & Queen	Will	1712	VG 50, p. 316
Fielding, Henry, of King & Queen Co.	London	Will	1712	N:PROB11/529
Fielding, Henry, of King & Queen Co.		Will	1712	VCRP, Survey #04361
Fielding, Joseph	Northumberland	Will Ref.	1698	OB5, p. 597
Fields, Leonard B., in NY	Hanover	Will	1891	CF1908-020
Fierer, Charles	D.C.	Will	1861	DCA:Box 29
Figg, Benjamin, of King William Co.	Henrico	Will	1839	CF1847-011
Figg, James	Prince George	Will	1832	SV 9:1, p. 23
Filbates, John, of Charles City Co.	Williamsburg	Will Abstract	1811	Crozier, p. 25
Filbates, William	New Kent	Will	1784	Note[2]
Filmer, Samuel		Will	1670	VCRP, Survey #03544
Finch, Agness	Charles City	Inventory	1773	Note[3]
Finch, Brothers	Charles City	Account	1767	Records, p. 19
Finch, William	Charles City	Division	1773	T: not Inventory
Finley, John	Augusta	Inventory	1791	Finley
Finley, John	Augusta	Will	1802	Finley
Finley, John	Augusta	Will	1807	Finley
Finley, Margaret	Albemarle	Will	1751	Finley
Finley, William	Augusta	Will	1836	Finley
Finney, John, in Patrick Co.	Henry	Will	1844	CF1875-015
Finney, Zachariah L., in Pittsylvania Co.	Franklin	Will	1863	CF1876-008

[1] From Duke University, William Patterson Smith Papers.
[2] LVA, Executive Communications, Box 5, 1789.
[3] LVA, Charles City County Records, 1766-1774, p. 457.

NAME	LOCATION	TYPE	YEAR	REFERENCE(S)
Fish, Francis	Fairfax	Inventory	1841	X
Fishback, John, in Culpeper Co.	Fauquier	Will	1828	CF1882-014
Fisher, Abraham, of Rockingham Co.	Augusta	Will	1828	CF1839-005
Fisher, George, in Richmond	Henrico	Will	1857	CF1867-001
Fisher, Philip	Northampton	Will Ref.	1701	Hening, Vol. 8, p. 440
Fisher, Susan Butler, of Hanover Co.	King William	Will	1904	CF1911-022
Fitzgerald, Elizabeth Ann, of F'burg.	Fauquier	Will	1881	CF1887-002
Fitzgerald, Francis	Nottoway	Will	1859	CF1900-002
Fitzgerald, James H., Buckingham Co.	Albemarle	Will	1893	CF1899-034
Fitzgerald, James H., Spotsylvania Co.	Fauquier	Will	1852	CF1873-051
Fitzgerald, John, in Fairfax Co.	Arlington	Will	1799	CF1832-015
Fitzgerald, William	Nottoway	Will	1818	LVA Acc. #41008, r4611
Fitzhugh, A.M., Mrs.	Alexandria	Will	1870	V: CT 275 F57
Fitzhugh, Francis C., in Bedford Co.	King George	Will	1858	CF1887-018
Fitzhugh, Henry	King George	Will	1783c	V:Mss1 F5785 b 6-9
Fitzhugh, John	King George	Account	1785	V:Mss10: no. 187
Fitzhugh, Meade	Fairfax	Will	1845	X
Fitzhugh, Mordecai	Fairfax	Plat	1859	X
Fitzhugh, Nicholas	Fairfax	Will	(nd)	V:Mss1 F5785 b 6-9
Fitzhugh, Richard, in Fairfax Co.	Fauquier	Will	1821	CF1872-041
Fitzhugh, Sarah	King George	Will	1820	BRCD
Fitzhugh, Sarah, in King George Co.	Fauquier	Will	1820	CF1829-044
Fitzhugh, Susannah, in Fairfax Co.	Fauquier	Will	1856	CF1872-041
Fitzhugh, Thomas, in Prince William Co.	Fairfax	Will	1829	X
Fitzhugh, Thomas, in Prince William Co.	Fairfax	Will	1830	CF1859-010
Fitzhugh, William	Stafford	Will	1701	WBZ, p. 92
Fitzpatrick, Joseph	Fluvanna	Will	1781	LVA Acc. #21823
Fiveash, John	Surry	Will	1688	T:D&W4, p. 41a
Fizer, John, in Bedford Co.	Campbell	Will	1853	CF1857-011
Flack, Andrew	Charles City	Inventory	1769	Records, p. 132
Flagg, Arthur I., of Fairfax Co.	D.C.	Will	1898	DCA:Box 175
Flanary, Elkanah, in Lee Co.	Wise	Will	1898	CF1900-060
Fleet, Edwin, of King & Queen Co.	Williamsburg	Will Abstract	1778	Fleet 2:332
Fleet, Edwin, of King & Queen Co.	Williamsburg	Will Abstract	1778	Crozier, p. 25
Fleet, Henry	Lancaster	Will	1735	LP
Fleet, Henry	Lancaster	Will	1827	LVA Acc. #35728
Fleet, Henry, of Lancaster Co.	Mecklenburg	Will	1735	CF1824-075
Fleet, James Robert	King & Queen	Will	1881c	V:Mss3 K5893 a 69-86
Fleet, James Robert, of *Goshen*	King & Queen	Will Ref.	1861	KQB:2
Fleet, M. Lou	King & Queen	Will	1903	LP
Fleet, William, of King & Queen Co.	Williamsburg	Will Abstract	1773	Fleet 2:332
Fleet, William, of King & Queen Co.	Williamsburg	Will Abstract	1773	Crozier, p. 25
Fleming, Alexander	Rappahannock*	Will Ref.	1668	Sweeny, p. 3
Fleming, John	Cumberland	Will Abstract	1767	VMHB 24, p. 94
Fleming, John, in Cumberland Co.	Powhatan	Will	1756	CF1805-012
Fleming, Thomas, in Goochland Co.	Powhatan	Will	1777	CF1805-012
Fleming, William	Chesterfield	Will	1824	V:Mss1 St242 a 104+
Fleming, William, in Hanover Co.	Louisa	Will	1744	CF1771-002
Fleming, William, in St. Paul's Parish	Hanover	Will	1744	WMQ2 15, p. 425; BRCD
Fleming, William N., Dr., in TN	Louisa	Will	1828	CF1852-093
Fletcher, Elijah, in Amherst Co.	Lynchburg	Will	1858	CF1875-033

NAME	LOCATION	TYPE	YEAR	REFERENCE(S)
Fletcher, John, in Culpeper Co.	Fauquier	Will	1827	CF1848-006
Fletcher, John, in Culpeper Co.	Rappahannock	Will	1827	CF1837-008
Fletcher, John, in Culpeper Co.	Rappahannock	Will	1827	CF1837-002
Fletcher, Sidney, in Amherst Co.	Staunton	Will	1898	CF1906-011
Fleyne, John		Inventory	1648	WOD2, p. 377
Flint, John	Northumberland	Will	1786	CF1815-013
Flint, Richard	Northumberland	Will	1701	V: BX5199.B53
Flint, Richard	Lancaster	Will	1715	V: BX5199.B53
Flint, Richard	Richmond	Will	1752	V: BX5199.B53
Flood, Joel W., in Appomattox Co.	Campbell	Will	1858	CF1898-001
Flook, Henry	Rockingham	Will	1841	CF1854-021
Florance, John	Prince William	Acct. Ref.	1844	CM:04 MAR 1844
Florance, John	Prince William	Acct. Ref.	1844	CM:02 JAN 1844
Flournoy, David, in KY	Powhatan	Will	1850	CF1851-014
Flournoy, John, in Chesterfield Co.	Powhatan	Will	1811	CF1845-017
Floyd, Charles	Brunswick	Will	1797	CF1833-019
Floyd, John, in Jefferson Co. KY		Will	1783	V:Mss2 F6693 a 1
Floyd, John, in Jefferson Co. KY		Inventory	1783c	V:Mss2 F6693 a 1
Fogerson, John	Southampton	Will	1778	WB3, p. 240
Fogg, Thomas		Will	1711	VCRP, Survey #04353
Foley, Enoch H.	Prince William	Will	1863	CF1898-001
Foley, James	Fauquier	Will	1793	CF1815-030
Foley, William	Prince William	Will	1868	CF1875-016
Follett, John, mariner		Will (N)	1692	VCRP, Survey #03752
Folson, Israel	Prince William	Will	1772	MVG 29:3, p. 191
Folson, Israel	Prince William	Will	1772	Land Office
Fontaine, Edmund	Hanover	Will	1869	CF1894-016
Fontaine, Edmund	Hanover	Will	1869	V:Mss1 M4618 d 14-19
Fontaine, Moses		Will	1764	CW(6)
Fontaine, Peter, Rev.		Will	1757	CW(6)
Fontaine, William	Hanover	Will	1810	VGSQ 11:4, p. 99
Foote, George	Fauquier	Will Ref.	1799	VMHB 38, p. 189
Foote, Richard, merchant		Will	1697	VCRP, Survey #04780
Foote, William H., in Fairfax Co.	Arlington	Will	1846	CF1850-020
Foote, William Henry	Hampshire	Will	1869	V:Mss2 F7397 a 2
Forbes, James	Surry	Will	1687	T:D&W4, p. 36a
Forbes, Samuel Austin, in Norfolk Co.	Portsmouth	Will	1855	CF1869-009
Forbess, Alice, widow	Essex	Will Ref.	1648	Winfree, p. 384
Forbush, George	Surry	Inventory	1694	T:D&W5, p. 39a
Forbush, James	Surry	Inventory	1688	T:D&W4, p. 60b
Force, Jacob	Botetourt	Will	1833	LVA Acc. #22676
Ford, Francis, in Spotsylvania Co.	Louisa	Will	1811	CF1844-001
Ford, James	Stafford	Will	1794	LVA Acc. #25809f
Ford, Joel	Buckingham	Will	1812	V:Mss1 F7345 a 875+
Ford, Reuben	Hanover	Will	1855	Cocke:56
Ford, Reuben	Hanover	Will	1855	CF1866-010
Ford, T., in Prince Edward Co.	Campbell	Will	1834	CF1837-007
Ford, Thomas, in Charlotte Co.	Campbell	Will	1834	CF1837-007
Ford, William H., Sr., in Lynchburg	Campbell	Will	1891	CF1907-051
Forrest, George	Mathews	Account	(nd)	V:Mss2 F7703 b
Forrest, James	Mathews	Account	(nd)	V:Mss2 F7703 b

NAME	LOCATION	TYPE	YEAR	REFERENCE(S)
Forrest, Philip	Mathews	Inventory	1797c	V:Mss2 F7703 b
Forrest, Phillip	Mathews	Will	1797c	V:Mss2 F7703 b
Forsee, Stephen	Powhatan	Will	1799	CF1829-006
Forsyth, Thomas	Surry	Inventory	1795	WB1, p. 85
Forsythe, Robert, heirs of	Fairfax	List	1858	X
Fort, Lewis, of *Fortsville*	Southampton	Will	1826	V:Mss1 M3816 c 1-2
Fort, Rebecca	Brunswick	Will	1767	CF1792-004
Forteney, George, in Loudoun Co.	Arlington	Will	1817	CF1818-011
Foster, Archibald, merchant	Williamsburg	Will	1830	VG 24, p. 110
Foster, Daniel	Prince William	Acct. Ref.	1844	CM:03 JUN 1844
Foster, Elizabeth		Will	1674	VCRP, Survey #03551
Foster, James, in Charlotte Co.	Lunenburg	Will	1771	CF1792-002
Foster, John, Jr.	Gloucester	Will Abstract	1784	Mason, Vol. 2, P. 72
Foster, Peter	Hanover	Will	1833	LVA Acc. #24677-25
Foster, Richard	Charles City	Inventory	1688	D&W1689, p. 77
Foster, Sarah A.	New Kent	Will	1875	CF1884-013
Foster, Thomas	Orange	Will	1791	V:Mss1 B2346 a 1154
Foster, William, of Caroline Co.	Halifax	Will	1768	CF1808-011
Fothergill, John, in Eng.	Orange	Will	1800	CF1804-009
Fotsch, Johannes	Rockingham	Will	1782	MVG 41:4, p. 271
Foulis, James, in Halifax Co.	Franklin	Will	1792	CF1794-007
Foulks, Thomas, of Princess Anne Co.	London	Will	1692	N:PROB11/410, 412
Foulks, Thomas, of Princess Anne Co.	London	Will	1692	VCRP, Survey #03754
Fowle, William, of Alexandria	Arlington	Will	1860	CF1878-036
Fowler, Henry, in MD	Bedford	Will	1861	CF1893-089
Fowler, Jacob, in Roanoke Co.	Bedford	Will	1860	CF1893-089
Fowler, James, late of Nansemond Co.	London	Will	1709	N:PROB11/508
Fowler, James, of Nansemond Co.		Will	1709	VCRP, Survey #04358
Fowler, John	Fairfax	Division	1821	X
Fowler, Samuel, in Sussex Co. NJ	Lynchburg	Will	1844	CF1844-003
Fowler, Thomas, in Botetourt Co.	Franklin	Will	1832	CF1849-037
Fowler, William, in Mecklenburg Co.	Lunenburg	Will	1856	CF1895-024
Fowler, William, of Essex Co.	London	Will	1745	N:PROB11/738
Fowlkes, Anderson J.	Nottoway	Will (N)	1846c	V:Mss1 N1786 a 8222+
Fowlkes, Henry, in Lunenburg Co.	Amelia	Will	1829	CF1885-009
Fowlkes, William	Nottoway	Will	1834	BRCD
Fowlkes, William, in Nottoway Co.	Lunenburg	Will	1835	CF1857-014
Fox, Ann	Gloucester	Will	1813	Note[1]
Fox, Ann	Fairfax	Inventory	1817	X
Fox, Ann, of *Greenwich*	Gloucester	Will	1813	TQ 25:2, p. 128
Fox, David, Gent.	Lancaster	Estate Ref.	1732	Winfree, p. 388
Fox, Elizabeth	King & Queen	Will	1839	Fleet 2:355, 356
Fox, Elizabeth	King & Queen	Will	1840	TQ 23:2, p. 107
Fox, Elizabeth	King & Queen	Will	1840	LP:08 FEB 1843
Fox, Gabriel	Fairfax	Inventory	1844	X
Fox, Hannah	Lancaster	Will	1709	MVG 51:52
Fox, Hannah	Lancaster	Will	1709	LP
Fox, John	Williamsburg	Will Ref.	1780	CW(2)

---

[1] LVA, U.S. Circuit Court Records, Box 24, *Bowden's Exors. v. Fox's Heirs* (1831).

NAME	LOCATION	TYPE	YEAR	REFERENCE(S)
Fox, John, Capt., of *Greenwich*	Gloucester	Will	1785	TQ 22:3, p. 171
Fox, John, of Gloucester Co.	Williamsburg	Will Abstract	1785	Crozier, p. 25
Fox, Margaret "Peggy"	Fairfax	Account	1836	X
Fox, Nathaniel	Hanover	Will	1817	LVA Acc. #26566
Fox, Nathaniel	Hanover	Will	1821	MVG 36:1, p. 43
Fox, Nathaniel, in Hanover Co.	Henrico	Will	1821	CF1833-001
Fox, Thomas	Spotsylvania	Will	(nd)	FDC L393-33
Fox, Thomas H.	Hanover	Will	1862	CF1903-002
Fox, Thomas H.	Hanover	Will	1868	CF1882-030
Foxall, John, of Washington Parish	Westmoreland	Will Abstract	1698	VMHB 44, p. 155
Foxhall, John, of Westmoreland Co.		Will	1704	VCRP, Survey #04140
France, Jacob, in Shenandoah Co.	Frederick	Will	1804	CF1817-113
Franceway, Joseph, in Berkeley Co.	Frederick	Will	1822	CF1832-132
Francis, Henry	Surry	Will	1691	T:D&W4, p. 242a
Francis, Henry [Frances]	Montgomery	Inventory	1781	D&W1773, p. 45
Francis, John	King William	Will	1805	BRCD
Francis, John B.	Hanover	Will	1843	Cocke:56
Francis, John B.	Hanover	Will	1843	CF1860-004
Francis, John, of King William Co.	Henrico	Will	1805	CF1817-027
Franckling, Thomas	Goochland	Estate	(nd)	UVA MSS 4756
Franckling, Thomas, shipwright		Will	1721	VCRP, Survey #04662
Franklin, James, in Amherst Co.	Lynchburg	Will	1813	CF1833-019
Franklin, James, in Amherst Co.	Lynchburg	Will	1813	CF1821-047
Franklin, Joel, in Amherst Co.	Lynchburg	Will	1807	CF1823-024
Franklin, Joel, in Amherst Co.	Lynchburg	Will	1807	CF1829-039
Frantz, Michael, in Botetourt Co.	Roanoke	Will	1833	CF1846-007
Fraser, Alexander, in Dinwiddie	Petersburg	Will	1828	CF1858-025
Fraser, Alexander, in Dinwiddie Co.	Petersburg	Will	1828	CF1860-047
Fraser, Anthony R., of Alexandria Co.	D.C.	Will	1881	DCA: Box 75
Fraser, Benjamin, of Richmond	Henrico	Will	1808	VGSQ 18:3, p. 79
Fraser, James, Sr.	D.C.	Will	1864	DCA: Box 33
Fravel, Henry, in Shenandoah Co.	Frederick	Will	1820	CF1828-218
Frazier, Alexander, of Urbanna	Middlesex	Will	1769	Fleet 2:200
Freeland, James	Buckingham	Will Ref.	1770	LP:15 NOV 1794
Freeman, Derry, of Botetourt Co.	Augusta	Will	1804	CF1824-015
Freeman, James, in Prince William Co.	Fauquier	Will	1751	CF1762-001
Freeman, Martha S., in Petersburg	Culpeper	Will	1866	CF1870-016
Freman, James	Prince William	Appraisal	1742	LVA Acc. #33797
French, Hugh	Stafford	Will	1737	FDC L572-60
French, Hugh	Stafford	Will	1739	FDC L572-60
French, J.B., Old Rappa. Co. NC	Fauquier	Will	1842	CF1869-049
French, Jacob, in Berkeley Co.	Frederick	Will	1826	CF1831-160
French, Jacob, in Berkeley Co.	Frederick	Will	1826	CF1828-042
French, James	Prince William	Will Ref.	1743	VGSQ 9, p. 56
French, James	Prince William	Will	1743	WBC, p. 42
French, James	Prince William	Will	1743	PWR 7:2, p. 50
French, John, in Nansemond Co.	Southampton	Will	1839	CF1844-023
French, Stephen	Prince William	Div. Ref.	1843	CM:02 OCT 1843
French, Stephen	Prince William	Acct. Ref.	1843	CM:07 AUG 1843
French, William	Stafford	Will Abstract	1790	VGSQ 9, p. 56
French, William	Prince William	Will	1792	LC 1793, p. 181

NAME	LOCATION	TYPE	YEAR	REFERENCE(S)
French, William, of Stafford Co.	Prince William	Will	1792	PWR 7:3, p. 72
Frere, Elizabeth, of *Mt. Gilead*	D.C.	Will	1899	DCA:Box 183
Frere, Hatley, Hon.		Will	1868	CW(2)
Freshwater, William, haberdasher		Will	1706	VCRP, Survey #04147
Fretwell, William	Cumberland	Will	1788	VGSQ 21:4, p. 147
Friel, Sophia	Wythe	Will	1836	V:Mss2 Sa565 b 1-7
Friend, Nathaniel, in Prince George Co.	Petersburg	Will	1842	CF1845-018
Friend, Susan G., in TX	Dinwiddie	Will	1867	CF1869-015
Frith, Anne	Henrico	Will	1740	Records, Vol. 4, p. 1093
Frizzle, Joshua	Isle of Wight	Will	1795	WB10, p. 346
Frobel, John Jacob	Fairfax	Will	1851	X
Fry, Elizabeth, in Madison Co.	Culpeper	Will	1843	CF1871-006
Fry, Elizabeth, in Madison Co.	Culpeper	Will	1844	CF1880-013
Frye, Joseph, in Shenandoah Co.	Frederick	Will	1781	CF1829-241
Fuchs, Edward, in Charlottesville	Albemarle	Will	1893	CF1897-041
Fulcher, Mary	Hanover	Will	1861	CF1878-030
Fulcher, Mary	Hanover	Will	1861	Cocke:57
Fulcher, William Joseph	Hanover	Will	1889	CF1890-031
Fulford, Robert	Arlington	Will	1794	CRA:144
Fulford, Robert	Arlington	Inventory	1795	CRA:172
Fuller, Hiram	Fairfax	Account	1851	X
Fuller, Hiram	Fairfax	Inventory	1851	X
Fuller, Hiram	Fairfax	Will	1851	X
Fuller, Jacob, in Rockbridge Co.	Culpeper	Will	1890	CF1903-015
Fuller, Joel W., in NY	Washington	Will	1868	CF1891-041
Fuller, Rachel S., in Rockbridge Co.	Culpeper	Will	1894	CF1903-015
Fuller, William	Henrico	Inventory	1744	Records, Vol. 4, p. 1303
Fuller, William	Fairfax	Will (U)	1872	X
Fulton, Edmund, in Bedford Co.	Campbell	Will	1872	CF1906-026
Fulton, John H., in Washington Co.	Russell	Will	1836	CF1893-020
Fulton, Robert	Arlington	Account	1797	CRA:283
Fulton, Robert	Arlington	Inventory	1797	CRA:239
Fulton, Robert	Arlington	Will	1797	CRA:235
Fulton, Thomas, of Rockingham Co.	Augusta	Will	1800	CF1821-016
Funkhouser, Abraham	Rockingham	Will	1863	CF1867-007
Funkhouser, Abraham	Rockingham	Will	1863	LVA:1159583
Fuqua, John, in Bedford Co.	Lynchburg	Will	1796	CF1823-062
Fuqua, John, in Bedford Co.	Lynchburg	Will	1796	CF1825-081
Furlong, William	King George	Will	1766	WB1, p. 237
Futrill, Thomas	Surry	Inventory	1693	T:D&W4, p. 302b
Fyst, George, in Clarke Co.	Frederick	Will	1842	CF1853-038

NAME	LOCATION	TYPE	YEAR	REFERENCE(S)

G

NAME	LOCATION	TYPE	YEAR	REFERENCE(S)
Gabby, William, in Loudoun Co.	Fauquier	Will	1841	CF1843-027
Gabby, William, in MD	Fauquier	Will	1841	CF1844-002
Gabriel, Jones	Rockingham	Will	1806	WBA, p. 60
Gaines, Eliza	Culpeper	Will	1868	CF1879-013
Gaines, Eliza	Culpeper	Will	1868	CF1869-028
Gaines, Harry, of King William Co.	King & Queen	Will	1766	Fleet 2:334
Gaines, Harry, of St. Stephen's Parish	King & Queen	Will	1785	Fleet 2:172
Gaines, Harry, of St. Stephen's Parish	King & Queen	Will	1789	LVA Acc. #23634-14
Gaines, John	Essex	Will Ref.	1722	Fleet 2:326
Gaines, John	King & Queen	Will	1848	LVA Acc. #24417c
Gaines, William H.	Culpeper	Will	(nd)	Note[1]
Gaines, William H.	Fauquier	Will	1885	CF1886-008
Gaines, William, in Stafford Co.	Fauquier	Will	1818	CF1838-008
Gains, Bernard	Richmond	Estate Ref.	1749	Winfree, p. 421
Gaither, Ephraim, in Berkeley Co.	Frederick	Will	1809	CF1823-340
Gaither, Ephraim, in Berkeley Co.	Frederick	Will	1809	CF1859-061
Gaither, Zachariah, of Howard Co. MD	Arlington	Heirs	1811	CF1860-004
Gallagher, Charles H., in MO	Fauquier	Will	1893	CF1903-072
Gallagher, Margaret S., in Pr. Wm. Co.	Fauquier	Will	1886	CF1903-072
Gallaher, Eliza A.R., of Fauquier Co.	D.C.	Will	1898	DCA:Box 176
Galt, Elizabeth	Prince George	Will	1833	SV 9:2, p. 54
Games, John, in Middlesex Co.	Essex	Will	1834	CF1835-021
Games, John, in Middlesex Co.	Essex	Will	1834	CF1838-009
Gantt, John	Fairfax	Account	1845	X
Gardner, Drusilla	King & Queen	Will	1857	CF1870-001
Gardner, James	King & Queen	Will	1788	FDC L559-26
Gardner, James	King & Queen	Will	1788	FDC V392-1
Gardner, James, of King & Queen Co.	Albemarle	Will	1792	MVG 31:4, p. 349
Gardner, John	Williamsburg	Will Abstract	1784	Fleet 2:346
Gardner, John	Hanover	Will	1825	Cocke:84
Gardner, John, heirs of	Fairfax	Account	1817	X
Gardner, John, of King & Queen Co.	Williamsburg	Will Abstract	1784	Crozier, p. 26
Gardner, Joseph, heirs of	Fairfax	Account	1817	X
Gardner, Joseph [Mary]	Fairfax	Dower	1817	X
Gardner, Mary	Louisa	Will	1795	BRCD
Gardner, Mary, of Louisa Co.	Albemarle	Will	1794	MVG 31:4, p. 350
Gardner, Reuben	Hanover	Will	1843	Fleet, Huntington Data
Gardner, Reuben	Hanover	Will	1843	LVA Acc. #28821
Gardner, Thomas	Hanover	Will	1858	CF1876-005
Gardner, Thomas	Hanover	Will	1858	Cocke:57
Gardner, William	King & Queen	Will	1854	CF1870-001
Garland, David	Lunenburg	Will	1782	CF1797-017
Garland, Edward		Will Ref.	1769	Hening, Vol. 8, p. 442
Garland, James	Hanover	Will	1857	CF1888-010
Garland, James, in Amherst Co.	Lynchburg	Will	1816	CF1818-024
Garland, John R., in NY	Lynchburg	Will	1898	CF1899-013

---

[1] David John Mays, ed., *The Letters and Papers of Edmund Pendleton, 1734-1803* (Charlottesville: University Press of Virginia, for the Virginia Historical Society, 1967), Vol. II, p. 486.

NAME	LOCATION	TYPE	YEAR	REFERENCE(S)
Garland, Mary M., in Richmond	Goochland	Will	1848	CF1852-004
Garland, Rice, in Albemarle Co.	Lynchburg	Will	1819	CF1829-006
Garlick, Camm, of King William Co.		Will	1783	VCRP, Survey #04704
Garlick, Mary C., in King William Co.	Hanover	Will	1856	Cocke:59
Garlick, Mary C., in King William Co.	Hanover	Will	1860	CF1884-013
Garlick, Mary C., of King William Co.	New Kent	Will	1856	CF1884-006
Garlick, Samuel	King William	Will	1765	UVA MSS 1067
Garlick, Samuel	King William	Will	1772	WMQ 16, p. 100
Garlick, Samuel	King William	Will	1772	V:Mss2 G18447 a 1
Garner, Bradley, of Westmoreland Co.	Williamsburg	Will Abstract	1770	Crozier, p. 27
Garner, Parish	Northumberland	Will	1769	CF1788-001
Garner, Thomas, in Stafford Co.	Fauquier	Will	1726	CF1793-012
Garner, Tristram, late of Alexandria	D.C.	Will	1866	DCA:Box 35
Garnett, Ann	Essex	Will	1788	CF1818-009
Garnett, Henry	Essex	Will	1811	MVG 29:3, p. 191
Garnett, James	Essex	Will	1765	LVA Acc. #20624e
Garnett, James	Essex	Estate Ref.	1790	Hening, Vol. 13, p. 221
Garnett, James, Gent., of Essex Co.	Williamsburg	Will Abstract	1765	Crozier, p. 26
Garnett, John	Essex	Will	1713	LVA Acc. #20624e
Garnett, John, Jr.	Essex	Will	1772	Fleet 2:342
Garnett, Muscoe	Essex	Will	1803	LVA Acc. #20624e
Garnett, Reuben	King & Queen	Will	1844	LVA Acc. #26342
Garnett, Robert Calvin, Sr.	Madison	Will	1873c	V:Mss1 G1875 c 486+
Garnett, Robert L.	King & Queen	Will	1832	LVA Acc. #26529-4
Garrat, John	Charles City	Will	1729	D&W1724, p. 259
Garrett, Alexander, in Albemarle Co.	Louisa	Will	1860	CF1900-067
Garrett, Edward, in Pittsylvania Co.	Henry	Will	1854	CF1903-010
Garrett, Evelina to William Brooks	King & Queen	Marriage	1838	LP
Garrett, Francis, in Pittsylvania Co.	Henry	Will	1873	CF1903-010
Garrett, Henrietta, in Prince George Co.	Petersburg	Will	1813	CF1842-042
Garrett, Ira, in Albemarle Co.	Albemarle	Will	1870	CF1881-042
Garrett, Iverson	King & Queen	Affadavit	1864	LP
Garrett, John	Nansemond	Will	1655	VG 20, p. 21
Garrett, John W., in MD	Arlington	Will	1884	CF1902-014
Garrett, John W., in MD	Arlington	Will	1884	CF1902-014
Garrett, Mary Winder		Will	1877	CW(7)
Garrett, Mary Winder		Will	1891	CW(7)
Garrett, Nancy, in Pittsylvania Co.	Henry	Will	1873	CF1903-010
Garrett, Robert L.	King & Queen	Will	1832	LVA Acc. #26529-4
Garth, Dabney, in MO	Albemarle	Will	(nd)	CF1887-049 CC
Garthright, Hutchings	Henrico	Will	1844	VGSQ 18:3, p. 80
Garthwright, John	Henrico	Will	1799	LVA Acc. #24642
Gartrell, Richard, in MD	Frederick	Will	1785	CF1822-090
Gary, George C., [of Prince George Co.]	Norfolk	Will	1840	SV 9:2, p. 57
Gary, Thomas S.	Prince George	Will	1848	SV 9:4, p. 156
Gatchell, Casandra	Caroline	Will	1859	W&D1794, p. 77
Gates, J.W. Beverly, in Chesterfield Co.	Henrico	Will	1869	CF1888-030
Gatewood, Charles, in Shenandoah Co.	Warren	Will	1832	CF1845-003
Gatewood, John	Essex	Will	1763	Fleet 2:331
Gatewood, John, in Page Co.	Warren	Will	1832	CF1844-006
Gaugh, William, Sr., in Campbell Co.	Bedford	Will	1863	CF1887-026

NAME	LOCATION	TYPE	YEAR	REFERENCE(S)
Gault, James, mariner		Will	1697	VCRP, Survey #04774
Geddy, William	New Kent	Will	1816	Swem(1):f162
Geddy, William	New Kent	Will	1817	V:Mss2 G2672 a 1
Gee, Henry	Prince George	Will Ref.	1746	VGSQ 15, p. 53
Gee, James S., in Prince George Co.	Petersburg	Will	1865	CF1873-047
Gee, William	Brunswick	Will	1797	CF1817-040
Gentry, David A.	Hanover	Will	1853	Cocke:62
Gentry, David A.	Hanover	Will	1853	CF1874-017
Gentry, Henry D.	Hanover	Will	1852	CF1874-017
Gentry, Henry D.	Hanover	Will	1853	Cocke:61
Gentry, Nicholas		Estate Ref.	1787	Hening, Vol. 12, p. 598
Gentry, Thomas J., in Madison Co.	Louisa	Will	1865	CF1891-028
Gentry, Turner W.	Hanover	Will Ref.	(nd)	Cocke:62
Gentry, William	Henrico	Will	1819	LVA Acc. #41008, r4610
Gentry, William	Henrico	Will	1819	Fleet, Huntington Data
George, Ann, in Goochland Co.	Louisa	Will	1838	CF1890-006
George, Cumberland, in Culpeper Co.	Fauquier	Will	1863	CF1872-002
George, Frederick, of Nansemond Co.	Williamsburg	Will Abstract	1812	Crozier, p. 26
George, H.H., in Albemarle Co.	Charlottesville	Will	1887	CF1905-011
George, John	Caroline	Appraisal	1784	BRCD
George, John	Caroline	Inventory	1784	LVA George Papers
George, John Dudley	Williamsburg	Will	1780	V:Mss1 G2937 a 5
George, John [of Fairford]	Caroline	Will	1784	FDC L672-19
George, Mary	Caroline	Account	1789	LVA George Papers
George, Reuben	Caroline	Will	1799	V:Mss1 G2937 a 6
George, Reuben	Caroline	Appraisal	1800	LVA George Papers
George, Reuben [of Fairford]	Caroline	Will	1799	CF1802-018
George, Robert	Caroline	Account	1790	LVA George Papers
George, William	King & Queen	Will	1821	BRCD
George, William, of King & Queen Co.	Essex	Will	1821	CF1847-020
George, William, of King & Queen Co.	Essex	Inventory	1821	CF1847-020
Gerecke, Charles, of Dinwiddie Co.	D.C.	Will	1893	DCA: Box 138
Gerrard, Henry		Will	1693	VCRP, Survey #03951
Gerrard, Henry, of Charles City Co.	London	Will	1693	N:PROB11/414
Gerrard, John, in Westmoreland Co.	Fairfax	Will	1711	X
Ghio, Enoch G., in Norfolk	Portsmouth	Will	1885	CF1887-006
Gibbons, Julia	Mathews	Will (U)	1857	LVA Wm. Smart Papers
Giberne, Mary, in Richmond Co.	Fauquier	Will	1820	CF1847-011
Gibson, Ann Eliz. Jones Gibson Bartlett	Richmond City	Will	1859	V:Mss2 G3597 c
Gibson, Ann G., in Orange Co.	Prince William	Will	1875	CF1882-009
Gibson, Churchill Jones	Petersburg	Will	1892	V:Mss1 C3552 c 2247+
Gibson, Edward	Charles City	Will	1727	D&W1724, p. 167
Gibson, Esther, in Loudoun Co.	Fauquier	Will	1825	CF1851-020
Gibson, Esther, in Loudoun Co.	Fauquier	Will	1828	CF1835-003
Gibson, Frances	Prince William	Will	1872	CF1882-009
Gibson, Gibby	Charles City	Will	1727	D&W1724, p. 161
Gibson, Gibby	Charles City	Inventory		D&W1724, p. 166
Gibson, Henry	Hanover	Will	1889	CF1895-012
Gibson, John		Will	1692	VCRP, Survey #03756

NAME	LOCATION	TYPE	YEAR	REFERENCE(S)
Gibson, John	Prince William	Will	1807	Note[1]
Gibson, John	Prince William	Will	1846	CF1882-009
Gibson, John, in Prince George Co.	Prince William	Will	1846	CF1881-018
Gibson, John, of Prince William Co.	Loudoun	Will	1806	CF1847-014
Gibson, Moses, in Rappahannock Co.	Warren	Will	1836	CF1842-007
Gibson, Thomas G.	Culpeper	Will	1863	CF1885-065
Gilbert, Francis		Will	1758	VCRP, Survey #04675
Gilbert, Hannah, in Westmoreland Co.	Frederick	Will	1800	CF1817-126
Gilbert, Robert		Estate Ref.	1788	Hening, Vol. 12, p. 689
Gilchrist, Daniel, in AL	Albemarle	Will	1870	CF1875-009
Gilchrist, John, Dr., of Norfolk Borough	Williamsburg	Will Abstract	1801	Crozier, p. 28
Giles, Mascall, clerk		Will	1653	VCRP, Survey #04108
Giles, William Branch	Amelia	Will	1830c	V:Mss1 N1786 a 8222+
Gill, Francis	Chesterfield	Will	1791	BRCD
Gill, William M., in Dinwiddie Co.	Lunenburg	Will	1873	CF1889-013
Gilliam, I.P., in Appomattox Co.	Prince Edward	Will	1866	CF1875-016
Gilliam, J.C.	New Kent	Will	(nd)	CF1914-007
Gilliam, John	Prince George	Will	1774c	V:Mss1 F9156 a 5
Gilliam, John	Prince George	Will	1801	LVA Acc. #21552
Gilliam, John	Prince George	Will	1820	BRCD
Gilliam, John	Prince George	Will	1823c	V:Mss1 F9156 a 5
Gilliam, John, in Prince George Co.	Petersburg	Will	1791	CF1834-022
Gilliam, John, in Prince George Co.	Petersburg	Will	1820	CF1845-051
Gilliam, John, Sr.	Prince George	Will	1801	LVA Acc. #21552
Gilliam, John W., in Dinwiddie Co.	Brunswick	Will	1854	CF1859-040
Gilliam, Joseph S.	Southampton	Will	1837	V:Mss1 M3816 c 1077+
Gilliam, Susan, in Brunswick Co.	Dinwiddie	Will	1855	CF1882-006
Gilliam, William	Prince George	Will	1800	BRCD
Gilliam, William	Prince George	Will	1800	V:Mss1 F9156 a 5
Gilliam, William, in Prince George Co.	Petersburg	Will	1800	CF1845-051
Gilliat, Thomas, of Richmond	London	Will	1810	N:PROB11/1517
Gillispie, David, of Halifax Co.	Mecklenburg	Will	1814	CF1832-018
Gillus, Jacob, of Greensville Co.	Brunswick	Will	1900	CF1904-097
Gilmer, David F.	Rockingham	Will	1853	CF1856-012
Gilmer, John H., in Richmond	Albemarle	Will	1879	CF1887-071
Gilmore, Joseph		Will	1863	UVA Acc. #640
Gilmore, William, in DC	Essex	Will	1826	CF1853-018
Gilmour, Robert, Gent., of Lancaster Co.	Williamsburg	Will Abstract	1782	Crozier, p. 28
Gilson, Andrew	Stafford	Will	1687	V:Mss2 B4598 c
Gilson, Behethland	Westmoreland	Will P.	1693	VMHB 38, p. 188
Gilson, Thomas	Stafford	Inventory	1707	V:Mss2 B4598 c
Gipson, Laban	Buckingham	Will	1818	LVA Patteson Papers
Gist, John, in Loudoun Co.	Fairfax	Will	1778	X
Gist, Samuel	Hanover	Will	1808	LP:14 DEC 1815
Glading, Ann	Fairfax	Account	1753	X
Glanvill, William		Will	1668	M: L8 f18
Glascock, Bushrod, in Loudoun Co.	Fauquier	Will	1853	CF1879-040
Glascock, Richard, of Richmond Co.	London	Will	1812	N:PROB11/1530

[1] LVA, U.S. Circuit Court Records, Box 200, *Hasty's Exors. v. Gibson's Exors.* (1832).

NAME	LOCATION	TYPE	YEAR	REFERENCE(S)
Glascock, Thomas	Fauquier	Will	1793	CF1837-047
Glassell, Andrew	Madison	Will	1827	V:Mss1 G8855 d 2-5
Glassell, John, in Culpeper Co.	Fauquier	Will	1850	CF1884-020
Glassell, Margaret C., in Culpeper Co.	Fairfax	Will	1843	CF1858-052
Glassell, Margaret C., in Culpeper Co.	Fairfax	Will	1846	CF1858-052
Glazebrook, John	Hanover	Will	1825	VG 23, p. 223
Gledhill, Mary, wid., of Isle of Wight Co.	London	Will	1721	N:PROB11/580
Glen, James	Hanover	Will	1762	UVA Acc. #5166
Glen, James	Hanover	Will	1763	V:Mss2 G4847 a 1
Glen, James	Hanover	Will	1763	LVA Acc. #21376
Glen, James, of St. Martin's Parish	Hanover	Will	1763	VGSQ 14:3, p. 84
Glen, James, of St. Martin's parish	Hanover	Will, 1763	1822	VMHB 47, p. 16
Glenn, Hannah	Hanover	Will	1830	CF1843-012
Glenn, Hannah	Hanover	Will	1830	Cocke:64
Glenn, John	Hanover	Will	1813	Cocke:64
Glenn, John	Hanover	Will	1813	CF1843-012
Glinn, German R.	Hanover	Will	1856	CF1875-031
Glover, Sarah	Surry	Will (U)	1838	VTG 13:3, p. 126
Glover, Sarah	Surry	Will Abstract	1838	VG 13, p. 53
Goddard, Anthony		Will	1663	M: L1 f179
Goddard, Edmund, cooper		Will	1681	VCRP, Survey #03727
Goddard, William	Arlington	Will	1816	CF1824-035
Goddin, Edmund	New Kent	Will	1804	Swem(1):f217
Goddin, Roxanna Ford	Henrico	Will	1864	LVA Acc. #25262
Godwin, Edmund	Nansemond	Will	(nd)	LVA Acc. #30183
Godwin, Edmund	Nansemond	Will	1755	LVA Acc. #30183
Godwin, Edmund	Isle of Wight	Will (U)	1818	SV 14:1, p. 19
Godwin, Isaac, of Blisland Parish	New Kent	Will	1758	Note[1]
Godwin, John, of Isle of Wight Co.	Williamsburg	Will Abstract	1790	Crozier, p. 27
Godwin, Susanna	Warwick	Will	1782	LVA Acc. #20029
Godwin, Thomas	Nansemond	Will	1676	LVA Acc. #30183
Godwin, Thomas	Nansemond	Will	1714	LVA Acc. #30183
Godwin, Thomas	Nansemond	Will	1747	LVA Acc. #30183
Godwin, Thomas	Nansemond	Will	1779	LVA Acc. #30183
Godwin, Thomas C., in Norfolk Co.	Portsmouth	Will	1839	CF1861-001
Goff, Horatio, in Appomattox Co.	Campbell	Will	1865	CF1898-024
Goff, John	Appomattox	Will	1865	BRCD
Golding, William	Orange	Inventory	1812	V:Mss1 B2346 a 704+
Golding, William	Orange	Will	1812	V:Mss1 B2346 a 704+
Goldrup, John	Fairfax	Inventory	1816	X
Goldrup, John	Fairfax	Sale	1816	X
Goldwell, Nicholas	New Kent	Will	1771	TVF 10:4, p. 234
Goldwell, Nicholas, of New Kent Co.	Cumberland	Will	1777	CF1783-007
Gondry, William		Will	1638	VCRP, Survey #03980
Gooch, Philip, in Amherst Co.	Lynchburg	Will	1805	CF1832-018
Gooch, Philip, in Amherst Co.	Lynchburg	Will	1805	CF1835-009
Goodall, Charles P.	Hanover	Will	1855	CF1883-027
Goodall, Isaac	Rockingham	Estate Ref.	1829	LP:11 DEC 1830

---

[1] LVA, Executive Communications, Box 5, 1789.

NAME	LOCATION	TYPE	YEAR	REFERENCE(S)
Goodall, Parke	Hanover	Will	1804	CF1835-002
Goodall, Parke, of St. Paul's Parish	Hanover	Will	1816	Cocke:66
Goode, Bennett	Cumberland	Will	1771	TQ 13:4, p. 269
Goode, Edward, of Caroline Co.	Williamsburg	Will Abstract	1763	Crozier, p. 26
Goode, Philip	Amelia	Will	1822	VMHB 30, p. 396
Goode, Richard	Dinwiddie	Will	1825	VG 16, p. 260
Goode, Richard Bland, of Manchester		Inventory	1813	V:Mss1 Sco846a 82-86
Goode, Robert	Chesterfield	Will	(nd)	V:Mss1 Sco846 a 82-86
Goode, Thomas	Powhatan	Will	1805	V:Mss1 N1786 a 6618+
Goode, Thomas	Powhatan	Will	1805	CF1868-019
Goode, Thomas, in Bath Co.	Albemarle	Will	1858	CF1888-004
Goodfellowe, Allen		Will	1638	VCRP, Survey #03981
Goodger, Francis	Warwick	Will	1688c	LVA Acc. #24853
Gooding, J. Peter, in Portsmouth	Fairfax	Will	1868	CF1894-033
Gooding, John	Fairfax	Inventory	1817	X
Gooding, Peter	Fairfax	Admin. Bond	1859	WB2:053
Gooding, Peter	Fairfax	Account	1859	WB2:052
Gooding, Peter	Fairfax	Inventory	1860	WB2:041
Gooding, Peter, in Portsmouth	Fairfax	Will	1885	CF1903-022
Gooding, Peter, in Portsmouth	Fairfax	Will	1885	CF1894-033
Goodman, James	Nansemond	Will	1861	CF1871-005
Goodman, Timothy	Hanover	Will	1805	Cocke:140
Goodman, Timothy	Hanover	Will	1805	CF1860-010
Goodrich, Briggs	Brunswick	Will	1788	CF1817-001
Goodrich, Mary	Brunswick	Will	1798	CF1817-001
Goodson, Thomas, in Montgomery Co.	Floyd	Will	(nd)	CF1860-016
Goodwin, Elizabeth, in York Co.	Lunenburg	Will	1780	CF1799-010
Goodwin, Mary W.	Hanover	Will	1871	CF1883-026
Goodwin, William D.	Hanover	Will	1828	CF1907-034
Goodwyn, E.M., in Appomattox Co.	Lunenburg	Will	1892	CF1893-005
Goolsby, Arthur, in Pittsylvania Co.	Lynchburg	Will	1819	CF1855-007
Gordan, John P.	James City	Admin.	1817	Swem(1):f148
Gordan, John P.	James City	Admin.	1820	Swem(1):f148
Gordon, Alexander, of Norfolk		Will	1799	VCRP, Survey #04805
Gordon, Ann, in Northumberland Co.	Arlington	Will	1818	CF1873-004
Gordon, Ann Isham	Prince George	Will	1790	WMQ 14, p. 211
Gordon, Ann Isham, of Prince George	Williamsburg	Will Abstract	1790	Crozier, p. 27
Gordon, Ann, wid., of Goochland Co.	London	Will	1808	N:PROB11/1477
Gordon, Archibald Turner, Buckingham	Cumberland	Will	1854	CF1856-011
Gordon, Chapman	Louisa	Will	1855	LVA Acc. #41008, r4610
Gordon, Chapman	Louisa	Will	1855	Fleet, Huntington Data
Gordon, Elizabeth	Lunenburg	Will Abstract	1818	VGS Bulletin VII, p. 21
Gordon, Elizabeth, in Petersburg	Essex	Will	1814	CF1841-010
Gordon, James	Fairfax	Will	1836	NVG 8, p. 1097
Gordon, James A., of Botetourt Co.	Augusta	Will	1825	CF1832-004
Gordon, James, of Lancaster Co.	London	Will	1808	N:PROB11/1477
Gordon, John	Northumberland	Will	1803	CF1821-007
Gordon, Robert A., in NC	James City	Will	1850	CF1878-012
Gordon, Susan	D.C.	Will	1866	DCA:Box 35
Gorrell, Jacob, in Berkeley Co.	Frederick	Will	1823	CF1825-134
Gouge, James	Caroline	Will	1781	FDC L673-57

NAME	LOCATION	TYPE	YEAR	REFERENCE(S)
Gough, Jane	King William	Will	1702	RB2, p. 1
Goul, William, of Rockingham Co.	Augusta	Will	1824	CF1830-082
Gouldman, Francis	Essex	Will	1716	Fleet 2:242
Gouldman, Richard	Essex	Will	1799	CF1818-007
Gouldman, Thomas	Essex	Will	1797	CF1810-022
Govan, Archibald	Hanover	Will Abstract	1848	Cocke:67
Govan, James	Hanover	Will Ref.	(nd)	Cocke:156
Govan, James	Hanover	Will	1831	Note[1]
Govan, James	Hanover	Will	1831	V:Mss2 H5568 b 5
Govan, James, the elder	Hanover	Will Abstract	1831	Fleet 2:359
Gover, Samuel, in Loudoun Co.	Frederick	Will	1820	CF1823-273
Gowl, Margaret	Rockingham	Will	1832	CF1857-014
Gowl, William	Rockingham	Will	1824	BRCD
Graham, Elizabeth	Prince William	Will	1795	LVA Steadman Coll.
Graham, Hugh	Fairfax	Account	1852	X
Graham, Isabella, in Bedford Co.	Amherst	Will	1830	CF1838-001
Graham, John	Augusta	Will	1771	V:Mss2 G76064 a 1
Graham, John	Henrico	Will	1820	LVA Acc. #41008, r4610
Graham, John	Prince William	Will	1850	CF1878-009
Graham, John, of Richmond	Henrico	Will	1820	LVA Acc. #28458
Graham, John, of Richmond	Henrico	Will	1820	Fleet, Huntington Data
Graham, John, of Rockingham Co.	Augusta	Will	1819	CF1854-042
Graham, Jonathan, in Montgomery Co.	Floyd	Will	(nd)	CF1834-001
Graham, Paul [of *Elson Green*]	Caroline	Will	1803	W&P1742, p. 69
Graham, Richard	Prince William	Will	1796	K
Graham, Sarah	Caroline	Will	1838	MVG 42:3, p. 183
Graham, Sarah, in Caroline Co.	Bath	Will	1838	CF1880-006
Graham, William	Prince William	Will	1821	LVA, Steadman Coll.
Graham, William, in MD	Albemarle	Will	1867	CF1925-001
Grammar, John	Prince George	Will	1853	SV 9:4, p. 159
Granberry, Moses	Norfolk	Will	1853	LVA Acc. #20931
Grant, John	Dinwiddie	Will	1801	LVA Acc. #27293-8
Grant, John	Dinwiddie	Will	1801	VG 16, p. 166
Grant, Thomas		Will	1828c	UVA MSS 5419
Grantham, Gabriel	Prince George	Will	1834	SV 9:2, p. 54
Grantland, Samuel	Hanover	Will	1824	CF1833-003
Grantland, Samuel	Hanover	Will	1824	Cocke:105
Grave, John		Will	1692	VCRP, Survey #03755
Graves, Beverley	Caroline	Guard. Appt.	1799	LVA George Papers
Graves, Claibourne	Orange	Will	1839	LVA Acc. #22618
Graves, Daingerfield	Caroline	Will Ref.	1810	LP:13 DEC 1811
Graves, Edmund V.	Charles City	Will	1827	Swem(1):f80
Graves, Herrian H., in MD	Hanover	Will	1880	CF1884-011
Graves, Joel S.	Rockingham	Will	1840	CF1840-004
Graves, John, in Louisa Co.	Hanover	Will	1837	CF1875-023
Graves, Joseph	Caroline	Will	1827	Weisiger 1:071
Graves, Joseph, aboard ship *Robert*	Charles City	Will	1731	D&W1724, p. 335
Gray, Adin, in Pittsylvania Co.	Lynchburg	Will	1816	CF1818-029

---

[1] Fleet, Beverly, *Virginia Colonial Abstracts*, King and Queen County County, 5th Collection, p. 100

NAME	LOCATION	TYPE	YEAR	REFERENCE(S)
Gray, Edwin, of Southampton Co.	Williamsburg	Will Abstract	1790	Crozier, p. 27
Gray, Jane Moore Cave, w/o John B.		Will	(nd)	V:Mss1 G7945 a 537+
Gray, John	Stafford	Inventory	1767	LVA Acc. #41008, r4614
Gray, John	Caroline	Will	1807	W&P1742, p. 82
Gray, John	Stafford	Will	1848	V:Mss2 G7933 a 1
Gray, Miles W., of Isle of Wight Co.	Williamsburg	Will Abstract	1821	Crozier, p. 28
Gray, Phebe	Caroline	Will	1831	W&D1794, p. 25
Gray, Stephen, of Overwharton Parish	Stafford	Will	1734	LVA Acc. #20487, p. 55
Gray, Theophilus	Alexandria	Will	1805	MVG 39:3, p. 209
Gray, Thomas		Will	1831	UVA Acc. #640
Gray, William	Essex	Will	1786	CF1803-014
Green, Abraham	Amelia	Will	1810	V:Mss1 Ea765a230-233
Green, Abraham, of Amelia Co.	Mecklenburg	Will	1810	CF1848-011 CSC
Green, Charles	Fairfax	Will	1765	CF1844-008
Green, Cloe, in Loudoun Co.	Frederick	Will	1814	CF1822-290
Green, Edward		Will	1698	VCRP, Survey #04784
Green, George, of St. Ann's Parish	Essex	Will Abstract	1763	Fleet 2:332
Green, George [off Sparta Rd.]	Caroline	Will	1852	LVA Acc. #26565
Green, Henry, of Alexandria	D.C.	Will	1897	DCA:Box 169
Green, Jane S., c/o William B.	Hanover	Guard.	1847	Cocke:58
Green, John	Westmoreland	Will	1795	LVA Acc. #36255-43
Green, John B.	Hanover	Will	1852	CF1868-031
Green, Lewis, of Prince George Co.	Surry	Will Ref.	1730	DB5, p. 44
Green, Mary Ann Munford	Prince George	Will	1843	SV 9:3, p. 108
Green, Peter, of Nansemond Co.	Williamsburg	Will Abstract	1770	Crozier, p. 27
Green, Ralph	Gloucester	Will Ref.	1685	TQ 22, p. 174
Green, Robert	Orange	Will Ref.	1748	VG 2, p. 90
Green, Robert, in LA	Rappahannock	Will	1858	CF1859-004
Green, Thomas	Amelia	Will	1792	LVA Acc. #21432
Green, Thomas M.	Hanover	Will	1876	CF1907-002
Green, Walker	Charles City	Will (N)	1726	D&W1724, p. 127
Green, Walker	Charles City	Inventory		D&W1724, p. 133, 164
Green, William	Westmoreland	Will	1785	LVA Acc. #36255-43
Green, William B.	Hanover	Will	1846	Cocke:68
Green, William, in Richmond	Culpeper	Will	1880	CF1882-010
Greene, John, of Gloucester Co.		Will	1694	VCRP, Survey #04709
Greene, William, in Bermuda	Fairfax	Will	1692	X
Greenhow, Robert, in Richmond	Frederick	Will	1840	CF1846-039
Greenway, James C., in Wash. Co.	Wise	Will	1888	CF1899-022
Gregg, Jane	Stafford	Will	1721	LVA, Steadman Coll.
Gregg, John	Prince William	Will	1743	LP
Gregory, James	Caroline	Will	1785	CF1802-019
Gregory, James	Charles City	Will	1859	BRCD
Gregory, James, in Charles City Co.	Henrico	Will	1859	CF1893-026
Gregory, John, Jr.	Charles City	Will	1777	WMQ 11, p. 266
Gregory, John, Jr., of Charles City Co.	Williamsburg	Will Abstract	1777	Crozier, p. 26
Gregory, Richard	Essex	Will Abstract	1700	Fleet 2:325
Gregory, Richard	Essex	Will Abstract	1700	Fleet 2:223
Gregory, Samuel, of Buckingham Co.	Prince Edward	Will	1836	LVA Acc. #25971d
Gregory, Thomas	Charles City	Inventory		D&W1724, p. 13, 199
Gregory, William	King William	Will	(nd)	LVA Acc. #25326

NAME	LOCATION	TYPE	YEAR	REFERENCE(S)
Gregory, William	King William	Will	1839	KWHSB, 11:3
Gregory, William	Albemarle	Estate	1840c	LVA Acc. #25327-7
Gregory, William, of Westover Parish	Charles City	Will	1776	V:Mss3 C3807 a 54
Grendon, Thomas	Charles City	Will	1683	V:Mss5:9 B9965:1
Grendon, Thomas	Charles City	Will	1683	V:Mss2 G8654 a 1
Grendon, Thomas, of Charles City Co.		Will	1685	VCRP, Survey #03732
Grendon, Thomas, of Westover Parish	Charles City	Will Abstract	1684	VMHB 50, p. 261
Grendon, Thomas, of Westover	London	Will	1685	N:PROB11/379
Gresham, Joseph	James City	Will	1845	Swem(1):148
Gresham, Samuel	King & Queen	Will	1846	CF1878-002
Gresham, Thomas	King & Queen	Will Abstract	1837	Fleet 2:354
Gresham, Thomas D.	King & Queen	Will	1838	Note[1]
Grey, Henry, of [New] Kent Co.		Will	1675	VCRP, Survey #03555
Greylock, William	Warwick	Will	1696	LVA Acc. #22057 p. 456
Grice, Edward, of Wilmington	Charles City	Will	1727	D&W1724, p. 169
Grice, Edward, of Wilmington	Charles City	Inventory		D&W1724, p. 183
Griffin, Cyrus	York	Will	1811	UVA MSS 107
Griffin, Fendall, in Richmond	Henrico	Will	1866	CF1904-054
Griffin, James, in Richmond	Henrico	Will	1852	CF1904-054
Griffin, Jean		Will	1661	VCRP, Survey #03527
Griffin, LeRoy, in Richmon Co.	Williamsburg	Will Abstract	1775	Crozier, p. 28
Griffin, Nathaniel, in TN	Brunswick	Will	1837	CF1876-023
Griffin, Thomas		Will	1697	VCRP, Survey #04769
Griffing, Mary	Essex	Will Abstract	1742	Fleet 2:302
Griffith, David, Rev.		Estate Ref.	1779	Hening, Vol. 13, p. 311
Griffith, John H., in DC	Alexandria	Will	1870	CF1891-028
Griffith, Sally Winslow	Arlington	Will	1858	V:Mss1 R1586 d 92-113
Griffiths, Jane, in NY	Albemarle	Will	1891	CF1892-014
Grifith, David, in Powhatan Co.	Portsmouth	Will	1875	CF1906-025
Grigg, William	Prince George	Will	1726	LVA Acc. #28515
Grigg, William, in Prince George Co.	Amelia	Will	1726	CF1738-001
Griggs, Frances H., in Clarke Co.	Warren	Will	1877	CF1909-048
Griggs, James, in Jefferson Co.	Warren	Will	1854	CF1909-048
Griggs, Michael, of Lancaster Co.	London	Will	1688	N:PROB11/392
Griggs, Michael, of Lancaster Co.		Will	1688	VCRP, Survey #03744
Griggs, Thomas, Sr., in Jefferson Co.	Warren	Will	1839	CF1909-048
Grigsby, Elisha	Page	Will	1846	V:Mss1 G8785 a 17-20
Grigsby, John	Rockbridge	Will	1794	V:Mss1 G8785 a 1-13
Grigsby, Lucian P.	Mercer	Will	1893	V:Mss1 G8785 a 139+
Grigsby, Reuben	Rockbridge	Will	1863	V:Mss1 G8785 a 110+
Grigsby, Thomas	Stafford	Will	1745	V:Mss1 G8785 a 1-13
Grinnan, Daniel	Culpeper	Will	(nd)	V:Mss1 G8855 d 1
Grissage, Richard, of St. Stephen's Par.	King William	Will Abstract	1703	LVA Acc. #30057
Groom, Nicholas, of King & Queen Co.	Middlesex	Will	1795	CF1798-001
Groome, Nicholas		Will	1652	VCRP, Survey #04102
Groome, Zachariah	King & Queen	Will	1785	Fleet 2:306
Grosjean, John, in KY	Hanover	Will	1819	CF1874-016
Grymes, Alice	Middlesex	Will	1710	VMHB 27, p. 403

---

[1] Beverly Fleet, *Virginia Colonial Abstracts*, King and Queen County County, Vol. 14, 5th Collection.

NAME	LOCATION	TYPE	YEAR	REFERENCE(S)
Grymes, John	Middlesex	Will	1709	VMHB 27, p. 186
Grymes, John, of *Brandon*	Middlesex	Will	1748	VMHB 27, p. 406
Grymes, Philip Ludwell, Middlesex Co.	Williamsburg	Will Abstract	1805	Crozier, p. 27
Grymes, Philip Ludwell, of *Brandon*	Middlesex	Will	1805	VMHB 28, p. 189
Grymes, Philip, of *Brandon*	Middlesex	Will	1762c	V:Mss1 T2478 b14-17
Grymes, Philip, of *Brandon*	Middlesex	Account	1762c	V:Mss1 T2478 b14-17
Grymes, Sarah Robinson	Orange	Will	1832c	V:Mss1 G9297 a 68-71
Grymes, Susan	Caroline	Will	1844	Weisiger 1:073
Guerrant, Peter, in Floyd Co.	Franklin	Will	1859	CF1883-050
Guillum, Peter, shipmaster		Will	1702	VCRP, Survey #04125
Gunn, Burwell	Nottoway	Will	1855	CF1885-003
Gunn, James, Sr.	Nottoway	Will	1807	SV 12:2, p. 68
Gunn, John	Henrico	Will	1772	Judgments 1785 FEB
Gunnell, Elizabeth, in Frederick Co.	Fairfax	Will	1827	X
Gunnell, Henry, in Fairfax Co.	Culpeper	Will	1822	CF1844-023
Gunnell, James, in Fauquier Co.	Fairfax	Will	1819	CF1835-002
Gunnell, James, in Fauquier Co.	Fairfax	Will	1819	X
Gunnell, Robert	Fairfax	Will	1817	X
Gunnell, William	Fairfax	Debts Due	1829	X
Gunnell, William	Fairfax	Account	1843	X
Guthrie, Major	King & Queen	Will	1858	CF1872-001
Gwaltney, Thomas, of Surry Co.	Williamsburg	Will Abstract	1798	Crozier, p. 28
Gwathmey, Joseph	King William	Will	1823	V:Mss1 G9957 a 1
Gwathmey, Joseph, in King William Co.	Petersburg	Will	1824	CF1860-024
Gwathmey, Joseph, of King William Co.	Petersburg	Will	1824	CF1860-024
Gwathmey, Richard	Hanover	Will	1866	CF1902-023
Gwathmey, Richard	Hanover	Will	1866	V:Mss1 G9957 a 78
Gwin, John, of James City Co.	London	Will	1684	N:PROB11/378
Gwin, John, of James City Co.		Will	1684	VCRP, Survey #03731
Gwynn, Edmund	Gloucester	Will Ref.	1683	Hening, Vol. 8, p. 483
Gwynn, Edmund	Gloucester	Will Ref.	1683	Hening, Vol. 8, p. 483

NAME	LOCATION	TYPE	YEAR	REFERENCE(S)

H

NAME	LOCATION	TYPE	YEAR	REFERENCE(S)
Hacker, John, planter		Will	1654	VCRP, Survey #04112
Hackett, Frederick, in PA	Henrico	Will	1895	CF1896-063
Hackley, Elizabeth	King George	Will	1756	FDC L563-52
Hackman, John, Sr., in Shenandoah Co.	Frederick	Will	1821	CF1833-025
Hackney, James W.	Prince George	Will	1853	SV 9:4, p. 159
Haddocke, William, planter		Will	1649	VCRP, Survey #03998
Hagner, Daniel R., Dr., in DC	Northumberland	Will	1893	CF1897-005
Hagner, Sarah A., in DC	Northumberland	Will	1895	CF1897-005
Hagood, Anderson, in Patrick Co.	Henry	Will	1854	CF1857-023
Hague, John, in Loudoun Co.	Frederick	Will	1767	CF1818-070
Hague, Joseph	New Kent	Estate Ref.	1820	LP:16 DEC 1822
Hague, Joseph	New Kent	Estate Ref.	1820	LP:07 JAN 1824
Haile, Richard Thomas	Essex	Will Abstract	1787	Fleet 2:347
Haile, Richard Thomas	Essex	Will	1795	CF1802-012
Haines, Frederick	Rockingham	Will	1780	BRCD
Haines, Henry, in Berkeley Co.	Frederick	Will	1777	CF1814-026
Hains, Frederick	Rockingham	Will	1780	CF1811-002
Hains, Frederick	Rockingham	Will	1784	MVG 31:4, p. 352
Hains, Frederick	Rockingham	Will	1784	LVA Acc. #26589-4
Hains, Sarah, in Berkeley Co.	Frederick	Will	1831	CF1835-108
Hair, William	Surry	Inventory	1693	T: correct from Hare
Hairston, Peter, in Stokes Co. NC	Henry	Will	1833	CF1858-038
Hairston, Robert, in MS	Henry	Will	1852	V:Mss1 H1274 a 15-17
Hairston, Robert, in MS	Henry	Will	1852	CF1855-019
Haislip, Henry	Fairfax	Survey	1831	X
Haislip, Henry [Sally]	Fairfax	Dower	1831	X
Hale, Charlotte, of West Point	King William	Will	1879	CF1887-021
Hale, Smith, in KY	Fauquier	Will	1817	CF1832-061
Hales, Thomas	Charles City	Inventory		D&W1724, p. 227
Hall, Annie	Hanover	Will	1879	CF1880-026
Hall, Archibald, heirs of	Fairfax	Plat	1884	X
Hall, Arthur E., in Norfolk	Nansemond	Will	1891	CF1901-005
Hall, Arthur E., of Norfolk	Nansemond	Will	1891	CF1901-005
Hall, Benjamin, in Halifax Co.	Franklin	Will	1803	CF1841-011
Hall, Cassander	Fairfax	Will	1854	NVG 8, p. 1098
Hall, Charles, fishmonger		Will	1699	VCRP, Survey #04787
Hall, David D.	King & Queen	Will	1914	LP
Hall, Elisha, in Fairfax Co.	Fauquier	Will	1751	CF1792-011
Hall, Henry, in Gloucester Co.	Henrico	Will	1801	CF1817-027
Hall, Henry, in Gloucester Co.	Henrico	Will	1801	CF1808-006
Hall, John	Gloucester	Will	1763	TVF 9:2, p. 122
Hall, John, of Gloucester Co.	Franklin	Will	1763	Deter. Papers 1799 APR
Hall, John, of Gloucester Co.	Franklin	Will	1763	MVG 31:4, p. 359
Hall, Joseph, in Berkeley Co.	Frederick	Will	1797	CF1813-076
Hall, Mary Seymour	Fauquier	Will	1853	CF1854-018
Halley, Francis		Will	1702	VCRP, Survey #04120
Halley, Henry S.	Fairfax	Sale	1839	X
Halley, Henry S.	Fairfax	Inventory	1839	X
Halley, John H.	Fairfax	Account	1853	X
Halley, Sally	Fairfax	Inventory	1853	X

NAME	LOCATION	TYPE	YEAR	REFERENCE(S)
Halley, Sarah	Fairfax	Account	1853	X
Halley, William	Fairfax	Will	1819	NVG 6, p. 628
Halley, William, in OH	Arlington	Will	1808	CF1836-007
Halsall, Benjamin, in Louisa Co.	Goochland	Will	1807	CF1851-003
Ham, George J., in Norfolk Co.	Portsmouth	Will	1827	CF1884-004
Ham, S.A., in NJ	Portsmouth	Will	1872	CF1884-004
Ham, Sarah A., in Norfolk Co.	Portsmouth	Will	1834	CF1884-004
Hambleton, Sarah, in Louisa Co.	Hanover	Will	1816	CF1843-002
Hambleton, Sarah, of Louisa Co.	Hanover	Will	1816	Cocke:71
Hamilton, James, of Botetourt Co.	Augusta	Will	1812	CF1831-015
Hamilton, John	Nansemond	Will	1711	LVA Acc. #26070
Hamilton, John	Nansemond	Will	1711	VG 11, p. 31
Hamilton, John, in Nicholas Co.	Bath	Will	1818	CF1832-021
Hamilton, John, in Nicholas Co.	Bath	Will	1818	CF1832-020
Hamilton, John, of Norfolk	London	Will	1817	N:PROB11/1588
Hamlet, John, in Charlotte Co.	Campbell	Will	1874	CF1883-005
Hamlett, James, in Charlotte Co.	Lunenburg	Will	1819	CF1838-002
Hamlin, Abraham	Charles City	Will	1700	D&W1724, p. 69
Hamlin, Charles, Jr.	Lunenburg	Will	1776	CF1798-006
Hamlin, John, in Dinwiddie Co.	Petersburg	Will	1824	CF1843-033
Hamme, Jacob, in Berkeley Co.	Frederick	Will	1822	CF1834-020
Hammitt, John	Prince William	Will	1800	PWR 6:1, p. 24
Hammock, George, in Nottoway Co.	Lunenburg	Will	1889	CF1898-002
Hammock, William	Lunenburg	Will	1785	CF1805-020
Hammond, James, in Jefferson Co.	Frederick	Will	1803	CF1819-114
Hammond, James, in Jefferson Co.	Frederick	Will	1803	CF1815-026
Hammond, Mildred D., in Jefferson Co.	Arlington	Will	1805	CF1837-019
Hammond, Mildred G., in Jefferson Co.	Frederick	Will	1800	CF1852-065
Hammond, Mildred G., in Jefferson Co.	Frederick	Will	1804	CF1852-061
Hamner, Jeremiah	Albemarle	Assignment	1813	MVG 31:4, p. 347
Hamphill, Samuel, of Rockingham Co.	Augusta	Will	1809	CF1819-051
Hampton, Henry	Prince William	Will	1778	LVA Acc. #26465
Hampton, James O.	Fairfax	Guard. Acct.	1860	X
Hampton, John	Caroline	Will	1803	W&P1842, p. 70
Hampton, John [of Hamptonsville]	Caroline	Will	1803	Note[1]
Hampton, Laura V., now Pettit	Fairfax	Guard. Acct.	1860	X
Hampton, Lucy E.	Fairfax	Guard. Acct.	1860	X
Hampton, Richard	Fauquier	Will	1766	CF1792-011
Hampton, Thomas		Will	1703c	GSTV 7, p. 120
Hampton, Thomas		Will		VTG 7:3, p. 10
Hampton, William H.	Fairfax	Guard. Acct.	1860	X
Hance, Peter, mariner [Hans]		Will	1708	VCRP, Survey #03901
Hancock, Benjamin, in Franklin Co.	Roanoke	Will	1860	CF1884-021
Hancock, Benjamin, in Franklin Co.	Roanoke	Will	1860	CF1876-006
Hancock, J.A., in Russell Co.	Tazewell	Will	1892	CF1902-085
Hancock, Martin	Charlotte	Will	1838	LVA Acc. #32910
Hancock, Samuel	Chesterfield	Will	1760	VMHB 33, p. 319
Hancock, Scarlet	Prince William	Will	1740	V:Mss1 T2118 d27684+

---

[1] Fredericksburg City Record of Cases Decided, No. 1, 1820, p. 228.

NAME	LOCATION	TYPE	YEAR	REFERENCE(S)
Hancock, William	Surry	Will	1693	LVA Acc. #20762
Hancock, Woodson W., in Chest. Co.	Powhatan	Will	1883	CF1888-016
Handford, Tobias, late of Gloucester Co.		Will	1677	VCRP, Survey #03714
Hanes, George B.	Hanover	Will	1865	CF1889-003
Hanes, Herbert, of Abingdon Parish	Gloucester	Will Abstract	1737	VMHB 32, p. 60
Hankins, Daniel	Charlotte	Will	1844	V:Mss1 B6638 a2812+
Hankins, John, of James City	Williamsburg	Will Abstract	1801	Crozier, p. 31
Hankins, William, in Pittsylvania Co.	Henry	Will	1824	CF1834-005
Hannah, George	Charlotte	Will	1855	V:Mss1 H1956 a 1117+
Hannan, Esom, in Botetourt Co.	Roanoke	Will	1843	CF1847-002
Hansard, John, in Amherst Co.	Lynchburg	Will	1825	CF1829-010
Hansborough, William, in Amherst Co.	Bedford	Will	1779	CF1795-016
Hansbrough, James P.	Amherst	Will	(nd)	V:Mss1 N1786 a 8222+
Hansbrough, Peter, in Culpeper Co.	King George	Will	(nd)	CF1883-008
Hansbrough, Peter, in Culpeper Co.	Fauquier	Will	1822	CF1866-002
Hansbrough, William, in Culpeper Co.	Fauquier	Will	1837	CF1840-005
Hansford, Elizabeth R.	Williamsburg	Will	1836	Swem(1):f199
Hansford, Richard, in Warwick Co.	York	Will	1808	CF1845-012
Hansford, Richard, in Warwick Co.	York	Will	1808	MVG 31:4, p. 357
Hardaway, David H.	Nottoway	Will	1853	CF1871-005
Hardaway, Frances	Dinwiddie	Will	1818	VG 16, p. 258
Hardaway, John, in Dinwiddie Co.	Petersburg	Will	1824	CF1835-033
Hardich, William, late of Westm. Co.		Will	1669	VCRP, Survey #03542
Harding, Elizabeth A.B., in Jefferson Co.	Frederick	Will	1825	CF1834-077
Harding, Robert, in Lunenburg Co.	Prince Edward	Will	1861	CF1868-020
Harding, William	King William	Will Partial	1702	RB2, p. 12
Harding, William		Will	1742	VCRP, Survey #04384
Harding, William	Goochland	Will	1768	CF1788-005
Harding, William	Northumberland	Will	1786	CF1805-027
Harding, William H., in Jefferson Co.	Frederick	Will	1809	CF1834-054
Harding, William H., in Lunenburg Co.	Prince Edward	Will	1862	CF1868-020
Harding, William, of *Springfield*	Northumberland	Will	1878	HHS 5, p. 40
Hardiway, John	Brunswick	Will	1780	CF1802-003
Hardwick, James	Westmoreland	Will	1737	D&W8 pt. 2, p. 325a
Hardy, Eliza J., w/o J.G., Barren Co. KY	Hanover	Will	1846	Cocke:97
Hardyman, Francis	Charles City	Will	1763	W&D1763, p. 299
Hardyman, Littleberry	Charles City	Inventory	1772	Records, p. 403
Hardyman, Littlebury	Charles City	Inventory	1772	Records, p. 403
Hare, William	Surry	Will (N)	1693	T:D&W4, p. 308b
Harford, Henry	Richmond	Will	1737c	V:Mss1 D3743 b
Hargrave, Anselm	Surry	Will	1797	WB1, p. 240
Hargrave, Benjamin	Surry	Will Abstract	1827	VG 13, p. 54
Hargrave, Benjamin	Surry	Will (U)	1827	VTG 13:3, p. 125
Hargrave, Samuel, in Caroline Co.	Bedford	Will	1777	CF1840-013
Hargrove, Tazewell L., in NC	Mecklenburg	Will	1891	CF1901-044 CC
Harle, John, mariner		Will	1696	VCRP, Survey #06051
Harlow, John	Henrico	Inventory	1763	Records, Vol. 6, p. 1879
Harlow, John	Henrico	Inventory	1763	Records, Vol. 6, p. 1879
Harlow, Nathaniel, in Nelson Co.	Lynchburg	Will	1815	CF1828-007
Harman, Jacob, merchant, Phila. PA	Arlington	Will	1780	CF1811-021
Harman, John, mariner		Will	1728	VCRP, Survey #04656

NAME	LOCATION	TYPE	YEAR	REFERENCE(S)
Harmon, Essie, of Washington DC	Dinwiddie	Will	1842	CF1944-020
Harnsberger, Jacob, Rockingham Co.	Augusta	Will	1861	CF1888-020
Harnsberger, Thomas K., Rockingham	Greene	Will	1894	CF1906-001
Harper, James	Mathews	Will	1795	LVA Acc. #25825
Harper, John, in Mecklenburg Co.	Lunenburg	Will	1815	CF1853-013
Harper, Robert, in Berkeley Co.	Fauquier	Will	1782	CF1848-011
Harrill, James	Prince William	Will	1756	LVA Acc. #25223
Harris, Ann N.	Hanover	Will	1866	CF1877-029
Harris, David B., in Goochland Co.	Louisa	Will	1865	CF1898-015
Harris, Frances, in Isle of Wight Co.	Nansemond	Will	1866	CF1883-003
Harris, Frances, of Isle of Wight Co.	Nansemond	Will	1866	CF1883-003
Harris, Francis	Henrico	Will	1743	Records, Vol. 4, p. 1231
Harris, Francis	Buckingham	Will	1827	UVA MSS 10644
Harris, Francis, in Wilcox Co. AL	Buckingham	Will	1827	VG 27, p. 209
Harris, George, late of Charles City Co.		Will	1674	VCRP, Survey #03552
Harris, George, of Charles City Co.	London	Will	1674	N:PROB11/345
Harris, George, of Louisa Co.	Albemarle	Will	1856	CF1860-059
Harris, James	Lancaster	Will	1787	LP
Harris, John	Lancaster	Will	1661	LP
Harris, John	Surry	Inventory	1687	T:D&W3, p. 82a
Harris, John	Northumberland	Will	1709	VMHB 23, p. 418
Harris, John	Northumberland	Will	1713	RB1710, p. 318
Harris, John	York	Will	1783	LVA Acc. #41008, r4614
Harris, John	Henrico	Will	1810	LVA Acc. #41008, r4610
Harris, John, in Williamsburg	York	Will	1783	Fleet, Huntington Data
Harris, John, in Williamsburg	D.C.	Will	1845	DCA:Box 17
Harris, John, of Northumberland Co.		Will	1723	VCRP, Survey #04369
Harris, John, of Richmond	Henrico	Will	1810	Fleet, Huntington Data
Harris, John T., in New Kent Co.	Albemarle	Will	1887	CF1904-026
Harris, Joseph, Sr.	King & Queen	Will	1919	LP
Harris, Lee	Amherst	Will	1792	CF1797-016
Harris, Martha Ann	Hanover	Will	1860	Cocke:72
Harris, Martha Ann	Hanover	Will	1860	CF1867-004
Harris, Michael		Will	1697	VCRP, Survey #06057
Harris, Sarah	Hanover	Will	1780c	HHS 33, p. 6
Harris, Sarah	Hanover	Will	1780c	V:Mss1 w8844 a 61-65
Harris, Stephen	Hanover	Will	1770	VG 22, p. 191
Harris, Stephen	Hanover	Will	1770	HHS 14, p. 6
Harris, Stephen	Hanover	Will	1770	V:Mss4 H1973 a 2
Harris, Thomas	Henrico	Will	1741	Records, Vol. 4, p. 1139
Harris, Thomas	Hanover	Will	1832	Cocke:73
Harris, Thomas, Gent.	Henrico	Estate Ref.	1730	Winfree, p. 344
Harris, Thomas, in PA	Culpeper	Will	1861	CF1904-018
Harris, William	Henrico	Will	1678	V:Mss5:9 B9965:1
Harris, William Eli	Hanover	Will Ref.	(nd)	Cocke:72
Harris, William, Maj.	Henrico	Will Abstract	1678	VMHB 50, p. 256
Harrison, Andrew	Essex	Will Abstract	1718	Fleet 2:326
Harrison, Ann R., in Albemarle Co.	Prince William	Will	1875	CF1895-004
Harrison, Barbara	Arlington	Will	1796	CRA:197
Harrison, Benjamin	Surry	Will	1712	WMQ 10, p. 109
Harrison, Benjamin	Charles City	Will	1791	VMHB 33, p. 413

NAME	LOCATION	TYPE	YEAR	REFERENCE(S)
Harrison, Benjamin, in Charles City Co.	Henry	Will	1799	CF1838-001
Harrison, Benjamin, of *Berkeley*	Charles City	Will	1745	BRCD
Harrison, Benjamin, of *Berkeley*	Charles City	Will	1745	LVA Acc. #29245
Harrison, Benjamin, of *Berkeley*	Charles City	Will	1745	VMHB 3, p. 124
Harrison, Benjamin, of *Berkeley*	Charles City	Will	1745	V:Mss2 H2451 a 1
Harrison, Benjamin, of *Berkeley*	Charles City	Will	1745	VMHB 32, p. 98
Harrison, Benjamin, of *Berkeley*	Charles City	Will	1780	V:Mss2 H2452 a 2
Harrison, Benjamin, of *Berkeley*	Charles City	Will	1787	LVA Acc. #20404
Harrison, Benjamin, the younger	Charles City	Estate Ref.	1710	Hening, Vol. 3, p. 538
Harrison, Catharine	Fairfax	Guard. Bond	1822	X
Harrison, Edmund		Will	1820	UVA Acc. #640
Harrison, Eliza M.	Richmond City	Will	1869	LVA Acc. #31473-248
Harrison, Elizabeth, Sr.	Brunswick	Will	1837	SV 3:3, p. 119
Harrison, George	James City	Will	1624	V:Mss2 B9966 c 1
Harrison, George E.	Prince George	Will	1839	BRCD
Harrison, George E., in Pr. Geo. Co.	Petersburg	Will	1839	CF1899-037
Harrison, George E., of *Brandon*	Prince George	Will	1839	LP:06 DEC 1839
Harrison, George Evelyn, Pr. Geo. Co.	Petersburg	Will	1839	CF1865-019
Harrison, Harriet Heileman, at *Ampthill*	Cumberland	Will Ref.	1885+	V:Mss1 H2485 g 33-36
Harrison, Hendrick		Will	1694	VCRP, Survey #04710
Harrison, Henry	Prince George	Inventory	1759	DB1759, p. 93
Harrison, Henry	Prince George	Inventory	1759	DB1759, p. 93
Harrison, Jeremiah	Northumberland	Will	1793	Note[1]
Harrison, Jeremiah, in Berkeley Co.	Frederick	Will	1793	CF1817-126
Harrison, Jesse, of Rockingham Co.	Augusta	Will	1826	CF1830-030
Harrison, John D., in Alexandria Co.	Fairfax	Will	1853	CF1856-011
Harrison, John D., in Alexandria Co.	Fairfax	Will	1853	X
Harrison, John, of Isle of Wight Co.	Williamsburg	Will Abstract	1791	Crozier, p. 29
Harrison, John, of Rockingham Co.	Augusta	Will	1819	CF1826-010
Harrison, John P., of Caswell Co., NC	Danville	Will	1849	DBB: 24
Harrison, Magdalene, Westmoreland Co.	Frederick	Will	1786	CF1817-126
Harrison, Mary	Surry	Will	1732	VMHB 31, p. 281
Harrison, Nathaniel	Amelia	Will	(nd)	V:Mss1 N1786 a 8222+
Harrison, Nathaniel	Surry	Inventory	1728	VMHB 31, p. 361
Harrison, Nathaniel	Amelia	Will	1852	LVA Acc. #41008, r4608
Harrison, Nathaniel	Amelia	Will Extract	1852	Fleet, Huntington Data
Harrison, Nathaniel, Martins Brandon	Prince George	Will	1792	DB1787, p. 635
Harrison, Nathaniel, of Southwark Par.	Surry	Will	1727	VMHB 31, p. 278
Harrison, Nicholas, planter		Will	1653	VCRP, Survey #03122
Harrison, Pleasant	Surry	Will	1799	T: correct from Harris
Harrison, Randolph	Arlington	Will	(nd)	CF1868-034
Harrison, Randolph, in Cumberland Co.	Goochland	Will	1839	CF1852-010
Harrison, Robert	York	Will	1668	DOW4, p. 180
Harrison, Robert H., in Caroline Co.	Essex	Will	1852	CF1879-024
Harrison, Samuel	Arlington	Will	1796	CRA:177
Harrison, Samuel, in Westmoreland Co.	Frederick	Will	1764	CF1817-126
Harrison, Sarah	Chesterfield	Will	1781	TQ 09:2, p. 132
Harrison, Thomas	Fauquier	Will Abstract	1774	VMHB 23, p. 332

[1] Northumberland County District Court Orders, Deeds, [Wills], 1789-1825, p. 319.

NAME	LOCATION	TYPE	YEAR	REFERENCE(S)
Harrison, Thomas N., in Madison Co.	Greene	Will	1889	CF1892-009
Harrison, Thomas, of Rockingham Co.	Augusta	Will	1799	CF1804-139
Harrison, Thomas, Sr., in NC	Lynchburg	Will	1790	CF1823-062
Harrison, Thomas W.	Prince George	Will	1859	SV 10:1, p. 14
Harrison, William	Chesterfield	Will	1753	TQ 09:2, p. 128
Harrison, William	Westmoreland	Will	1788	Wills #33
Harrison, William A.	Prince George	Will	1824	Note[1]
Harrison, William Allen, in Pr. Geo. Co.	Petersburg	Will	1824	CF1842-042
Harrison, William Allin, in Pr. Geo. Co.	Petersburg	Will	1824	CF1837-026
Harrison, William, Col., Charles Co. MD	Alexandria	Will	1786	NVG 3:4, p. 161
Harrison, William H.	Prince George	Will	1824	LVA Acc. #22296
Harrison, William Henry		Will	1841	Note[2]
Harrison, Wm. Allen, Prince George Co.	Petersburg	Will	1824	CF1832-006
Harriss, John, in Lancaster Co.	Northumberland	Will	1786	CF1827-003
Harrod, Thomas	Lancaster	Will	1709	LP
Harrod, William, in OH	Dinwiddie	Will	1890	CF1892-005
Hart, Andrew, mariner		Will	1723	VCRP, Survey #04370
Hart, Frances, in Richmond	Amelia	Will	1881	CF1895-005
Hart, Silas, of Rockingham Co.	Augusta	Will	1795	CF1823-065
Hart, William	Surry	Admin.	1695	T:D&W5, p. 43b
Harte, Thomas	Surry	Account	1674	T: correct from Haite
Hartley, Henry		Will	1699	VCRP, Survey #04788
Hartley, James	Richmond	Will	1719	WB4, p. 78
Hartley, James	Richmond	Will	1719	T: not Inventory
Hartshorne, William	Fairfax	Plat	1791	X
Hartwell, John, of Nansemond Co.	Isle of Wight	Will	1806	Judgments 1811 OCT
Harvey, Henry	Charles City	Account	1728	D&W1724, p. 204
Harvey, Isham, in Charlotte Co.	Prince Edward	Will	1842	CF1877-035
Harvey, John	Stafford	Will	1700c	V:Mss1 T2118 d27684+
Harvey, John, Sir		Will	1650	VCRP, Survey #04000
Harvey, Matthew, in Botetourt Co.	Bedford	Will	1823	CF1855-033
Harvey, Mungo, of Westmoreland Co.	Williamsburg	Will Abstract	1794	Crozier, p. 30
Harvey, Robert	Botetourt	Will	1830	V:Mss1 B7425 b36-41
Harvey, Thomas	Charlotte	Will	1812	LVA Acc. #21624
Harvey, Thomas	Charlotte	Will	1812	LVA Acc. #22543
Harvey, William	Surry	Will	1704	T: correct from Harwy
Harvey, William, Jr., in Campbell Co.	Lynchburg	Will	1813	CF1830-149
Harvie, John	Henrico	Will	1807	LVA Acc. #23531b
Harvie, John	Richmond City	Will	1807	Note[3]
Harvie, John, of Henrico Co.	Chesterfield	Will	1807	Dead Papers 1802-1815
Harvie, Lewis Edwin	Amelia	Will	1866	V:Mss1 H2636 c 2913+
Harvill, Richard	Prince George	Will	1827	SV 9:1, p. 22
Harwar, Thomas, of Essex Co.	London	Will	1704	N:PROB32/46/15 & 17
Harwell, James, in Mecklenburg Co.	Brunswick	Will	1770	CF1783-009
Harwell, Manson	Brunswick	Will	1823	CF1840-030
Harwell, Mary	Dinwiddie	Will	1828	CF1860-005

---

[1] LVA, U.S. Circuit Court Records, Virginia District, Box 150, *Christian & Wife v. Harrison* (1845).
[2] Library of Congress, William Henry Harrison Papers, Series 1 (Reel 2), Item Nos. 1467-1470.
[3] LVA, James River and Kanawha Co. Deed Book No. 2, p. 42.

NAME	LOCATION	TYPE	YEAR	REFERENCE(S)
Harwell, Mary	Dinwiddie	Will	1828	CF1884-001
Harwell, Thomas	Greensville	Will	1825	SV 13:1, p. 21
Harwood, Arthur, mechant		Will	1642	VCRP, Survey #03990
Harwood, Humphrey, Sr., of York Co.	Williamsburg	Will Abstract	1789	Crozier, p. 31
Harwood, Samuel	Charles City	Will Ref.	1778	VG 14, p. 184
Harwood, Samuel		Inventory	1778	Misc. reel 547; Note[1]
Harwood, Samuel	Charles City	Inventory		D&W1724, p. 271
Harwood, Thomas, in Stafford Co.	Essex	Will	1845	CF1899-001
Harwood, Thomas S.	Gloucester	Will	1856	CF1886-005
Harwood, William	Williamsburg	Will Abstract	1794	Crozier, p. 30
Harwood, William	Williamsburg	Will	1794	CW M-1561
Harwood, William J., in Richmond	Henrico	Will	1872	CF1891-043
Harwood, William, of Warwick Co.	York	Will	1780	CF1787-001
Harwood, William, of Warwick Co.	York	Will	1781	MVG 31:4, p. 355
Haskew, Henry, of Amelia Co.	Cumberland	Will	1845	CF1851-012
Hastings, John, mariner		Will	1707	VCRP, Survey #03899
Hatcher, Henry		Account	1746	DB1744, p. 144
Hatcher, James	Henrico	Will	1757	Records, Vol. 5, p. 1751
Hatcher, James	Henrico	Will	1757	Records, Vol. 5, p. 1751
Hatcher, Jonah, in Loudoun Co.	Culpeper	Will	1887	CF1906-059
Hatcher, Sarah	Goochland	Will	1798	CF1803-012
Hatcher, Thomas	Goochland	Will	1797	CF1803-012
Hatcher, Thomas A., in AR	Mecklenburg	Will	1892	CF1894-011 CC
Hathaway, James H.	Fauquier	Will	1892	CF1906-020
Hattel, Henry	Rockingham	Will	1815	BRCD
Hatton, John, salter		Will	1663	VCRP, Survey #03533
Haviland, Anthony	Surry	Will	1687	T:D&W4, p. 35a
Hawes, Samuel	Essex	Will	1786	CF1800-001
Hawkins, Nat	James City	Will	1838	Swem(1):150
Hawkins, Sarah	Shenandoah	Will	1835	LVA Acc. #21734
Hawkins, Thomas	Essex	Will	1786	CF1810-018
Hawkins, William	Essex	Will	1769	CF1809-008
Hawthorne, Hannah	Fairfax	Will	1785	X
Hawthorne, Thomas	Goochland	Will	1824	Fleet, Huntington Data
Haxall, Bolling Walker	Richmond City	Will	1885	V:Mss1 H3203 c 197+
Haxall, Henry, in Richmond	Bedford	Will	1889	CF1900-051
Haxall, William	Petersburg	Will	1834	V:Mss1 H3203 d 82-84
Hay, Ann		Will	1753	LVA Acc. #19793-10
Hay, John	York	Will	1777	CF1784-006
Hay, John	York	Will	1788	CF1804-006
Hay, John	York	Will	1788	CF1790-001
Hay, Joseph, in Nansemond Co.	Southampton	Will	1798	CF1838-005
Haydon, Charles, in Botetourt Co.	Roanoke	Will	1837	CF1844-009
Haydon, Charles, in Botetourt Co.	Roanoke	Will	1839	CF1844-009
Haydon, Mary	Lancaster	Will	1787	LP
Hayes, Joseph, of Gloucester Co.		Will	1678	VCRP, Survey #03717
Hayes, Joseph, of Gloucester Co.	London	Will	1687	N:PROB11/357
Hayes, Robert, in TN	Lunenburg	Will	1860	CF1873-033

---

[1] University of Chicago, Weyanoke Plantation Papers, Folder 28.

NAME	LOCATION	TYPE	YEAR	REFERENCE(S)
Haynes, Betty, of Princess Anne Co.	Williamsburg	Will Abstract	1808	Crozier, p. 29
Haynes, Herbert, of Gloucester Co.	London	Will	1737	N:PROB11/686
Haynes, Herbert, of Gloucester Co.		Will	1737	VCRP, Survey #04375
Haynes, James	Lancaster	Will	1712	LP
Haynes, Thomas	Warwick	Will	1746	V:Mss2 H3338 a 1
Haynes, Thomas	Warwick	Will Abstract	1746	TQ 1:1, p. 68.
Haynes, Thomas	Warwick	Will	1746	LVA Acc. #23920a
Haynes, Thomas, of Warwick Co.	London	Will	1746	NGSQ Vol. 64, p. 286
Haynes, Thomas, of Warwick Co.	London	Will	1746	N:PROB11/749
Haynes, Thomas, of Warwick Co.		Will	1746	VCRP, Survey #04634
Haynie, Anthony	Northumberland	Will	1711	VMHB 23, p. 417
Haynie, Bridgar	Northumberland	Will	1791	CF1806-016
Haynie, Sarah	Northumberland	Will	1831	Note[1]
Haynie, Warner R., in Lancaster Co.	Richmond	Will	1871	CF1876-003
Hays, Andrew	Rockbridge	Will	1786	Land Office
Hays, Andrew	Rockbridge	Will	1786	MVG 29:3, p. 191
Hays, Andrew	Rockbridge	Will	1786	WB1, p. 258
Hays, Samuel	Smyth	Will	1851	MVG 29:3, p. 191
Hayward, John	Stafford	Will	1701	WBZ, p. 117
Hayward, Joseph	Stafford	Admin.	1690	OB: 12 MAR 1690
Hayward, Martha	Stafford	Will	1697	LVA Acc. #22622
Hayward, Martha Washington	Stafford	Will	1697	TQ 28:3, p. 165
Hayward, Samuel	Stafford	Will	1684	TQ 28:1, p. 18
Hayward, Samuel	Stafford	Will	1696	LVA Acc. #22508
Hazzard, Jos. R., Northumberland Co.	Richmond	Will	1866	CF1878-004
Heaberd, John	Stafford	Estate Ref.	1690	OB: 19 JUL 1690
Headley, William, in Frederick Co.	Warren	Will	1836	CF1838-001
Heale, Ellen	Lancaster	Will	1713	T: correct from 1710
Heale, George, of Lancaster	London	Will	1709	N:PROB11/507
Hearn, S.W., in NC	Essex	Will	1890	CF1900-009
Heater, John	Rockingham	Will	1823	CF1845-008
Heater, John, of Rockingham Co.	Loudoun	Will	1823	CF1842-013
Heath, Adam	Dinwiddie	Will	1819	V:Mss1 B4325 a 85-89
Heath, Elizabeth	Surry	Will	1751	T: correct from 1750
Heath, Joseph	Prince George	Will	1834	BRCD
Heath, Joseph, in Prince George Co.	Petersburg	Will	1834	CF1850-024
Heblethwaite, Robert	Dinwiddie	Estate Ref.	1797	LP:12 DEC 1808
Hedgeman, Nathaniel	Lancaster	Will	1699	LP
Heffernan, Henry, of Middlesex Co.	Williamsburg	Will Abstract	1814	Crozier, p. 30
Heidon, Mary	Surry	Will (N)	1680	T: correct from Herdon
Heiskell, Adam, in Hampshire Co.	Frederick	Will	1822	CF1829-166
Helm, Frances, in Frederick Co.	Essex	Will	1820	CF1845-022
Hemphill, Samuel, of Rockingham Co.	Augusta	Will	1809	CF1819-051
Henderson, Alexander	Prince William	Will	1815	BRCD
Henderson, Alexander	Prince William	Will Ref.	1843	CM:07 AUG 1843
Henderson, Alexander	Prince William	Acct. Ref.	1843	CM:07 AUG 1843
Henderson, Alexander, in Pr. Wm. Co.	Frederick	Will	1815	CF1825-194
Henderson, Frances, in Orange Co.	Louisa	Will	1834	CF1839-005

---

[1] Northumberland County District Court Orders, Deeds, [Wills], 1789-1825 [1849], p. 465.

NAME	LOCATION	TYPE	YEAR	REFERENCE(S)
Henderson, Harry, of New Kent Co.	London	Will	1674	N:PROB11/346
Henderson, Henry		Will	1674	VCRP, Survey #03553
Henderson, Isaiah, in Richmond	Henrico	Will	1888	CF1904-030
Henderson, James	Williamsburg	Will	1818	V:Mss6:1 H3833:1
Henderson, James	Williamsburg	Will	1818	LVA Acc. #28458
Henderson, James, Rev., Williamsburg	James City	Will	1820	VG 29, p. 208
Henderson, John	Augusta	Will	1766	Finley
Henderson, John	Greenbrier	Inventory	1787	V:Mss2 H38356 b
Henderson, John	Greenbrier	Will	1787	V:Mss2 H38356 b
Henderson, John	Albemarle	Will	1799c	V:Mss1 M3855 a 5499+
Henderson, Joseph M., in Orange Co.	Louisa	Will	1900	CF1904-001
Henderson, Nathaniel	Buckingham	Estate Ref.	1831	Note[1]
Hendrick, John	Buckingham	Will	1814	BRCD
Hendrick, John, in Buckingham Co.	Campbell	Will	1814	CF1823-002
Hendricks, J.R., in Russell Co.	Washington	Will	1896	CF1900-102
Hendry, Eleanor, in MD	Staunton	Will	1883	CF1888-003
Hendry, George	Frederick	Will	1782	WB4, p. 635
Heninger, Rees T., in UT	Tazewell	Will	1888	CF1893-046
Henley, Charles	Princess Anne	Will Ref.	1703	DB1, p. 432
Henley, Leonard	James City	Sale	1813	BRCD
Henley, Leonard	James City	Will	1831	Swem(1):f152
Henley, Richardson L.	James City	Will	1897	CF1898-010
Henley, S.W., in NC	Essex	Will	1890	CF1902-005
Henley, S.W., in NC	Essex	Will	1890	CF1900-009
Henley, William D., in Norfolk	Isle of Wight	Will	1838	CF1844-086
Henning, David, in Frederick Co.	Greene	Will	1847	CF1871-008
Henop, Mary, of Norfolk Co.	Williamsburg	Will Abstract	1820	Crozier, p. 31
Henry, Edward	Northumberland	Inventory	1824	Note[2]
Henry, James, of Northumberland Co.	Williamsburg	Will Abstract	1805	Crozier, p. 30
Henry, John	Arlington	Will	1800	CRA:328
Henry, John, of Richmond	London	Will	1809	N:PROB11/1506
Henry, Judith	Prince William	Will	1862	LP
Henry, Patrick	Charlotte	Will	1799	LVA Acc. #26340
Henry, Patrick	Charlotte	Will	1799	V:Mss3 C3815 a 6
Henry, Patrick, Negro caretaker	Rockbridge	Will	1829	VMHB 58, p. 134
Henry, Patrick, Rev.	Hanover	Will	1777	HHS 9, p. 4
Henry, Patrick, Rev., of St. Paul's Parish	Hanover	Will	1777	VMHB 58, p. 120
Henry, Patrick, Sr.	Hanover	Will	1777	Valentine
Henry, Patrick, Sr.	Hanover	Will	1777	HHS 9, p. 4
Henry, Rebecca, in Frederick Co.	Warren	Will	1830	CF1905-001
Henry, Sarah Winston Syme	Amherst	Will	1784	LVA Acc. #28785
Henry, Sarah Winston Syme	Amherst	Will	1784	Valentine
Henry, Sarah Winston Syme	Amherst	Will	1785	WMQ2 8, p. 117
Henshaw, Philip, in Caroline Co.	Essex	Will	1814	CF1824-004
Henshaw, Philip, of Caroline Co.	Essex	Will	1814	LP:15 DEC 1825
Henshaw, Samuel, in Essex Co.	Bedford	Will	1758	CF1774-003
Henson, John	Fairfax	Will	1816	X

---

[1] LVA, Revolutionary War Rejected Claims, John Baskerville, Folder 7.

[2] Northumberland County District Court Orders, Deeds, [Wills], 1789-1825 [1849], p. 462.

NAME	LOCATION	TYPE	YEAR	REFERENCE(S)
Henton, John	Rockingham	Estate Ref.	1790	LP:20 OCT 1790
Hentzel, Michael, in Berkeley Co.	Frederick	Will	1781	CF1827-209
Herbert, Christopher, of Norfolk Co.	Williamsburg	Will Abstract	1774	Crozier, p. 29
Herbert, John	Chesterfield	Inventory	1761	VMHB 18, p. 181
Herbert, Jonas, of Norfolk Co.	Williamsburg	Will Abstract	1782	Crozier, p. 29
Herbert, Mary L., in Jefferson Co.	Fairfax	Will	1827	CF1839-033
Herbert, Mary Lee, in NY	Fairfax	Will	1827	CF1887-041
Herdman, John, of Rockingham Co.	Augusta	Will	1826	CF1837-013
Herefoot, Ann, of Charles Co. MD and	Prince William	Account	1767	M: L56 f191
Herefoot, Henry, Charles Co. MD and	Prince William	Account	1767	M: L56 f191
Hereford, Alice Thornton, Loudoun Co.	Fairfax	Will	1843	CF1859-010
Hereford, James	Fairfax	Will	1744	X
Hereford, James	Fairfax	Partition	1799	X
Hereford, James	Fairfax	Will	1802	V:Mss1 H2485 e 85-88
Hermard, Peter, weaver		Will	1719	VCRP, Survey #04342
Herndon, Alexander, Spotsylvania Co.	Culpeper	Will	1876	CF1898-033
Herndon, Alexander, Spotsylvania Co.	Culpeper	Will	1876	CF1898-032
Herndon, Edward	Spotsylvania	Will	1799	FDC V566-83
Herndon, Sarah, in Pittsylvania Co.	Lynchburg	Will	1819	CF1821-070
Herndon, Virginia L., Spotsylvania Co.	Culpeper	Will	1893	CF1898-033
Herndon, Virginia L., Spotsylvania Co.	Culpeper	Will	1893	CF1898-032
Heron, James, in Frankfort KY	Richmond City	Will	1801	LVA Acc. #23531a
Heron, John E., in Henderson Co. TN	Henrico	Will	1832	CF1834-006
Heron, John E., of Richmond	Henrico	Will	1829c	VGSQ 18:3, p. 80
Herring, Daniel, of Isle of Wight Co.	Williamsburg	Will Abstract	1823	Crozier, p. 31
Herring, John	Isle of Wight	Will (U)	1815	SV 14:1, p. 19
Herron, Walter	Norfolk City	Will	1838	V:Mss1 D7784 a 3-7
Herron, Walter, of Norfolk	D.C.	Will	1867	DCA:Box 37
Hess, Christian, in Augusta Co.	Staunton	Will	1848	CF1908-003
Hess, Jacob, in Augusta Co.	Staunton	Will	1897	CF1908-003
Hester, Jacob, in Montgomery Co.	Floyd	Will	(nd)	CF1845-003
Heth, Andrew, of Jefferson Co.	Augusta	Will Abstract	1788	VMHB 42, p. 276
Heth, Henry	Chesterfield	Will	1824	V:Mss1B4678 b929-17,193
Heth, Henry G.	Henrico	Will Ref.	1816	VMHB 42, p. 276
Heth, William	Richmond City	Will	1807	Note[1]
Hewitt, Robert	Stafford	Will P.	1692	OB: 12 MAY 1692
Hewitt, Susanna, of Stafford Co.	Fredericksburg	Will	1797	DCWA, p. 80
Hewlett, William	Caroline	Estate Ref.	1807	LP:11 DEC 1807
Hewlett, William	Richmond City	Will	1820	Fleet, Huntington Data
Hewson, George	Surry	Inventory	1696	T: correct from Newsom
Hibble, Ann	Gloucester	Will	1855	CF1879-002
Hickman, John, of St. David	King William	Will	1788	Note[2]
Hicks, Charles	Brunswick	Will	1821	SV 3:3, p. 110
Hicks, Edward Brodnax	Brunswick	Will	1852	V:Mss7:1 B8646:2
Hicks, Edward Brodnax, planter	Brunswick	Will	1858	LVA Acc. #29690
Hicks, John	Brunswick	Will	1825	SV 3:3, p. 112

---

[1] LVA, Treasurer's Office Material, 7th Stack (E5), Box "James River and Kanawha Co. Guaranteed Bonds. Wills and Certificates..." Accession #28458.

[2] LVA, U.S. Circuit Court Records, Box 115, *Donald & Scott v. Hickman* (1824), also LVA Acc. #28458.

NAME	LOCATION	TYPE	YEAR	REFERENCE(S)
Hierholzer, Joseph, in Richmond	Henrico	Will	1869	CF1896-013
Hiett, Isabella Jane, in Clarke Co.	Frederick	Will	1847	CF1854-038
Higby, Lot, a free man of color	Henrico	Will	1854	TVF 1:4, p. 174
Higdon, Daniel	Prince George	Will	1735	LVA Acc. #28514
Higdon, Daniel, of Prince George Co.	Amelia	Will	1735	MVG 31:4, p. 351
Higdon, Daniel, of Prince George Co.	Goochland	Will	1735	Judgments 1736
Higgason, Walter, of Culpeper Co.	Loudoun	Will	1825	OB14 (cover)
Higginbotham, Aaron, in Amherst Co.	Lynchburg	Will	1785	CF1815-012
Higginbotham, Jesse Alexander	Amherst	Will	1849c	V:Mss1 T2123 a 33-38
Higgins, John, in Hardy Co.	Frederick	Will	1802	CF1822-265
High, Thomas	Surry	Will	1688	T:D&W4, p. 59b
Hightower, Joshua	Nottoway	Will	1794	WB1, p. 125
Hill, Ann Cox, in Culpeper Co.	Fairfax	Will	1825	CF1843-011
Hill, Caroline	King & Queen	Heirs	(nd)	LP
Hill, Castillo, of Northumberland Co.	Cumberland	Will	1850	CF1772-009
Hill, Edward, Col.	Charles City	Account	1725	D&W1724, p. 54
Hill, Elizabeth, in Augusta Co.	Staunton	Will	1883	CF1887-004
Hill, Francis, of Isle of Wight Co.	Williamsburg	Will Abstract	1791	Crozier, p. 30
Hill, Henry	Henrico	Will	1719	Records, Vol. 2, p. 465
Hill, Henry	Henrico	Will	1719	Records, Vol. 2, p. 465
Hill, Humphrey	King & Queen	Will	1775	V:Mss2 H5526 a 1
Hill, Humphrey, Col., of *Hillsborough*	King & Queen	Will	1774	Fleet 2:343
Hill, Humphrey, Col., St. Stephen's Par.	King & Queen	Will	1775	VMHB 4, p. 369
Hill, Humphrey, Col., St. Stephen's Par.	King & Queen	Will	1775	WMQ 16, p. 97
Hill, James, Sr.	Hanover	Will Abstract	1849	Cocke:74
Hill, James, Sr.	Hanover	Will	1849	LP
Hill, John	King William	Will	(nd)	V:Mss4 K5898 b
Hill, John	Essex	Will	1777	CF1806-002
Hill, John, in Franklin Co.	Roanoke	Will	1838	CF1847-010
Hill, Joseph, of Isle of Wight Co.	Williamsburg	Will Abstract	1776	Crozier, p. 31
Hill, Richard	Essex	Will	1764	Fleet 2:333
Hill, Richard	Essex	Will	1784	CF1806-002
Hill, Robert W., in Buckingham Co.	Prince Edward	Will	1890	CF1904-033
Hill, Russell, in Petersburg	Culpeper	Will	1838	CF1840-004
Hill, Samuel	Caroline	Will	1808	Note[1]
Hill, Samuel, merchant		Will	1695	VCRP, Survey #04715
Hill, Thomas, of St. Stephen's Parish	King & Queen	Will	1799	LVA Acc. #23634-6:30
Hill, William	Brunswick	Will Ref.	1791	VMHB 45, p. 87
Hill, William	Brunswick	Will	1799	CF1804-030
Hill, William	Brunswick	Will	1799	CF1833-028
Hill, Willoughby, mariner		Will	1703	VCRP, Survey #04123
Hillard, John, of James City Co.	Charles City	Will Ref.	1711	D&W1724, p. 208
Hillard, Richard	Charles City	Will	1774	LVA Acc. #23307
Hilliard, Benjamin F., in MD	Henrico	Will	1841	CF1848-003
Hillyard, Joseph	King William	Will	1830	BRCD
Hillyard, Joseph, in King William Co.	Henrico	Will	1830	CF1834-016
Hinds, Matthew	Fairfax	Account	1747	X
Hinds, Matthew	Fairfax	Admin. Bond	1750	X

---

[1] Fredericksburg City District, Superior Court Wills, Bk. A (A-3), 1789-1831, p. 291.

NAME	LOCATION	TYPE	YEAR	REFERENCE(S)
Hines, Thomas, in Prince Edward Co.	Lunenburg	Will	1849	CF1855-002
Hinton, Samuel, in Dinwiddie Co.	Lunenburg	Will	1789	CF1833-013
Hinton, Samuel, of Lancaster Co.	Mecklenburg	Will	1771	CF1824-075
Hite, Isaac		Will	1827	Fleet, Huntington Data
Hite, John, of Rockingham Co.	Augusta	Will	1822	CF1826-045
Hite, Joost	Frederick	Will	1761	LVA Acc. #24663
Hite, Margaret	D.C.	Will	1846	DCA:Box 18
Hitt, Nancy, in Madison Co.	Culpeper	Will	1876	CF1894-001
Hix, James, in Bedford Co.	Lynchburg	Will	1813	CF1839-008
Hix, James, of Prince Edward Co.	Cumberland	Will	1837	CF1845-042
Hix, Meshack	Goochland	Estate	(nd)	UVA MSS 4756
Hix, William	Surry	Inventory	1711	T:D&W6, p. 59
Hixon, Timothy, in Loudoun Co.	Frederick	Will	1812	CF1828-089
Hixon, Timothy, in Loudoun Co.	Frederick	Will	1812	CF1820-124
Hixon, Timothy, in Loudoun Co.	Frederick	Will	1812	CF1820-120
Hixson, Timothy, in Loudoun Co.	Frederick	Will	1812	CF1831-054
Hoard, William	Bedford	Will	1781	WB1, p. 398
Hoback, Levi, in Russell Co.	Wise	Will	1897	CF1916-008
Hobbs, Bernard	Prince George	Will	1823	SV 9:1, p. 19
Hobbs, Lamma W.	Dinwiddie	Will	1855	CF1879-018
Hobbs, Mary C.	Prince George	Will	1854	SV 9:4, p. 161
Hobbs, Thomas	Dinwiddie	Will	1872	CF1901-007
Hobbs, W.L.	Dinwiddie	Will	1877	CF1879-018
Hobson, John	Henrico	Inventory	1670	Records, Vol. 1, p. 53
Hobson, John	Henrico	Inventory	1769	Records, Vol. 6, p. 2029
Hobson, Mathew, in Halifax Co.	Franklin	Will	1814	CF1843-021
Hobson, Matthew	Henrico	Will	1772	Note[1]
Hobson, William	Henrico	Inventory	1718	Records, Vol. 2, p. 409
Hockaday, John	New Kent	Will	1799	Note[2]
Hockaday, Warwick	Charles City	Will Partial	1758	D&W1766, p. 174
Hodnett, Philip, in Buckingham Co.	Lynchburg	Will	1822	CF1826-016
Hoe, Elizabeth, of Rockingham Co.	Augusta	Will	1816	CF1829-004
Hoffman, Christian, in Shenandoah Co.	Frederick	Will	1825	CF1829-147
Hogg, Peter, in Rockingham Co.	Augusta	Will	1782	CF1805-031
Hoggard, Thurmer	Princess Anne	Will	1779	DB16, p. 64
Holbourne, William	Richmond	Will	1810	V:Mss1 T2118 d 996
Holbourne, William, in Richmond Co.	Essex	Will	1820	CF1842-012
Holden, George, of Gloucester Co.	Williamsburg	Will Abstract	1777	Crozier, p. 31
Holder, John	James City	Will	1687c	V:Mss1 Am167b
Holdsworth, Charles	Surry	Inventory	1792	WB12, p. 325
Holdsworth, Rebecca	Surry	Will	1790	T: correct from 1789
Holeman, Jacob	Shenandoah	Will	1784	LVA Acc. #39709
Holladay, Frances Ann, of *Prospect Hill*	Spotsylvania	Will	1878	V:Mss1 H7185 b 4240+
Holladay, James Minor	Spotsylvania	Will	1873	V:Mss1 H7185 b 8955+
Holladay, James Minor	Spotsylvania	Account	1893	V:Mss1 H7185 b 8955+
Holladay, John	Spotsylvania	Will	1742	V:Mss2 H7186 a1
Holladay, John	King William	Will	1842	V:Mss6:1 H7185:3

---

[1] Henrico County Proceedings of Commissioners ..., 1774-1782, p. 21.

[2] LVA, John K. Martin Papers, Box 6, Revolutionary War Claims H-J, Folder John Hockaday.

NAME	LOCATION	TYPE	YEAR	REFERENCE(S)
Holladay, John, in King William Co.	Spotsylvania	Will	1742	FDC L574-62
Holladay, Joseph	Spotsylvania	Will	1765	FDC L574-62
Holladay, Josiah	Nansemond	Will	1795	VTG 12:4, p. 143
Holladay, Josiah	Nansemond	Will	1795	SV 17:1, p. 33
Holladay, Josiah, of Nansemond Co.	Isle of Wight	Will (U)	1795	LVA:1161459
Holladay, Mary Waller, of *Prospect Hill*	Spotsylvania	Will	(nd)	V:Mss1 H7185 b 4240+
Holladay, Samuel	Isle of Wight	Appraisal	1716	W&D2, p. 608
Holland, Daniel	Northumberland	Inventory	1673	M: Box 3 folder 4
Holland, Michael	Louisa	Will	1746	V:Mss2 H7194 a1
Holland, Mills H.	Nansemond	Will	1897	BRCD
Hollar, Augustine, in Shenandoah Co.	Rockingham	Will	1830	CF1893-098
Hollings, John	King William	Inventory	1704	RB2, p. 27
Hollingshurst, Elizabeth	Charles City	Inventory		D&W1724, p. 223
Hollingshurst, Thomas	Charles City	Inventory	1725	D&W1724, p. 39
Hollins, Ann, in Campbell Co.	Lynchburg	Will	1877	CF1879-045
Hollinshurst, Elizabeth	Charles City	Inventory	1728	D&W1724, p. 233
Hollinshurst, Elizabeth, of Westover P.	Charles City	Will	1728	D&W1724, p. 213
Holloman, William	Surry	Inventory	1704	T: correct from 1706
Holloway, John	Caroline	Will	1770	W&P1742, p. 13
Holloway, Thomas	Nansemond	Will	1798	VG 38, p. 127
Holloway, Thomas	Nansemond	Will	1798	LVA Acc. #34696
Holloway, William	Spotsylvania	Will	1746	WBA, p. 431
Holloway, William	Brunswick	Will	1784	MVG 25:2, cover
Holman, James	Cumberland	Will	1763c	V:Mss1 H7315 a 1-6
Holman, James	Goochland	Will	1823c	V:Mss1 H7315 a 1-6
Holman, William Miller	Goochland	Will	1838	CF1853-015
Holman, William Miller	Goochland	Will	1838	V:Mss1 H7315 a 1-6
Holmes, Betsy, in CN	Lynchburg	Will	1878	CF1882-016
Holmes, David	Frederick	Will	1832	V:Mss1 C7637 a 302+
Holmes, Hugh, of Frederick Co.	D.C.	Will	1888	DCA:Box 108
Holmes, Thomas	Henrico	Inventory	1768	Records, Vol. 6, p. 2025
Holmes, William		Will	1649	VCRP, Survey #03997
Holt, Francis	Surry	Account	1769	T: correct from will
Holt, John H.	Richmond City	Will	1788	T:HCD1, p. 207
Holt, John, of Surry Co.	Williamsburg	Will Abstract	1783	Crozier, p. 31
Holt, Leonidas D., in Norfolk	Nansemond	Will	1900	CF1901-004
Holt, Leonidas D., of Norfolk	Nansemond	Will	1900	CF1901-004
Holt, Richard	Essex	Will	1791	CF1796-008
Holt, William	Williamsburg	Will	1791	Swem(3)
Holt, William	Williamsburg	Will Abstract	1791	Crozier, p. 30
Holt, William, in Williamsburg	Henrico	Will	1791	BRCD
Homan, Godleb	Rockingham	Will	1810	CF1850-005
Homes, John	Isle of Wight	Will (U)	1795	LVA:1161459
Homes, John	Isle of Wight	Will (U)	1795	SV 13:2, p. 85
Honyman, Robert	Hanover	Will	1824	CF1882-003
Honyman, Robert, Dr.	Hanover	Will Abstract	1824	Cocke:74
Hooe, Fanny, in King George Co.	Culpeper	Will	1830	CF1871-034
Hooe, James H., in Fairfax Co.	Arlington	Will	1824	CF1827-016
Hooe, John	Stafford	Will	1766	WBO, p. 506
Hooe, John	Stafford	Will	1766	TQ 09:3, p. 204
Hooe, John	Stafford	Will	1766	LVA Allason Letter Book

NAME	LOCATION	TYPE	YEAR	REFERENCE(S)
Hooe, John, in Prince William Co.	Arlington	Will	1798	CF1825-021
Hooe, Nathaniel		Will	(nd)	UVA Acc. #4492
Hooe, Nathaniel Harris	King George	Will	1844	UVA MSS 10548-a
Hooe, Thomas P.	Prince William	Will	1836	CF1844-004
Hooe, William F.	Fairfax	Guard. Bond	1822	X
Hooe, William F.	Fairfax	Guard. Acct.	1822	X
Hooe, William H., in King George Co.	Culpeper	Will	1818	CF1871-034
Hooff, Moore	Prince William	Will	1825	NVG 8, p. 1205
Hoofman, Valentine	Rockingham	Will	1803	LVA:1159583 t
Hoofman, Valentine [Hoffman, Huffman]	Rockingham	Will	1803	MVG 47:1, p. 71
Hook, John, in Franklin Co.	Bedford	Will	1808	CF1853-026
Hooker, Peter, tallow chandler		Will	1639	VCRP, Survey #03986
Hoomes, Benjamin	King & Queen	Will	1812	V:Mss3 K5893 a 69-86
Hoomes, Benjamin	King & Queen	Will	1812	LVA Acc. #24824
Hoomes, John	Caroline	Will	1806	LVA Acc. #24284
Hoomes, John, of Bowling Green Farm	Caroline	Will	1805	VMHB 38, p. 74
Hoomes, Thomas C.	King & Queen	Will	1821	LVA Acc. #24824
Hooper, John, in Berkeley Co.	Frederick	Will	1818	CF1828-033
Hoops, Adam, of Bucks Co. PA	Hanover	Will	1771	G2:64
Hoover, John	Lee	Will	1795	DB1, p. 54
Hoover, John, of Rockingham Co.	Augusta	Will	1830	CF1865-002
Hope, John	New Kent	Estate Ref.	1659	Hening, Vol. 1, p. 548
Hope, William, in Richmond	Louisa	Will	1837	CF1898-010
Hopegood, Peter	Rappahannock*	Will	1677	T: Note[1]
Hopkins, Archebald, Sr.	Rockingham	Will	1799	LVA Acc. #23772, 3-34
Hopkins, Archebald, Sr.		Will	1799	LVA Acc. #23772-3/34
Hopkins, James, in Amherst Co.	Lynchburg	Will	1803	CF1824-063
Hopkins, James, in Amherst Co.	Lynchburg	Will	1803	CF1849-010
Hopkins, John	Hanover	Inventory	1766	BRCD
Hopkins, John		Will	1766c	VCR 6, p. 286
Hopkins, John, of Hanover Co.	Louisa	Will	1766	Judgments 1825 JUN
Hopkins, John, of *Hill and Dale*	Frederick	Will	1822	V:Mss1 L51 f529-530
Hopkins, Joshua, of Princess Anne Co.	Williamsburg	Will Abstract	1795	Crozier, p. 29
Hopkinson, Daniell		Will	1637	VCRP, Survey #03976
Hopson, Elizabeth, in Pittsylvania Co.	Lynchburg	Will	1817	CF1830-061
Hord, Peter, of Brunswick Parish	Stafford	Will	1787	TQ 27:2, p. 109
Hord, Thomas, in LA	Fauquier	Will	1855	CF1876-046
Hord, Thomas, in Mecklenburg Co.	Lunenburg	Will	1799	CF1833-022
Hornbe, Robert, mariner		Will	1704	VCRP, Survey #04141
Horne, Isaac	Washington	Will	1875	CF1902-058
Horner, Gustavus B., in Fauquier Co.	Culpeper	Will	1815	CF1850-012
Horner, Gustavus B., in Fauquier Co.	Culpeper	Will	1815	CF1856-012
Horner, Gustavus Richard Brown	Fauquier	Will	1892	CF1896-043
Horner, William Edmonds, in PA	Fauquier	Will	1853	CF1872-065
Hornsby, Thomas	Patrick	Will	1808	LVA Acc. #41328
Hornsby, William	Williamsburg	Will Abstract	1805	Crozier, p. 29
Horsell, Judith	Stafford	Will	1699	WBZ, p. 18
Horseman, William, in Loudoun Co.	Frederick	Will	1815	CF1817-025

---

[1] Refer to Sweeny, pp. 9, 179, where the compiler lists wills given in *Torrence* that have not been found of record in Rappahannock County.

NAME	LOCATION	TYPE	YEAR	REFERENCE(S)
Horton, Daniel	Nansemond	Estate Ref.	1693	Hening, Vol. 4, p. 528
Horton, Jane	Northampton	Will	1666	D&W1657, p. 245
Horton, John	Stafford	Will	1792	FDC V559-72
Horton, Roy W.	Prince William	Will	1864	CF1885-009
Horton, Roy W.	Prince William	Will	1864	CF1870-009
Horton, Roy W.	Prince William	Will	1865	CF1906-013
Hoskins, William	King & Queen	Inventory	1802	LVA Webb-Smith Papers
Hotopp, William, in Albemarle Co.	Charlottesville	Will	1898	CF1900-005
Hottel, Henry, of Rockingham Co.	Augusta	Will	1815	CF1826-006
Hotzenpeller, Stephen	Frederick	Will	1776	WB4, p. 321
Hough, Joseph, in Loudoun Co.	Frederick	Will	1777	CF1822-077
Hough, William, in Loudoun Co.	Arlington	Will	1815	CF1873-003
Hough, William, in Loudoun Co.	Frederick	Will	1815	CF1818-065
Houke, Jacob, in Berkeley Co.	Frederick	Will	1814	CF1824-219
Houlsworth, Ann	Surry	Will	1675	T: correct from 1673
Houpt, George A., in PA	Bedford	Will	1893	CF1906-071
House, Henry	Brunswick	Will	1790	CF1809-028
Houston, Robert, in Caroline Co.	Essex	Will	1834	CF1836-005
Houston, Robert [of *Dogwood Grove*]	Caroline	Will	1827	W&P1742, p. 120
Howard, Benjamin	Charles City	Inventory	1726	D&W1724, p. 123, 162
Howard, Benjamin	Charles City	Inventory	1726	D&W1724, p. 123
Howard, Benjamin	Charles City	Inventory	1727	D&W1724, p. 162
Howard, Benjamin, of James City Co.	Charles City	Will	1725	D&W1724, p. 52
Howard, James C., in Bedford Co.	Campbell	Will	1845	CF1859-016
Howard, John Beale	Fairfax	Will	1835	X
Howard, John Beale, of Baltimore Co.	Fairfax	Will	1836	CF1869-008
Howard, Major, in Floyd Co.	Franklin	Will	1859	CF1876-008
Howard, Margaret, in MD	Fairfax	Will	1844	CF1869-008
Howard, Margaret, of Baltimore Co. MD	Fairfax	Will	1845	CF1869-008
Howard, Mary, in Clarke Co.	Frederick	Will	1854	CF1859-075
Howard, Reuben	Hanover	Estate Ref.	1820	LP:20 JAN 1824
Howard, Samuel	Fairfax	Will	1860	X
Howard, Sarah M., in Williamsburg	James City	Will	1856	CF1896-014
Howard, Thomas, Sr.	York	Will	1824	CF1837-003
Howell, George	Richmond	Inventory	1699	V:Mss4 R4143 a 1
Howell, Samuel, in IL	Roanoke	Will	1835	CF1839-007
Howerton, Ann W., of King & Queen Co.	Halifax	Will	1846	CF1849-036
Howerton, Robert G.	King & Queen	Will	1854	CF1872-004
Howerton, Robert G.	King & Queen	Will	1854	LVA Acc. #41853
Howerton, Thomas, in NC	Mecklenburg	Will	1824	CF1840-006 CSC
Howett, John, of Elizabeth City Co.	London	Will	1659	N:PROB11/294
Howett, John, of Elizabeth City Co.	London	Will	1659	VCRP, Survey #03521
Howison, Allen	Prince William	Will	1875	CF1884-003
Howison, Catherine M.	Prince William	Acct. Ref.	1843	CM:04 SEP 1843
Howison, Catherine M.	Prince William	Acct. Ref.	1843	CM:06 NOV 1843
Howison, Jane	Prince William	Will	1866	CF1878-017
Howison, Stephen	Prince William	Will	1854	CF1878-017
Howison, Thomas	Culpeper	Will	1769	FDC L673-96
Howle, Pulaski	New Kent	Estate Ref.	1842	LP:03 MAR 1842
Howsing, Judah	Northumberland	Will	1772	CF1791-002
Hoye, William	Arlington	Inventory	1800	CRA:317

NAME	LOCATION	TYPE	YEAR	REFERENCE(S)
Hoye, William	Arlington	Will	1800	CRA:305
Hoyle, Samuel	Essex	Will	1707	DB13, p. 36
Hubball, William	Fairfax	Account	1844	X
Hubbard, Bowles	New Kent	Will	1848	Note [1]
Hubbard, James	Gloucester	Will	1785	Note [2]
Hubbard, Jesse	Lancaster	Will	1849	CF1111-008
Hubbard, John	Gloucester	Will	1779	Note [3]
Hubbard, Matthew	New Kent	Will	1814	Swem(1):f218
Hubbard, William Hedges	Richmond City	Will	1865c	V:Mss1 G1774 a 86-92
Hubberd, Filmer M.	York	Will	1835	CF1847-003
Huberd, Mathew	Charles City	Division S.	1724	D&W1724, p. 17
Huckstep, John, in Greene Co.	Albemarle	Will	1853	CF1882-052
Huckstep, Samuel, of King & Queen Co.	London	Will	1696	N:PROB11/433
Huckstep, Samuel, of King & Queen Co.		Will	1696	VCRP, Survey #04718
Hudgins, Archibald	Mathews	Will	1843	TVF 4:4, p. 256
Hudgins, Archibald	Mathews	Will	1851	BRCD
Hudgins, Houlder	Mathews	Will	1815	TVF 8:3, p. 170
Hudgins, Houlder	Mathews	Will	1816	Note [4]
Hudgins, Houlder	Mathews	Will	1816	Note [5]
Hudgins, James	Cumberland	Will	1823	V:Mss6:1 H8664:1
Hudgins, Johnson	Mathews	Will	1863	LVA Acc. #25302
Hudgins, Ransom	Nottoway	Will	1803	SV 14:3, p. 123
Hudnall, Thomas	Prince William	Will	1740	LVA Acc. #24961-3
Hudson, Bryan	Rappahannock*	Will Ref.	1687	Sweeny, p. 5
Hudson, Charles, of St. Paul's Parish	Hanover	Will	1748	VGSQ 20:2, p. 59
Hudson, Christopher, in Amelia Co.	Powhatan	Will	1789	CF1839-007
Hudson, George	Hanover	Will	1773	VMHB 66, p. 85
Hudson, George	Hanover	Will	1773	V:Mss2 H8678 a 1
Hudson, Isaac	Rappahannock*	Will	1687	Sweeny, p. 138
Hudson, Jesse	Kanawha	Will	1869	V:Mss1 P4299 g 64-69
Hudson, John	Accomack	Will Original	1677	M: Box H folder 139
Hudson, John	Albemarle	Will	1769	V:Mss2 H8681 a 1
Hudson, John, in Albemarle Co.	Bedford	Will	1801	CF1811-025
Hudson, Joshua	Amherst	Will	1799	CF1805-014
Hudson, Peter	Halifax	Will	1752	LVA Acc. #27547
Hudson, Peter	Halifax	Will	1752	V:Mss2 H8687 a 1
Hudson, Peter	Halifax	Will	1753	LVA Acc. #26196
Hudson, Robert	Culpeper	Will	1872	Swem
Hudson, William	Dinwiddie	Will	1790	Note [6]
Hudson, William	Halifax	Will	1802	V:Mss1 R5595 a 4,241+
Hudspeath, Ralph	Henrico	Will	1719	Records, Vol. 2, p. 469
Hudspeth, Ralph	Henrico	Will	1719	V:Mss2 H8695 a 1
Hues, Richard	Fredericksburg	Will	1713	Note [7]

---

[1] New Kent County Wills, Bk. 2, 1880-1938, p. 7, at the courthouse only.

[2] LVA, U.S. Circuit Court Records, Bk. 17 (Richmond), p. 518.

[3] LVA, U.S. Circuit Court Records, Bk. 17 (Richmond), p. 519.

[4] LVA, U.S. Circuit Court Records, Box 136, *Cay's Exors. v. Hudgins' Exors.* (1833)

[5] LVA, U.S. Circuit Court Records, Bk. 20, p. 539.

[6] LVA, Land Office Certificates, Box 30, Folder 25; also Virginia Land Office Military Certificates, Reel 17.

[7] Fredericksburg Superior Court of Chancery, Land Causes and Appeals, 1814-1815, p. 245.

NAME	LOCATION	TYPE	YEAR	REFERENCE(S)
Hues, Richard	Northumberland	Will	1713	FDC V569-1
Huffman, Jacob, in Botetourt Co.	Roanoke	Will	1814	CF1849-006
Hughes, Frances Thruston, *Benvenue*	Gloucester	Will	1849	V:Mss2 H8749 b 15
Hughes, Frances Thruston, *Benvenue*	Gloucester	Will	1852	V:Mss2 H8749 b 16
Hughes, Frances Thruston, *Benvenue*	Gloucester	Will	1853	V: Mss1 M7607 a 309
Hughes, John	Warwick	Will	1823	BRCD
Hughes, John, of St. Paul's Parish	Hanover	Will	1815	Cocke:75
Hughes, Mary	Hanover	Will	1850	V:Mss2 F9599 b 40-42
Hughes, Rachel	King William	Will	1876	LVA Acc. #38260
Hughes, Ralph	Frederick	Will	1767	MVG 29:3, p. 191
Hughes, Reubin	Hanover	Will	1814	LVA Acc. #20301a
Hughes, Robert, mariner		Will	1727	VCRP, Survey #04644
Hughes, Thomas, in Culpeper Co.	Rappahannock	Will	1833	CF1844-012
Hughes, William, in Amherst Co.	Lynchburg	Will	1802	CF1833-032
Huidekoper, Frank C., in MA	Washington	Will	1890	CF1906-136
Hull, Peter, of Pendleton Co.	Augusta	Will	1818	CF1823-071
Hull, Richard	Northumberland	Will Ref.	1693	OB5, pp. 511, 608
Hull, Robert	Arlington	Inventory	1799	CRA:282
Hull, Thomas T., in Smyth Co.	Tazewell	Will	1851	CF1874-012
Hulls, George	Fairfax	Will	1854	NVG 8, p. 1100
Hume, Charles, in Madison Co.	Culpeper	Will	1831	CF1836-005
Humphrey, Joseph	Essex	Will	1706	DB12, p. 332
Hundley, Charles	Hanover	Will	1797	CF1838-002
Hundley, Charles	Hanover	Will	1797	Cocke:17
Hundley, George K., in Hanover Co.	King & Queen	Will	1866	CF1879-009
Hundley, Matthew [of *Catalpa Grove*]	Caroline	Will	1829	Weisiger 1:075
Huniford, Phill	Surry	Inventory	1687	T:D&W4, p. 10a
Hunley, John	Essex	Will	1796	CF1818-005
Hunley, Wilkinson, in Gloucester Co.	Amelia	Will	1772	CF1817-029
Hunley, Wilkinson, of Kingston Parish	Gloucester	Will Abstract	1747	Mason, Vol. 2, p. 67
Hunnicutt, Lemuel, in Prince George Co.	Petersburg	Will	1848	CF1868-030
Hunnicutt, Lemuel, of Pr. Geo. Co.	Prince Edward	Will	1848	Free Negro Records Box 2
Hunt, David, in Pittsylvania Co.	Lynchburg	Will	1826	CF1835-002
Hunt, George	Charles City	Will	1725	D&W1724, p. 59
Hunt, George	Charles City	Inventory	1725	D&W1724, p. 63
Hunt, George	Charles City	Account	1728	D&W1724, p. 201
Hunt, John	Charles City	Will	1731	D&W1724, p. 339
Hunt, John	Charles City	Will	1731	D&W1724, p. 339
Hunt, John	Charles City	Will	1731	D&W1724, p. 339
Hunt, Mimucan, in Granville Co. NC	Henry	Will	1808	CF1846-003
Hunt, Tabitha	Charles City	Inventory	1725	D&W1724, p. 20
Hunt, Thomas		Will	1813	UVA Acc. #1228
Hunt, William	Charles City	Inventory	1715	D&W1724, p. 20
Hunt, William	Charles City	Division	1716	D&W1724, p. 20
Hunter, Absolem M., in Montgomery Co.	Campbell	Will	1851	CF1858-020
Hunter, Adam, of Stafford Co.	Fredericksburg	Will	1798	DCWA, p. 94
Hunter, Alexander, of *Abingdon*	D.C.	Will	1849	DCA:Box 20
Hunter, Anne	Essex	Will Abstract	1717	Fleet 2:326
Hunter, Dangerfield	Augusta	Will	1856	V:Mss2 H9167 a 1

NAME	LOCATION	TYPE	YEAR	REFERENCE(S)
Hunter, Ichabod	Richmond City	Will	1799	Note[1]
Hunter, Ichabod	Richmond City	Will	1799	T:HCD2, p. 554
Hunter, James	Stafford	Will	1784	Note[2]
Hunter, James	Stafford	Will	1784	FDC L392-76
Hunter, John	Fairfax	Will	1815	X
Hunter, John	Fairfax	Inventory	1817	X
Hunter, John, in Westmoreland Co.	Richmond	Will	1855	CF1869-005
Hunter, John, of Norfolk	London	Will	1783	N:PROB11/1102
Hunter, Josiah W., in Norfolk Co.	Princess Anne	Will	1811	CF1835-022
Hunter, Louisa, in Richmond	Arlington	Will	1864	CF1880-002
Hunter, Louisa, of Washington DC	Arlington	Will	1866	WB8:300; File #641A
Hunter, Peter, Sr., in Bedford Co.	Campbell	Will	1835	CF1909-044
Hunter, Robert H., in Alexandria Co.	Alexandria	Will	1858	CF1872-001
Hupp, Elizabeth, in IN	Rockingham	Will	1884	CF1896-012
Hurley, Margaret Jane, in Lynchburg	Campbell	Will	1898	CF1900-018
Hurry, John	Fairfax	Will	1804	M:LAL2 f22
Hurst, Henry	Northumberland	Will	1798	CF1804-021
Hurst, John	Fairfax	Will	1789	CF1849-005
Hurst, Joseph	Northumberland	Will	1789	CF1812-025
Hurst, Kemp	Northumberland	Will	1794	CF1809-018
Hurt, Benjamin	Caroline	Will	1835	W&D1794, p. 34
Hurt, Benjamin [of Thornhill]	Caroline	Will	1781	LVA Acc. #22591a
Hurt, Moses, in Amelia Co.	Lunenburg	Will	1814	CF1814-011
Husband, Edward	Henrico	Inventory	1683	Records, Vol. 1, p. 61
Hussey, Giles		Will	1669	Note[3]
Huston, Archibald, of Augusta Co.	Rockingham	Will	1774	LVA:1159583
Hutcherson, David H.	Charlotte	Will	1813	V:Mss1 H3968 a 897+
Hutcherson, Sarah R.	Louisa	Will	1873	CF1908-012
Hutcheson, John [of *Locust Hill*]	Caroline	Will	1812	LVA Acc. #30739
Hutchings, John		Will Ref.	1790	Hening, Vol. 13, p. 226
Hutchison, Elizabeth, in Loudoun Co.	Fairfax	Will	1875	CF1875-005
Hutchison, John	Prince William	Inv. Ref.	1844	CM:04 MAR 1844
Hutchison, John	Prince William	Sale Ref.	1844	CM:04 MAR 1844
Hutchison, Joshua	Fairfax	Inventory	1842	X
Hutchison, Joshua	Fairfax	Account	1844	X
Hutchison, Joshua, Capt.	Fairfax	Sale	1842	X
Hutchison, Mary Ann	Fairfax	Inventory	1845	X
Hutson, William, Stratton Major Parish	King & Queen	Will	1815	LP:19 DEC 1815
Hutton, Arthur	Washington	Will	1873	LVA Acc. #33608
Hutton, Dixon	Washington	Will	1835	LVA Acc. #33608
Hyde, Henry, Sir		Will	1660	VCRP, Survey #03525
Hylton, George	Floyd	Will	1845	V:Mss1 J6496 a 1 151-1
Hylton, George, in Nelson Co.	Lynchburg	Will	1813	CF1826-076
Hylton, John, of Chesterfield Co.	Cumberland	Will	1774	CF1792-006

[1] Richmond City Hustings Court Deeds, No. 2, 1792-1799, p. 554.
[2] LVA, U.S. Circuit Court Records, Box 131, *Backhouse's Admin. v. Hunter's Admin.* (1831), Folder 5.
[3] Northern Neck Land Grants, Bk. 1, 1690-1692, p. 131.

NAME	LOCATION	TYPE	YEAR	REFERENCE(S)

I

NAME	LOCATION	TYPE	YEAR	REFERENCE(S)
Iden, Jacob J.	Fairfax	Sale	1860	X
Indan, Willoughby		Will Ref.	1853	CW(5)
Ingo, James, Gent.	Richmond	Will Ref.	1722	Winfree, p. 376
Ingram, Ann	Northumberland	Will	1733	LVA Acc. #25878
Ingram, Ann	Northumberland	Will	1733	CF1789-003
Ingram, Ann		Will	1733	LVA Acc. #25878
Ingram, John	Brunswick	Will	1763	CF1791-010
Ingram, Joseph		Will	1653	VCRP, Survey #03121
Ingram, William	Charles City	Inventory	1729	D&W1724, p. 275
Innes, Rebecca	Gloucester	Inventory	1827	LVA, misc. Reel #547
Innes, Rebecca (Lewis)	Gloucester	Will	1826	VGS Bulletin V, p. 10
Innis, Rebecca	Gloucester	Will	1800	CF1898-035
Insull, John, cook		Will	1694	VCRP, Survey #06048
Irby, Edmund, Martins Brandon	Prince George	Will	1733	LVA Acc. #22465
Irby, Hardyman, of Charles City Co.	Williamsburg	Will Abstract	1798	Crozier, p. 32
Irbye, Walter, of Northampton Co.	London	Will	1652	N:PROB11/222
Irbye, Walter, of Northampton Co.		Will	1652	VCRP, Survey #04103
Ironmonger, John	Surry	Will (N)	1691	T:D&W4, p. 242b
Ironmonger, Mary	Surry	Inventory	1693	T:D&W4, p. 307a
Ironmonger, Thomas	Surry	Inventory	1691	T:D&W4, p. 213a
Irvine, Walter	Buckingham	Estate Ref.	1807	LP:24 DEC 1807
Irwin, Bedford Morris, of Warwick Co.	Williamsburg	Will Abstract	1779	Crozier, p. 32
Isaacson, William deStuteville, Rev.	Albemarle	Will	1874	VMHB 37, p. 165
Isabell, James [Isbell]	Caroline	Guard. Appt.	1799	BRCD
Isbell, Daniel, of Caroline Co.	Halifax	Will	1768	CF1808-011
Isbell, Daniel [Isbel]	Caroline	Will	1767	LVA Acc. #24642-7
Isbell, James D., in Cumberland Co.	Powhatan	Will	1862	CF1871-020
Isham, Henry, of Henrico Co.		Will	1680	VCRP, Survey #03722
Ishman, Henry, of Henrico Co.	London	Will	1680	N:PROB11/363
Isman, John	Charles City	Inventory	1725	D&W1724, p. 58
Isman, John	Charles City	Inventory	1725	D&W1724, p. 58
Ives, Thomas, of Ipswich		Will	1663	VCRP, Survey #07815
Ivy, John	Norfolk	Will	1777	LVA Acc. #26080
Ivy, Martha Ann, in Norfolk Co.	Portsmouth	Will	1873	CF1882-011

NAME	LOCATION	TYPE	YEAR	REFERENCE(S)
J				
Jackman, Joseph John, of Surry Co.	London	Will	1714	N:PROB11/540
Jackson, David, in Charles City Co.	Chesterfield	Will	1803	CF1843-015
Jackson, Elvira S., of Hooper's Rock	Cumberland	Will	1892	Fleet, Huntington Data
Jackson, Fips	York	Will	1770	V:Mss1 L51 b27-28
Jackson, Francis, II	Amelia	Will	1811	LVA Acc. #36255-43
Jackson, Francis, Sr.	Amelia	Will	1792	LVA Acc. #36255-43
Jackson, Henry	Warwick	Will	1661	Miscellany 1648, p. 46
Jackson, Henry	Brunswick	Will	1789	CF1819-055
Jackson, Henry	Brunswick	Will	1789	CF1795-016
Jackson, Henry Clay	Fairfax	Guard. Bond	1840	X
Jackson, Henry, Sr.	Warwick	Will	1659	Miscellany 1648, p. 54
Jackson, Henry, Sr.	Warwick	Will	1756	Note[1]
Jackson, Jane	Nottoway	Will	1856	BRCD
Jackson, Jane, in Nottoway Co.	Petersburg	Will	1856	CF1860-022
Jackson, John	Lancaster	Will	1661	LP
Jackson, John, Sr.	Isle of Wight	Will	1762	T: correct from Henrico
Jackson, John, Sr., in Loudoun Co.	Frederick	Will	1821	CF1822-275
Jackson, John Thomas Jefferson	Fairfax	Will	1851	X
Jackson, Joseph	Dinwiddie	Will	179_	LVA Acc. #27293b
Jackson, Joseph	Dinwiddie	Will	179_	VG 16, p. 165
Jackson, Joseph John, of Surry Co.		Will	1714	VCRP, Survey #04362
Jackson, Julia Ann	Fairfax	Guard. Bond	1840	X
Jackson, Mary	Isle of Wight	Will	1761	T: correct from Henrico
Jackson, Molly E., wid., in Baltimore MD	Gloucester	Will	1862	CF1882-017
Jackson, Patsy, of Richmond	Henrico	Will	1812	VGSQ 18:3, p. 81
Jackson, Richard	Chesterfield	Will	(nd)	V: BX5199.B53
Jackson, Richard	Chesterfield	Inventory	(nd)	V: BX5199.B53
Jackson, Richard	Isle of Wight	Will	1703	T: not Henrico Co.
Jackson, Richard	Isle of Wight	Will	1741	T: not Henrico Co.
Jackson, Richard	Fairfax	Division	1870	X
Jackson, Robert, in Charlotte Co.	Lunenburg	Will	1791	CF1808-015
Jackson, Robert W.	Fairfax	Guard. Bond	1840	X
Jackson, Spencer	Fairfax	Inventory	1831	X
Jackson, Spencer	Fairfax	Account	1852	X
Jackson, Turner	Charles City	Inventory	1770	Records, p. 241
Jackson, William	Henrico	Will	1739	Records, Vol. 4, p. 1095
Jackson, William	Brunswick	Will	1741	WB2, p. 30
Jacob, Rosamond		Will	1688	V:Mss1 B4678 a 4788
Jacobs, Alfred	Fairfax	Guard. Acct.	1840	X
Jacobs, Harrison	Fairfax	Guard. Acct.	1840	X
Jacobs, John, Sr., in Nelson Co.	Lynchburg	Will	1819	CF1824-055
Jago, John (C), cook		Will	1739	VCRP, Survey #04654
James, Ann	Charles City	Will	1673	OB1672, p. 539
James, Francis	King George	Will	1721	DB1, p. 6
James, Henry	Charles City	Will	1673	OB1672, p. 538
James, John, of James City Co.	Williamsburg	Will Abstract	1818	Crozier, p. 33

---

[1] LVA, Warwick County Miscellany, 1648-1875, p. 54.

NAME	LOCATION	TYPE	YEAR	REFERENCE(S)
James, Mary	Stafford	Will	1833	Note[1]
James, Susannah	Caroline	Will	1831	W&D1794, p. 27
James, Thomas	King George	Will	1851	CF1898-034
James, [blank]	Fauquier	Will	(nd)	CF1849-014
James, [blank]	Fauquier	Will	(nd)	CF1850-008
Jameson, Alexander	Dinwiddie	Estate Ref.	1797	LP:18 DEC 1797
Jameson, James	Essex	Will	1736	Fleet 2:300
Janey, Joseph, of *Bowler's Wharf*	Essex	Will	1832	V:Mss1 H7935 a 1
Janney, Blackston, in Loudoun Co.	Frederick	Will	1812	CF1833-136
Janney, Daniel, in Loudoun Co.	Fairfax	Will	1859	CF1860-010
Janney, Sarah S., in Alexandria	Frederick	Will	1853	CF1884-015
Jaquelin, Martha	Richmond City	Will	1793	T:HCD2, p. 70
Jardine, Robert S., of Madison Co.	London	Will	1815	N:PROB11/1575
Jarrat, W.N., of Sussex Co.	Nansemond	Will	1881	CF1896-017
Jarratt, Ann	Surry	Will	1784	WB12, p. 26
Jarratt, Ann	Surry	Will	1784	WB12, p. 26
Jarratt, W.N., in Sussex Co.	Nansemond	Will	1881	CF1896-017
Jarrell, James	Culpeper	Account	1795	WBC, p. 434
Jarrell, Olivia, in Albemarle Co.	Greene	Will	1876	CF1920-003
Jarrell, Thomas	Surry	Will	1713	T: correct from Farrell
Jarvis, Thomas, merchant		Will	1684	VCRP, Survey #03729
Jarvis, William, of York Co.	Williamsburg	Will Abstract	1824	Crozier, p. 33
Jefferies, Thomas	King & Queen	Will	1827	WMQ2 15, p. 79
Jefferson, Field	Mecklenburg	Will	1765	WB1, p. 4
Jefferson, Jane	Albemarle	Will	1778c	UVA MSS 830
Jefferson, Peter	Albemarle	Inventory	(nd)	UVA MSS 1364
Jefferson, Peter	Albemarle	Will	1757c	UVA MSS 1364
Jefferson, Thomas	Henrico	Will	1731c	UVA MSS 825
Jefferson, Thomas	Albemarle	Will	1826	LVA Acc. #21505
Jefferson, Thomas	Albemarle	Will	1826	UVA MSS 5145
Jeffress, Jennings M., of Charlotte Co.	Mecklenburg	Will	1852	CF1859-007
Jeffreys, William, mariner		Will	1694	VCRP, Survey #06046
Jeffreys, William, mariner		Will	1715	VCRP, Survey #04364
Jeffries, Marcey Godfrey, Mecklenburg	Essex	Will	1795	CF1812-001
Jeffries, Nathaniel	Buckingham	Will	1793	SV 3:3, p. 122
Jeffries, Nathaniel	Buckingham	Will	1795	TQ 27:1, p. 57
Jenifer, Walter Hanson, in MD	Fauquier	Will	1786	CF1851-002
Jenkins, Aaron	Frederick	Will	1759	MVG 29:3, p. 191
Jenkins, Charles	Westmoreland	Inventory	1707	OB1705, p. 76
Jenkins, Charles Tyler	Fairfax	Will	1857	WB2:009
Jenkins, Exum, in Nansemond Co.	Southampton	Will	1866	CF1868-020
Jenkins, Exum, of Nansemond Co.	Southampton	Will	1866	CF1868-011
Jenkins, Henry	Fairfax	Will	1860	X
Jenkins, John, of Chesterfield Co.	Cumberland	Will	1818	CF1860-020
Jenkins, Samuel	Fairfax	Account	1826	X
Jenkins, Sarah	Elizabeth City	Will	1842	LP:18 JAN 1843
Jenkins, Silas, in Culpeper Co.	Rappahannock	Will	1832	CF1884-005
Jenkins, Silas, in Culpeper Co.	Rappahannock	Will	1832	CF1847-006

---

[1] LVA, U.S. Circuit Court Records, Virginia District, Box 142, *Buchan v. Buchan & Seddon* (1838).

NAME	LOCATION	TYPE	YEAR	REFERENCE(S)
Jenkins, William, Capt., in Cabell Co.	Lynchburg	Will	1860	CF1870-029
Jennings, Allen, in Prince Edward Co.	Campbell	Will	1821	CF1853-007
Jennings, Daniel, in Loudoun Co.	Arlington	Will	1783	CF1817-024
Jennings, Lewis T.S., in TN	Fauquier	Will	1854	CF1855-035
Jennings, Mary	Cumberland	Will	1791	Note[1]
Jennings, Mary	Hanover	Will	1791	LVA Acc. #28460
Jennings, Mary, of Hanover Co.	Cumberland	Will	1791	CF1861-005
Jennings, Needler Robinson	Richmond City	Will	1892	V:Mss1 M9924 a 139+
Jennings, Robert, of St. Paul's Parish	Hanover	Will	1758	LVA Acc. #21035
Jennings, Robert P., in Nottoway Co.	Prince Edward	Will	1862	CF1868-008
Jennings, Sarah, in Louisa Co.	Goochland	Will	1828	CF1847-007
Jennings, Theodocia	Hanover	Will	1725	Note[2]
Jennings, William	Henrico	Will	1851	CF1905-033
Jerdone, Elizabeth		Will	1623	Swem(3)
Jerdone, Francis	Louisa	Will	1770	WMQ2 11, p. 7
Jerdone, Francis	Louisa	Will	1770	Swem(3)
Jerdone, Francis		Inventory	1841	Swem(3)
Jerdone, George		Will	1633	Swem(3)
Jerdone, John		Will	1627	Swem(3)
Jerdone, Sarah		Will	1813	Swem(3)
Jerdone, Sarah	Louisa	Will	1818	CW(1)
Jesse, William, in Middlesex Co.	Essex	Will	1840	CF1888-032
Jeter, Henry, in Bedford Co.	Lynchburg	Will	1807	CF1830-123
Jeter, James M., in Amelia Co.	Powhatan	Will	1844	CF1851-012
Jett, Francis	Stafford	Will	1791	FDC L563-52
Jett, Francis	Stafford	Will	1794	TQ 20:4, p. 234
Jett, Francis	Stafford	Will	1794	FDC L574-60
Jett, John	Westmoreland	Inventory	1762	T: not Richmond
Jett, Margaret	Westmoreland	Will	1739	T: not Richmond
Jett, Peter	Westmoreland	Will	1739	T: not Richmond
Jett, Susan, in Rappahannock Co.	Fauquier	Will	1850	CF1886-022
Jewett, Mollie J., in Chesterfield Co.	Henrico	Will	1887	CF1888-001
Jewett, Thomas, Sr., in Chesterfield Co.	Henrico	Will	1851	CF1888-001
Jewry, William	Isle of Wight	Will Abstract	1651	VMHB 6, p. 248
John, Daniel, in Pittsylvania Co.	Campbell	Will	1850	CF1853-023
John, Polly	Rockingham	Will	1856	CF1859-030
Johns, Richard	King William	Will	1703	RB2, p. 21
Johnson, Anderson W., in Louisa Co.	Goochland	Will	1832	CF1837-012
Johnson, Andrew, mariner		Will	1708	VCRP, Survey #03900
Johnson, Benjamin	Prince William	Will	1881	CF1883-007
Johnson, Caroline	Chesterfield	Will	1849	Fleet, Huntington Data
Johnson, Edward	Lancaster	Will	1688	LP
Johnson, Francis	Charles City	Account	1770	Records, p. 203
Johnson, Isaac, in Chesterfield Co.	Lynchburg	Will	1807	CF1827-002
Johnson, James	Lunenburg	Will	1787	CF1789-001
Johnson, James	Louisa	Will (N)	1792	Note[3]

---

[1] Cumberland County Loose Papers, Box 30, cause *Bailey v. Foster* (March 1861).
[2] William H. Dabney, *Sketch of the Dabneys of Virginia* (1888), p. 38.
[3] Louisa County Wills Not Fully Proven, 1757-1902, p. 29.

NAME	LOCATION	TYPE	YEAR	REFERENCE(S)
Johnson, James	Louisa	Will	1792	Note[1]
Johnson, James, in Pittsylvania Co.	Bedford	Will	1817	CF1828-028
Johnson, James, in Pittsylvania Co.	Lynchburg	Will	1817	CF1836-004
Johnson, James, in Pittsylvania Co.	Lynchburg	Will	1817	CF1827-064
Johnson, Jeffery, of Hamilton Parish	Prince William	Will	1758	Land Office
Johnson, Jeoffry	Prince William	Will	1758	MVG 29:3, p. 191
Johnson, John	Northumberland	Will	1720	FDC V569-1
Johnson, John	Charles City	Inventory	1729	D&W1724, p. 275
Johnson, John	Washington	Admin. Bond	1795	LVA Acc. #42953
Johnson, John, mariner		Will	1682	VCRP, Survey #03728
Johnson, John, of Westover Parish	Charles City	Will	1730	D&W1724, p. 272
Johnson, Joshua	Sussex	Will	1794	WBE, p. 354
Johnson, Luke, planter		Will	1659	VCRP, Survey #03522
Johnson, Martin	Orange	Will	1820	V:Mss1 B2346 a 1155
Johnson, Michael	Henrico	Inventory	1719	Records, Vol. 2, p. 437
Johnson, Peter, mariner		Will	1693	VCRP, Survey #03954
Johnson, Peyton	Buckingham	Will	1845	LVA Acc. #26247
Johnson, Rebecca, of King William Co.	New Kent	Will	1844	Swem(1):f221
Johnson, Richard	King & Queen	Will Ref.	1695	Hening, Vol. 5, p. 114
Johnson, Richard	King William	Inventory	1704	RB1, p. 240
Johnson, Richard	King & Queen	Will Ref.	1733	Hening, Vol. 8, p. 455
Johnson, Richard	Buckingham	Will	1831	Election[2]
Johnson, Richard	Buckingham	Will	1831	SV 5:1, p. 4
Johnson, Richard H.	Hanover	Will	1849	LVA Acc. #41008, r4609
Johnson, Richard H.	Hanover	Will	1849	Fleet, Huntington Data
Johnson, Richard, in Buckingham Co.	Lynchburg	Will	1831	CF1866-012
Johnson, Robert	Frederick	Will	1863	MVG 29:3, p. 191
Johnson, Samuel, in MD		Will	1741	VCRP, Survey #04381
Johnson, Sarah	Henrico	Will (N)	1660	VG 20, p. 6
Johnson, Sarah	Henrico	Inventory	1660	Records, Vol. 1, p. 13
Johnson, Sarah	Henrico	Will (N)	1660	Records, Vol. 1, p. 13
Johnson, Solomon	Nansemond	Will	1853	LVA, Kilby Family Papers
Johnson, Thomas		Estate Ref.	1740	Hening, Vol. 5, p. 115
Johnson, William		Will cod.	1849	V:Mss1 G8626 a 135+
Johnson, William Quarles, in TN	Louisa	Will	1855	CF1860-001
Johnston, James	Northumberland	Will	1717	RB8, p. 139
Johnston, James	Northumberland	Will	1717	RB8, p. 139
Johnston, James	Isle of Wight	Will	1805	UVA Acc. #38-463
Johnston, John	Caroline	Will	1786	W&P1742, p. 37
Johnston, Mary	Henrico	Will	1825	VGSQ 18:3, p. 81
Johnston, Peter	Washington	Inventory	1832	LVA Acc. #20389
Johnston, Rebecah	Surry	Will (U)	1821	VTG 13:3, p. 124
Johnston, Rebeccah	Surry	Will Abstract	1821	VG 13, p. 54
Johnston, Robert	Caroline	Will	1780	LVA Acc. #30172
Johnston, William	Fairfax	Account	1801	X
Jolly, Edward	Charles City	Account	1727	D&W1724, p. 173
Jolly, Edward	Charles City	Account	1727	D&W1724, p. 173

---

[1] Louisa County Wills Not Fully Proven, 1757-1902, p. 29.
[2] LVA, Contested Election Papers, Buckingham County, 1840/41.

NAME	LOCATION	TYPE	YEAR	REFERENCE(S)
Jolly, Sophia, in PA	Louisa	Will	1851	CF1899-031
Jones, Abraham	Prince George	Will	1743	Swem(2)
Jones, Abraham	Isle of Wight	Will	1758	TQ 08:4, p. 280
Jones, Abraham, Jr., of Pr. George Co.	Mecklenburg	Will	1744	CF1794-014
Jones, Allbridgton	Warwick	Will	1718	VGSQ 50:4, p. 264
Jones, Allen, of Bourbon	London	Will	1792	N:PROB11/1224
Jones, Alpheus M., in Lunenburg Co.	Prince Edward	Will	1850	CF1868-003
Jones, Ann	Dinwiddie	Will	1809	BRCD
Jones, Ann	Dinwiddie	Will	1811	SV 2:1, p. 6
Jones, Ann, in Dinwiddie Co.	Brunswick	Will	1809	CF1828-058
Jones, Anne, wid.	Isle of Wight	Will	1704	TQ 08:4, p. 279
Jones, Anthony	Isle of Wight	Will	1649	VMHB 6, p. 245
Jones, Anthony	Isle of Wight	Will	1649	TQ 08:4, p. 278
Jones, Arthur, of Bermuda		Will	1692	VG 43, p. 227
Jones, Benjamin, in Greensville Co.	Brunswick	Will	1821	CF1857-029
Jones, Bennet	Caroline	Will	1834	Weisiger 1:073
Jones, Binnes	Brunswick	Will	1791	CF1839-033
Jones, Cadwaller, in Clark Co. KY	Fairfax	Will	1862	CF1903-027
Jones, Catherine H.	Henrico	Will	1837	VGSQ 18:3, p. 82
Jones, Christopher T., of Dinwiddie Co.	Lancaster	Will	1819	LP 1843
Jones, David, in OH	Mecklenburg	Will	1879	CF1890-054 CC
Jones, Dorothy, in Amelia Co.	Lynchburg	Will	1782	CF1835-023
Jones, Edward	York	Inventory	1689	DOW8, p. 277 (aft. 179)
Jones, Edward	York	Will	1689	DOW8, p. 258
Jones, Edward	Buckingham	Will	1820	LVA Acc. #33216
Jones, Edward	Buckingham	Will	1820	MVG 31:4, p. 342
Jones, Edward, of Buckingham Co.	Albemarle	Will	1820	BRCD
Jones, Elizabeth	Essex	Will Abstract	1746	Fleet 2:326
Jones, Elizabeth Lee		Will		HSF 25, p. 45
Jones, Fauntleroy, in KY	Fairfax	Will	1897	CF1903-027
Jones, Fielding, in Appomattox Co.	Lynchburg	Will	1855	CF1873-004
Jones, Francis, of Nansemond Co.	Williamsburg	Will Abstract	1806	Crozier, p. 32
Jones, Frederick, in Dinwiddie Co.	Lunenburg	Will	1792	CF1839-012
Jones, Gabriel	Rockingham	Will	1804	V:Mss2 J7162 a 1
Jones, Gabriel	Rockingham	Will	1806	WBA, p. 60
Jones, Gabriel	Rockingham	Will	1806	LVA Acc. #21278[1]
Jones, Henry B., in Fauquier Co.	Culpeper	Will	1861	CF1885-097
Jones, Hezekiah, in Nelson Co.	Campbell	Will	1862	CF1879-003
Jones, Hezekiah, in Nelson Co.	Campbell	Will	1862	CF1880-009
Jones, Honoria	Rappahannock*	Will	1685	V:Mss1 T2118 d27684+
Jones, Humphrey	Middlesex	Will	1684	WB1675, p. 20
Jones, James	Nottoway	Will	1848	Judgments 1868
Jones, Jane, in Warren Co. KY	Culpeper	Will	1857	CF1874-041
Jones, Jesse W., in Albemarle Co.	Charlottesville	Will	1888	CF1891-004
Jones, Joel	Hanover	Will	1829	LVA Acc. #30399
Jones, Joel	Hanover	Will	1835	CF1884-034
Jones, Joel	Hanover	Will	1835	LVA Acc. #30399
Jones, Joel	Hanover	Will	1837	CF1855-006

[1] The copy found in Rockingham Co. Will Book A, 1803-1863, pp. 60-63, is incomplete.

NAME	LOCATION	TYPE	YEAR	REFERENCE(S)
Jones, Joel, of St. Paul's Parish	Hanover	Will	1835	Cocke:76
Jones, John	Isle of Wight	Will	1697	TQ 08:4, p. 283
Jones, John	Hanover	Will	1785	FDC L387-20
Jones, John	Richmond	Will	1796	TVF 10:3, p. 169
Jones, John	York	Will	1803	TVF 2:1, p. 30
Jones, John	York	Will	1804	CF1820-001
Jones, John, in Campbell Co.	Lynchburg	Will	1816	CF1827-006
Jones, John, in Richmond	Rockingham	Will	1867	CF1892-047
Jones, John, in Williamsburg	York	Will	1804	MVG 31:4, p. 359
Jones, John, of Gloucester Co.	Williamsburg	Will Abstract	1751	Crozier, p. 33
Jones, John, Sr., in Amelia Co.	Powhatan	Will	1819	CF1842-006
Jones, Josias, in Buckingham Co.	Lynchburg	Will	1815	CF1828-038
Jones, Katherine	Warwick	Account	1648	Miscellany, p. 46
Jones, Lankerston	Henrico	Will	1813	VGSQ 18:3, p. 82
Jones, Lettice Corbin	Fairfax	Will	1804	X
Jones, Lettice Corbin, in Northld. Co.	Fairfax	Will	1805	CF1831-002
Jones, Lewis, in Lancaster Co.	Essex	Will	1800	CF1845-012
Jones, Lucy	Middlesex	Will	1788	V:Mss2 J7207 a 1
Jones, Ludwell	Sussex	Will Ref.	(nd)	VGSQ Vol. 50:4, p. 279
Jones, Ludwell	Dinwiddie	Will	1760	SV 3:1, p. 3
Jones, Martha	Prince George	Will	1742	V:Mss2 J7212 a 1
Jones, Martha	Prince George	Will	1743	LVA Acc. #43887
Jones, Mary Ann	Hanover	Will	1829	Fleet, Huntington Data
Jones, Mary, of Gloucester Co.	Lancaster	Will	1837	CF1843-016
Jones, Matthew	Isle of Wight	Will	1728	TQ 08:4, p. 282
Jones, Orlando	York	Will	1719	WMQ 8, p. 191
Jones, Peter	Dinwiddie	Will	1771	Swem(2)
Jones, Peter, of Dinwiddie Co.	Petersburg	Will	1771	Land Ejectments 1852
Jones, Peter, Sr., of Bristol Parish	Prince George	Will	1726	VMHB 4, p. 272
Jones, Philip de Catesby	Frederick	Will	1873	V:Mss1 J735 c 1-4
Jones, Philip Edwards, of Mathews Co.	Williamsburg	Will Abstract	1801	Crozier, p. 32
Jones, Reps	Lunenburg	Will	1778	CF1816-022
Jones, Rice	Essex	Will	1767	CF1823-011
Jones, Richard	Amelia	Will Ref.	1758	Hening, Vol. 8, p. 276
Jones, Richard, in Halifax Co.	Lynchburg	Will	1817	CF1826-033
Jones, Robert	Northumberland	Will	1675	RB1706, p. 244
Jones, Robert	Charles City	Will	1690	D&W1689, p. 85
Jones, Robert	Charles City	Will	1690	D&W1689, p. 85
Jones, Robert	Amelia	Accounts	1805+	LVA Acc. #1104171
Jones, Robert C.	Dinwiddie	Will	1838	BRCD
Jones, Roger	Middlesex	Inventory	1741	LVA Acc. #41008, r4611
Jones, Roger	Fairfax	Inventory	1852	X
Jones, Rowland	York	Inventory	1689	DOW8, p. 362
Jones, Rowland	York	Account	1690	DOW8, p. 495
Jones, Samuel	Buckingham	Will	1837	MVG 41:1, p. 39
Jones, Samuel, in Buckingham Co.	Powhatan	Will	1838	CF1846-007
Jones, Samuel, in Prince William Co.	Frederick	Will	1776	CF1837-053
Jones, Samuel, mariner		Will	1693	VCRP, Survey #03952
Jones, Samuel, of Buckingham Co.	Cumberland	Will	1838	Judgments 1859 AUG
Jones, Sarah, of Southampton Co.	Williamsburg	Will Abstract	1798	Crozier, p. 32
Jones, Scervant, Capt., Warwick Co.	York	Will	1773	MVG 31:4, p. 355

NAME	LOCATION	TYPE	YEAR	REFERENCE(S)
Jones, Scervant, of Warwick Co.	York	Will	1773	CF1790-002
Jones, Scervant, of Warwick Co.	York	Account	1782	CF1790-002
Jones, Scervant, Rev.		Will	1852	CW(8)
Jones, Servant	Warwick	Will	1773	BRCD
Jones, Servant, in Warwick Co.	York	Will	1773	CF1790-002
Jones, Servant, Rev., in Williamsburg	James City	Will	1854	CF1881-006
Jones, Susan, in Amelia Co.	Brunswick	Will	1849	CF1875-023
Jones, Thomas		Will	1698	VCRP, Survey #04785
Jones, Thomas	Hanover	Will	1865	Cocke:78
Jones, Thomas ap Catesby	Fairfax	Sale	1858	X
Jones, Thomas ap Catesby	Fairfax	Inventory	1858	X
Jones, Thomas, in Campbell Co.	Lynchburg	Will	1816	CF1822-035
Jones, Thomas, in Campbell Co.	Lynchburg	Will	1819	CF1827-006
Jones, Thomas, in Campbell Co.	Lynchburg	Will	1826	CF1833-034
Jones, Thomas, of Southampton Co.	Williamsburg	Will Abstract	1800	Crozier, p. 32
Jones, Walter, mariner		Will	1776	VCRP, Survey #04801
Jones, William	Essex	Will	1791	CF1823-010
Jones, William D., in PA	Washington	Will	1890	CF1891-141
Jones, William, in Campbell Co.	Lynchburg	Will	1824	CF1828-004
Jones, William, in Rappahannock Co.	Culpeper	Will	1856	CF1893-037
Jones, William M.	James City	Will	1857	CF1874-007
Jones, William M.	James City	Will	1857	CF1902-010
Jones, William M.	James City	Will	1857	CF1890-003
Jones, William O., in PA	Wise	Will	1891	CF1894-013
Jones, William, of Buckingham Co.	Prince Edward	Will	1850	LVA Acc. #25791g
Jones, William, of Hungar's Parish	Northampton	Will	1669	VMHB 49, p. 293
Jones, William, shipwright		Will	1718	VCRP, Survey #04340
Jones, William, Sr., of Warwick Co.	York	Will	1824	MVG 31:4, p. 357
Joplin, Thomas B., in Bedford Co.	Franklin	Will	1867	CF1882-002
Jordan, Ann, in Nansemond Co.	Isle of Wight	Will	1829	CF1845-049
Jordan, Benjamin	Henrico	Will	1791	LVA Acc. #23305a
Jordan, Benjamin	Norfolk City	Will	1791	LVA Acc. #23305a
Jordan, George, Lt.-Col.	Surry	Will	1678	WMQ 16, p. 288
Jordan, Isham	Isle of Wight	Will	1834	V:Mss7:1 J7635:1
Jordan, James		Will	1835	UVA Acc. #640
Jordan, John	Powhatan	Will	1844	V:Mss2 J7643 a 1
Jordan, John Morton, of Annapolis MD		Will	1772	VCRP, Survey #04685
Jordan, Josiah M., in Prince George Co.	Petersburg	Will	1835	CF1843-031
Jordan, Richard	Surry	Inventory	1687	T:D&W3, p. 86a
Jordan, Robert	Powhatan	Will	1791	V:Mss2 J7663 a 1
Jordan, Robert	Powhatan	Will	1791	CF1835-002
Jordan, Robert	Powhatan	Will	1791	CF1838-010
Jordan, Samuel	New Kent	Will	(nd)	V:Mss4 L9303 a 1
Jordan, Samuel	New Kent	Will	1719	TQ 20:3, p. 170
Jordan, Samuel	Amelia	Will	1861	LVA Acc. #21628
Jordan, Samuel F., in Rockbridge Co.	Louisa	Will	1872	CF1897-044
Jordan, Samuel, in New Kent Co.	Louisa	Will	1719	CF1788-004
Jordan, Thomas	Surry	Inventory	1686	T: correct from 1681
Jordan, Thomas	Prince William	Will	1744	LVA Allason Letter Book
Jordan, William, in Amelia Co.	Lunenburg	Will	1780	CF1820-014
Jordon, Isaac	Essex	Will	1786	CF1810-023

NAME	LOCATION	TYPE	YEAR	REFERENCE(S)
Jouett, Matthew, of Hanover Co.	Louisa	Will	1743	DBA, p. 237
Joyne, Abel, of Accomack Co.	Williamsburg	Will Abstract	1782	Crozier, p. 33
Joyner, Eli, in Southampton Co.	Isle of Wight	Will	1855	CF1886-019
Joyner, George, Sr., in Norfolk Co.	Portsmouth	Will	1879	CF1909-034
Joyner, Harrison, in Southampton Co.	Isle of Wight	Will	1861	CF1871-020
Joynes, Levin Smith, Dr.	Richmond City	Will	1880	V:Mss1 J8586 Sect. 24
Joynes, Levin Smith, Dr.	Richmond City	Inventory	1881	V:Mss1 J8586 Sect. 24
Judkins, Robert	Surry	Will	1693	T:D&W4, p. 344a
Judkins, Samuel	Surry	Will	1672	T:D&W2, p. 13
Julian, Phebe	Fredericksburg	Will	1794	DCWBA, p. 39
Junegal, Ignatius	Arlington	Will	1810	CF1821-023

NAME	LOCATION	TYPE	YEAR	REFERENCE(S)
K				
Kandler, [blank]	Warwick	Inventory	1654	Miscellany, p. 52
Kauffman, John	King & Queen	Will	1795	LVA Acc. #28513
Kaufman, Hiram, in MD	Henrico	Will	1881	CF1882-003
Kautzman, John V.	D.C.	Will	1839	DCA:Box 14
Kay, Andrew	Essex	Will	1863	V:Mss1 B3445 b 131+
Kay, James	Essex	Will	1865	V:Mss1 B3445 c 44-45
Kay, Joseph Wiley	Caroline	Will	1854	V:Mss1 B3445 b 131+
Kean, William, in Cumberland Co.	Powhatan	Will	1794	CF1835-016
Kearsey, Mary T., in Albemarle Co.	Charlottesville	Will	1863	CF1894-012
Keeble, Grace	Fauquier	Will	1796	BRCD
Keeble, Walter	Gloucester	Will	1748	TQ 23:2, p. 117
Keeble, Walter, of Gloucester Co.	Cumberland	Will	1743	CF1761-002
Keech, Simon, d. in Accomack Co.	London	Will	1688	N:PROB11/392
Keeling, Edward, Gent.	Rappahannock*	Will	1687	Sweeny, p. 133
Keeling, Jacob, Sr., in Nansemond Co.	Portsmouth	Will	1853	CF1889-055
Keen, James	Fairfax	Will	1761	X
Keen, Thomas	Northumberland	Will Ref.	1722	Winfree, p. 231
Keen, William, in Halifax Co.	Lynchburg	Will	1805	CF1827-036
Keene, John, in Loudoun Co.	Frederick	Will	1777	CF1822-285
Keene, Newton	Fairfax	Division	1803	X
Keene, Newton, of Northumberland Co.	Williamsburg	Will Abstract	1771	Crozier, p. 34
Keene, William, in Halifax Co.	Campbell	Will	1804	CF1838-005
Keens, Mathew	Stafford	Will	1731	BRCD
Keens, Mathew, of Stafford Co.	Fauquier	Inventory	1732	CF1789-011
Keesee, Sally, in Caroline Co.	Essex	Will	1872	CF1909-008
Keeth, Simon		Will (N)	1688	VCRP, Survey #03743
Keith, James, in DC	Alexandria	Will	1874	CF1884-013
Keith, James, in DC	Arlington	Will	1874	CF1884-013
Keith, Marshall, in GA	Fauquier	Will	1842	CF1854-067
Keith, Marshall, in GA	Fauquier	Will	1866	CF1882-027
Keith, Thomas, in KY	Fauquier	Will	1844	CF1866-031
Kells, Richard, of Southampton Co.	Williamsburg	Will Abstract	1790	Crozier, p. 34
Kelly, John, in Fauquier Co.	Culpeper	Will	1820	CF1849-004
Kelly, John, of Sussex Co.	Williamsburg	Will Abstract	1790	Crozier, p. 33
Kelly, John P., in Culpeper Co.	Fauquier	Will	1871	CF1903-006
Kelly, John P., in Culpeper Co.	Fauquier	Will	1871	CF1899-011
Kelsick, Elizabeth, of Princess Anne Co.	Williamsburg	Will Abstract	1789	Crozier, p. 34
Kelsick, Richard	Norfolk	Will	1773	LVA-LP:25 JAN 1836
Kemp, Parker, in MA	Princess Anne	Will	1893	CF1897-007
Kemp, Robert	Lancaster	Will	1664	LP
Kemp, Thomas, of Middlesex Co.	Williamsburg	Will Abstract	1772	Crozier, p. 34
Kemp, Thomas, of Petsworth Parish	Gloucester	Will	1812	Swem(1):f22
Kempe, Richard	James City	Will	1656	LVA Acc. #42425
Kempe, Richard, of Kick Neck	London	Will	1676	N:PROB11/260
Kempe, Richard, of Kickneck		Will	1656	VCRP, Survey #03514
Kemper, William	Fauquier	Will	1834	V:Mss1 B3658 a 5-20
Kendall, John	Henrico	Inventory	1763	Records, Vol. 6, p. 1899
Kendall, Samuel, barber chirurgeon		Will	1696	VCRP, Survey #06052
Kenline, John	Princess Anne	Will	1782	DB18, p. 65
Kennedy, Charles, in Hanover Co.	Louisa	Will	1784	CF1812-027

NAME	LOCATION	TYPE	YEAR	REFERENCE(S)
Kennedy, Charles, in Hanover Co.	Louisa	Will	1784	CF1812-022
Kennedy, Hugh, in KY	Frederick	Will	1821	CF1839-051
Kennedy, Joseph	Amherst	Will	1820	Fleet, Huntington Data
Kennedy, Martin	Hanover	Will	1847	CF1869-015
Kennedy, Martin	Hanover	Will	1847	Cocke:79
Kenner, Rodham	Fauquier	Will	1793	CF1846-008
Kenney, John, of Botetourt Co.	Augusta	Will	1813	CF1827-015
Kennon, Agnes Bolling	Chesterfield	Will	1763c	V: F221V85v.37no.4
Kennon, Ann, of Chesterfield Co.	Williamsburg	Will Abstract	1769	Crozier, p. 33
Kennon, Elizabeth	Henrico	Will	1743	Records, Vol. 4, p. 1225
Kenny, Joseph		Will	1745	VCRP, Survey #04628
Kenny, William	Rappahannock*	Will Abstract	1677	VMHB 5, p. 287
Kent, Jacob	Botetourt	Will	1777	LVA Acc. #22676
Kent, William	Northumberland	Will	1789	CF1848-052
Keplinger, John A., in TN	Washington	Will	1888	CF1903-079
Ker, David, of Middlesex Co.	Williamsburg	Will Abstract	1772	Crozier, p. 33
Ker, George		Estate Ref.	1788	Hening, Vol. 12, p. 681
Kerby, William	York	Will	1782	CF1795-004
Kerr, Francis	King & Queen	Will	1833	CF1868-005
Kerr, Francis	King & Queen	Account	1838	CF1868-005
Kersey, Ann	Charles City	Inventory	1727	D&W1724, p. 185
Kersey, J. Henry	Hanover	Will	1867	CF1888-008
Ketchum, Israel, Sr., in NY	Norfolk	Will	1865	CF1872-004
Kibble, George	Lancaster	Will	1666	LVA Wills/Admin. DB
Kidd, Ann	King & Queen	Will	1838	CF1840-001
Kidd, Pitman	Hanover	Will	1808	Weisiger 1:001
Kidd, Pitman	Hanover	Will	1808	CF1845-015
Kidd, Pitman	Hanover	Will	1808	Cocke:80
Kidd, Pittman	Hanover	Will	1806	LVA Acc. #41008, r4609
Kidd, Pittman	Hanover	Will	1806	Fleet, Huntington Data
Kidd, Willis [of *Cedar Grove*]	Caroline	Will	1843	Weisiger 1:075
Kidwell, Levi	Fairfax	Guard. Acct.	1859	X
Kietly, St. Clair	Rockingham	Will	1846	LVA:1159583
Kimbrough, Lewis P.	Hanover	Will	1865	CF1884-004
Kincaid, Robert	Buckingham	Will	1810	LP:25 OCT 1814
Kincheloe, John, in Loudoun Co.	Fauquier	Will	1826	CF1838-021
Kincheloe, John, in Loudoun Co.	Fauquier	Will	1826	CF1838-022
Kincheloe, William	Fairfax	Inventory	1845	X
King, Ann	Prince William	Inv. Ref.	1844	CM:03 JUN 1844
King, Basil	Prince William	Will	1843	CF1875-049
King, Basil	Prince William	Will Ref.	1844	CM:06 MAY 1844
King, Basil	Prince William	Sale Ref.	1844	CM:01 JUL 1844
King, Basil	Prince William	Will (U)	1844	PWR 6:3, p. 55
King, Basil	Prince William	Inv. Ref.	1844	CM:03 JUN 1844
King, Elizabeth, in Richmond	Smyth	Will	1864	CF1892-040
King, Eusebius, of Prince George Co.	London	Will	1711	N:PROB11/523
King, Eusebius, of Prince George Co.		Will	1711	VCRP, Survey #04354
King, Henry	Elizabeth City	Will	1787	W1701, p. 403
King, Henry, in Richmond	Hanover	Will	1837	CF1866-007
King, Henry, of Richmond	Richmond City	Will	1837	Cocke:82
King, James	Washington	Will	1809	LVA Acc. #23432

NAME	LOCATION	TYPE	YEAR	REFERENCE(S)
King, John	Loudoun	Will	1784	LVA Acc. #41008, r4610
King, John Curle, of Hampton	London	Will	1763	N:PROB11/893
King, John, of Norfolk Borough	Williamsburg	Will Abstract	1784	Crozier, p. 34
King, Miles	Nansemond	Will	1772	VG 21, p. 278
King, Miles, Sr., of Norfolk Borough	Williamsburg	Will Abstract	1815	Crozier, p. 34
King, Nathaniel	Brunswick	Will	1803	SV 3:3, p. 115
King, Robert	Stafford	Will Ref.	1690	VMHB 44, p. 300
King, Thomas	Surry	Inventory	1680	T: correct from 1679
King, Thomas	Surry	Will Abstract	1816	VG 13, p. 54
King, William	Washington	Will	1808	LVA Acc. #23432
King, William	Washington	Will	1808	V:Mss1 Sh394 a 65-85
King, William, in King George Co.	Essex	Will	1857	CF1874-023
King, William, of Christ Church Parish	Lancaster	Will	1716	TVF 6:2, p. 105
Kingston, Nicholas		Will Ref.	1697	LVA Acc. #22028
Kinnear, John, in Rockbridge Co.	Lynchburg	Will	1828	CF1857-016
Kirby, Agnn C.	Fairfax	Will	(nd)	CF1837-010
Kirby, James H., in York Co.	James City	Will	1871	CF1878-013
Kirk, Bridget	Arlington	Will	1798	CRA:270
Kirk, Randol	Westmoreland	Will	1792	Note[1]
Kirk, William, in Lancaster Co.	Northumberland	Will	1820	CF1836-001
Kirtley, Francis	Augusta	Will	1774	V:Mss1 B2346 a 1163
Kitchen, Sarah	Westmoreland	Will	1780	Wills #19
Kitchen, Thomas	Southampton	Will	1767	WB2, p. 217
Klipple, Michel, in Shenandoah Co.	Warren	Will	1802	CF1838-003
Klug, Michael	Madison	Will	1812	V:Mss1 B2346 a 1161
Klugh, Samuel, in Middlesex Co.	Essex	Will	1794	CF1810-040
Knapton, John	Warwick	Admin.	1669	Miscellany 1648, p. 53
Knight, Henry	Mathews	Will	1821	V:Mss2 K7445 a 1
Knight, James V., in Lynchburg	Campbell	Will	1874	CF1882-037
Knight, William, of Williamsburg	London	Will	1711	N:PROB11/963
Knight, William, of Williamsburg	London	Will	1771	VCRP, Survey #04688
Knott, Elander	Westmoreland	Will	1787	Wills #28
Knott, James	Nansemond	Will	1653	LVA Acc. #28720
Knowles, John	Henrico	Will	1676	Records, Vol. 1, p. 49
Knupp, John Jacob, in Shenandoah Co.	Rockingham	Will	1872	CF1896-012
Knupp, John Jacob, in Shenandoah Co.	Rockingham	Will	1891	CF1892-025
Koker, John Michael	Grayson	Will	(nd)	DB1:235
Koogler, Jacob	Rockingham	Will	1854	CF1858-003
Koon, John L., in NY	Fairfax	Will	1876	CF1882-029
Koon, Matthew, of Stafford Co.	Fauquier	Will	1731	CF1789-011
Kosciuszko, Tadeusz	Albemarle	Will	1798	UVA MSS 10459-a
Kosciuszko, Tadeusz		Will	1817	V:Mss2 C5794 a 2
Krantz, Michael, in Bedford Co.	Lynchburg	Will	1796	CF1834-033
Kring, John, Sr., of Rockingham Co.	Augusta	Will	1802	CF1827-055
Kringer, Harman		Will	1699	VCRP, Survey #06066
Kuykendall, Abraham, in Hampshire Co.	Frederick	Will	1777	CF1813-042
Kyle, William, of Botetourt Co.	Augusta	Will	1820	CF1822-037

---

[1] LVA, Westmoreland County Wills, 1755-1800, Reel 28a, #40.

NAME	LOCATION	TYPE	YEAR	REFERENCE(S)
L				
Lacey, Israel, in Loudoun Co.	Frederick	Will	1816	CF1840-048
Lackey, William	Amherst	Will	1772	T: correct from Lacey
Lackland, Samuel Watkins	Jefferson	Will	1857	V:Mss1 L1188 a 86
Lacy, Patrick		Will	1700	VCRP, Survey #06068
Ladd, James	Charles City	Inventory	1771	Records, p. 277
Ladd, Joseph	Charles City	Will	1814	TVF 4:1, p. 35
Lafeber, Zilpha	Loudoun	Will	1850	Judgments Dec. 1852
Laine, William [Layne], Westover Par.	Charles City	Will	1725	D&W1724, p. 53
Laird, David	Augusta	Will	1800	WB1A, p. 38
Lake, Ann E.	Williamsburg	Will	1833	Swem(1):f200
Lake, William	Essex	Will	1700	T: correct from Leake
Lambert, Sterling, in Nottoway Co.	Lunenburg	Will	1827	CF1839-036
Lambert, Sterling, in Nottoway Co.	Lunenburg	Will	1827	CF1888-019
Lambeth, George K., in Campbell Co.	Lynchburg	Will	1833	CF1859-044
Lambeth, John	Norfolk	Will	1746	W&DH, p. 256
Lambeth, Meredith, in Campbell Co.	Lynchburg	Will	1835	CF1852-026
Lamkin, Matthew	Westmoreland	Will	1769	Wills #4
Lamkin, Peter, in Fauquier Co.	Frederick	Will	1823	CF1838-094
Lamont, John, in Amherst Co.	Lynchburg	Will	1778	CF1838-011
Lamont, John, in Bedford Co.	Lynchburg	Will	1823	CF1851-011
Land, Joshua, Sr.	Princess Anne	Will	1800	SV 15:2, p. 85
Landman, James, in Richmond	Essex	Will	1761	CF1798-005
Landrum, Alexander L., in Richmond	Louisa	Will	1856	CF1889-015
Landrum, John	Essex	Will	1708	DB13, p. 103
Landrum, Richard, in Amherst Co.	Washington	Will	1858	CF1873-015
Lane, David	Fairfax	Account	1817	X
Lane, Francis W.	Fairfax	Guard. Acct.	1845	X
Lane, James, mariner		Will	1743	VCRP, Survey #04623
Lane, Lydia	Fairfax	Will	1818	NVG 8, p. 1093
Lane, Lydia, in Fairfax Co.	Frederick	Will	1820	CF1833-041
Lane, Mary D.	Prince William	Admin. Ref.	1844	CM:06 MAR 1844
Lane, Philo R.	Fairfax	Account	1829	X
Lane, Presley Carr, in KY	Fairfax	Will	1819	CF1846-036
Lane, Richard	Surry	Will	1687	T:D&W3, p. 83b
Lane, Richard	Fairfax	Will	1817	X
Lane, Samuel, of Rockingham Co., NC	Danville	Will	1845	DBA:231
Laneave, John C., in Nottoway Co.	Prince Edward	Will	1840	CF1867-012
Lanford, Edward, in Westmoreland Co.	Northumberland	Will	1786	CF1793-001
Langborn, William	King William	Will	1821	TVF 9:1, p. 48
Langborn, William	King William	Will	1821	TVF 8:1, p. 36
Langborne, William	King William	Will	1823	LVA Tazewell Papers
Langfitt, John, in Stafford Co.	Fauquier	Will	1813	CF1846-076
Langhorne, Catharine Callaway	Botetourt	Will	1871	V:Mss1 J6496 a 1 151-1
Langhorne, William	Warwick	Will	1797	Note[1]
Langhorne, William	King William	Will	1821	BRCD
Langhorne, William	Botetourt	Will	1854	V:Mss1 J6496 a 1 151-1
Langhorne, William B., of NC	Cumberland	Will	1841	CF1856-016

[1] LVA, Tazewell Papers, Box 26.

NAME	LOCATION	TYPE	YEAR	REFERENCE(S)
Langley, Lemuel, in Norfolk	Portsmouth	Will	1835	CF1889-018
Langston, William	Elizabeth City	Will	1773	Note[1]
Langstone, Mary, of York Co.	Williamsburg	Will Abstract	1794	Crozier, p. 35
Lanier, John	Surry	Account	1781	not Inventory
Lankford, Elizabeth, Westover Parish	Charles City	Will	1778	LP, box 51, folder 251
Lankford, Sarah	Hanover	Will	1842	CF1874-010
Lankford, Sarah	Hanover	Will	1842	CF1875-033
Lankford, Sarah	Hanover	Will	1842	Cocke:18
Lankford, Sterling	Hanover	Will	1829	Cocke:83
Lankford, Sterling	Hanover	Will	1829	CF1881-024
Lankford, Sterling	Hanover	Will	1829	CF1839-004
Lansdell, William	Northumberland	Will	1791	CF1797-011
Lare, Anthony, in PA	James City	Will	1898	CF1903-005
Lare, Emily R., in PA	James City	Will	1899	CF1903-005
Largiant, John	Orange	Will	1738	WB1, p. 71
Larkin, Thomas	Prince William	Admin. Ref.	1843	CM:04 SEP 1843
Larkins, Henry, of Botetourt Co.	Augusta	Will	1772	CF1830-063
Larrance, John	Prince George	Estate Ref.	1733	DB1733, p. 564
Larred, Mary	Richmond City	Will	1797	T:HCD2, p. 364
Lashly, Mary, of Sussex Co.	Williamsburg	Will Abstract	1795	Crozier, p. 34
Lashly, William, of Sussex Co.	Williamsburg	Will Abstract	1788	Crozier, p. 35
Latham, Nancy, in Fauquier Co.	Culpeper	Will	1831	CF1835-010
Lathbury, John, pewterer		Will	1655	VCRP, Survey #03128
Lathom, Susanna	King & Queen	Will	1838	LP ur
Latimore, John, in Prince William Co.	Fauquier	Will	1761	CF1868-190
Laughton, William	Surry	Will (N)	1789	WB12, p. 258
Laurence, Elizabeth	Nansemond	Will	1739	SV 1:1, p. 65
Laurence, John	Nansemond	Will	1796	SV 1:1, p. 27
Lawi, James	Lancaster	Will	1713	T: correct from Lowry
Lawrence, Elizabeth	Nansemond	Will	1739	BRCD
Lawrence, John	Hanover	Inventory	1798	G1:73
Lawrence, John, in Nansemond Co.	Southampton	Will	1796	CF1827-005
Lawrence, John, of St. Martin's Parish	Hanover	Will	1781	Note[2]
Lawrence, John, of St. Martin's Parish	Hanover	Will, 1788	1805	G1:71
Lawrence, John, Rev., in Little Creek	Norfolk	Will	1684	VMHB 2, p. 176
Lawrence, Joseph J.	Nansemond	Will	1864	CF1875-029
Lawrence, Mills, of Isle of Wight Co.	Williamsburg	Will Abstract	1816	Crozier, p. 36
Lawrence, Peter, in Culpeper Co.	Rappahannock	Will	1826	CF1838-008
Lawrence, Peter, in Culpeper Co.	Rappahannock	Will	1826	CF1837-011
Laws, Cuthbert		Will	1732	VCRP, Survey #04659
Lawson, Isaac, of Rockbridge Co.	Augusta	Will	1821	CF1838-017
Lawson, Richard	Rappahannock*	Will Abstract	1658	VMHB 5, p. 284
Lawson, Robert	Fredericksburg	Bond	1800	Note[3]
Lawson, Thomas	Princess Anne	Inventory	1714	DB3, p. 13
Lawson, Thomas, in Hampshire Co.	Frederick	Will	1796	CF1820-233
Lawton, Adelaide C., in Richmond	Henrico	Will	1895	CF1905-001

---

[1] Elizabeth City County Loose Wills, 1701-1859, Nos. 1-396, p. 175; Elizabeth City County Reel #16a.

[2] LVA, U.S. Circuit Court Records, Box 82, *Anderson's Exors. v. Lawrence's Exors.* (1811).

[3] Fredericksburg District Superior Court Wills, Book A, p. 147.

NAME	LOCATION	TYPE	YEAR	REFERENCE(S)
Lay, Joseph	Fairfax	Will	1803	LVA Acc. #343683, 2:38
Lay, Joseph	Fairfax	Will	1809	LVA Acc. #343683, 2:38
Lay, Joseph	Fairfax	Will	1818	NVG 6, p. 627
Layne, William [Laine]	Charles City	Inventory	1725	D&W1724, p. 59
Lea, John, in Louisa Co.	Goochland	Will	1843	CF1847-012
Leacey, George C.	Prince George	Will	1818	LVA Acc. #27394
Leach, James P., in Cumberland Co.	Prince Edward	Will	1866	CF1904-041
Leamon, Mary	Gloucester	Will	1843	Swem(1):f22
Leane, Simon	Arlington	Inventory	1790	CRA:14
Lear, John	Nansemond	Will	1695	LVA Acc. #26074
Lear, John	Nansemond	Will	1695	TVF 12:2, p. 110
Lear, John	Nansemond	Will	1695	VG 11, p. 30
Lear, John, of Nansemond Co.	Henrico	Will	1695	Records, Vol. 1, p. 95
Leath, Peters	Prince George	Inventory	1759	DB1759, p. 124
Leath, Stephen, in Prince George Co.	Petersburg	Will	1825	CF1837-027
Leaton, Robert		Will	1699	VCRP, Survey #06065
Leavell, Burwell, in Spotsylvania Co.	Rappahannock	Will	1848	CF1882-002
Leavell, Burwell, in Spotsylvania Co.	Rappahannock	Will	1848	CF1869-002
Leavell, Edward	Culpeper	Will	1782c	Fleet, Huntington Data
Leavell, Edward	Culpeper	Will	1783	LVA Acc. #41008, r4608
Leavet, Thomas	Gloucester	Will	1771	TVF 9:2, p. 123
Leavit, Thomas	Gloucester	Will	1771	MVG 31:4, p. 345
Leavit, Thomas, of Gloucester Co.	York	Will	1771	LP 1784-1858 Box 15
Leavit, William F.	Gloucester	Will	1854	CF1887-007
Leckie, Robert, in Washington DC	Mecklenburg	Will	1834	CF1867-024 CC
Ledbetter, Susannah	Dinwiddie	Will	1815	VGSQ 10:1, p. 4
Lee, Ambrose, in Amherst Co.	Lynchburg	Will	1764	CF1848-012
Lee, Ann R., in Hardy Co.	Westmoreland	Will	1840	MVG 29:3, p. 191
Lee, Arthur	Middlesex	Will	1792	V:Mss2 L5102 a 1
Lee, Betsy, in Northumberland Co.	Richmond	Will	1860	CF1872-013
Lee, Charles, Gen., of Berkeley Co.		Will	1785	VCRP, Survey #04705
Lee, Charles, Maj.-Gen.	Berkeley	Will	1782c	WVHM 2:4, p. 10
Lee, Charles, of Berkeley Co.	London	Will	1785	N:PROB11/1131
Lee, Elizabeth	Prince George	Will	1840	SV 9:2, p. 57
Lee, Fielding	Essex	Will	1850	LP ur
Lee, Francis	York	Will	1799	CF1811-002
Lee, Francis L.	Fairfax	Guard. Acct.	1816	X
Lee, Francis L.	Fairfax	Account C.	1828	X
Lee, Francis L.	Fairfax	Account C.	1829	X
Lee, Francis L.	Fairfax	Account	1830	X
Lee, Frank, in Amherst Co.	Lynchburg	Will	1791	CF1848-012
Lee, Hancock	Culpeper	Will	1842	V:Mss2 L51148 a 1
Lee, Henry, in Hardy Co.	Westmoreland	Will	1840	MVG 29:3, p. 192
Lee, Isaac, of Rappahannock River	London	Will	1727	N:PROB11/618
Lee, Isaac, of Rappahannock River		Will	1727	VCRP, Survey #04649
Lee, John	Prince William	Will	1848	LVA Steadman Coll.
Lee, John, in Campbell Co.	Bedford	Will	1819	CF1857-058
Lee, John, in Radford	Bedford	Will	1819	CF1858-058
Lee, John, of Westmoreland Co.	Augusta	Will	1767	CF1827-015
Lee, Mary	Petersburg	Will	1841	V:Mss1 Ad198 b 19-41
Lee, Mary Anna Randolph Custis	Fairfax	Will	1865	V:Mss1 L5114 d 156+

NAME	LOCATION	TYPE	YEAR	REFERENCE(S)
Lee, Nathan, of Prince George Co.	Petersburg	Will	1823	CF1842-044
Lee, Richard	Northumberland	Will	1664c	TVF 27:3, p. 91
Lee, Richard		Will Ref.	1665	VCRP, Survey #03535
Lee, Richard	Westmoreland	Will	1715	V:Mss10: no. 122
Lee, Richard, Col.	Northumberland	Will	1664c	VMHB 74, p. 23
Lee, Richard, Col., of Eng.		Will	1663	Swem(2)
Lee, Richard Henry	Westmoreland	Will	1794	LVA Acc. #21465
Lee, Richard, in Bedford Co.	Lynchburg	Will	1814	CF1830-142
Lee, Robert Eden, in Rankin Co. MS	Fauquier	Will	1844	LVA Acc. #30825
Lee, Robert Edward		Will	1846	V:Mss2 L515 a 18
Lee, Robert Edward		Inventory	1846c	V:Mss2 L515 a 18
Lee, Samuel	Prince George	Will	1759	DB1759, p. 96
Lee, Thomas	Middlesex	Will Ref.	1709	Fleet 2:326
Lee, Thomas	Westmoreland	Will	1751	V:Mss1 P3374 b 68
Lee, Thomas	Westmoreland	Will	1751	V:Mss1 L51 f240-242
Lee, Thomas, of *Stratford*	Westmoreland	Will	1751	FDC L572-60
Lee, William	York	Will	1728	V:Mss2 L5162 a 1
Lee, William		Will	1796	BRCD, GC
Lee, William	Prince George	Will	1831	SV 9:1, p. 22
Lee, William, in James City Co.	Frederick	Will	1796	CF1822-268
Lee, William Ludwell	James City	Will	1775	BRCD
Lee, William Ludwell, in James City Co.	Arlington	Will	1803	CF1814-019
Leet, Frances F., in KY	Henrico	Will	1819	CF1823-018
Leeth, Thomas, mariner		Will	1711	VCRP, Survey #04352
Leethe, George	Frederick	Will	1768	WB3, p. 460
Lefevre, Madelence	Henrico	Will	1720	Records, Vol. 2, p. 489
Leftwich, Thomas, in Bedford Co.	Lynchburg	Will	1815	CF1857-009
Leftwich, Thomas, in Bedford Co.	Lynchburg	Will	1815	CF1826-054
Leftwich, William, Sr., in Bedford Co.	Lynchburg	Will	1820	CF1844-008
Leftwich, William, Sr., in Bedford Co.	Roanoke	Will	1820	CF1850-015
Leggett, Aaron	Fairfax	Will	1856	X
Legrand, Paulina	Charlotte	Will	1845	MVG 29:3, p. 192
Legrand, Peter	Goochland	Will	1736	DB3, p. 45
LeGrand, Baker	Prince Edward	Will	(nd)	LVA Acc. #41008, r4611
LeGrand, Baker	Prince Edward	Will Partial	(nd)	Fleet, Huntington Data
LeGrand, Peter	Goochland	Will Ref.	1736	VMHB 44, p. 258
Leigh, Ferdinando	Dinwiddie	Will	1784	MVG 31:4, p. 344
Leigh, Ferdinando, of Dinwiddie Co.	Albemarle	Will	1784	LP
Leigh, John	Gloucester	Will	1860	CF1881-030
Leigh, Richard, of Gloucester Co.	Williamsburg	Will Abstract	1800	Crozier, p. 35
Leigh, Walter	Henrico	Will	1751	D&W1750, p. 89
Leister, Aaron	Henrico	Will	1720	Records, Vol. 2, p. 487
Leister, Henry	Henrico	Will	1723	Records, Vol. 2, p. 569
Lemar, William B., in MD	Frederick	Will	1812	CF1827-178
Lemay, William, of St. Paul's Parish	Hanover	Will	1784	TQ 32:1, p. 30
Lemont, James	Norfolk	Will (N)	1687	DB5, p. 7
Lennel, William	Lancaster	Will	1683	WB5, p. 88
Lennig, Charles, in PA	Louisa	Will	1891	CF1904-027
Lenox, Thomas, Dr.	King & Queen	Will	1826	V:Mss1 T5996 c 243+
Leonard, Abraham F., in Norfolk	Alexandria	Will	1871	CF1882-023
Leonard, Chauncey B., in OH	Dinwiddie	Will	1878	CF1881-008

NAME	LOCATION	TYPE	YEAR	REFERENCE(S)
Leonard, Samuel, Sir		Will	1618	VCRP, Survey #08227
Leonberger, John	Frederick	Will Abstract	1757	VGS Bulletin VIII, p. 64
Lescure, Peter	Buckingham	Will	1822	LP:16 JUL 1843
Lester, Benjamin, of York Co.	Williamsburg	Will Abstract	1795	Crozier, p. 35
Lester, Bryant	Lunenburg	Will	1796	CF1820-017
Lester, James, in Tazewell Co.	Washington	Will	1887	CF1905-008
Lester, Susanna	James City	Will	1801	Swem(1):f129
Lester, William	Charles City	Will	1728	D&W1724, p. 225
Lester, William	Charles City	Inventory	1728	D&W1724, p. 229
Letchworth, Thomas, fishmonger		Will	1657	VCRP, Survey #03515
Leven, Richard	Henrico	Inventory	1743	Records, Vol. 5, p. 1447
Levy, Ezekiel	Richmond	Will	1813	TQ 10:1, p. 33
Lewellin, Charles, in Campbell Co.	Lynchburg	Will	1804	CF1832-013
Lewellin, Charles, in Campbell Co.	Lynchburg	Will	1804	CF1835-027
Lewellin, Daniel		Will	1711	LVA Acc. #27033-d
Lewelling, Stephen W., in TN	Norfolk	Will	1851	CF1857-007
Lewis, Andrew, of Botetourt Co.	Augusta	Will	1782	BRCD
Lewis, Ann	Westmoreland	Will	1791	Wills #38
Lewis, Benjamin, in Brunswick Co.	Lunenburg	Will	1828	CF1833-001
Lewis, Benjamin, in Brunswick Co.	Lunenburg	Will	1828	CF1829-001
Lewis, Charles	Rockingham	Estate Ref.	1840	LP:02 JAN 1858
Lewis, Charles, of St. James Northam	Goochland	Will	1779	VMHB 7, p. 294
Lewis, Edward	Arlington	Will	1800	CRA:297
Lewis, Fielding	Spotsylvania	Will	1781c	V:Mss1 T2197 a 54-61
Lewis, Francis	King & Queen	Will	1919	LP
Lewis, Huldah	Spotsylvania	Will	1891	V:Mss1 H7185 d 159+
Lewis, James	Gloucester	Will	1789	Note[1]
Lewis, John	Hanover	Will Ref.	1726	Note[2]
Lewis, John	Northumberland	Will	1746	BRCD
Lewis, John	Prince George	Will	1756	LVA Acc. #19941
Lewis, John	Augusta	Will	1762	LVA Acc. #23826a
Lewis, John	Augusta	Will	1762	V:Mss1 L5896 b 1
Lewis, John	Williamsburg	Will Abstract	1785	Crozier, p. 35
Lewis, John	Gloucester	Will	1828	LVA Acc. #29518
Lewis, John	Gloucester	Will	1828	Duke Acc. #29518
Lewis, John, in Augusta Co.	Bath	Will	1790	CF1805-003
Lewis, John, of Abingdon Parish	Gloucester	Will Ref.	1725	Hening, Vol. 8, p. 59
Lewis, John, of Hanover Co.	Henrico	Will	1780	Judgments 1795 Box 44
Lewis, Joseph	Goochland	Will	1783	CF1823-003
Lewis, Joseph	Goochland	Will	1783	CF1822-003
Lewis, Judith Walker Browne	Spotsylvania	Will	1829c	V:Mss1 C5217 b 118+\
Lewis, Lawrence, of Fairfax Co.	D.C.	Will	1874	DCA:Box 54
Lewis, Malinda	Fauquier	Will	1841	CF1846-038
Lewis, Mary P.	Essex	Will	(nd)	UVA Acc. #6053
Lewis, Permelia	Dinwiddie	Will	1852	CF1935-019
Lewis, Richard	Stafford	Will	1777	LP:12 DEC 1808
Lewis, Samuel Hance	Rockingham	Will	1869	V:Mss1 L5896 b 15-21

---

[1] Misc. Reel #547, from University of Chicago, Weyanoke Plantation Papers, Folder 29; LVA Fielding Lewis Business Papers.
[2] William Terrell Lewis, *Genealogy of the Lewis Family* (1893), p. 56.

NAME	LOCATION	TYPE	YEAR	REFERENCE(S)
Lewis, Thomas	Gloucester	Will	1789	LVA Fielding Lewis Papers
Lewis, Thomas	Gloucester	Will	1797	LVA, misc. reel #547
Lewis, Thomas		Will	1800c	DAR MSS 13 b4 f12
Lewis, Thomas	Rockingham	Estate Ref.	1840	LP:02 JAN 1858
Lewis, Thomas, of Rockingham Co.	Augusta	Will	1790	CF1806-087
Lewis, Warner	Gloucester	Will	1784	CF1898-035; HC
Lewis, Warner, the younger	Gloucester	Estate Ref.	1801	VGS Bulletin V, pp. 1, 7
Lewis, William	Dinwiddie	Will	1810	VGSQ 10:1, p. 7
Lewis, William, in TN	Scott	Will	(nd)	CF1889-016
Lewis, Zirkle, of Rockingham Co.	Augusta	Will	1806	CF1825-083
Lewis, [blank]	Scott	Will	(nd)	CF1892-029
Ley, Humphrie		Will	1663	VCRP, Survey #03531
Leyburn, Geo. Wm., in Rockbridge Co.	Bedford	Will	1875	CF1883-037
Lide, Robert	Charles City	Inventory	1725	D&W1724, p. 36
Lide, Robert, of Wilmington	Charles City	Will	1725	D&W1724, p. 19
Lifsey, Sally, in Greensville Co.	Brunswick	Will	1857	CF1867-018
Light, George	Lancaster	Will	1748	LP
Light, Peter, in Berkeley Co.	Frederick	Will	1807	CF1816-056
Light, Peter, Sr., in Berkeley Co.	Frederick	Will	1807	CF1822-203
Lightfoot, Francis	Charles City	Will	1727	D&W1724, p. 193
Lightfoot, Francis		Will Ref.	1727	Hening, Vol. 5, p. 112
Lightfoot, Francis	Charles City	Will Cod.	1728	D&W1724, p. 194
Lightfoot, Francis	Charles City	Inventory	1730	D&W1724, p. 299
Lightfoot, George B.	James City	Will	1839	Swem(1):f159
Lightfoot, Henry Benskin, of Antigua	New Kent	Will	1805	VG 30, p. 195
Lightfoot, John	James City	Will	1777	BRCD
Lightfoot, John	James City	Will	1777	MVG 31:4, p. 348
Lightfoot, Nicholas, of James City Co.	Williamsburg	Will Abstract	1809	Crozier, p. 35
Lightfoot, Philip	James City	Will Ref.	1708	Hening, Vol. 5, p. 111
Lightfoot, Philip	York	Will Ref.	1747	Hening, Vol. 8, p. 457
Lightfoot, Philip	Culpeper	Will	1865	CF1885-079
Ligon, Richard	Henrico	Inventory	1724	Records, Vol. 2, p. 595
Limbrey, John	Prince George	Will	1712	SV 10:1, p. 9
Linberger, John, in Page Co.	Roanoke	Will	1874	CF1894-068
Lindsay, James, in Louisa Co.	Albemarle	Will	1856	CF1900-002
Lindsay, William, Jr., Prince Edward Co.	Cumberland	Will	1825	CF1831-016
Lindsey, John, in SC	Frederick	Will	1787	CF1820-245
Lingo, John A., in DE	Gloucester	Will	1900	CF1903-046
Link, Adam	Jefferson	Will	1835	V:Mss1 T6895 a 3,844
Link, John Nicholas	Augusta	Will	1816	V:Mss2 L6585 b 1
Linnard, Mary	Henrico	Will	1807	VGSQ 18:3, p. 82
Linscott, Edward, in Norfolk Co.	Portsmouth	Will	1827	CF1876-004
Linton, Moses	Prince William	Will	1729	Note[1]
Lionbarger, John, in Shenandoah Co.	Frederick	Will	1806	CF1826-139
Lipford, Henry, of Powhatan Co.	Cumberland	Will	1841	CF1855-018
Lipford, Henry, of Powhatan Co.	Cumberland	Will	1841	CF1859-017
Lipscomb, Anderson	King William	Will Ref.	1773	RB2, pt. 3, p. 41

---

[1] Prince William County Land Causes, 1793-1811, p. 351.

NAME	LOCATION	TYPE	YEAR	REFERENCE(S)
Lipscomb, Bernard	King William	Will	1833	Note[1]
Lipscomb, Bernard	King William	Will	1833	LVA Acc. #20703
Lipscomb, Daniel		Estate Ref.	1781	Note[2]
Lipscomb, John	King William	Will	1777	LVA Acc. #21815
Lipscomb, John	King William	Will	1777	LVA Acc. #20009
Lipscomb, John	King William	Will	1777	WMQ2 10, p. 183
Lipscomb, John	Richmond City	Will	1784	TQ 33:3, p. 179
Lipscomb, John, or Richmond	Hanover	Will	1784	TQ 33, p. 179
Lipscomb, Madison	King William	Will	1815	LVA Acc. #20954
Lipscomb, Nathaniel C.	Hanover	Will Ref.	(nd)	Cocke:84
Lipscomb, Nathaniel C.	Hanover	Will	1847	LP 1860
Lipscomb, Nathaniel C.	Hanover	Will	1847	TQ 33:3, p. 179
Lipscomb, Nathaniel C.	Hanover	Will	1847	Huntington Data
Lipscomb, Philip	King William	Will Ref.	1805	Note[3]
Lipscomb, Reuben	King William	Will	1779	LVA Acc. #20703
Lipscomb, William C., in Augusta Co.	Albemarle	Will	1856	CF1895-332
Lipscomb, Wyatt, in SC	Louisa	Will	1840	CF1843-013
Lister, John, of Gloucester Co.	Elizabeth City	Will	1734	Wills 1701, p. 3
Littlepage, Edmund	King & Queen	Bond	1813	LP
Littlepage, Edmund	King William	Will	1813	LP:19 DEC 1825
Littlepage, Edmund, in King William Co.	King & Queen	Will	1813	CF1885-002
Littlepage, James	Hanover	Will	1807	Cocke:149
Littlepage, James	Hanover	Will	1807	CF1841-013
Littlepage, James	Hanover	Will	1817	CF1841-013
Littlepage, James, of St. Paul's Parish	Hanover	Will	1766	TQ 23:1, p. 57
Littlepage, James, of St. Paul's Parish	Hanover	Will	1766	V:Mss1 H7185 b 330+
Littlepage, James, of St. Paul's Parish	Hanover	Will	1817	Cocke:132
Littlepage, Lewis	Fredericksburg	Will	1802	V:Mss1 H7185 d 159+
Littlepage, Lewis	King William	Will	1863	Fleet, Huntington Data
Littlepage, Lewis	King William	Will	1863	LVA Acc. #41008, r4610
Littlepage, Sarah, in Richmond	Hanover	Will	1820	CF1841-013
Littleton, Ann Southey Harmer	Northampton	Will	1656	V:Mss2 L7345 a 1
Littleton, Ann, w/o Col. Nathaniel	Northampton	Will	1656	VMHB 75, p. 11
Liverett, Thomas	Lunenburg	Will	1783	CF1784-005
Lloyd, Elizabeth		Admin. Ref.	1694	WMQ2 14, p. 264
Lloyd, Elizabeth, of Lower Norfolk Co.		Will	1657	VCRP, Survey #03517
Lloyd, Simon, mariner		Will	1657	VCRP, Survey #03519
Lloyd, William, of Westover Parish	Charles City	Will	1724	D&W1724, p. 12
Lloyd, William [Loyd]	Charles City	Inventory	1724	D&W1724, p. 17
Lockhart, Joseph	Norfolk	Will	1770	T: correct from James
Lockheart, Samuel	New Kent	Will	1836	Swem(1):f217
Lockley, William, of Pr. George Co.		Will	1745	VCRP, Survey #04631
Loe, Charles	Northumberland	Will	1786	CF1848-050
Lofft, Capel, in Eng.	Amelia	Will	1874	CF1878-009
Logwood, Archibald	Chesterfield	Account	1799	LVA:104594
Logwood, Edward	Powhatan	Will	1799	CF1808-002

---

[1] LVA, Land Office Revlutionary War Military Certificate Papers, Reuben Lipscomb, Folder 4.

[2] LVA, Land Office Revolutionary War Military Certificate Papers, Daniel Lipscomb, Folder 31.

[3] King William County Records, Bk. 4, p. 351.

NAME	LOCATION	TYPE	YEAR	REFERENCE(S)
Loker, Thomas	Rockingham	Will	1795	Note[1]
Loker, Thomas	Rockingham	Will	1795	MVG 44:3, p. 192
Loker, Thomas, of Rockingham Co.	Augusta	Will	1795	CF1818-054
Lomax, Thomas [of Portabago]	Caroline	Will	1811	TQ 23:1, p. 60
Long, Bloomfield	Spotsylvania	Will	1763	WBD, p. 47
Long, Charles, in Botetourt Co.	Bedford	Will	1814	CF1837-014
Long, Gabriel, in Culpeper Co.	Rappahannock	Will	1824	CF1858-008
Long, Gabriel, in Culpeper Co.	Rappahannock	Will	1827	CF1859-013
Long, Henry, of Rockingham Co.	Augusta	Will	1779	Note[2]
Long, Robert	Surry	Inventory	1752	T: correct from King
Longest, Elizabeth	King & Queen	Will	1828c	V:Mss1 M1752a92-108
Loomis, Josiah	Fairfax	Will	1853	X
Lothrup, Seth, Jr.	Arlington	Will	1800	CRA:318
Lounds, Henry	Henrico	Will Abstract	1708	VGS Bulletin IV, p. 94
Loury, Thomas, in Amelia Co.	Lunenburg	Will	1767	CF1780-002
Loury, Thomas, in Amelia Co.	Lunenburg	Will	1767	CF1812-017
Love, Allan	Brunswick	Will	1788	CF1815-001
Love, Allen	Brunswick	Will	1799	CF1799-005
Love, Daniel		Will	1790	LVA Acc. #25204
Love, Samuel	Prince William	Will	1787	Note[3]
Love, William	Stafford	Estate Ref.	1786	Hening, Vol. 12, p. 408
Lovejoy, Margaret	Fairfax	Will	1834	NVG 8, p. 1096
Loven, Edwin B.	King & Queen	Will	(nd)	V:Mss10: no. 244
Lovett, John	Norfolk	Inventory	1687	DB5, p. 29
Loving, Maria Pettis	Nelson	Will	1856	UVA MSS 11488
Loving, William	Amherst	Will	1792	V:Mss1 B2346 a 656+
Lowe, Micajah, of Charles City Co.	London	Will	1703	N:PROB11/469
Lowry, Charles B.	Bath	Will	1796	UVA Acc. #1253i
Lowry, John, of Elizabeth City Co.	Williamsburg	Will Abstract	1790	Crozier, p. 35
Lowry, Mathew	Goochland	Will	1794	CF1842-006
Lowry, Thomas, in Amelia Co.	Lunenburg	Will	1767	CF1807-016
Lowther, Gerard	Stafford	Will (N) P.	1690	OB: 11 MAR 1690
Loyd, Elizabeth		Will	1694	WMQ 14, p. 264
Loyd, Lewis, planter	Rappahannock*	Will	1690	Sweeny, p. 147
Loyd, William	Charles City	Will	1725	D&W1724, p. 12
Loyd, William [Lloyd]	Charles City	Inventory	1724	D&W1724, p. 17
Lucas, Anthony	Prince William	Will	1796	CF1903-001
Lucas, Fieldilng, in Spotsylvania Co.	Culpeper	Will	1841	CF1885-049
Lucas, Fielding, in Fredericksburg	Culpeper	Will	1841	CF1852-004
Lucas, Fielding, in Fredericksburg	Culpeper	Will	1841	CF1850-005
Lucas, Fielding, in Spotsylvania Co.	Culpeper	Will	1861	CF1880-031
Lucas, Francis		Will	1740	LVA Acc. #24961-3
Lucas, Monica, of Alexandria	Arlington	Will	1864	CF1871-009
Lucas, Robert, in Warwick Co.	York	Will	1782	CF1790-006
Lucas, Robert, of Warwick Co.	York	Will	1782	MVG 31:4, p. 356
Lucas, Samuel	Hanover	Will	1884	CF1888-018

---

[1] Rockingham County Land Causes 1 & 2, p. 75, *John Loker v. Sarah Loker* (1819).
[2] Augusta County District Court Orders, Bk. 1797-1803, p. 6.
[3] LVA, U.S. Circuit Court Records, box 233, *Bird & Roberts v. Watson & Love* (1816).

NAME	LOCATION	TYPE	YEAR	REFERENCE(S)
Lucas, William	Jefferson	Will	1877	V:Mss1 L9625 b 3-4
Lucas, William, in Orange Co.	Henry	Will	1813	CF1850-032
Lucas, William, joiner		Will	1738	VCRP, Survey #04650
Lucke, Gustavous, elder, in Richmond	Henrico	Will	1834	CF1898-032
Luckett, Ludwell, in Loudoun Co.	Bath	Will	1875	CF1893-012
Luckett, Virlinda, in MD	Frederick	Will	1828	CF1831-214
Luckett, William, in MD	Frederick	Will	1783	CF1831-214
Ludeman, William	Richmond City	Will	1786	T:HCD1, p. 50
Ludlowe, George	York	Will	1655	VMHB 29, p. 353
Ludlowe, George, of York Co.		Will	1656	VCRP, Survey #03131
Ludwell, Thomas	Williamsburg	Will	1676	CW(8)
Ludwell, Thomas		Will	1679	VCRP, Survey #03719
Lumpkin, Achilles	Hanover	Will	1859	CF1869-010
Lumpkin, Archilles	Hanover	Will	1859	Cocke:85
Lumpkin, John	King & Queen	Will	1826c	V:Mss3 K5893 a 69-86
Lumpkin, Richard	King & Queen	Sale	1830	BRCD
Lumpkin, Richardson	King & Queen	Will	1863	LVA Acc. #28458
Lumsden, David	Prince George	Will	1854	SV 9:4, p. 159
Lutz, Balser, in Augusta Co.	Rockingham	Will	1850	CF1880-054
Lutz, Philip	Jefferson	Estate Ref.	1791	Hening, Vol. 13, p. 303
Luxon, Henry		Will	1768	VCRP, Survey #04696
Lyddall, George, Capt.	New Kent	Will	1703	UVA MSS 5241-a
Lyde, James		Will	1731	VCRP, Survey #08286
Lyell, Jonathan, of Dinwiddie Co.	Mecklenburg	Will	1759	CF1798-013
Lyle, James	Bath	Will	1885	CF1909-006
Lyle, James, Sr.	Chesterfield	Will	1812	LVA Acc. #36336
Lyle, James, Sr.	Chesterfield	Will	1812	Note[1]
Lyle, John, in Berkeley Co.	Frederick	Will	1798	CF1829-153
Lyle, John, in Berkeley Co.	Frederick	Will	1798	CF1851-114
Lyles, Nancy Eleanor	Fairfax	Guard. Bond	1790	X
Lynch, Anselm, in Campbell Co.	Lynchburg	Will	1826	CF1835-001
Lynch, Charles H., in Campbell Co.	Lynchburg	Will	1875	CF1887-043
Lynch, Charles Henry, in Campbell Co.	Lynchburg	Will	1875	CF1881-013
Lynch, Charles Henry, in Campbell Co.	Lynchburg	Will	1875	CF1882-005
Lynch, John		Will	1743	VCRP, Survey #04619
Lynch, John, in Lynchburg	Campbell	Will	1820	CF1852-028
Lynch, Patrick, in Hardy Co.	Frederick	Will	1803	CF1823-209
Lyne, Henry	King & Queen	Will	1798	TVF 12:4, p. 224
Lyne, Henry, in Henry Co.	Lynchburg	Will	1807	CF1857-026
Lyne, John	Richmond City	Will	1799	T:HCD2, p. 525
Lyne, John, in Richmond	Essex	Will	1799	CF1833-031
Lyne, Robert B., in Richmond	Henrico	Will	1881	CF1913-002
Lyne, William	King & Queen	Will	1808	LP
Lyne, William Henry	Orange	Will	1887	V:Mss1 L9933 a 2-3
Lyne, William, in King & Queen Co.	Essex	Will	1808	CF1831-044
Lynn, Benson	Prince William	Will	1858	CF1880-017
Lynton, John	Prince William	Will Ref.	1727	WBK, p. 283

---

[1] LVA, Crittenden, Jones, Tyler Families Papers, 1768-1809, as found on Misc. Reel #6. Pages are unnumbered, and will begins on the 17th page of the manuscript material.

NAME	LOCATION	TYPE	YEAR	REFERENCE(S)
Lynton, John	Stafford	Will	1728	V:Mss1 T2118 d27684+
Lynton, John	Stafford	Will	1728	VGSQ 10:4, p. 98
Lynton, Moses	Prince William	Will Ref.	1729	WBK, p. 321
Lynton, Moses	Stafford	Will	1729	V:Mss1 T2118 d27684+
Lynton, Moses, of Overwharton Parish	Stafford	Will	1729	VGSQ 10:4, p. 98
Lyon, Elisha, in Franklin Co.	Lynchburg	Will	1787	CF1822-010
Lyon, Sarah, in Franklin Co.	Lynchburg	Will	1789	CF1822-010
Lyon, Walter	Princess Anne	Will	1775	DB14, p. 149a
Lyons, James	Hanover	Will	1835	V:Mss1 H3968 a 903+
Lyons, John	Hanover	Will	1819	Cocke:86
Lyons, John	Hanover	Will	1819	CF1840-007
Lyons, Peter	Hanover	Will	1837	CF1840-007
Lyons, Peter, in Richmond	Hanover	Will	1837	Cocke:87

NAME	LOCATION	TYPE	YEAR	REFERENCE(S)

M

NAME	LOCATION	TYPE	YEAR	REFERENCE(S)
Maben, John, in Richmond	Gloucester	Will	1880	CF1910-005
Macbee, William, of Prince George Co.	Amelia	Account	1735	LP 1730-1740s
Machen, Henry	Prince William	Will	1752	MVG 28:3, p. 191
Machen, Henry	Prince William	Will	1752	MVG 48:4, p. 264
Machir, Alexander	Shenandoah	Will	1790	V:Mss1 G8855 b 124+
Macintosh, Martha	Surry	Will (U)	1825	VTG 13:3, p. 123
Macintosh, Martha	Surry	Will Abstract	1825	VG 13, p. 54
Mackall, John, of Rockingham Co.	Augusta	Will	1799	CF1805-105
Mackenzie, Donald	Petersburg	Will	1841	LVA Acc. #23709d-j
Mackey, Nelley	Isle of Wight	Will (U)	1808	SV 14:1, p. 19
Mackghee, John, in Hanover Co.	Franklin	Will	1828	CF1850-027
Mackghee, John, of Hanover Co.	Floyd	Will	1828	CF1828-frame 464
Mackie, Andrew, Sr., of Surry Co.	Williamsburg	Will Abstract	180-	Crozier, p. 40
Mackie, Josias, Rev., of Norfolk Co.	Princess Anne	Will	1716	VMHB 7, p. 358
MacNair, Ralph	Richmond City	Will	1785	T:HCD1, p. 41
Macon, Elizabeth Moore	King William	Will	1779	Swem(2)
Macon, Elizabeth, wid., St. John's Par.	King William	Will	1779	WMQ 14, p. 265
Macon, Gideon	New Kent	Will	1767	TVF 1:2, p. 88
Macon, Gideon, in New Kent Co.	Amelia	Will	1769	CF1792-025
Macon, Henry, of Powhatan Co.	Cumberland	Will	1809	CF1830-004
Macon, John, of Powhatan Co.	Cumberland	Will	1793	CF1807-005
Macon, Sarah, of *Mount Prospect*	New Kent	Will	1849	CF1881-008
Macon, Thomas	Hanover	Will	1886	CF1891-014
Macon, William Hartwell	New Kent	Will	1843	Swem(1):f218
Macrae, Philip	Richmond City	Will	1794	T:HCD2, p. 145
Maddox, Allison	Prince William	Will Ref.	1843	CM:07 AUG 1843
Maddox, Robert	Henrico	Inventory	1771	Records, Vol. 7, p. 2135
Maddox, Sarah	Prince William	Will Ref.	1844	CM:06 MAY 1844
Maddox, William	Buckingham	Will	1801	Note[1]
Maddox, William	Buckingham	Will	1801	VGSQ 16:1, p. 28
Maddox, William	Buckingham	Will	1801	TQ 14:3, p. 161
Maddox, William G.	Hanover	Will	1890	CF1893-008
Maddox, William, of Buckingham Co.	Prince Edward	Will	1801	TQ 14, p. 161
Madison, Ambrose, of St. Mark's Parish	Spotsylvania	Will	1732	VG 26, p. 286
Madison, Ambrose, of St. Mark's Parish	Spotsylvania	Will	1732	VMHB 6, p. 434
Madison, George W.	Caroline	Will	1855	BRCD
Madison, George W., in Caroline Co.	Louisa	Will	1855	CF1864-001
Madison, George W. [of *Poplar Grove*]	Caroline	Will	1855	V:Mss1 M7445 a 4311+
Madison, James	Orange	Will	1836	LVA Acc. #21638
Madison, James	Orange	Will	1836	V:Mss10: no. 167
Madison, James, of Orange Co.	D.C.	Will	1883	DCA:Box 83
Madison, James, Rev.	James City	Will	1812	VMHB 38, p. 373
Madison, John, of Botetourt Co.	Augusta	Will	1784	CF1796-009
Madison, Thomas	Botetourt	Will	1798	LVA Acc. #20716
Maffitt, John		Will	1684	T: not Rappahannock[2]
Maffitt, William	Fairfax	Account	1844	X

---

[1] Also see Prince Edward County District Court Wills, Bk. 2, p. 21.

[2] Refer to Sweeny, p. 9, where the compiler lists wills given in *Torrence* that have not been found of record in Rappahannock County.

NAME	LOCATION	TYPE	YEAR	REFERENCE(S)
Magarety, Patrick	Surry	Account	1725	T: not inventory
Magart, Christian	Shenandoah	Will	1828c	V:Mss3 Sh453 a 44-73
Maget, Samuel	Surry	Will	1693	T:D&W4, p. 302a
Magruder, Rebecca, in MD	Albemarle	Will	1796	CF1813-049
Magruder, Robert P., in WV	Albemarle	Will	1881	CF1881-002
Magruder, Thomas	Fairfax	Appraisal	1785	X
Maib, William	Albemarle	Will	1762	T: correct from Mail
Major, Barnard	Charles City	Will	1777	LVA Acc. #19933
Major, Bernard	Charles City	Will	1777	LVA Acc. #24384
Major, Edward		Will	1661	Note[1]
Major, John	Charles City	Inventory	1769	Records, p. 118
Major, Nicholas	Charles City	Inventory	1728	D&W1724, p. 228
Major, Richard	Middlesex	Will	1750	Fleet 2:328
Major, Samuel	York	Will	1785	BRCD
Major, Samuel	York	Will	1785	CF1835-001
Major, Samuel	Dinwiddie	Will Ref.	1808	LP:12 DEC 1808
Major, Susannah		Will	1663	Note[2]
Majors, Edward	Nansemond	Will	1654	Note[3]
Makely, B.T.	Fairfax	Will	1860	X
Malden, Joseph		Inventory	1688	LVA Wills/Admin. DB
Malin, David	Frederick	Will	1761	MVG 29:3, p. 192
Malle, Daniel	Rappahannock*	Will (N)	1686	Sweeny, p. 132
Mallicote, John	Warwick	Will	1719	Note[4]
Mallicote, Thomas	Surry	Will	1792	T: correct from Millicote
Mallicote, Thomas, of Warwick Co.	York	Will	1826	MVG 31:4, p. 353
Mallory, Charles King	Norfolk City	Will	1872	V:Mss1 M2976 a 52-64
Mallory, Diana	Elizabeth City	Will	1782	V:Mss1 M2976 a 52-64
Mallory, Florisbella, of King Wm. Co.	London	Will	1769	N:PROB11/951
Mallory, Francis	Elizabeth City	Will	1742	V:Mss1 M2976 a 52-64
Mallory, Francis	Elizabeth City	Will	1744	VMHB 14, pp. 219, 322
Mallory, Francis		Inventory	1788	V:Mss1 M2976 a 52-64
Mallory, John	Orange	Inventory	(nd)	UVA MSS 38-140
Mallory, John	Orange	Will	1774	UVA MSS 38-140
Mallory, John, of Isle of Wight Co.	Williamsburg	Will Abstract	1789	Crozier, p. 39
Mallory, Johnson	Elizabeth City	Will	1760	V:Mss1 M2976 a 52-64
Mallory, Johnson	Elizabeth City	Will	1762	VMHB 14, pp. 218, 323
Mallory, Nathan	Orange	Will	1875	UVA MSS 38-140
Mallory, Philip, clerk		Will	1661	VCRP, Survey #03529
Mallory, William	Elizabeth City	Will	1720	V:Mss1 M2976 a 52-64
Mallory, William, of Eliz. City Co.		Will	1769	VCRP, Survey #04698
Malone, Jones	Mecklenburg	Will	1784	WB2, p. 72
Man, Mary Elizabeth, in NY	Louisa	Will	1896	CF1905-032
Maners, John	Surry	Inventory	1698	T:D&W5, p. 167a
Manfield, George, merchant		Will	1670	VCRP, Survey #03545
Manger, Peter F., in Fredericksburg	Culpeper	Will	1805	CF1831-003

---

[1] James B. Cabell, *The Majors and Their Marriages*, p. 25.

[2] James B. Cabell, *The Majors and Their Marriages*, p. 24.

[3] James B. Cabell, *The Majors and Their Marriages*, p. 24.

[4] Warwick County Records, Bk. 1719, p. 256.

NAME	LOCATION	TYPE	YEAR	REFERENCE(S)
Manifee, Jonas	Culpeper	Will	1782	WBB, p. 533
Mankin, William	Arlington	Estate Ref.	(nd)	CF1874-003
Manlove, Christopher, of Dinwiddie Co.	Petersburg	Will	1804	Judgments 1844
Manlove, Mary Eppes	Dinwiddie	Will	1820	LVA Acc. #41008, r4608
Manlove, Mary Eppes, Sr.	Dinwiddie	Will	1820	Fleet, Huntington Data
Manlove, Mary Eppes, Sr.	Dinwiddie	Will	1820	LVA Acc. #28517
Manlove, Robert	Norfolk	Will	1824	LVA Acc. #41008, r4611
Manlove, Robert	Norfolk	Will	1824	Fleet, Huntington Data
Mann, Eliza V., in Scott Co.	Wise	Will	1898	CF1900-089
Mann, Hugh C., in Middlesex Co.	King & Queen	Will	1851	CF1868-001
Mann, John	Gloucester	Will	1694	Mason, Vol. 2
Mann, John	Gloucester	Will	1694	WMQ2 6, p. 136
Mann, Joseph		Account	1817c	V:Mss1 H7935 a 1
Mann, Mary, of Abingdon Parish	Gloucester	Will	1704	WMQ2 6, p. 138
Mann, Mary, of Abingdon Parish	Gloucester	Will	1704	Mason, Vol. 2
Mann, Robert	Essex	Will	1797	CF1823-019
Mann, Robert	King & Queen	Estate Ref.	1800+	Fleet, 2nd Collection
Mann, Robert	King & Queen	Will	1827	LP
Mann, Robert, in King & Queen Co.	Essex	Will	1827	CF1901-026
Mann, Robert, of South Farnham Par.	Essex	Will	1797	Fleet 2:351
Mann, Thomas, in King & Queen Co.	Gloucester	Will	1857	CF1903-036
Mann, William, of Botetourt Co.	Augusta	Will	1778	CF1818-064
Manning, William	New Kent	Will	1834	Note[1]
Manning, William	New Kent	Will	1834	LVA Acc. #33141
Manson, Peter	Dinwiddie	Will	1793	SV 11:4, p. 186
Marable, Mathew, in Mecklenburg Co.	Lunenburg	Will	1786	CF1795-007
March, Bernard, of Nansemond Co.	Williamsburg	Will Abstract	1815	Crozier, p. 39
Marden, Jesse, in MD	Hanover	Will	1877	CF1902-033
Marders, Barbara	King George	Will	1843	LVA Acc. #42107
Marin, Elizabeth	York	Will	1805	CF1839-002
Mariwether, Francis	Essex	Estate Ref.	1713	Land Trials 1741, p. 188
Mariwether, Martha	Louisa	Will	1787	Note[2]
Mariwether, Nicholas		Will Ref.	1678	LVA Acc. #26900
Markey, Nicolas, in Botetourt Co.	Roanoke	Will	1824	CF1850-008
Markham, Jane Waller	Stafford	Will	1815	TQ 31:4, p. 264
Markham, John		Inventory	1804	LVA Acc. #42842
Markham, John	Stafford	Will	1804	Fleet, Huntington Data
Markham, John	Stafford	Will	1804	TQ 31:3, p. 180
Markham, John	Stafford	Will	1804	LVA Acc. #22956
Markham, John	York	Will	1804	LVA Acc. #41008, r4614
Markle, Charles, Sr., in MO	Bedford	Will	1827	CF1870-166
Markle, Charles, Sr., in MO	Bedford	Will	1828	CF1847-025
Markle, Charles, Sr., in MO	Bedford	Will	1828	CF1846-013
Marks, Edward, in Prince George Co.	Petersburg	Will	1823	CF1855-033
Marks, Edward, Jr.	Prince George	Will	1823	LVA Acc. #22296
Marks, Elisha, in Loudoun Co.	Frederick	Will	1805	CF1832-085
Marks, Mary H.	Prince George	Will	1843	SV 9:3, p. 108

---

[1] See *The Southside Virginian*, Vol. VIII No. 1 (January 1990), pp. 10-11. Source identity and location is not shown.

[2] Louisa County Wills Not Fully Proved, 1757-1902, p. 32.

NAME	LOCATION	TYPE	YEAR	REFERENCE(S)
Marks, Richard	Prince George	Will	1828	BRCD
Marks, Richard E.	Prince George	Will	1851	BRCD
Marks, Richard E., in Prince George Co.	Petersburg	Will	1851	CF1854-011
Marks, Richard, in Prince George Co.	Petersburg	Will	1828	CF1854-036
Marquess, Anthony, d. 15 DEC 1821	Stafford	Will	1822	TQ 24:2, p. 110
Marr, Alexander, in Amherst Co.	Lynchburg	Will	1807	CF1818-013
Marrable, Charles, of Charles City Co.	Williamsburg	Will Abstract	1778	Crozier, p. 38
Marrow, Daniel		Will	1748	DB5, p. 522
Marshall, George, mariner		Will	1720	VCRP, Survey #04642
Marshall, James	Fairfax	Will	1815	NVG 6, p. 626
Marshall, James	Fairfax	Appraisal	1816	NVG 6, p. 626
Marshall, James Eben, Charles Co. MD	Arlington	Will	1812	CF1848-006
Marshall, James M., in Frederick Co.	Fauquier	Will	1848	CF1849-003
Marshall, James Pulliam	Charlotte	Will	1864	V:Mss1 H3968 a 133+
Marshall, John	Lancaster	Will	1726	LP
Marshall, John	Lancaster	Will	1726	LP
Marshall, John	Richmond City	Will	1835	LVA Acc. #24903
Marshall, John	Richmond City	Will	1835	V:Mss2 M3567 a 2
Marshall, John, in Richmond	Fauquier	Will	1835	CF1850-002
Marshall, John, in Richmond	Fauquier	Will	1835	CF1848-033
Marshall, John J., of Hanover Co.	Henrico	Will	1844	CF1846-002
Marshall, John, mariner		Will	1717	VCRP, Survey #04337
Marshall, Lucy, in Fauquier Co.	Culpeper	Will	1825	CF1838-009
Marshall, Thomas	Northumberland	Account	1752	M: L32 f340
Marshall, Thomas	Northumberland	Will	1761	M: L31 f250
Marshall, Thomas	Northampton	Account	1762	M: L48 f187
Marshall, Thomas	Richmond City	Will Cert.	1817	V:Mss2 D9567 b
Marshall, Thomas	Bedford	Will	1819	UVA MSS 4306
Marshall, Thomas, carpenter	Westmoreland	Will	1704	VMHB 2, p. 343
Marshall, Thomas, of Woodford Co. KY	Richmond City	Will Cert.	1802	V:Mss2 D9567 b
Marshall, Thomas T.	Fairfax	Account C.	1860	X
Marshall, William, in Gloucester Co.	Culpeper	Will	1796	CF1834-016
Marshall, William, of Abingdon Parish	Gloucester	Will	(nd)	VMHB 38, p. 74
Marshall, William, of Richmond City	Augusta	Will	1817	CF1866-050
Marsteller, Samuel A.	Prince William	Will	1869	CF1904-007
Marston, John, of Surry Co.	Williamsburg	Will Abstract	1798	Crozier, p. 38
Marston, John Soane	Charles City	Inventory	1771	Records, p. 265
Martin, Elizabeth Ann Winfree	Richmond City	Will	1863	V:Mss1 M3644 a 11-15
Martin, Elizabeth Aphra	Richmond City	Will	1872	V:Mss1 M3644 a 11-15
Martin, Elizabeth, of Rockingham Co.	Augusta	Will	1798	CF1821-033
Martin, George	Frederick	Will	1752	WB2, p. 73
Martin, Hudson, in Eng.	Goochland	Will	1755	CF1818-004
Martin, James, in Amherst Co.	Lynchburg	Will	1775	CF1835-007
Martin, John	King William	Will	1748	LVA Acc. #26035ah
Martin, John		Will	1756	Note[1]
Martin, John	Fairfax	Will	1757	CF1858-040
Martin, John	Goochland	Will	1856	Fleet, Huntington Data
Martin, John [of *Clifton*]	Caroline	Will	1738	CF1808-023

---

[1] *Journals of the House of Burgesses, 1752-1758*, p. 356.

NAME	LOCATION	TYPE	YEAR	REFERENCE(S)
Martin, John [of *Clifton*]	Caroline	Will	1783	W&P1742, p. 33
Martin, Joseph T., in MO	Henry	Will	1880	CF1889-006
Martin, Mary Ann	Westmoreland	Will	1791	Wills #39
Martin, Mildred Pollard	King William	Will	1826	LVA Acc. #21309
Martin, Peter	Surry	Inventory	1688	T:D&W4, p. 60a
Martin, Richard, merchant		Will	1721	VCRP, Survey #04663
Martin, Samuel H., in MO	Henry	Will	1873	CF1889-006
Martin, Stephen, in Bedford Co.	Lynchburg	Will	1849	CF1858-019
Martin, Thomas B.	King William	Will	1853	CF1912-004
Martin, Thomas Bryan	Frederick	Will		V:Mss2 H2463 d
Martin, Vallentine	Cumberland	Will	1760	WB1, p. 203
Martin, William	Chesterfield	Division	1811	LVA Acc. #23219
Martin, William	Chesterfield	Plat	1811	LVA Acc. #23219
Martin, William, mariner		Will	1705	VCRP, Survey #04146
Martsh, Caroline, in NY	Fairfax	Will	1862	CF1879-034
Martyn, Nicholas		Will	1656	VCRP, Survey #03132
Martz, Sebastian	Rockingham	Will Ref.	1818	LVA:1159583
Mary, John	Rockingham	Will	1833	CF1859-037
Marye, James	Spotsylvania	Will	1780	FDC L568-66
Mason, Ann	Prince William	Will Partial	1762	Note[1]
Mason, Armistead T.		Will	1818	Mason
Mason, David	Williamsburg	Admin.	1839	Swem(1):f164
Mason, Edward	Stafford	Will P.	1690	OB: 10 SEP 1690
Mason, Edward	Stafford	Admin.	1691	OB: 08 OCT 1691
Mason, Francis		Will	1696	TQ 24:4, p. 230
Mason, George	Fairfax	Will	(nd)	CF1903-026
Mason, George	Stafford	Will	1715	Note[2]
Mason, George	Fairfax	Will	1792	V:Mss2 M3813 a 3
Mason, George	Arlington	Will	1795	CRA:180
Mason, George	Arlington	Inventory	1796	CRA:189
Mason, George, in Alexandria	Fairfax	Will	1888	CF1903-026
Mason, George, of *Gunston Hall*	Fairfax	Will	1792	HSF 6, p. 1
Mason, George, of *Lexington*	Fairfax	Will	1787	Gunston Hall
Mason, George, Sr.	Stafford	Will	1715	Note[3]
Mason, George, Sr.	Stafford	Will	1716	LVA Acc. #20487 p. 249
Mason, James	Surry	Inventory	1752	T: correct from John
Mason, James, of Botetourt Co.	Augusta	Will	1808	CF1855-052
Mason, John	Caroline	Will	1780	BRCD
Mason, John, in Greensville Co.	Brunswick	Will	1793	CF1804-031
Mason, John, of *Clermont*	D.C.	Will	1866	DCA:Box 36
Mason, John Young	Southampton	Will	1859c	V:Mss1 M3816 c 1327+
Mason, Josiah	Rappahannock*	Will	1687	Sweeny, p. 135
Mason, Lewis Edmunds	Southampton	Will	1878	V:Mss1 M3816 c 4813+
Mason, Peter	Hanover	Inventory	1766	V:Mss4 F2944 b
Mason, Peter	Hanover	Inventory	1766	LVA Acc. #25116
Mason, Peter, in Fayette Co. KY	Hanover	Will	1766	V:Mss4 F2944 b

[1] Prince William County Land Causes, 1793-1811, p. 21.
[2] Kate Mason Rowland, *Life of George Mason* (1892), Vol. 1, p. 376.
[3] Fairfax County Land Causes, 1812-1832, p. 13.

NAME	LOCATION	TYPE	YEAR	REFERENCE(S)
Mason, Peter, of St. Martin's Parish	Hanover	Will	1766	LVA Acc. #25116
Mason, Richard	Southampton	Will	1836	V:Mss1 M3816 b 71-72
Mason, Sarah, of Overwharton Parish	Stafford	Will	1716	Note[1]
Mason, Stephen Thomson, Loudoun Co.	Frederick	Will	1803	CF1823-221
Mason, Stephens Thomson, in Loudoun	Frederick	Will	1815	CF1820-238
Mason, Stevens Thomson	Frederick	Will	1803	Mason
Mason, Stevens Thomson	Frederick	Will	1815	Mason
Mason, William, in Charles Co. MD	Fairfax	Will	1818	CF1857-028
Mason, William, in Charles Co. MD	Fairfax	Will	1818	X
Mason, William, in Charles Co. MD	Fairfax	Inventory	1827	X
Massenburgh, John, of Elizabeth City	London	Will	1749	N:PROB11/772
Massey, John, in Madison Co.	Culpeper	Will	1833	CF1840-022
Massey, Sigismund	Stafford	Will P.	1692	OB: 10 MAY 1692
Massey, Thomas [Massy]	New Kent	Will Ref.	1731	Note[2]
Massie, John, of Goochland Co.	Hanover	Will	1748	G2:23
Massie, John W.	Fairfax	Will	1840	X
Massie, Maria Catherine Effinger	Nelson	Will	1887	V:Mss1 M3855 g 692+
Massie, Maria Catherine Effinger	Nelson	Inventory	1889	V:Mss1 M3855 g 692+
Massie, Sarah Cocke	Nelson	Will	1834	V:Mss1 M3855 g 809+
Massie, Thomas	Fauquier	Will	1801	TQ 13:2, p. 124
Massie, Thomas	Fauquier	Will	1834	V:Mss1 M3855 g 118+
Massie, Thomas	Nelson	Will	1834	LVA Acc. #41008, r4300
Massie, Thomas	Nelson	Will	1834	Fleet, Huntington Data
Massie, Thomas, in Nelson Co.	Albemarle	Will	1864	CF1893-048
Massie, William	New Kent	Will	1793	V:Mss2 C3557 b 1-4
Massie, William	Nelson	Will	1844	V:Mss1 M3855 g 524+
Massie, William, of St. Peter's Parish	New Kent	Will	1751	WMQ 13, p. 199
Massie, William, of St. Peter's Parish	New Kent	Will	1751c	V:Mss1 M3855 a 5499+
Massie, William, of St. Peter's Parish	New Kent	Will	1793	WMQ 27, p. 244
Masters, Henry B.	New Kent	Will	1885	CF1890-003
Mateer, James	Fairfax	Division	1869	X
Mateer, James	Fairfax	Plat	1869	X
Mathers, Sarah, late of Washington DC	Arlington	Will	1821	File #61A
Mathewes, Thomas, of *Merchant's Hope*	London	Will (N)	1645	N:Guildhall
Mathews, James S., in Norfolk Co.	Portsmouth	Will	1819	CF1901-011
Mathews, Robins Kendal	Accomack	Will	1780	T: correct from Kendall
Matthews, Edwin, in Lynchburg	Bedford	Will	1855	CF1867-014
Matthews, James S., in Norfolk Co.	Portsmouth	Will	1819	CF1889-042
Matthews, John, of Gloucester Co.	Williamsburg	Will Abstract	1767	Crozier, p. 36
Matthews, Stafford	Prince William	Acct. Ref.	1843	CM:04 SEP 1843
Matthews, Thomas, Northumberland Co.	London	Will	1707	N:PROB11/492
Matthias, Hilliary	Princess Anne	Will	1799	SV 11:1, p. 30
Matthis, Edward	Southampton	Will	1761	BRCD
Mattox, Sally	Prince George	Will	1833	SV 9:2, p. 54
Maule, Margaret	Henrico	Will	1835	LVA Acc. #41008, r4610
Maule, Margaret, of Richmond	Henrico	Will	1835	Fleet, Huntington Data
Maupin, Catherine M.	James City	Will	1879	CF1899-005

---

[1] LVA, Acc. #20487, p. 252, John Mercer's Land Book.
[2] LVA, Colonial Papers, folder 37, 1733-1735, No. 4, 1 NOV 1733.

NAME	LOCATION	TYPE	YEAR	REFERENCE(S)
Maupin, Catherine M.	James City	Will	1879	CF1897-007
Maupin, Gabriel, of Williamsburg	James City	Will	1719	LVA Acc. #28374h
Maupin, Gabriel, of Williamsburg	James City	Will	1720	Note[1]
Maupin, John M.	James City	Will	1851	Swem(1):f164
Mauzey, David	Lancaster	Will	1713	LP
Mauzy, Henry	Fauquier	Will	1804	V:Mss1 G8274a293-294
Maxwell, James	Norfolk City	Will	1795	WB1
May, Agnes, in Campbell Co.	Bedford	Will	1805	CF1846-021
May, William	James City	Will Ref.	1677	LVA Wills/Admin. DB
Mayberry, Rebecca, in Berkeley Co.	Louisa	Will	1873	CF1899-031
Mayberry, Sarah Ann, in Berkeley Co.	Louisa	Will	1873	CF1899-031
Mayers, Stephen, in Berkeley Co.	Frederick	Will	1827	CF1836-047
Maylard, Poynes	Charles City	Inventory	1727	D&W1724, p. 184
Maynard, Henry, merchant		Will	1727	VCRP, Survey #04646
Maynard, Nathaniel	Charles City	Will	1769	Records, p. 139
Mayo, Abigail DeHart	Richmond City	Will	1843	V:Mss1 M4544 a 15-18
Mayo, James, in Norfolk Co.	Portsmouth	Will	1855	CF1881-006
Mayo, John	Chesterfield	Will	1786	V:Mss1 M4544 a 15-18
Mayo, John	Henrico	Will	1818	V:Mss1 M4544 a 15-18
Mayo, Joseph	Henrico	Will Ref.	1780	Hening, Vol. 12, p. 611
Mayo, Joseph	Henrico	Will Ref.	1780	Washington, p. 45
Mays, James, in Nelson Co.	Lynchburg	Will	1825	CF1831-012
Mays, Zachariah, in Nelson	Lynchburg	Will	1825	CF1830-094
Mazaret, John, in Westmoreland Co.	Essex	Will	1794	CF1845-018
Mazaret, John, in Westmoreland Co.	Essex	Will	1794	CF1845-017
McAdam, John	Northumberland	Will	1807	BRCD
McAdam, Joseph	Northumberland	Will	1788	CF1848-049
McAdams, John	Northumberland	Will	1787	TVF 4:2, p. 106
McAllister, Elijah	Rockingham	Will Ref.	1795	LVA:1159583
McCabe, William, in Bedford Co.	Campbell	Will	1856	CF1859-007
McCall, Catharine Flood, of Richmond	London	Will	1831	N:PROB11/784
McCall, Catherine Flood, Richmond Co.	Essex	Will	1828	CF1836-014
McCandless, William A., in PA	Henrico	Will	1892	CF1896-015
McCandlish, Robert, in James City Co.	Gloucester	Will	1859	CF1912-054
McCannon, Christopher	Richmond City	Will	1793	T:HCD2, p. 87
McCarty, Daniel, in Fairfax Co.	Frederick	Will	1792	CF1833-027
McCarty, Susan, in Norfolk	Campbell	Will	1899	CF1900-010
McCarty, Thaddeus	Lancaster	Will	1787	LP
McCarty, Thaddeus, in Loudoun Co.	Frederick	Will	1812	CF1830-154
McCarty, Thadeus, in Loudoun Co.	Frederick	Will	1812	CF1829-046
McClanahan, Mary, in Augusta Co.	Bedford	Will	1855	CF1858-020
McClanahan, Mary W., in Augusta Co.	Roanoke	Will	1855	CF1858-017
McClanahan, William, in Botetourt Co.	Augusta	Will	1819	CF1832-037
McClanahan, William, in Botetourt Co.	Bedford	Will	1820	CF1858-020
McClanahan, William, in Botetourt Co.	Roanoke	Will	1821	CF1839-011
McClean, Daniel, in DC	Fauquier	Will	1823	CF1866-006
McClenachan, Alexander, Col.	Augusta	Inventory	1797	WB1A, p. 27
McClenachan, John	Augusta	Will	1774	MVG 29:3, p. 192

[1] Nell Watson Sherman, *The Maupin Family* (1962), copied by Dr. Socrates Maupin, c.1850.

NAME	LOCATION	TYPE	YEAR	REFERENCE(S)
McClintic, Alexander H.	Bath	Will	1869	CF1906-023
McCloud, Joseph	Richmond City	Will	1791	T:HCD1, p. 523
McClure, Malcom, of Botetourt Co.	Augusta	Will	1781	CF1836-037
McClure, William, in IN	Bedford	Will	1843	CF1863-009
McComb, Janetta B., in Augusta Co.	Staunton	Will	1885	CF1895-010
McCook, Neal	Hanover	Will	1838	CF1868-012
McCook, Neal	Hanover	Will	1838	Cocke:89
McCord, William, in Shenandoah Co.	Prince Edward	Will	1838	CF1866-006
McCoy, Lewis A.	Prince William	Will	1861	CF1883-025
McCrabb, William	Washington	Will	1831c	V:Mss1 P9267 e 2185+
McCraw, James Harvey, Botetourt Co.	Bedford	Will	1832	CF1836-027
McCredie, George, in Henrico Co.	Lynchburg	Will	1807	CF1816-009
McCuin, William	Prince William	Will Ref.	1844	CM:01 JUL 1844
McCullock, Jeremiah, in Pittsylvania Co.	Lynchburg	Will	1849	CF1882-047
McCullugh, Thomas	Washington	Will	1780	Finley
McCune, John, of Rockingham Co.	Augusta	Will	1820	CF1827-099
McCutchan, Cyrus A., in Augusta Co.	Bath	Will	1890	CF1908-006
McCutchan, Jane	Augusta	Will	(nd)	UVA Acc. #3334
McDonald, Alexander	Fairfax	Will	1793	CF1847-002
McDonald, Ann, in Charles Co. MD	Fairfax	Will	1773	CF1847-002
McDonald, Ann, in Charles Co. MD	Fairfax	Will	1773	X
McDonald, Colin	Dinwiddie	Will	1772	LVA Acc. #28657-11
McDonald, Daniel, in Nelson Co.	Lynchburg	Will	1812	CF1848-008
McDonald, Duncan, of Norfolk Borough	Williamsburg	Will Abstract	1806	Crozier, p. 38
McDonald, Henrietta	Fairfax	Will	1794	X
McDonald, Mary	Fairfax	Will	1794	CF1847-002
McDonald, Ronald, Rockingham Co. NC	Henry	Will	1834	CF1846-003
McFarland, Jonathan F.	Fairfax	Inventory	1853	X
McFarland, Jonathan F.	Fairfax	Sale	1853	X
McFarlane, Thomas	Westmoreland	Will	1755	Finley
McFarlane, Thomas	Westmoreland	Will	1755c	VTG 30:2, p. 9
McGavock, James	Wythe	Will	1800	V:Mss2 K4165 b
McGavock, James, in Wythe Co.	Smyth	Will	1839	CF1853-002
McGee, Edward H.	Hanover	Will	1845	CF1885-018
McGehee, Samuel	Louisa	Will	1795	OB1792, p. 188
McGehee, Thomas, of St. John's Par.	King William	Will	1727	LVA Acc. #20266
McGeorge, William	King William	Will	1822	CF *McGeorge v. McGeorge*
McGhee, John, in Hanover Co.	Floyd	Will	(nd)	CF1864-002
McGhee, John, in Hanover Co.	Franklin	Will	1828	CF1851-010
McGuire, Edmund, of Norfolk Borough	Williamsburg	Will Abstract	1819	Crozier, p. 37
McGuire, Judith Carter Lewis	King George	Will	1882	V:Mss1 M1795 c 1-13
McHenry, James	Arlington	Inventory	1798	CRA:256
McIlhaney, John, in Loudoun Co.	Frederick	Will	1809	CF1821-243
McIntosh, Martha	Surry	Will Abstract	1825	VG 13, p. 54
McIntosh, Richard, of Warwick Co.	Williamsburg	Will Abstract	1803	Crozier, p. 38
McIntosh, Robert, in Surry Co.	Williamsburg	Will Abstract	1815	Crozier, p. 37
McKay, Donald, in Dinwiddie Co.	Henrico	Will	1819	CF1827-007
McKay, Donald, in Dinwiddie Co.	Henrico	Will	1819	CF1824-007
McKay, Richard	Richmond	Will	1699	V:Mss4 R4143 a 1
McKay, Richard	Richmond	Inventory	1699	V:Mss4 R4143 a 1
McKeand, John	Richmond City	Will	1792	T:HCD2, p. 2

NAME	LOCATION	TYPE	YEAR	REFERENCE(S)
McKee, A.R., in KY	Albemarle	Will	1894	CF1914-020
McKee, Adam, in Wythe Co.	Smyth	Will	1847	CF1866-015
McKenney, William	Stafford	Will P.	1692	OB:13 DEC 1692
McKenzie, William, Jr.	New Kent	Will	1806	Swem(1):f218
McKinney, William, in Campbell Co.	Lynchburg	Will	1833	CF1852-011
McKinsie, John, in NC		Will	1754	LVA Acc. #26073
McKinzie, Alexander	Albemarle	Will	1798	BRCD
McKinzie, John	Nansemond	Will	1754	LVA Acc. #26073
McKinzie, John, minister of Suffolk Par.	Nansemond	Will	1754	VG 11, p. 32
McKinzie, Thomas, of Rockingham Co.	Augusta	Will	1812	CF1823-027
McLain, Samuel	Fairfax	Inventory	1793	X
McLaurine, James	Cumberland	Will	1848	V:Mss7:2 Ed355:1
McLaurine, James	Cumberland	Inventory	1849	V:Mss7:2 Ed355:1
McLaurine, James	Cumberland	Account	1849	V:Mss7:2 Ed355:1
McLean, Honore Ann	D.C.	Will	1848	DCA:Box 19
McMasters, Mary	Alexandria	Inventory	1797	WBA, p. 4
McNally, John	Fairfax	Account	1853	X
McNeal, Elizabeth Martin, of Rock'ham.	Augusta	Will	1798	CF1821-033
McNeal, Martin	Rockingham	Will	1798	BRCD
McPhatridge, Malcom, in Wythe Co.	Smyth	Will	1820	CF1847-012
McPhatridge, Malcom, in Wythe Co.	Smyth	Will	1820	CF1842-007
McPherson, Daniel	Arlington	Will	1791	CRA:30
McQuown, Isaac, in TN	Washington	Will	1863	CF1869-007
McRobert, Alexander	Richmond City	Will	1798	T:HCD2, p. 453
Meace, John [Meade]	Warwick	Will Partial	1685	Records 1685
Mead, William, in Loudoun Co.	Lynchburg	Will	1816	CF1830-126
Meade, Andrew	Nansemond	Will	1744	SV 7:1, p. 12
Meade, Andrew	Nansemond	Will	1744	LVA Acc. #26674-166
Meade, Andrew, of Upper Parish	Nansemond	Will	1767	UVA MSS 800
Meade, Everard	Amelia	Will	1803	V:Mss2 M46197 b 1-3
Meade, Jane Eliza	Richmond City	Will	1879	V:Mss2 M46197 b 18+
Meade, John, of *Mulberry Island*	Warwick	Will Partial	1684	Note[1]
Meade, John [Meace]	Warwick	Will Partial	1685	Records 1685
Meade, Susanna M.	Clarke	Will	1820	V:Mss2 C9695 b 5-6
Meader, Jonas	Cumberland	Will (N)	1773	OB1772, p. 492
Meador, Ambrose	Bedford	Will	1795	WB2, p. 161
Means, Robert	King & Queen	Will Ref.	1808	Note[2]
Means, Robert	Richmond City	Will	1808	Note[3]
Means, Robert	Richmond City	Will	1808	LVA Acc. #28118
Meaux, James	Caroline	Will	1823	W&P1742, p. 112
Meazle, Luke	Surry	Will (N)	1693	T:D&W4, p. 308b
Medley, John	Culpeper	Will	1763	FDC L571-106
Medley, John	Culpeper	Will	1763	V:Mss1 B2346 a 768+
Medlicott, Samuel R.	Gloucester	Will	1857	CF1884-015
Medlicott, Samuel [R.]	Gloucester	Will	1857	TVF 3:3, p. 179
Meeks, Richard	Richmond	Will	1729	LVA Acc. #38561

---

[1] LVA, Warwick County Court Records, 1685.

[2] LVA, Land Office Revolutionary War Military Certificate Papers, Thomas Lipscomb, Folder 5.

[3] U.S. District Court, Ended Cases, 1824, Box 110, Part 2.

NAME	LOCATION	TYPE	YEAR	REFERENCE(S)
Mefford, Gasper, of Rockingham Co.	Augusta	Will	1805	CR1818-005
Megeagh, Joseph, in Loudoun Co.	Frederick	Will	1761	CF1821-162
Megginson, William	Buckingham	Estate Ref.	1833	Note[1]
Melson, Isaac, of Accomack Co.	Williamsburg	Will Abstract	1785	Crozier, p. 38
Melson, Levin, of Accomack Co.	Williamsburg	Will Abstract	1795	Crozier, p. 38
Melton, David	Henrico	Inventory	1765	Records, Vol. 6, p. 1975
Mendenhall, William	Arlington	Inventory	1800	CRA:351
Menefee, George, of _Buckland_	Prince William	Will	1845	LVA Acc. #40922
Menefie, George, of _Buckland_		Will	1647	VCRP, Survey #03994
Menefie, George, of _Buckland_	London	Will	1747	N:PROB11/199
Menifee, Thomas K., in Augusta Co.	Staunton	Will	1876	CF1877-010
Mennis, Charles	York	Will	1773	T: correct from Elias
Mercer, Ann	Stafford	Will	1771	LVA Acc. #23762a
Mercer, George	Loudoun	Will Ref.	1770	Hening, Vol. 12, p. 366
Mercer, George	Loudoun	Estate Ref.	1786	Hening, Vol. 12, p. 365
Mercer, Hugh, in Fredericksburg	Spotsylvania	Will	1777	V:Mss2 M53465 a 2
Mercer, Hugh, in Fredericksburg	Spotsylvania	Will	1777	V:Mss2 M5346 a1
Mercer, James	Isle of Wight	Will	1816	SV 16:1, p. 32
Mercer, John	Stafford	Will	1768	LVA Acc. #23762a
Mercer, John F., in Loudoun Co.	Frederick	Will	1811	CF1820-237
Mercer, William	Fredericksburg	Will	1829	Filson
Meredeth, Samson	Charles City	Inventory	1730	D&W1724, p. 303
Meredith, Edward P., in Richmond	Hanover	Will	1894	CF1908-011
Meredith, James	Hanover	Will	1832	LVA Acc. #27159
Meredith, James, in Amherst Co.	Lynchburg	Will	1819	CF1826-002
Meredith, John	Lancaster	Will	1737	LP
Meredith, Samuel	New Kent	Will	1838	CF1868-011
Meredith, Samuel, Dr., in Richmond	Bedford	Will	1866	CF1883-005
Meredith, Samuel, in Amherst Co.	Lynchburg	Will	1809	CF1821-009
Meredith, Samuel, in Amherst Co.	Lynchburg	Will	1809	CF1826-002
Meredith, Thomas	Stafford	Estate Ref.	1693	OB:05 APR 1693
Meriwether, Ann	Hanover	Will	1804	Note[2]
Meriwether, Catharine E., in Bedford Co.	Lynchburg	Will	1827	CF1884-002
Meriwether, David	Hanover	Estate Ref.	1752	Hening, Vol. 6, p. 301
Meriwether, Francis, in Bedford Co.	Lynchburg	Will	1834	CF1884-002
Meriwether, George	Louisa	Will	1775	V:Mss2 M5454 a1
Meriwether, Nicholas, in Goochland Co.	Hanover	Will	1744	G2:68
Meriwether, Nicholas, the younger	Hanover	Will Ref.	1738	Hening, Vol. 8, p. 54
Meriwether, Thomas	Henrico	Will	1709c	V:Mss4 V8 g
Meriwether, Thomas	Essex	Estate Ref.	1753	Hening, Vol. 6, p. 405
Meriwether, Thomas, So. Farnam Par.	Essex	Will	1708	TVF 2:2, p. 69
Merritt, John	Warwick	Appraisal	16__	Miscellany, p. 95
Merritt, Mary	Brunswick	Will	1789	SV 3, p. 37
Merriwether, William D.		Will		UVA MSS 2831
Merry, Prettyman	Buckingham	Will	1818	LVA Acc. #42116
Merry, Prettyman	Buckingham	Will	1818	VG 50, p. 70
Merryman, Thomas, convict, s/o Jesse		Estate Ref.	1806	Shepherd, Vol. 3, p. 241

---

[1] LVA, Land Office Revlutionary War Military Certificate Papers, William Megginson, Folder 19.

[2] LVA, U.S. Circuit Court Records, Box 116, _Donald, Scott & Co. v. Winston's Exor's et al._ (1829).

NAME	LOCATION	TYPE	YEAR	REFERENCE(S)
Merryweather, William, Jr., mariner		Will	1742	VCRP, Survey #04379
Metcalf, Vernon, in Bedford Co.	Lynchburg	Will	1817	CF1823-021
Metcalfe, John, of King & Queen Co.	London	Will	1762	N:PROB11/874
Metcalfe, Margaret, in Madison Co. TN	Lynchburg	Will	1865	CF1871-028
Meteer, Mary A., in LA	Fauquier	Will	1877	CF1880-036
Meux, William	King William	Will	1826	MVG 22:4, p. 30
Meux, William	King William	Will	1826	Note[1]
Michael, Adam	Rockingham	Will	1836	CF1872-032
Michaux, Abraham	Henrico	Will	1717	WMQ2 17, p. 96
Michaux, Abraham	Henrico	Will	1717	VMHB 44, p. 373
Michaux, James	Goochland	Will	1744	VHMB 45, p. 213
Michaux, Joseph, in Cumberland Co.	Prince Edward	Will	1807	CF1877-014
Michaux, Susanne	Goochland	Will	1744	VMHB 44, p. 374
Michie, Alexander H., in Albemarle Co.	Louisa	Will	1855	CF1891-028
Michie, Ann Watson	Louisa	Will	1830	V:Mss1 G8274a150-154
Michie, Charles, in Goochland Co.	Louisa	Will	1845	CF1891-028
Michie, David	Albemarle	Will	1836	V:Mss1 G8274a150-154
Michie, David, in Albemarle Co.	Louisa	Will	1841	CF1891-028
Michie, James, in Albemarle Co.	Louisa	Will	1850	CF1891-028
Michie, Mary A., in Petersburg	Louisa	Will	1882	CF1900-044
Michie, Mary G., in Albemarle Co.	Louisa	Will	1852	CF1891-028
Michie, Pamela A., in Albemarle Co.	Louisa	Will	1879	CF1900-044
Michie, Robert	Louisa	Will	1793	V:Mss1 G8274a150-154
Michie, Sarah H., in Albemarle Co.	Louisa	Will	1862	CF1891-028
Michie, William Watson	Hanover	Will	1842	Cocke:91
Mickleburrough, Robert	Caroline	Will	1788	MVG 31:4, p. 343
Micou, James [of Port Royal]	Caroline	Will	1781	Note[2]
Middleton, Benjamin	Westmoreland	Will	1790	Wills #37
Middleton, John	Henrico	Inventory	1764	Records, Vol. 6, p. 1911
Middleton, Robert		Will	1627	VCRP, Survey #03116
Middleton, Robert	Westmoreland	Will	1773	Wills #7
Middleton, Walter	Lee	Will	1795	DB1, p. 53
Midleton, Thomas	Surry	Inventory	1688	T:D&W4, p. 58a
Milby, Thomas, of Surry Co.	Prince George	Will	1854	SV 9:4, p. 160
Mildmay, Richard	Stafford	Will P.	1691	OB: 06 OCT 1691
Miles, John	Surry	Inventory	1698	T: correct from 1697
Miles, John	Lunenburg	Will	1848	BRCD
Miles, John, of Cumberland Parish	Lunenburg	Will	1748	MVG 31:4, p. 350
Millan, John	Fairfax	Account	1839	X
Millan, William	Fairfax	Account	1813	X
Millan, William	Fairfax	Appraisal	1813	X
Millan, William W.	Fairfax	Guard. Acct.	1844	X
Miller, Charles Fenton, in MS	Dinwiddie	Will	1878	CF1886-018
Miller, D.M.	Louisa	Inventory	1873	V:Mss2 M6196 b1-2
Miller, D.P., of Amelia Co.	Cumberland	Will	1835	CF1849-004
Miller, Dabney, of Amelia Co.	Cumberland	Will	1831	CF1849-004
Miller, Elizabeth H.	Buckingham	Will	1856	MVG 41:2, p. 99

[1] LVA, Legislative Petitions, New Kent County, 18 DEC 1826
[2] Caroline County Appeals and Land Causes, 1777-1807, p. 396.

NAME	LOCATION	TYPE	YEAR	REFERENCE(S)
Miller, Elizabeth H., of Buckingham Co.	Cumberland	Will	1856	Judgments 1859 AUG
Miller, Elon, in Berkeley Co.	Frederick	Will	1821	CF1827-125
Miller, Francis, in MD	Prince William	Will	1888	CF1900-019
Miller, Henry Clay, in MD	Franklin	Will	1880	CF1881-048
Miller, Henry, of Augusta Co.	Staunton	Will	1796	LVA Acc. #23826a
Miller, Jacob C., in Roanoke	Bedford	Will	1880	CF1888-030
Miller, Jacob O., in PA	Staunton	Will	1898	CF1909-012
Miller, James	Fairfax	Account	1859	X
Miller, James, in Nottoway Co.	Amelia	Will	1875	CF1901-029
Miller, James L., in Shenandoah Co.	Warren	Will	1866	CF1866-003
Miller, James, of St. Mary's Parish	Caroline	Will	1808	TQ 19:2, p. 102
Miller, James, of St. Mary's Parish	Caroline	Will	1808	Note[1]
Miller, James, of St. Mary's Parish	Caroline	Will	1808	W&P1742, p. 85
Miller, John	Prince Edward	Will	1795	WB3, p. 4
Miller, John	Culpeper	Will	1832	LP:31 DEC 1847
Miller, John, in Culpeper Co.	Rappahannock	Will	1832	CF1852-006
Miller, M. Erskine	Staunton	Will	1897	CF1899-007
Miller, M. Erskine	Staunton	Will	1897	CF1907-012
Miller, Mordecai, in Alexandria Co.	Fairfax	Will	1832	NVG 8, p. 1091
Miller, Morrell, in PA	Bath	Will	1837	CF1896-009
Miller, Morrell, in PA	Bath	Will	1837	CF1879-005
Miller, Peter	Botetourt	Will	1810	LVA Acc. #22676
Miller, Robert	Caroline	Will	1812	TQ 19:2, p. 105
Miller, Robert, of Port Royal	Caroline	Will	1813	TQ 21:2, p. 121
Miller, Samuel, of Rockingham Co.	Augusta	Will	1811	CF1829-012
Miller, Simon	Stafford	Will	1800	LVA Acc. #41008, r4614
Miller, Simon	Stafford	Will	1800	LVA Acc. #22962
Miller, Simon, of Essex Co.	Williamsburg	Will Abstract	1792	Crozier, p. 40
Miller, Simon, of Hanover Parish	Richmond	Will Ref.	1719	Winfree, p. 362
Miller, Simon, of Stafford Co.	Fredericksburg	Will	1800	Fleet, Huntington Data
Miller, Symon	Rappahannock*	Will	1684	LVA Acc. #20955
Miller, Thomas, in HI	Essex	Will	1864	CF1888-027
Miller, William, of Essex Co.	Williamsburg	Will Abstract	1793	Crozier, p. 41
Miller, William, of St. Anne's Parish	Essex	Will	1793	Note[2]
Miller, William, of St. Anne's Parish	Essex	Will	1793	CF1823-007
Miller, William, of St. Anne's Parish	Essex	Will	1793	CF1823-006
Miller, William R., in MD	Bedford	Will	1889	CF1890-016
Mills, Ann, in Norfolk Co.	Portsmouth	Will	1843	CF1890-006
Mills, Charles, Sr.	Hanover	Will	1828	Cocke:93
Mills, Charles, Sr., of Hanover Co.	Louisa	Will	1828	Ejectments Holloway/Pigges
Mills, Fortune	Surry	Inventory	1669.	T:D&W1, p. 342
Mills, James, Gent., of Middlesex Co.	Williamsburg	Will Abstract	1782	Crozier, p. 41
Mills, John	Henrico	Inventory	1670	Records, Vol. 1, p. 53
Mills, John	Fairfax	Estate Ref.	1785	Hening, Vol. 12, p. 203
Mills, John	Middlesex	Will Ref.	1785	Hening, Vol. 12, p. 204
Mills, John, of Nottoway Co.	Mecklenburg	Will	1823	CF1849-033
Mills, Margaret	Prince William	Sale Ref.	1843	CM:02 OCT 1843

---

[1] Fredericksburg Superior Court of Chancery, Land Causes and Appeals, 1817-1819, p. 452.

[2] See also Louis A. Burgess, *Virginia Soldiers of 1776* (1927), Vol. 3, p. 1119; Essex Co. Orders, Bk. 32, pp. 265, 278, April 1793.

NAME	LOCATION	TYPE	YEAR	REFERENCE(S)
Mills, Margaret	Prince William	Inv. Ref.	1843	CM:02 OCT 1843
Mills, Mathew	Caroline	Will	1753	OB1746, p. 408
Mills, Mathew	Caroline	Will	1753	VGS Bulletin VII, p. 8
Mills, Mathew, of St. Margaret's Parish	Caroline	Will	1753	VGS Bulletin VII, p. 8
Mills, Matthew	Caroline	Will	1753	LVA Acc. #28295
Mills, Matthew	Caroline	Will	1753	VGS Bulletin VII, p. 8
Mills, Matthew	Caroline	Will	1753	LVA Acc. #28403
Mills, Matthew	Caroline	Will	1753	VGS Bulletin VII, p. 8
Mills, Peter	Fairfax	Will	1826	X
Mills, Thompson	Caroline	Will	1808	CF1832-002
Mills, Thompson	Caroline	Will	1808	W&P1742, p. 93
Mills, William H., in KY	Louisa	Will	1860	CF1895-015
Mills, William H., in KY	Louisa	Will	1860	CF1899-002
Milner, Luke	Richmond	Will	1746	WB5, p. 511
Milstead, John		Estate Ref.	1789	Hening, Vol. 13, p. 94
Milstead, John	Prince William	Will Ref.	1843	CM:07 AUG 1843
Milton, Henry, of Alexandria DC	London	Will	1821	N:PROB11/1647
Ming, Victoria, in Prince William Co.	Fauquier	Will	1869	CF1881-032
Minge, David, of Charles City Co.	Williamsburg	Will Abstract	1781	Crozier, p. 40
Minge, George, of Charles City Co.	Williamsburg	Will Abstract	1782	Crozier, p. 40
Minge, John	Charles City	Will	1772	VG 48, p. 157
Minge, John	Dinwiddie	Will	1801	VGSQ 10:1, p. 8
Minge, Valentine	Charles City	Account	1727	D&W1724, p. 196
Minge, Valentine	Charles City	Account	1728	D&W1724, p. 226
Minness, John, of Pendleton Co.	Augusta	Will	1824	CF1827-016
Minnick, John	Rockingham	Will	1852	CF1855-006
Minor, Daniel, in Alexandria Co.	Fairfax	Will	1865	CF1898-024
Minor, Daniel, in Alexandria Co.	Fairfax	Will	1865	X
Minor, Lucius H.	Hanover	Will	1863	Cocke:87
Minor, Lucy Landon, in Fredericksburg	Lynchburg	Will	1854	CF1860-002
Minor, Mary	Fairfax	Will	1858	X
Minor, Robert Dabney	Richmond City	Will	1871	V:Mss1 M6663 c 3,393
Minor, Vivion [of *Springfield*]	Caroline	Will	1791	W&P1742, p. 49
Minor, William, in Alexandria	Fairfax	Will	1859	X
Minthorne, Richard	Stafford	Admin.	1689	OB:12 DEC 1689
Mitcham, James	Fredericksburg	Will	1791	DCWBA, p. 14
Mitchell, Charles C.	Hanover	Will	1842	CF1907-035
Mitchell, Charles C.	Hanover	Will	1852	Cocke:95
Mitchell, David	Westmoreland	Will	1776	Wills #14
Mitchell, Francis J., in Henrico Co.	Louisa	Will	1830	CF1898-020
Mitchell, Frank	Fairfax	Guard. Acct.	1851	X
Mitchell, Hugh	Fairfax	Guard. Acct.	1851	X
Mitchell, James	Brunswick	Will	1791	CF1801-003
Mitchell, James, of King & Queen Co.	Williamsburg	Will Abstract	1794	Crozier, p. 41
Mitchell, James, of King & Queen Co.	Williamsburg	Will Abstract	1794	Fleet 2:351
Mitchell, John	Brunswick	Will	1770	CF1801-003
Mitchell, John	Caroline	Will	1807	CF1812-019
Mitchell, John P., in King Wiliam Co.	Gloucester	Will	1855	CF1870-018
Mitchell, Philo	Fairfax	Guard. Acct.	1851	X
Mitchell, Richard, of Lancaster Co.	Williamsburg	Will Abstract	1781	Crozier, p. 40
Mitchell, Richard T.	Prince William	Acct. Ref.	1843	CM:04 DEC 1843

NAME	LOCATION	TYPE	YEAR	REFERENCE(S)
Mitchell, Richard T.	Prince William	Acct. Ref.	1844	CM:05 FEB 1844
Mitchell, Robert J., in NC	Lynchburg	Will	1898	CF1913-066
Mitchell, William	Essex	Will	1771	Fleet 2:341
Mitchell, William, in Lancaster Co.	Richmond	Will	1804	CF1855-005
Mitchell, William, in Richmond	Louisa	Will	1822	CF1898-020
Mitchell, William, in Richmond	Louisa	Will	1836	CF1849-014
Mitchell, William, in Richmond	Louisa	Will	1836	CF1850-003
Mitchell, William, in Scott Co.	Roanoke	Will	1828	CF1840-005
Mitchell, William, of York Co.	Williamsburg	Will Abstract	1786	Crozier, p. 39
Mize, Stephen	Lunenburg	Will	1792	CF1802-004
Mizell, Luke	Surry	Admin.	1673	T: correct from 1695
Moffett, Horatio G., Rappahannock Co.	Culpeper	Will	1892	CF1901-060
Mohr, Christian	Campbell	Will	1867	V:Mss1 B6638 a2812+
Mollory, Florisabella, of King William Co.		Will	1769	VCRP, Survey #04699
Moncure, Henry W., in Richmond	Bath	Will	1866	CF1891-006
Monger, John, of Rockingham Co.	Augusta	Will	1803	DF1824-038
Monk, Richard	Surry	Will	1688	T:D&W4, p. 42b
Monroe, Alexander	Fauquier	Inventory	1786	WB2, p. 91
Monroe, Andrew	Westmoreland	Division	1784	Wills #24
Monroe, George	Westmoreland	Division	1778	Wills #20
Monroe, Jamima	Westmoreland	Will	1785	Wills #27
Monroe, Jesse, in Westmoreland Co.	Essex	Will	1826	CF1894-026
Monroe, John, in Richmond Co.	Frederick	Will	1807	CF1833-020
Monroe, John, in Richmond Co.	Frederick	Will	1807	CF1827-032
Monroe, Rachel	Westmoreland	Will	1773	Wills #8
Monroe, Thomas, in Alexandria Co.	Fairfax	Will	1839	CF1859-034
Monroe, William	Orange	Will	1769	LP:18 FEB 1839
Monroe, William	Westmoreland	Division	1781	Wills #21
Montague, Thomas Ball	Gloucester	Division	1874c	V:Mss1 M7607 a 309
Montague, Thomas Ball	Gloucester	Will	1874c	V:Mss1 M7607 a 309
Montague, William	Middlesex	Will	1753	CW(13)
Montague, William	Middlesex	Will	1763	CW(13)
Montgomerie, Thomas	Prince William	Will	1792	Note[1]
Montgomery, Francis, in Pr. Wm. Co.	Fauquier	Will	1814	CF1866-007
Montgomery, James, of James River		Will	1697	VCRP, Survey #04779
Montgomery, John	Amherst	Will	1784	WB2, p. 176
Montgomery, William, in Pr. Wm. Co.	Fauquier	Will	1804	CF1866-007
Moody, Horatio Gates, James City Co.	York	Will	1801	CF1816-004
Moody, James	Mathews	Estate Ref.	1840	Note[2]
Moody, John M.	Hanover	Will	1866	CF1878-023
Moody, John Mills, of *Bee Hive*	Hanover	Will	1873c	V:Mss1 M7765 a 130+
Moody, Laura A.	Prince George	Will	1861	BRCD
Moody, Laura A., in Prince George Co.	Petersburg	Will	1861	CF1871-039
Moody, Samuel	Charles City	Inventory	1727	D&W1724, p. 185
Moody, Samuel	Charles City	Inventory	1773	Note[3]
Moody, Thomas	Charles City	Account	1772	Records, p. 381

---

[1] LVA, U.S. Circuit Court Records, Box 73, *Dunlop's Lessee v. Elisha J. Hall* (1808).
[2] LVA, Land Office Revlutionary War Military Certificate Papers, James Moody, Folder 4
[3] LVA, Charles City County Records, 1766-1774, p. 477.

NAME	LOCATION	TYPE	YEAR	REFERENCE(S)
Moody, Thomas	New Kent	Will	1813	LP:18 DEC 1818
Moody, Thomas, in Prince George Co.	Petersburg	Will	1827	CF1850-015
Moon, Arthur H., of Buckingham Co.	Campbell	Will	1853	CF1860-020
Moon, George, mariner		Will	1680	VCRP, Survey #03557
Moon, John	Isle of Wight	Will	1655	VMHB 6, p. 33
Moon, John	Fairfax	Will	1824	NVG 8, p. 1117
Moon, John, Capt.	Isle of Wight	Will Ref.	(nd)	VMHB 6, p. 249
Moon, John S., in Buckingham Co.	Albemarle	Will	1876	CF1880-022
Moon, Littleberry	Buckingham	Division	1828	MVG 31:4, p. 343
Moon, Littleberry	Buckingham	Division	1828	BRCD
Mooney, Virinda, in Greene Co.	Albemarle	Will	1881	CF1895-292
Moor, Edward	Stafford	Will	1806	TQ 28:2, p. 107
Moore, Andrew L., in King William Co.	King & Queen	Will	1828	CF1885-002
Moore, Augustine	King William	Will Ref.	1742	Hening, Vol. 8, p. 285
Moore, Augustine	King William	Will Ref.	1742	Hening, Vol. 8, p. 476
Moore, Augustine	Elizabeth City	Will	1824	Note[1]
Moore, Augustine, of King William Co.	Caroline	Will	1744	W&P1742, p. 3
Moore, Bernard, of St. Thomas Parish	Orange	Will	1775	TQ 09:1, p. 52
Moore, Daniel	York	Will	1767	CF1804-009
Moore, Elizabeth, of York Co.	Williamsburg	Will Abstract	1804	Crozier, p. 36
Moore, Frances	Lancaster	Will	1700	LP
Moore, Francis	Fredericksburg	Will	1799	Note[2]
Moore, Francis	Fredericksburg	Will	1799	DCWA, p. 126
Moore, Garland, in Jefferson Co.	Frederick	Will	1827	CF1828-127
Moore, Henry, in Fairfax Co.	Arlington	Will	1773	CF1809-026
Moore, Henry, in Fairfax Co.	Arlington	Will	1773	CF1809-026
Moore, Horatio, in Prince George Co.	Petersburg	Will	1830	CF1839-051
Moore, Hugh, in Halifax Co.	Lynchburg	Will	1760	CF1828-036
Moore, J. Augustine		Will	(nd)	Swem(2)
Moore, James	Augusta	Will	1791	WB1A, p. 8
Moore, Jesse Marian	Lunenburg	Will	1842	SV 12:4, p. 172
Moore, John	Nansemond	Will Ref.	1738	Hening, Vol. 5, p. 75
Moore, John	King George	Will	1759	VMHB 52, p. 64
Moore, John	Warwick	Inventory	1767	Note[3]
Moore, John	Warwick	Inventory	1767	Note[4]
Moore, John	Elizabeth City	Will	1803	Note[5]
Moore, John, in Loudoun Co.	Frederick	Will	1806	CF1835-142
Moore, John J., in WV	Fairfax	Will	1882	CF1910-050
Moore, John, of Elizabeth City Co.	Williamsburg	Will Abstract	1803	Crozier, p. 39
Moore, John, of Rockingham Co.	Augusta	Will	1820	CF1824-017
Moore, Joseph	Caroline	Will	1808	W&P1742, p. 88
Moore, Judith	Westmoreland	Will	1779	Wills #17
Moore, Mary	York	Will	1782	CF1791-001
Moore, Mary Anne	Halifax	Estate Ref.	1804	Shepherd, Vol. 3, p. 43

---

[1] LVA, U.S. Circuit Court Records, Box 136, *Cay's Exors. v. Hudgins' Exors* (1833).

[2] Fredericksburg District Court Wills, Bk. A, 1789-1831, p. 126.

[3] Warwick County Miscellaneous Court Papers, p. 137.

[4] Warwick County Miscellaneous Court Papers, p. 137.

[5] LVA, U.S. Circuit Court Records, Box 136, *Cay's Exors. v. Hudgins' Exors* (1833).

NAME	LOCATION	TYPE	YEAR	REFERENCE(S)
Moore, Pheby [late wife of David Arell]	Fairfax	Dower	1803	X
Moore, Rebecca Catlett	King George	Will	1760	VMHB 52, p. 66
Moore, Robert, in Buckingham Co.	Powhatan	Will	1875	CF1908-012
Moore, Robert, of Petersburg	Dinwiddie	Will	1804	LP:15 DEC 1819
Moore, William, in Lunenburg Co.	Franklin	Will	1806	CF1834-007
Moorman, Charles	Louisa	Will Ref.	1778	Hening, Vol. 12, p. 613
Moory, George	Warwick	Division	1685	Note[1]
Moran, William, in Fairfax Co.	Alexandria	Will	1849	CF1879-008
Mordant, George		Will	1633	VCRP, Survey #03967
Mordland, George	Fairfax	Inventory	1857	WB2:023
Mordland, George	Fairfax	Sale	1857	WB2:023
Morecroft, Edmund, merchant		Will	1639	VCRP, Survey #03984
Morehead, Charles	Fauquier	Will	1783	FC 8, p. 101
Morgan, Andrew, in Rockbridge Co.	Bedford	Will	1837	CF1840-024
Morgan, Daniel, in Westmoreland Co.	Richmond	Will	1782	CF1847-009
Morgan, Daniel, of Westmoreland Co.	Williamsburg	Will Abstract	1789	Crozier, p. 40
Morgan, Elizabeth	Surry	Inventory	1676	T:D&W3, p. 53a
Morgan, George		Will	1669	VCRP, Survey #03543
Morgan, George, now at Norfolk	Williamsburg	Will Abstract	1812	Crozier, p. 39
Morgan, John, mariner		Will	1719	VCRP, Survey #04345
Morgan, Robert	Goochland	Will	1746	CF1765-003
Morgan, William, in Middlesex Co.	Fauquier	Will	1764	CF1784-012
Moring, Christopher	Surry	Inventory	1790	WB12, p. 274
Morris, Ann C., in Albemarle Co.	Louisa	Will	1863	CF1895-004
Morris, Barton M., in Caroline Co.	Hanover	Will	1863	CF1895-001
Morris, Barton W., in Caroline Co.	Hanover	Will	1863	CF1874-002
Morris, Edmund, in Caroline Co.	Hanover	Will	1865	CF1895-001
Morris, Elizabeth	James City	Will	1763	LVA, WPA Inventory
Morris, George W., Dr.	New Kent	Will	1835	Swem(1):f218
Morris, Jacob, of Albemarle Co.	Augusta	Will	1806	CF1824-051
Morris, John	Fairfax	Will	1825	X
Morris, Thomas, of Gloucester Co.	Williamsburg	Will Abstract	1782	Crozier, p. 37
Morris, William	Hanover	Will	1746	V:Mss6:1 D1123:2
Morris, William	Hanover	Will	1746	LVA Acc. #19988
Morris, William	Kanawha	Estate Ref.	1804	Shepherd, Vol. 3, p. 50
Morris, William	Bath	Will	1808	LVA Acc. #39797
Morris, William, mariner, of Mathews Co.	Williamsburg	Will Abstract	1794	Crozier, p. 37
Morrisett, David	Chesterfield	Will	1793	WB4, p. 357
Morrisett, John	Chesterfield	Will	1782	WB3, p. 392
Morrison, Henry A., in Scott Co.	Washington	Will	1892	CF1893-036
Morrison, John	James City	Will	1807	Swem(1):165
Morrison, William, in Albemarle Co.	Bedford	Will	1761	CF1820-020
Morriss, Henry	Brunswick	Will	1783	CF1800-017
Morriss, Richard G., in Richmond	Henrico	Will	1884	CF1891-006
Morriss, Zachariah	Amelia	Will	(nd)	V:Mss1 N1786 a 8222+
Morrissett, William	Goochland	Will	1797	DB17, p. 166
Morrow, David	Caroline	Will	1807	Note[2]

[1] LVA, Warwick County Records, 1685.
[2] LVA, Land Office Revlutionary War Military Certificate Papers, Robert Morrow, Folder 22.

NAME	LOCATION	TYPE	YEAR	REFERENCE(S)
Morse, Henry		Will	1775	CW M-1561
Morse, Henry, of Williamsburg	London	Will	1775	N:PROB11/1014
Morse, Henry, of Williamsburg		Will	1775	VCRP, Survey #04802
Morsham, Margaret, in Mecklenburg Co.	Brunswick	Will	1823	CF1837-027
Morton, Elizabeth W.	Charlotte	Will	1861	UVA MSS 8979-p
Morton, Hezekiah	Prince Edward	Will	1831	MVG 29:3, p. 192
Morton, Joseph	King George	Will	1759	OB1751, p. 1202
Morton, Joseph, of James City Co.	King George	Will	1758	MVG 29:4, p. 324
Morton, Patty	Prince Edward	Will	1834	MVG 29:3, p. 192
Morton, Richard	Stafford	Will Ref.	1812	WBAA, p. 334
Morton, Samuel D.	Charlotte	Will	1858	UVA MSS 8979-p
Morton, William, in Charlotte Co.	Prince Edward	Will	1895	CF1904-040
Morton, William, of Baltimore MD and	York	Will	1751	M: L28 f30
Mosby, Micajah, in Cumberland Co.	Powhatan	Will	1772	CF1804-009
Mosby, Robert	Powhatan	Will	1798	CF1852-009
Moseby, John	Henrico	Will	1718	Records, Vol. 2, p. 365
Moseby, John	Henrico	Will	1718	Records, Vol. 2, p. 365
Moseley, Arthur	Cumberland	Estate	(nd)	UVA MSS 4756
Moseley, Benjamin	Buckingham	Plat	1811	UVA Acc. #1173
Moseley, Christopher, in Pr. Anne Co.	Norfolk	Will	1800	CF1824-002
Moseley, Elizabeth Thompson Catlett	Essex	Will	1710c	V:Mss2 M5348 a1
Moseley, Francis	Buckingham	Will	1783	V:Mss1 St242 a 882+
Moseley, Tully, in Pr. Anne Co.	Norfolk	Will	1833	CF1846-015
Moseley, William	Essex	Will	1700	V:Mss1 B4678 a 4788
Moseley, William, Jr.	Powhatan	Will	1807	VGSQ 13:3, p. 76
Moseley, William, of Hanover Co.	Powhatan	Will	1826	CF1841-014
Mosher, Samuel	Charles City	Will	1693	D&W1692, p. 178
Mosher, Samuel, of James City Co.	Charles City	Will	1693	VGSQ 17:4, p. 128
Mosier, Nicholas	Charles City	Will (N)	1728	D&W1724, p. 222
Moss, Alfred	Fairfax	Bond R.	1857	WB2:011
Moss, Alfred, clerk	Fairfax	Bond	1858	WB2:035
Moss, Benjamin, Sr.	York	Will	1735	CF1778-006
Moss, Hugh	Goochland	Will	1780c	V:Mss1 G8855 c 778+
Moss, Jean	Louisa	Will	1772	Note[1]
Moss, John	Fairfax	Will	1809	NVG 6, p. 623
Moss, Margaret Tabb, in Petersburg	Northumberland	Will	1804	CF1813-010
Moss, Rebecah	Goochland	Will	1771c	V:Mss1 G8855 c 778+
Moss, Robert	Rappahannock*	Will	1689	Sweeny, p. 141
Moss, Samuel D., in Goochland Co.	Louisa	Will	1848	CF1860-001
Moss, Thomas T.	Rappahannock*	Will	1678	UVA Acc. #3136
Moss, William	Henrico	Will	1810	VGSQ 18:3, p. 83
Moss, William	Fairfax	Account	1854	X
Motley, Edwin	King & Queen	Will	1808	TVF 12:3, p. 181
Motley, Edwin	King & Queen	Will	1809	LVA Acc. #24541
Motley, Edwin	King & Queen	Will	1809	LP
Motley, Edwin	King & Queen	Will Ref.	1808	KQB:2
Motley, Edwin Joseph	King & Queen	Will	1791c	V:Mss3 K5893 a 69-86
Motley, Elizabeth A., in Nottoway Co.	Amelia	Will	1886	CF1905-006

---

[1] Louisa County Wills Not Fully Proved, 1757-1902, p. 35.

NAME	LOCATION	TYPE	YEAR	REFERENCE(S)
Moulden, George	Fairfax	Admin. Bond	1857	WB2:012
Moult, William, of Accomack Co.	London	Will	1657	N:PROB11/265
Moulte, William		Will	1657	VCRP, Survey #03518
Mount, Thomas C.	Prince William	Will	1828	CF1834-002
Mount, Thomas, in Prince William Co.	Fauquier	Will	1828	CF1836-013
Mount, William, in Prince William Co.	Fauquier	Will	1816	CF1836-013
Mountcastle, Joab [Jacob]	Charles City	Will	1773	Note[1]
Mountcastle, W.H., in Amherst Co.	Lynchburg	Will	1884	CF1891-069
Mountfort, Zachariah	York	Will	1745	Note[2]
Mountjoy, William	Stafford	Will	1777	BRCD
Mountjoy, William		Will	1777	Note[3]
Mountjoy, William, Capt.	Stafford	Will	1777	TQ 26:1, p. 99
Mountjoy, William, in Stafford Co.	Fauquier	Will	1777	CF1830-148
Mouring, Henry, in Gloucester Co.	King & Queen	Will	1838	CF1869-001
Mowatt, Walter, mariner		Will	1742	VCRP, Survey #04383
Moxley, William	Fairfax	Will	1752	X
Moyers, Michael, in Greene Co.	Rockingham	Will	1849	CF1896-006
Mozingo, Charles, in Culpeper Co.	Rappahannock	Will	1830	CF1885-004
Mugget, Ann	Surry	Will	1690	T:D&W4, p. 144b
Muir, Ann Downman	Dinwiddie	Will	1805	VG 19, p. 085
Muir, Francis	Dinwiddie	Will	1810	V:Mss1 N1786 a 5772+
Muir, Francis, in Dinwiddie Co.	Petersburg	Will	1810	CF1851-021
Muire, Absolum to Rutha Ann Oliver	King & Queen	Marriage	1840	LP
Muire, Richard W.	King & Queen	Will	1810	LP
Muire, Thacker	King & Queen	Will	1866	Note[4]
Muire, Thomas, of Walkerton	King & Queen	Will	1866	Fleet 2:394
Mullen, Patrick	Arlington	Inventory	1797	CRA:196
Mullen, Patrick	Arlington	Inventory	1797	CRA:196
Munday, Richard, mariner		Will	1738	VCRP, Survey #04652
Munday, Thomas	Essex	Will	1703	V:Mss1 B4678 a 4788
Munden, Rachel	Henrico	Inventory	1762	Records, Vol. 6, p. 1877
Munden, William M., in Norfolk Co.	Princess Anne	Will	1857	CF1882-006
Munford, Robert	Gloucester	Estate Ref.	(nd)	LP:14 NOV 1816
Munford, Robert	Charles City	Will	1799	LVA Fielding Lewis Papers
Munford, Robert	Charles City	Will	1800	WMQ 11, p. 262
Munford, Robert, of Bristol Parish	Prince George	Will Ref.	1743	Note[5]
Munford, Robert, of Bristol Parish	Prince George	Will	1745	TQ 12:1, p. 88
Munford, Robert, of Bristol Parish	Prince George	Will	1745	DCW1&2, p. 106
Munford, Robert, of Prince George Co.	Mecklenburg	Will	1745	CF1794-014
Munford, Samuel, of Abingdon Parish	Gloucester	Will	1817	Fleet, Huntington Data
Munford, William Greene, Charles City	Williamsburg	Will Abstract	1786	Crozier, p. 41
Munford, William Greene, Col.	Charles City	Will	1786	WMQ 11, p. 260
Munger, John, of Rockingham Co.	Augusta	Will	1803	CF1824-038
Murdaugh, James	Nansemond	Will	1794	VG 21, p. 273

---

[1] Charles City County Deeds, Wills, Orders, etc., 1766-1774, p. 447.
[2] York County Land Causes, 1746-1769, p. 13 (2nd).
[3] Fauquier County Land Causes 1, 1809-1815, p. 200.
[4] Fleet, King and Queen County, 6th Collection.
[5] LVA, Bristol Parish Vestry Book.

NAME	LOCATION	TYPE	YEAR	REFERENCE(S)
Murray, Abigail	Princess Anne	Will	1799	SV 11:3, p. 83
Murray, Ann	Amelia	Will	1810c	V:Mss1 N1786 a 8222+
Murray, Anthony	Stafford	Inventory	1750	BRCD
Murray, Anthony	Stafford	Will	1750	BRCD
Murray, Anthony, of Stafford Co.	Cumberland	Will	1750	CF1762-006
Murray, David	Nansemond	Will	1777	LVA Acc. #27745
Murray, James, of Prince George Co.	Petersburg	Will	1764	CF1805-007
Murray, Richard	Buckingham	Will	1772	LVA Acc. #25971j
Murray, Richard	Buckingham	Will	1772	SV 3:3, p. 122
Murray, Richard, of Buckingham Co.	Cumberland	Will	1772	CF1784-009
Murray, Thomas, of Prince George Co.	Goochland	Will	1783	Judgments 1828 APR
Murray, William, of Middlesex Co.	Williamsburg	Will Abstract	1787	Crozier, p. 36
Murry, William	Charles City	Inventory	(nd)	D&W1724, p. 261
Murry, William, of Westover Parish	Charles City	Will	1729	D&W1724, p. 248
Murtaugh, James	Fairfax	Will	1899	CF1903-014
Muschett, Louisa C.	Prince William	Will	1858	CF1883-009
Muschett, Louise C.	Prince William	Will	1858	CF1887-022
Muse, Ann	Westmoreland	Will Ref.	1726	VMHB 53, p. 135
Muse, David, of Lunenburg Parish	Richmond	Will Abstract	1784	VMHB 53, p. 225
Muse, Edward, in Loudoun Co.	Frederick	Will	1808	CF1832-090
Muse, Edward, Sr.	Westmoreland	Will Ref.	1782	VMHB 53, p. 221
Muse, Hudson	Middlesex	Will	1799	V:Ms22 M9725 a1
Muse, Hudson, of Middlesex Co.	Williamsburg	Will Abstract	1799	Crozier, p. 37
Muse, John, in Botetourt Co.	Roanoke	Will	1828	CF1840-005
Muse, John, in Botetourt Co.	Roanoke	Will	1838	CF1894-009
Muse, John, Sr.	Westmoreland	Will Ref.	1723	VMHB 53, p. 134
Muse, Thomas, in Middlesex Co.	Essex	Will	1812	CF1845-024
Muse, Thomas, of Washington Parish	Westmoreland	Will Ref.	1734	VMHB 53, p. 223
Musgrave, Michael		Will	1698	VCRP, Survey #04781
Musgrave, Michael, of Middlesex Co.	London	Will	1698	N:PROB11/443
Musgrave, Michael, of Pienketank Par.	Middlesex	Will	1697	VMHB 14, p. 93
Mutter, Thomas, of York Co.	Williamsburg	Will Abstract	1812	Crozier, p. 38
Myn, Robert, of Abingdon Parish	Gloucester	Will	1718	Mason, Vol. 2, p. 51
Myne, Deborah	Gloucester	Will	1671	Mason, Vol. 2, p. 52

NAME	LOCATION	TYPE	YEAR	REFERENCE(S)

N

NAME	LOCATION	TYPE	YEAR	REFERENCE(S)
Nair, Martin [Near]	Rockingham	Will	1844	CF1851-001
Nair, Mary	Rockingham	Will	1849	CF1853-023
Naish, William	Mecklenburg	Will	(nd)	V:Mss1 Sp716 a 252+
Nash, Aaron H., in Russell Co.	Scott	Will	1880	CF1886-024
Nash, Aaron H., in Russell Co.	Wise	Will	1880	CF1890-039
Nash, Aaron, in Russell Co.	Wise	Will	1880	CF1904-103
Nash, Abner, Dr.	Amelia	Will	1843	V:Mss1 N1786 a 7823+
Nash, Lora, in NY	Fauquier	Will	1860	CF1867-036
Nash, Paul, of Petersburg	London	Will	1823	N:PROB11/1665
Nash, Robert, of Abingdon Parish	Gloucester	Will Ref.	1702	Winfree, p. 267
Nash, Travers	Fauquier	Will	1816c	V:Mss1 N1786 a 1-7
Neal, Armistead, in Roanoke Co.	Amelia	Will	1856	CF1882-011
Neal, Charles	Montgomery	Estate Ref.	1806	Shepherd, Vol. 3, p. 270
Neal, John	Lunenburg	Will	1789	CF1795-008
Neal, Owney, in Roanoke Co.	Amelia	Will	1854	CF1882-011
Neale, John	Fairfax	Inventory	1809	NVG 6, p. 624
Neale, Presley	Lancaster	Will (N)	1792	LP
Neale, Robert		Will	1835	CW(10)
Neaveill, Thomas	Isle of Wight	Will (U)	1794	LVA:1161459
Neavill, George	Fauquier	Will	1774	CF1791-024
Neavill, George	Fauquier	Will	1774	CF1803-067
Neavill, George, of Fauquier Co.	Frederick	Will (U)	1774	LVA:1117621
Necks, Robert, mariner, of Norfolk		Will	1775	VCRP, Survey #04797
Neeve, Mary, spinster		Will	1674	VCRP, Survey #03550
Neff, Henry	Rockingham	Will	1842	CF1850-015
Neighbors, Abraham	Buckingham	Will	1856	UVA Acc. #1173
Neill, George S., of Georgetown DC	Arlington	Heirs	(nd)	CF1866-010
Nelms, Peter	Northumberland	Will	1828	CF1839-003
Nelms, William [Helms]	Northumberland	Will	1719	T: correct from Helms
Nelson, Ann Rosalie	Clarke	Will	1849	V:Mss1 B9963 c 82-88
Nelson, Edward S., in Henrico Co.	Hanover	Will	1855	CF1867-016
Nelson, Elizabeth	Henrico	Will	1837	VGSQ 18:3, p. 83
Nelson, Francis	Hanover	Will	1833	CF1841-011
Nelson, Francis, of *Mount Air*	Hanover	Will	1833	Cocke:98
Nelson, George, in Fauquier Co.	Culpeper	Will	1860	CF1893-010
Nelson, Hugh		Will	1826c	UVA MSS 2831
Nelson, Hugh, of York Co.	Williamsburg	Will Abstract	1800	Crozier, p. 43
Nelson, James, in Augusta Co.	Essex	Will	1854	CF1871-005
Nelson, John, in Jefferson Co.	Frederick	Will	1805	CF1823-315
Nelson, Joshua	Northumberland	Will	1744	T: not Northampton
Nelson, Thomas	King William	Will	1804	MVG 29:3, p. 192
Nelson, Thomas	Richmond City	Will	1850	LVA Acc. #35627
Nelson, Thomas, in Augusta Co.	Louisa	Will	1870	CF1910-005
Nelson, Thomas, in Fauquier Co.	Rappahannock	Will	1851	CF1872-006
Nelson, Thomas, in York Co.	Frederick	Will	1789	CF1815-061
Nelson, Thomas, of Newport Parish	Isle of Wight	Will	1779	SV 11:2, p. 68
Nelson, Thomas, of Newport parish	Isle of Wight	Will (U)	1779	LVA:1161459
Nelson, Thomas, of York Co.	Williamsburg	Will Abstract	1789	Crozier, p. 42
Nelson, William	York	Will	1775	Swem
Nelson, William	Hanover	Inventory	1794	LVA Acc. #21367

NAME	LOCATION	TYPE	YEAR	REFERENCE(S)
Nelson, William	New Kent	Will	1846c	V:Mss1 C1118 a 196+
Nelson, William, Jr., of York Co.	Williamsburg	Will Abstract	1803	Crozier, p. 43
Netherland, George S., in Richmond	Henrico	Will	1879	CF1903-011
Netherland, Margaret, in TN	Washington	Will	1841	CF1874-003
Nevell, John		Will	1697	VCRP, Survey #04778
Nevett, Hugh		Will	1680	VCRP, Survey #03725
Nevil, James, in St. Ann's Parish	Albemarle	Will	1752	LVA Wills/Admin. DB
Nevil, James, of Albemarle Co.	Williamsburg	Will Abstract	1752	Crozier, p. 42
Nevill, James, of St. Anns's Parish	Albemarle	Will	1752	VMHB 37, p. 166
New, Daniel, of Gloucester Co.	Williamsburg	Will Abstract	1776	Crozier, p. 42
New, Robert	Charles City	Inventory	1729	D&W1724, p. 266
Newberry, Samuel	Montgomery	Will	1788	VAN 2, p. 92
Newbill, Nathaniel	Essex	Will Abstract	1743	Fleet 2:302
Newbill, William	Essex	Will	1815	V:Mss1 M1752a92-108
Newby, Nathan	Nansemond	Will Ref.	1733	Hening, Vol. 4, p. 530
Newby, William, in Lancaster Co.	Northumberland	Will	1815	CF1841-009
Newcomb, Nancy	King & Queen	Will Ref.	1848	KQB:2
Newcomb, Nancy	King & Queen	Will	1848	V:Mss1 B6108 c32-36
Newcomb, Nancy	King & Queen	Will	1848	LVA Acc. #24097
Newcomb, Nancy	King & Queen	Will	1853	CF1866-004
Newcomb, Nancy	King & Queen	Will	1853	LVA Acc. #22548
Newland, John, in Wythe Co.	Smyth	Will	1833	CF1843-014
Newman, Thomas	Prince William	Will	1821	CF1835-007
Newman, Thomas, in Prince William Co.	Fauquier	Will	1821	CF1840-027
Newman, Thomas, in York Co.	James City	Will	1853	CF1873-008
Newman, Walter, in Shenandoah Co.	Frederick	Will	1815	CF1822-097
Newman, William, in Orange Co.	Greene	Will	1857	CF1872-006
Newman, William J.	Prince William	Will	1824	CF1835-007
Newman, William J.	Prince William	Will	1824	NVG 8, p. 1207
Newsum, William	Surry	Will	1691	T:D&W4, p. 226a
Newsum, William to Sary Cary	King & Queen	Marriage	1823	LP
Newton, Francis, grocer		Will	1662	VCRP, Survey #03530
Newton, Henry	Essex	Will	1718	V:Mss1 B4678 a 4604+
Newton, John	Westmoreland	Will	1679	LVA Tazewell Papers
Newton, Joseph		Will	1694	VCRP, Survey #06047
Newton, Polly	Caroline	Will	1842	W&D1794, p. 43a
Newton, William, Maj.	Stafford	Will	1789	TQ 23:4, p. 222
Nicely, James, of Rockingham Co.	Orange	Will	1836	Judgments 1854 OCT
Nicewander, Elizabeth, in MD	Rockingham	Will	1857	CF1895-006
Nicholas, George	Fairfax	Account	1762	X
Nicholas, George	Buckingham	Will	1812	V:Mss1 F7345 a 740+
Nicholas, John	Buckingham	Will	1795	LVA Acc. #28458
Nicholas, John	Buckingham	Will	1795	Note[1]
Nicholas, John, of Rockingham Co.	Augusta	Will	1794	CF1824-050
Nicholas, Lewis	Westmoreland	Will	1698	T: correct reverse entry
Nicholas, William		Will	1734	VCRP, Survey #04668
Nicholls, George	Rappahannock*	Will Abstract	1677	VMHB 5, p. 286
Nichols, Isaac, Sr., in Loudoun Co.	Frederick	Will	1829	CF1828-259

[1] LVA, Treasurer's Office Material, "James River and Kanawha County Guaranteed Bonds, Wills and Certificates," Acc. #28458.

NAME	LOCATION	TYPE	YEAR	REFERENCE(S)
Nichols, John	Lancaster	Will	1669	LP
Nichols, Lewis, in Campbell Co.	Lynchburg	Will	1824	CF1857-001
Nichols, Michael, in Jefferson Co.	Frederick	Will	1815	CF1821-102
Nichols, Thomas	King William	Inventory	1704	RB2, p. 35
Nicholson, Francis, Gov.		Will Ref.	1732	CW(11)
Nicholson, Francis, Gov.		Account Ref.	1865	CW(11)
Nicholson, Robert	Brunswick	Will	1773c	GSTV 10, p. 189
Nicholson, Robert, merchant		Will	1652	VCRP, Survey #04106
Nicholson, Robert, of London, Eng.	Warwick	Will	1652	LVA Acc. #23920
Nicholson, William, mariner		Will	1745	VCRP, Survey #04629
Nickolls, James Bruce, of Alexa. DC	London	Will	1831c	N:PROB11/1800
Nicolson, Andrew	Chesterfield	Will	1810	V:Mss5:3 N5484:1
Nicolson, Andrew	Chesterfield	Inventory	1810c	V:Mss5:3 N5484:1
Nicolson, Robert	Brunswick	Will		VTG 10:4, p. 189
Niemeyer, Henry V., in Norfolk Co.	Portsmouth	Will	1883	CF1899-032
Niemeyer, Henry V., in Norfolk Co.	Portsmouth	Will	1883	CF1883-011
Nimmo, William		Will Abstract	1748	WMQ 5, p. 135
Nininger, Christian, in Botetourt Co.	Roanoke	Will	1838	CF1853-001
Nisewander, Jacob, in Giles Co.	Bland	Will	1848	CF1891-013
Nivins, Samuel	Chesterfield	Will	1782c	Fleet, Huntington Data
Nivision, John		Will	1820	LVA Acc. #24194
Nivision, John	Norfolk	Account	1821	LVA Acc. #24194
Nivision, John, in Northampton Co.	Norfolk	Inventory	1820	LVA Acc. #24194
Nivision, John, in Princess Anne Co.	Norfolk	Inventory	1820	LVA Acc. #24194
Nivision, Sarah	Norfolk	Inventory	1830	LVA Acc. #24194
Nivision, Sarah		Will	1830	LVA Acc. #24194
Nivision, William T.		Will	1820	LVA Acc. #24194
Nixon, George, in Hampshire Co.	Frederick	Will	1793	CF1817-042
Nixon, George, in Loudoun Co.	Frederick	Will	1797	CF1816-094
Noble, Allison B., in Amelia Co.	Roanoke	Will	1833	CF1850-010
Noble, John, of Danville	Pittsylvania	Will	1855	LVA Acc. #21357
Noblin, John	Warwick	Inventory	1702	Miscellany 1648, p. 72
Noel, Samuel F.	Caroline	Will	1859	W&D1794, p. 80
Noell, Cornelius, in Bedford Co.	Henry	Will	1820	CF1850-045
Noland, Charles	Fairfax	Account	1817	X
Noore, John, mariner		Will	1693	VCRP, Survey #03953
Norborne, Lord Botetourt		Will	1771	VCRP, Survey #04687
Norfleet, Cordall, of Southampton Co.	Williamsburg	Will Abstract	1788	Crozier, p. 43
Norfleet, Elisha	Nansemond	Will	1870	LVA Acc. #22601
Norfleet, John, Sr.	Nansemond	Will	1867	BRCD
Norfleet, Rebecca J.	Nansemond	Will	1870	BRCD
Norgrave, Joseph, Capt.	Stafford	Division Ref.	1691	OB: 10 JUN 1691
Norman, Isaac, in Culpeper Co.	Louisa	Will	1855	CF1863-008
Norman, Mary S., in OH	Fairfax	Will	1888	CF1902-036
Normanshell, Richard		Will	1684	Note[1]
Norment, Josue	King William	Inventory	1706	RB2, p. 59
Norment, Samuel [of *Mount View*]	Caroline	Will Ref.	1846	LP:21 JAN 1846
Norris, Daniel, in Nelson Co.	Amherst	Will	1824	CF1856-001

---

[1] Fairfax County Land Causes, 1788-1824, p. 42.

NAME	LOCATION	TYPE	YEAR	REFERENCE(S)
Norris, James, in Lancaster Co.	Richmond	Will	1812	CF1855-005
Northal, William	Stafford	Will	1671	RB1671, p. 455
Northam, James, Sr., in Accomack Co.	Henrico	Will	1886	CF1893-031
Northsworthy, George	Norfolk	Will	1705	OB1755, p. 249a
Norton, Patrick		Will	1677	T: not Rappahannock[1]
Norton, Patrick	Rappahannock*	Will	1688	Sweeny, p. 138
Norvell, James M., in Nelson Co.	Albemarle	Will	1859	CF1879-009
Norvell, Thomas, in Richmond	Lynchburg	Will	1817	CF1830-130
Norvell, William, of James City Co.	Richmond City	Will	1802	Hustings 1813 MAR
Norvell, William of James City Co.	Richmond City	Will	1802	MVG 31:4, p. 349
Norvell, William, of James City Co.	Williamsburg	Will Abstract	1802	Crozier, p. 41
Nott, Edward, Lt. Gov. of Va.		Will	1706	VCRP, Survey #03892
Notwell, Arthur		Will	1699	LVA Acc. #21285
Nowlin, David	Buckingham	Will	1819	V:Mss2 N8675 a 1
Nuckolls, James	Hanover	Will	1730	Note[2]
Nuckolls, James	Hanover	Will	1730	MVG 48:4, p. 288
Nuckolls, Samuel	Louisa	Will	1757	Note[3]
Nuckols, Ann W.	Hanover	Will	1848	LP 1850
Nuckols, William, of Hanover Co.	Goochland	Will	1819	Fiduciaries 1800-1899
Nuckols, William W.	Hanover	Will	1864	Cocke:100
Nunn, James		Will Ref.	1786	Note[4]
Nunn, Richard		Estate Ref.	1776	Note[5]
Nunnally, Daniel, in Dinwiddie Co.	Brunswick	Will	1762	CF1798-005
Nunnally, John W.	Chesterfield	Will	1862	LVA Acc. #24652
Nutt, Ann E., in Prince William Co.	Fauquier	Will	1893	CF1898-063
Nutt, Moseley, of Northumberland Co.	Williamsburg	Will Abstract	1801	Crozier, p. 42
Nuttall, Ireson, of Gloucester Co.	Williamsburg	Will Abstract	1799	Crozier, p. 42
Nuttall, John	Gloucester	Estate Ref.	1822	Note[6]

---

[1] Refer to Sweeny, p. 9, where the compiler lists wills given in *Torrence* that have not been found of record in Rappahannock County.

[2] LVA, Colonial Records Project, Reel #252; also in Coldham's *Loyalist Claims* under Nickolls.

[3] Louisa County Wills Not Fully Proved, 1757-1902, p. 37.

[4] LVA, Land Office Revolutionary War Military Certificate Papers, Richard Nunn, Folder 8.

[5] LVA, Land Office Revolutionary War Military Certificate Papers, Richard Nunn, Folder 8.

[6] LVA, Land Office Revolutionary War Military Certificate Papers, John Nuttall, Folder 3.

NAME	LOCATION	TYPE	YEAR	REFERENCE(S)
O				
O'Ferrall, John, in OH	Frederick	Will	1810	CF1827-107
O'Meara, Michael	Fairfax	Account	1818	NVG 6, p. 627
O'Neal, Arthur	Hampshire	Will	1761	Land Office
O'Neal, Arthur	Hampshire	Will	1761	MVG 29:3, p. 192
O'Toole, George, in Albemarle Co.	Charlottesville	Will	1856	CF1899-001
O'Toole, John, in Albemarle Co.	Charlottesville	Will	1872	CF1899-001
O'Toole, John L., in Albemarle Co.	Charlottesville	Will	1872	CF1899-001
Obanion, Bryan	Fauquier	Will Ref.	1778	Hening, Vol. 9, p. 576
Ocheltree, Michael, of Botetourt Co.	Augusta	Will	1799	CF1808-023
Odell, James	New Kent	Will	1840	CF1896-004
Odenell, Thomas [Anne]	Stafford	Dower	1691	OB: 11 FEB 1691
Odeon, William, Sr.	Norfolk	Will (N)	1687	DB5, p. 33
Odonell, Thomas	Stafford	Will	1690	Land Office
Odonelle, Thomas	Stafford	Will	1690	MVG 29:3, p. 192
Oelschlagle, John Ehard	Culpeper	Will	1793	FDC L560-115
Offutt, Alfred	Fairfax	Guard. Bond	1816	X
Ogden, Thomas, mariner		Will	1704	VCRP, Survey #04142
Oker, Abraham		Will	1667	VCRP, Survey #03539
Oldess, William	Surry	Will P.	1677	T:D&W2, p. 129a
Oldham, William, Sr.	Northumberland	Will	1791	CF1811-014
Olinger, J.C., Sr., in Lee Co.	Wise	Will	1889	CF1889-047
Olinger, John C., in Lee Co.	Wise	Will	1866	CF1891-018
Oliver, Ann A., in Hanover Co.	Henrico	Will	1846	CF1889-108
Oliver, Benjamin	Hanover	Will	1815	LVA Acc. #22725 a-c
Oliver, Benjamin	Hanover	Will	1820	LVA Acc. #22725
Oliver, David	Hanover	Will	1822	CF1855-007
Oliver, David	Hanover	Will	1822	Cocke:100
Oliver, David	Hanover	Will	1822	LVA Acc. #22813 a-k
Oliver, James	Fairfax	Partition	1879	X
Oliver, James	Fairfax	Plat	1879	X
Oliver, James	Fairfax	Partition	1879	X
Oliver, James	Fairfax	Plat	1879	X
Oliver, James	Fairfax	Will	1887	CF1893-033
Oliver, James H.	Gloucester	Will	1840	Note[1]
Oliver, John	Isle of Wight	Will	1652	VMHB 6, p. 249
Oliver, John	Hanover	Will	1815	LVA Acc. #27286
Oliver, John	Hanover	Will	1815	Fleet, Huntington Data
Oliver, Robert, in MD	Rockingham	Will	1835	CF1896-018
Oliver, Rutha Ann to Absolum Muire	King & Queen	Marriage	1840	LP
Oliver, Sarah E.	Fairfax	Will	1888	X
Oliver, William	Lancaster	Will	1750	LP
Oliver, William, Capt.	Essex	Will	1843	UVA MSS 4627
Omohundro, John, in Fluvanna Co.	Albemarle	Will	1845	CF1876-006
Opie, Lindsy, of Northumberland Co.	Williamsburg	Will Abstract	1785	Crozier, p. 43
Opie, Thomas, of Northumberland Co.	Williamsburg	Will Abstract	1785	Crozier, p. 43
Organ, Lucy E., in Floyd Co.	Bedford	Will	1895	CF1898-061
Osborne, Robert	Orange	Will	(nd)	V:Mss1 B2346 a 1156

---

[1] LVA, Land Office Revolutionary War Military Certificate Papers, Thomas Ransone, #9265, 9266

NAME	LOCATION	TYPE	YEAR	REFERENCE(S)
Osburn, Abner, in Loudoun Co.	Frederick	Will	1802	CF1834-057
Oslin, William L.	Mecklenburg	Will	1820	BRCD
Osling, Jesse		Will	1814c	DAR MSS 13 b5 f4
Osmun, Elisha, in NJ	Prince William	Will	1868	CF1879-010
Oswin, Thomas, of York River		Will	1721	VCRP, Survey #04666
Otterback, Philip, in DC	Fauquier	Will	1858	CF1883-023
Otterson, James, of Philadelphia PA	Arlington	Will	1891	WB10:181; File #749A
Ould, Robert	Richmond City	Will	1882	V:Mss2 Ou55 b
Ould, Robert, in Richmond	Henrico	Will	(nd)	CF1895-025 CC
Ould, Robert, in Richmond	Henrico	Will	1881	CF1895-025
Outten, Purnell	Accomack	Will	1796	LVA Acc. #27615
Overbey, Elizabeth, in WV	Mecklenburg	Will	1893	CF1898-017 CC
Overbey, Hezekiah, in LA	Mecklenburg	Will	1869	CF1884-065 CC
Overton, Elizabeth W., Appomattox Co.	Prince Edward	Will	1852	CF1871-019
Overton, James, Capt.		Will		HHS 31, p. 7
Overton, James, of St. Martin's Parish	Hanover	Will	1747	Note[1]
Overton, John, planter	Rappahannock*	Will	1691	Sweeny, p. 148
Overton, Rebecca, in Richmond	Gloucester	Will	1868	CF1912-054
Overton, Samuel	Hanover	Will	(nd)	HHS 60, p. 5
Overton, Samuel	Hanover	Will	1812	VG 45, p. 123
Overton, Samuel	Hanover	Will	1812	LP:21 OCT 1814
Overton, Samuel, in Hanover Co.	Louisa	Will	1812	CF1837-001
Overton, Samuel, in Hanover Co.	Louisa	Will	1812	CF1832-060
Overton, Samuel, of St. Martin's Parish	Hanover	Will	1812	VGS Bulletin VII, p. 72
Owen, Ann	Prince Edward	Will	1822	LVA Acc. #28154
Owen, Ann	Prince Edward	Inventory	1825	LVA Acc. #28154
Owen, Ann Crawford	Prince Edward	Will	1825	V:Mss1 Ow25 a 1-2
Owen, Ann Crawford	Prince Edward	Inventory	1825	V:Mss1 Ow25 a 1-2
Owen, David [Owin]	Charles City	Inventory	1730	D&W1724, p. 290
Owen, Jesse	Prince Edward	Will	1792	DCW2, p. 1
Owen, Robert	Henrico	Will	(nd)	Records, Vol. 7, p. 2355
Owen, William	Henrico	Will	1775	Records, Vol. 7, p. 2259
Owen, William	Arlington	Will	1800	CRA:328
Owen, William L., of Halifax Co.	Mecklenburg	Will	1888	CF1889-029 CC
Owens, Levi, in Nelson Co.	Lynchburg	Will	1828	CF1829-036
Owin, David [Owen]	Charles City	Account	1730	D&W1724, p. 334
Owin, Thomas	Henrico	Will	1744	Records, Vol. 4, p. 1283
Ozburn, Jonathan, in Berkeley Co.	Frederick	Will	1778	CF1818-092

---

[1] Tennessee State Archives, Claybrooke Collection, Box 14, Folder 8.

NAME	LOCATION	TYPE	YEAR	REFERENCE(S)

P

NAME	LOCATION	TYPE	YEAR	REFERENCE(S)
Pace, John	Goochland	Will	1790	CF1816-040
Packe, Graves, mariner		Will	1731	VCRP, Survey #04658
Packerill, William		Will	1702	LVA Wills/Admin. DB
Page, John	Gloucester	Will	1718	Note[1]
Page, John	Middlesex	Will	1720	WB1713, p. 173
Page, John	Lunenburg	Will	1786	CF1811-012
Page, John	Elizabeth City	Will	1800	Note[2]
Page, John B., in Norfolk Co.	Frederick	Will	1832	CF1843-038
Page, John C., in Cumberland Co.	Prince Edward	Will	1853	CF1907-046
Page, John, in Elizabeth City Co.	Frederick	Will	1800	CF1843-038
Page, John, of Elizabeth City Co.	Williamsburg	Will Abstract	1800	Crozier, p. 45
Page, John, of Gloucester Co.	London	Will	1719	N:PROB11/567
Page, John, of Gloucester Co.		Will	1719	VCRP, Survey #04341
Page, John, of Gloucester Co.	Fredericksburg	Will Partial	1774	Note[3]
Page, John, of *North End*	Gloucester	Will	1772	VMHB 34, p. 275
Page, Mann	Gloucester	Will	1731	LVA Wills/Admin. DB
Page, Mann	Gloucester	Will	1731	VMHB 32, p. 32
Page, Mann, in Gloucester Co.	Frederick	Will	1778	CF1843-038
Page, Mann, of *Rosewell*	Gloucester	Will Ref.	1730	Hening, Vol. 5, p. 277
Page, Mann, of *Rosewell*	Gloucester	Will Ref.	1730	Hening, Vol. 7, p. 480
Page, Mann, of *Rosewell*	Gloucester	Will Ref.	1730	Winfree, p. 359
Page, Media Ann, in Richmond	Nansemond	Will	1892	CF1933-105
Page, Robert	Hanover	Will	1767	Note[4]
Page, Robert	Hanover	Will	1794	Note[5]
Page, Robert		Will	1796	Note[6]
Page, Robert Carter	Hanover	Will	1782	HHS 5, p. 1
Page, Robert Carter		Will	1782	Note[7]
Page, Robert Carter	Hanover	Will, 1782	1798	G1:79
Page, Robert, of *Broadneck*	Hanover	Will	1767	VMHB 34, p. 275
Page, William, of Overwharton Parish	Stafford	Will Ref.	1715	DB1780, p. 56
Paine, John	Charles City	Inventory	1727	D&W1724, p. 161
Paine, Nicholas	Middlesex	Will	1693	WB1679, pt. 1, p. 83
Paine, Samuel	Henrico	Appraisal	1822	LVA Acc. #41008, r4610
Paine, William, mariner		Will	1710	VCRP, Survey #04351
Palistone, John	Surry	Inventory	1707	T:D&W5, p. 383b
Pallin, Thomas, mariner		Will	1718	VCRP, Survey #04338
Palmer, Joseph H., in LA	Brunswick	Will	1854	CF1857-034
Palmer, Joseph, in Richmond Co.	Fauquier	Will	1852	CF1870-007
Palmer, Joseph, of Richmond Co.	Williamsburg	Will Abstract	1750	Crozier, p. 44
Palmer, Thomas		Will	1630	VCRP, Survey #03959
Palmer, Thomas, of King William Co.	London	Will	1768	N:PROB11/943
Palmore, Benjamin, of Powhatan Co.	Cumberland	Will	1849	CF1854-006

---

[1] R.C.M. Page, *Genealogy of the Page Family of Virginia* (1893), p. 47.

[2] LVA, U.S. Circuit Court Records, Box 25, A-P (Restored), *Campbell's Exors. V. Page et al* (1832).

[3] Fredericksburg Superior Court Chancery Order Book, 1816-1818, p. 175.

[4] Fredericksburg Superior Court Chancery Order Book, 1816-1818, p. 175.

[5] LVA, U.S. Circuit Court Records, Bk. 17 (Richmond), p. 62.

[6] LVA, U.S. Circuit Court Records, Bk. 17 (Richmond), p. 62.

[7] LVA, U.S. Circuit Court Records, Bk. 20 (Richmond), p. 263.

NAME	LOCATION	TYPE	YEAR	REFERENCE(S)
Pancoast, Joseph T., in MD	Henrico	Will	1882	CF1896-022
Pannell, Thomas	Rappahannock*	Will	1677	V:Mss1 B4678 b38-189
Pannill, David		Will Ref.	1795	Note[1]
Parfitt, Elizabeth	Lancaster	Will (N)	1709	LP
Parham, Ephraim, in Dinwiddie Co.	Brunswick	Will	1779	CF1826-058
Parham, Ephraim, of Bristol Parish	Dinwiddie	Will	1779	SV 2:1, p. 5
Parham, Simon	Prince George	Will	1828	LP:06 DEC 1828
Parham, William	Brunswick	Will	1780	CF1803-004
Parham, William	Brunswick	Will	1780	CF1802-004
Parish, David, of Elizabeth City Co.	Williamsburg	Will Abstract	1805	Crozier, p. 47
Parish, John, of Elizabeth City Co.	Williamsburg	Will Abstract	1803	Crozier, p. 47
Parish, Mary R.	New Kent	Will	1866	CF1890-006
Park, Patty, alias Cole	Henrico	Will	1807	VGSQ 18:3, p. 84
Parke, Daniel	James City	Will Ref.	1679	VMHB 50, p. 254
Parke, Daniel	James City	Will Abstract	1679	VMHB 14, p. 174
Parke, Daniel		Will	1679	VCRP, Survey #03720
Parke, Daniel, in London, Eng.	James City	Will	1679	V:Mss2 P2204 a 1
Parke, Daniel, Jr.	James City	Estate Ref.	1711	Hening, Vol. 6, p. 319
Parke, Daniel, Sr.	James City	Will Ref.	1670	Hening, Vol. 6, p. 319
Parke, William		Will	1634	VCRP, Survey #03969
Parker, Elizabeth, in Westmoreland Co.	Essex	Will	1855	CF1867-011
Parker, George	Fairfax	Will	1829	NVG 8, p. 1091
Parker, George S., of Washington DC	Arlington	Will	1896	WB10:329; File #772A
Parker, James	Caroline	Will	1817	W&D1794, p. 13a
Parker, John, in Richmond		Will	1701	VCRP, Survey #04117
Parker, John [Judah]	Surry	Admin.	1679	LVA Wills/Admin. DB
Parker, Josiah, of Isle of Wight Co.	Williamsburg	Will Abstract	1810	Crozier, p. 44
Parker, Patrick, in Norfolk Co.	Princess Anne	Will	1795	CF1811-001
Parker, Patrick, of Norfolk Co.	Williamsburg	Will Abstract	1795	Crozier, p. 44
Parker, Richard	Surry	Admin.	1677	T:D&W2, p. 141a
Parker, Richard	Nansemond	Will	1764	VTG 12:4, p. 142
Parker, Richard, of Nansemond Co.	Isle of Wight	Will (U)	1764	LVA:1161459
Parker, Richard, of Upper Parish	Nansemond	Will	1764	SV 10:4, p. 159
Parker, Thomas	Isle of Wight	Will	1663	V:Mss2 P2285 a 1
Parker, Thomas	Isle of Wight	Will	1663	LVA Acc. #29980
Parkes, Andrew, haberdasher		Will	1630	VCRP, Survey #03957
Parkinson, James	Henrico	Will	1828	LVA Acc. #41008, r4610
Parkinson, James	Henrico	Will	1828	Fleet, Huntington Data
Parks, Richard, in Culpeper Co.	Rappahannock	Will	1817	CF1840-009
Parks, William, in Amherst Co.	Lynchburg	Will	1778	CF1829-050
Parks, William, printer, of Williamsburg	York	Will	1750	WMQ2 2, p. 92
Parnel, Elizabeth	Isle of Wight	Will (U)	1786	LVA:1161459
Parratt, William	Richmond City	Will	1797	T:HCD2, p. 376
Parrett, Henry	Rockingham	Will	1826	CF1860-025
Parrill, Edward, in Hampshire Co.	Frederick	Will	1826	CF1832-086
Parrish, Constance, in Fluvanna Co.	Hanover	Will	1872	CF1875-003
Parrish, Constance M., in Fluvanna Co.	Louisa	Will	1872	CF1893-018
Parrish, George W., in Louisa Co.	Hanover	Will	1859	CF1861-030

[1] LVA, Land Office Revolutionary War Military Certificate Papers, David Pannill, Folder 16.

NAME	LOCATION	TYPE	YEAR	REFERENCE(S)
Parrish, George W., in Louisa Co.	Hanover	Will	1859	CF1875-003
Parrish, Humphrey	Goochland	Will	1823	LVA Acc. #28827
Parrish, James, in Pittsylvania Co.	Lynchburg	Will	1818	CF1821-035
Parrish, James, of Brunswick Co.	Mecklenburg	Will	1754	CF1817-001
Parrish, John	Goochland	Will	1786	CF1817-005
Parrot, Ruth	Brunswick	Will	1798	DB1, p. 83
Parrott, Henry	Rockingham	Will	1826	CF1845-004
Parrott, Richard, of *Ellerslie*, in DC	Arlington	Will	1823	CF1838-023
Parrott, Richard, of *Ellerslie*, in DC	Arlington	Will	1823	CF1838-038
Parry, John		Will (N)	1638	VCRP, Survey #03982
Parsley, William	Hanover	Will	1836	CF1857-005
Parsley, William	Hanover	Will	1836	Cocke:102
Parson, Anthony, in Southampton Co.	Norfolk	Will	1798	CF1844-009
Parsons, Alee, in Pendleton Co.	Frederick	Will	1824	CF1830-158
Parsons, James, Capt., in Hardy Co.	Frederick	Will	1813	CF1825-179
Parsons, John	Rappahannock*	Will	1689	Sweeny, p. 143
Parsons, Joseph	Henrico	Will	1762	LVA Acc. #29598
Parsons, Joseph	Henrico	Will	1762	LVA Acc. #41008, r4610
Parsons, Joseph	Henrico	Inventory	1770	Records, Vol. 7, p. 2089
Parsons, Joseph	Henrico	Inventory	1770	LVA Acc. #29598
Parsons, Joseph, of Henrico Parish	Henrico	Will	1762	Fleet, Huntington Data
Parsons, Sarah	Henrico	Will	1770	Records, Vol. 7, p. 2099
Parsons, Solomon, in Loudoun Co.	Fairfax	Will	1830	X
Parsons, Thomas, in Hardy Co.	Frederick	Will	1804	CF1830-158
Partin, Lucy	Brunswick	Will	1837	SV 3:3, p. 117
Pasteur, William	Williamsburg	Will	1791	V:Mss1 An245 b24
Pate, Samuel	Halifax	Will	1867	LVA Acc. #26969
Paterson, Gilbert, mariner [Petterson]		Will	1724	VCRP, Survey #04676
Patillo, James, of Dinwiddie Co.	Brunswick	Will	1754	CF1808-015
Paton, William, of Alexandria	Arlington	Will	1825	CF1854-005
Patrick, Richard		Will	1675	LVA Wills/Admin. DB
Patterson, Agnes	Giles	Will	1843	THS 9:1, p. 3
Patterson, Elizabeth, in Buckingham Co.	Albemarle	Will	1857	CF1889-009
Patterson, Frances	Essex	Will	1876	LP ur
Patterson, James	Hanover	Will	1826	Cocke:103
Patterson, James	Hanover	Will	1826	CF1845-011
Patterson, Robert F., in TN	Culpeper	Will	1895	CF1910-018
Patterson, Thomas	Fairfax	Will	1792	X
Patterson, Timothy M., in Botetourt Co.	Roanoke	Will	1828	CF1840-003
Patteson, David	Albemarle	Will	1745	BRCD
Patteson, David	Buckingham	Will	1846	LVA Patteson Papers
Patteson, James M.	Buckingham	Will	1858	LVA Patteson Papers
Patteson, John H., in Danville	Lynchburg	Will	1889	CF1895-030
Patteson, Jonathan, in New Kent Co.	Lunenburg	Will	1774	LVA Acc. #29368
Patteson, Thomas	Albemarle	Will	1747	LVA, Patteson Papers
Patteson, William		Admin. Bond	1735	LVA Acc. #22483a
Pattison, George, mariner		Will	1722	VCRP, Survey #04669
Patton, Hugh	Richmond City	Will	1790	T:HCD1, p. 390
Patton, John M., in Richmond	Albemarle	Will	1858	CF1899-008
Patton, William	Augusta	Inventory	1793	LVA Acc. #23826a
Paul, William, of Fredericksburg	Spotsylvania	Will	1774	VMHB 15, p. 215

NAME	LOCATION	TYPE	YEAR	REFERENCE(S)
Paulett, John	Charlotte	Will	1795	V:Mss1 B6638 a2812+
Paulett, Thomas	Charles City	Will	(nd)	V:Mss5:9 B9965:1
Pawlett, Thomas		Will	1643	VMHB 47, p. 194
Pawlett, William		Will	1695	VCRP, Survey #06050
Paxton, Elisha	Rockbridge	Will	1866	UVA MSS 658-a
Payne, Albert, in Madison Co.	Culpeper	Will	1854	CF1900-041
Payne, Albert Washington	Culpeper	Will	1854c	V:Mss1 P2936 c 195+
Payne, Archer, Jr., in Bedford Co.	Lynchburg	Will	1806	CF1842-005
Payne, Daniel, of Stafford Co.	Fredericksburg	Will	1779	DCWA, p. 48
Payne, Daniel, of Stafford Co.	Fredericksburg	Inventory	1796	DCWA, p. 48
Payne, Enoch, in Hancock Co. TN	Russell	Will	1863	CF1873-007
Payne, Frank, in Rappahannock Co.	Fauquier	Will	1837	CF1839-038
Payne, Isabella J., in SC	Albemarle	Will	1885	CF1890-021
Payne, Jean, of Goochland Co.	London	Will	1808	N:PROB11/1481
Payne, Jesse, of Goochland Co.	Williamsburg	Will Abstract	1771	Crozier, p. 46
Payne, John	Charles City	Account	1727	D&W1724, p. 173
Payne, John	Bedford	Will	1798	LVA Acc. #36255-43
Payne, John C.	Fauquier	Will	1867	CF1889-017
Payne, Marion Andrew Morson Love	Fauquier	Will	1837	V:Mss1 H9267 a 3
Payne, Philip, in Campbell Co.	Lynchburg	Will	1840	CF1857-029
Payne, William	Fairfax	Will	1782	LVA Acc. #26121
Payton, Anthony	Westmoreland	Will	1788	Wills #34
Peachy, Judith	Northumberland	Will	1755	RB3, p. 183
Peachy, Mary, of King & Queen Co.	London	Will	1717	N:PROB11/556
Peachy, Mary, of King & Queen Co.		Will	1717	VCRP, Survey #04335
Peachy, Samuel	Essex	Will	1784	CF1819-001
Peachy, Samuel	Richmond	Will	1795	MVG 29:3, p. 193
Peachy, Thomas Griffin	Williamsburg	Will Abstract	1802	Crozier, p. 44
Peachy, William	Essex	Will	1803	MVG 29:3, p. 193
Peachy, William	Essex	Will	1803	CF1813-002
Peachy, William, of Essex Co.	Williamsburg	Will Abstract	1803	Crozier, p. 46
Peacock, Thomas J.	Fairfax	Will	1897	CF1908-024
Peacock, William [Pecock]	Surry	Will	1724	T: correct from 1722
Pearce, Baldwin		Inventory	1801	V:Mss1 Ad198 b 19-41
Pearce, Christopher	King William	Will	1704	RB2, p. 33
Pearson, Charles	James City	Will	1761	BRCD
Pearson, John	Prince William	Will	1888	LP
Pearson, Samuel	Hanover	Inventory	1802	G1:82
Pearson, Samuel	Hanover	Will, 1790	1802	G1:81
Pearson, Simon	Fairfax	Account	1769	X
Peasley, Henry	Gloucester	Will Ref.	1675	Hening, Vol. 7, p. 41
Peatross, Matthew [of Horse Pasture]	Caroline	Will	1805	W&P1742, p. 76
Peatross, William	Caroline	Will	1808	W&P1742, p. 89
Peck, Anna, in Richmond Co.	Northumberland	Will	1829	CF1832-004
Peck, Jacob, of Botetourt Co.	Augusta	Will	1837	CF1842-017
Peck, John	Giles	Will	1848	MVG 29:3, p. 193
Peebles, Robert S.J., in Richmond	Henrico	Will	1873	CF1889-015
Peebles, William	Prince George	Will	1839	SV 9:2, p. 56

NAME	LOCATION	TYPE	YEAR	REFERENCE(S)
Peek, Jeffery	Buckingham	Will	1800	Note[1]
Peele, John	Lancaster	Will	1677	LP
Peeples, Joseph	Prince George	Estate Ref.	1759	DB1759, p. 118
Pegram, James West	Richmond City	Will	1849	V:Mss1 P3496 a 355+
Peirce, Francis	Henrico	Will	1717	Records, Vol. 1, p. 337
Peirce, Thomas	Warwick	Will	1697	Records 1695, p. 453
Peirce, Thomas [Pierce]	Warwick	Will	1696	TVF 3:4, p. 227
Peirsey, Abraham	James City	Will	1627	TQ 8, p. 212
Peirsey, Abraham	James City	Will	1627	VMHB 11, p. 174
Pell, Joseph	Norfolk	Will	1804	Fleet, Huntington Data
Pell, Joseph	Norfolk	Will	1833	LVA Acc. #41008, r4611
Peltus, Thomas	James City	Will	1684	M: L4 f120
Pemberton, Thomas	Goochland	Will	1828	CF1853-004
Pemberton, Thomas	Goochland	Will	1828	V:Mss1 F7345 a 888+
Pemberton, Thomas, in Goochland Co.	Powhatan	Will	1828	CF1832-008
Pemberton, Thomas, in Goochland Co.	Powhatan	Will	1828	CF1860-015
Pemberton, Thomas, of Goochland Co.	Cumberland	Will	1828	CF1859-025
Pemberton, Wilson Coleman	King William	Will	1855	V:Mss1 Ay445 b902
Pence, John	Rockingham	Estate Ref.	1823	LP:18 DEC 1823
Pence, John H.	Rockingham	Marriage A.	1821	LVA:1159583
Pence, Malinda	Rockingham	Will Ref.	1825	LVA:1159583
Pendleton, Edmund	Caroline	Will	1799	BRCD
Pendleton, Edmund, of *Edmundsburg*	Caroline	Will	1803	LVA Acc. #20450
Pendleton, Edmund, of *White Plains*	Caroline	Will	1827	LVA Acc. #20449
Pendleton, Edmund [of *Edmundton*]	Caroline	Will	1824	BRCD
Pendleton, Elizabeth	King & Queen	Will	1847	LVA Acc. #22043
Pendleton, Elizabeth	King & Queen	Will	1847	Fleet 2:392
Pendleton, F.H., in Norfolk Co.	Louisa	Will	1894	CF1894-029
Pendleton, Henry	Louisa	Will	1822	V:Mss2 W7336 b 4
Pendleton, Isabella, c/o Philip B.	King & Queen	Guard. Acct.	1864	Fleet 2:467
Pendleton, Lillian G., c/o Philip B.	King & Queen	Guard. Acct.	1864	Fleet 2:467
Pendleton, Mary C., c/o Philip B.	King & Queen	Guard. Acct.	1864	Fleet 2:467
Pendleton, Philip B.	King & Queen	Will	1840	CF1860-004
Pendleton, Philip B.	King & Queen	Account	1865	Fleet 2:467
Peniston, Elizabeth	Prince George	Will	1769	VMHB 48, p. 104
Peniston, Elizabeth	Prince George	Will	1769	VMHB 48, p. 104
Peniston, Elizabeth	Prince George	Exor. Bond	1773	VMHB 48, p. 105
Penn, Gabriel	Amherst	Will	1798	LP:12 DEC 1833
Penn, Gabriel, in Amherst Co.	Lynchburg	Will	1794	CF1825-034
Penn, Gabriel, in Amherst Co.	Lynchburg	Will	1798	CF1836-001
Penn, Gabriel, in Amherst Co.	Lynchburg	Will	1798	CF1819-010
Penn, George	Amherst	Will	1794	CF1803-002
Penn, John, in Amherst Co.	Bedford	Will	1845	CF1852-007
Pennell, Joseph, in PA	Bath	Will	1820	CF1854-005
Pennington, Howell, in Mecklenburg Co.	Brunswick	Will	1819	CF1833-035
Penniston, Anthony C.	Prince George	Will	1774	BRCD
Penniston, Anthony C.	Prince George	Inventory	1783	BRCD
Penniston, Anthony Collins	Prince George	Will	1772	MVG 31:4, p. 351

---

[1] Prince Edward County District Court Wills, Bk. 2, p. 18.

NAME	LOCATION	TYPE	YEAR	REFERENCE(S)
Penticost, Scarbrough	Brunswick	Will	1795	CF1801-015
Pepper, George, in PA	Wise	Will	1890	CF1894-023
Pepper, Nathan, in Brunswick Co.	Smyth	Will	1836	CF1837-002
Percey, Richard		Will	1654	VCRP, Survey #03123
Perkey, Jacob, of Rockingham Co.	Augusta	Will	1809	CF1815-049
Perkins, Christopher, of Norfolk		Will	1765	VCRP, Survey #04681
Perkins, Elizabeth	Dinwiddie	Will	1805	VGSQ 10:1, p. 9
Perkins, Hardin, of Buckingham Co.	Albemarle	Will	1821	CF1837-034
Perkins, Humphrey	Rappahannock*	Will Ref.	1687	Sweeny, p. 5
Perkins, Isaac O.	Fluvanna	Admin.	1862	LVA Acc. #41008, r4608
Perkins, John, of Tillotson Parish	Buckingham	Will	1803	LP:22 DEC 1807
Perkins, Lewis	Dinwiddie	Will	1811	VGSQ 10:1, p. 9
Perkins, Richard, in Campbell Co.	Lynchburg	Will	1860	CF1870-005
Perkins, Thomas	Henrico	Will	1761	Records, Vol. 6, p. 1833
Perkins, William, in Patrick Co.	Floyd	Will	(nd)	CF1856-008
Perkinson, John	Henrico	Will	1736	Records, Vol. 3, p. 985
Perrin, Isaac	Hanover	Will	1821	Weisiger 1:001
Perrin, Isaac		Will		HHS 11, p. 5
Perrin, John	Henrico	Inventory	1675	Records, Vol. 1, p. 47
Perrin, Mathurin	Arlington	Will	1814	CF1822-023
Perrott, Francis		Will	1654	VCRP, Survey #04115
Perry, Augusta B., in NY	Princess Anne	Will	1891	CF1894-010
Perry, Nicholas	Charles City	Inventory	1770	Records, p. 243
Perry, Nicholas	Charles City	Will	1770	Records, p. 226
Perry, Pierce, in Culpeper Co.	Fauquier	Will	1856	CF1873-059
Perry, William, Capt.		Will Ref.	1637	Note[1]
Persey, Abraham	Elizabeth City	Will	1628c	V:Mss1 K6315 b
Persey, Abraham		Will	1633	VCRP, Survey #03966
Persey, Abraham, of Persey's Hundred	London	Will	1633	N:PROB11/163
Person, John, of Southampton Co.	Williamsburg	Will Abstract	1767	Crozier, p. 47
Person, Philip, of Southampton Co.	Williamsburg	Will Abstract	1782	Crozier, p. 44
Peter, Peter, in Hampshire Co.	Frederick	Will	1773	CF1821-119
Peterkin, Emma R., in MD	Fauquier	Will	1879	CF1880-036
Peters, Don T.C., in Lynchburg	Campbell	Will	1871	CF1883-027
Peters, Don T.C., in Lynchburg	Bedford	Will	1877	CF1892-046
Peters, Elisha E., in Nelson Co.	Bedford	Will	1886	CF1892-046
Peters, John	Nansemond	Will Ref.	1719	Hening, Vol. 4, p. 528
Peters, Matthew, in Warwick Co.	York	Will	1813	CF1838-002
Peterson, Jonas	King William	Inventory	1706	RB2, p. 58
Peterson, Thomas, in Prince George Co.	Cumberland	Will	1809	Judgments 1816 FEB
Peterson, Thomas, in Prince George Co.	Petersburg	Will	1809	CF1842-032
Peteway, William	Surry	Account	1711	T: from Inventory
Petterson, Gilbert, mariner [Paterson]		Will	1724	VCRP, Survey #04676
Pettit, Laura V., late Hampton	Fairfax	Guard. Acct.	1860	X
Pettit, Samuel, in Amherst Co.	Bedford	Will	1863	CF1906-113
Pettit, Thomas, of Farnham Parish	Rappahannock*	Will	1665	Sweeny, p. 157
Pettit, Thomas, of South Farnham P.	Essex	Will Abstract	1719	Fleet 2:222
Pettiver, John	King William	Inventory	1704	RB1, pp. 220, 229

---

[1] Virginia Land Office Patents, Bk. 1, p. 702.

NAME	LOCATION	TYPE	YEAR	REFERENCE(S)
Pettus, James G., in Richmond	Louisa	Will	1838	CF1869-005
Pettus, Leroy O., in TN	Louisa	Will	1878	CF1891-013
Pettus, Sarah	Lunenburg	Will	1798	CF1828-061
Pettus, Stephen	Hanover	Estate Ref.	1788	LP:31 OCT 1788
Pettus, Thomas	Henrico	Inventory	1691	Records, Vol. 1, p. 73
Pettus, Thomas	Lunenburg	Will	1780	V:Mss2 P4558 a 1
Pettus, Thomas B., of KY	Louisa	Will	1849	CF1869-005
Pettway, Edward	Surry	Will	1690	T:D&W4, p. 182b
Pettway, Thomas	Surry	Will (N)	1700	T:D&W5, p. 215b
Peugh, Spencer, in Loudoun Co.	Frederick	Will	1816	CF1831-212
Peyton, Craven, in Loudoun Co.	Arlington	Will	1781	CF1833-010
Peyton, Craven, in Loudoun Co.	Arlington	Will	1781	CF1833-010
Peyton, Elizabeth Bronaugh	Fauquier	Will	1839	LVA Acc. #30824
Peyton, Elizabeth Bronaugh	Fauquier	Will	1839	V:Mss2 P4684 a 1
Peyton, Henry	Fauquier	Will	1814	V:Mss1 P4686 c 4-5
Peyton, Henry, in Prince William Co.	Frederick	Will	1781	CF1827-157
Peyton, Henry, in Prince William Co.	Frederick	Will	1781	CF1822-082
Peyton, John	Stafford	Will	1760	V:Mss1 P4686 c 1-3
Peyton, John	Prince William	Will	1774	Note[1]
Peyton, John	Fluvanna	Will	1801	V:Mss1 F7345 a 883+
Peyton, John	Fluvanna	Will	1801	Fleet, Huntington Data
Peyton, John, Sir	Gloucester	Estate Ref.	1790	LP:20 NOV 1790
Peyton, John, Sir	Gloucester	Will	1790	Note[2]
Peyton, T., in KY	Frederick	Will	1788	CF1827-157
Peyton, Timothy, in Prince William Co.	Frederick	Will	1788	CF1827-157
Peyton, Wm. Madison, in Roanoke Co.	Albemarle	Will	1868	CF1886-068
Pfahler, Sarah A., in IN	Portsmouth	Will	1877	CF1882-006
Phelps, Eli, in Loudoun Co.	Frederick	Will	1804	CF1816-018
Phelps John Wolcott, in MA	Alexandria	Will	1884	CF1887-014
Phelps, John Wolcott, in MA	Arlington	Will	1884	CF1887-014
Philips, Thomas	York	Will	1781	CF1793-001
Philipson, Robert, in York Co.	Brunswick	Will	1745	CF1805-042
Phillips, Ann	Charles City	Will (N)	1769	Records 1766, p. 139
Phillips, Charles C., in TN	Mecklenburg	Will	1851	CF1851-013 CSC
Phillips, Dibdul T.	Hanover	Will	1848	LP 1846
Phillips, George	Lunenburg	Will	1786	CF1799-010
Phillips, James	Lancaster	Will	1689	FDC L564-128
Phillips, John	Surry	Will	1690	T:D&W4, p. 185b
Phillips, John	Hanover	Will	1793	BRCD, damaged
Phillips, John, in Prince George Co.	Petersburg	Will	1820	CF1841-041
Phillips, Richard	King William	Inventory	1702	RB2, p. 6
Phillips, William	Surry	Will	1721	T: correct from 1720
Phillips, William	Prince George	Will	1842	SV 9:3, p. 106
Phillips, William, of York Co.	Williamsburg	Will Abstract	1785	Crozier, p. 46
Phillips, William Wesley	Fauquier	Will	1876	CF1888-042
Pickerell, William		Will	1702	LVA Wills/Admin. DB
Picket, Joyce	Stafford	Will	1703	WBZ, p. 171

---

[1] Prince William County Land Causes, 1793-1811, p. 289.
[2] LVA, U.S. Circuit Court Records, Box 195, *Murdock, Donald & Co. v. Dixon's Reps* (1824).

NAME	LOCATION	TYPE	YEAR	REFERENCE(S)
Pickett, Martin	Fauquier	Will Abstract	1804	VMHB 49, p. 188
Pickett, Martin, in Fauquier Co.	Frederick	Will	1803	CF1835-119
Pickett, Sanford, in Saline Co. MO	Fauquier	Will Abstract	1846	VGS Bulletin VIII, p. 14
Pickett, William	Essex	Will Abstract	1748	VMHB 49, p. 186
Pickett, William	Fauquier	Will Abstract	1766	VMHB 49, p. 188
Pickett, William, in Fauquier Co.	Frederick	Will	1766	CF1835-119
Picot, Amelia V.H., in Richmond	Henrico	Will	1868	CF1888-033
Picot, Edward Joseph, in Richmond	Henrico	Will	1860	CF1888-033
Picot, Josephine M., in NJ	Hanover	Will	1869	CF1888-002
Pictoe, Henry	Stafford	Will Ref.	1666	OB:10 OCT 1666
Pidington, Thomas	Surry	Will	1702	T:D&W5, p. 246b
Pierce, Ann	Charles City	Will	1784	LP, box 51, folder 271
Pierce, Ann	Charles City	Will	1784	MVG 35:2, p. 143
Pierce, Ann, in Charles City Co.	Henrico	Will	1784	CF1799-015
Pierce, Thomas	Warwick	Will	1696	LVA Acc. #22057 p. 453
Pierce, Thomas [Peirce]	Warwick	Will	1696	TVF 3:4, p. 227
Piernett, Peter	New Kent	Will	1810	LP:07 DEC 1810
Pierson, John	Prince George	Will	1855	SV 10:1, p. 11
Piggott, Fielding D.	James City	Will	1854	LVA Acc. #41537
Piggott, Francis	James City	Will	1830	BRCD
Piggott, Pearson, of James City Co.	Williamsburg	Will Abstract	1787	Crozier, p. 47
Pike, George	Henrico	Will	1752	Records, Vol. 5, p. 1567
Piles, John	Essex	Will	1759	WB11, p. 33
Piles, Samuel	Essex	Will	1779	CF1831-028
Pinchard, John	Lancaster	Will	1689	LP
Pinckard, John	Henry	Will	1782	WB1, p. 52
Pinckard, Thomas, of Lancaster Co.	Williamsburg	Will Abstract	1782	Crozier, p. 46
Pinkard, Thomas, in TX	Culpeper	Will	1846	CF1868-001
Pinner, Margaret, in Norfolk	Portsmouth	Will	1876	CF1894-009
Pirkey, John, of Rockingham Co.	Augusta	Will	1794	CF1827-105
Pirkey, John, of Rockingham Co.	Augusta	Will	1794	CF1858-017
Pitman, Lawrence	Shenandoah	Will	1850c	DAR MSS 13 b5 f5
Pitt, Robert, of Accomack Co.	Williamsburg	Will Abstract	1756	Crozier, p. 45
Pittillo, James, in Dinwiddie Co.	Brunswick	Will	1754	CF1800-015
Pittman, John	Buckingham	Will	1830	SV 5:1, p. 4
Pittman, John	Buckingham	Will	1830	Election[1]
Pittman, William		Estate Ref.	1794	Shepherd, Vol. 1, p. 335
Pitts, Frances, in Norfolk Co.	Portsmouth	Will	1871	CF1889-028
Pitts, Thomas	Essex	Will	1806	LVA Acc. #21087
Pitts, Thomas	Essex	Will	1806	CF1827-004
Platt, Ralph	Stafford	Will P.	1691	OB:10 FEB 1691
Pleasants, Archibald	Richmond City	Will	1864c	V:Mss1 J8586 b 187+
Pleasants, Archibald	Richmond City	Exor. Bond	1864c	V:Mss1 J8586 b 187+
Pleasants, Jane, of *Curles*	Henrico	Will	1709	VMHB 18, p. 450
Pleasants, John	Henrico	Will	1690	HCHS 28:3, p. 5
Pleasants, John		Will	1771	Note[2]
Pleasants, John, in Henrico Co.	Lynchburg	Will	1771	CF1837-015

---

[1] LVA, Contested Election Papers, Buckingham Co., 1840/41.

[2] Virginia Journal of the House of Delegates, 1790, p. 58.

NAME	LOCATION	TYPE	YEAR	REFERENCE(S)
Pleasants, John, in Williamsburg	James City	Will	1867	CF1872-004
Pleasants, John, of *Curles*	Henrico	Will	1690	VMHB 18, p. 101, 229
Pleasants, Jonathan		Will	1776	Note[1]
Pleasants, Jonathan, in Henrico Co.	Powhatan	Will	1776	CF1821-009
Plecker, Adam W., in MD	Rockingham	Will	1892	CF1892-113
Plecker, Jacob	Augusta	Will	1855	UVA MSS 13688
Plecker, Jacob, in Augusta Co.	Rockingham	Will	1855	CF1892-113
Pledge, John	Henrico	Will	1720	Records, Vol. 2, p. 509
Plume, William	Norfolk City	Will	1807	V:Mss1 D7784 a 1-2
Plummer, Ann, in Richmond Co.	Northumberland	Will	1843	CF1859-001
Poindexter, Elizabeth	Louisa	Will Ref.	1802	VMHB 20, p. 110
Poindexter, James D.	Hanover	Will	1895	CF1897-012
Poindexter, James L., in Pittsylvania Co.	Louisa	Will	1853	CF1870-015
Poindexter, John	Louisa	Will Abstract	1753	VMHB 19, p. 439
Poindexter, John Lewis	New Kent	Will	1835	LVA Acc. #21421
Poindexter, Parke, in Chesterfield Co.	Prince Edward	Will	1847	CF1870-003
Poindexter, Sarah	Mecklenburg	Will	1791	T: correct from 1790
Poindexter, Thomas	Louisa	Will Ref.	1796	VMHB 20, p. 110
Poindexter, Thomas, in Bedford	Lynchburg	Will	1851	CF1877-013
Poindexter, Thomas, in Franklin Co. KY	Louisa	Will Ref.	1796	VMHB 21, p. 215
Pointer, John A., in Gloucester Co.	Henrico	Will	1866	CF1868-005
Pointer, Thomas	Richmond City	Will	1797	T:HCD2, p. 335
Polk, Charles Peale	D.C.	Will	1822	DCA:Box 7
Pollard, Joseph	King & Queen	Will	1791c	V:Mss3 K5893 a 69-86
Pollard, Peter Thornton, of *Millford*	King & Queen	Will	1843	CF1892-002
Pollard, Robert	King & Queen	Will	1757	V:Mss3 K5893 a 69-86
Pollard, Robert	New Kent	Will	1835	LVA Acc. #41008, r4611
Pollard, Robert	New Kent	Will	1835	Fleet, Huntington Data
Pollard, Robert, Jr.	King & Queen	Will Partial	1757	LVA Acc. #23553
Pollard, William	Hanover	Will	1832	Cocke:107
Pollard, William	Hanover	Will	1832	CF1853-006
Pollard, William C.	King William	Will	1865	CF1917-003
Pollard, William T.H.	Hanover	Will	1856	Cocke:108
Pollard, William T.H.	Hanover	Will	1856	CF1867-007
Pollitt, Susan	D.C.	Will	1837	DCA:Box 13
Pollock, David	Charles City	Inventory	1726	D&W1724, p. 125
Polock, David	Charles City	Will	1726	D&W1724, p. 112
Pond, Samuel, of Skittle's Creek		Will	1717	Note[2]
Pool, Thomas, of Fauquier Co.	Loudoun	Will	1803	CF1852-00
Poole, Thomas, of Fauquier Co.	Loudoun	Will	1803	CF1852-002
Pope, Ann E., in TN	Washington	Will	1885	CF1904-107
Pope, Betty Grymes		Will		UVA MSS 2831
Pope, John	Northumberland	Will	1723	CF1806-012
Pope, Sampson	Southampton	Will	1839	SV 1:1, p. 30
Pope, Sampson	Southampton	Will	1848	BRCD
Pope, Thomas, in Bristol, Eng.	Westmoreland	Will	1686	VMHB 3, p. 422
Popejoy, William	Prince William	Inventory	1779	T: correct from 1799

---

[1] *Virginia Journal of the House of Delegates*, 1790, p. 60.
[2] Virginia Colonial Records Project, Survey Report #4889 (4658), will of Graves Packe, of London, Eng.

NAME	LOCATION	TYPE	YEAR	REFERENCE(S)
Porter, Charity	Stafford	Will	1830	LVA Acc. #31053
Porter, Charles	Stafford	Will	1788	LVA Acc. #22515-27
Porter, Jacob	Stafford	Admin.	1664	OB:15 JUN 1664
Porter, James P., in Pulaski Co.	Rappahannock	Will	1869	CF1872-013
Porter, John	Henrico	Will	1722	Records, Vol. 2, p. 553
Porter, John	Rockbridge	Will	1794	CF1805-013
Porter, John, in Berkeley Co.	Frederick	Will	1848	CF1849-028
Porter, Martin	Fauquier	Will	1835	NVG 5, p. 480
Porter, Sinah B.	Fairfax	Will	1853	X
Porter, Sinal Ball, in Alexandria Co.	Fairfax	Will	1853	CF1857-004
Porter, William, of Culpeper Co.	Rappahannock	Will	1815	CF1841-013
Porter, William, of Culpeper Co.	Rappahannock	Will	1815	VGSQ Vol. 50:4, p. 320
Porterfield, Charles, in Berkeley Co.	Frederick	Will	1828	CF1831-020
Porteus, Edward		Will	1700	VCRP, Survey #04793
Portlock, David, in Norfolk Co.	Portsmouth	Will	1892	CF1896-011
Portlock, Nathaniel	Norfolk City	Will	1752	LVA-LP:10 OCT 1792
Portlock, Nathaniel	Norfolk City	Account	1792	LVA-LP:10 OCT 1792
Portlock, Tapley, in Norfolk Co.	Portsmouth	Will	1862	CF1869-024
Portman, Robert, bound for Ire.		Will	1654	VCRP, Survey #03126
Posey, John Price, of New Kent Co.	Cumberland	Account	1793	Judgments 1793
Pottie, Edith	Hanover	Will	1880	BRCD
Pottie, George		Will	1784	Swem(3)
Potts, Eleanor M., in MD	Louisa	Will	1882	CF1900-047
Pound, Reuben, in Page Co.	Culpeper	Will	1859	CF1893-017
Povall, Charles	Henrico	Inventory	1719	Records, Vol. 2, p. 467
Powell, D. Lee, of Richmond	James City	Will	1871	CF1884-011
Powell, Elizabeth P., Prince George Co.	Petersburg	Will	1837	CF1875-033
Powell, Elizabeth [Harrison], of *Brandon*	Prince George	Will	1837	SV 9:2, p. 55
Powell, George, in SC	Lunenburg	Will	1842	CF1859-001
Powell, Jacob	Isle of Wight	Will (U)	1773	LVA:1161459
Powell, Jennet, of Rockingham Co.	Augusta	Will	1807	CF1809-007
Powell, John		Will	1771	VCRP, Survey #01617
Powell, John	Brunswick	Will	1791	CF1805-042
Powell, Levin M., in DC	Rockingham	Will	1884	CF1898-052
Powell, Lewis G., in Orange Co.	Greene	Will	1823	CF1846-003
Powell, Lewis G., in Orange Co.	Greene	Will	1823	CF1868-008
Powell, Lucy, of Warwick Co.	Williamsburg	Will Abstract	1814	Crozier, p. 45
Powell, Robert, in Greensville Co.	Brunswick	Will	1791	CF1822-020
Powell, Thomas	Lancaster	Will	1669	LP
Powell, William H., in Greensville Co.	Brunswick	Will	1841	CF1891-030
Powell, William H., in Brunswick Co.	Dinwiddie	Will	1841	CF1856-005
Power, Frederick B., in York Co.	James City	Will	1843	CF1880-012
Powers, John, in Norfolk Co.	Portsmouth	Will	1828	CF1870-011
Powers, Urias	Roanoke	Will	1869	V:Mss1 J6496 a 1 151-1
Powers, William	Goochland	Estate	(nd)	UVA MSS 4756
Poythress, Francis	Dinwiddie	Will	1796	VGSQ 10:1, p. 5
Poythress, Joshua, Martins Brandon	Prince George	Will	1740	LVA Acc. #23849
Poythress, Mary	Prince George	Inventory	1760	DB1759, p. 158
Poythress, Mary	Dinwiddie	Will	1772	VGSQ 10:1, p. 4
Poythress, Mary, Martins Brandon	Prince George	Will	1788	DB1787, p. 112
Poythress, Patrick H.	Dinwiddie	Will	1818	VGSQ 10:1, p. 5

NAME	LOCATION	TYPE	YEAR	REFERENCE(S)
Poythress, Peter	Prince George	Will	1786	Note[1]
Poythress, Robert	Prince George	Will	1743	SV 8:4, p. 147
Poythress, Robert, in Prince George Co.	Chesterfield	Will	1743	CF1798-023
Poythress, Robert, of Prince George Co.	Petersburg	Will	1743	Ejectments 1852
Poythress, William		Division	1771	LVA Acc. #22483
Poythress, William		Division	1776	LVA Acc. #22483d
Pratt, John	York	Will	1677	DWO6, p. 32
Pratt, John	King George	Will	1724	OB1766, p. 294
Pratt, Thomas	Stafford	Appraisal	1766	LVA Acc. #41008, r4614
Predix, Gabriel, mariner		Will	1697	VCRP, Survey #04770
Prentis, Joseph	Williamsburg	Will	1807	Swem(4)
Prentis, Joseph	Williamsburg	Sale	1809	Swem(4)
Prentis, Joseph	Williamsburg	Account	1815	Swem(4)
Presson, Daniel	York	Will	1782	CF1804-006
Presson, Thomas, of Warwick Co.	Williamsburg	Will Abstract	1814	Crozier, p. 45
Presson, William, of York Co.	Williamsburg	Will Abstract	1817	Crozier, p. 45
Presstman, Stephen W., Abbeville NC	Arlington	Will	1868	WB9:134; File #666A
Preston, George	King William	Inventory	1704	RB2, p. 29
Preston, John	Washington	Will	1790	V:Mss1 P9267 b 52
Preston, Thomas, of Botetourt Co.	Augusta	Will	1808	CF1820-041
Preston, William	Montgomery	Will	1777	V:Mss1 P9267 b 17
Preston, William	Montgomery	Account	1805	V:Mss1 P9267 b 12-16
Preston, William Campbell	Albemarle	Will	1860	V:Mss1 P9267 c 189+
Price, Alexander Pope	Bedford	Will	1861c	V:Mss7:1 P9316:1
Price, Daniel	Henrico	Will	1770	Records, Vol. 6, p. 2001
Price, Daniel	Henrico	Will	1770	T: correct from 1783
Price, Daniel, in Halifax Co.	Campbell	Will	1802	CF1853-017
Price, Elizabeth	Henrico	Will	1786	WB1 1781, p. 315
Price, Hopkin, of Middlesex Co.	London	Will	1679	N:PROB11/361
Price, Hopkin, of Middlesex Co.		Will	1679	VCRP, Survey #03721
Price, John	Westmoreland	Will	1788	Wills #35
Price, John	Henrico	Will, 1783	1812	WB4, p. 200
Price, John F., in Augusta Co.	Albemarle	Will	1888	CF1893-013
Price, John, mariner		Will	1677	VCRP, Survey #03712
Price, John, of Essex Co.	Cumberland	Will	1772	CF1792-002
Price, John W., in Washington Co.	Russell	Will	1863	CF1893-016
Price, John W., of Fincastle	Botetourt	Will	1855	UVA MSS 10605
Price, Leonard	Goochland	Will	1772	MVG 29:3, p. 193
Price, Mary	Northumberland	Will	1726	RB1718, p. 388
Price, Roger, leatherseller		Will	1672	VCRP, Survey #03547
Price, Thomas	Hanover	Will	1838	Cocke:110
Price, Thomas	Hanover	Will	1838	CF1872-016
Price, Thomas, in Hanover Co.	Henrico	Will	1838	CF1904-031
Price, William W., in Danville	Louisa	Will	1850	CF1887-021
Priddy, John		Will	1841	BRCD, CA
Priddy, Nancy D.	Henrico	Will	1858	CF1906-060
Priddy, Thomas, in Richmond	Hanover	Will	1832	CF1832-009
Priddy, Thomas, of Richmond	Richmond City	Will	1832	Cocke:113

---

[1] LVA, U.S. Circuit Court Records, Box 159, *Randolph v. Randolph's Exors.* (1857).

NAME	LOCATION	TYPE	YEAR	REFERENCE(S)
Pride, John	Henrico	Will	1742	Records, Vol. 4, p. 1222
Pride, William	Henrico	Inventory	1724	Records, Vol. 2, p. 571
Primus, John, mariner		Will	1697	VCRP, Survey #04776
Prince, Richard	Sussex	Will	1816c	V:Mss2 P9358 b
Prindle, Parrott A., in DC	Lynchburg	Will	1861	CF1870-038
Prinn, Nichlas, mariner		Will	1684	VCRP, Survey #03730
Prior, William		Will	1647	VCRP, Survey #03995
Prior, William W., of Caswell Co., NC	Danville	Will	1860	WBA:213
Pritchett, Henry J., in Dinwiddie Co.	Brunswick	Will	1887	CF1896-009
Pritchett, William	Brunswick	Will	1795	CF1805-017
Provost, Elias, carpenter, of NY		Will	1691	VCRP, Survey #03750
Pruden, Henry	Nansemond	Will (U)	1792	SV 13:2, p. 84
Pryor, William S.	Hanover	Will	1840	Cocke:109
Pryor, William S.	Hanover	Will	1840	CF1873-021
Puckett, John	Henrico	Account	1679	Records, Vol. 1, p. 52
Puckett, John	Henrico	Will	1719	Records, Vol. 2, p. 429
Puckett, William	Henrico	Inventory	1719	Records, Vol. 2, p. 463
Pugh, Jonathan, in Hampshire Co.	Frederick	Will	1794	CF1819-084
Pullen, William	Lancaster	Will	1767	LP
Puller, Thomas	King William	Will Ref.	1826	LP:20 DEC 1826
Pulliam, Stephen T.	Hanover	Will	1851	CF1868-015
Pulliam, Stephen T.	Hanover	Will Abstract	1851	Cocke:114
Pulliam, Stephen T.	Hanover	Will	1851c	V:Mss1 D1124 b 2725+
Pulliam, William	Hanover	Will	1813	LVA Acc. #32974
Pulliam, William	Hanover	Will	1813	HHS 40, p. 2
Pully, Mary, of Halifax Co.	Mecklenburg	Will	1857	CF1860-050 CC
Pulman, Henry	Lancaster	Will	1670	LP
Purcell, Thomas, in Bedford Co.	Lynchburg	Will	1856	CF1870-039
Purdie, George, of Isle of Wight Co.	Williamsburg	Will Abstract	1803	Crozier, p. 44
Purdie, Mary, of Isle of Wight Co.	Williamsburg	Will Abstract	1809	Crozier, p. 44
Purkins, Henry	Essex	Will	1780	CF1817-010
Purkins, Tabitha	Essex	Will Abstract	1738	Fleet 2:301
Purks, William	Caroline	Will	1850	W&D1794, p. 64
Purnell, Arthur	Warwick	Will Ref.	1650	Note[1]
Purnell, William		Will	1749	VCRP, Survey #04636
Purris, William	Augusta	Will	1791	CF1823-021
Pursel, Phillip	Henrico	Will	1720	Records, Vol. 2, p. 497
Pursell, Elizabeth, Northumberland Co.	Richmond	Will	1848	CF1879-012
Pursell, Elizabeth, Northumberland Co.	Richmond	Will	1848	CF1889-002
Pursell, Maria L., c/o James W.	King & Queen	Guard. Acct.	1865	Fleet 2:467
Pursell, Marya L., c/o James W.	King & Queen	Guard. Acct.	1865	Fleet, 8th Collection
Puryear, William	Henrico	Will	1769	Records, Vol. 6, p. 2043
Putnam, Thomas		Will	1657	VCRP, Survey #03516
Putney, Caroline F., in Kanawha Co.	Louisa	Will	1858	CF1894-019
Pyland, Nicholas	Surry	Will	1778	T: correct from 1777

---

[1] Warwick County Court Orders, 1648-1651, p. 16.

NAME	LOCATION	TYPE	YEAR	REFERENCE(S)
Q				
Quarles, Aaron, of King William Co.	London	Will	1771	VCRP, Survey #04692
Quarles, Aaron, of King William Co.	London	Will	1771	N:PROB11/973
Quarles, Aaron, of St. John Parish	King William	Will	1771	VMHB 45, p. 192
Quarles, Betty	Fauquier	Will Abstract	1772	VMHB 23, p. 332
Quarles, Henry, in Orange Co.	Louisa	Will	1865	CF1869-012
Quarles, John, in Bedford Co.	Lynchburg	Will	1810	CF1825-090
Quarles, Lucy, in Orange Co.	Louisa	Will	1841	CF1851-018
Quarles, Nathaniel	Chesterfield	Will	1816	Fleet 2:204
Quarles, Nathaniel	Chesterfield	Will	1816	Fleet, 2nd Collection
Quarles, William, in Orange Co.	Louisa	Will	1827	CF1852-050
Quarles, Wilson [of *Jerusalem*]	Caroline	Will	1850	W&D1794, p. 66
Queen, John, of Nansemond Co.	Williamsburg	Will Abstract	1769	Crozier, p. 47
Quinn, James, in Berkeley Co.	Frederick	Will	1804	CF1822-187
Quinn, James, in Berkeley Co.	Frederick	Will	1804	CF1828-249
Quinn, Lucy	Williamsburg	Will	1833	Swem(1):f146

NAME	LOCATION	TYPE	YEAR	REFERENCE(S)

R

NAME	LOCATION	TYPE	YEAR	REFERENCE(S)
Radwell, Thomas, of Nansemond Co.	Williamsburg	Will Abstract	1825	Crozier, p. 49
Ragdale, William	Nansemond	Will Ref.	1719	Hening, Vol. 4, p. 528
Ragland, Evan, in Halifax Co.	Lynchburg	Will	1795	CF1819-015
Ragland, Gideon	Hanover	Will	1795	CF1837-008
Ragland, Gideon, of St. Paul's Parish	Hanover	Will	1795	Cocke:115
Ragland, John, of St. Paul's Parish	Hanover	Will Partial	1750	LVA Acc. #25628-5
Ragland, Pettus	Hanover	Will	1807	Cocke:116
Ragland, Pettus	Hanover	Will	1807	CF1861-014
Ragland, William James	Richmond City	Will	1860	Fleet, Huntington Data
Ragsdale, Drury	Chesterfield	Account	1749	LVA:104594
Ragsdale, Drury	King William	Will	1804	V:Mss6:1 R3993:1
Ragsdale, Joseph	Lunenburg	Will	1796	CF1800-016
Raines, Ann, of Caroline Co.	King William	Will	1798	LP:05 DEC 1806
Raines, Ann, of Caroline Co.	King William	Will	1798	LP:18 DEC 1810
Raines, Giles	Caroline	Will	1806	SV 4:3, p. 100
Raines, Giles	Caroline	Will	1806	LVA[1]
Raines, Grayce, in Prince Edward Co.	Campbell	Will	1856	CF1857-025
Raines, Shands, Jr.	Prince George	Account	1760	DB1759, p. 166
Rains, Henry	Caroline	Will	1767	FDC L561-113
Ramsay, George, Dr.		Will	1756	Swem
Ramsay, John	Norfolk City	Will	(nd)	Swem
Ramsay, John, of Norfolk Borough	Williamsburg	Will Abstract	1780	Crozier, p. 48
Ramsay, William	Arlington	Will	1795	CRA:169
Ramsay, William, of Alexandria	Arlington	Will	1785	CF1851-002
Ramsey, Elizabeth, in Richmond	Henrico	Will	1861	CF1886-005
Ramsey, Francis	Essex	Will	1767	CF1808-016
Randall, John	Fauquier	Will	1812	NVG 8, p. 1123
Randle, Josias	King William	Will	1703	RB2, p. 25
Randolph, Ann, in Goochland Co.	Louisa	Will	1825	CF1852-036
Randolph, Beverley	Powhatan	Will	1838	UVA MSS 2450
Randolph, Charles H.	Powhatan	Will	1840	V:Mss2 R15273 a 1
Randolph, Edward, of Acquamat	London	Will	1703	N:PROB11/473
Randolph, Edward, surveyor		Will	1703	VCRP, Survey #04124
Randolph, Jacob, of Nansemond Co.	Isle of Wight	Will	1798	CF1808-015
Randolph, Jacob, of Nansemond Co.	Isle of Wight	Account	1801	CF1808-015
Randolph, Jane	Henrico	Will	1767	Records, Vol. 6, p. 1995
Randolph, Jane, of *Curles*	Henrico	Will Abstract	1766	VMHB 22, p. 443
Randolph, John	Roanoke	Will	1821	UVA MSS 4358
Randolph, John	Roanoke	Will	1832	UVA MSS 4358
Randolph, John		Will	1837	BRCD, GC
Randolph, John Edmund	Southampton	Will	1823	V:Mss2 C5214 b 34-36
Randolph, John, in Richmond	Petersburg	Will	1836	CF1857-039
Randolph, John, Sir	Williamsburg	Will	1737	LVA Acc. #19819
Randolph, John, Sir	Williamsburg	Will	1737	VMHB 36, p. 376
Randolph, John, Sr.		Will	1774	UVA MSS 3881
Randolph, Judith	Prince Edward	Will	1816	LVA Acc. #23868
Randolph, Judith, of Prince Edward Co.	Mecklenburg	Will	1816	CF1857-002 CC

---

[1] LVA, Halifax County Chancery Papers, Box 14.

NAME	LOCATION	TYPE	YEAR	REFERENCE(S)
Randolph, Martha, in MA	Albemarle	Will	1836	CF1892-033
Randolph, Mary	Prince William	Will Ref.	1844	CM:05 MAR 1844
Randolph, Peter, Hon., of *Chatsworth*	Henrico	Will	1768	VG 02, p. 3
Randolph, Peter, Hon., of Henrico Co.	London	Will	1768	N:PROB11/943
Randolph, Peyton	Henrico	Will	1784	V:Mss6:1 R152:7
Randolph, Peyton	Henrico	Will	1784	LVA Tazewell Papers
Randolph, Richard	Henrico	Will	1748	LVA Acc. #36380, r19
Randolph, Richard	King & Queen	Will Abstract	1799	Fleet, 9th Collection
Randolph, Richard, in Cumberland Co.	Prince Edward	Will	1797	V:Mss2 R1572 a 1
Randolph, Richard, in James City Co.	Powhatan	Will	1799	CF1845-012
Randolph, Richard, Jr., of *Bizarre*	Cumberland	Will	1796	UVA MSS 3882
Randolph, Richard, Jr., of *Bizarre*	Prince Edward	Will	1797	VMHB 34, p. 72
Randolph, Richard, of *Curles*	Henrico	Will	1742	CW M-1561
Randolph, Richard, of *Curles*	Henrico	Will Abstract	1749	VMHB 22, p. 442
Randolph, Richard Ryland	Prince George	Will	1834	SV 9:2, p. 55
Randolph, Richard Ryland, Pr. Geo. Co.	Petersburg	Will	1834	CF1835-025
Randolph, Robert	Henrico	Will	1839	V:Mss6:1 R152:7
Randolph, Robert	Richmond City	Will	1839	BRCD Superior Court
Randolph, Robert Beverley, of *Norwood*	Powhatan	Will	1839	V:Mss2 R15728 a 2
Randolph, Sarah N., in MD	Albemarle	Will	1892	CF1896-032
Randolph, William	Henrico	Will	1711	V:Mss6:1 R152:7
Randolph, William	Henrico	Will	1711	V:Mss1 Am167b
Randolph, William	Henrico	Will	1742	V:Mss6:1 R152:7
Randolph, William	Goochland	Will Ref.	1743	VMHB 45, p. 62
Randolph, William	Henrico	Will	1762	V:Mss6:1 R152:7
Randolph, William	Henrico	Will	1815	V:Mss6:1 R152:7
Randolph, William		Inventory	1815	V:Mss1 C7833 a 125+
Randolph, William		Will	1825	UVA MSS 2093
Randolph, William	Princess Anne	Will	1828	LVA Acc. #20969
Ranes, Ephraim	Prince George	Will	1849	SV 9:4, p. 157
Rankin, Benjamin, in Berkeley Co.	Frederick	Will	1787	CF1815-026
Rankin, James, of Rockingham Co.	Augusta	Will	1827	CF1846-057
Ransdell, Edward, of Westmoreland Co.	Williamsburg	Will Abstract	1773	Crozier, p. 51
Ransome, Flamstead	Buckingham	Will	1796	Note[1]
Ransone, Thomas	Mathews	Estate Ref.	1818	Note[2]
Ratcliff, John	Henrico	Inventory	1738	Records, Vol. 4, p. 1077
Ratcliffe, Barbara, w/o Richard	Fairfax	Dower	1788	X
Ratcliffe, Charles	Fairfax	Will	1835	NVG 8, p. 1096
Ratcliffe, George B.	James City	Will	1867	CF1878-009
Ratcliffe, James W.	Hanover	Will	1878	CF1879-004
Ratcliffe, John [Siclemore]		Will	1611	VCRP, Survey #03105
Ratcliffe, Richard	Fairfax	Will	1825	X
Raub, John P.	Fairfax	Will	1884	CF1893-035
Ravenscroft, John T.	Lunenburg	Will	1817	Swem
Ravenscroft, Robert, of Petersburg	Dinwiddie	Will	1778	VGSQ 10:1, p. 12
Rawlings, William, of St. John's Parish	King William	Will	1704	RB2, p. 30
Rawlins, Albin	Caroline	Will	1807	W&P1742, p. 84

---

[1] LVA, U.S. Circuit Court Records, Box 77, *Hopkirk v. Ransome's Heirs* (1809).

[2] LVA, Land Office Revolutionary War Military Certificate Papers, Thomas Ransone, Folders 19, 22-24.

NAME	LOCATION	TYPE	YEAR	REFERENCE(S)
Rawlins, Jeremiah	Caroline	Will	1806	W&P1742, p. 80
Rayfield, William	Gloucester	Will	1878	CF1909-030
Rayment, John		Will (N)	1630	VCRP, Survey #03963
Read, Alexander	Lancaster	Will	1669	LP
Read, Benjamin	York	Will	1692	Fleet 2:227
Read, Clement H., in Henrico Co.	Roanoke	Will	1845	CF1872-020
Read, Edmund	Charlotte	Will	1803	MVG 29:3, p. 193
Read, George	York	Will P.	1671	DB5, p. 3
Read, George, mariner		Will	1685	VCRP, Survey #03835
Read, John, mariner		Will	1688	VCRP, Survey #03741
Read, John, of Bristol	London	Will	1688	N:PROB11/392
Read, Margaret	Surry	Admin.	1688	T:D&W4, p. 67b
Read, Robert	Augusta	Estate Ref.	1789	Hening, Vol. 13, p. 95
Read, Samuel	Prince William	Will	1855	CF1891-002
Reade, Alexander, of Middlesex Co.	London	Will	1767	N:PROB11/930
Reade, Alexander, of Middlesex Co.		Will	1767	VCRP, Survey #04695
Reade, John	King & Queen	Will	1744	V:Mss2 R2242 a 1
Reade, Margaret	Surry	Inventory	1693	T:D&W4, p. 346a
Reade, Thomas		Will	1663	VCRP, Survey #03532
Reade, William	Surry	Inventory	1687	T:D&W4, p. 9a
Reader, Adam	Augusta	Will	1773	WB5, p. 82
Reames, Simon, in Dinwiddie Co.	Petersburg	Will	1813	CF1851-035
Reamy, Daniel, in Henry Co.	Lynchburg	Will	1805	CF1840-004
Reardon, Yelverton	Fairfax	Will	1814	NVG 6, p. 625
Reardon, Yelverton	Fairfax	Will	1814	X
Reardon, Yelverton	Fairfax	Exor. Bond	1814	X
Rector, Jane	Fauquier	Appraisal	1847	NVG 7, p. 943
Redd, Elizabeth, in Richmond	Henrico	Will	1855	CF1875-012
Redd, James, in Culpeper Co.	Fauquier	Will	1853	CF1895-018
Redd, James M., in Patrick Co.	Henry	Will	1837	CF1877-049
Redd, Philip D., in Spotsylvania Co.	Culpeper	Will	1826	CF1857-025
Redd, Sally	Hanover	Will	1863	CF1907-009
Redd, Thomas	Prince Edward	Will	1801	VMHB 51, p. 205
Redd, Thomas, of Halifax Co.	Cumberland	Will	1825	CF1835-016
Redd, William [of *Cedar Vale*]	Caroline	Will	1802	W&P1742, p. 64
Reddick, James	Surry	Inventory	1693	T:D&W4, p. 350a
Reddick, William	Grayson	Appraisal		DB1:242
Redfield, Herman J., in NY	Albemarle	Will	1876	CF1891-056
Redfield, Herman J., in NY	Albemarle	Will	1878	CF1884-017
Redman, Samuel, of Pendleton Co.	Augusta	Will	1808	CF1829-028
Redmond, Andrew, in Loudoun Co.	Frederick	Will	1807	CF1830-260
Redwood, William	James City	Will	1816	Swem(1):f175
Reed, Jacob, in Rockingham Co.	Frederick	Will	1848	CF1859-022
Reed, James, in Hampshire Co.	Frederick	Will	1810	CF1838-007
Reed, James, in Hampshire Co.	Frederick	Will	1811	CF1823-256
Reed, James, in Norfolk Co.	Portsmouth	Will	1854	CF1889-041
Reed, James, in Norfolk Co.	Portsmouth	Will	1854	CF1861-005
Reed, Mary	Frederick	Will	1782	Finley
Reed, William, of James River	London	Will	1703	N:PROB11/470
Reems, Simon, in Dinwiddie Co.	Petersburg	Will	1813	CF1851-035
Rees, Thomas, in Berkeley Co.	Frederick	Will	1819	CF1828-223

NAME	LOCATION	TYPE	YEAR	REFERENCE(S)
Rees, Thomas, Sr., in Berkeley Co.	Frederick	Will	1819	CF1820-083
Reese, Esther, in Shenandoah Co.	Frederick	Will	1818	CF1828-179
Reese, Herbert		Will	1848c	DAR MSS 13 b5 f6
Reese, Sarah	Prince George	Will	1768	LVA Acc. #19940
Reese, Thomas	Dinwiddie	Will	1775	LVA Acc. #28657-17
Reeve, Payson, in Richmond	Hanover	Will	1898	CF1912-009
Reeve, Peter, in PA	Frederick	Will	1799	CF1833-111
Reeves, George, merchant		Will	1689	VCRP, Survey #03745
Reeves, Henry	Rappahannock*	Will Ref.	1687	Sweeny, p. 8
Reeves, Henry, Sr.		Will	1687	LVA Wills/Admin. DB
Reeves, John, of Rockingham Co.	Augusta	Will	1799	CF1827-004
Regan, Daniel	Surry	Will	1687	T:D&W3, p. 88a
Reid, Alexander	Amherst	Will	1804	Finley
Reid, Alexander, in Amherst Co.	Lynchburg	Will	1804	CF1827-081
Reid, Ann E.	Fairfax	Guard. Acct.	1857	X
Reid, Benjamin F.	Fairfax	Will	1890	CF1896-048
Reid, Charles J.	Fairfax	Guard. Acct.	1853	X
Reid, George	York	Will	1792	LP:16 DEC 1805
Reid, James, of Urbanna, Middlesex Co.	Williamsburg	Will Abstract	1764	Crozier, p. 48
Reid, James S.	Fairfax	Guard. Acct.	1853	X
Reid, John N.	Amherst	Will	1799	CF1805-010
Reid, John N.	Fairfax	Inventory	1853	X
Reid, John N.	Fairfax	Sale	1853	X
Reid, John N.	Fairfax	Account	1854	X
Reid, Robert S. [Catharine]	Fairfax	Dower	1865	X
Reid, Robert S. [Catharine]	Fairfax	Plat	1865	X
Reid, William	Prince William	Will	1860	CF1899-009
Reid, William W., in NC	Princess Anne	Will	1842	CF1880-012
Relfe, James, in MD	Frederick	Will	1788	CF1822-265
Remnant, John, waterman		Will	1743	VCRP, Survey #04621
Render, Lewis	Madison	Will (U)	1813	BRCD
Render, Lewis	Madison	Will	1813	V:MssG1875c651-680
Render, Lewis	Madison	Will	1813	LVA Acc. #40766
Rennolds, Elizabeth	Essex	Will	1761	WB11, p. 305
Renoe, Francis	Prince William	Will	1797	WBH, p. 224
Renoe, Strother	Prince William	Acct. Ref.	1843	CM:06 NOV 1843
Renoe, Strother	Prince William	Acct. Ref.	1843	CM:03 JUL 1843
Renoe, Strother	Prince William	Acct. Ref.	1843	CM:07 NOV 1843
Renolds, William	Warwick	Will	1672	Note[1]
Renshall, John, Jr.	Charles City	Account	1727	D&W1724, p. 160
Renshall, Joseph	Charles City	Inventory	1726	D&W1724, p. 99
Renshall, Joseph	Charles City	Will	1726	D&W1724, p. 77
Renshall, Joseph	Charles City	Account	1727	D&W1724, p. 160
Renshall, Joseph, Jr.	Charles City	Inventory	1726	D&W1724, p. 100
Renton, Joseph, chirurgeon		Will	1742	VCRP, Survey #04382
Respess, Henry	Mathews	Estate Ref.	1809	LP:11 DEC 1818
Respess, Henry, of Mathews Co.	Williamsburg	Will Abstract	1807	Crozier, p. 49
Respess, Richard H.	Mathews	Will	1851	TVF 5:1, p. 39

[1] LVA, Warwick County Miscellaneous Court Records, 1648-1875, p. 61.

NAME	LOCATION	TYPE	YEAR	REFERENCE(S)
Respess, Richard H.	Mathews	Will	1851	LP 1877
Reuben, George	Caroline	Will	1799	BRCD
Reveley, Mary	Surry	Will	1793	LVA Acc. #21701
Revely, Mary	Surry	Will	1793	T: correct from Beverly
Reverly, Mary		Will	1793	LVA Acc. #21701
Rex, Willoughby M., in PA	Louisa	Will	1879	CF1899-031
Reynolds, Ailce	Richmond	Will	1842	V:Mss1 T2118 d27684+
Reynolds, Charles B., in Amherst Co.	Franklin	Will	1876	CF1892-050
Reynolds, Christopher	Isle of Wight	Will Abstract	1654	VMHB 6, p. 252
Reynolds, George, in Richmond Co.	Frederick	Will	1777	CF1817-006
Reynolds, Jemima, in Norfolk	Portsmouth	Will	1874	CF1880-012
Reynolds, Jemima, in Norfolk	Portsmouth	Will	1874	CF1883-009
Reynolds, John	Arlington	Inventory	1797	CRA:241
Reynolds, John, in Caroline Co.	Lynchburg	Will	1755	CF1823-039
Reynolds, John M., Rockingham Co. NC	Henry	Will	1860	CF1882-014
Rice, James, in Loudoun Co.	Frederick	Will	1817	CF1824-195
Rice, John	Rockingham	Will	1797	MVG 42:1, p. 49
Rice, John	Rockingham	Will	1805	VGSQ 21:1, p. 49
Rice, Mary O., in Petersburg	Dinwiddie	Will	1860	CF1860-007
Richardon, Frances, in MO	Greene	Will	1848	CF1895-010
Richards, Catharine	Fauquier	Will	1794	CF1868-098
Richards, James, in Fairfax Co.	Frederick	Will	1811	CF1824-199
Richards, John	Stafford	Will	1785	FDC L392-76
Richards, John, in Alexandria Co.	Fairfax	Will	1843	CF1886-002
Richards, John, in Alexandria	Fairfax	Will	1843	X
Richards, Samuel, in Pendleton Co.	Bath	Will	1798	CF1833-004
Richards, William	Rappahannock*	Will	1686	TVF 2:2, p. 69
Richards, William	Henrico	Will	1687c	V:Mss4 V8 g
Richards, William	Fairfax	Account	1817	X
Richardson, Elizabeth, in PA	Louisa	Will	1876	CF1899-031
Richardson, Henry B.M.	James City	Will	(nd)	CF1886-016
Richardson, John	Cumberland	Will	1753	VMHB 46, p 65
Richardson, John	Essex	Will	1791	CF1822-004
Richardson, John	Hanover	Will	1800	LVA Acc. #27286f
Richardson, John	Hanover	Will	1800	Fleet, Huntington Data
Richardson, John	Hanover	Will	1800	LVA Acc. #23953
Richardson, John	Charlotte	Will	1822	VMHB 46, p. 72
Richardson, John	Hanover	Will (N)	1825	Cocke:118
Richardson, John	Grayson	Will		DB1:129
Richardson, John	Cumberland	Will Partial		VMHB 45, p 410
Richardson, John, B.H.	Charlotte	Will	1822	VMHB 46, p. 70
Richardson, John H.	Hanover	Will Ref.	(nd)	Cocke:120
Richardson, John, in Norfolk Co.	Portsmouth	Will	1836	CF1883-008
Richardson, John, in Norfolk Co.	Portsmouth	Will	1836	CF1892-001
Richardson, Miles J., in Norfolk Co.	Portsmouth	Will	1843	CF1883-008
Richardson, Moses, in Norfolk Co.	Portsmouth	Will	1854	CF1883-008
Richardson, Sallie Barron, Augusta Co.	Staunton	Will	1882	CF1875-003
Richardson, Samuel	Henrico	Will	1742	Records, Vol. 4, p. 1199
Richardson, Thomas, in Norfolk Co.	Portsmouth	Will	1803	CF1883-008
Richardson, W., in Norfolk Co.	Portsmouth	Will	1868	CF1883-008
Richardson, William, in Norfolk Co.	Portsmouth	Will	1839	CF1883-008

NAME	LOCATION	TYPE	YEAR	REFERENCE(S)
Richeson, Holt	King William	Will	1800	LVA Acc. #22870
Richeson, Holt	King William	Will	1800	TQ 33:1, p. 49
Richeson, John	King William	Heirs Ref.	1852	Fleet 2:533
Richman, William, Dr., of *Kittiewan*	Charles City	Will	1778	Swem
Rick, William	Arlington	Account	1793	CRA:137
Rick, William	Arlington	Inventory	1793	CRA:119
Ricketts, Anthony, in Shenandoah Co.	Warren	Will	1826	CF1844-002
Rickman, John	Charles City	Will	1789	LP, box 51 folder 271
Rickman, William	Charles City	Will	1778	BRCD
Ricks, Edwin	Nansemond	Will	(nd)	VG 22, p. 36
Riddick, Edward	Nansemond	Will	1873	BRCD
Riddick, Henry	Nansemond	Will	1785	V:Ms11 R4313 a 1
Riddick, James, Sr.	Surry	Inventory	1693	T:D&W4, p. 339a
Riddick, Jean	Nansemond	Will	1752	LVA Acc. #23846
Riddick, Josiah	Nansemond	Will	1838	CF1877-011
Riddick, Willis	Nansemond	Will Partial	1782	Note[1]
Riddle, Josephine Craig	Petersburg	Will	1890	V:Mss1 R4315 a 202+
Riddlehurst, John, of Westover Parish	Charles City	Will	1772	TVF 6:3, p. 157
Riddlehurst, Richard	Warwick	Will	1685	Note[2]
Ridenig, Richard	King William	Inventory	1704	RB1, p. 233
Rider, James K.	Bath	Will	1880	CF1899-013
Ridley, John D., in Montgomery Co.	Bedford	Will	1869	CF1870-028
Ridley, Matthew, of Southampton Co.	Williamsburg	Will Abstract	1795	Crozier, p. 49
Riely, William, in Jefferson Co.	Frederick	Will	1840	CF1859-049
Rigden, Edward	Fairfax	Will	1772	X
Rigg, Sarah	Westmoreland	Will	1771	Wills #5
Riggs, Francis		Will	1664	M: L1 f220
Riley, Edmond, of Farnham Parish	Rappahannock*	Will	1689	Sweeny, p. 144
Riley, Edward	Hanover	Will	1866	CF1904-001
Riley, John, Sr.	Fairfax	Will	1869	LVA Acc. #343683, 2:38
Riley, Terence	New Kent	Will	1876	CF1898-020
Rind, James		Estate Ref.	1806	Shepherd, Vol. 3, p. 249
Ring, John		Will	1637	VCRP, Survey #03977
Ritter, Benjamin I., in PA	Fairfax	Will	1872	CF1911-011
Ritter, Benjamin I., in PA	Fairfax	Will	1894	CF1911-011
Ritter, Emily I., in DC	Fairfax	Will	1900	CF1911-011
Rives, Elizabeth	Prince George	Inventory	1759	DB1759, p. 83
Rives, Peyton	Prince George	Will	1842	SV 9:3, p. 107
Rives, Robert	Appomattox	Will Ref.	1848	LP:03 JAN 1848
Rives, William	Sussex	Will	1777	UVA MSS 2532
Rives, William E.	Prince George	Will	1841	SV 9:2, p. 58
Rixey, Samuel, in Culpeper Co.	Fauquier	Will	1866	CF1890-036
Rixey, Samuel, in Culpeper Co.	Fauquier	Will	1866	CF1890-053
Rixey, Thomas C., in Caroline Co.	Culpeper	Will	1834	CF1880-032
Roach, John	Charles City	Will	1731	D&W1724, p. 337
Roach, William L., in Madison Co.	Culpeper	Will	1857	CF1880-031
Roan, Will	Henrico	Will	1771	Records, Vol. 7, p. 2109

---

[1] Fillmore Norfleet, *Bible Records of Suffolk and Nansemond County*, p. 195, citing a cluse quoted in the Kilby Papers at Duke University.

[2] LVA, Warwick County Court Records, 1685.

NAME	LOCATION	TYPE	YEAR	REFERENCE(S)
Roane, Alexander	Gloucester	Will	1785	V:Mss1 C8177 a 1-3
Roane, Alexander	Gloucester	Will	1785	VG 14, p. 121
Roane, Alexander, of Caroline Co.	Frederick	Will	1790	CF1826-1829 misc
Roane, John, of *Newington*	King & Queen	Will	1810	Note[1]
Roane, Sarah	King & Queen	Will	1831	LVA Acc. #26529-61
Roane, Spencer, Hon.	Richmond City	Will	1822	Fleet, 3rd Collection
Roane, Spencer, Hon.	Richmond City	Will	1822	Fleet 2:260
Roane, Thomas	King & Queen	Will	1799	LP
Roane, Thomas	King & Queen	Will	1799	TVF 12:4, p. 237
Roane, Thomas, in King & Queen Co.	Essex	Will	1799	CF1832-036
Roane, Thomas, of St. Stephen's Parish	Essex	Will	1799	WMQ 18, p. 259
Roane, William	Essex	Will	1785	CF1793-002
Robb, James	Caroline	Will	(nd)	V:Mss1 G7945 a 537+
Robb, James	Caroline	Will	1805	W&P1742, p. 74
Roberdeau, Daniel, in Frederick Co.	Arlington	Will	1795	CF1813-014
Roberts, Benjamin	Culpeper	Will	1782	CF1857-030
Roberts, Boanerges, in Fauquier Co.	Culpeper	Will	1847	CF1851-014
Roberts, Enoch, in Lynchburg	Campbell	Will	1819	CF1852-028
Roberts, Humphrey, of Portsmouth	London	Will	1793	N:PROB11/1231
Roberts, John	Isle of Wight	Will	1809	UVA MSS 10511
Roberts, John	Isle of Wight	Will	1830	UVA MSS 10511
Roberts, John, in Madison Co.	Culpeper	Will	1812	CF1855-010
Roberts, John, in York Co.	James City	Will	1812	CF1889-008
Roberts, Mary I., in Louisa Co.	Bath	Will	1848	CF1906-007
Roberts, Matilda, in Lynchburg	Campbell	Will	1831	CF1852-028
Roberts, Michael	Elizabeth City	Will (N)	1718	Records 1715, p. 155
Roberts, Morris	Henrico	Will	1722	Records, Vol. 2, p. 639
Roberts, Nancy	Dinwiddie	Will	1868	CF1871-029
Roberts, Nathaniel	Surry	Will	1693	T:D&W4, p. 323b
Roberts, Thomas		Will	1683	T: not Rappahannock[2]
Roberts, Thomas	Amelia	Inventory	1737	WB1, p. 5
Roberts, Thomas, of Prince George Co.	Amelia	Will	1737	WB1, p. 4
Roberts, William	Nansemond	Will	1796	VG 21, p. 274
Roberts, William, of King & Queen Co.	Essex	Will	1728	Fleet 2:248
Roberts, Wirt, in Richmond	Henrico	Will	1889	CF1904-045
Robertson, Ann F., in Richmond	Campbell	Will	1887	CF1900-009
Robertson, B.T., in TX	Culpeper	Will	1899	CF1907-024
Robertson, David, of Appomattox Co.	Goochland	Will	1856	BRCD
Robertson, Henry, in Amelia Co.	Lunenburg	Will	1782	CF1817-027
Robertson, James	Stafford	Will Ref.	1768	Washington, p. 36
Robertson, James, of Allegany Co. MD	Arlington	Will	1866	WB8:415
Robertson, James, Sr., in Fairfax Co.	Arlington	Will	1768	CF1845-007
Robertson, James, Sr., in Fairfax Co.	Arlington	Will	1769	CF1812-020
Robertson, John	Nottoway	Will	1865	CF1888-003
Robertson, Powhatan	Mathews	Will	1882	BRCD
Robertson, Powhatan, in Mathews Co.	Campbell	Will	1882	CF1900-009

---

[1] Provided to the compiler by Mrs. Neil (Betsy) Ware of *Bellevue Farm*, Ware's Wharf, Essex County. The testator of this fragmented will was accused of murder after he was apparently found intoxicated and slit the throat of his new bride. While in the King & Queen County jail he died of laudanum poisoning.

[2] Refer to Sweeny, p. 9, where the compiler lists wills given in *Torrence* that have not been found of record in Rappahannock County.

NAME	LOCATION	TYPE	YEAR	REFERENCE(S)
Robertson, Walter	Halifax	Will Ref.	1784	Hening, Vol. 11, p. 363
Robey, Henry Richard, of *Hopewell*	Spotsylvania	Will	1876	V:Mss1 R5497 a 28-40
Robins, Christopher		Estate Ref.	17__	Hening, Vol. 4, p. 462
Robins, John, of *Robins' Neck*	Gloucester	Will Ref.	1655	Hening, Vol. 4, p. 462
Robins, Joshua, of Northampton Co.	Williamsburg	Will Abstract	1789	Crozier, p. 48
Robins, Obedience	Northampton	Will (N)	1662	V:Mss2 R5578 a 1
Robins, Thomas	Gloucester	Will	1821c	V:Mss1 R5595 a 546+
Robins, Thomas	Gloucester	Inventory	1822	V:Mss1 R5595 a 546+
Robins, William		Estate Ref.	16__	Hening, Vol. 4, p. 462
Robins, William	Gloucester	Will	1786	VG 12, p. 8
Robins, William Augustus	Gloucester	Will	1887	V:Mss1 R5595 a 4,041+
Robins, William David Sims	King William	Will	1841	V:Mss1 R5595 a 904+
Robins, William, of Gloucester Co.	Williamsburg	Will Abstract	1786	Crozier, p. 47
Robinson, Abner, in Richmond	Henrico	Will	1842	CF1868-001
Robinson, Alexander, in Washington Co.	Smyth	Will	(nd)	CF1849-008
Robinson, Ann C.	Hanover	Will	1839	CF1871-013
Robinson, Ann C.	Hanover	Will	1856	CF1897-006
Robinson, Benjamin	Caroline	Will	1805	W&P1742, p. 72
Robinson, Christopher	Middlesex	Will	1692	LVA Acc. #24193
Robinson, Christopher	Middlesex	Will	1692	CW(14)
Robinson, Christopher	Middlesex	Will	1693	V:Mss1 T2478 b1-2
Robinson, Christopher	Middlesex	Will	1693	VMHB 7, p. 17
Robinson, Christopher		Will, Partial	1700	CW(14)
Robinson, Christopher	Middlesex	Will	1768	CW(3, 14)
Robinson, Christopher		Will	1775	CW(14)
Robinson, Christopher, of *Hewick*		Will	1751	CW(14)
Robinson, Edward	Charles City	Inventory	1689	D&W1689, p. 86
Robinson, Edward Clack	Amelia	Will	1866	V:Mss1 Ep275 a 53-63
Robinson, Eliza S.	Richmond City	Will	1842c	V:Mss1 R5685 d 241+
Robinson, George	Prince William	Acct. Ref.	1843	CM:04 DEC 1843
Robinson, George	Prince William	Acct. Ref.	1843	CM:02 OCT 1843
Robinson, George, in DE	Frederick	Will	1784	CF1813-062
Robinson, Henry	Amelia	Will	1825	V:Mss1 Ep275 a 53-63
Robinson, Henry	Hanover	Will	1832	V:Mss2 W7336 b 5
Robinson, James	Louisa	Will	1748	V:Mss1 B2346 a 1159
Robinson, Joanna	Hanover	Will	1847	CF1897-006
Robinson, John	Middlesex	Will	1785	CW(14)
Robinson, John	Middlesex	Will Ref.	1787	VMHB 17, p. 206
Robinson, John, Bishop of London		Will	1722	CW(14)
Robinson, John, Maj., of Christ Church	Middlesex	Will	1785	Fleet 2:346
Robinson, John, of Middlesex Co.	Williamsburg	Will Abstract	1787	Crozier, p. 50
Robinson, Judith		Will	1774	CW(14)
Robinson, Judith	King William	Will	1826	V:Mss1 G9297 a 1-65
Robinson, Judith, of Middlesex Co.	Williamsburg	Will Abstract	1806	Crozier, p. 51
Robinson, Mary	Hanover	Will	1848	V:Mss2 R5642 a 1
Robinson, Mary, of Gloucester Co.	Williamsburg	Will Abstract	1803	Crozier, p. 50
Robinson, Neddler, of New Kent Co.	Williamsburg	Will Abstract	1823	Fleet 2:354
Robinson, Needler, of New Kent Co.	Williamsburg	Will Abstract	1823	Crozier, p. 51

NAME	LOCATION	TYPE	YEAR	REFERENCE(S)
Robinson, Peter		Will	1765	Note[1]
Robinson, Peter		Account	1791	CW(14)
Robinson, Peter		Will Ref.	1792	CW(14)
Robinson, Peter	Hanover	Will	1886	CF1889-017
Robinson, Peter, in Nottoway Co.	Brunswick	Will	1814	CF1829-014
Robinson, Robert, in Charlotte Co.	Lynchburg	Will	1805	CF1830-105
Robinson, Sarah	Middlesex	Will	1771	CW(14)
Robinson, Sarah	Middlesex	Will Ref.	1772	VMHB 17, p. 93
Robinson, Starkey	York	Will	1815	MVG 31:4, p. 357
Robinson, William	Brunswick	Inventory	1784	WB2, p. 413
Robinson, William	Middlesex	Will	1807	V:Mss1 T2478 b 28-29
Robinson, William	Fairfax	Inventory	1816	X
Robinson, William, of Middlesex Co.	Williamsburg	Will Abstract	1807	Crozier, p. 51
Robson, Isaac, mariner		Will	1710	VCRP, Survey #04350
Roby, James	Fairfax	Will	1872	CF1890-003
Roch, John Fitz	Charles City	Will Partial	1727	D&W1724, p. 187
Roch, John Fitz	Charles City	Account	1728	D&W1724, p. 211
Roche, James, of Isle of Wight Co.	London	Will	1652	N:PROB11/224
Roche, James, of Isle of Wight Co.		Will	1652	VCRP, Survey #04107
Rodehefer, Conrad	Rockingham	Will	1856	LVA:1159583
Rodes, Ryland, in Nelson Co.	Albemarle	Will	1854	CF1895-108
Rodes, V.H., in Augusta Co.	Lynchburg	Will	1879	CF1884-052
Rodgers, John, in Charles City Co.	Henrico	Will	1788	CF1832-034
Rodgers, Thomas	Dinwiddie	Will	1759	LVA Wm. Allason Papers
Roff, William, in KY	Rappahannock	Will	1884	CF1878-010
Roger, Achillis	Caroline	Guard. Appt.	1801	BRCD
Rogers, John	Charles City	Will	1788	LP, box 51, folder 271
Rogers, John	Charles City	Will	1788	TVF 4:3, p. 182
Rogers, John	Charles City	Will	1788	VG 31, p. 57
Rogers, John, of Charles City Co.	Henrico	Will	1788	CF1832-034
Rogers, John, of Westover Parish	Charles City	Will	1730	D&W1724, p. 298
Rogers, Lewis, in Fra.	Albemarle	Will	1867	CF1911-003
Rogers, Mary	Fredericksburg	Will	1802	FDC L540-48
Rogers, Ralph, of Princess Anne Co.	Albemarle	Will	1856	CF1860-061
Rogers, William	Fairfax	Account	1817	X
Rogers, William D.	York	Will	1832	CF1837-001
Rogers, William M., in King George Co.	Arlington	Will	1836	CF1839-011
Roler, Peter, of Rockingham Co.	Augusta	Will	1798	CF1822-089
Rolfe, John	Surry	Will	1621	SV 12:3, p. 123
Rolfe, John	James City	Will	1622	LVA Acc. #34381
Rolfe, John, in Jamestown	James City	Will	1821	V:Mss5:7 D2655:1
Rolfe, John, in London, Eng.		Will	1621	VCRP Survey #4159
Rolfe, John, of James City Co.	London	Will	1630	N:PROB11/157
Rolfe, John, of James City Co.		Will	1630	VCRP, Survey #03960
Rollie, Francis, of MD		Will	1724	VCRP, Survey #04678
Rollison, G.W.	King & Queen	Will	1904	LP
Rolph, Jonathan, cooper		Will	1708	VCRP, Survey #03902
Roney, Jane, w/o Michael	Fairfax	Admin. Bond	1818	NVG 6, p. 627

[1] An abstract appeared in the *Richmond Standard*, 19 MAR 1881; also see *Richmond Standard*, 1 MAY 1880, Notes and Queries.

NAME	LOCATION	TYPE	YEAR	REFERENCE(S)
Roosevelt, Elliott, in Washington Co.	Wise	Will	1894	CF1899-022
Rootes, Philip	King & Queen	Will	1756	Fleet 2:166
Rootes, Philip	King & Queen	Will	1756	Fleet, 1st Collection
Roper, Nicholas, Jefferson Co.	Frederick	Will	1817	CF1828-142
Roper, Thomas	Charles City	Inventory	1769	Records, p. 133
Roscow, William	Warwick	Will Ref.	1700	Hening, Vol. 8, p. 301
Rose, Alexander Fontaine	Stafford	Will	1832	LVA Acc. #31985
Rose, Alexander Fontaine, *Hampstead*	Stafford	Will	1832	VG 29, p. 50
Rose, Catherine, in Fairfax Co.	King George	Will	1808	CF1857-002
Rose, Charles	Sussex	Will	1795	WBE, p. 353
Rose, Charles		Will	1803	Fleet, Huntington Data
Rose, Duncan, in Shelby Co. KY	Dinwiddie	Will	1785	V:Mss2 R7202 a 1
Rose, Duncan, in Shelby Co. KY	Dinwiddie	Will	1785	VG 40, p. 146
Rose, Duncan, in Shelby Co. KY	Dinwiddie	Will	1785	LVA Acc. #35633
Rose, Henry, in Fairfax Co.	King George	Will	1810	CF1857-002
Rose, Hugh	Amherst	Will	1795	CF1803-018
Rose, Hugh, Col., of *Geddes*	Amherst	Will	1794	Fleet, Huntington Data
Rose, John	Northumberland	Will	1743	LVA Acc. #26249
Rose, John		Will	1743	LVA Acc. #26249
Rose, John, in Westmoreland Co.	King George	Will	1803	CF1857-002
Rose, William	Prince William	Will	1841	CF1869-005
Rose, William, of Prince William Co.	Loudoun	Will	1841	CF1842-021
Roseberry, Kline, in Warren Co. NJ	Prince William	Will	1864	CF1899-006
Rosenbaum, Joseph, in Richmond	Henrico	Will	1885	CF1901-016
Rosier, John	Westmoreland	Will	1660	D&W1, p. 127
Ross, David	Henrico	Will	1817	LVA Acc. #23318
Ross, David, in Henrico Co.	Franklin	Will	1817	CF1861-003
Ross, David, of *Mount Ida*	Buckingham	Will	1819	V:Mss1 F7345 a 852+
Ross, David, of *Mount Ida*	Buckingham	Inventory	1821	V:Mss1 F7345 a 852+
Ross, David, of New Kent Co.	Williamsburg	Will Abstract	1797	Crozier, p. 49
Ross, David, of Richmond	London	Will	1722	N:PROB11/1656
Ross, Edward	Fredericksburg	Will	1789	DCWBA, p. 2
Ross, Francis	Elizabeth City	Guard.	1809	TVF 3:2, p. 102
Ross, James	Fluvanna	Will	1800	LVA Acc. #23341
Ross, Mary Breckinridge McDowell	Albemarle	Will	1890c	V:Mss1 M1485 b 22-23
Ross, Peter	Fluvanna	Will	1818	LVA Acc. #23341
Ross, William	Dinwiddie	Will	1841	BRCD
Ross, William, of *Mount Ida*	Buckingham	Will	1804	V:Mss1 F7345 a 840+
Rosse, Robert	Lancaster	Will	1667	LP
Rosser, John	Fauquier	Will	1783	CF1788-005
Rosser, Michael	Prince George	Inventory	1759	DB1759, p. 131
Rosser, Thomas, in Campbell Co.	Bedford	Will	1847	CF1859-021
Rothrock, Mary R., in Fredericksburg	Fauquier	Will	1859	CF1888-052
Rothwell, Benjamin, in MO	Albemarle	Will	1839	CF1878-032
Roudabush, Samuel	Bath	Will	1882	CF1895-011
Roundtree, William, of Isle of Wight Co.	Williamsburg	Will Abstract	1796	Crozier, p. 49
Rountree, Nancy	Hanover	Will	1852	Cocke:135
Rountree, Nancy	Hanover	Will	1852	CF1868-016
Rout, John	Northumberland	Will	1759	V:Mss2 R7656 a 2
Routledge, Robert	Prince Edward	Estate Ref.	1794	Shepherd, Vol. 1, p. 315
Routt, Harriet E., in Fauquier Co.	Franklin	Will	1892	CF1895-004

NAME	LOCATION	TYPE	YEAR	REFERENCE(S)
Rovieree, Claude	Henrico	Will	1740	Records, Vol. 4, p. 1127
Row, Clack, of Caroline Co.	Williamsburg	Will Abstract	1804	Crozier, p. 49
Row, Clack, of Caroline Co.	Williamsburg	Will Abstract	1809	Fleet 2:350
Row, Thomas, of King & Queen Co.	Williamsburg	Will Abstract	1789	Fleet 2:350
Row, Thomas, of King & Queen Co.	Williamsburg	Will Abstract	1789	Crozier, p. 48
Rowan, George, in Loudoun Co.	Frederick	Will	1805	CF1818-020
Rowen, John	Henrico	Will	1662	Records, Vol. 1, p. 15
Rowin, Francis	Henrico	Will	1718	Records, Vol. 2, p. 417
Rowland, James	Botetourt	Will	1805	V:Mss1 P9267 e 2298+
Rowland, William, in Botetourt Co.	Roanoke	Will	1833	CF1848-016
Rowles, Julianna	Fairfax	Guard. Acct.	1816	X
Rowley, William	King George	Will	1754	FDC L564-128
Rowley, William	King George	Will	1774	FDC L564-128
Rowzie, Edward	Rappahannock*	Will Abstract	1677	VMHB 5, p. 288
Roy, Augustus G.D., in Essex Co.	King & Queen	Will	1873	CF1887-002
Roy, Beverly	King & Queen	Will	1820	Note[1]
Roy, Beverly	King & Queen	Will	1820	Fleet 2:171
Roy, Eliljah, in Shenandoah Co.	Warren	Will	1826	CF1861-002
Royall, Elizabeth	Prince George	Will	1866	BRCD
Royall, Elizabeth, in Prince George Co.	Petersburg	Will	1866	CF1867-020
Royall, John J., in Fauquier Co.	Culpeper	Will	1856	CF1885-018
Royer, John	Rockingham	Will	1831	CF1842-002
Royster, Charles, of Henry Co.	Mecklenburg	Will	1806	CF1826-045
Royster, Edward, of Henry Co.	Mecklenburg	Will	1810	CF1848-003
Royster, John, in Richmond	Bedford	Will	1850	CF1854-032
Royster, John W.	Hanover	Will	1865	CF1877-037
Royster, Mary R.	Hanover	Will	1866	CF1877-037
Royster, Peter	Charles City	Will	1766	V:Mss3 C3807 a 53
Rozer, Francis Hall, in Pr. Geo. Co. MD	Arlington	Will	1803	CF1835-015
Rozer, Henry, in Pr. Geo. Co. MD	Arlington	Will	1802	CF1835-015
Ruble, George, in OH	Frederick	Will	1813	CF1830-115
Rucker, James B., in Amherst Co.	Lynchburg	Will	1863	CF1886-029
Rudd, Hezekiah	Chesterfield	Guard. Acct.	1803	Note[2]
Ruffin, Francis	Surry	Will	1803	Fleet, Huntington Data
Ruffin, John, of Mecklenburg Co.	Williamsburg	Will Abstract	1775	Crozier, p. 50
Ruffin, Robert, of King William Co.	Williamsburg	Will Abstract	1777	Crozier, p. 50
Ruffin, Thomas	Dinwiddie	Will	1776	LVA Acc. #41008, r4608
Ruffin, Thomas, clerk	Dinwiddie	Will	1776	Fleet, Huntington Data
Ruffin, William	Surry	Inventory	1802	VG 13, p. 54
Ruffin, William, of Surry Co.	Williamsburg	Will Abstract	1774	Crozier, p. 51
Ruffin, William, of Surry Co.	Williamsburg	Will Abstract	1809	Crozier, p. 51
Rumsey, James, of Berkeley Co.		Will	1793	VCRP, Survey #04772
Runkle, Jacob, of Rockingham Co.	Augusta	Will	1791	CF1817-002
Runnels, William, in Hampshire Co.	Frederick	Will	1794	CF1827-042
Ruple, Elizabeth, in Augusta Co.	Bath	Will	1835	CF1858-008
Rush, Benjamin	Prince William	Will Ref.	1767	Note[3]

---

[1] Beverly Fleet, *Virginia Colonial Abstracts*, King and Queen County County, Vol. 14, 1st Collection, p. 090

[2] Chesterfield County Wills, Bk. 6, p. 190.

[3] *Journal of North Carolina Genealogy*, Vol. 12, p. 1661.

NAME	LOCATION	TYPE	YEAR	REFERENCE(S)
Rush, William, in Berkeley Co.	Frederick	Will	1820	CF1830-146
Rush, William, in Berkeley Co.	Frederick	Will	1820	CF1831-189
Russell, Robert, in Campbell Co.	Lynchburg	Will	1791	CF1829-011
Russell, Thomas	York	Will	1783c	V:Mss1 R5685 d 24-33
Russell, William, in Loudoun Co.	Frederick	Will	1813	CF1822-035
Russell, William, of Princess Anne Co.	Williamsburg	Will Abstract	1790	Crozier, p. 50
Rust, Benjamin, in Richmond Co.	Essex	Will	1754	CF1846-013
Rust, Benjamin, in Richmond Co.	Frederick	Will	1754	CF1806-022
Rust, Jeremiah, in KY	Frederick	Will	1821	CF1822-231
Rust, Peter, in Westmoreland Co.	Fauquier	Will	1782	CF1803-016
Rust, Samuel, of Westmoreland Co.	Augusta	Will	1799	CF1811-140
Rutherford, Joseph	Prince Edward	Will	1785	DCW1, p. 82
Rutherford, Thomas	Hanover	Will	1853	V:Mss1 D7598 a 51-52
Rutherford, Thomas, in Berkeley Co.	Frederick	Will	1796	CF1825-131
Rutherford, Thomas, in Berkeley Co.	Frederick	Will	1819	CF1826- 118
Rutter, John, in Norfolk Co.	Portsmouth	Will	1845	CF1868-012
Ryan, James, in Hardy Co.	Frederick	Will	1816	CF1820-081
Ryan, Margaret, in Hardy Co.	Frederick	Will	1816	CF1825-108
Ryan, William P.	Fairfax	Account	1853	X
Ryland, Joseph	Essex	Will	1771	Fleet 2:340
Ryland, Joseph	Essex	Division S.	1773	Fleet 2:341
Ryland, Josiah	King & Queen	Will	1842	Note[1]
Ryland, Josiah	King & Queen	Will	1842	Fleet 2:356
Ryland, William S.	King William	Will	1861	CF1889-021

---

[1] Beverly Fleet, *Virginia Colonial Abstracts*, King and Queen County County, Vol. 14, 5th Collection, p. 97

NAME	LOCATION	TYPE	YEAR	REFERENCE(S)

S

NAME	LOCATION	TYPE	YEAR	REFERENCE(S)
Sadler, John		Will	1716	VCRP, Survey #04143
Sale, Charlotte, in Bedford Co.	Campbell	Will	1880	CF1901-032
Sale, Cornelius	Essex	Will	1775	CF1810-012
Sale, Thomas, in Amherst Co.	Lynchburg	Will	1798	CF1838-007
Sallard, Simon, of Richmond Co.	Williamsburg	Will Abstract	1770	Crozier, p. 55
Salle, Abraham	Henrico	Will	1719	Records, Vol. 2, p. 513
Sallé, John	Chesterfield	Bond	1797	LVA:104594
Salyer, Shanklin, in Russell Co.	Wise	Will	1867	CF1867-006
Samford, William K.	Brunswick	Will	1795	CF1799-006
Sampson, Edwin D., in NY	Culpeper	Will	1882	CF1893-020
Sampson, Mary, in Madison Co.	Culpeper	Will	1824	CF1834-001
Sampson, Rosalie P., in Albemarle Co.	Charlottesville	Will	1883	CF1895-008
Samuel, Andrew B., in Orange Co.	Essex	Will	1842	CF1874-034
Samuel, George W.	Caroline	Will	1822	Weisiger 1:073
Samuel, Leonard	Caroline	Will	1821	W&P1742, p. 111
Samuel, Philip [of *Pleasant Hill*]	Caroline	Will	1843	Weisiger 1:073
Samuel, Thomas [of *Bath*]	Caroline	Will	1771	FDC L567-38
Samuell, John		Will	1745	VCRP, Survey #04630
Sanborne, Phinias, in NC	Norfolk	Will	1840	CF1858-023
Sanders, Hugh	Spotsylvania	Will	1781	T: from Westmoreland
Sanders, John	Goochland	Will	1736	DB2, p. 270
Sanders, John, in Chesterfield Co.	Powhatan	Will	1803	CF1821-007
Sanders, Robert	Warwick	Inventory	1685	Records 1684
Sanders, William	Westmoreland	Will	1726	MVG 29:3, p. 193
Sanders, William, Sr., of Lunenburg Co.	Richmond	Will	1793	TVF 1:3, p. 139
Sanderson, John	Stafford	Will	1761	DBO, p. 389
Sandford, Samuell, of Accomack Co.		Will	1710	VCRP, Survey #04348
Sandidge, John	King William	Will	1750	BRCD
Sandidge, John, in King William Co.	Lunenburg	Will	1751	CF1790-011
Sandifur, John, in Charlotte Co.	Lynchburg	Will	1804	CF1834-035
Sanford, Joseph	Westmoreland	Will	1741	D&W9, p. 155
Sanger, Annie E., in Rockingham Co.	Fairfax	Will	1897	CF1913-070
Sanger, Annie E., in Rockingham Co.	Fairfax	Will	1899	CF1913-070
Sangster, Mary, now Ferguson	Fairfax	Dower	1803	X
Sangster, Thomas	Fairfax	Plat	1803	X
Sangster, Thomas [Mary]	Fairfax	Dower	1803	X
Satterwhite, Robert	Caroline	Will	1847	Note[1]
Saufly, Martha, in KY	Fauquier	Will	1875	CF1895-001
Saunders, Alexander, of Essex Co.	Williamsburg	Will Abstract	1778	Crozier, p. 54
Saunders, David, Sr., in Bedford Co.	Lynchburg	Will	1842	CF1858-027
Saunders, Elizabeth	Fairfax	Account	1837	X
Saunders, Ellis G.	King & Queen	Will	1859	CF1868-008
Saunders, George, of St. Martin's Par.	Hanover	Will	1808	VGS Bulletin VII, p. 68
Saunders, Jane J., in Pittsylvania Co.	Franklin	Will	1862	CF1883-049
Saunders, John	Fairfax	Division	1823	X
Saunders, John C.	Hanover	Will	1864	CF1883-024
Saunders, Lucy B. Page, of *Rosewell*	D.C.	Will	1886	DCA:Box 99

[1] Caroline County Land Causes, 1835-1893, Vol. 1, p. 97.

NAME	LOCATION	TYPE	YEAR	REFERENCE(S)
Saunders, Margaret, in Loudoun Co.	Frederick	Will	1828	CF1831-136
Saunders, Robert	Williamsburg	Will	1835	LVA Acc. #28458
Saunders, Robert, in Lunenburg Co.	Brunswick	Will	1857	CF1879-006
Saunders, Robert, in Williamsburg	James City	Will	1869	CF1881-006
Saunders, W.H., in Mecklenburg Co.	Lunenburg	Will	1890	CF1896-009
Savage, John	Northampton	Will Ref.	1732	Winfree, p. 369
Savage, John	Northampton	Estate Ref.	1766	Hening, Vol. 8, p. 222
Savage, John	Northampton	Will Ref.	1767	Hening, Vol. 8, p. 468
Savage, Nathaniel L.	New Kent	Estate Ref.	1794	LP:17 NOV 1794
Savidge, John	Surry	Will	1795	WB1, p. 99
Sawyer, Sarah F., in MD	Henrico	Will	1898	CF1898-006
Sawyers, Sampson, of Botetourt Co.	Augusta	Will	1817	CF1823-072
Sayers, Robert, in Wythe Co.	Smyth	Will	1833	CF1840-004
Sayre, Harvey, in Livingston Co. NY	Fairfax	Will	1877	X
Sayre, Harvey, in Livingston Co. NY	Fairfax	Will	1886	CF1887-041
Scarborough, John Pompey	Prince George	Will	1854	SV 9:4, p. 160
Scarburgh, Mary	Accomack	Will	1691	VMHB 11, p. 222
Scarlett, Ann	Stafford	Will	1698	VGSQ 10:4, p. 97
Scarlett, Ann	Stafford	Will	1698	V:Mss1 T2118 d27684+
Scarlett, Martin	Stafford	Will	1686	VGSQ 10:4, p. 97
Scarlett, Martin	Stafford	Will	1686	V:Mss1 T2118 d27684+
Scearce, William B., in Alexandria Co.	Fairfax	Will	1861	CF1867-023
Schermerhorn, John P.	Henrico	Will	1850	V:Mss1 C5217 b 813+
Schminke, Frederick, in MD	Richmond	Will	1885	CF1917-004
Schmucker, Joseph, in Shenandoah Co.	Rockingham	Will	1876	CF1894-043
Schofield, William, in Amherst Co.	Lynchburg	Will	1791	CF1837-013
Scholfield, Andrew, of Alexandria	D.C.	Will	1841	DCA:Box 15
Scholfield, Catharine, in Berkeley Co.	Fairfax	Will	1850	CF1854-035
Scholfield, Catherine, in Frederick Co.	Warren	Will	1849	CF1860-006
Schoolbred, John, of London		Will	1801	VCRP, Survey #06892
Schoolfield, Benjamin	Campbell	Will	1857	V:Mss2 M381372 b
Schoolfield, William M., in Amherst Co.	Lynchburg	Will	1855	CF1872-009
Schools, George	King & Queen	Will	1836	CF1861-001
Schools, Rebecca	King & Queen	Will	1857	CF1861-001
Schools, Waller	King & Queen	Will	1844	CF1861-001
Schreve, Mary Ann		Will	1839	BRCD, GC
Schreve, Mary Ann, in NY	Petersburg	Will	1839	CF1845-057
Schulhofer, Gustave, in Richmond	Henrico	Will	1881	CF1890-013
Sclater, John	York	Will	1797	CF1841-007
Sclater, Richard	York	Will	1777	CF1841-007
Scott, Adelaid	King & Queen	Will	1892	LP
Scott, Benjamin	King & Queen	Will	1795	V:Mss1 T2118 d27684+
Scott, Benjamin	King & Queen	Will	1795	VGSQ 10:4, p. 99
Scott, Carey, in Rockbridge Co.	Staunton	Will	1868	CF1882-001
Scott, Daniel Roe	Accomack	Inventory	1786	WB 1784, p. 216
Scott, Edward	Prince Edward	Will	1817	UVA Acc. #9929
Scott, Francis	Williamsburg	Will	1738	BRCD, GC
Scott, Francis	Williamsburg	Will	1738	SV 1:4, p. 158
Scott, Francis, in James City Co.	Southampton	Will	1738	CF1766-003
Scott, Henry		Will	1858	V:Mss1 Sco866 c
Scott, Henry	Fairfax	Plat	1868	X

NAME	LOCATION	TYPE	YEAR	REFERENCE(S)
Scott, Henry	Fairfax	Division	1868	X
Scott, Jacob K., in Hinds Co. MS	Powhatan	Will	1836	CF1848-009
Scott, James		Estate Ref.	1791	Hening, Vol. 13, p. 306
Scott, James, Gent.	Fauquier	Estate Ref.	1786	Hening, Vol. 12, p. 382
Scott, John	Fauquier	Will	1785	V:Mss1 4686 c 12-13
Scott, John	Prince Edward	Will	1791	WB2, p. 134
Scott, John	Albemarle	Will	1798	V:Mss2 N5149 b
Scott, John, Jr.	Prince George	Inventory	1733	DB1733, p. 566
Scott, John, of Westmoreland Co.	London	Will	1702	N:PROB11/467
Scott, John, of Westmoreland Co.		Will	1702	VCRP, Survey #04122
Scott, Joseph	Albemarle	Will	1778	LVA Acc. #21824
Scott, Joseph Bailey, Sr.	Henrico	Will	(nd)	LVA Acc. #41008, r4610
Scott, Joseph Bailey, Sr.	Henrico	Will	(nd)	Fleet, Huntington Data
Scott, Matthew, in Montgomery Co.	Floyd	Will	(nd)	CF1840-002
Scott, Nicholas	Charles City	Inventory	1728	D&W1724, p. 198
Scott, Rebecca	Dinwiddie	Will	1813	VG 16, p. 171
Scott, Richard	Princess Anne	Will	1753	SV 12:1, p. 15
Scott, Richard	Princess Anne	Will	1753	MVG 31:4, p. 352
Scott, Richard	Princess Anne	Will	1767	BRCD
Scott, Richard Marshall	Fairfax	Will	1833	NVG 8, p. 1094
Scott, Richard Marshall, of *Bush Hill*	Fairfax	Will	1833	V:Mss1 B2105 a 892+
Scott, Richard Scott, in Fairfax Co.	Arlington	Will	1833	CF1848-006
Scott, Robert, in Campbell Co.	Lynchburg	Will	1810	CF1838-016
Scott, Samuel B., in Lynchburg	Campbell	Will	1880	CF1904-005
Scott, Samuel B., in Richmond	Prince Edward	Will	1884	CF1904-055
Scott, Samuel, in Campbell Co.	Lynchburg	Will	1821	CF1827-084
Scott, Samuel, in Campbell Co.	Lynchburg	Will	1821	CF1849-008
Scott, Sarah	Fauquier	Will	1799	CF1884-022
Scott, Thomas	Middlesex	Inventory	1767	WBE, p. 311
Scott, Thomas [of *Greenwood*]	Caroline	Will	1773	LVA Acc. #20632
Scott, W.H., in Nottoway Co.	Lunenburg	Will	1885	CF1907-021
Scott, William	Fairfax	Will	1787	X
Scott, William E., in Campbell Co.	Lynchburg	Will	1855	CF1879-009
Scott, William, in Campbell Co.	Lynchburg	Will	1817	CF1827-012
Scott, William, in Campbell Co.	Lynchburg	Will	1817	CF1830-146
Scott, William, in Dinwiddie Co.	Amelia	Will	1795	CF1805-007
Scrosby, James, of Mathews Co.	Williamsburg	Will Abstract	1792	Crozier, p. 55
Scrosby, John, of Gloucester Co.	Williamsburg	Will Abstract	1791	Crozier, p. 52
Scrubbs, John, in TN	Henrico	Will	1831	CF1846-001
Scruggs, Grove	Buckingham	Will	1827	Weisiger 1:061
Scruggs, Mary, in Buckingham Co.	Bedford	Will	1860	CF1848-035
Scruggs, Rebecca, in Anderson Co. TN	Henrico	Will	1843	CF1846-003
Scruggs, Thomas, Sr., in Bedford Co.	Lynchburg	Will	1804	CF1824-003
Seacatt, Charles, in Botetourt Co.	Roanoke	Will	1837	CF1859-013
Seal, David	Caroline	Will	1820	W&P1742, p. 109
Seaman, Jonathan, in Berkeley Co.	Frederick	Will	1785	CF1818-092
Searne, Richard	Surry	Inventory	1684	T: correct from Learne
Sears, James, of Alexandria	D.C.	Will	1853	DCA:Box 22
Sears, Thomas	King & Queen	Will	1850	CF1875-002
Sears, William, of St. Ann's Parish	Essex	Will	1752	Fleet 2:330
Seat, Robert	Surry	Will	1708	T: correct from Leal

NAME	LOCATION	TYPE	YEAR	REFERENCE(S)
Seaton, Betty, of King William Co.	Henrico	Will	1790	Judgments 1804 APR
Seaton, John A., in Alexandria	Fauquier	Will	1898	CF1908-002
Seavers, Augustus, in MD	Gloucester	Will	1875	CF1892-009
Seawell, Frances	Gloucester	Will	1832	BRCD
Seawell, Francis, of Gloucester Co.	Mecklenburg	Will	1813	CF1858-029
Seawell, John, of Gloucester Co.	Mecklenburg	Will	1806	CF1858-029
Seay, Flurry	Caroline	Will	1829	W&D1794, p. 23
Seay, George N., in Lunenburg Co.	Amelia	Will	1887	CF1912-014
Seay, James	King William	Will	1752	TVF 12:3, p. 173
Seay, James, of King William Co.	Amelia	Will	1752	LP 1757-1758
Sebastian, Benjamin, Breckenridge KY	Fairfax	Will	1834	X
Seddon, James Alexander	Goochland	Will	1878	V:Mss1 B8306 b1349+
Seddon, Sarah Bruce	Goochland	Will	1882	V:Mss1 Se275 a
Seddon, Susan Pearson Alexander	Richmond City	Will	1844	V:Mss1 B8306 b1349+
Seddon, Thomas, in Fredericksburg	Culpeper	Will	1831	CF1888-022
Seddon, Thomas, Sr.	Stafford	Will	1811	Note[1]
Seevers, Ann C.	Frederick	Will (U)	1885	LVA:1117621
Segar, Randolph	King & Queen	Will	1795	Fleet 2:305
Seguine, James S., in Norfolk Co.	Portsmouth	Will	1868	CF1874-005
Selden, Henry	Norfolk City	Will	1855	LVA Acc. #41008, r4611
Selden, Henry	Norfolk City	Will	1855	Fleet, Huntington Data
Selden, Samuel, of Overwharton Par.	Fredericksburg	Will	1791	DCWBA, p. 9
Semmes, Sophia Wilson Potts	Arlington	Will	1839c	V:Mss1 R2723 a 13-22
Semmes, Thomas	Arlington	Will	1833c	V:Mss1 R2723 a 13-22
Semple, John	Prince William	Will	1783	Note[2]
Semple, Robert Baylor, Spotsylvania Co.	Essex	Will	1831	CF1832-003
Senckler, John, mariner		Will	1697	VCRP, Survey #04771
Settle, Merriman, in Culpeper Co.	Rappahannock	Will	1814	CF1841-010
Settle, William, in Richmond Co.	Essex	Will	1834	CF1845-022
Seward, Benjamin, in Middlesex Co.	Essex	Will	1816	CF1846-026
Seward, Edward, in Middlesex Co.	Essex	Will	1840	CF1858-018
Seward, John	Surry	Account	1702	T: not Inventory
Seward, John, mechant		Will	1651	VCRP, Survey #04100
Seward, William Caufell, of Surry Co.	Williamsburg	Will Abstract	1782	Crozier, p. 54
Sexsmith, Rebecca	Prince William	Will	1881	CF1881-006
Sexton, Isaac, in Norfolk	James City	Will	1796	CF1886-011
Shackelford, Daniel	Culpeper	Will	1815	CF1869-004
Shackelford, Richard, Stratton Major P.	King & Queen	Will	1773	Fleet 2:168
Shackelford, Samuel J., in Frederick Co.	Warren	Will	1835	CF1845-008
Shackelford, William	King & Queen	Inventory	1788	Fleet 2:169
Shackleford, George D.	James City	Will	1821	Swem(1):f178
Shackleford, Lyne, of *Curle*, Henrico Co.	Williamsburg	Will Abstract	1806	Crozier, p. 52
Shackleford, Zachary, of Rock'ham. Co.	Augusta	Will	1822	CF1832-009
Shacklett, Elizabeth	Fauquier	Will	1848	NVG 7, p. 938
Shaffer, Nicholas, of Rockingham Co.	Augusta	Will	1790	CF1809-125
Shands, Augustin, Sr.	Prince George	Will	1814	SV 9:1, p. 18
Shands, William	Prince George	Will	1860	SV 10:1, p. 14

---

[1] LVA, U.S. Circuit Court Records, Box 142, *Buchan v. Buchan & Seddon* (1838).

[2] LVA, U.S. Circuit Court Records, Box 71, *James Lawson v. Lockhead's Admin.* (1807).

NAME	LOCATION	TYPE	YEAR	REFERENCE(S)
Shankland, Ellanor		Will	1775	LVA Acc. #23772-3/35
Shanks, David, in Botetourt Co.	Roanoke	Will	1834	CF1847-006
Sharp, Henry	Henrico	Inventory	1757	Records, Vol. 5, p. 1747
Sharp, James H.	Hanover	Will	1830c	V:Mss1 D1124 b 2802+
Sharp, John	Stafford	Will P.	1683	OB:08 NOV 1683
Sharp, John, in Jefferson Co.	Frederick	Will	1816	CF1823-059
Sharp, Matthew	Augusta	Will	1750	WB1, p. 271
Sharp, Robert	Henrico	Inventory	1720	Records, Vol. 2, p. 491
Sharpe, Robert	Henrico	Will	1772	MVG 30:3, p. 155
Sharpe, Robert, Sr.	Henrico	Will	1772	MVG 30:3, p. 155
Sharrot, Daniel, in Pendleton Co.	Bath	Will	1807	CF1832-013
Shaw, John, in Halifax Co. NC	Mecklenburg	Will	1832	CF1852-041
Shaw, Richard		Will	1700	VCRP, Survey #04791
Shawen, Cornelius, in Loudoun Co.	Frederick	Will	1820	CF1832-081
Shearer, William, in Appomattox Co.	Lynchburg	Will	1859	CF1870-036
Sheares, George	Nansemond	Will	1657	VG 19, p. 183
Shearman, Adam, in Shenandoah Co.	Frederick	Will	1797	CF1821-152
Shearman, Adam, in Shenandoah Co.	Frederick	Will	1814	CF1832-095
Sheasler, George [Sheaster]		Will	1749	LVA Wills/Admin. DB
Sheaster, George [Sheasler]		Will	1749	LVA Wills/Admin. DB
Sheild, Robert	James City	Will	1840	Swem(1):f178
Sheilds, James, of James City Co.	York	Will	1795	MVG 31:4, p. 349
Shelburn, Silas	Hanover	Will	(nd)	LVA Acc. #25880
Shell, John	Brunswick	Will	1794	CF1802-012
Shell, John	Brunswick	Will	1794	CF1803-012
Shelor, John, Sr., in Orange Co.	Greene	Will	1825	CF1846-008
Shelton, Henry [Chelton]		Will	1730	LVA Wills/Admin. DB
Shelton, Nicholas [Chelton]		Will	1738	LVA Wills/Admin. DB
Shelton, Ralph, of St. Mary's Parish	King William	Will	1744	Note[1]
Shelton, Richard, in Amherst Co.	Lynchburg	Will	1821	CF1830-114
Shelton, William	King & Queen	Will	1804	V:Mss1 G1873 a 18-24
Shepheard, William	Surry	Admin.	1699	T:D&W5, p. 188a
Shepherd, Augustine	Amherst	Will	1796	CF1796-002
Shepherd, Augustine, in Amherst Co.	Lynchburg	Will	1795	CF1825-074
Shepherd, Augustine, in Nelson Co.	Lynchburg	Will	1816	CF1825-074
Shepherd, Lemuel	Princess Anne	Will	1804	V:Mss1 Sh485 a 27-30
Shepherd, Lemuel	Princess Anne	Will	1805	V:Mss1 Sh485 a 27-30
Shepherd, Samuel, of King & Queen	Middlesex	Will	1751	Fleet 2:303
Shepherd, Samuel, of King & Queen	Middlesex	Will	1752	CF1791-002
Shepherd, Sarah	Princess Anne	Inventory	(nd)	V:Mss1 Sh485 a 27-30
Shepherd, Smith	Princess Anne	Will	1795	V:Mss1 Sh485 a 24-26
Shepherd, Smith, Sr.	Princess Anne	Will	1799	SV 11:4, p. 172
Shepherd, Thomas, in Berkeley Co.	Frederick	Will	1792	CF1830-175
Sheppard, Eliza	Fairfax	Guard.	1830	X
Sheppard, Eliza	Fairfax	Account	1852	X
Sheppard, John	Fairfax	Account	1816	X
Sheppard, Philip	Hanover	Will	1815	CF1852-003
Sheppard, Philip	Hanover	Will	1815	Cocke:29

---

[1] *The Amherst Enterprise*, 7 AUG 1879; LVA Acc. #30057.

NAME	LOCATION	TYPE	YEAR	REFERENCE(S)
Sheppard, Sarah Ann	Fairfax	Guard.	1830	X
Sheppard, William	Fairfax	Account	1816	X
Shepperson, William, in Chesterfield Co.	Henrico	Will	1884	CF1889-012
Sherley, William		Will	1750	VCRP, Survey #04638
Sherman, Thomas, of New Kent Co.	Williamsburg	Will Abstract	1801	Crozier, p. 52
Sherman, William, of New Kent Co.	Williamsburg	Will Abstract	1796	Crozier, p. 52
Shermer, John, in James City Co.	York	Will	1775	CF1794-009
Shermer, John, in New Kent Co.	York	Will	1774	MVG 31:4, p. 350
Sherrard, Denis	Surry	Inventory	1690	T:D&W4, p. 186a
Sherwood, Philip	Rappahannock*	Will	(nd)	TQ 23:2, p. 114
Sherwood, William	James City	Will	1687	WMQ 17, p. 268
Sherwood, William	James City	Will	1697	V:Mss1 Am167b
Sherwood, William, of Jamestown	James City	Will	1697	WMQ 13, p. 138
Shields, James, in James City Co.	York	Will	1795	CF1808-001
Shields, Thomas	Henrico	Inventory	1719	Records, Vol. 2, p. 459
Shimer, Samuel, in NJ	Prince William	Will	1889	CF1899-006
Ship, Lemuel, of St. Mary's Parish	Caroline	Will	1788	VMHB 47, p. 177
Ship, Samuel [of Port Royal]	Caroline	Will	1788	W&P1742, p. 45
Shipp, Simon	Princess Anne	Will	1795	SV 14:2, p. 70
Ships, James, in Frederick Co.	Rappahannock	Will	1835	CF1847-007
Shirley, Ann D., of Norfolk	D.C.	Will	1873	DCA:Box 52
Shirley, Jarvis, in Jefferson Co.	Frederick	Will	1819	CF1830-058
Shirley, Ralph	Surry	Will	1693	T:D&W4, p. 327a
Short, James		Will	1774	VCRP, Survey #01907
Short, John	Culpeper	Will	1734	CF1848-009
Short, John	Stafford	Will	1794	TQ 32:3, p. 208
Short, Judith Ball	Culpeper	Will	1843	V:Mss2 Sh814 a 1
Short, Judith Ball	Culpeper	Inventory	1843	V:Mss2 Sh814 a 1
Short, Landman	Westmoreland	Will	1800	Note[1]
Short, Landman	Westmoreland	Will	1800	Note[2]
Short, William		Will Ref.	(nd)	Hening, Vol. 11, p. 148
Short, William	Surry	Will	1659	V:Mss2 Sh817 a 1
Short, William	Surry	Will	1676	T: correct from 1675
Short, William		Estate Ref.	1788	Hening, Vol. 12, p. 681
Shorte, Robert	Charles City	Will	1690	D&W1689, p. 82
Shreve, Benjamin	Arlington	Will	1801	CF1823-019
Shreve, Mary Ann		Will	1839	BRCD, GC
Shumate, John, Sr.	Fauquier	Will	1814	NVG 9, p. 1332
Sibert, Elizabeth J. Smoot Payne	Culpeper	Will	1853	V:Mss1 P2936 c 208+
Sicklemore, John [Ratcliffe]		Will	1611	VCRP, Survey #03105
Sidniham, Lee Andrew, in Richmond	Henrico	Will	1874	CF1891-046
Sidway, Mary	Surry	Will	1688	T:D&W4, p. 41b
Sikes, John, in Halifax Co.	Lynchburg	Will	1784	CF1827-018
Simmons, Cary	Floyd	Will	1868	MVG 29:3, p. 193
Simmons, Elizabeth	Fairfax	Account	1816	X
Simmons, Henry		Will Ref.	1803	UVA MSS 3347
Simmons, Joel	Prince George	Will	1858	SV 10:1, p. 13

---

[1] Westmoreland County Original Wills, 1755-1800, Reel 28a, #46; card reference at LVA.
[2] Westmoreland County Original Wills, 1755-1800, Reel 28a, #46.

NAME	LOCATION	TYPE	YEAR	REFERENCE(S)
Simmons, Rebecca	Surry	Inventory	1792	WB12, p. 335
Simmons, William	Stafford	Will	1807	LP:15 DEC 1809
Simms, James	Richmond City	Will	1794	T:HCD2, p. 98
Simms, Nancy	Fairfax	Guard. Bond	1845	X
Simons, Henry	Brunswick	Will	1781	CF1792-018
Simons, James	Rappahannock*	Will	1687	Sweeny, p. 137
Simons, William	Surry	Inventory	1697	T:D&W5, p. 143a
Simpson, Alexander	Norfolk	Will	1771	UVA
Simpson, Alexander, of Norfolk	London	Will	1771	N:PROB11/968
Simpson, Alexander, of Norfolk		Will	1771	VCRP, Survey #04689
Simpson, John	Fairfax	Plat	1824	WBN, p. 277
Simpson, Mary, in Loudoun Co.	Frederick	Will	1814	CF1828-139
Simpson, Nancy	Fairfax	Account	1860	X
Simpson, Thomas, in Prince William Co.	Fairfax	Will	1734	X
Sims, David	Hanover	Will	1817	CF1837-015
Sims, David, of St. Martin's Parish	Hanover	Will	1817	Cocke:122
Sims, John	Halifax	Will	1825	V:Mss1 C2355 a
Sims, Patrick H.	Hanover	Will	1824	CF1880-030
Sims, Patrick H., of Louisa Co.	Hanover	Will	1834	Cocke:123
Sims, William	Hanover	Will	1809	LVA Acc. #33203
Sims, William, in Hanover Co.	Louisa	Will	1814	CF1822-027
Sims, William, of James City Co.	Louisa	Will Ref.	1710	DBB 1754 end
Sinclair, Alexander	Prince William	Will	1749	PWR 6:1, p. 6
Sinclair, Arthur	Norfolk City	Will	1831	V:Mss2 Si622 b 1
Sinclair, Henry Clay	Fairfax	Guard. Bond	1845	X
Sinclair, Julia Elizabeth	Fairfax	Guard. Bond	1845	X
Sinclair, Robert, of Dettingen Parish	Prince William	Will	1750	PWR 6:1, p. 8
Sinclair, Robert Walker	Fairfax	Guard. Bond	1845	X
Sinclair, William Z., in Jefferson Co.	Frederick	Will	1840	CF1850-029
Singleton, Anthony	Richmond City	Will	1795	T:HCD2, p. 215
Singleton, Joshua, in Richmond Co.	Frederick	Will	1772	CF1818-018
Singleton, Mary L., in Albemarle Co.	Charlottesville	Will	1887	CF1901-001
Singleton, Robert	Gloucester	Will	1725	LVA Acc. #32488
Singleton, Robert	Gloucester	Will	1725	VMHB 61:103
Sipe, John	Rockingham	Will	1842	CF1849-007
Sipe, Margaret	Rockingham	Will	1832	CF1844-010
Sipel, George, in WV	Rockingham	Will	1876	CF1893-080
Sister, John [Lister], of Gloucester	Elizabeth City	Will	1734	Wills 1701, p. 3
Sizer, John	King William	Account	1861	LVA Acc. #21292
Sizer, John	King William	Will	1861	LVA Acc. #21292
Skeeter, Alexander, in Norfolk Co.	Portsmouth	Will	1896	CF1913-002
Skeeter, Alexander, in Norfolk Co.	Portsmouth	Will	1896	CF1910-013
Skelton, Bathurst, in Albemarle, etc.	Charles City	Inventory	1773	Note[1]
Skelton, Eliza	Hanover	Will	1869	CF1879-014
Skelton, Powell, in KY	Mecklenburg	Will	1829	CF1839-020 CSC
Skillern, George, of Botetourt Co.	Augusta	Will	1814	CF1820-086
Skilton, Reuben		Will	1759	Note[2]

---

[1] LVA, Charles City County Records, 1766-1774, p. 524.

[2] Copy pasted to the back of the Douglas Register, according to page 364 of the printed version, which copies it.

NAME	LOCATION	TYPE	YEAR	REFERENCE(S)
Skinker, Samuel	Hanover	Will	1752	LVA Tazewell Papers
Skinnell, William H., in Bedford Co.	Franklin	Will	1862	CF1870-025
Skinner, Peter	Westmoreland	Will	1722	LVA Acc. #41008, r4614
Skinner, Peter	Westmoreland	Will	1722	LVA Acc. #36102, r444a
Skinner, Peter, of Washington Parish	Westmoreland	Will	1722	Fleet, Huntington Data
Skipwith, Fulwar	Dinwiddie	Will	1765	LVA Acc. #27293-2
Skipwith, Fulwar	Dinwiddie	Will	1765	VG 16, p. 164
Skipwith, Fulwar	Dinwiddie	Will	1765	LVA Acc. #28757-18
Skipwith, Henry	Powhatan	Will	1807	LVA Acc. #24194
Skipwith, Peyton	Mecklenburg	Will	1805	UVA MSS 7574
Skipwith, Peyton, Sir	Mecklenburg	Will	1805	V:Mss1 Sk366 a 9-11
Skipwith, William, Sir	Prince George	Will	1764	LVA Acc. #23423d
Slate, Edward	Surry	Will	1750	T: not Brunswick
Slate, John	Surry	Inventory	1761	T: from Brunswick
Slater, John	New Kent	Will	1865	CF1872-005
Slater, Sarah, wid/o Merideth, in AL	New Kent	Estate Ref.	1846	VGS Bulletin VIII, p. 13
Slaughter, Amelia, in Berkeley Co.	Frederick	Will	1822	CF1835-181
Slaughter, Francis	Rappahannock*	Will Abstract	1656c	VMHB 5, p. 283
Slaughter, Henry T.	King William	Will	1817	V:Mss1 B9468 a 12-16
Slaughter, John L. to Cornelia Boulware	King & Queen	Marriage	1864	LP
Slaughter, Patrick H.	King William	Will	1881	CF1888-014
Slaughter, Robert, in Rappahannock Co.	Culpeper	Will	1841	CF1869-029
Slaughter, Smith, in Jefferson Co.	Frederick	Will	1824	CF1821-144
Slaughter, William, in Culpeper Co.	Rappahannock	Will	1821	CF1842-007
Slusser, George	Rockingham	Will	1833	CF1838-006
Smallay, Robert, Capt., Bermuda 100		Will	1621	VCRP, Survey #03112
Smallwood, William	Fredericksburg	Inventory	1792	DCWBA, p. 25
Smart, William	Gloucester	Will	1839	LVA Wm. Smart Papers
Smelly, John, in GA	Isle of Wight	Will	1821	CF1826-002
Smets, Eliza W.M.	Fairfax	Will	1861	X
Smith, Abraham	Dinwiddie	Will	1782	Note[1]
Smith, Adam	Botetourt	Will	1785c	V:Mss3 P9465aSec1s-v
Smith, Albert G.	Fauquier	Will	1892	CF1899-012
Smith, Alexander	Middlesex	Will	1696	V:Mss2 Sm513 a 1
Smith, Alexander	Middlesex	Will	1696	WB 1675, p. 101
Smith, Alexander	Essex	Will	1773	Fleet 2:343
Smith, Alexander		Estate Ref.	1797	Shepherd, Vol. 2, p. 130
Smith, Ann	Middlesex	Will Abstract	1749	Fleet 2:327
Smith, Anne	Essex	Will	1753	Fleet 2:328
Smith, Arthur	Isle of Wight	Will Ref.	1645	Hening, Vol. 6, p. 308
Smith, Arthur	Nansemond	Appraisal	1849	BRCD
Smith, Arthur, of Suffolk Co.	Nansemond	Will	1849	BRCD
Smith, Arthur, of Warrisquiake	Isle of Wight	Will	1645	VMHB 6, p. 113
Smith, Augustine, in Middlesex Co.	Frederick	Will	1774	CF1814-049
Smith, Caster, in Montgomery Co.	Floyd	Will	(nd)	CF1852-002
Smith, Cealey	Hanover	Will	1839	CF1875-031
Smith, Cealey	Hanover	Will	1839	Cocke:123
Smith, Charles	New Kent	Will	1834	Swem(1):f220

[1] LVA, U.S. Circuit Court Records, Box 127, *Hamilton Trustees v. Smith* (1829).

NAME	LOCATION	TYPE	YEAR	REFERENCE(S)
Smith, Charles	New Kent	Will	1846	Swem(1):f220
Smith, Christopher, of Rockingham Co.	Augusta	Will	1799	CF1823-052
Smith, Delia, in Fredericksburg	Prince William	Will	1841	CF1875-017
Smith, Denwood, of Somerset Co. MD		Will	1800	LVA Acc. #24194
Smith, Drury	Prince George	Will	1854	SV 9:4, p. 160
Smith, Edward H.	Rockingham	Will Ref.	1852	LVA:1159583
Smith, Elizabeth C.	Prince George	Will	1856	SV 10:1, p. 12
Smith, Elsi O., in Bath Co. KY	Fairfax	Will	1847	CF1860-001
Smith, Francis	Essex	Will	1762	TQ 14:1, p. 18
Smith, Francis	Hanover	Will	1775	V:Mss1 P9267 b 12-16
Smith, Francis	Washington	Will	1844c	V:Mss10: no. 109
Smith, George	Frederick	Will	1777	LVA Acc. #24062
Smith, George	Prince William	Will	1822	CF1875-017
Smith, Granville, in Goochland Co.	Powhatan	Will	1836	CF1839-002
Smith, Guy, in Bedford Co.	Franklin	Will	1781	CF1834-025
Smith, Guy, in Bedford Co.	Franklin	Will	1783	CF1834-025
Smith, Henry	Rockingham	Will	1827	MVG 41:3, p. 221
Smith, Henry	Rockingham	Will	1831	LVA:1159583
Smith, Henry	Rockingham	Will	1831	LP:07 DEC 1848
Smith, Hiram, in Scott Co.	Washington	Will	1888	CF1893-060
Smith, Humphrey	Floyd	Will	1840	V:Mss2 Sm588 a 1
Smith, Humphrey, in Cumberland Co.	Powhatan	Will	1766	CF1811-004
Smith, Isaac	Charles City	Inventory	1772	Records, p. 359
Smith, Jacob, in Amherst Co.	Lynchburg	Will	1801	CF1820-002
Smith, James		Will	1744	VCRP, Survey #04626
Smith, James, in Alexandria	Fairfax	Will	1871	CF1907-007
Smith, James, in KY	Fauquier	Will	1826	CF1892-058
Smith, John		Will	1631	LVA Wills/Admin. DB
Smith, John	Surry	Inventory	1689	T:D&W4, p. 114b
Smith, John		Will	1698	VCRP, Survey #06061
Smith, John		Estate Ref.	1753	Hening, Vol. 6, p. 409
Smith, John	Stafford	Admin. Bond	1754	LVA Acc. #41008, r4614
Smith, John	Hanover	Will	1773	LVA Acc. #28973
Smith, John	King & Queen	Will Ref.	1834	Note[1]
Smith, John	Prince William	Will Ref.	1843	CM:07 AUG 1843
Smith, John	Prince William	Acct. Ref.	1844	CM:06 MAY 1844
Smith, John, Capt.	Augusta	Will	1755	V:Mss7:1 Sm616:1
Smith, John H.	Nansemond	Will	1890	BRCD
Smith, John H., in Essex Co.	King & Queen	Will	1849	CF1858-004
Smith, John, in Mecklenburg Co.	Brunswick	Will	1798	CF1807-035
Smith, John, in Richmond Co.	Essex	Will	1794	CF1845-023
Smith, John, in Richmond Co.	Essex	Will	1797	CF1845-022
Smith, John, Jr., in MS	Bedford	Will	1853	CF1866-025
Smith, John, Jr., in Lynchburg	Bedford	Will	1854	CF1866-025
Smith, John, of Fauquier Co.	Prince William	Will	1811	LP
Smith, John, of Hanover	Prince George	Will Partial	1759	DB1759, p. 113
Smith, John, of Hanover	Prince George	Inventory	1760	DB1759, p. 113
Smith, John, of Petsworth Parish	Gloucester	Will Ref.	1735	Hening, Vol. 5, p. 397

---

[1] LVA, Land Office Revlutionary War Military Certificate Papers, John Smith, Folder 26.

NAME	LOCATION	TYPE	YEAR	REFERENCE(S)
Smith, John, planter	Essex	Will Ref.	1703	Winfree, p. 233
Smith, John, Sr.	Hanover	Will Extract	1746	G2:22
Smith, John T.	Loudoun	Inventory	1825	UVA MSS 4325
Smith, John T.	Loudoun	Sale	1836	UVA MSS 4325
Smith, Joseph	Lancaster	Will (N)	1664	LP
Smith, Joseph		Will	1728	V:Mss1 B4678 a 4788
Smith, Joseph	Lunenburg	Will	1794	CF1804-015
Smith, Joseph, Jr., in Rockingham Co.	Bath	Will	1896	CF1901-009
Smith, Joseph, of Alexandria	Arlington	Will	1846	CF1868-003
Smith, Lawrence, of Abingdon Parish	Gloucester	Estate Ref.	1753	Hening, Vol. 6, p. 407
Smith, Lawrence, of York Co.	Williamsburg	Will Abstract	1779	Crozier, p. 56
Smith, Margaret, in Middlesex Co.	Frederick	Will	1777	CF1814-049
Smith, Martha	Prince George	Will	1849	SV 9:4, p. 157
Smith, Mary	Williamsburg	Will Abstract	1816	Crozier, p. 54
Smith, Mary, in GA	Essex	Will	1799	CF1845-023
Smith, Mary, in King & Queen Co.	Frederick	Will	1797	CF1810-019
Smith, Maurice	Middlesex	Will	1795	Wills 1795, p. 11
Smith, Mortimer	King & Queen	Will	1861c	V:Mss1 El275 a 17-22
Smith, Nicholas	Essex	Will	1757	TQ 14:1, p. 17
Smith, Oliver, mariner		Will	1686	VCRP, Survey #03738
Smith, Parke	Hanover	Sale	1775	BRCD
Smith, Peter	Surry	Will Abstract	1814	VG 13, p. 55
Smith, Peter	Surry	Will (U)	1814	VTG 13:2, p. 56
Smith, Philip, in Amherst Co.	Lynchburg	Will	1814	CF1830-133
Smith, Presley Alexander L.	Fauquier	Will	1837	V:Mss1 P4686 a 301+
Smith, Presley N., in Madison Co.	Culpeper	Will	1850	CF1874-001
Smith, Ralph, in Campbell Co.	Lynchburg	Will	1848	CF1869-007
Smith, Richard G.	Hanover	Will	1854	CF1858-006
Smith, Richard G., of *Eastern View*	Hanover	Will	1854	Cocke:124
Smith, Richard, mariner		Will	1680	VCRP, Survey #03723
Smith, Robert	Caroline	Will	1743	OB1741, p. 201
Smith, Robert	Caroline	Will Ref.	1752	Hening, Vol. 6, p. 316
Smith, Robert, Maj.-Gen.	Middlesex	Will	1683	TQ 19:2, p. 101
Smith, Robert, mariner, of York Co.	Williamsburg	Will Abstract	1814	Crozier, p. 56
Smith, Robert S.	King & Queen	Will	1860	CF1866-003
Smith, Samuel	Essex	Will Abstract	1734	Fleet 2:301
Smith, Samuel	Fairfax	Division	1845	X
Smith, Samuel	Fairfax	Plat	1845	X
Smith, Samuel N., in Essex Co.	King & Queen	Will	1855	CF1858-004
Smith, Sarah	Prince George	Will	1759	DB1759, p. 127
Smith, Sarah	Prince George	Inventory	1760	DB1759, p. 178
Smith, Sarah, in Westmoreland Co.	Frederick	Will	1779	CF1810-019
Smith, Susanna	Essex	Will	1766	Fleet 2:333
Smith, Susanna W.	Hanover	Will	1889	CF1899-002
Smith, Thomas	Lancaster	Will	1662	LP
Smith, Thomas	Prince George	Will	1865	BRCD
Smith, Thomas A., in Prince William Co.	Fauquier	Will	1889	CF1893-028
Smith, Thomas, in Prince George Co.	Petersburg	Will	1865	CF1871-040
Smith, Thomas, of Isle of Wight Co.	Williamsburg	Will Abstract	1799	Crozier, p. 56
Smith, Thomas, of Westmoreland Co.	Williamsburg	Will Abstract	1789	Crozier, p. 56
Smith, Thompson	Fauquier	Will	1835	NVG 5, p. 479

NAME	LOCATION	TYPE	YEAR	REFERENCE(S)
Smith, Toby	Rappahannock	Will Abstract	1757	VMHB 5, p. 283
Smith, W.A.B.	Prince William	Will	1883	CF1887-019
Smith, William C.	New Kent	Will	1880	CF1886-006
Smith, William, in King William Co.	New Kent	Will	1784	CF1848-001
Smith, William, in NC	Princess Anne	Will	1865	CF1878-006
Smither, Gabriel, in Richmond Co.	Northumberland	Will	1785	CF1806-001
Smither, James	King & Queen	Will	1839	CF1871-001
Smither, William	Essex	Will	1782	CF1800-022
Smither, William T.	Gloucester	Will	1858	CF1905-026
Smithson, William	Lunenburg	Will	1797	CF1804-017
Smutz, John W., in Shenandoah Co.	Warren	Will	1866	CF1877-017
Snapp, Philip, in Shenandoah Co.	Frederick	Will	1812	CF1823-201
Snapp, Philip, in Shenandoah Co.	Frederick	Will	1812	CF1823-198
Snead, Edwin	Hanover	Will	1846	CF1860-008
Snead, Edwin	Hanover	Will	1846	Cocke:125
Snead, Evan, in Bedford Co.	Lynchburg	Will	1841	CF1857-023
Snead, Hawkins	Stafford	Admin.	1692	OB:14 DEC 1692
Snead, John	Hanover	Will	1881	CF1903-032
Snead, Robert	Hanover	Will	1841	Note[1]
Snead, Samuel	Stafford	Will	1686	TQ 21, p. 55
Snodgrass, Catharine T.	Berkeley	Will	1832	V:Mss2 R5687 b
Snodgrass, Robert	Berkeley	Will	1834	V:Mss2 R5687 b
Snow, William W.	Prince George	Will	1855	SV 9:4, p. 161
Snuggs, Charles	Henrico	Will	1718	Records, Vol. 2, p. 425
Snyder, Elizabeth A., of Alexandria	Arlington	Will	1865	CF1867-012
Snyder, James, in Norfolk Co.	Portsmouth	Will	1856	CF1873-002
Snydor, Elizabeth, in Nottoway Co.	Lunenburg	Will	1815	CF1833-011
Soane, Henry, of Charles City Co.	Chesterfield	Appraisal	1755	Dead Papers 1797 Part V
Sollner, Elizabeth, in Richmond	Henrico	Will	1882	CF1898-025
Sollner, John M., in Richmond	Henrico	Will	1861	CF1898-025
Somers, George, Sir		Will	1611	VCRP, Survey #03106
Somervill, John, in Mecklenburg Co.	Brunswick	Will	1831	CF1845-024
Somerville, James	Fredericksburg	Will	1798	DCWA, p. 84
Somerville, James	Spotsylvania	Will Extract	1798	Swem
South, George	Westmoreland	Will	1702	D&W1761, p. 99
South, John	Westmoreland	Will	1792	LVA Acc. #22337
South, John	Northumberland	Will	1793	Note[2]
Southall, Peyton A.	James City	Will	1854	CF1871-014
Southall, Philip	Charles City	Will	1815	LVA Acc. #21491(4)
Southall, Sarah, of Westover Parish	Charles City	Will	1764	W&D1763, p. 314
Southall, Stephen O., in Albemarle Co.	Amelia	Will	1885	CF1913-006
Southcott, Leonard, in York River		Will	1677	VCRP, Survey #03711
Southell, Seth, of Albemarle Co. NC		Will	1697	VCRP, Survey #04773
Southerland, Fendall	King William	Will	1789	KWHSB, 8:1
Southerland, Fendall	King William	Will	1789	LVA Acc. #28659
Southerland, Fendall	King William	Will	1789	V:Mss2 So885 a 1
Southerland, John, mariner, in NC	Dinwiddie	Will	1771	LVA Acc. #26072

[1] LVA, John K. Martin papers, Revolutionary War papers, Folder Robert Snead
[2] Northumberland County District Court Orders, Deeds, [Wills], 1789-1825, p. 288.

NAME	LOCATION	TYPE	YEAR	REFERENCE(S)
Southerland, John, mariner, in NC	Dinwiddie	Will	1771	VG 11, p. 35
Southerland, William, of St. John's Par.	King William	Will	1789	LVA Acc. #28659
Southgate, Wright	Henrico	Will	1811	LVA Acc. #41008, r4610
Southgate, Wright, of Richmond	Henrico	Will	1811	Fleet, Huntington Data
Southwick, Thomas, mariner		Will	1743	VCRP, Survey #04624
Sowerby, Thomas	Surry	Will P.	1696	T:D&W5, p. 110b
Spady, Massy, of Portsmouth, Norfolk	Williamsburg	Will Abstract	1826	Crozier, p. 52
Spain, Peter	Richmond City	Will	1840	V:Mss1 C5217 b 811+
Sparding, Jasper	Henrico	Inventory	1750	Records, Vol. 5, p. 1511
Sparke, Michael, stationer		Will	1654	VCRP, Survey #04113
Sparks, Henry	Culpeper	Will	1770	MVG 29:3, p. 193
Speak, Lucretia	Fairfax	Will	1816	X
Spears, James	Buckingham	Will	1833	Cocke:126
Spears, James, in Buckingham Co.	Hanover	Will	1833	CF1874-021
Speermaine, Launce, mariner		Will	1700	VCRP, Survey #06067
Spellman, Thomas		Will	1628	VCRP, Survey #03118
Spellman, Thomas [Spelman]		Will	1627	VCRP, Survey #03115
Spence, John	Prince William	Will	1829	V:Mss2 Sp328 a 1
Spence, John	Prince William	Will	1829	Note[1]
Spence, Patrick, form. Cople Parish	London	Will	1710	NGSQ Vol. 62, p. 209
Spence, Patrick, form. Westmoreland	London	Will	1710	N:PROB11/515
Spence, Patrick, of Westmoreland Co.		Will	1710	VCRP, Survey #04349
Spence, Wilson, in Pasquotank Co. NC	Nansemond	Will	1872	CF1887-005
Spence, Wilson, of NC	Nansemond	Will	1872	CF1887-005
Spencer, Abraham	Nansemond	Will Ref.	1790	VG 22, p. 113
Spencer, Elizabeth W., Cumberland Co.	Prince Edward	Will	1859	CF1875-022
Spencer, Gideon, in Charlotte Co.	Powhatan	Will	1822	CF1882-010
Spencer, Hannah W.	Williamsburg	Inventory	1853	Swem(1)
Spencer, Isaac, in Albemarle Co.	Powhatan	Will	1875	CF1882-010
Spencer, John	King & Queen	Will	1859	CF1866-002
Spencer, John, in Greensville Co.	Brunswick	Will	1854	CF1869-015
Spencer, Mary	Buckingham	Will	1783	LVA Acc. #20241
Spencer, Mottrom, of Westmoreland Co.	London	Will	1703	N:PROB11/471
Spencer, Nicholas, Westmoreland Co.	London	Will	1700	N:PROB11/454
Spencer, Nicholas, Westmoreland Co.	London	Will	1700	VCRP, Survey #04790
Spencer, Sarah Ann	New Kent	Will	1827	LVA Acc. #25327
Spencer, Sharp, Sr., in Pr. Edward Co.	Lynchburg	Will	1814	CF1820-030
Spicer, Arthur, of Richmond Co.	London	Will	1700	NGSQ Vol. 63, p. 136
Spicer, Arthur, of Richmond Co.	London	Will	1700	N
Spicer, James	Brunswick	Will	1783	CF1783-001
Spiegle, Michael, in Shenandoah Co.	Frederick	Will	1804	CF1825-123
Spigle, William	Shenandoah	Will	1853	V:Mss2 Sp445 b1 6
Spilman, Baldwin H., Rappa. Co.	Fauquier	Will	1893	CF1900-033
Spilman, Clement	Westmoreland	Will	1676	DB1665, p. 360
Spiltimber, Anthony	Surry	Will	1672	T:D&W2, p. 11
Spindle, Fanny	Essex	Will	1837	Cocke:127
Spindle, Fanny, in Essex Co.	Hanover	Will	1837	CF1880-016
Spinks, John	Elizabeth City	Will	1687	LVA Acc. #30880

---

[1] LVA, U.S. Circuit Court Records, Box 200, *Hasty's Exors. v. Gibson's Exors.* (1832).

NAME	LOCATION	TYPE	YEAR	REFERENCE(S)
Spinny, Roger	Northampton	Will	1663	D&W1657, p. 193
Spotswood, Alexander	Orange	Will	1740	V:Mss1 Sp687 a
Spotswood, Alexander	Orange	Will	1740	V:Mss1 Sp687 a 7
Spotswood, Alexander, of Orange Co.	London	Will	1742	N:PROB11/716
Spotswood, Alexander, of Orange Co.	London	Will	1742	VCRP, Survey #04380
Spotswood, John	Spotsylvania	Will	1756	V:Mss1 Sp687 a 8
Spotswood, John, of Orange Co.	Fredericksburg	Will	1801	LVA Acc. #23427
Spraggin, Rebecca, of James City Co.	Williamsburg	Will Abstract	1804	Crozier, p. 53
Spraggins, Thomas, in Halifax Co.	Lynchburg	Will	1794	CF1825-073
Spragins, Thomas	Halifax	Will	1792	V:Mss1 Sp716 a 21
Spratt, Daniel, of Urbanna, Middlesex	Williamsburg	Will Abstract	1807	Crozier, p. 53
Spratt, James	Princess Anne	Will	1799	SV 13:2, p. 90
Spratt, Robert Beverley, of Middlesex	Williamsburg	Will Abstract	1805	Crozier, p. 53
Sprowl, John	Bath	Will	1796	CF1820-007
Sprowle, Andrew, of Norfolk	London	Will	1782	N:PROB11/1089
Spurling, Jeremiah	Fairfax	Account	1817	X
Squiggins, Sey, alias Cyrus	Henrico	Will	1813	VGSQ 18:3, p. 84
St. John, William, in Middlesex Co.	Essex	Will	1811	CF1835-019
Stackhouse, Sally	Prince George	Will	1855	SV 10:1, p. 11
Stafford, Catherine, in Hampshire Co.	Frederick	Will	1810	CF1834-060
Stainaker, Boston	Randolph	Will	1826	Finley
Stainback, George	Brunswick	Will	1796	CF1802-003
Stallard, David, in Culpeper Co.	Rappahannock	Will	1829	CF1853-008
Stalling, Richard R.	Nansemond	Will	1864	CF1873-008
Stalnaker, Boston	Randolph	Will	1826	Finley
Stamper, James	New Kent	Will	1853	WB1, p. 134
Stamper, James	New Kent	Will	1856	CF1882-006
Stamper, James	New Kent	Will	1868	CF1881-015
Stamps, William	Fauquier	Will	1772	CF1813-019
Stanard, Beverley	Spotsylvania	Will	1765c	V:Mss2 St2413 b
Stanard, Beverley	Spotsylvania	Inventory	1765c	V:Mss2 St2413 b
Stangle, John A.	Prince William	Will	1831	CF1841-001
Stangle, John A.	Prince William	Will	1831	CF1843-007
Stanhope, Lewis R.	Fairfax	Account	1837	X
Stanhope, Margaret A.	Fairfax	Guard. Acct.	1853	X
Stanley, Frances	Hanover	Will Ref.	(nd)	Cocke:128
Stansberry, Mary Jane, Cumberland Co.	Prince Edward	Will	1878	CF1893-045
Stanton, John	Dinwiddie	Will	1827	SV 1:1, p. 28
Stanton, John, in Dinwiddie Co.	Southampton	Will	1827	CF1827-032
Staples, David, in Amherst Co.	Lynchburg	Will	1861	CF1874-009
Staples, Samuel, in Patrick Co.	Roanoke	Will	1825	CF1845-006
Staples, Waller Redd	Montgomery	Will	1897	UVA MSS 1000
Stapp, Abraham	Essex	Will	1714	D&W14, p. 234
Starke, Flurry	Williamsburg	Will Abstract	1753	Fleet 2:330
Starke, Flurry, of King & Queen Co.	Williamsburg	Will Abstract	1753	Crozier, p. 53
Starke, Philemon	Williamsburg	Will Abstract	1756	Fleet 2:330
Starke, Philemon, of King & Queen Co.	Williamsburg	Will Abstract	1756	Crozier, p. 53
Starke, Robert B., in Norfolk	Brunswick	Will	1839	CF1884-027
Starke, William	Prince George	Will Ref.	1755	Hening, Vol. 8, p. 289
Starn, Jacob, in Hampshire Co.	Frederick	Will	1797	CF1823-265
Staton, John, in Adair Co. KY	Buckingham	Will	1820	LVA Acc. #32001

NAME	LOCATION	TYPE	YEAR	REFERENCE(S)
Staton, John, of Tillotson Parish	Buckingham	Will	1789	LVA Acc. #32001
Steagall, Thomas	Brunswick	Will	1820	CF1836-029
Stearns, Franklin, in Richmond	Henrico	Will	1888	CF1912-039
Steed, Juliana M., in NC	Alexandria	Will	1863	CF1882-023
Steele, David	Rockingham	Will	1841	CF1863-015
Steele, John, merchant		Will	1638	VCRP, Survey #03983
Steele, Mary	Rockingham	Will	1847	CF1863-015
Steenbergen, Elizabeth Peale	Shenandoah	Will	1842	V:Mss2 St325 a 1
Steenbergen, William, Shenandoah Co.	Fauquier	Will	1840	CF1866-055
Steger, Nancy Ashley, St. Louis Co. MO	Powhatan	Will	1844c	V:Mss1 N1786 a 6303+
Stegge, Thomas		Will	1652	VCRP, Survey #04104
Stegge, Thomas	Henrico	Will	1670	VMHB 48, p. 31
Stegge, Thomas, in Eng.	Henrico	Will	1671c	V:Mss5:9 B9965:1
Stegge, Thomas, of Henrico Co.	London	Will	1671	N:PROB11/336
Stegge, Thomas, of Henrico Co.		Will	1671	VCRP, Survey #03546
Steinback, Louisa, in Mecklenburg Co.	Brunswick	Will	1815	CF1832-037
Stephen, Alexander, of Frederick Co.		Will	1770	VCRP, Survey #04682
Stephen, Robert, in Berkeley Co.	Frederick	Will	1811	CF1816-075
Stephens, Alexander, of Frederick Co.	London	Will	1770	N:PROB11/958
Stephens, Anthony	Lancaster	Will	1663	LP
Stephens, Brian M., in Frederick Co.	Warren	Will	1847	CF1858-004
Stephens, Mary L., in DC	Richmond	Will	1897	CF1909-014
Stephens, Matthew	Warwick	Inventory	1697	Records 1695, p. 457
Stephens, Matthew, shipmaster	Warwick	Inventory	1696	TVF 3:4, p. 228
Stephens, Robert, in Berkeley Co.	Frederick	Will	1811	CF1828-150
Stephens, Thomas	Buckingham	Will	1802	VGSQ 14:3, p. 88
Stephens, Thomas	Buckingham	Will	1806	LVA Acc. #28193
Stepkin, Charles		Will	1689	VCRP, Survey #03746
Steptoe, Elizabeth, Westmoreland Co.	Williamsburg	Will Abstract	1802	Crozier, p. 55
Stern, David, of St. Mary's Parish	Caroline	Will	1797	TQ 30:4, p. 257
Stern, David [of *Hickory Grove*]	Caroline	Will	1797c	TQ 30:4, p. 256
Stern, Peyton, St. Mary's Parish	Caroline	Will	1800	TQ 30:4, p. 256
Sterne, David, of Sittingborne Parish	Rappahannock*	Will	1691	Sweeny, p. 149
Stevens, James	Halifax	Will	1795	V:Mss2 St478 b
Stevens, John	Caroline	Will	1753c	MVG 38:4, p. 295
Stevens, Mary	Mecklenburg	Will	1791	WB3, p. 76
Stevens, Mary B.	Hanover	Will	1848	BRCD
Stevens, Mary B.	Hanover	Will Abstract	1848	Cocke:128
Stevens, William, of Hampton	London	Will	1803	N:PROB11/1389
Stevenson, William	York	Will	1776	CF1785-008
Steward, Alexander		Will	1758	LVA Wills/Admin. DB
Steward, Anderson	Lunenburg	Will	1874	CF1876-022
Steward, Hannah	Surry	Will (U)	1768	VTG 13:2, p. 52
Steward, Hannah	Surry	Will (U)	1768	LVA:1048937
Steward, Michael	Henrico	Will	1719	Records, Vol. 2, p. 439
Steward, Nathaniel, in Culpeper Co.	Frederick	Will	1812	CF1816-034
Stewart, Brannum A.	Fairfax	Guard. Acct.	1852	X
Stewart, Caroline E.	Fairfax	Guard. Acct.	1852	X
Stewart, Charles	Dinwiddie	Will	1831	VGSQ 16, p. 258
Stewart, Charles	Fairfax	Division	1873	X
Stewart, Charles	Fairfax	Plat	1873	X

NAME	LOCATION	TYPE	YEAR	REFERENCE(S)
Stewart, Daniel	Hanover	Will	1866	CF1879-015
Stewart, Frances A.	Fairfax	Guard. Acct.	1852	X
Stewart, John [Cisly]	Fairfax	Dower	1801	X
Stewart, Richard	Surry	Will	1759	T: from account
Stewart, Thomas	Dinwiddie	Will	1810	VG 16, p. 255
Stewart, William	Fauquier	Will	(nd)	V:Mss2 H7847 b
Sthreshley, Thomas, of Caroline Co.	King & Queen	Will	1825	CF1868-003
Stiff, Thomas, of Middlesex Co.	Williamsburg	Will Abstract	1816	Crozier, p. 55
Stiles, John	Isle of Wight	Will Abstract	1652	VMHB 6, p. 250
Stinson, James, in Shenandoah Co.	Warren	Will	1831	CF1853-012
Stinson, James, Sr., in Shenandoah Co.	Warren	Will	(nd)	CF1850-003
Stith, Anderson	Charles City	Will Ref.	1764	VG 14, p. 181
Stith, Drury	Brunswick	Will	1789	CF1810-018
Stith, Elizabeth, of Southwark Parish	Surry	Will	1774	WMQ 5, p. 114
Stith, Griffin, of Northampton Co.	Williamsburg	Will Abstract	1799	Crozier, p. 54
Stith, John, in Westover Parish	Charles City	Will	1764	D&W1763, p. 313
Stith, John, Sr., of Westover Parish	Charles City	Will	1694	VGSQ 17:4, p. 131
Stith, John, Sr., of Westover Parish	Charles City	Will	1694	D&W1692, p. 185
Stith, Richard, in Campbell Co.	Bedford	Will	1802	CF1838-015
Stocker, A.J., in PA	Albemarle	Will	1866	CF1870-027
Stockton, William, in Bedford Co.	Lynchburg	Will	1795	CF1823-061
Stoddard, William, in MD	Prince William	Will	1885	CF1909-026
Stodghill, James	Essex	Will	1784	CF1802-012
Stokes, Allen	Lunenburg	Will	1787	CF1815-018
Stokes, Allen	Dinwiddie	Will	1821	V:Mss1 Ea765a234-239
Stokes, Colin, in Lunenburg Co.	Henrico	Will	1865	CF1898-024
Stokes, Henry	Henrico	Will	1766	WB3, p. 1
Stokes, Martha, in Dinwiddie Co.	Lunenburg	Will	1788	CF1796-007
Stokes, Richard		Will	1711	V:Mss1 B4678 a 4788
Stolpes, John, mariner		Will	1692	VCRP, Survey #03753
Stone, Ann, in Richmond Co.	Frederick	Will	1774	CF1817-126
Stone, Ann, in Richmond Co.	Frederick	Will	1774	CF1821-196
Stone, Caleb F.	Fairfax	Account	1852	X
Stone, Charles S., in Alexandria Co.	Fairfax	Will	1875	CF1878-024
Stone, Daniel, in Fluvanna Co.	Albemarle	Will	1854	CF1902-006
Stone, George W., in Culpeper Co.	Fauquier	Will	1877	CF1880-075
Stone, Mary, w/o Simon, Princess Anne	Williamsburg	Will Abstract	1819	Crozier, p. 54
Stone, Nancy	Fairfax	Will (U)	1864	X
Stone, Robert	Arlington	Inventory	1797	CRA:230
Stone, Thomas, of Henrico Co.	Cumberland	Will	1781	CF1790-011
Stone, William A., in Montgomery Co.	Floyd	Will	(nd)	CF1875-006
Stone, William A., in Franklin Co.	Floyd	Will	(nd)	CF1875-022
Stone, William, of Albemarle Co.	Cumberland	Will	1779	CF1801-009
Stone, William, of Fluvanna Co.	Cumberland	Will	1778	CF1790-011
Stone, William P.	Hanover	Will	1868	CF1882-032
Stonebanks, Thomas	Charles City	Inventory	1725	D&W1724, p. 57
Stonestreet, Bazil, in Loudoun Co.	Frederick	Will	1811	CF1826-095
Stonnell, Richard D.	Prince William	Will	1857	CF1896-021
Stonnell, Robert F.	Prince William	Will	1857	CF1885-014
Stookey, Jacob, in Hardy Co.	Frederick	Will	1802	CF1816-008
Storer, Priscilla C.	Fairfax	Will	1860	X

NAME	LOCATION	TYPE	YEAR	REFERENCE(S)
Storke, Elizabeth, in Westmoreland Co.	King George	Will	1879	CF1906-004
Storke, Henry D., in Westmoreland Co.	King George	Will	(nd)	CF1874-011
Storke, Henry D., in Westmoreland Co.	King George	Will	(nd)	CF1874-011
Storke, Nehemiah	Westmoreland	Will P.	1693	VMHB 38, p. 188
Storrs, Martha Trueheart	Henrico	Will	1860	V:Mss2 St7557 a 1
Story, John	King & Queen	Will Ref.	1717	KQB:2
Story, John	King & Queen	Will	1718c	V:Mss3 K5893 a 69-86
Story, John, of Stratton Major Parish	King & Queen	Will	1717	UVA MSS 3615-a
Story, Ralph, mariner		Will	1664	VCRP, Survey #06534
Story, Thomas, chirurgeon's mate		Will	1698	VCRP, Survey #06059
Stote, Sarah, in Lancaster Co.	Richmond	Will	1832	CF1855-005
Stott, Kealey	Charles City	Will	1788	TVF 12:3, p. 186
Stott, Kealey, of Charles City Co.	Northampton	Will	1788	CF1797-012
Stott, Oliver, in Richmond Co.	Northumberland	Will	1817	CF1827-003
Stott, Sarah F., in Lancaster Co.	Northumberland	Will	1832	CF1854-009
Stoutemyre, Jacob, of Rockingham Co.	Augusta	Will	1802	BCRD
Stoutenburgh, Seymour B.	Alexandria	Will	1892	CF1896-030
Stovall, Bartholomew	Henrico	Will	1721	Records, Vol. 2, p. 541
Stovall, John, in Granville Co. NC	Mecklenburg	Will	1820	CF1852-076
Stover, Christian, in Shenandoah Co.	Frederick	Will	1818	CF1835-091
Stover, Joseph, in Shenandoah Co.	Frederick	Will	1820	CF1826-040
Strang, John		Will	1718	V:Mss1 B4678 a 4788
Strange, John, in Campbell Co.	Lynchburg	Will	1815	CF1830-023
Stratford, Thomas		Will	1706	VCRP, Survey #03890
Stratton, Edward	Henrico	Will Abstract	1689	VGS Bulletin IV, p. 74
Stratton, Edward, Sr.	Henrico	Will	1689	D&W1688, p. 37
Stratton, Elizabeth, in Richmond	Powhatan	Will	1870	CF1881-004
Stratton, Henry, in Bedford Co.	Lynchburg	Will	1799	CF1819-009
Stratton, John		Will	1801	LVA Acc. #24194
Stratton, Martha, wid.	Henrico	Will Abstract	1695	VGS Bulletin IV, p. 74
Stratton, William, in Cumberland Co.	Powhatan	Will	1852	CF1875-015
Strayer, Adam, in Berkeley Co.	Frederick	Will	1818	CF1829-119
Strayer, Adam, in Berkeley Co.	Frederick	Will	1818	CF1827-106
Strayer, Adam, Jr., in Berkeley Co.	Frederick	Will	1818	CF1851-027
Street, Anthony	Hanover	Will	1842	CF1850-003
Street, Anthony	Hanover	Will	1844	Cocke:131
Street, Bailey, in Halifax Co.	Campbell	Will	1846	CF1876-009
Street, Charles P.	Hanover	Will	1843	CF1883-027
Street, Charles P.	Hanover	Will	1868	CF1881-002
Street, James H., in NC	Mecklenburg	Will	1856	CF1859-012 CC
Street, John	Hanover	Will	1801	CF1842-014
Street, John, of St. Paul's Parish	Hanover	Will	1801	Cocke:129
Street, Parke, in MS	Hanover	Will	1843	CF1881-002
Street, Parke, Jr.	Hanover	Will	1844	CF1883-027
Street, Robert	Stafford	Will P.	1692	OB:06 NOV 1692
Street, William	Henrico	Will	1776	Note[1]
Streshley, Thomas, in Caroline Co.	King & Queen	Will	1825	CF1868-003
Strickler, Daniel, in Shenandoah Co.	Frederick	Will	1807	CF1822-250

[1] Henrico County Proceedings of Commissoiners ..., 1774-1782, p. 15.

NAME	LOCATION	TYPE	YEAR	REFERENCE(S)
Strickler, Isaac, in Shenandoah Co.	Frederick	Will	1817	CF1831-146
Strickler, Joseph, in Shenandoah Co.	Frederick	Will	1795	CF1822-250
Strider, Christiana, in Jefferson Co.	Frederick	Will	1818	CF1827-228
Stringer, Hillary	Northampton	Will	1695	LVA Acc. #24194
Stringer, Hillary	Northampton	Will	1695	O&W13, p. 360
Stringer, Hillary	Northampton	Will	1744	W&I19, p. 129
Stringer, John	Elizabeth City	Will	1718	D&W1715, p. 120
Stringer, William	Surry	Inventory	1714	T:D&W6, p. 214
Stringfellow, Henry, of Bromfield Parish	Culpeper	Will	1815	TQ 27:1, p. 39
Stringfellow, James, in Fauquier Co.	Culpeper	Will	1847	CF1905-034
Strode, James, in Berkeley Co.	Frederick	Will	1795	CF1822-291
Stroder, James, in Berkeley Co.	Frederick	Will	1795	CF1823-270
Strong, Jane	Hanover	Will	1852	CF1861-020
Strong, Jane	Hanover	Will	1853	Cocke:133
Strong, Judith	Hanover	Will	1851	CF1861-020
Strong, Judith	Hanover	Will	1852	Cocke:133
Strother, George, in Fauquier Co.	Fairfax	Will	1879	CF1887-034
Strother, James, in Frederick Co.	Fauquier	Will	1829	CF1850-011
Strother, Mary	Fauquier	Will	1847	V:Mss1 P4686 c 1246+
Strutton, Peter	King William	Inventory	1702	RB2, p. 10
Stuart, Alexander	Frederick	Will	1758	MVG 29:3, p. 193
Stuart, C.C.	Fairfax	Account	1854	WB2:013
Stuart, C.C.	Fairfax	Account	1857	WB2:016
Stuart, Catharine, in King George Co.	Fauquier	Will	1805	CF1846-001
Stuart, Cornelia Lee	Fairfax	Will	1883	CF1891-030
Stuart, David	Henrico	Inventory	1737	Records, Vol. 3, p. 1057
Stuart, Henry, Sr.	Caroline	Will	1801	W&P1742, p. 62
Stuart, Isabella V.	Fairfax	Guard. Acct.	1860	WB2:065
Stuart, Jeb	Wythe	Will	1865	V:Mss2 St922 a 11
Stuart, Jeb	Wythe	Will	1865	V:Mss1 St923 d108-111
Stuart, John	King George	Will	1842c	V:Mss1 G7605a341-344
Stuart, John Alexander	King George	Will	1808	V:Mss1 G7605a341-344
Stuart, John, in King George Co.	Fauquier	Will	1843	CF1881-027
Stuart, Mary, in King George Co.	Fauquier	Will	1805	CF1846-001
Stuart, Sarah, in King George Co.	Fauquier	Will	1813	CF1846-001
Stubblefield, Mary, of Gloucester Co.	Williamsburg	Will Abstract	1823	Crozier, p. 56
Stubblefield, Thomas, of Gloucester Co.	Williamsburg	Will Abstract	1823	Crozier, p. 56
Stubbs, John, of Petsworth Parish	Gloucester	Will	1760	LVA Acc. #24235
Stump, John [Cassandra]	Fairfax	Dower	1817	X
Stump, John [Cassandra]	Fairfax	Dower	1830	X
Stump, Peter, in Hampshire Co.	Frederick	Will	1815	CF1827-103
Sturdevant, Joel, mariner	Prince George	Will	1777	Fleet, Huntington Data
Sturdevant, John, Sr., of Pr. Geo. Co.	Petersburg	Will	1820	CF1834-022
Sturdey, William, of Stafford Co.		Will	1715	VCRP, Survey #04365
Sturdivant, Joel	Prince George	Will	1777	LVA Acc. #28517
Sturdivant, Joel	Prince George	Will	1777	LVA Acc. #41008, r4612
Sturdivant, Joel	Dinwiddie	Will	1841	CF1873-013
Sturdivant, Joel, mariner	Prince George	Will	1777	LVA Acc. #28517
Sturdivant, John	Prince George	Will	1795	LVA Acc. #28009
Sturdivant, John	Prince George	Will	1795	Fleet, Huntington Data
Sturdivant, John	Prince George	Will	1795	LVA Acc. #28517

NAME	LOCATION	TYPE	YEAR	REFERENCE(S)
Sturdivant, John, Jr.	Prince George	Will	1795	LVA Acc. #41008, r4612
Sturdivant, John, Sr.	Prince George	Will	1793	LVA Acc. #28517
Sturdivant, John, Sr.	Prince George	Will	1793	LVA Acc. #41008, r4612
Sturdivant, John, Sr.	Prince George	Will	1820	BRCD
Sturdivant, John, Sr., in Bristol Parish	Prince George	Will	1793	LVA Acc. #28517
Sturdivant, John, Sr., of Bristol Parish	Prince George	Will	1793	Fleet, Huntington Data
Sturdivant, John, Sr., Prince George Co.	Petersburg	Will	1820	CF1849-031
Sturdivant, Richard	Prince George	Will	1850	SV 9:4, p. 158
Sturdivant, William, in Bath Parish	Dinwiddie	Will	1769	Note[1]
Sturdy, William, of Stafford Co.	London	Will	1715	N:PROB11/546
Sturman, Elliott	Essex	Will	1792	V:Mss2 St973 a 1
Sturman, Richard, of Westm. Co.		Will	1672	VCRP, Survey #03549
Sturton, Samuel, shipwright		Will	1699	VCRP, Survey #06064
Sublett, Abram	Chesterfield	Will	1820	Fleet, Huntington Data
Sublett, Edith, wid/o Abram	Chesterfield	Will	1828	Fleet, Huntington Data
Sublett, T.C., in Roanoke Co.	Franklin	Will	1896	CF1912-002
Sublette, Abraham	Chesterfield	Will	1820	VMHB 69, p. 62
Suggitt, John, of Northampton Co.		Will	1771	VCRP, Survey #04690
Suggitt, John, planter	Rappahannock*	Will	1690	Sweeny, p. 145
Sullivan, Daniel	Nansemond	Estate Ref.	1744	Hening, Vol. 5, p. 243
Sullivan, Daniel, in Norfolk Co.	Portsmouth	Will	1843	CF1872-023
Sullivan, George, Montgomery Co. OH	Lynchburg	Will	1825	CF1829-046
Sullivan, Murtho, in Loudoun Co.	Frederick	Will	1814	CF1830-041
Sullivan, Murtho, of Loudoun Co.	D.C.	Will	1886	DCA:Box 100
Sullivan, Timothy	Arlington	Inventory	1798	CRA:255
Summer, Andrew, in MD	Rockingham	Will	1851	CF1895-006
Summer, Jacob, in MD	Rockingham	Will	1886	CF1895-006
Summer, Magdalena, in MD	Rockingham	Will	1880	CF1895-006
Summerell, Henry, of Southampton Co.	Williamsburg	Will Abstract	1801	Crozier, p. 54
Summers, George, Col.	Fairfax	Sale	1806	X
Summers, William, of Alexandria	Fairfax	Will	1797	X
Summerson, George		Estate Ref.	1792	Note[2]
Sumner, Ezekiah, in Montgomery Co.	Floyd	Will	(nd)	CF1840-004
Supinger, John, in Shenandoah Co.	Frederick	Will	1804	CF1833-100
Sutherland, Aeneas, surgeon		Will	1721	VCRP, Survey #04664
Sutherlin, James, in Pittsylvania Co.	Lynchburg	Will	1812	CF1828-003
Sutton, James [of Chesterfield]	Caroline	Will	1795	W&P1742, p. 55
Sutton, John C.	Caroline	Will	1847	W&D1794, p. 51
Sutton, Moses	Northumberland	Will	1796	CF1812-020
Sutton, Richard G.	Hanover	Will	1891	CF1906-007
Sutton, Robbie Magruder	Hanover	Will	1895	CF1906-007
Sutton, Rowland	Williamsburg	Will Abstract	1782	Fleet 2:345
Sutton, Rowland, of Middlesex Co.	Williamsburg	Will Abstract	1782	Crozier, p. 55
Sutton, Stephen C.	King William	Will	1864	LVA Acc. #31280
Sutton, William [of Chesterfield]	Caroline	Will	1797	W&P1742, p. 57
Swan, Thomas	Northumberland	Will Ref.	1668	OB3, p. 26
Swan, Thomas	King William	Will Ref.	1704	VMHB 24, p. 391

---

[1] LVA, Land Office Military Certificates, Capt. Joel Sturdivant, Certificate #8164.
[2] LVA, Land Office Revolutionary War Military Certificate Papers, George Summerson, Folder 23.

NAME	LOCATION	TYPE	YEAR	REFERENCE(S)
Swan, Thomas, of St. John's Parish	King William	Will	1704	RB2, p. 40
Swartz, William	Rockingham	Will	1864	CF1889-009
Swearingen, Benoni, in MD	Frederick	Will	1798	CF1827-159
Swearingen, Thomas, in Berkeley Co.	Frederick	Will	1811	CF1819-078
Sweeney, George William	Fairfax	Guard. Acct.	1848	X
Sweeney, Martin, in Henrico Co.	New Kent	Will	1871	CF1879-001
Sweeney, Sarah E.	Fairfax	Guard. Acct.	1848	X
Sweeny, Moses, Sr.	Buckingham	Will	1833	SV 5:1, p. 5
Sweeny, Moses, Sr.	Buckingham	Will	1833	Election[1]
Swillevant, Daniel	Northumberland	Will	1704	RB1743, p. 266b
Swink, Francis Ann	Fairfax	Guard. Bond	1842	X
Swink, John William	Fairfax	Guard. Bond	1842	X
Swink, Josephine	Fairfax	Guard. Bond	1842	X
Swinton, George		Will	1798	LVA Wills/Admin. DB
Swinton, George, of King & Queen Co.	Caroline	Will	1789	Fleet 2:254
Swinton, James, of Richmond	Henrico	Will	1803	Fleet, Huntington Data
Sword, John, in Loudoun Co.	Arlington	Will	1814	CF1820-002
Sybrantyson, Gabriel, mariner		Will	1744	VCRP, Survey #04627
Sydnor, Ann, of Hanover Co.	Augusta	Will	1817	CF1841-036
Sydnor, Anthony	Northumberland	Will	1779	CF1809-021
Sydnor, Edward	Hanover	Will	1865	CF1879-013
Sydnor, Elizabeth	Nottoway	Will	1843	BRCD
Sydnor, Elizabeth, in Nottoway Co.	Lunenburg	Will	1815	CF1840-010
Sydnor, Fortunatus	Northumberland	Will	1781	CF1809-021
Sydnor, Sarah E.	Hanover	Will	1895	CF1905-002
Sydnor, William	Lancaster	Will	1794	UVA MSS 6405
Sydnor, William		Estate Ref.	1795	Shepherd, Vol. 1, p. 420
Sydnor, William	Nottoway	Will	1819	LVA Acc. #20861
Sydnor, William B.	Hanover	Will	1862	CF1886-020
Syme, John	Hanover	Will	1739	Note[2]
Syme, Martha H.	Hanover	Will	1824	G2:77
Symes, Benjamin	Elizabeth City	Will, 1634	1715	LP:18 DEC 1830
Symes, Benjamin	Elizabeth City	Will, 1634	1715	WMQ2 20, p. 21

---

[1] LVA, Contested Election Papers, Buckingham County, 1840/41.

[2] See Louisa County Deeds, Bk. A, p. 374; Goochland County Deeds, Bk. 5, p. 185.

NAME	LOCATION	TYPE	YEAR	REFERENCE(S)

T

NAME	LOCATION	TYPE	YEAR	REFERENCE(S)
Tabb, Elizabeth B., in AL	Mecklenburg	Will	1836	CF1840-002
Tabb, Evelina Mary	Gloucester	Will	1862	CF1884-013
Tabb, Evelina Mary	Gloucester	Will	1862	LVA Acc. #28458
Tabb, Henry Wythe, Dr.	Mathews	Will	1864c	V:Mss1 T5996 c 355+
Tabb, John, Col.	Elizabeth City	Will	1762	D&W1758, p. 309
Tabb, John, of *White Marsh*	Gloucester	Will	1859	TVF 6:4, p. 232
Tabb, John, Sr.	James City	Will	(nd)	CF1876-009
Tabb, Thomas, in NC	Norfolk	Will	1834	CF1856-003
Tabb, William, of Gloucester Co.	Augusta	Will	1765	CF1810-135
Taber, Evan	Henrico	Inventory	1713	Records, Vol. 1, p. 221
Taberner, Joshua	Isle of Wight	Will	1656	VMHB 6, p. 117
Taff, Thomas	Middlesex	Will	1786	WB 1675, p. 503
Tait, Bacon	Richmond City	Will	1871	Fleet, Huntington Data
Taite, Anne	Northumberland	Will	1777	Note[1]
Talbert, Thomas	Fairfax	Will	1852	NVG 8, p. 1098
Talbott, Edward, in MD	Frederick	Will	1778	CF1798-001
Talbott, Edward, in MD	Frederick	Will	1793	CF1804-024
Talbott, Henry	Westmoreland	Will	1671	DB1665, p. 117a
Talbott, Thomas	Fairfax	Account	1859	WB2:039
Talbott, Thomas	Fairfax	Sale	1859	WB2:037
Talbott, William Smith	Fairfax	Will	1816	X
Taliaferro, Benjamin	James City	Will	1801	LVA Acc. #24194
Taliaferro, Charles	Caroline	Will	1735c	V:Mss1 G8855 b 121+
Taliaferro, Charles, in St. Mary's Parish	Caroline	Will	1735	LVA Wills/Admin. DB
Taliaferro, Frances	Hanover	Will	1860	CF1880-008
Taliaferro, Frances G.	Hanover	Will	1859	CF1865-001
Taliaferro, Frances G.	Hanover	Will	1860	Cocke:136
Taliaferro, John	Essex	Will	1744	UVA MSS 38-418
Taliaferro, John	Spotsylvania	Will	1744	V:Mss1 G8855 a 305+
Taliaferro, John	Spotsylvania	Will	1805	V:Mss1 G8855 a 305+
Taliaferro, Lawrence	Essex	Will	1726	VMHB 12, p. 104
Taliaferro, Louisa G., in Caroline Co.	Fauquier	Will	1844	CF1880-045
Taliaferro, Rebecca	James City	Will	1810	LVA John K. Martin Papers
Taliaferro, Richard	James City	Will	1779	WMQ 12, p. 124
Taliaferro, Richard	James City	Will	1791	LVA John K. Martin Papers
Taliaferro, Richard	James City	Will	1792	LVA Tazewell Papers
Taliaferro, Richard, of James City Co.	Williamsburg	Will Abstract	1779	Crozier, p. 57
Taliaferro, Robert	James City	Will	1789	LVA Acc. #24194-26
Taliaferro, William	King & Queen	Will	1760	V:Mss2 T1437 a 1
Taliaferro, William	King & Queen	Will	1760	LVA Acc. #24477
Taliaferro, William	King & Queen	Will	1760	V:Mss3 K5893 a 69-86
Taliaferro, William, at *Hockly*	King & Queen	Will	1805	MVG 46:1, p. 231
Talley, Charles, Sr., in Hanover Co.	Henrico	Will	1823	CF1848-013
Talley, Didbral	Hanover	Will Ref.	(nd)	Cocke:137
Talley, Henry	Hanover	Will	1842	CF1874-019
Talley, Henry	Hanover	Will	1842	Cocke:138
Tally, John, of Prince George Co.	Amelia	Will	1740	WB1, p. 10

---

[1] Northumberland County District Court Orders, Deeds, [Wills], 1789-1825, p. 325.

NAME	LOCATION	TYPE	YEAR	REFERENCE(S)
Tankard, Charity	Isle of Wight	Will Ref.	1821	LVA Acc. #21400
Tann, Jacob	Surry	Will	1781	T: correct from Fann
Tanner, Christopher	Madison	Will	1797	CF1818-001
Tanner, Edward	Henrico	Will	1719	Records, Vol. 2, p. 443
Tantel, William	York	Will	1677	DWO6, p. 24
Tapscot, Edney	Lancaster	Will	1782	T: not Northumberland
Tapscot, Henry	Lancaster	Will	1781	T: not Northumberland
Tapscott, Martin	Westmoreland	Will	1805	Note[1]
Tapscott, Martin, in Westmoreland Co.	Albemarle	Will	1805	CF1893-069
Tapscott, Martin, of Westmoreland Co.	Augusta	Will	1805	CF1819-100
Tarent, Leonard	Essex	Will	1718	M: L14 f487
Tarpley, Elizabeth Ripping, of W'burg.	James City	Will Ref.	1722	VGSQ 49:3, p. 241
Tarpley, Travers	Richmond	Will	1768	WB7, p. 11
Tarry, Samuel, of Amelia Co.	London	Will	1768	N:PROB11/944
Tarry, Samuel, of Amelia Co.		Will	1768	VCRP, Survey #04697
Tate, J. William, in Washington Co.	Smyth	Will	1830	CF1859-003
Tate, Jesse, in Bedford Co.	Lynchburg	Will	1805	CF1815-013
Tate, Jesse, in Bedford Co.	Lynchburg	Will	1805	CF1871-001
Tate, Mitchell B., in Smyth Co.	Lynchburg	Will	1892	CF1894-069
Tate, Thomas M., in Smyth Co.	Fauquier	Will	1872	CF1894-061
Tate, William, in Jefferson Co.	Frederick	Will	1818	CF1821-233
Tatem, James, in Norfolk Co.	Portsmouth	Will	1845	CF1889-002
Tatem, James, of Chesapeake	Norfolk	Will	1821	LVA Acc. #44102
Tatem, Nathaniel P., in Norfolk Co.	Portsmouth	Will	1836	CF1877-025
Tatem, Stephen B., in Norfolk Co.	Portsmouth	Will	1872	CF1890-017
Tatum, Henry Augustus	Richmond City	Will	1862	V:Mss2 T1892 a 1
Tatum, Josiah, in Chesterfield Co.	Powhatan	Will	1797	CF1846-006
Tatum, Robert	Prince George	Will	1759	DB1759, p. 118
Tatum, Robert	Prince George	Inventory	1759	DB1759, p. 131
Taurman, William, of Botetourt Co.	Goochland	Will	1842	CF1859-021
Tavernor, Robert, merchant		Will	1677	VCRP, Survey #03563
Tayler, John	Surry	Will	1687	T:D&W4, p. 8a
Tayler, Walter	Surry	Will	1689	T:D&W4, p. 105b
Tayloe, John	Richmond	Will	1747	V:Mss1 T2118 d 149
Tayloe, John	Richmond	Will	1779	V:Mss1 T2118 d 166
Tayloe, John, of *Mt. Airy*, in DC	Richmond	Will	1828	V:Mss1 T2118 d 539+
Tayloe, Joseph	Lancaster	Will	1716	LP
Tayloe, William	Lancaster	Will	1770	LP
Tayloe, William	Lancaster	Will	1770	V:Mss1 T2118 d27684+
Tayloe, William Henry	Richmond	Will	1869	V:Mss1 T2118 d 8683
Taylor, Abraham	Greene	Will	1882	V:Mss2 F6355 c 32-38
Taylor, Alsop, in Bedford Co.	Lynchburg	Will	1814	CF1855-005
Taylor, Amey	Williamsburg	Will	1797	LP:21 DEC 1809
Taylor, Ann, in Norfolk	Portsmouth	Will	1854	CF1901-020
Taylor, Archibald	Buckingham	Will	1833	MVG 24:1, p. 84
Taylor, Archibald, d. 5 APR 1833	Gloucester	Will	1833	Note[2]
Taylor, Archibald, of Buckingham Co.	Gloucester	Will	1833	LVA Fielding Lewis Papers

---

[1] Northumberland County District Court Orders, Deeds, Wills, 1789-1825, p. 396.

[2] LVA Microfilm, Miscellaneous Reel #547, Weyanoke Plantation records, Folder 29.

NAME	LOCATION	TYPE	YEAR	REFERENCE(S)
Taylor, Argale	Northumberland	Will	1758	CF1789-006
Taylor, Charles C., in Smyth Co.	Tazewell	Will	1881	CF1888-006
Taylor, Chastain	Hanover	Will	1885	CF1888-028
Taylor, Dareas	Henrico	Inventory	1741	Records, Vol. 4, p. 1143
Taylor, Edmund	Hanover	Will	1822	CF1886-034
Taylor, Edmund	Hanover	Will	1822	Weisiger 1:001[1]
Taylor, Edmund	James City	Will	1828	BRCD
Taylor, Edmund, Sr., in James City Co.	York	Will	1828	CF1837-002
Taylor, Edwin Wharton	Accomack	Will	1888	LVA Acc. #28954
Taylor, Elizabeth	Nottoway	Will	1815	BRCD
Taylor, Ethelred	Surry	Will	1716	TQ 24:3, p. 230
Taylor, Francis	King & Queen	Will	1774	BRCD
Taylor, George	Louisa	Will	1782	Note[2]
Taylor, Henry		Will	1756	VCRP, Survey #04673
Taylor, Henry H.	New Kent	Will	1847	Swem(1):f222
Taylor, James	Surry	Account	1655	T: not Inventory
Taylor, James	James City	Will	1831	LVA Acc. #24601c
Taylor, James, in TN	Albemarle	Will	1833	CF1846-026
Taylor, John	Prince George	Will	1707	V:Mss2 F6692 b
Taylor, John	Fairfax	Exor. Bond	1748	X
Taylor, John	Northumberland	Will Abstract	1751	VMHB 47, p. 83
Taylor, John	Southampton	Will Abstract	1806	VMHB 23, p. 324
Taylor, John	Caroline	Will	1853	Note[3]
Taylor, John, in Berkeley Co.	Frederick	Will	(nd)	CF1814-030
Taylor, John, in Berkeley Co.	Frederick	Will	1792	CF1818-162
Taylor, Joseph	Essex	Will	1769	Fleet 2:340
Taylor, Joseph	Northumberland	Will Abstract	1778	VMHB 47, p. 83
Taylor, Joseph Chalkley, in Norfolk Co.	Portsmouth	Will	1896	CF1900-006
Taylor, Joseph, in Fauquier Co.	Culpeper	Will	1806	CF1837-002
Taylor, Josiah, in Chesterfield Co.	Powhatan	Will	1840	CF1851-009
Taylor, Letitia H., w/o Archibald	Henrico	Will	1832	VGSQ 18:3, p. 84
Taylor, Mathew	Henrico	Will	1748	Records, Vol. 5, p. 1467
Taylor, Nancy, in Clarke Co.	Frederick	Will	1867	CF1881-001
Taylor, Richard	Lancaster	Will Abstract	1774	VMHB 47, p. 82
Taylor, Richard	James City	Will	1788	Note[4]
Taylor, Richard	Stafford	Will	1808	MVG 26:2, p. 101
Taylor, Richard B.	New Kent	Will	1858	LVA Acc. #41008, r4611
Taylor, Richard B.	New Kent	Will	1858	Fleet, Huntington Data
Taylor, Richard B.	New Kent	Will	1872	CF1884-011
Taylor, Richard, of James City Co.	Nansemond	Will	1788	LP:18 JAN 1832
Taylor, Richard, of Norfolk	D.C.	Will	1881	DCA:Box 77
Taylor, Richard, of Prince George Co.	Williamsburg	Will Abstract	1801	Crozier, p. 58
Taylor, Robert	Lancaster	Will	1662	LP
Taylor, Robert I., in DC	Fauquier	Will	1840	CF1871-096
Taylor, Robert P.	James City	Will	1866	CF1879-017

---

[1] Weisiger, Benjamin B. III, *Burned County Data, 1809-1848, as Found in the Virginia Contested Election Files* (Athens, Ga.: Iberian Publishing Co., 1986).

[2] Louisa County Wills Not Fully Proved, 1757-1902, p. 44.

[3] Caroline County Land Causes, 1835-1913, Vol. 1, p. 121.

[4] Military Certificates from the Virginia Land Office, 1782-1876, file 5921, Richard Taylor; Reel 33 frame 964.

NAME	LOCATION	TYPE	YEAR	REFERENCE(S)
Taylor, Sally, in Smyth Co.	Russell	Will	1840	CF1877-033
Taylor, Samuel, in Clarke Co.	Frederick	Will	1845	CF1858-016
Taylor, Sarah	Richmond City	Will	1792	T:HCD1, p. 606
Taylor, Sarah, in Middlesex Co. MA	Arlington	Will	1843	CF1852-004
Taylor, Thomas	Henrico	Will	1724	Records, Vol. 2, p. 454
Taylor, Thomas	James City	Will	1831	LVA Acc. #24601c
Taylor, Thomas	James City	Will	1831	LVA Acc. #24601
Taylor, Thomas	Accomack	Will	1851	LVA Acc. #28954
Taylor, Thoroughgood, in Lancaster Co.	Fauquier	Will	1874	CF1899-011
Taylor, William	Accomack	Will	1686	LVA Acc. #28954
Taylor, William	Charles City	Will (N)	1693	D&W1692, p. 153
Taylor, William	Essex	Will Abstract	1756	Fleet 2:330
Taylor, William	Augusta	Will	1768	WB4, p. 84
Taylor, William	King & Queen	Will	1846	CF1863-004
Taylor, William, of Overwharton Parish	Stafford	Will	1789	TQ 25:2, p. 131
Tazewell, Henry	James City	Will	1799	LVA Acc. #24194-26
Tazewell, John	Williamsburg	Inventory	1782	LVA Acc. #24194
Tazewell, Littleton	Williamsburg	Will	1815	Swem(1):f146
Teas, William, in Augusta Co.	Lynchburg	Will	1778	CF1833-031
Tee, William, in Norfolk Co.	Portsmouth	Will	1849	CF1872-014
Telcourt, Christian	Rockingham	Estate Ref.	1823	LP:07 JAN 1846
Telford, Alexander	Rockbridge	Will	1790	Swem
Temple, Allen	Prince George	Will	1839	SV 9:2, p. 55
Temple, Ann	King William	Will	1781	WMQ 13, p. 140
Temple, Ann	King William	Will	1781	V:Mss1 T2478 b 30-32
Temple, Benjamin	King William	Will	1802	V:Mss1 T2478 b 33-42
Temple, Benjamin	King William	Admin.	1802c	V:Mss1 T2478 b 33-42
Temple, Benjamin	Spotsylvania	Will	1852	V:Mss1 T2478 a 45
Temple, Benjamin	Middlesex	Will	1872	V:Mss1 T2478 a
Temple, Benjamin, in King William Co.	Frederick	Will	1802	CF1815-045
Temple, Elizabeth Skyren, w/o Robert	Richmond City	Will	1862	V:Mss1 H2485 a 444+
Temple, Elizabeth Skyren, w/o Robert	Richmond City	Inventory	1867	V:Mss1 H2485 a 444+
Temple, Joseph, of King William Co.	London	Will	1762	N:PROB11/872
Temple, Peter, in Richmond Co.	Essex	Will	1808	CF1832-020
Temple, Robert, of *Ampthill*	Chesterfield	Inventory	1837	V:Mss1 H2485 a 332+
Temple, Robert, of *Ampthill*	Chesterfield	Will	1837	V:Mss1 H2485 a 332+
Temple, William	King & Queen	Will	1835c	V:Mss3 K5893 a 69-86
Temple, William A.	Prince George	Will	1853	BRCD
Temple, William A., Prince George Co.	Petersburg	Will	1853	CF1871-042
Temple, William, of King William Co.		Will	1767	VCRP, Survey #04694
Tenant, James, of Princess Anne Co.	London	Will	1727	N:PROB11/634
Tench, Robert C., in Prince George Co.	Petersburg	Will	1833	CF1835-015
Tenent, James, Rev., Pr. Anne Co.		Will	1729	VCRP, Survey #04372
Tenniss, Aaron, of York Co.	Williamsburg	Will Abstract	1813	Crozier, p. 57
Terrell, Ann, in Albemarle Co.	Hanover	Will	1844	MVG 31:4, p. 347
Terrell, David		Will Abstract	1759	WMQ 18, p. 106
Terrell, David		Will	1759	Note[1]
Terrell, David, in Campbell Co.	Lynchburg	Will	1806	CF1816-014

---

[1] Celeste Jane Terrell Barnhill, *William Richmond and Timothy Terrell, Colonial Virginians* (Greenfield, Ind.: The Mitchell Co., 1934).

NAME	LOCATION	TYPE	YEAR	REFERENCE(S)
Terrell, Elizabeth	Hanover	Will	1832	LCH 5:2, p. 7
Terrell, Henry		Will	1760	LVA Wills/Admin. DB
Terrell, James	Cumberland	Will	1766	LP, box 40
Terrell, John, orphans of	Hanover	Guard.	1841	Cocke:139
Terrell, Samuel	Caroline	Will	1842	LVA Acc. #22467
Terrill, James	Caroline	Will	1766	TVF 11:1, p. 21
Terrill, James	Caroline	Will	1766	LVA Acc. #27899
Terrill, James, of Caroline Co.	Cumberland	Will	1766	LP 1760-1850
Terrill, James, planter	Caroline	Will	1766	MVG 33:3, p. 231
Terrill, Robert, of St. Thomas Parish	Orange	Will	1786	VMHB 31, p. 175
Terry, Joseph, in Pittsylvania Co.	Lynchburg	Will	1815	CF1817-020
Terry, Thomas, in Fluvanna Co.	Louisa	Will	1804	CF1817-004
Tevebough, Daniel, in Hardy Co.	Frederick	Will	1801	CF1830-269
Thacker, Edwin	Middlesex	Estate Ref.	1745	Hening, Vol. 7, p. 343
Thacker, Edwin	Middlesex	Estate Ref.	1745	Hening, Vol. 6, p. 314
Thacker, Louisa A.	Hanover	Will	1841	VGS Bulletin VII, p. 69
Thacker, Louisa A.	Hanover	Will	1841	VGS Bulletin VII, p. 69
Thacker, Louisa A.	Hanover	Will	1841	LVA Acc. #24677a
Thacker, Samuel		Will	1712	VMHB 18, p. 329
Thatcher, Thomas	King George	Will	1750	WBA1, p. 253
Thatcher, Thomas	King George	Will	1750	TQ 18, p. 234
Thatcher, Thomas	King George	Will	1751	TQ 18:4, p. 234
Thilman, Paul	Hanover	Estate Ref.	1791	LP:03 NOV 1791
Thom, William	Fairfax	Will	1773c	PGM 29, p. 62
Thomas, Addison N.	Prince William	Will	1871	CF1891-015
Thomas, Amelia	Fairfax	Will	1845	X
Thomas, Anna	Dinwiddie	Will	1860	VGSQ 10:1, p. 12
Thomas, Catlett	Caroline	Will	1849	W&D1794, p. 56
Thomas, Charles	Nansemond	Will	1787	Note[1]
Thomas, David	King William	Inventory	1703	RB1, p. 190
Thomas, Frederick, of St. Paul's Parish	Henrico	Will	1809	VGSQ 18:3, p. 85
Thomas, George, in Prince William Co.	Fauquier	Will	1781	CF1815-037
Thomas, Jacob	Halifax	Will	1849	V:Mss1 B6638 a2812+
Thomas, James	Essex	Will	1845	LP ur
Thomas, James, Sr.	Caroline	Will	1853	Note[2]
Thomas, Meziah	Fairfax	Inventory	1859	WB2:059
Thomas, Meziah	Fairfax	Admin. Bond	1859	WB2:038
Thomas, Meziah	Fairfax	Sale	1860	WB2:062
Thomas, Robert	Fairfax	Exor. Bond	1769	X
Thomas, Thomas, of Buckingham Co.	Albemarle	Will	1802	CF1839-014
Thomas, William		Will	1660	VCRP, Survey #03526
Thomas, William	Lancaster	Will	1667	LP
Thomas, William	Southampton	Will	1794	LVA Acc. #27394
Thomas, William ap	Elizabeth City	Will	1679	TQ 22:4, p. 229
Thomas, William ap	Elizabeth City	Will Partial	1679	LVA Acc. #23316
Thomasson, William	Louisa	Will	1793	Note[3]

---

[1] LVA, Revolutionary War Bounty Warrants, Charles Thomas, Folder 8.
[2] Caroline County Land Causes, 1835-1913, Vol. 1, p. 116.
[3] Louisa County Wills Not Fully Proved, 1757-1902, p. 46.

NAME	LOCATION	TYPE	YEAR	REFERENCE(S)
Thompson, A., in Loudoun Co.	Frederick	Will	1805	CF1821-197
Thompson, Amos, in CT	Frederick	Will	1787	CF1821-197
Thompson, Anderson, in Bedford Co.	Lynchburg	Will	1835	CF1857-003
Thompson, Cornelia, in Berkeley Co.	Frederick	Will	1815	CF1828-133
Thompson, Cornelius, in Berkeley Co.	Frederick	Will	1815	CF1822-240
Thompson, Garland, in Culpeper Co.	Louisa	Will	1808	CF1849-013
Thompson, Garland, in Culpeper Co.	Louisa	Will	1827	CF1849-013
Thompson, Garland, in Culpeper Co.	Louisa	Will	1844	CF1849-014
Thompson, Henry	Stafford	Will	1691	Note[1]
Thompson, Henry, Gent.	Stafford	Will	1691	TQ 21, p. 57
Thompson, James	Charles City	Inventory	1689	D&W1689, p. 90
Thompson, James	Charles City	Inventory	1773	Note[2]
Thompson, James P., in Wash. Co.	Tazewell	Will	1813	CF1838-004
Thompson, James P., in Wash. Co.	Tazewell	Will	1814	CF1845-015
Thompson, Jane, in Loudoun Co.	Frederick	Will	1807	CF1821-197
Thompson, Jane, in Loudoun Co.	Frederick	Will	1807	CF1820-174
Thompson, John	Campbell	Will	1792	Fleet, Huntington Data
Thompson, John	Campbell	Will	1792	LVA Acc. #41008, r4608
Thompson, John, in Berkeley Co.	Frederick	Will	1818	CF1831-184
Thompson, John, in Botetourt Co.	Lynchburg	Will	1822	CF1826-066
Thompson, John, in Cumberland Co.	Lunenburg	Will	1785	CF1833-042
Thompson, John, of Surry Co.		Will	1699	VCRP, Survey #04786
Thompson, Julia, in James City Co.	Louisa	Will	1875	CF1898-020
Thompson, Margaret	Westmoreland	Will	1790	Note[3]
Thompson, Phillip Montague	James City	Will	1893	CF1900-011
Thompson, Rebecca, in Nelson Co.	Albemarle	Will	1872	CF1879-009
Thompson, Robert T.	Fairfax	Will (U)	1866	X
Thompson, Roger		Estate Ref.	1790	Hening, Vol. 13, p. 224
Thompson, Thomas, Sr., in Franklin Co.	Bedford	Will	1833	CF1849-001
Thompson, William	Norfolk	Will Ref.	1685	Hening, Vol. 6, p. 446
Thompson, William, in PA	Frederick	Will	1815	CF1835-095
Thomson, David		Will	1749	VCRP, Survey #04637
Thomson, George, mariner		Will	1706	VCRP, Survey #03895
Thomson, John	Hanover	Will	1759	LVA Acc. #30723
Thomson, John, in Hanover Co.	Louisa	Will	1759	CF1819-018
Thomson, John, of St. Paul's Parish	Hanover	Will	1759	MVG 31:4, p. 346
Thomson, John, of St. Paul's Parish	Hanover	Will, 1759	1807	G2:80
Thomson, Mary		Will	1706	Mason
Thomson, Samuel		Will	1694	VCRP, Survey #04713
Thomson, Stephen	Rappahannock*	Will Ref.	1686	Sweeny, p. 5
Thomson, William		Will	1739	Mason
Thornberry, Samuel	Fauquier	Will	1797	CF1830-147
Thornhill, Absolem	Buckingham	Will	1834	VMHB 48, p. 172
Thornhill, Elizabeth, w/o Jesse	Campbell	Will	1842	VMHB 48, p. 168
Thornhill, Jesse	Campbell	Will	1837	VMHB 48, p. 72
Thornhill, Sarah	Buckingham	Will	1843	VMHB 48, p. 173

---

[1] Prince William County Land Causes, 1789-1793, p. 49.

[2] LVA, Charles City County Records, 1766-1774, p. 474.

[3] Westmoreland County Wills, 1755-1800, reel 28a, #36.

NAME	LOCATION	TYPE	YEAR	REFERENCE(S)
Thornley, William [of *Hampstead*]	Caroline	Will	1837	W&D1794, p. 38
Thornley, Winnifred, in Caroline Co.	Louisa	Will	1842	CF1845-025
Thornton, Anthony	Stafford	Will	1757	V:Mss1 T2118 d27684+
Thornton, Anthony	Stafford	Will	1757	VGSQ 10:4, p. 98
Thornton, Anthony	Stafford	Will	1757	DB1748, p. 331
Thornton, Anthony	Hanover	Will	1822	CF1849-001
Thornton, Anthony	Hanover	Will	1822	Cocke:144
Thornton, Boswell	Fredericksburg	Will	1799	DCWA, p. 134
Thornton, Francis	Spotsylvania	Will	1795	V:Mss1 G8368 a 1-2
Thornton, John	King George	Will	1800c	V:Mss1 H2463 e
Thornton, John	Hanover	Will	1822	CF1842-019
Thornton, John	Hanover	Will	1822	CF1849-001
Thornton, John	Hanover	Will	1829	CF1849-001
Thornton, John A., in Culpeper Co.	Rappahannock	Will	1818	CF1844-007
Thornton, John, Jr.	Hanover	Will	1829	Cocke:143
Thornton, John, Sr.	Hanover	Will	1822	Cocke:142
Thornton, John [of *Fox Springs*]	Caroline	Estate Ref.	1778	Hening, Vol. 9, p. 573
Thornton, Peter Presley	Northumberland	Inventory	1781	T: correct from Presley
Thornton, Reuben	Caroline	Will Abstract	(nd)	VMHB 43, p. 252
Thornton, Reuben		Will	1768	LVA Wills/Admin. DB
Thornton, Rowland, of Hanover Parish	King George	Will	1741	TQ 22:4, p. 231
Thornton, Sterling, of Petsworth Parish	Gloucester	Will	1790	WMQ 8, p. 57
Thornton, Thomas	Richmond	Will	1729	VG 47, p. 293
Thornton, Thomas		Will	1741c	DAR MSS 13 b5 f8
Thornton, Thomas, of Fredericksburg	Prince William	Will	1792	Note[1]
Thornton, William	King George	Will	1743	FDC L575-132
Thornton, William, the elder	Gloucester	Will Ref.	1726	Winfree, p. 374
Thoroughgood, Adam	Princess Anne	Will Abstract	1719	VMHB 26, p. 414
Thoroughgood, John	Princess Anne	Will Abstract	1701	VMHB 26, p. 416
Thoroughgood, John	Princess Anne	Will Abstract	1719	VMHB 26, p. 414
Thorowgood, Adam	James City	Will	1640	Note[2]
Thorowgood, Adam	James City	Will	1640c	V:Mss6:1 T3978:2
Thorowgood, Adam	Princess Anne	Will	1685c	C 39, p. 14
Thorowgood, Argall	Princess Anne	Will	1700c	V:Mss6:1 T3978:2
Thorowgood, John	Princess Anne	Will	1763	V:Mss6:1 T3978:2
Thorowgood, John Harper	Princess Anne	Will	1796c	V:Mss6:1 T3978:2
Thorowgood, John, Princess Anne Co.	Williamsburg	Will Abstract	1803	Crozier, p. 58
Thorowgood, John Wainhouse	Princess Anne	Will	1803	V:Mss6:1 T3978:2
Thorowgood, John Wm., Princess Anne	Williamsburg	Will Abstract	1804	Crozier, p. 57
Thorp, Timothy	Southampton	Will	1763	LVA Acc. #38262
Thorp, Timothy	Southampton	Will	1789	V:Mss1 M3618 b 1-5
Thorpe, Thomas, s/o John		Will	1724	VCRP, Survey #04677
Thresh, Clement	Rappahannock*	Will Abstract	1656	VMHB 5, p. 282
Thrift, Ann, c/o Hamilton	Fairfax	Guard. Bond	1817	X
Thrift, Charles, Sr.	Fairfax	Will	1788	LVA Acc. #343683, 2:38
Thrift, Kerron H., c/o Hamilton	Fairfax	Guard. Bond	1817	X
Throckmorton, John, in Berkeley Co.	Frederick	Will	1775	CF1829-167

---

[1] James R. Robertson, *Petitions of Early Inhabitants of Kentucky* (1914), p. 182.

[2] *The Standard*, 26 NOV 1881.

NAME	LOCATION	TYPE	YEAR	REFERENCE(S)
Throckmorton, Mordecai		Will	1760	PRO T 79/7, r174
Throckmorton, Robert, in Berkeley Co.	Frederick	Will	1796	CF1835-172
Thruston, John	Gloucester	Will	1675	WMQ 8, p. 115
Thruston, John	Gloucester	Will	1765	Mason, Vol. 2, p. 58
Thruston, Robert, of Abingdon Parish	Gloucester	Will	1805	Note[1]
Thruston, William S., in Mathews Co.	Gloucester	Will	1861	CF1887-014
Thruston, William S., in Mathews Co.	Gloucester	Will	1861	CF1881-003
Thurman, Josephine, in Campbell Co.	Albemarle	Will	1879	CF1899-047
Thurston, Robert, armorer		Will	1678	VCRP, Survey #03715
Thurston, Samuel	King & Queen	Will	1830	Note[2]
Thurston, Seth	Henrico	Inventory	1727	Records, Vol. 3, p. 743
Thweatt, Henry, in Greene Co. AL	Dinwiddie	Will	1839	LVA Acc. #32908
Thweatt, James [Mary]	Charles City	Dower	1693	VGSQ 17:3, p. 104
Thweatt, John	Prince George	Will	1759	DB1759, p. 84
Thweatt, John James, in Pr. Geo. Co.	Petersburg	Will	1821	CF1843-044
Thweatt, Lucretia	Prince George	Will	1848	SV 9:4, p. 157
Thweatt, Miles	Prince George	Will	1767	LVA Acc. #19942
Thweatt, Sarah	Charles City	Dower	1700	MVG 23:1, p. 64
Thweatt, Thomas	Dinwiddie	Will	1845	MVG 29:3, p. 193
Thweatt, Thomas	Dinwiddie	Will	1845	Note[3]
Tidwell, William Carr	Westmoreland	Will	1774	Wills #9
Tilly, George		Will	1743	VCRP, Survey #04620
Tilton, Joseph B., in MA	Henrico	Will	1882	CF1895-031
Timberlake, Ann	Caroline	Will	1833	W&D1794, p. 31a
Timberlake, Benjamin	Hanover	Will	1820	CF1861-004
Timberlake, Benjamin	Hanover	Will	1820	Cocke:145
Timberlake, Benjamin [Timerlake]	New Kent	Will	1863	CF1900-003
Timberlake, Frances	New Kent	Will	1794	TVF 11:1, p. 24
Timberlake, Frances, of New Kent Co.	Richmond City	Will	1795	MVG 31:4, p. 351
Timberlake, Frances, of New Kent Co.	Richmond City	Will	1795	Hustings 1818 Box 83
Timberlake, Francis	Hanover	Will	1807	CF1841-005
Timberlake, Francis	Hanover	Will	1808	Cocke:146
Timberlake, Francis	Hanover	Will	1808	CF1843-009
Timberlake, Francis	James City	Will	1833	Swem(1):182
Timberlake, Henry, of St. Paul's Parish	Hanover	Will	1805	LVA Acc. #21930
Timberlake, John C., in York Co.	James City	Will	1888	CF1894-003
Timberlake, John, of Bristol Parish	New Kent	Will	1787	Note[4]
Timberlake, Nancy	Warren	Will	1846	UVA Acc. #8712-d
Timberlake, Sally H.	New Kent	Will	1860	LVA Acc. #31121
Timberlake, Sally H.	New Kent	Will	1860	WB1, p. 86
Timberlake, Sally H.	New Kent	Will	1866	CF1882-023
Timberlake, Sally H.	New Kent	Will	1866	CF1895-004
Timberlake, William H.	Hanover	Will	1883	CF1890-002
Timberlake, William I.	New Kent	Will	1866	CF1887-007

---

[1] Polly Cary Mason, *Records of Colonial Gloucester*, Vol. 2, p. 64.
[2] Beverly Fleet, *Virginia Colonial Abstracts*, King and Queen County County, Vol. 14, 1st Collection, p. 92.
[3] LVA, Land Office Caveats, Box 1858-1896.
[4] LVA, Executive Communications, 17 DEC 1789.

NAME	LOCATION	TYPE	YEAR	REFERENCE(S)
Timpson, Samuel	James City	Estate Ref.	1832	Note[1]
Timson, John, of York Co.		Will	1736	VCRP, Survey #04373
Timson, William, of York Co.	London	Will	1736	N:PROB11/677
Timson, William, of York Co.		Will	1736	VCRP, Survey #04374
Tinsley, Charles	Hanover	Will Abstract	1842	Cocke:147
Tinsley, Charles	Hanover	Will	1842	LP 1842 APR
Tinsley, Charles C.	Hanover	Will	1862	CF1888-025
Tinsley, John	Hanover	Will	1795	Cocke:43
Tinsley, John	Hanover	Will	1795	CF1838-005
Tinsley, John B.	Hanover	Will	1819	CF1865-003
Tinsley, John, in Amherst Co.	Lynchburg	Will	1817	CF1836-023
Tinsley, Joshua	Culpeper	Will	1876	CF1894-012
Tinsley, Nathaniel	Hanover	Estate Ref.	1841	LP:12 JAN 1841
Tinsley, Philip	Hanover	Will	1793	CF1865-003
Tinsley, Sophia	Hanover	Will	1883	CF1888-025
Tinsley, Thomas	New Kent	Will	1702	Note[2]
Tinsley, Thomas	New Kent	Will	1702	LVA Acc. #28877
Tinsley, Thomas	New Kent	Will	1702	V:Mss2 T4973 a 1
Tinsley, William, in Amherst Co.	Lynchburg	Will	1812	CF1818-027
Tinsley, William, in Amherst Co.	Lynchburg	Will	1816	CF1825-075
Tinsley, William, in Amherst Co.	Lynchburg	Will	1816	CF1833-013
Tiplady, Ruth [Ralph]		Will	1697	LVA Wills/Admin. DB
Tisdal, John	Henrico	Inventory	1797	VGSQ 10:1, p. 13
Tisdale, Jane M.	Lunenburg	Will	1876	CF1885-003
Tisdale, John	Dinwiddie	Inventory	1797	LVA Acc. #2867-19
Toake, John [William]		Inventory	1721	LVA Wills/Admin. DB
Toancel, Edward	Westmoreland	Will	1755	T: correct from Joncel
Tobert, Nancy, in MO	Fauquier	Will	1859	CF1903-063
Tobert, Nancy, in MO	Fauquier	Will	1860	CF1860-004
Toby, Catherine	Louisa	Will	1767	Note[3]
Todd, Bernard	King & Queen	Will	1810	V:Mss3 K5893 a 69-86
Todd, Bernard	King & Queen	Will	1810	LVA Acc. #24038
Todd, Bernard	King & Queen	Will Ref.	1810	KQB:2
Todd, John	Fayette	Estate Ref.	1782	Hening, Vol. 12, p. 369
Todd, John		Estate Ref.	1787	Hening, Vol. 12, p. 628
Todd, John		Estate Ref.	1790	Hening, Vol. 13, p. 231
Todd, John	Louisa	Will	1792	LP:04 DEC 1811
Todd, Thomas, Gent.	Gloucester	Will Ref.	1722	Hening, Vol. 5, p. 395
Todd, Thomas, the younger, Baltimore	King & Queen	Will	1715	Fleet 2:175
Todd, William	King & Queen	Will Ref.	1736	Hening, Vol. 8, p. 57
Todd, William		Estate Ref.	1761	Hening, Vol. 7, p. 484
Toler, Absalom, of Powhatan Co.	Cumberland	Will	1818	CF1854-025
Toler, Annie	Hanover	Will	1881	CF1881-004
Toler, Benjamin	Hanover	Will	1808	Cocke:149
Toler, Benjamin A.	Hanover	Will	1808	CF1867-011
Toler, George	Goochland	Will	1823	CF1856-002

---

[1] LVA, Land Office Revlutionary War Military Certificate Papers, Samuel Timpson, Folder 30.
[2] Published in the *Richmond News Leader*, 13 MAR 1908, p. 8, cols. 1-2.
[3] Louisa County Wills Not Fully Proven, 1757-1902, p. 49.

NAME	LOCATION	TYPE	YEAR	REFERENCE(S)
Toler, J. Anderson, in Henrico Co.	Hanover	Will	1841	CF1873-008
Tolles, Samuel L., in NJ	Princess Anne	Will	1870	CF1888-002
Tomkies, Charles, Dr., Gloucester Co.	Williamsburg	Will Abstract	1737	Crozier, p. 57
Tomkies, Mordecai	Charlotte	Will	1807	MVG 43:1, p. 1
Tomkies, Morgan	Gloucester	Will	(nd)	VG 27, p. 282
Tomlin, Elizabeth R.	Hanover	Will	1896	CF1904-016
Tomlin, Elizabeth R.	Hanover	Will	1896	CF1911-024
Tomlin, Robert	Rappahannock*	Will Ref.	1688	Sweeny, p. 8
Tomlin, Robert	Rappahannock*	Will	1688	LVA Wills/Admin. DB
Tomlin, Robert, in Richmond Co.	Essex	Will	1795	CF1846-013
Tomlinson, Benjamin	Lunenburg	Will	1789	CF1826-003
Tomlinson, Edward, mariner		Will	1743	VCRP, Survey #04622
Tompkins, Bailey	Caroline	Will	1847	W&D1794, p. 47
Tompkins, Robert	Fredericksburg	Will	1796	DCWA, p. 55
Tompson, Jacob, mariner		Will	1699	VCRP, Survey #04789
Toms, William, mariner		Will	1681	VCRP, Survey #03726
Toncray, J.C., in TN	Washington	Will	1874	CF1891-033
Toone, James	Rappahannock*	Will Abstract	1677	VMHB 5, p. 287
Topping, George W., in Norfolk Co.	Portsmouth	Will	1857	CF1901-034
Torbert, John, in OH	Fauquier	Will	1852	CF1860-004
Torkington, Joseph, planter		Will	1653	VCRP, Survey #04109
Torver, Thomas	Surry	Will	1712	T:D&W6, p. 111
Towersey, William		Will	1698	VCRP, Survey #06060
Towler, William, in Mecklenburg Co.	Brunswick	Will	1856	CF1879-006
Townes, Edmund, in Granville Co. NC	Mecklenburg	Will	1861	CF1870-054 CC
Townes, Edmund, in NC	Mecklenburg	Will	1859	CF1875-074 CC
Townsend, James	Fairfax	Sale	1853	X
Townsend, James	Fairfax	Inventory	1853	X
Trabue, John, in Chesterfield Co.	Powhatan	Will	1791	CF1795-010
Tracey, James Francis [Frances Maria]	Fairfax	Renounce	1831	X
Tracey, Thomas, in Alexandria Co. DC	Fairfax	Will	1821	CF1842-024
Trainham, Joshua	Caroline	Estate Ref.	1780	LP:02 NOV 1793
Trammel, John, in MD	Frederick	Will	1784	CF1111-066
Travalyon, John, of Hampton		Will	1741	VCRP, Survey #04377
Traverse, Giles	Prince William	Will	1717	Note[1]
Traverse, Giles	Stafford	Will	1717	FDC L572-60
Travis, Edward	James City	Will	1784	VGS Bulletin V, p. 42
Travis, Edward	James City	Will	1784	Land Office
Travis, Edward	James City	Will	1784	MVG 29:3, p. 194
Travis, Margaret, of Stafford Co.	Fredericksburg	Will	1794	DCWA, p. 44
Travis, Samuel	Williamsburg	Will Abstract	1821	Crozier, p. 58
Trench, C. Stewart, in Amelia Co.	Henrico	Will	1886	CF1893-014
Trice, James	Louisa	Will	1820	V:Mss2 T7316 a 1
Trice, James, of King William Co.	Louisa	Appraisal	1769	CF1804-006
Trice, John, in TN	Louisa	Will	1808	CF1835-013
Trice, Richard A.	Goochland	Will	1864	LVA Acc. #27618
Trick, James M., in Richmond	Rockingham	Will	1876	CF1894-052
Trigg, A.B., in MS	Washington	Will	1879	CF1882-015

---

[1] Prince William County Land Causes, 1789-1793, p. 335.

NAME	LOCATION	TYPE	YEAR	REFERENCE(S)
Trimble, James, of Botetourt Co.	Augusta	Will	1776	CF1835-012
Triplett, Franklin	Fauquier	Account	1847	NVG 7, p. 941
Triplett, Reuben, in Frederick Co.	Rappahannock	Will	1854	CF1859-014
Triplett, William	Prince William	Will	1749	LC 1789, p. 2
Triplett, William	Prince William	Will	1749	TQ 24, p. 299
Triplett, William W.	Fairfax	Account	1859	X
Trisler, Peter, in Richmond	Fairfax	Will	1865	X
Trisler, Peter, in Richmond	Fairfax	Will	1866	CF1881-022
Trisler, Peter, of Fairfax Co.	Richmond City	Will	1864	CCW2, p. 438
Trott, Samuel	Fairfax	Will	(nd)	V:Mss1 H4214 a 30-41
Trotter, Hannah	Brunswick	Will (U)	1797	SV 3:1, p. 35
Try, Ralph, cooper, of Yorktown		Will	1701	VCRP, Survey #04116
Tuck, John	Caroline	Will	1807	V:Mss1 C5217 b 793+
Tucker, Drury, in Amherst Co.	Lynchburg	Will	1801	CF1855-003
Tucker, Henry, in Buckingham Co.	Prince Edward	Will	1859	CF1882-032
Tucker, John	Norfolk	Will	1736	SV 11:1, p. 19
Tucker, Mary	Dinwiddie	Will	1812	SV 1:1, p. 28
Tucker, Mary, in Dinwiddie Co.	Southampton	Will	1815	CF1830-021
Tucker, Nathaniel B., in James City Co.	Petersburg	Will	1851	CF1863-041
Tucker, Richard, in Prince George Co.	Petersburg	Will	1847	CF1857-027
Tucker, Robert	Elizabeth City	Will	1763	D&W1758, p. 515
Tucker, Robert, Jr., of Norfolk Co.	Williamsburg	Will Abstract	1779	Crozier, p. 57
Tucker, Robert, of Norfolk Borough	Williamsburg	Will Abstract	1769	Crozier, p. 58
Tucker, Robert, of Norfolk	Williamsburg	Will	1769	Fleet 2:333
Tucker, Robert, of Southwark Parish	Surry	Will Abstract	1770	VG 13, p. 55
Tucker, Robert, of Southwark Parish	Surry	Will (U)	1770	VTG 13:2, p. 53
Tucker, Robert, of Southwark Parish	Surry	Will (U)	1770	LVA:1048937
Tucker, Thomas Tudor		Account	1832	LVA Acc. #41008
Tucker, William	Caroline	Will	1844	Weisiger 1:073
Tucker, William, of Prince George Co.	Petersburg	Will	1847	CF1808-030
Tuder, Robert	Brunswick	Will	1827	SV 3:3, p. 114
Tunis, J.E., in Norfolk	Portsmouth	Will	1866	CF1883-013
Tunis, John, in Norfolk	Portsmouth	Will	1855	CF1883-013
Tunstall, Molly	King & Queen	Will	1784	LVA Acc. #24193
Tunstall, Molly	King & Queen	Will	1796	Fleet 2:201
Tunstall, Thomas B.	New Kent	Will	1892	CF1948-006
Tupman, Francis	Fredericksburg	Will	1798	DCWA, p. 100
Turberville, John, in Westmoreland Co.	Arlington	Will	1799	CF1811-003
Turberville, John, in Westmoreland Co.	Northumberland	Will	1799	CF1815-002
Turberville, Martha	Fairfax	Dower	1806	X
Turberville, Martha	Fairfax	Dower	1806	X
Turman, Benjamin, of Botetourt Co.	Augusta	Will	1784	CF1808-036
Turner, Ann, in Fredericksburg	Fauquier	Will	1825	CF1846-030
Turner, Anthony, in Jefferson Co.	Frederick	Will	1814	CF1827-155
Turner, Fielding, in Loudoun Co.	Fairfax	Division	1811	X
Turner, Francina, in Fairfax Co.	Arlington	Will	1804	CF1807-040
Turner, George	King William	Will	1772	Note[1]
Turner, Harriet, in MA	Fairfax	Will	1879	CF1896-016

---

[1] LVA, U.S. Circuit Court Records, Box 115, *Cockran, Donald & Co. v. Turner's Exors.* (1824).

NAME	LOCATION	TYPE	YEAR	REFERENCE(S)
Turner, Henry	Henrico	Will	1712	LVA Acc. #26071
Turner, Henry	New Kent	Will	1880	CF1884-012
Turner, Henry	New Kent	Will	1896	CF1905-008
Turner, Henry D., in NC	Mecklenburg	Will	1869	CF1875-075 CC
Turner, Henry, in Amherst Co.	Bedford	Will	1829	CF1834-011
Turner, Henry, planter	Henrico	Will	1712	VG 11, p. 33
Turner, Jackson	Charles City	Inventory	1770	Records, p. 241
Turner, John	Norfolk	Will (N)	1687	DB5, p. 35
Turner, Lewis	Sussex	Will	1818	V:Mss2 T8552 b
Turner, Robert, in Charles City Co.	Bath	Will	1818	CF1829-003
Turner, Robert, in Charles City Co.	Bath	Will	1818	CF1836-005
Turner, Samuel, in Amherst Co.	Lynchburg	Will	1829	CF1842-015
Turner, Samuel, in Amherst Co.	Lynchburg	Will	1829	CF1835-013
Turner, Terisha, in Nelson Co.	Bedford	Will	1841	CF1890-051
Turner, Thomas	Hanover	Will	1842	Cocke:155
Turner, Thomas	Hanover	Admin.	1842c	V:Mss2 M2375 b
Turner, Thomas, Col.	Caroline	Will Ref.	1787	VMHB 52, p. 7
Turner, Thomas S.	Hanover	Will	1869	CF1892-014
Turner, William, of James City Co.	Williamsburg	Will Abstract	1809	Crozier, p. 57
Turner, William S., in Amherst Co.	Campbell	Will	1852	CF1885-003
Turner, William W.	Hanover	Will	1837	LP 1837
Turner, William W.	New Kent	Will	1894	CF1909-006
Turner, William W., in Hanover Co.	Lynchburg	Will	1837	CF1859-012
Turpin, James, tobacconist		Will	1678	VCRP, Survey #03716
Turpin, Josiah	Chesterfield	Will	1768	WB2, p. 212
Turpin, Martha	Chesterfield	Will	1825	BRCD
Turpin, Obedience		Will	1746c	DAR MSS 13 b5 f8
Turpin, Philip	Henrico	Will	1718	Records, Vol. 2, p. 372
Turpin, Thomas, in Chesterfield Co.	Powhatan	Will	1858	CF1888-019
Tute, John, of James River		Will	1738	VCRP, Survey #04651
Tweedy, Joseph, in Campbell Co.	Lynchburg	Will	1810	CF1824-036
Twiford, Sarah	Accomack	Will	1788	W1788, p. 37
Twine, Thomas	Portsmouth	Receipt	1854	LVA Acc. #19951
Twine, Thomas	Portsmouth	Receipt	1855	LVA Acc. #19954
Twyman, George	Spotsylvania	Will	1773	UVA MSS 7808
Twyman, George		Estate Ref.	1818	UVA Acc. #1261
Tye, Lambert, in Westover Parish	Charles City	Will	1728	D&W1724, p. 205
Tye, Mary	Charles City	Inventory	1729	D&W1724, p. 260
Tye, Richard, Capt., orphans	Charles City	Estate	1663	VMHB 43, p. 148
Tyler, George Gray	Prince William	Will	1811	CF1833-003
Tyler, John	Charles City	Will	1813	V:Mss2 T9714 a 1
Tyler, John	Charles City	Will	1813	V:Mss1 C9434 a 269+
Tyler, John	Charles City	Will	1863	LVA Acc. #22546
Tyler, John, Hon.	Charles City	Inventory	(nd)	WMQ 17, p. 231
Tyler, John, Hon.	Charles City	Will	1813	WMQ 17, p. 231
Tyler, Richard	Caroline	Will	1802	V:Mss2 T9717 a 1
Tyler, Richard	Caroline	Will	1802	W&P1742, p. 68
Tyler, Samuel	Williamsburg	Estate Ref.	1815	LP:29 DEC 1815
Tyler, William	Charles City	Account	1727	D&W1724, p. 174
Tyler, William		Will	1791	LVA Acc. #24145
Tyler, William	Caroline	Will	1794	LVA Acc. #24145

NAME	LOCATION	TYPE	YEAR	REFERENCE(S)
Tyler, William, Capt.	Caroline	Will	1791	LVA Acc. #24253
Tyler, William E.	Hanover	Will	1891	CF1906-041
Tyree, Francis	Charles City	Will P.	1754	OB1751, p. 49
Tyree, Francis	Charles City	Inventory	1771	Records, p. 269
Tyree, Mary	New Kent	Will	1836	WB1, p. 224
Tyree, Mary	New Kent	Will	1858	CF1878-001

NAME	LOCATION	TYPE	YEAR	REFERENCE(S)
U				
Umstadter, Jacob, in Norfolk	Portsmouth	Will	1872	CF1889-052
Underwood, Jane	Hanover	Will	1821	LVA Acc. #28393
Underwood, Jane	Hanover	Will	1821	G1:86
Underwood, Jane	Hanover	Will	1821	Note[1]
Underwood, Jane	Hanover	Inventory	1821	G1:94
Underwood, Nathan	Madison	Will	1804	FDC L567-87
Underwood, Thomas	Hanover	Will	1815	LVA Acc. #28393
Underwood, Thomas	Hanover	Will	1815	G1:88
Underwood, Thomas	Hanover	Will	1815	Note[2]
Underwood, William	Rappahannock*	Will Ref.	1672	Sweeny, p. 5
Unknown, of Overwharton Parish	Stafford	Will	1776	Note[3]
Upchurch, Francis	Surry	Inventory	1691	T:D&W4, p. 258b
Upchurch, James	Brunswick	Will	1783	CF1808-015
Upchurch, Michael	Surry	Inventory	1681	T:D&W2, p. 294b
Updike, Abraham, in Albemarle Co.	Warren	Will	1868	CF1885-002
Updike, Rufus	Loudoun	Will Ref.	1838c	V:Mss1 Up13 a 18-20
Upton, John, Capt.	Isle of Wight	Will	1652	VMHB 6, p. 36
Upton, Thomas, of Kanawha Co.	Augusta	Will	1794	CF1808-133
Urquhart, Charles, in Caroline Co.	Culpeper	Will	1867	CF1885-060

---

[1] LVA, U.S. Circuit Court Records, Bk. 19 (Richmond), p. 266.

[2] LVA, U.S. Circuit Court Records, Bk. 19 (Richmond), pp. 263, 268-269.

[3] LVA, Land Office Military Certificates No. 2.

NAME	LOCATION	TYPE	YEAR	REFERENCE(S)
V				
Vaas, Anna E., in Culpeper Co.	Fauquier	Will	1890	CF1906-051
Vadin, Henry	Henrico	Will	1747	DB1744, p. 344
Vaiden, George W.	Charles City	Division	1858	CF1859-054
Vaiden, John, of New Kent Co.	Goochland	Appraisal	1783	Fiduciaries 1728-1799
Vaiden, William H., Sr.	New Kent	Will	1832	Swem(1)
Valentine, Howard	Dinwiddie	Will	1809	VG 16, p. 170
Valentine, John, planter	Isle of Wight	Will	1652	VMHB 6, p. 118
Valentine, Mann S., in Richmond	Powhatan	Will	1899	CF1908-007
Valentine, Mary, in Richmond	Powhatan	Will	1899	CF1908-007
Vallandingham, John	D.C.	Will	1849	DCA:Box 20
Van Horne, Cornelius T.E.	James City	Will	1873	CF1874-009
Van Horne, Cornelius T.E.	James City	Will	1873	CF1884-014
Vance, William B., in Webster Co. WV	Bath	Will	1889	CF1894-012
Vandewell, Nathaniel	Henrico	Will	1769	Proceedings, p. 24
Vanmeter, Abraham, in Berkeley Co.	Frederick	Will	1783	CF1819-069
Vanmeter, Abraham, in Hardy Co.	Frederick	Will	1823	CF1827-210
Vanmeter, Henry, in Hampshire Co.	Frederick	Will	1778	CF1852-062
Vanmeter, John, in Berkeley Co.	Frederick	Will	1818	CF1830-299
Vansant, James, in Alexandria Co.	Fairfax	Will	1866	CF1893-036
Vansyckel, Sarah, in PA	Henrico	Will	1872	CF1903-053
Vanvacter, Absalom	Loudoun	Inventory	1831	WBT, p. 259
Varnal, George	Fairfax	Inventory	1818	X
Vass, Fanny	King & Queen	Will	1799	Fleet, 1st Series
Vass, Vincent	Essex	Will	1727	Fleet 2:248
Vasser, John	Isle of Wight	Will	1650	VMHB 6, p. 247
Vaughan, Cornelius, of King & Queen	Amherst	Inventory	1735	CF
Vaughan, Cornelius, of King & Queen	Amherst	Will	1735	Causes 1793
Vaughan, I.N., in Hanover Co.	Henrico	Will	1898	CF1901-024
Vaughan, James	York	Estate Ref.	1790s	Note[1]
Vaughan, James	Charles City	Will	1820	TVF 4:1, p. 32
Vaughan, James	Nansemond	Will	1832	BRCD
Vaughan, Joseph	Hanover	Will	1849	CF1868-006
Vaughan, Joseph	Hanover	Will	1849	Cocke:157
Vaughan, Ledford	Gloucester	Will	1838	CF1895-003
Vaughan, Lemuel	Hanover	Will	1868	CF1878-013
Vaughan, Peter, in Dinwiddie Co.	Petersburg	Will	1816	CF1835-021
Vaughan, Rabley	Charles City	Inventory	1772	Records, p. 369
Vaughan, Rabley, of King William Co.	Williamsburg	Will Abstract	1787	Crozier, p. 59
Vaughan, Robert B., of York Co.	Williamsburg	Will Abstract	1822	Crozier, p. 59
Vaughan, Sarah, in Elizabeth City Co.	York	Will	1847	CF1856-009
Vaughan, Thomas, in TN	Lynchburg	Will	1818	CF1819-025
Vaughan, Timothy	New Kent	Will	1759	Note[2]
Vaughan, William, in Brunswick Co.	Bedford	Will	1809	CF1840-020
Vaughan, William, in Brunswick Co.	Dinwiddie	Will	1809	CF1847-001
Vaughan, Willis	Dinwiddie	Will	1819	VGSQ 10:1, p. 13
Vaughn, Almond, in Culpeper Co.	Rappahannock	Will	1842	CF1858-005

[1] York County Land Causes, 1795-1854, p. 28.
[2] Decisions of Cases in Virginia By the High Court of Chancery ..., Richmond 1795, p. 4.

NAME	LOCATION	TYPE	YEAR	REFERENCE(S)
Vaulx, Robert	Westmoreland	Will	1721	VMHB 44, p. 152
Vaulx, Robert		Will	1757	LVA Acc. #21570
Vea, William	Albemarle	Will	1783	WB2, p. 408
Vele, Morris	Prince William	Will	1750	MVG 29:3, p. 194
Vele, Morris	Prince William	Will	1750	Land Office
Venable, Abraham, in Pr. Edward Co.	Lynchburg	Will	1778	CF1826-047
Venable, Abraham, of Buckingham Co.	Prince Edward	Will	1798	DCW2, p. 8
Venable, Elizabeth, in Pr. Edward Co.	Lynchburg	Will	1811	CF1826-047
Venable, Samuel, of Prince Edward Co.	Cumberland	Will	1821	CF1839-013
Venable, William	Prince Edward	Will	(nd)	UVA MSS 8979-p
Verell, John	Dinwiddie	Will	1826	LP:07 DEC 1826
Verlander, James	King & Queen	Affadavit	1911	LP
Vermillion, Charles	Prince William	Will	1873	CF1910-037
Vernon, Daniel, in Loudoun Co.	Frederick	Will	1824	CF1827-128
Vest, Ann S.	Hanover	Will	1868	CF1882-033
Vest, Charles	Hanover	Will	1869	CF1899-013
Vest, Charles	Hanover	Will	1869	CF1875-010
Vest, William W.	James City	Will	1893	CF1924-008
Vezey, George	Lancaster	Will	1665	LP
Via, Gibson	Hanover	Will	1864	CF1875-014
Vickers, Margaret, of Fauquier Co.	Arlington	Will	1849	File #77A
Vinson, John	Surry	Will	1699	T:D&W5, p. 172a
Violett, Elizabeth	Fairfax	Plat	1873	X
Violett, Elizabeth	Fairfax	Division	1873	X
Violett, John, in Loudoun Co.	Frederick	Will	1814	CF1817-052
Violett, John, Sr., in Loudoun Co.	Frederick	Will	1814	CF1821-058
Violett, John, Sr., in Loudoun Co.	Frederick	Will	1814	CF1819-191
Vivion, John	Middlesex	Will	1705	VMHB 46, p. 357
Vowell, John C., of Alexandria	Arlington	Will	1853	LVA Acc. #34683, 1:8
Vowles, James	Prince William	Will	1873	CF1880-016
Vowles, John, in Albemarle Co.	Louisa	Will	1871	CF1899-018
Vowles, Lucy Ann, in Albemarle Co.	Louisa	Will	1885	CF1899-018

NAME	LOCATION	TYPE	YEAR	REFERENCE(S)

W

NAME	LOCATION	TYPE	YEAR	REFERENCE(S)
Waddey, Edward S., of Norfolk Borough	Williamsburg	Will Abstract	1819	Crozier, p. 62
Waddey, John R., of Northampton Co.	Williamsburg	Will Abstract	1815	Crozier, p. 63
Waddy, Samuel, Jr.	Louisa	Will	1786	LVA Acc. #41008, r4610
Wade, Ambrose	Henrico	Will	1820	VGSQ 18:3, p. 85
Wade, Henry, in Pittsylvania Co.	Campbell	Will	1824	CF1855-013
Wade, Henry, in Pittsylvania Co.	Campbell	Will	1824	CF1852-026
Wade, James	James City	Will	1803	Swem(1):f184
Wade, John	York	Will	1774	T: correct from 1744
Wade, Miles P., in Richmond	Henrico	Will	1874	CF1896-014
Wade, Robert, in WV	Hanover	Will	1871	CF1882-013
Wadlow, Thomas	Goochland	Will	1773	CF1785-005
Wagener, Peter, in Fairfax Co.	Fauquier	Will	1795	CF1848-032
Wagener, Sinah, in Fairfax Co.	Fauquier	Will	1810	CF1848-032
Waggy, Margaret, in WV	Rockingham	Will	1876	CF1889-071
Wail, Thomas	Isle of Wight	Will	1777	SV 11:2, p. 68
Wail, Thomas, of Newport parish	Isle of Wight	Will (U)	1778	LVA:1161459
Waite, Jane	Fauquier	Will	1794	CF1802-044
Waits, James	Augusta	Will	1781	Note[1]
Wake, Richard	Norfolk	Inventory	1648	LVA Wills/Admin. DB
Walden, Charles, in Pittsylvania Co.	Campbell	Will	1830	CF1845-009
Walden, Elizabeth, in Bedford Co.	Rappahannock	Will	1864	CF1936-001
Walden, John [of *Walden Towers*]	Caroline	Will	1794	W&D1794, p. 1
Walden, Richard, Sr.	King & Queen	Will	1845	CF1860-001
Walden, Samuel	King William	Estate Ref.	1812	LP:13 DEC 1813
Walden, Samuel	King William	Estate Ref.	1812	LP:12 DEC 1815
Walden, William, in Bedford Co.	Rappahannock	Will	1863	CF1936-001
Waldrop, Sarah M.	Louisa	Will	1897	CF1909-031
Waldrop, William	Hanover	Will	1881	CF1889-011
Wales, Andrew, of Alexandria	Arlington	Will	1800	CF1816-001
Walke, Anthony		Estate Ref.	1792	Hening, Vol. 13, p. 613
Walke, Anthony	Princess Anne	Will	1814	LVA Acc. #24194
Walke, Anthony, Col.	Princess Anne	Will	1768	VMHB 5, p. 142
Walke, Mary, rel/o Wm., Princess Anne	Williamsburg	Will Abstract	1798	Crozier, p. 62
Walke, Thomas	Princess Anne	Will	1693	VMHB 5, p. 139
Walke, Thomas	Princess Anne	Will	1704	LVA Acc. #29136, r12
Walke, Thomas, Col., merchant	Princess Anne	Will	1723	VMHB 26, p. 412
Walke, Thomas, Maj.	Princess Anne	Will	1761	VMHB 26, p. 412
Walke, William, of Princess Anne Co.	Williamsburg	Will Abstract	1795	Crozier, p. 61
Walker, Alexander	Charles City	Account	1729	D&W1724, p. 237
Walker, Bolling M.	Dinwiddie	Will	1814c	V:Mss1 M6154 a 66-70
Walker, Bolling M., in Dinwiddie Co.	Petersburg	Will	1815	CF1836-030
Walker, Charles, c/o Samuel	Fairfax	Guard. Bond	1845	X
Walker, David	Brunswick	Will	1786	CF1794-011
Walker, David, Dr.	Petersburg	Will	1816c	V:Mss1 M6154 a 66-70
Walker, David, Sr.	Goochland	Will Partial	1774	VMHB 48, p. 68
Walker, Edward	Northumberland	Will	1656	MVG 29:3, p. 194
Walker, Edward, of Dinwiddie Co.	Williamsburg	Will Abstract	1781	Crozier, p. 61

[1] Augusta County District Court Order Book, 1797-1803, p. 417.

NAME	LOCATION	TYPE	YEAR	REFERENCE(S)
Walker, Elizabeth, in Dinwiddie Co.	Petersburg	Will	1828	CF1836-030
Walker, Elizabeth Starke	Dinwiddie	Will	1828	V:Mss1 M6154 a 66-70
Walker, Fanny, in Madison Co.	Albemarle	Will	1845	CF1895-122
Walker, George, mariner		Will	1719	VCRP, Survey #04344
Walker, Henry, in KY	Mecklenburg	Will	(nd)	CF1875-065 CC
Walker, Henry, in KY	Mecklenburg	Will	1838	CF1848-029 CSC
Walker, John	Rappahannock*	Will Ref.	1668	Sweeny, p. 161
Walker, John, c/o Samuel	Fairfax	Guard. Bond	1845	X
Walker, John, now of Nassau, Bahama	Williamsburg	Will Abstract	1784	Crozier, p. 61
Walker, Littleberry	James City	Will	1804	Swem(1)
Walker, Mary Allen, in PA	Bedford	Will	1857	CF1858-022
Walker, Peter, in Goochland Co.	Lynchburg	Will	1806	CF1866-012
Walker, Ralph	Stafford	Will (N)	1707	WB1699, p. 394
Walker, Rebeccah	Elizabeth City	Will	1697	D&W1689, p. 228
Walker, Robert	Charles City	Will	1780	LP, box 12, folder 102
Walker, Robert, in Dinwiddie Co.	Petersburg	Will	1798	CF1836-030
Walker, Robert, in Dinwiddie Co.	Petersburg	Will	1830	CF1857-038
Walker, Robert, of James City Co.	Williamsburg	Will Abstract	1804	Crozier, p. 61
Walker, Robert, seaman		Will	1782	VCRP, Survey #04702
Walker, Samuel	Fairfax	Will	1845	X
Walker, Sarah	Rappahannock*	Will	(nd)	TQ 23:2, p. 114
Walker, Sarah	Stafford	Will Ref.	1708	WB1699, p. 413
Walker, Temple	King & Queen	Will	1868	LVA Acc. #24038
Walker, Temple	King & Queen	Will	1868	V:Mss3 K5893 a 69-86
Walker, Temple	King & Queen	Will Ref.	1868	KQB:2
Walker, Thomas	Richmond City	Will	1796	T:HCD2, p. 271
Walker, Thomas	King & Queen	Will	1850	V:Mss3 K5893 a 69-86
Walker, Thomas	King & Queen	Will	1850	LVA Acc. #25253
Walker, Thomas, c/o Samuel	Fairfax	Guard. Bond	1845	X
Walker, William	Charles City	Will	1787	LP, box 51, folder 271
Walker, William	James City	Will	1820	Weisiger 1:053
Walker, William Hart, in Campbell Co.	Lynchburg	Will	1810	CF1828-056
Walker, William, Sr.	James City	Will	1819	Weisiger 1:054
Wall, David F.	Halifax	Estate Ref.	1804	Shepherd, Vol. 3, p. 44
Wall, Edward, in Richmond Co.	Northumberland	Will	1813	CF1841-009
Wall, Isaac	Dinwiddie	Will	1794	MVG 31:4, p. 344
Wall, Isaac, of Dinwiddie Co.	Brunswick	Will	1794	Judgments 1819 SEP
Wall, Joel, of Surry Co.	Williamsburg	Will Abstract	1801	Crozier, p. 61
Wall, Richard, in Richmond Co.	Northumberland	Will	1819	CF1841-008
Wallace, Howson Hooe	Fredericksburg	Will	1844	V:Mss1 Ar554 c 23-30
Wallace, James	Elizabeth City	Will Ref.	1754	VMHB 78, p. 228
Wallace, John Robert, in DC	Fauquier	Will	1849	CF1866-011
Wallace, Michael		Will	1753	Note[1]
Wallace, Michael	Prince George	Inventory	1759	DB1759, p. 73a
Wallace, Michael	King George	Will	1766	UVA MSS 38-150
Wallace, Robert	Bath	Will	1895	CF1910-020
Waller, Allen, of Overwharton Parish	Stafford	Will	1777	TQ 31:4, p. 263
Waller, Barsheba	Stafford	Will	1815	TQ 31:4, p. 263

---

[1] *The Researcher*, Vol. 2, p. 102.

NAME	LOCATION	TYPE	YEAR	REFERENCE(S)
Waller, Benjamin, in Williamsburg	James City	Will	1865	CF1886-018
Waller, Edmund		Will	1687	CL M228
Waller, Edward	Gloucester	Will	1745	TQ 28:3, p. 168
Waller, Lucy	Surry	Inventory	1791	WB12, p. 316
Waller, Robert Hall	James City	Will	1808	V:Mss1 B6235a234-241
Walley, Mary, of Williamsburg	London	Will	1743	N:PROB11/724
Wallice, Brocas	Charles City	Will	1668	D&W1724, p. 21
Walls, Francis	Lancaster	Will	1714	LP
Walrond, John, in Pittsylvania Co.	Bedford	Will	1832	CF1870-198
Walsh, Samuel Hyde, Brunswick Co. NC	Powhatan	Will	1827	V:Mss1 Sa878 a 3,550
Walston, Ann	Norfolk	Will (N)	1687	DB6, p. 13a
Walston, Joseph	Norfolk	Will (N)	1687	DB5, p. 22a
Walten, John	Hanover	Will	1772	TVF 11:4, p. 222
Walters, Walter	Isle of Wight	Will	1732	WB3, p. 297
Walthall, Archard	Chesterfield	Will	(nd)	V:Mss1 N1786 a 8222+
Walthall, James Knox	Prince George	Will	1861	SV 10:1, p. 15
Walthall, Susan A.	James City	Will	1893	CF1911-005
Walthall, William	Powhatan	Will	1847	V:Mss1 N1786 a 8222+
Walthall, William	Powhatan	Will	1847	CF1874-011
Walthoe, Nathaniel	Williamsburg	Will Ref.	(nd)	Hening, Vol. 8, p. 627
Walthoe, Nathaniel, of Williamsburg	London	Will	1722	N:PROB11/979
Walthoe, Nathaniel, of Williamsburg	London	Will	1772	VCRP, Survey #04684
Walton, Agnes	Hanover	Will	1854	CF1884-025
Walton, Agnes D.	Hanover	Will	1854	Cocke:160
Walton, Elizabeth	Isle of Wight	Will	1676	RB2, p. 141
Walton, George	Prince Edward	Will	1796c	V:Mss2 W1796 b
Walton, George A., in TN	Campbell	Will	1847	CF1856-024
Walton, Joel	Louisa	Will	1840	LVA Acc. #33203
Walton, John	Hanover	Will	1772	V:Mss2 W1764 a 1
Walton, John	Hanover	Will	1772	VGSQ 9, p. 19
Walton, John	Hanover	Will	1772	Note[1]
Walton, John C.	King & Queen	Will	1860	CF1860-003
Walton, Thomas	Prince Edward	Will	1817c	V:Mss2 W1796 b
Walton, Walter		Will	1650	VCRP, Survey #04099
Walton, William, in Botetourt Co.	Roanoke	Will	1825	CF1848-010
Walton, William, in Botetourt Co.	Roanoke	Will	1825	CF1848-010
Wamack, Samuel, of Broadway	Prince George	Will	1858	SV 10:1, p. 13
Wamsley, John		Will	1698	VCRP, Survey #06058
Warburton, William	Henrico	Inventory	1753	Records, Vol. 5, p. 1627
Ward, Anna Maria	Fairfax	Will	1853	X
Ward, Anna Maria, in Prince William Co.	Fairfax	Will	1852	CF1858-018
Ward, Anna Maria, in Prince William Co.	Fairfax	Will	1854	CF1887-004
Ward, Annie, in Prince William Co.	Fairfax	Will	1852	CF1887-004
Ward, John R., in TX	Campbell	Will	1885	CF1909-017
Ward, John, Sr., in Pittsylvania Co.	Lynchburg	Will	1827	CF1827-071
Ward, Maria, in Prince William Co.	Fairfax	Will	1854	CF1858-018
Ward, Martha, in Culpeper Co.	Fauquier	Will	1863	CF1881-032
Ward, Richard	Henrico	Inventory	1724	Records, Vol. 2, p. 597

---

[1] William H. Black and William J. Jones, *Walton-Sims of Eastern Virginia* (1961), p. 2.

NAME	LOCATION	TYPE	YEAR	REFERENCE(S)
Ward, William	Surry	Will	1782	WB12, p. 15
Ward, Zachariah	Fairfax	Will	1822	X
Ward, Zachariah, in Prince William Co.	Fairfax	Will	1822	CF1858-018
Ward, Zachariah, in Prince William Co.	Fairfax	Will	1822	CF1887-004
Ward, [blank]	Fauquier	Will	(nd)	CF1894-057
Warden, Philip	Prince William	Will Ref.	1844	CM:05 MAR 1844
Warden, William, in Brunswick Co.	Prince Edward	Will	1871	CF1893-031
Warder, Philip	Prince William	Inv. Ref.	1844	CM:03 JUN 1844
Wardrop, John, in Nansemond Co.	Isle of Wight	Will	1766	CF1797-007
Ware, Betsey, in Amherst Co.	Lynchburg	Will	1818	CF1828-021
Ware, Charity [Weir]	Prince William	Acct. Ref.	1843	CM:07 AUG 1843
Ware, Mary	King & Queen	Will	1839	Swem(1):f205
Ware, Mildred, in Louisa Co.	Goochland	Will	1829	CF1841-005
Ware, Mildred, in Louisa Co.	Goochland	Will	1841	CF1841-004
Ware, Nathaniel	Caroline	Will	1848	W&D1794, p. 53
Ware, Nathaniel	Charles City	Will	1852	V:Mss2 W2254 a 1
Ware, Robert	King & Queen	Will Abstract	1781	Fleet 2:305
Ware, Thomas	King & Queen	Will	1822	LP
Ware, Thomas, of King William Co.	Essex	Will	1822	TVF 11:3, p. 164
Ware, Thomas, of King William Co.	Essex	Will	1825	CF1853-031
Ware, William	King William	Will	1884	CF1868-001
Warick, William, in Amherst Co.	Bedford	Will	1832	CF1872-076
Waring, E.L., in Westmoreland Co.	Essex	Will	1821	CF1853-023
Waring, Francis	Essex	Will	1770	Fleet 2:340
Waring, Horace	King William	Will	1832	LP
Waring, Thomas	Essex	Will	1754	Fleet 2:327
Waring, William Lowry, in Essex Co.	King & Queen	Will	1841	CF1884-007
Warinner, Daniel	Henrico	Will	1773	Records, Vol. 7, p. 2216
Warner, Augustine	Gloucester	Will Ref.	1679	Hening, Vol. 8, p. 630
Warner, Augustine, II	Gloucester	Will Ref.	(nd)	VMHB 3, p. 11
Warner, Mildred		Will Ref.	169_	Note[1]
Warnett, Thomas, in London, Eng.	James City	Will	1630	Note[2]
Warnett, Thomas, of James City Co.	London	Will	1630	N:PROB11/158
Warnett, Thomas, of James City Co.		Will	1630	VCRP, Survey #03965
Warren, Dawson, in Surry Co.	Isle of Wight	Will	1849	CF1889-010
Warren, John	Surry	Will	1790	WB12, p. 267
Warren, Lucy	Surry	Will	1795	WB12, p. 86
Warren, Martha	Surry	Will	1784	WB12, p. 46
Warren, Michael S.	James City	Will	1891	CF1905-014
Warren, William A.	James City	Will	1887	CF1895-014
Warren, Willis D.	Surry	Will (U)	1827	VTG 13:3, p. 124
Warren, Willis D.	Surry	Will Abstract	1827	VG 13, p. 55
Warrick, William, in Amherst Co.	Bedford	Will	1833	CF1849-026
Warrock, Lodowick	Richmond City	Will	1794	T:HCD2, p. 74
Warthen, James	Prince George	Will	1841	Note[3]
Warthen, James	Prince George	Will	1841	SV 9:2, p. 57

---

[1] LVA, *Papers of George Washington*, Ser. 4, Reel 101, #254-48.

[2] H.F. Waters, *Genealogical Gleanings in England*, p. 39.

[3] LVA, John K. Martin Papers, Box 17, War of 1812, Folder James Warthen.

NAME	LOCATION	TYPE	YEAR	REFERENCE(S)
Warthen, Thomas	Prince George	Will	1847	SV 9:4, p. 156
Warwell, Thomas [John]		Admin.	1675	LVA Wills/Admin. DB
Warwick, Byrd	Richmond City	Will	1882	V:Mss2 W2685 a 1
Warwick, John	Amherst	Will	1848	V:Mss2 W2687 a 1
Wash, Dickinson, in Louisa Co.	Hanover	Will	1856	CF1877-015
Wash, Dickinson, of Louisa Co.	Hanover	Will	1857	Cocke:70
Wash, Edmund	Hanover	Will	1858	Cocke:158
Wash, Edmund	Hanover	Will	1858	CF1878-010
Wash, Edmund, in Hanover Co.	Louisa	Will	1858	CF1900-069
Washington, Anne	Westmoreland	Will	1772	Wills #6
Washington, Augustine	King George	Will	1743	Note[1]
Washington, Augustine	King George	Will	1743	TQ 09:1, p. 35
Washington, Augustine	Williamsburg	Will	1858	BRCD
Washington, Augustine, in D.C.	Williamsburg	Will Abstract	1810	Crozier, p. 59
Washington, Corbin, in Fairfax Co.	Frederick	Will	1799	CF1832-176
Washington, Edward	Fairfax	Account	1813	X
Washington, Edward	Fairfax	Sale	1814	X
Washington, Edward	Fairfax	Account	1816	X
Washington, George	Fairfax	Will	1800	LVA Acc. #23761
Washington, George Alexander, in DC	Arlington	Will	1817	CF1821-012
Washington, George, Gen.	Fairfax	Inventory	1810	X
Washington, H., in Fairfax Co.	Frederick	Will	1802	CF1832-176
Washington, Hannah	Fairfax	Will	1801	X
Washington, Hannah, in Westmoreland	Frederick	Will	1801	CF1832-176
Washington, Henry Augustine	Williamsburg	Will	1858	LVA Acc. #31277
Washington, James, Northampton NC	Southampton	Will	1766	CF1786-001
Washington, John	Westmoreland	Will	1677	LVA Acc. #22047
Washington, John	Westmoreland	Will	1697	WMQ 13, p. 145
Washington, John	Westmoreland	Will	1697	LVA Acc. #41008, r4614
Washington, John	Westmoreland	Will	1698	Fleet, Huntington Data
Washington, John	Stafford	Will	1742	TQ 08:2, p. 113
Washington, John	Westmoreland	Will	1787	Wills #29
Washington, John, Gent.	Westmoreland	Will Partial	1677	DB1665, p. 365a
Washington, Lawrence		Will	1675	Fleet, Huntington Data
Washington, Lawrence, of Westm. Co.	London	Will	1700	N:PROB11/458
Washington, Lawrence, of Westm. Co.		Will	1700	VCRP, Survey #04796
Washington, Martha	Fairfax	Will	1802	LVA Acc. #23761
Washington, Martha	Fairfax	Inventory	1802	X
Washington, Mary	Fredericksburg	Will	1789	FDC V569-1
Washington, Mary Ball	Fredericksburg	Will	1778	V:Mss1 H3297 a 147+
Washington, Mary Ball	Fredericksburg	Will	1788	V:Mss2 W2785 a 1
Washington, Mary Ball	Fredericksburg	Will	1788	UVA MSS 951
Washington, Mary Ball	Fredericksburg	Will	1789	V:Mss1 B2105 b 105+
Washington, Mary Ball	Fredericksburg	Will	1804	LVA Acc. #23402
Washington, Olivia H., in MD	Fauquier	Will	1847	CF1875-074
Washington, Richard H.L.	Fairfax	Appraisal	1817	NVG 6, p. 627
Washington, Richard H.L.	Fairfax	Appraisal	1818	NVG 6, p. 627
Washington, Townshend, of St. Paul's	Stafford	Will	1744	TQ 08:2, p. 115

---

[1] *New England Historical and Genealogical Register*, Vol. 45 (1891), pp. 209-213, from an attested copy sold in 1891.

NAME	LOCATION	TYPE	YEAR	REFERENCE(S)
Washington, William	Caroline	Will	1843	Note[1]
Washington, William Augustine	Williamsburg	Will	1810	V:Mss1 B4678 a 4498
Waterland, Michaell	Charles City	Will (N)	1678	OB1677, p. 316
Waterman, Augustus, Rockingham Co.	Augusta	Will	1858	CF1895-119
Waters, Benjamin	Arlington	Will	1863	LVA Acc. #23305c
Waters, Edward	Elizabeth City	Will	1630c	V:Mss1 K6315 b
Waters, Edward, of Elizabeth City Co.	London	Will	1630	N:PROB11/158
Waters, Edward, of Elizabeth City Co.		Will	1630	VCRP, Survey #03964
Waters, William	Northampton	Will Ref.	1665	Hening, Vol. 8, p. 470
Waters, William	Northampton	Will	1689	LVA Acc. #24194
Waters, William, Lt. Col.	Botetourt	Will	1689	LVA Acc. #22676
Waters, William, of Northampton Co.	London	Will	1722	N:PROB11/587
Waters, William, of Northampton Co.	London	Will	1722	VCRP, Survey #04671
Waterson, John	Northampton	Will	1733	Note[2]
Watkin, Gifford, merchant		Will	1637	VCRP, Survey #03979
Watkins, Abner, of Lunenburg Co.	Cumberland	Will	1835	CF1854-001
Watkins, Benjamin P., in Goochland Co.	Henrico	Will	1824	CF1830-007
Watkins, Benjamin P., in Goochland Co.	Henrico	Will	1824	CF1830-007
Watkins, Benjamin Pride	Goochland	Will	1824	V:Mss1 D1124 a 285+
Watkins, Edward, in Culpeper Co.	Frederick	Will	1787	CF1810-025
Watkins, Edward, in Culpeper Co.	Frederick	Will	1787	CF1851-029
Watkins, Edward, of St. Mark's Parish	Culpeper	Will	1787	VMHB 43, p. 173
Watkins, Elizabeth	Buckingham	Will	1834	VGSQ 9, p. 17
Watkins, George, in Charlotte Co.	Lynchburg	Will	1820	CF1855-001
Watkins, Henry A.	Charlotte	Will	1848	V:Mss2 W3245 a 1
Watkins, James	Surry	Will	1692	T:D&W4, p. 285a
Watkins, Joel	Buckingham	Inventory	1824	VGSQ 9, p. 17
Watkins, John	Henrico	Will	1744	Records, Vol. 4, p. 1291
Watkins, John	Buckingham	Will	1768	VGSQ 9, p. 17
Watkins, John	Chesterfield	Will	1855	V:Mss1 D1124 a 285+
Watkins, John, in Dinwiddie Co.	Petersburg	Will	1820	CF1839-062
Watkins, John, in Dinwiddie Co.	Petersburg	Will	1820	CF1851-021
Watkins, John, Jr.	Surry	Will	1797	LVA Wills/Admin. DB
Watkins, Joseph, in Goochland Co.	Henrico	Will	(nd)	CF1830-007
Watkins, Martha S.B.	Surry	Will (U)	1835	VTG 13:3, p. 126
Watkins, Martha S.B.	Surry	Will Abstract	1835	VG 13, p. 55
Watkins, Mary, in Goochland Co.	Henrico	Will	1824	CF1830-007
Watkins, Mayo C., in Goochland Co.	Henrico	Will	1812	CF1830-007
Watkins, Sarah	Culpeper	Will Abstract	1807	VMHB 43, p. 175
Watkins, Silas	Buckingham	Inventory	1799	Note[3]
Watkins, Stephens		Will	1754	UVA Acc. #38-106+
Watkins, Thomas	Hanover	Will	1835	LVA Acc. #30400
Watkins, Thomas	Hanover	Will Ref.	1835	Cocke:159
Watkins, William	Essex	Will	1789	CF1808-019
Watlington, Nathaniel	Gloucester	Will	1816	LVA Acc. #22130
Watson, Andrew	Stafford	Will	1679	MVG 29:3, p. 194

---

[1] Caroline Co. Land Causes, 1835-1913, Vol. 1, p. 97.

[2] Northampton County Land Causes, 1731-1754, p. 234.

[3] LVA, Acc. #24813, George Brown Goode Papers, Box 3, correspondence folder, letter of 17 OCT 1859.

NAME	LOCATION	TYPE	YEAR	REFERENCE(S)
Watson, Andrew	Stafford	Will	1679	Land Office
Watson, Andrew	Norfolk City	Will	1801	LVA Acc. #24194
Watson, Anna, in McCracken Co. KY	Powhatan	Will	1835	CF1868-012
Watson, David	Louisa	Will	1883	UVA MSS 38-79
Watson, Elizabeth Shelton	Louisa	Will	1863	UVA MSS 38-79
Watson, George, Dr.	Richmond City	Will	1853c	V:Mss1 W3395 a 151+
Watson, James	Amherst	Will	1792	MVG 47:3, p. 249
Watson, James	Louisa	Will	1823	UVA MSS 38-79
Watson, James	Prince Edward	Will	1824	LVA Acc. #21781
Watson, Robert	Isle of Wight	Will	1651	VMHB 6, p. 120
Watts, Anna	Brunswick	Will	1822	LVA Wills/Admin. DB
Watts, Anna	Brunswick	Will	1822	SV 3:1, p. 38
Watts, Arthur, in Dinwiddie Co.	Lynchburg	Will	1755	CF1816-007
Watts, Edward, in Roanoke Co.	Bedford	Will	1859	CF1863-008
Watts, Edward Moore, in Norfolk Co.	Portsmouth	Will	1849	CF1910-003
Watts, Eliz. Breckenridge, Roanoke Co.	Bedford	Will	1862	CF1863-008
Watts, Hugh	Middlesex	Will	1720	TVF 12:2, p. 108
Watts, Jane, of Elizabeth City Co.	Williamsburg	Will Abstract	1798	Crozier, p. 61
Watts, John, of Caroline Co.	Mecklenburg	Will	1775	CF1786-002
Watts, Martha Christian	Nelson	Will	1833	UVA MSS 795
Watts, Mary, in Campbell Co.	Roanoke	Will	1836	CF1854-006
Watts, Samuel	Elizabeth City	Will	1798	Note[1]
Watts, Shadrack	Hanover	Will	1792	Note[2]
Watts, Stephen	Nelson	Will	1831	UVA MSS 795
Watts, Thomas	Elizabeth City	Will	1727	Note[3]
Watts, Thomas	Essex	Will	1767	Fleet 2:303
Watts, Thomas	Elizabeth City	Will	1815	Note[4]
Watts, William	Dinwiddie	Estate Ref.	1802	LP:20 DEC 1802
Watts, William, in Campbell Co.	Roanoke	Will	1798	CF1854-006
Watts, Winchester, in Norfolk Co.	Portsmouth	Will	1857	CF1859-004
Waugh, David		Will	1694	VCRP, Survey #04714
Waugh, David, of Stafford Co.	London	Will	1694	N:PROB11/422
Waugh, Gowry	Stafford	Will	1781	V:Mss1 P3374 b 78
Waugh, John A., of Dinwiddie Co.	Amelia	Will	1815	LP 1810-1816 Box 2
Wax, Henry, Capt.	Botetourt	Will	1796	LVA Acc. #22676
Wayland, Adam	Culpeper	Will Ref.	1782	UVA MSS 7653
Wayles, John	Charles City	Will	1773	OB
Wayne, Anthony		Will	1796c	V:Mss1 G7945 a 537+
Wease, Michael, in Hampshire Co.	Frederick	Will	1780	CF1830-145
Weatherly, Mathias, in Loudoun Co.	Frederick	Will	1822	CF1830-267
Weatherspoon, John	Charles City	Inventory	1726	D&W1724, p. 101
Weatherspoon, John, in Westover Par.	Charles City	Will	1726	D&W1724, p. 76
Weatherspoon, John, of Westover Par.	Charles City	Will	1726	D&W1724, p. 76
Weaver, John George	Augusta	Will	1790	LVA Acc. #36280-45
Webb, Frances	Lancaster	Will	1781	LP

---

[1] Elizabeth City County Superior Court Land Causes, 1809-1813, p. 22.
[2] LVA, U.S. Circuit Court Records, Box 187, *Donald, Scott & Co. v. Watts* (1820).
[3] Elizabety City County Superior Court Land Causes, 1809-1813, p. 19.
[4] Elizabeth City County Superior Court Land Causes, 1809-1813, p. 23.

NAME	LOCATION	TYPE	YEAR	REFERENCE(S)
Webb, Herdiman	Prince George	Will	1842	SV 9:3, p. 107
Webb, Isaac, of South Farnham Parish	Essex	Will Ref.	1729	Fleet 2:202
Webb, James, of Nansemond Co.	Isle of Wight	Account	1785	CF1809
Webb, James, of Norfolk Co.	Williamsburg	Will Abstract	1792	Crozier, p. 62
Webb, James, of Southfarnham Parish	Essex	Will	1716	TQ 07:3, p, 197
Webb, James, of Southfarnham Parish	Essex	Will	1771	TQ 07:4, p. 270
Webb, James, of Southfarnham Parish	Essex	Will Abstract	1773	Fleet 2:343
Webb, James, of Southfarnham Parish	Essex	Will	1774	TQ 07:4, p. 273
Webb, Jesse, in Campbell Co.	Bedford	Will	1843	CF1851-036
Webb, John	Henrico	Inventory	1726	Records, Vol. 2, p. 665
Webb, John	Henrico	Will	1736	Records, Vol. 3, p. 991
Webb, John, of South Farnham Parish	Essex	Will	1767	Fleet 2:335
Webb, Lillian	Essex	Will	1792	Fleet 2:336
Webb, Lilly Ann	Essex	Will	1792	CF1798-006
Webb, Mary, in Norfolk Co.	Portsmouth	Will	1858	CF1875-010
Webb, Mary, in Norfolk Co.	Portsmouth	Will	1858	CF1860-009
Webb, Mary, of Turkey Island	Henrico	Will	1809	VGSQ 18:3, p. 86
Webb, Matthias, of Isle of Wight Co.	Williamsburg	Will Abstract	1785	Crozier, p. 60
Webb, Motley	Northumberland	Will (U)	1779	NHS 25, p. 91
Webb, Notley, of Northumberland Co.	Williamsburg	Will Abstract	1785	Crozier, p. 60
Webb, Samuel, Dr.	New Kent	Will	1853	LVA Acc. #41008, r4611
Webb, Samuel, Dr.	New Kent	Will	1853	Fleet, Huntington Data
Webb, William	Buckingham	Will	1830	LVA Acc. #21322
Webb, William	Buckingham	Will	1830	Weisiger 1:039
Webb, William, of Northumberland Co.	Williamsburg	Will Abstract	1763	Crozier, p. 59
Webb, William, of Richmond Co.	Middlesex	Will	1765	BRCD
Weblin, Sarah	Princess Anne	Will	1769	V:Mss1 Sh485 a 24-26
Weblin, Sarah	Princess Anne	Will	1771	DB12, p. 92
Webster, Samuel	Northampton	Will	1665	D&W1657, p. 227
Weedon, A.B.	Prince William	Will	1878	CF1903-013
Weedon, George, of Washington Parish	Westmoreland	Will Ref.	1703	Winfree, p. 371
Weeks, John	Prince George	Will	1811	SV 9:2, p. 18
Weeks, William	Prince George	Will	1843	SV 9:3, p. 107
Wehmeier, Bernard	Fairfax	Will	1859	X
Weir, Bladen	Fairfax	Inventory	1853	X
Weir, Charity	Prince William	Acct. Ref.	1843	CM:02 OCT 1843
Weir, Charity [Ware]	Prince William	Acct. Ref.	1843	CM:07 AUG 1843
Weire, John	Rappahannock*	Will Ref.	1671	Sweeny, p. 7
Weitzell, John, Sr.	Rockingham	Will	1827	LVA Acc. #37710
Welch, Daniel	Lancaster	Will	1661	LP
Welch, Lucy Martin	Fauquier	Will	1856	V:Mss1 P4686 c 1246+
Welch, Nathaniel	Madison	Will	1815	V:Mss1 B2346 a 1162
Welch, Reuben, of Hanover Co.	Essex	Inventory	1729	Fiduciaries 1729
Welch, Walter	Rappahannock*	Will	1689	Sweeny, p. 143
Welles, Philip, of James City Co.	Henrico	Will	1694	Records, Vol. 1, p. 89
Wellford, Robert	Fredericksburg	Will	1823	V:Mss2 W4595 a 4
Wells, Amy	Dinwiddie	Will	1791	LVA Acc. #27293-9
Wells, Joseph	Prince William	Will Ref.	1843	CM:04 DEC 1843
Wells, Joseph, in Lee Co.	Wise	Will	1855	CF1873-010
Wells, Phillip	Henrico	Will	1694	Records, Vol. 1, p. 89
Welsh, Richard	Rappahannock*	Will	1691	Sweeny, p. 150

NAME	LOCATION	TYPE	YEAR	REFERENCE(S)
West, Benjamin C., of Caswell Co., NC	Danville	Will	1850	DBB:019
West, Charles	King William	Will Ref.	1734	Hening, Vol. 7, p. 488
West, Drury	Henrico	Will Ref.	1791	Fleet 2:350
West, Francis		Will	1634	VCRP, Survey #03968
West, Hugh	Fairfax	Will	1754	X
West, Hugh	Fairfax	Division	1783	X
West, Hugh, of Truro Parish	Fairfax	Will	1754	CF1869-008
West, Isaac, in Montgomery Co.	Floyd	Will	(nd)	CF1839-002
West, Isham	Henrico	Will	1771	Records, Vol. 7, p. 2131
West, John	New Kent	Will Ref.	1689	Hening, Vol. 6, p. 321
West, John	Northumberland	Will	1759	CF1807-003
West, John	Charles City	Will Partial	1764	W&D1763, p. 313
West, John	Fairfax	Will	1776	X
West, John	Fairfax	Will	1806	X
West, John, Maj.	Stafford	Will	1716	TQ 20:2, p. 102
West, John, of Stafford Co.	Fairfax	Will	1717	Note[1]
West, Mary, of Gloucester Co.	Williamsburg	Will Abstract	1784	Crozier, p. 59
West, Nathaniel	King William	Will Ref.	1727	Hening, Vol. 5, p. 297
West, Nathaniel	King & Queen	Estate Ref.	1752	Hening, Vol. 6, p. 322
West, Ralph	Williamsburg	Will Abstract	1798	Crozier, p. 62
West, Sarah	Surry	Will	1793	WB1, p. 41
West, Thomas	King William	Estate Ref.	1761	Hening, Vol. 7, p. 488
West, Thomas, in Campbell Co.	Lynchburg	Will	1829	CF1830-062
West, Thomas Wade, in Norfolk Co.	Arlington	Will	1800	CF1812-004
West, William		Will	1616	VCRP, Survey #03110
West, William	Charles City	Inventory	1772	Records, p. 351
West, William, of Baltimore Town MD	Fairfax	Will	1791	CF1869-008
West, William, of Baltimore Town MD	Fairfax	Will	1791	X
Westbrooke, William, of Southampton	Williamsburg	Will Abstract	1805	Crozier, p. 62
Westhrope, John, merchant		Will	1656	VCRP, Survey #03130
Westmore, William B., King William Co.	Essex	Will	1839	CF1841-008
Westmoreland, Richard	King William	Inventory	1706	RB1, p. 301
Weston, Lewis	Arlington	Will	1795	CRA:151
Whaley, Alexander	Fairfax	Account	1845	X
Whaley, George	Fairfax	Sale	1843	X
Whaley, George	Fairfax	Will	1843	X
Whaley, Gibson	Fairfax	Division	1822	X
Whaplett, Thomas		Will	1636	VCRP, Survey #03975
Wharton, Ann	Accomack	Will	1766	T: from Lancaster
Wharton, Charlotte A., in Goochland Co.	Hanover	Will	1841	CF1868-012
Wharton, Charlotte A., in Goochland Co.	Hanover	Will	1841	Cocke:90
Wharton, John	Accomack	Will	1814	LVA Acc. #28954
Wharton, John	Gloucester	Estate Ref.	1852	Note[2]
Wharton, Richard, of Williamsburg	London	Will	1712	N:PROB11/532
Wharton, Richard, s/o William		Will	1713	VCRP, Survey #04359
Wharton, William, in Culpeper Co.	Fauquier	Will	1858	CF1894-082

---

[1] Fairfax County Land Records (of Long Standing), 1742-1770, p. 208.

[2] LVA, Land Office Revlutionary War Military Certificate Papers, John Wharton, Folders 6 and 7.

NAME	LOCATION	TYPE	YEAR	REFERENCE(S)
Whayne, Benjamin	King & Queen	Estate Ref.	1834	Note[1]
Wheat, A.J., in Augusta Co.	Fairfax	Will	1873	X
Wheeler, Francis, merchant		Will	1660	VCRP, Survey #03524
White, Alice L.	Hanover	Will	1864	CF1886-012
White, C.O., in Roanoke Co.	Bedford	Will	1859	CF1877-062
White, Caroline Battaile, in Fauquier Co.	Fairfax	Will	1853	CF1869-003
White, Celie, in Campbell Co.	Lynchburg	Will	1892	CF1894-058
White, Charles	Prince George	Will	1850	SV 9:4, p. 158
White, Elisha	Hanover	Will	1860	Cocke:165
White, Elisha	Hanover	Will	1870	CF1877-010
White, Elisha	Hanover	Will	1870	CF1887-013
White, Elisha	Hanover	Will	1870	CF1884-019
White, Elizabeth F.	Hanover	Will	1876	CF1887-013
White, Frances	Caroline	Will	1859	W&D1794, p. 82
White, Francis, in Hampshire Co.	Frederick	Will	1826	CF1840-051
White, Hannah	Surry	Will (N)	1785	WB12, p. 55
White, Henry, in DE	Roanoke	Will	1857	CF1857-008
White, James, in Fauquier Co.	Warren	Will	1849	CF1852-003
White, Jeremiah	Pittsylvania	Will	1788	D&W1, p. 169
White, John	Surry	Will	1679	T:D&W2, p. 209a[2]
White, John	Orange	Will	1788	WB3, p. 178
White, John	Henrico	Will	1809	Fleet, Huntington Data
White, John	Henrico	Will	1809	LVA Acc. #41008, r4610
White, John, in Berkeley Co.	Frederick	Will	1793	CF1815-053
White, John, in Fauquier Co.	Rappahannock	Will	1841	CF1844-013
White, John [of *Pleasant Grove*]	Caroline	Will	1813	V:Mss2 W58409 a 1
White, John [of *Pleasant Grove*]	Caroline	Will	1820	W&D1794, p. 14
White, Joseph	Orange	Will	1773	WB2, p. 475
White, Joseph, Somerset Co. MD and	Spotsylvania	Will	1743	M: L23 f162
White, Mary	Hanover	Will	1859	CF1887-013
White, Mary	Hanover	Will	1859	CF1913-006
White, Mary J.	Hanover	Will	1859	CF1886-040
White, Matthew J., in Nansemond Co.	Isle of Wight	Will	1840	CF1845-049
White, Mildred	Hanover	Will	1850	Cocke:163
White, Mildred	Hanover	Will	1850	CF1860-006
White, Moses	Hanover	Will	1842	LVA Acc. #41008, r4609
White, Moses	Hanover	Will	1877	CF1887-013
White, Moses, of St. Paul's Parish	Hanover	Will	1842	Fleet, Huntington Data
White, Moses, of St. Paul's Parish	Hanover	Will	1842	Cocke:164
White, Nathaniel	Hanover	Will	1836	Cocke:166
White, Nathaniel	Hanover	Will	1836	CF1851-002
White, Oliver	King & Queen	Will	1863	LVA Acc. #24522
White, Oliver	King & Queen	Will	1863	V:Mss3 K5893 a 69-86
White, Oliver	King & Queen	Will Ref.	1863	KQB:2
White, Richard	Orange	Will	1849	UVA MSS 702
White, Richard B.	Caroline	Will	1859	Note[3]

---

[1] LVA, Land Office Revlutionary War Military Certificate Papers, Benjamin Whayne, Folder 9

[2] Refer to *Sweeny*, p. 9, where the compiler lists wills given in *Torrence* that have not been found of record in Rappahannock County.

[3] Caroline Co. Land Causes, 1835-1913, Vol. 1, p. 132.

NAME	LOCATION	TYPE	YEAR	REFERENCE(S)
White, Robert B.	Prince William	Will	1881	CF1895-023
White, Silas	Hanover	Will	1866	Cocke:163
White, Smith J.R., in Caroline Co.	Essex	Will	1893	CF1905-013
White, Tarpley	Henrico	Will	1811	LVA Acc. #41008, r4610
White, Tarpley	Henrico	Will	1811	Fleet, Huntington Data
White, Thomas	Hanover	Will	1894	CF1906-036
White, William	Hanover	Will	1812	CF1860-006
White, William	Hanover	Will	1812	Cocke:162
White, William	Hanover	Estate Ref.	1850	Note[1]
White, William, mariner		Will	1697	VCRP, Survey #04775
White, William, of Fauquier Co.	Prince William	Will	1804	Haymarket District
White, Willis, Sr.	Orange	Will	1830	UVA MSS 702
Whitehead, Dudley, in Pr. Anne Co.	Norfolk	Will	1833	CF1845-014
Whitehead, John, in Orange Co.	Fairfax	Will	1869	CF1885-029
Whitehurst, Tanor C., Princess Anne Co.	Portsmouth	Will	1894	CF1909-053
Whitescarver, Betty, in IA	Rappahannock	Will	1895	CF1898-005
Whithelme, Christian, galleypotmaker		Will	1630	VCRP, Survey #03958
Whithers, James, in Fauquier Co.	Culpeper	Will	1808	CF1857-008
Whiting, Francis, in Jefferson Co.	Frederick	Will	1818	CF1836-031
Whiting, Francis, of Gloucester Co.	Williamsburg	Will Abstract	1826	Crozier, p. 62
Whiting, Mary Ann DeButts Dulany	Fauquier	Will	1894	V:Mss1 D3545a794-800
Whiting, Peter Beverley	Gloucester	Will	1783	V:Mss2 W5895 a 1
Whiting, Thomas	Gloucester	Estate Ref.	1798	LP:22 DEC 1802
Whiting, Thomas, in Abingdon Parish	Gloucester	Will	1782	Note[2]
Whiting, Thomas, of Abingdon Parish	Gloucester	Will	1782	Fleet, Huntington Data
Whitlock, David	Hanover	Will	1798	CF1860-010
Whitlock, David	Hanover	Will	1798	CF1860-003
Whitlock, David, of St. Paul's Parish	Hanover	Will	1798	TQ 18:3, p. 173
Whitlock, David, of St. Paul's Parish	Hanover	Will	1798	Cocke:167
Whitlock, James	Hanover	Will	1736	TQ 18:4, p. 231
Whitlock, James, of Hanover Co.	Prince Edward	Will Abstract	1736	VGS Bulletin V, p. 43
Whitlock, James, of St. Charles	Hanover	Will	1736	LVA Wills/Admin. DB
Whitlock, Martha	Hanover	Will	1839	CF1860-003
Whitlock, Martha	Hanover	Will	1839	Cocke:168
Whitlock, Thomas	Rappahannock*	Will Abstract	1659	VMHB 5, p. 285
Whitlocke, Frances	King William	Will	(nd)	V:Mss4 K5898 b
Whitloe, William	Henrico	Will	1777	Note[3]
Whitmore, Abraham, of Rockingham Co.	Augusta	Will	1835	CF1853-020
Whitmore, Ann	Prince George	Will	1857	SV 10:1, p. 13
Whitmore, Charles	Dinwiddie	Will	1785	VGSQ 10:1, p. 6
Whitnall, William	Rappahannock*	Will (N)	1686	Sweeny, p. 152
Whitney, Chares B., of Campbell Co.	Danville	Will	1862	WBA:285
Whitney, Jeremiah	Buckingham	Division	1783	LVA Acc. #30721
Whitney, John	Richmond City	Will	1798	T:HCD2, p. 384
Whitney, John	Richmond City	Account	1799	Note[4]

---

[1] LVA, Land Office Revlutionary War Military Certificate Papers, William White, Folder 24.

[2] John Bigelow, *Memoir of the Life and Public Services of John Charles Fremont* (New York, 1856), p. 14.

[3] Henrico County Proceedings of Commissioners ..., 1774-1782, p. 14.

[4] Richmond City Hustings Court Deeds, No. 2, 1792-1799, p. 524.

NAME	LOCATION	TYPE	YEAR	REFERENCE(S)
Whitney, Susanna	Buckingham	Will	1802	LVA Acc. #30721
Whitney, Susannah	Buckingham	Will	1794	V:Mss2 W6165 a 1
Whittacre, George		Will	1654	VCRP, Survey #03125
Whittall, Francis	Louisa	Will	1751	V:Mss1 B2346 a 1160
Whitton, Wlliam, of Drysdale Parish	Caroline	Will	1730	TQ 21:2, p. 123
Whowell, Andrew	York	Will	1631	NNHM 15:1, p. 1390
Wiatt, Peter	Gloucester	Will	1815	LVA Acc. #20890
Wiatt, Peter	Gloucester	Will	1815	LVA Acc. #21105
Wicker, Bentley, in Hanover Co.	Henrico	Will	1865	CF1868-001
Wiggins, Wiley, in Gates Co. NC	Nansemond	Will	1897	CF1935-018
Wigginton, Henry	Prince William	Acct. Ref.	1844	CM:05 FEB 1844
Wigginton, Henry	Prince William	Inv. Ref.	1844	CM:05 FEB 1844
Wigginton, Roger	Westmoreland	Will	1717	V:Mss10: no. 121
Wigginton, Roger	Westmoreland	Will	1718	WB6, p. 349
Wight, Grace Hughes	Goochland	Will	(nd)	V:Mss2 W6393 b
Wight, Hezekiah Lord	Goochland	Will	(nd)	V:Mss2 W6393 b
Wight, William Leeds	Goochland	Will	(nd)	V:Mss2 W6393 b
Wilcocks, John, Capt., of Accomack Co.	London	Will	1628	N:PROB11/153
Wilcocks, John, Capt., of Accomack Co.	London	Will	1628	VCRP, Survey #03117
Wilcocks, Richard	Rappahannock*	Will (N)	1688	Sweeny, p. 141
Wilcox, Edmund	Amherst	Will	1781	TQ 13:4, p. 268
Wild, Daniel		Will Ref.	1691	VCRP, Survey #03751
Wilder, Amherst H., of St. Paul MN	Arlington	Will	1895	WB10:270; File #763A
Wiles, Jesse	Dinwiddie	Account	1822	BRCD
Wiley, John	Essex	Will Abstract	1762	Fleet 2:304
Wiley, John, of King William Co.	Halifax	Will	1790	CF1824-020
Wilhoit, John, in Madison Co.	Culpeper	Will	1823	CF1836-017
Wilhoit, Joseph	Madison	Will	1838	LVA Acc. #41008, r4611
Wilhoit, Larance	Richmond City	Will	1849	Fleet, Huntington Data
Wilkerson, Stith	Prince George	Will	1859	SV 10:1, p. 14
Wilkes, Colston, in Washington DC	Brunswick	Will	1835	CF1838-027
Wilkins, Edmund	Prince George	Will	1844	SV 9:3, p. 109
Wilkins, John L., in OH	Brunswick	Will	1898	CF1906-040
Wilkins, Joseph, in Greensville Co.	Brunswick	Will	1816	CF1822-024
Wilkins, Joseph, in MD	Albemarle	Will	1850	CF1891-043
Wilkins, Mary	Prince George	Will	1711	SV 10:2, p. 56
Wilkins, Nathaniel	Northampton	Estate Ref.	1792	Hening, Vol. 13, p. 617
Wilkinson, Benjamin	Prince William	Will Abstract	1770	VGS Bulletin VII, p. 23
Wilkinson, John	Prince William	Will	1814	CF1831-003
Wilkinson, John D., of James City Co.	Williamsburg	Will Abstract	1814	Crozier, p. 60
Wilkinson, Mills, of Nansemond Co.	Williamsburg	Will Abstract	1804	Crozier, p. 60
Wilkinson, Thomas	York	Will	1668	MVG 29:4, p. 321
Wilkinson, William	James City	Will	1800	LVA John K. Martin Papers
Wilkinson, William, of Nansemond Co.	Williamsburg	Will Abstract	1807	Crozier, p. 60
Will, George		Will	(nd)	UVA MSS 10543-a
Willabee, Hugh	Amherst	Will	1769	CF1796-006
Williams, A.C., of Fairfax Co. VA	Arlington	Will	1899	WB10:371; File #087A
Williams, Adolph Dill	Richmond City	Will	1884c	V:Mss2 W6767c
Williams, Alar	Fairfax	Will	1804	X
Williams, Bazil, of *Prince Seaton*	Arlington	Will	1854	CF1857-001
Williams, Benjamin	Prince George	Will	1851	SV 9:4, p. 158

NAME	LOCATION	TYPE	YEAR	REFERENCE(S)
Williams, Daniel	Nansemond	Will	1768	LVA Acc. #28516
Williams, Daniel	Nansemond	Will	1768	VG 23, p. 109
Williams, Daniel, in Nansemond Co.	Southampton	Will	1768	CF1808-015
Williams, David G., in Lunenburg Co.	Henrico	Will	1858	CF1887-025
Williams, Ebenezer, in Hardy Co.	Frederick	Will	1818	CF1859-041
Williams, Elias, in NC	Princess Anne	Will	1805	CF1829-001
Williams, Eliza J.	Nottoway	Will	1853	CF1882-001
Williams, Frederick, in Petersburg	Lynchburg	Will	1829	CF1876-048
Williams, George	Stafford	Will	1750	BRCD
Williams, George	Prince William	Acct. Ref.	1844	CM:03 JUN 1844
Williams, George	Fairfax	Will	1845	X
Williams, George, in Nelson Co.	Albemarle	Will	1849	CF1895-147
Williams, George, in Stafford Co.	Fauquier	Will	1750	CF1807-041
Williams, George, of Sittingbourne Par.	Rappahannock*	Will	1688	Sweeny, p. 139
Williams, Henry H., in MD	Fauquier	Will	1873	CF1874-001
Williams, James	Charles City	Will	1790	LP, box 51, folder 271
Williams, James	Petersburg	Will	1818	LVA Acc. #24194
Williams, Jesse	Chesterfield	Will	1874	V:Mss1 C7833 a 125+
Williams, Jesse	Richmond City	Will	1874c	V:Mss2 W6767c
Williams, John	Henrico	Will	1766	LVA Acc. #35482
Williams, John	Henrico	Will	1766	LVA Acc. #41008, r4610
Williams, John	Henrico	Will	1766	MVG 35:4, p. 314
Williams, John	Henrico	Will	1766	Fleet, Huntington Data
Williams, John	Henrico	Will	1776	Note[1]
Williams, John	Lunenburg	Will	1795	CF1806-009
Williams, John	Lunenburg	Will	1797	CF1809-013
Williams, John	Gloucester	Inventory	1807	V:Mss1 R5595 a 4,241+
Williams, John B., in Prince George Co.	Petersburg	Will	1828	CF1841-033
Williams, John, in Brunswick Co.	Henry	Will	1772	CF1810-004
Williams, John, orphans of	Gloucester	Guard. Bond	1810	V:Mss1 R5595 a 4,241+
Williams, L.E., in Campbell Co.	Lynchburg	Will	1889	CF1897-081
Williams, Mary, in Lunenburg Co.	Bedford	Will	1857	CF1902-063
Williams, Philip	Brunswick	Will	1823	LVA Wills/Admin. DB
Williams, Philip	Brunswick	Will	1823	SV 3:1, p. 37
Williams, Rachel	Dinwiddie	Will	1793	VGSQ 10:1, p. 11
Williams, Rachel	Dinwiddie	Will	1793	LVA Acc. #27293-10
Williams, Richard		Will	1653	VCRP, Survey #03120
Williams, Richard, Sr., in Pr. Geo. Co.	Petersburg	Will	1811	CF1841-033
Williams, Richard, Sr., in Pr. Geo. Co.	Prince Edward	Will	1811	Judgments
Williams, Roger	Surry	Will	1708	T: correct from 1709
Williams, Samuel, of Kingston Parish	Gloucester	Will	1789	LVA Acc. #22963
Williams, Thomas	Nottoway	Will	1798	BRCD
Williams, Thomas	Mathews	Inventory	1823	LVA Acc. #22963
Williams, Thomas C.	Chesterfield	Will	1888	V:Mss1 C7833 a 125+
Williams, Thomas R., in Nottoway Co.	Lynchburg	Will	1798	CF1833-010
Williams, Travis H.	Prince George	Will	1861	SV 10:1, p. 15
Williams, William	Brunswick	Will	1800	SV 3:3, p. 114
Williamson, Beverly, in Amherst Co.	Lynchburg	Will	1806	CF1825-079

---

[1] Henrico County Proceedings of Commissioners ..., 1774-1782, p. 4.

NAME	LOCATION	TYPE	YEAR	REFERENCE(S)
Williamson, Edward	Essex	Will Abstract	1748	Fleet, 5th Collection
Williamson, Edward	Essex	Will Ref.	1748	Fleet 2:327
Williamson, George	Henrico	Inventory	1768	Records, Vol. 6, p. 2031
Williamson, John		Will	1701	V:Mss1 B4678 a 4788
Williamson, John	Hanover	Will	1774	LCH 2, p. 15
Williamson, John	Hanover	Will Ref.	1786	Hening, Vol. 12, p. 381
Williamson, John	Essex	Will	1791	CF1809-007
Williamson, John G., in Williamsburg	James City	Will	1865	CF1871-008
Williamson, John, in Hanover Co.	Henrico	Will	1769	CF1893-009
Williamson, John, in Henrico Co.	Hanover	Will	1807	CF1840-001
Williamson, John, of St. Paul's Parish	Hanover	Will	1767	LCH 8:2, p. 54
Williamson, John, of St. Paul's Parish	Hanover	Will	1769	LVA Acc. #29327
Williamson, Martha A., Nansemond Co.	Dinwiddie	Will	1874	CF1882-020
Williamson, Richard	Henrico	Will	1771	Records, Vol. 7, p. 2101
Williamson, Richard, in Henrico Co.	Goochland	Will	1771	CF1812-004
Williamson, Richard, merchant tailor		Will	1646	VCRP, Survey #03993
Williamson, Susanna	Henrico	Will	1811	VGSQ 18:3, p. 87
Williamson, Thomas		Estate Ref.	1794	Shepherd, Vol. 1, p. 332
Williamson, William	Essex	Will Abstract	1742	Fleet 2:326
Willing, Abigail		Will	1791c	V:Mss1 B9963 c 9-11
Willingham, Jarred	Halifax	Will	1792	WB2, p. 505
Willis, Francis, of Gloucester Co.		Will	1691	VCRP, Survey #03749
Willis, Francis, of Ware Parish	Gloucester	Will	1764	Note[1]
Willis, Henry	Williamsburg	Will	1740	FDC L566-115
Willis, Joel, in PA	Fauquier	Will	1793	CF1804-051
Willis, John, in Culpeper Co.	Rappahannock	Will	1848	CF1868-006
Willoughby, John, of Norfolk Co.	Williamsburg	Will Abstract	1791	Crozier, p. 63
Wills, Amy, of Bath Parish	Dinwiddie	Will	1791	VGSQ 10:1, p. 10
Wills, Elias	Fluvanna	Will Abstract	1805	VGS Bulletin VI, p. 36
Wills, Elizabeth Bernard	Buckingham	Will	1855	V:Mss1 B4568 a 47-48
Wills, Elizabeth, of Warwick Co.	Isle of Wight	Will	1774	Judgments 1790 AUG
Wills, George G., of King William Co.	Williamsburg	Will Abstract	1785	Crozier, p. 64
Wills, George G., of King William Co.	Williamsburg	Will Abstract	1785	Crozier, p. 64
Wills, James, in Nelson Co.	Lynchburg	Will	1821	CF1821-055
Wills, John	Charles City	Will	1791	V:Mss5:3 W6857:1
Wills, John	Charles City	Will	1813	LVA Acc. #24523a
Wills, John, of Warwick Co.	Williamsburg	Will Abstract	1803	Crozier, p. 60
Wills, John, of Westover Parish	Charles City	Will	1791	LVA Acc. #24523c
Wills, John, of Westover Parish	Charles City	Will	1791	VGSQ 15, p. 68
Wills, Lawrence	Amelia	Will	1785c	DAR MSS 13 b5 f10
Wills, Mary, in Warwick Co.	Elizabeth City	Will	1766	D&WF, p. 78b
Wills, Mary, w/o Thomas, Warwick Co.	Albemarle	Will	1752	MVG 31:4, p. 354
Wills, Mary, w/o Matthew, Warwick Co.	Elizabeth City	Will Abstract	1766	VGS Bulletin VI, p. 37
Wills, Nathaniel, of Isle of Wight Co.	Williamsburg	Will Abstract	1823	Crozier, p. 64
Wills, Thomas, of Warwick Co.	York	Will	1766	MVG 31:4, p. 354
Wills, Thomas, the Elder, Warwick Co.	York	Will	1766	CF1794-005
Wills, Willis	Fluvanna	Will	1782	WB1, p. 50
Willson, Anne	Surry	Will	1702	T:D&W5, p. 246b

---

[1] LVA, U.S. Circuit Court Records, Box 79, *Cockran, Donald & Co. v. Willis' Exors.* (1810).

NAME	LOCATION	TYPE	YEAR	REFERENCE(S)
Willson, Henry, of Farnham Parish	Rappahannock*	Will	1688	Sweeny, p. 140
Willson, Samuel, Sr., in Rockbridge Co.	Frederick	Will	1805	CF1822-017
Willson, William	Lunenburg	Will	1796	CF1856-038
Wilmoth, Edward	Isle of Wight	Will Abstract	1647	VMHB 6, p. 244
Wilsher, John	Amherst	Will	1782	WB2, p. 51
Wilson, Ann, in Norfolk Co.	Princess Anne	Will	1851	CF1880-012
Wilson, Benjamin	Cumberland	Will	1814	Note[1]
Wilson, Charles, in Nottoway Co.	Dinwiddie	Will	1819	CF1849-005
Wilson, Charles, in Nottoway Co.	Lunenburg	Will	1819	CF1857-012
Wilson, Charlotte F., in Loudoun Co.	Fairfax	Will	1873	CF1875-018
Wilson, David J., in Botetourt Co.	Washington	Will	1881	CF1893-081
Wilson, David, of Stephensburg	D.C.	Will	1818	DCA:Box 173
Wilson, Edley		Will	1858	BRCD
Wilson, Edward R., in DE	Amelia	Will	1894	CF1901-046
Wilson, Emily G., in Madison Co. TN	Isle of Wight	Will	1895	CF1916-007
Wilson, Ephraim	Chesterfield	Will	1864	LVA Acc. #37460
Wilson, Goodrich, of Norfolk Co.	Williamsburg	Will Abstract	1785	Crozier, p. 65
Wilson, Goodrich [Willson]	Portsmouth	Will	1785	V:Mss2 P3575 a 1
Wilson, Henry	Prince William	Will	1778	LVA Acc. #36254-442
Wilson, James	Rockbridge	Will	1825	LVA Acc. #36280-4545
Wilson, James, of Norfolk Co.	Williamsburg	Will Abstract	1820	Crozier, p. 64
Wilson, John, in TN	Bland	Will	1887	CF1903-001
Wilson, Josiah		Will	1794	LVA Acc. #22069
Wilson, Margaret	Norfolk City	Will	1852	V:Mss1 C2358 d 640+
Wilson, Margaret B., in MD	Culpeper	Will	1896	CF1900-018
Wilson, Matthew	Cumberland	Will	(nd)	V:Mss1 N1786 a 6652+
Wilson, Robert	Campbell	Will	1830	Fleet, Huntington Data
Wilson, Robert	Campbell	Will	1830	LVA Acc. #41008, r4608
Wilson, Robert B., of Lunenburg Co.	Mecklenburg	Will	1849	CF1861-002
Wilson, Robert, s/o Robert		Will	1651	VCRP, Survey #04101
Wilson, Ruth S., in Pittsylvania Co.	Henry	Will	1889	CF1899-034
Wilson, Samuel	Cumberland	Will	1842c	V:Mss1 N1786 a 8222+
Wilson, Samuel, in Berkeley Co.	Frederick	Will	1816	CF1821-203
Wilson, Sarah		Will	1795	LVA Acc. #22069
Wilson, Thomas	Mason	Will	1822	V:Mss1 A d454 a 1
Wilson, Thomas, mariner		Will	1655	VCRP, Survey #03127
Wilson, William, Jr., of Norfolk Co.	Williamsburg	Will Abstract	1787	Crozier, p. 64
Wilson, William, of Botetourt Co.	Augusta	Will	1823	CF1856-050
Wilson, Willis, of Norfolk Co.	Williamsburg	Will Abstract	1798	Crozier, p. 63
Wilson, Woodroof	Botetourt	Will	1811	LVA Acc. #22676
Wilson, Zachariah	Caroline	Will	1825	LVA Acc. #24642(7)
Wilson, Zachariah	Caroline	Appraisal	1826	BRCD
Windsor, Richard, in Alexandria	Fairfax	Will	1876	CF1888-030
Wine, W.T., in Fauquier Co.	Culpeper	Will	1893	CF1902-024
Winfeild, Thomas, currier		Will	1722	VCRP, Survey #04670
Winfree, Valentine, in Chesterfield Co.	Powhatan	Will	1824	CF1878-013
Winfree, William W., in Chesterfield Co.	Powhatan	Will	1840	CF1855-003
Wingard, John, in Jefferson Co.	Frederick	Will	1816	CF1830-171

[1] Cumberland County Loose Papers, Box 40, Deeds and Wills Not Recorded.

NAME	LOCATION	TYPE	YEAR	REFERENCE(S)
Wingfield, Isaac	Hanover	Will Ref.	1864	Cocke:170
Wingfield, Isaac W.	Hanover	Will	1867	CF1870-014
Wingfield, Joseph S.	Hanover	Will	1887	CF1889-009
Wingfield, Martha R.	Hanover	Will	1871	CF1892-007
Wingfield, Robert	Louisa	Will	1767	LCH 8:2, p. 86
Wingfield, Thomas	Hanover	Will	1830	CF1849-002
Wingfield, Thomas	Hanover	Will	1830	Cocke:171
Wingfield, William	Hanover	Will Ref.	1843	Cocke:170
Wingfield, William, Jr.	Hanover	Will	1843	BRCD
Wingo, John, in Amelia Co.	Bedford	Will	1828	CF1867-013
Wingo, John, in Amelia Co.	Powhatan	Will	1828	CF1845-009
Wingo, John K.M., in Amelia Co.	Bedford	Will	1831	CF1855-044
Winn, Daniel	Lunenburg	Will	1799	LVA Acc. #22078
Winn, Gloucester	King William	Division	1800c	V:Mss4 K5898 b
Winn, Jane	Nottoway	Will	1851	BRCD
Winn, Jesse	Hanover	Will	1878	CF1880-018
Winn, Joseph	Lunenburg	Will	1800	CF1813-018
Winn, Joseph	Lunenburg	Will	1800	LVA Acc. #22078
Winn, Minor, in Fauquier Co.	Rappahannock	Will	1813	CF1849-010
Winn, Peter	Nottoway	Will	1839	BRCD
Winn, Polly	King William	Will	(nd)	V:Mss4 K5898 b
Winn, Susanna	Nottoway	Will	1795	WB1, p. 161
Winn, Thomas	Brunswick	Will	1799	SV 3:1, p. 36
Winn, W.H.C., in AR	Lunenburg	Will	1881	CF1902-001
Winslow, Benjamin	Essex	Will	1751	LVA Acc. #28958
Winslow, Benjamin	Essex	Will	1751	FDC L387-69
Winslow, Fortunatus, in Orange Co.	Greene	Will	1824	CF1844-002
Winslow, Fortunatus, in Orange Co.	Greene	Will	1824	CF1844-003
Winston, Edmund	Caroline	Will	1833	W&D1794, p. 32
Winston, Edmund	Hanover	Will	1875	V:Mss1 W8844 a 545+
Winston, Isaac	Hanover	Will	1760	Note[1]
Winston, John, Capt.	Hanover	Will	1797	VG 43, p. 291
Winston, John, of Hanover Co.	Louisa	Will	1798	CF1833-007
Winston, Peter	Hanover	Will	1829	LVA Acc. #24677
Winston, Philip B.	Hanover	Will	1852	CF1873-001
Winston, Philip B.	Hanover	Will	1853	Cocke:173
Winston, Thomas	Hanover	Will	1785	LVA Acc. #28459
Winston, Thomas, of Hanover Co.	Goochland	Will	1785	CF1810-001
Winston, Thomas, of Hanover Co.	Goochland	Will	1785	VGS Bulletin VII, p. 12
Winston, William C.	Hanover	Will	1880	CF1899-018
Winston, William, Maj., in St. Paul's P.	Hanover	Will	1781	TQ 19:4, p. 219
Winston, William O.	Hanover	Will	1862	CF1874-023
Winston, William O.	Hanover	Will	1864	CF1880-008
Winston, William O.	Hanover	Will Abstract	1867	Cocke:137
Winston, William S.	Louisa	Will	1847	UVA MSS 4762
Winston, William, Sr., of St. Paul's Par.	Hanover	Will, 1781	1811	G1:99
Winston, William, Sr., St. Paul's Parish	Hanover	Will Ref.	1781	VGS Bulletin VII, p. 13
Winter, William	Northumberland	Will	1733	M: L20 f749

---

[1] *The Huguenot*, Publication No. 6 (1933), p. 180.

NAME	LOCATION	TYPE	YEAR	REFERENCE(S)
Winterton, William, in Hampshire Co.	Frederick	Will	1804	CF1833-066
Wise, John		Will	1685	VCRP, Survey #03734
Wise, Ollo William	Accomack	Will	1748	M: L27 f62
Wishart, John	King George	Will	1774	FDC L564-61
Wishart, John	King George	Will	1774	UVA MSS 38-150
Wishart, William	Norfolk City	Inventory	1785	LVA-LP:08 DEC 1808
Wishart, William, of Princess Anne Co.	Norfolk City	Will	1783	LVA-LP:08 DEC 1808
Witcher, Nannie E., in Pittsylvania Co.	Franklin	Will	1897	CF1900-009
Witcher, Nathaniel N., Sr., Pittsylvania	Franklin	Will	1896	CF1900-009
Witcher, William A., in Pittsylvania Co.	Franklin	Will	1887	CF1895-053
Withers, Andrew F., c/o H.C.	Fairfax	Guard. Bond	1840	X
Withers, Elizabeth	Stafford	Will	1798	Note[1]
Withers, Elizabeth S., c/o H.C.	Fairfax	Guard. Bond	1840	X
Withers, Erasmus	Northumberland	Will (N)	1681	OB4, p. 94
Withers, James & wife Eliz., Stafford Co.	Fauquier	Inventory	1746	CF1789-011
Withers, James & wife Eliz., Stafford Co.	Fauquier	Inventory	1768	CF1789-011
Withers, James, in Stafford Co.	Fauquier	Will	1746	CF1794-018
Withers, James, of Stafford Co.	Fauquier	Will	1784	Note[2]
Withers, John	Stafford	Will Ref.	1698	Hening, Vol. 6, p. 513
Withers, John, Sr., in Stafford Co.	Fauquier	Will	1794	CF1815-041
Withers, John, Sr., of Overwharton Par.	Stafford	Will	1794	DAR Mag. 68, p. 493
Withers, Sarah	Stafford	Will	1797	Note[3]
Withers, Susannah, c/o H.C.	Fairfax	Guard. Bond	1840	X
Withers, William, Dr.	Sussex	Will	1824c	V:Mss1 M6154 a 66-70
Withers, William, in Fauquier Co.	Rappahannock	Will	1804	CF1834-004
Withrow, Joel	Roanoke	Will	1867c	V:Mss1 J6496 a939-973
Witmer, Nancy, in MD	Rockingham	Will	1857	CF1895-006
Witmore, Charles	Dinwiddie	Will	1785	LVA Acc. #27293-7
Witney, Augustine	Rappahannock*	Will Abstract	1659	VMHB 5, p. 285
Witten, William H., in WV	Tazewell	Will	1895	CF1896-060
Witzel, Martin	Augusta	Will	1795	WB1A, p. 20
Wodard, Lancelot [Woodward]	Charles City	Inventory	1731	D&W1724, p. 340
Woddrop, Ann, of Nansemond Co.	Williamsburg	Will Abstract	1789	Crozier, p. 63
Woddrop, Anne, in Nansemond Co.	Isle of Wight	Will	1789	CF1797-007
Woddrop, John, of Charles City Co.	Williamsburg	Will Abstract	1779	Crozier, p. 63
Woddrop, John, of Nansemond Co.	Williamsburg	Will Abstract	1766	Crozier, p. 63
Wodrow, Alexander		Will Ref.	1771	Hening, Vol. 11, p. 150
Wodrow, Alexander		Estate Ref.	1785	Hening, Vol. 12, p. 220
Wolfe, Jonas	Scott	Account	1857c	LVA Acc. #28951
Wolfe, Oliver	Scott	Account	1862c	LVA Acc. #28951
Womack, Charles, in Cumberland Co.	Amelia	Will	1838	CF1837-013
Womak, William	Henrico	Will	1718	Records, Vol. 2, p. 369
Womble, Matthew, convicted murderer		Estate Ref.	1785	Hening, Vol. 12, p. 201
Wood, Abraham, of Ft. Henry	Charles City	Will Partial	1682	LVA Acc. #24325a
Wood, Edward	Charles City	Inventory	1727	D&W1724, p. 159
Wood, Elizabeth, in Madison Co.	Culpeper	Will	1803	CF1838-005

---

[1] LVA, Stafford County Loose Papers, 1671-1797, Folder 20; recorded in now lost Stafford County Wills, Bk. Y, p. 498.
[2] Fauquier County Land Causes 1, 1809-1815, p. 287.
[3] LVA, Stafford County Court Records, 1671-1797, Folder 20.

NAME	LOCATION	TYPE	YEAR	REFERENCE(S)
Wood, Frances A., in TN	Albemarle	Will	1889	CF1890-014
Wood, Henry, in Kanawha Co.	Bath	Will	1814	CF1827-001
Wood, James, in Henrico Co.	Frederick	Will	1804	CF1840-058
Wood, James, in Henrico Co.	Frederick	Will	1813	CF1829-175
Wood, John	Orange	Will	1785	WB3, p. 90
Wood, John, in Lynchburg	Campbell	Will	1871	CF1887-027
Wood, John Scott	Culpeper	Will	1778	FDC L562-26
Wood, Josiah	Surry	Inventory	1690	T:D&W4, p. 147a
Wood, Richard	Amelia	Will	1884	Fleet, Huntington Data
Wood, Thomas	Henrico	Inventory	1771	Records, Vol. 7, p. 2137
Wood, Thomas [Word]		Will	1717	LVA Wills/Admin. DB
Wood, William	Warwick	Inventory	1703	Miscellany 1648, p. 77
Wood, William	Nottoway	Will	1798	WB1, p. 300
Wood, William		Will	1850	Valentine
Woodard, Albert, in Rappahannock Co.	Culpeper	Will	1887	CF1897-007
Woodbridge, Elizabeth	Richmond	Will	1746	TQ 17:1, p. 102
Woodbridge, Paul	Rappahannock*	Will	1691	TQ 17:1, p. 101
Woodbridge, Paul, of Farnham Parish	Rappahannock*	Will	1691	Sweeny, p. 151
Woodfolk, Pichegrue, in Caroline Co.	Henrico	Will	1863	CF1896-005
Woodhouse, Ann	Charles City	Inventory	1728	D&W1724, p. 210
Woodhouse, Ann	Charles City	Will	1728	D&W1724, p. 204
Woodhouse, Henry, Lower Norfolk Co.	London	Will	1688	VCRP, Survey #03742
Woodhouse, Henry, of Norfolk Co.	London	Will	1688	N:PROB11/392
Wooding, Susanna Christopher	Pittsylvania	Will	1850	V:Mss1 W8585 a 15-16
Woodlief, Edward	Prince George	Will	1759	DB1759, p. 94
Woodlief, Edward	Prince George	Inventory	1759	DB1759, p. 123
Woodlief, Francis E.	Petersburg	Will	1810	MVG 29:3, p. 194
Woodrow, Alexander	Stafford	Will	1777	Note[1]
Woodrow, Alexander	Stafford	Will	1777	LP:30 MAY 1782
Woods, Eliza, in Albemarle Co.	Charlottesville	Will	1845	CF1892-001
Woods, George H.	Franklin	Will	1853	V:Mss1 H1274 b 21-24
Woods, Joseph, in Roanoke Co.	Rockingham	Will	1849	CF1888-060
Woods, Sarah, in Roanoke Co.	Rockingham	Will	1849	CF1888-060
Woods, Wiley P.	Franklin	Will	1859	V:Mss1 Ea765 b 75-94
Woods, William M., in Buckingham Co.	Albemarle	Will	1862	CF1883-050
Woodside, John, of Norfolk Borough	Williamsburg	Will Abstract	1801	Crozier, p. 64
Woodson, Benjamin	Fluvanna	Will	1778	LVA Acc. #21825
Woodson, Charles, in Powhatan Co.	Lynchburg	Will	1796	CF1834-012
Woodson, George	Chesterfield	Will	1800	LVA Acc. #29437
Woodson, John	Cumberland	Will	1793	Fleet, Huntington Data
Woodson, Joseph, in Powhatan Co.	Lynchburg	Will	1791	CF1824-059
Woodson, Josephine A.	Hanover	Will	1895	CF1908-042
Woodson, Miller, in Henrico Co.	Lunenburg	Will	1849	CF1894-014
Woodson, Tarleton	Chesterfield	Will	1763	LVA Acc. #29437
Woodward, Fanny B.	King & Queen	Account	1832	BRCD
Woodward, Fanny B.	King & Queen	Sale S.	1839	LP
Woodward, Fanny B.	King & Queen	Appraisal	1864	CF1868-007
Woodward, Fanny B., of Middlesex Co.	King & Queen	Will	1864	CF1868-007

[1] LVA, Allason Papers, William Allason Letterbook, 1770-1787, p. 414.

NAME	LOCATION	TYPE	YEAR	REFERENCE(S)
Woodward, Jeremiah, in Goochland Co.	Hanover	Will	1863	CF1908-043
Woody, John	Hanover	Will	1784	LVA, WPA #17
Woodyard, Jeremiah	Fairfax	Inventory	1816	X
Woodyard, Jeremiah	Fairfax	Sale	1816	X
Wooldridge, John	Chesterfield	Will	1759	LVA Acc. #21305
Wooldridge, John	Chesterfield	Will	1759	LVA Acc. #33683
Woolfolk, J. Thomas, in Orange Co.	Louisa	Will	1848	CF1866-015
Woolfolk, John George, *Shepherd's Hill*	Caroline	Will	1819c	V:Mss1 W8844 a 146+
Woolfolk, Jourdan	Caroline	Inventory	1868	V:Mss1 W8844 a 416+
Woolfolk, Jourdan [of *Mulberry Place*]	Caroline	Will	1868	V:Mss1 W8844 a 416+
Woolves, Thomas	Surry	Will (N)	1691	T:D&W4, p. 213a
Wootten, Willis, in York Co.	James City	Will	1859	CF1888-014
Wootten, Willis, Sr., in Warwick Co.	York	Will	1847	CF1857-002
Wootton, Simeon H., in Pr. Edward Co.	Lunenburg	Will	1876	CF1899-027
Wormeley, Carter Warner	King William	Inventory	(nd)	V:Mss1 W8945 b 1035+
Wormeley, Carter Warner	King William	Will	1892	V:Mss1 W8945 a 201
Wormeley, Eleanor, of *Rosegill*	Middlesex	Will	1815	Fleet, Huntington Data
Wormeley, Elizabeth	Middlesex	Will Ref.	1744	Hening, Vol. 8, p. 452
Wormeley, Elizabeth, of *Rosegill*	Middlesex	Will Abstract	1761	Fleet 2:221
Wormeley, John	Middlesex	Will Ref.	1725	Hening, Vol. 5, p. 86
Wormeley, John	Middlesex	Will Ref.	1725	Hening, Vol. 8, p. 260
Wormeley, Ralph	Middlesex	Will	1806	LVA #1153274
Wormley, Eleanor	Middlesex	Will	1815	LVA Acc. #41008, r4611
Wormley, John	Middlesex	Appraisal	1830	LVA Acc. #41008, r4611
Wormley, Ralph	Middlesex	Appraisal	1830	LVA Acc. #41008, r4611
Worsham, Daniel	Amelia	Will	1781	CF1800-027
Worsham, Lucy, of Dinwiddie Co.	Mecklenburg	Will	1783	CF1803-023
Worsham, Philip, of Dinwiddie Co.	Mecklenburg	Inventory	1754	Judgments 1803 AUG
Wortham, Richard C., in Richmond	Henrico	Will	1896	CF1906-063
Worthington, Ephraim, in Berkeley Co.	Frederick	Will	1797	CF1813-079
Worthington, Robert		Will	1735	M: L21 f516
Wotton, William		Will	1656	VCRP, Survey #03129
Wraxhall, William, joiner		Will	1630	VCRP, Survey #03961
Wren, James	Fairfax	Will	1815	LVA Acc. #22078
Wren, James	Fairfax	Will	1843	X
Wren, James	Fairfax	Division	1880	X
Wren, James, in Fairfax Co.	Frederick	Will	1815	CF1826-066
Wren, Richard	Lancaster	Will	1676	LP
Wren, Robert	Powhatan	Will	1857	LVA Acc. #21819
Wren, Robert	Powhatan	Bond	1857	LVA Acc. #21819
Wrenn, James	Fairfax	Will	1843	LVA Acc. #343683, 2:38
Wrenn, John	Fairfax	Sale	1817	X
Wrenn, Minor, in Fauquier Co.	Rappahannock	Will	1813	CF1837-013
Wrenn, Sarah	Fairfax	Will	1816	X
Wright, Ann Hassie	Caroline	Will	1870	V:Mss2 M6196 b1-2
Wright, Anthony, in Loudoun Co.	Frederick	Will	1818	CF1832-060
Wright, Benjamin		Will	1707	VCRP, Survey #03896
Wright, Benjamin	York	Will	1794	CW M-1561
Wright, Edward	Nansemond	Will Ref.	1786	LP:03 NOV 1786
Wright, Harry	Caroline	Will	1823	W&P1742, p. 114
Wright, Isaac, in Amherst Co.	Lynchburg	Will	1808	CF1826-044

NAME	LOCATION	TYPE	YEAR	REFERENCE(S)
Wright, James S.	Nottoway	Will	1856	CF1921-006
Wright, John, in Bedford Co.	Lynchburg	Will	1803	CF1843-007
Wright, John, Sr.	Caroline	Will	1785	CF1797-001
Wright, Lewis A., in Pittsylvania Co.	Henry	Will	1862	CF1881-027
Wright, Patrick, of Richmond City	Williamsburg	Will Abstract	1787	Crozier, p. 64
Wright, Thomas, in Campbell Co.	Lynchburg	Will	1805	CF1825-027
Wright, Thomas, in Campbell Co.	Lynchburg	Will	1805	CF1873-014
Wright, Thomas, in MS	Essex	Will	1859	CF1888-030
Wroe, Originall, in Washington Parish		Will	1774	LVA Wills/Admin. DB
Wyatt, John, of Drysdale Parish	King & Queen	Will	1789	LVA Wyatt Family Papers
Wyatt, John V.	Hanover	Will	1889	CF1893-007
Wyatt, Nicholas, of Prince George Co.	Goochland	Will	1720	CF1806-015
Wyatt, Peter	Gloucester	Will	1815	LVA Acc. #21105
Wyatt, Peter	Gloucester	Will	1815	LVA Acc. #20890
Wyld, Daniel, formerly York Co.	London	Will	1676	N:PROB11/352
Wyld, Daniel, late of York Co.	London	Will	1676	VCRP, Survey #03561
Wynne, Humphrey H.	Warwick	Will	1822	BRCD
Wynne, Joshua	Dinwiddie	Will	1811	SV 3:1, p. 5
Wynne, Joshua, of Dinwiddie Co.	Sussex	Will	1811	LVA[1]
Wynne, Mary, in Greensville Co.	Brunswick	Will	1788	CF1805-042
Wynne, Robert, of Charles City Co.		Will	1678	VCRP, Survey #03718
Wynne, Robert, of Charles City Co.	London	Will	1687	N:PROB11/357
Wynne, Robert, of Jordan's Parish	Charles City	Will	1678	VMHB 14, p. 173
Wynne, Robert, of Jordans, in Eng.	Charles City	Will	1678	V:Mss2 W9894 a 1
Wynne, Thomas	James City	Will	1875	CF1890-010
Wynne, Thomas	James City	Will	1875	CF1888-013
Wythe, George	Richmond City	Will	1806	LVA Acc. #39197, r115
Wythe, George	Richmond City	Will	1806	LVA Acc. #25664
Wythe, Nathaniel	Warwick	Will	1751	VGSQ Vol. 50:4, p. 273

---

[1] LVA, Sussex County Loose Papers, 1754-1870, Box 243, filed with the bill of complaing in chancery cause of *William K. Parham & Salley his wife 'late Salley Malone, formerly Salley Wynne' and Martha Ann Elizabeth Parham, infant, v. Thomas Malone, Executor of Daniel Malone, dec.*

NAME	LOCATION	TYPE	YEAR	REFERENCE(S)
Y				
Yager, Nicholas, in Culpeper Co.	Madison	Will	1793	CF1873-029
Yancey, David	Louisa	Will	1808	LCH 1:2, p. 72
Yancey, Stephen, convicted murderer		Estate Ref.	1784	Hening, Vol. 11, p. 508
Yancy, Major, in Culpeper Co.	Fauquier	Will	1849	CF1873-053
Yarbrough, Benjamin	Caroline	Will	1800	Note[1]
Yarbrough, Henry	Caroline	Will	1793	W&P1742, p. 51
Yarbrough, Jesse G.	Hanover	Will	1858	Cocke:177
Yarbrough, Jesse G.	Hanover	Will	1858	CF1868-029
Yarbrough, Joseph	Lunenburg	Will	1827	V:Mss2 Y203 a 1
Yardley, George, Sir	Jamestown	Will	1627	Note[2]
Yardley, George, Sir	Jamestown	Will	1629	VCRP, Survey #03119
Yates, Benjamin P.	Dinwiddie	Will	1817	BRCD
Yates, Benjamin P., in Dinwiddie Co.	Petersburg	Will	1817	CF1839-049
Yates, Benjamin P., in Dinwiddie Co.	Petersburg	Will	1817	CF1851-021
Yates, Charles, of Spotsylvania Co.	London	Will	1809	N:PROB11/1503
Yates, James, in Culpeper Co.	Rappahannock	Will	1829	CF1833-003
Yates, John [of *Forest Springs*]	Caroline	Will	1812	W&P1742, p. 96
Yates, Mary, in Middlesex Co.	Essex	Will	1799	CF1838-004
Yates, William	James City	Will	1764	LVA Acc. #26024
Yates, William	James City	Will	1764	LVA Acc. #41008, r4610
Yates, William	James City	Will	1764	V:Mss2 Y275 a 1
Yates, William, of Bruton Parish	James City	Will	1764	Fleet, Huntington Data
Yeamans, Mary	Hanover	Will	1879	CF1886-017
Yeamans, Pleasant	Hanover	Will	1865	CF1884-025
Yeamans, Pleasant	Hanover	Will	1866	Cocke:161
Yeardley, George, Sir	James City	Will	1627	V:Mss2 Y327 a 1
Yeates, John	Nansemond	Will	1731	GSTV 8, p. 3
Yeates, John	Nansemond	Will	1732	UVA MSS 38-546
Yeates, John, of Upper Parish	Nansemond	Will	1731	VTG 8:1, p. 3
Yeates, John, of Upper Parish	Nansemond	Will	1731	LVA Acc. #20019
Yeats, John, of Upper Parish	Nansemond	Will	1731	V:Mss7:1 Y345:1
Yelverson, Jacob	Fairfax	Will	1869	CF1900-018
Yelverton, Jacob	Fairfax	Will	1876	CF1900-018
Yerby, George, of Richmond Co.	Williamsburg	Will Abstract	1793	Crozier, p. 65
Young, Edwin, in Shenandoah Co.	Warren	Will	1820	CF1839-004
Young, Frederick	Rockingham	Will	1837	CF1846-010
Young, Henry	Charles City	Inventory	1726	D&W1724, p. 152
Young, Henry	Essex	Will	1749	Fleet 2:327
Young, James, in Halifax Co.	Lynchburg	Will	1795	CF1831-041
Young, John	Surry	Will	1715	T: correct from 1714
Young, John	Albemarle	Will	1867	LVA Acc. #35955
Young, Nathaniel	Caroline	Will	1781	LVA Acc. #24642
Young, Nathaniel	Caroline	Will	1781	BRCD
Young, Nathaniel, in Tazewell Co.	Smyth	Will	1853	CF1866-033
Young, Richard	Caroline	Will	1778	V:Mss1 B2346 a 1164
Young, Susan M., in Fauquier Co.	Culpeper	Will	1874	CF1879-007

---

[1] Fredericksburg District Superior Court Wills, Bk. A, p. 137.
[2] *New England Historical and Genealogical Register*, Vol. 38, p. 69.

NAME	LOCATION	TYPE	YEAR	REFERENCE(S)
Z				
Zaines, John	Surry	Admin.	1658	T:D&W1, p. 117
Zimerman, Abraham	Rockingham	Will	1815	CF1848-004
Zimmerman, Henry	Fairfax	Sale	1807	X
Zimmerman, Henry	Fairfax	Account	1810	X
Zirkle, Ludwick, of Rockingham Co.	Augusta	Will	1812	CF1825-083
Zittey, Peter, of Rockingham Co.	Augusta	Will	1800	CF1819-053
Zouch, John, Sir		Will	1639	VCRP, Survey #03987

NAME	LOCATION	TYPE	YEAR	REFERENCE(S)
No Surname				
[ ], Mahala	Hanover	Will	1824	CF1834-003
[ ], Mahala, a free woman of color	Hanover	Will	1831	Cocke:22

Heritage Books by Wesley E. Pippenger:

Alexander Family: Migrations from Maryland

Alexandria (Arlington) County, Virginia Death Records, 1853–1896

Alexandria City and Arlington County, Virginia Records Index: Vol. 1

Alexandria City and Arlington County, Virginia Records Index: Vol. 2

Alexandria County, Virginia Marriage Records, 1853–1895

Alexandria Virginia Marriage Index, January 10, 1893 to August 31, 1905

Alexandria, Virginia Marriages, 1870–1892

Alexandria, Virginia Town Lots, 1749–1801
Together with the Proceedings of the Board of Trustees, 1749–1780

Alexandria, Virginia Wills, Administrations and Guardianships, 1786–1800

Alexandria, Virginia 1808 Census (Wards 1, 2, 3, and 4)

Alexandria, Virginia Death Records, 1863–1896

Alexandria, Virginia Hustings Court Orders, Volume 1, 1780–1787

*Connections and Separations: Divorce, Name Change and Other
Genealogical Tidbits from the Acts of the Virginia General Assembly*

Daily National Intelligencer *Index to Deaths, 1855–1870*

Daily National Intelligencer, *Washington, District of Columbia
Marriages and Deaths Notices (January 1, 1851 to December 30, 1854)*

*Dead People on the Move: Reconstruction of the Georgetown Presbyterian
Burying Ground, Holmead's (Western) Burying Ground, and
Other Removals in the District of Columbia*

Death Notices from Richmond, Virginia Newspapers, 1841–1853

*District of Columbia Ancestors,
A Guide to Records of the District of Columbia*

District of Columbia Death Records: August 1, 1874–July 31, 1879

District of Columbia Foreign Deaths, 1888–1923

District of Columbia Guardianship Index, 1802–1928

*District of Columbia Interments (Index to Deaths)
January 1, 1855 to July 31, 1874*

District of Columbia Marriage Licenses, Register 1: 1811–1858

District of Columbia Marriage Licenses, Register 2: 1858–1870

*District of Columbia Marriage Records Index
June 28, 1877 to October 19, 1885: Marriage Record Books 11 to 20*
Wesley E. Pippenger and Dorothy S. Provine

*District of Columbia Marriage Records Index
October 20, 1885 to January 20, 1892: Marriage Record Books 21 to 30*

*District of Columbia Marriage Records Index
January 20, 1892 to August 30, 1896: Marriage Record Books 31 to 40*

*District of Columbia Marriage Records Index
August 31, 1896 to December 17, 1900: Marriage Record Books 41 to 65*

District of Columbia Probate Records, 1801–1852

District of Columbia: Original Land Owners, 1791–1800

Early Church Records of Alexandria City and Fairfax County, Virginia

Essex County, Virginia Guardianship and Orphans Records, 1707–1888: A Descriptive Index

Essex County, Virginia Marriage Bonds, 1804–1850, Annotated

Essex County, Virginia Newspaper Notices, 1738–1938

www.ingramcontent.com/pod-product-compliance
Lightning Source LLC
Chambersburg PA
CBHW080416270326
41929CB00018B/3054